Mainstreaming Corporate Responsibility

"Expectations that business will respond to the social, environmental and governance challenges of the 21st century are growing. Those expectations are now the subject of teaching and research, and are being hotly debated at business schools.

London Business School became a founding partner of the European Academy of Business in Society (EABIS) in 2003. My predecessor, Laura Tyson, took the view that corporate responsibility and ethics are integral to all business functions. The whole curriculum needed to be infused with the issue of how business manages its relationship with society.

At the time, very few teaching materials for subjects such as finance, accounting and marketing included non-financial performance issues. The quality of available case studies was questionable. The theoretical grounding of corporate responsibility in these business disciplines was considered weak.

In the five years since, business schools including London Business School, have made substantial progress. EABIS has made huge steps through its research outputs, colloquia, educational exchanges and curriculum design programmes.

Together, London Business School and EABIS set up a Curriculum Development Project. It was led by N. Craig Smith, then Associate Dean of the MBA programme at the School.

This book, co-edited by EABIS President Gilbert Lenssen, is one of the excellent outputs of that project. It is a collection of texts and cases for use in both core and specialized courses.

We are delighted to see our initial investment in this growing field come to fruition. This book will benefit both faculty and students. I hope it will prove a major contribution to making corporate responsibility a staple element across the curriculum."

Robin Buchanan, President of London Business School

"This book is a welcome resource for businesses and for business schools like Ashridge that are integrating corporate responsibility issues into front-line executive education. Business schools must provide the leaders of tomorrow with a better understanding of the issues, opportunities and urgency for making sustainability central to corporate strategy and practice. The articles and cases presented here offer a thoughtful introduction to sustainability for strategic advantage."

Kai Peters, CEO, Ashridge Business School

"The cases and insights in this book are a vital resource for those in charge of shaping their firm's general management curriculum and leadership programmes. Unilever has been proud to support this EABIS initiative and its goal of integrating personal and corporate responsibility into executive learning worldwide."

Sandy Ogg, Chief Human Resources Officer, Unilever

"This book is a valued resource for teaching corporate responsibility issues. At IBM, our model of corporate citizenship is being transformed by the emergence of a global economy — and the enormous challenges and opportunities it presents. Corporate citizenship today plays a key role in addressing some of society's most complex problems. The articles and cases presented offer an insightful introduction to tackling global sustainability to make the world work better."

Michael Burkhardt, VP Human Resources, Northeast Europe, IBM

"This book is an important resource for any company with a serious commitment to responsible management. The external issues confronting business today have a direct impact across core functions and stakeholder relations, which management must acknowledge and address. The EABIS case studies offer valuable material to build new capabilities at any level of executive development and learning."

Garmt Louw, VP Learning & Organisation Effectiveness, Royal Dutch Shell

Mainstreaming Corporate Responsibility

Edited by N. Craig Smith, INSEAD and
Gilbert Lenssen, EABIS

WILEY

A John Wiley and Sons, Ltd, Publication

Other Wiley Editorial Offices

John Wiley & Sons Inc., 111 River Street, Hoboken, NJ 07030, USA

Jossey-Bass, 989 Market Street, San Francisco, CA 94103-1741, USA

Wiley-VCH Verlag GmbH, Boschstr. 12, D-69469 Weinheim, Germany

John Wiley & Sons Australia Ltd, 42 McDougall Street, Milton, Queensland 4064, Australia

John Wiley & Sons (Asia) Pte Ltd, 2 Clementi Loop #02-01, Jin Xing Distripark, Singapore 129809

John Wiley & Sons Canada Ltd, 6045 Freemont Blvd. Mississauga, Ontario, L5R 4J3 Canada

Wiley also publishes its books in a variety of electronic formats. Some content that appears in print may not be available
in electronic books.

Library of Congress Cataloging-in-Publication Data
Smith, N. Craig, 1958-
  Mainstreaming corporate responsibility
N. Craig Smith and Gilbert Lenssen.
     p. cm.
  Includes bibliographical references and index.
  ISBN 978-0-470-75394-1 (pbk.)
  1. Social responsibility of business—Study and teaching. 2. Social responsibility of business—Case studies.
  3. Business education—Curricula. I. Lenssen, Gilbert. II. Title.
  HD60.S58 2009
  658.4'080711—dc22

                                                                                    2009009684

British Library Cataloguing in Publication Data

A catalogue record for this book is available from the British Library

ISBN 978-0-470-75394-1 (pbk)

Typeset in 10/12 pt Optima by Thomson Digital, India
Printed and bound in Great Britain by Bell & Bain, Glasgow.

This book is dedicated to the memory of Thomas W. Dunfee (1941–2008), a wonderful human being as well as a key contributor to the field of corporate responsibility.

Contents

About the Editors

N. Craig Smith is the INSEAD Chaired Professor of Ethics and Social Responsibility at INSEAD, France and the Academic Director of the Corporate Social Responsibility and Ethics Research Group in the INSEAD Social Innovation Centre. He was previously on the faculties of London Business School, Georgetown University and Harvard Business School. His current research examines ethical consumerism/consumer activism, marketing ethics, deception in marketing, mainstreaming corporate responsibility and strategic drivers of corporate responsibility/sustainability. His recent publications appear in *Business Ethics Quarterly, California Management Review, Journal of the Academy of Marketing Science, Journal of Consumer Psychology, Journal of Marketing* and *Journal of Public Policy & Marketing*. He has another recent book (with Bhattacharya, Vogel and Levine) on *Global Challenges of Responsible Business* (Cambridge University Press, 2010). He consults with various organizations on business and marketing ethics and corporate responsibility/sustainability, and serves on the Scientific Committee of Vigeo (a social responsibility rating agency), the Advisory Board of Carbon Clear (a carbon management consultancy), and the Ethics Advisory Board of SNS Asset Management.

Gilbert Lenssen is President of the European Academy of Business in Society, a former Professor at the College of Europe, former fellow at Templeton College Oxford University and visiting Professor at the Management Schools of Henley and Cranfield. He is a member of the Academic Advisory Boards of several Business Schools and a member of the Board of EFMD.

Acknowledgements

This book advances a new and innovative approach to the task of equipping future business leaders and managers to address today's challenging issues of corporate responsibility. It is in large measure the product of a three-year project on Curriculum Development for Mainstreaming Corporate Responsibility, sponsored by the European Academy of Business in Society (EABIS) and led by London Business School initially and then by the INSEAD Social Innovation Centre. As such, it is truly the work of many hands.

We would like to acknowledge our thanks to all the various people who have contributed to the EABIS project, including but certainly not limited to the following. First, the former London Business School Dean, Laura Tyson (now S. K. and Angela Chan Professor of Global Management at the Haas School of Business, University of California, Berkeley), for her vision as an early advocate of the need to better embed attention to corporate responsibility throughout the business school curriculum and her support of the initial proposal to EABIS from London Business School to develop the mainstreaming project. Second, the project's tireless administrators who as well as making the project happen, also championed the project within London Business School and INSEAD, and externally: Gay Haskins (formerly of London Business School, now with Saïd Business School, University of Oxford); Sophie Linguri (formerly of London Business School, now with IMD in Lausanne); and Roisin Kelly of INSEAD. We are also grateful for the support of INSEAD and more specifically the Dean, J. Frank Brown, and Luk Van Wassenhove, Academic Director of the INSEAD Social Innovation Centre. Their support has been crucial to the successful conclusion of the project. The continued support of London Business School under its President, Robin Buchanan and Dean Andrew Likierman is also much appreciated, not least in ensuring access to the London Business School cases included in this volume (with the kind assistance of Richard Frost, School Secretary).

We owe a particular debt of gratitude to the EABIS Executive Director (2003–2007), Peter Lacy (now with Accenture as Managing Director, Sustainability Practice for Europe, Africa and Latin America) and Simon Pickard, Director General of EABIS (from 2008). Peter was a key thought leader at the project's inception, a mantle that Simon readily assumed, and both have exhibited unflagging enthusiasm for the project over the years—not to mention seemingly unlimited patience with its many contributors.

Both were also members of the project's Steering Committee, a key advisory body. The other members of the committee who deserve recognition were: Elena Bonfiglioli, Director for Corporate Citizenship, Microsoft Europe; Joan Fontrodona, Associate Professor and Head, Business Ethics Department, IESE Business School; Celia Moore, Corporate Citizenship and Corporate Affairs Executive, IBM EMEA; Alex Nevill, Biofuels Agronomy Manager, Shell; Mette Morsing, Professor of Corporate Social Responsibility, Copenhagen Business School; and Mark Wade,

Corporate Advisor, Sustainability and Value Creation (formerly with Shell). This group made a major commitment to the project, meeting regularly to ensure that the project kept on track both academically and relative to the challenges of corporate responsibility in business practice today. We also thank Bart Neerscholten, Associate Director Education & EU Affairs, for his adminis-tration of the project at EABIS as well as the five corporate founding partners of EABIS – IBM, Johnson & Johnson, Microsoft, Shell and Unilever – without whose financial support the project would not have been possible.

The book builds on the EABIS "Mainstreaming Corporate Responsibility" project but also extends it, not least in the development of the chapters describing how corporate responsibility is relevant to the different core subjects of the business school curriculum. We are grateful to these contribu-tors for their willingness to devote time and intellectual energy to formulating a critical set of guid-ing contributions to the book. Roisin Kelly of INSEAD deserves a second mention here because of her role not only in administering the EABIS project but also in making the book happen, including chasing up our various contributors as well as the book's editors.

We offer our thanks to Wiley for its vision in backing an innovative publishing project. Specifically, we thank our original Sponsoring Editor Sarah Booth; our current Sponsoring Editor Mark Styles; Production Editor Céline Durand; Publishing Assistant Georgia King; and Proofreader Fliss Watts. We look forward to being able to thank Wiley Marketing Manager, Peter Hudson, once the book has been adopted by business schools around the world!

Finally, we thank our families for their forbearance and understanding of a lengthy and demanding project. We hope it makes a difference.

N. Craig Smith
Gilbert Lenssen

Foreword

Transforming Business and Business Education by Embedding Corporate Responsibility throughout the Curriculum

The year 2008 was far more difficult for the world's economies than we might have anticipated at its outset, despite knowing then of the sub-prime mortgage crisis. As we write, the world's stock markets remain highly volatile, with the major markets down by more than a third year-on-year. Credit is in short supply for the 'real economy' of consumers and businesses, as well as for financial institutions – government interventions notwithstanding. It is likely that we have witnessed the largest-ever destruction of shareholder value, with estimates of three to four trillion dollars lost in the United States alone. The *Financial Times* reports that more than 130 000 financial services jobs have been lost worldwide since the credit squeeze began a year ago. These job losses include our alumni, and the prospects for our current students seeking jobs in finance and other sectors are less positive than ever before. However, the crisis has significant implications not only for our students, alumni and corporate partners, but also for the curricula of business schools.

An impending recession has led some commentators to suggest that interest in corporate social responsibility (CSR) will wane, with companies focused solely on short-term financial performance. We don't think so. If anything, a recession with roots in the financial crisis should prompt business and business schools to give greater attention to CSR. The jury is still undecided on precisely why the credit crunch emerged and with such profoundly negative effects on the world's economies, but it is clear that changes are required in our financial institutions. British Prime Minister Gordon Brown has said that we 'must have a new Bretton Woods . . . a new international financial architecture for the years ahead'. Forward-looking business schools have a part to play in these changes.

Testifying to US lawmakers examining the causes of the financial crisis, former US Federal Reserve Chairman Alan Greenspan commented: 'Those of us who have looked to the self-interest of lending institutions to protect shareholders' equity (myself especially) are in a state of shocked disbelief'. The failure of the banks to price risk correctly, thereby ultimately destroying huge quantities of shareholder value, is a failure of management. As the late Peter Drucker observed in his book *Management: Tasks, Responsibilities, Practices* (1974, Heinemann), CSR is a key management task. It is relevant here if only because of the patent absence of social responsibility on the part of many executives involved in creating the crisis.

More fundamentally, Greenspan's remarks call into question a central idea underpinning deregulation, business practice and, indeed, business school teaching itself – that market discipline will ensure the best economic outcomes. The large-scale destruction of shareholder value of recent months has come at a time when markets have never been more unfettered and when the mantra of shareholder value maximization has never been more loudly proclaimed. Clearly, something more – something new – is required. As the deans of two of the world's leading business schools, we have concluded that we must examine our existing assumptions and our school curricula.

How timely, then, that we have a book advocating the mainstreaming of CSR into business school curricula. What we see in this book is an opportunity for schools to address CSR in every course in the core curriculum – be it strategy, accounting, entrepreneurship, marketing or even finance – as well as CSR foundations as a core course. Here are the subject-specific cases and readings that will enable a rich discussion and embedded learning of how CSR is relevant to all the major courses in the typical business school curriculum.

For most companies today, CSR can no longer be treated as a peripheral activity left to compliance or public affairs. It has to be embedded within the day-to-day activities of the business. As managers find that they must grapple with increasingly complex social and environmental problems as an integral part of business strategy and operations, they require different knowledge, skills and competencies than in the past. We believe it is the role of business schools to equip future business leaders and managers with the knowledge, skills and competencies to meet the current challenges. Corporate responsibility must be mainstreamed into business schools as well as into business. The recent financial crisis clearly highlights both the importance of this and the need for much more work to be done as we reflect on how we might strengthen business school curricula.

J. Frank Brown, Dean, INSEAD, Fontainebleau, France.
Thomas S. Robertson, Dean, Wharton School, Philadelphia, USA.

PART ONE

INTRODUCTION

CHAPTER ONE

Mainstreaming Corporate Responsibility: An Introduction

N. Craig Smith, INSEAD, and Gilbert Lenssen, EABIS

Corporate social responsibility (CSR) has never been more prominent on the corporate agenda. The financial crisis and its effects across the global economy have once more made it obvious that the stability of our global market system depends on responsible behaviour, sustainable business models and proactive management of business impacts on society, as well as regulatory frameworks. Responding to the challenges of global climate change and growing social inequities also remain imperatives on the global corporate citizenship agenda. Public policy leadership by leading corporate players is now in sharp demand at the global and industry sector level. It is being claimed that a new paradigm of global governance is emerging in which government, business and civil society can engage in co-regulation (Lenssen, Arenas and Lacy, 2008).

Sometimes also referred to as corporate responsibility or corporate citizenship, CSR encompasses issues such as sustainability (meeting the needs of the present without compromising the ability of future generations to meet their needs), stakeholder management and corporate governance, as well as corporate philanthropy, although the latter is increasingly seen as a peripheral consideration.[1]

The *case for business* to engage in addressing environmental, social and governance issues is based on the realization that a new global social contract between business, government and society is needed to enhance stability and long-term wealth creation (Davis, 2005). The *business case* at the level of the firm is becoming increasingly clear as more companies are coming to understand that, aside from any moral obligation, it is in their economic interest to address environmental, social and governance issues and in a manner that is integrated with their strategy and operations. But only a few companies have achieved deep organizational integration. Spending money on CSR programmes is often a tactical response to pressure from activists. However, society is typically more interested in the way profit is made (and with what impacts and externalities) rather than the way it is spent on CSR programmes.

Many companies have treated corporate responsibility as a peripheral issue – a bolt-on to a business-as-usual approach. This criticism was widespread five years ago. Commentators provocatively suggested that 'CSR in most companies is in a ghetto: it is a marginalized and marginal activity, often left to a dedicated department with the task of getting the message out about a company's good works' (Smith and Cohon, 2004, p. 21). Indeed, civil society and the broader public are often sceptical of CSR and companies that have expressed a strong commitment to corporate responsibility have sometimes become the target of more attacks, not fewer.

The Polaris Institute, a nongovernmental organization (NGO), makes a Corporate Greenwashing Award to companies 'that have pushed profits higher while investing millions of dollars into covering up environmentally damaging practices with corporate social responsibility projects'. Coca-Cola, the first award winner in 2005, was selected 'after careful consideration, (because) the Coca-Cola Company stood out as the company that has worked the hardest this year to present itself as socially and environmentally responsible – while continuing to harm environments and communities through the production and distribution of its products.'[2] In its report, *Behind the Mask: The Real Face of Corporate Social Responsibility*, Christian Aid, another NGO, concluded that 'the corporate world's commitments to responsible behaviour are not borne out by the experience of many who are supposed to benefit from them' (2004, p. 2).

As Smith and Cohon (2004, p. 21) suggested, one of the main aims of corporate responsibility programmes is seemingly 'to build goodwill as a sort of insurance policy to be redeemed in case something goes badly wrong in the main part of the business. But the social effects of these core business operations are left largely unexamined'. We believe this is changing today. As Dunfee (2008, p. 346) asserted: 'Discretionary social responsibility actions by corporations benefit needy stakeholders around the globe. These actions have a total value in the billions of dollars on an annual basis.' Nonetheless, we agree that 'mainstreaming has become the key challenge for the corporate social responsibility movement' (Katsoulakos and Katsoulacos, 2007, p. 356) – and not only for the CSR movement, but also for business and policymakers. Mainstreaming requires a good understanding of the business case as well as the case for business to engage seriously with CSR beyond enlightened profit maximization.

WHAT IS MAINSTREAMING CORPORATE RESPONSIBILTY?

While writing primarily about corporate ethics programmes, Weaver, Trevino and Cochran (1999, p. 539) observed that 'corporations can respond to expectations for socially responsible processes and outcomes in organizationally integrated ways or in [an] easily decoupled fashion'. The greenwashing or 'window dressing' claims of Polaris and other NGOs are indicative of a decoupled approach to corporate responsibility. As Weaver, Trevino and Cochran (1999, p. 541, emphasis in original) explained:

> An *easily decoupled* structure or policy provides the appearance of conformity to external expectations while making it easy to insulate much of the organization from those expectations. Although the structure or policy exists, there is no guarantee that it will regularly interact with other organizational policies and functions or that employees will be accountable to it.

In contrast, they wrote (1999, p. 540, emphasis in original) that:

> *Integrated* structures and policies affect everyday decisions and actions; decisions are made in light of these policies, and people occupying these specialized structures have the confidence of and regular interaction with other departments and their managers. An integrated structure or policy is likely to be supported by other organizational policies and programs. Thus, managers and employees are held accountable to it, take note of it, and see it as having a valued role in the organization's operations.

As Berger, Cunningham and Drumwright (2007, p. 133) have observed in relation to CSR specifically:

> if something is mainstream, it is clearly seen to be on the company's agenda in a legitimate, credible, and ongoing manner, and it is incorporated into day-to-day activities in appropriate and relevant ways. For an issue to be mainstreamed within an organization, it needs to be included in the policy development, technical tools, performance measures, and political agenda-setting processes of the organization.

By contrast, they note that a cause-related marketing campaign is typically short-term in nature, easily terminated and not diffused through other aspects of the company. The same can be said of much corporate philanthropy and thus some observers suggest it should be seen as falling outside the domain of corporate responsibility.

Thus, *mainstreaming corporate responsibility is the embedding of attention to corporate social and environmental impacts throughout the business as an integrated policy affecting the day-to-day decision-making and actions of the organization at all levels.*

Much like corporate efforts to integrate attention to quality or customer orientation, mainstreaming corporate responsibility is easier said than done. However, this volume contains detailed illustrations of companies attempting to achieve this goal (see, for example, the case studies on Novo Nordisk, innocent and Hydro Polymers, in Chapters 9, 18 and 22 respectively). These companies realise that corporate responsibility and sustainability is becoming part of competitiveness (Lenssen, Gasparkski and Rok 2006). Perhaps they are also sensing that after the customer revolution, the quality revolution and the information revolution of the late 20th century, the sustainability revolution could well be the next major change to which business needs to adapt in transformational ways (Lenssen, Tyson and Pickard, 2009). If mainstreaming means organizational transformation, it requires a process of planned and emergent change.

De Wit, Wade and Schouten's (2006) study of Shell's mainstreaming of sustainable development (SD), to use Shell's preferred term, suggests that this process requires both 'hardwiring' and 'softwiring'. Hardwiring is 'aligning key business processes within a governance framework of commitments, policies, standards and guidelines consistent with contributing to SD' (2006, pp. 491–492), with stakeholder engagement as a core activity.[3] However, hardwiring is not enough; softwiring is also required. De Wit *et al.* (2006, p. 497) note:

> It is one thing to write a manual of recommended procedures, but if that is all that happens, the manual will simply sit on the shelf. At best, a culture of minimum acceptance will be achieved; at worst, one of avoidance. What is also needed is to touch the hearts and minds of people, so that they feel it is the right way to do business and can see how business value can be derived. It is therefore vital that people at all levels are convinced of the strength of the business case and the practicality of your approach. In reality, this means translating SD into something that is tangible and relevant to both business teams and individuals.

Hardwiring is about integration of CSR into organizational systems, processes and structures: it reconditions the 'brain of the firm'. Softwiring is about integration into organizational culture, skills and competencies: it affects the 'heart of the enterprise'. Both require equal attention in organizational transformation. Clearly, mainstreaming by organizational transformation is not a quick re-engineering effort. It must manifest itself as a learning journey based on a strategic intent (Lenssen *et al.*, 2007).

MAINSTREAMING AND THE BUSINESS SCHOOL CURRICULUM

Following the shock of the corporate scandals early in the 21st century, many business schools responded by adding more ethics and CSR courses to the curriculum. This move was lamented by the late Sumantra Ghoshal (2005, p. 75), a professor of strategy and management luminary, in an article entitled 'Bad Management Theories Are Destroying Good Management Practices', where he observed:

> Business schools do not need to do a great deal more to help prevent future Enrons; they need only to stop doing a lot they currently do . . . business school faculty need to own up to our own role in creating Enrons. It is our theories and ideas that have done much to strengthen the management practices that we are all now so loudly condemning.

Ghoshal referred to the cynical ('bad') theories underlying mainstream courses in strategy, finance and economics, which he claimed were disconnected from any moral reasoning or societal implications and needed to be de-masked as a root cause of the ethical deficiencies in business education. Ghoshal argued that theories grounded in a neo-liberal conception of economics – such as agency theory, rational choice theory, transaction cost theory and game theory – advanced the relentless pursuit of self interest and profit, the externalization of as many costs as possible to society and the exploitation of natural and social resources, if possible with a strict minimum of regulation. Ethics courses would change little, according to Ghoshal, if the mainstream curriculum remained unchanged and stuck in its old ideologies. Adding an ethics course in response to the corporate ethics scandals could be seen as comparable to creating a CSR department and CSR programmes in response to challenges from civil society activists, while continuing with business as usual elsewhere in the organization. Both responses often amount to little more than window dressing.

Ghoshal's paper is a landmark in the debate on the deficiencies in the business curriculum. He pleaded for revolutionizing the business curriculum. We propose incremental change and evolution. Various commentators have suggested that the financial crisis is doing its work in de-masking the deficiencies of the old theories (Krugman, 2008). We suspect that new theories will emerge that better grasp the new contexts, complexities and connectedness of global markets and global business.

For business schools, mainstreaming means that CSR needs to become integral to the range of subject areas covered, at least in core courses, rather than being limited to a Business Ethics, Corporate Responsibility or Environmental Management course. This book seeks to enhance the integration of corporate responsibility issues into the core educational programmes for the next generation of corporate managers. To that end, it provides a fascinating set of case studies of mostly well-known organizations addressing critical issues of business and society that can be used in business and management degree programmes (MBA and final year undergraduate) as well as executive education. The book is structured around the major subject areas in the business school curriculum: strategy, accounting, finance, economics, entrepreneurship, marketing, organizational behaviour and human resource management, and operations management.

Two-thirds of the cases in the book have been developed as part of a major three-year curriculum development project on mainstreaming corporate responsibility, sponsored by EABIS (the European Academy of Business in Society)[4] and led by Craig Smith, initially from London Business School and subsequently from the INSEAD Social Innovation Centre, with the support of a project steering committee comprising businesspeople and academics, as well as Gilbert Lenssen and other representatives of EABIS. The EABIS project cases have been supplemented by six further cases, four of which are award winners for their treatment of corporate responsibility.[5]

Formal requirements of integration, however, that are expected of faculty across subject areas will only go so far in mainstreaming. The soft-wiring of faculty embracing corporate responsibility is also required. With this in mind, the introductory chapter for each subject-specific module attempts to identify key points of connection with that subject. For example, Pettigrew (in Chapter 3) and Gabel (Chapter 14) show how corporate responsibility enters into strategy and economics. Bhattacharya and Sen (Chapter 20) show how consumer behaviour analysis in marketing is informed by corporate responsibility, and Oswald (Chapter 7) shows how the role of the financial accountant is now being extended beyond traditional financial reporting to include the measurement of performance relative to corporate responsibility metrics.

The cases and other materials in this book shed new and important light on how companies today are navigating their way towards a genuine mainstreaming of corporate responsibility. They provide a vehicle for exploring this topic in both traditional corporate responsibility courses and, more innovatively, in the standard core courses of the business school curriculum where, in most schools to date at least, too little attention is being given to these critically important issues of business in society.

NOTES

1. The terms corporate social responsibility and corporate responsibility are used interchangeably throughout this book. Although corporate social responsibility is the more established term, the term corporate responsibility is often preferred today because it does not appear to suggest a focus on corporate social impacts to the exclusion of environmental impacts.

2. See http://www.polarisinstitute.org/coca_cola_company_wins_corporate_greenwashing_award (accessed 30 October 2008).

3. A stakeholder is 'any group or individual who can affect or is affected by the achievement of a corporation's purpose' (Freeman, Harrison and Wicks, 2007, p. 6). Primary stakeholders are typically identified as shareholders/financiers, customers, employees, suppliers and the local community; secondary stakeholders include the government, media, competitors, NGOs/consumer advocacy groups and special interest groups (Freeman, Harrison and Wicks, 2007).

4. In 2002, deans from leading European business schools, together with business leaders, founded the European Academy of Business in Society, with the explicit aim to mainstream corporate responsibility into business theory and business practice. It is increasingly viewed as Europe's reference point for corporate responsibility knowledge development and learning. Gilbert Lenssen has been its President since inception. For more information on members and activities, visit: www.eabis.org.

5. Co-operative Group: Fair-Trade Chocolate won the European Foundation for Management Development (EFMD) award, Corporate Social Responsibility category, 2004; TPG-WFP Partnership won the EFMD award, Corporate Social Responsibility category, 2005. GlaxoSmithKline won the European Case Clearing House (ECCH) award, Ethics and Social Responsibility category, 2006; Wal-Mart won the ECCH award, Ethics and Social Responsibility category, 2008. As the book goes to press, it has just been announced that the following EABIS project cases have won awards: illycaffè, won the 2008 EFMD award in the Supply Chain Management category and innocent: Values and Value, won the 2008 award in the Corporate Social Responsibility category.

REFERENCES

Berger, I.E., Cunningham, P.H. and Drumwright, M.E. (2007) Mainstreaming corporate social responsibility: Developing markets for virtue. *California Management Review*, **49** (4), 132–57.

Christian Aid (2004) *Behind the Mask: The Real Face of Corporate Social Responsibility*, Christian Aid, London. Available at: http://www.risc.org.uk/readingroom/csr/csr_behindthemask.pdf (accessed 11 February 2009).

Davis, I. (2005) The biggest contract. *The Economist*, 28 May.

De Wit, M., Wade, M. and Schouten, E. (2006) Hardwiring and softwiring corporate responsibility: A vital combination. *Corporate Governance*, **6** (4), 491–505.

Dunfee, T.W. (2008) Stakeholder theory: Managing corporate social responsibility in a multiple actor context, in *The Oxford Handbook of Corporate Social Responsibility* (eds A. Crane, A. McWilliams, D. Matten, J. Moon and D. Siegel), Oxford University Press, Oxford, pp. 346–62.

Freeman, R.E., Harrison, J.S. and Wicks, A.C. (2007) *Managing for Stakeholders: Survival, Reputation, and Success*. Yale University Press, New Haven.

Ghoshal, S. (2005) Bad management theories are destroying good management practices. *Academy of Management Learning and Education*, **4** (1), 75–91.

Katsoulakos, T. and Katsoulacos, Y. (2007) Integrating corporate responsibility principles and stakeholder approaches into mainstream strategy: A stakeholder-oriented and integrative strategic management framework. *Corporate Governance*, **7** (4), 355–69.

Krugman, P. (2008) *The Return of Depression Economics and the Crisis of 2008*, Norton, New York.

Lenssen, G., Gasparski, W. and Rok, B. (2006) Corporate responsibility, competitiveness and human/social capital, a special issue of *Corporate Governance, The International Journal of Business in Society*, Volume 6.

Lenssen, G., Perrini, F., Tencati, A. and Lacy, P. (2007) Corporate responsibility and strategic management, a special issue of *Corporate Governance, The International Journal of Business in Society*, Volume 7.

Lenssen, G., Arenas, D. and Lacy, P. (2008) Corporate responsibility and the emerging global governance paradigm, a special issue of *Corporate Governance, The International Journal of Business in Society*, Volume 8.

Lenssen, G., Tyson, S. and Pickard, S. (forthcoming 2009) Corporate responsibility, leadership and organisational change, a special issue of *Corporate Governance, The International Journal of Business in Society*, Volume 9.

Smith, N.C. and Cohon, C. (2004) Good works in a corporate ghetto. *Financial Times*, 8 December, p. 21.

Weaver, G.R., Trevino, L.K. and Cochran, P.L. (1999) Integrated and decoupled corporate social performance: Management commitments, external pressures, and corporate ethics practices. *Academy of Management Journal*, **42** (5), 539–52.

CHAPTER TWO

Business as Usual is Not the Answer to Society's Problems[1]

N. Craig Smith, INSEAD and Halina Ward, IIED

Britain is a leader in the field of corporate social responsibility (CSR), and home to many of its foremost thinkers, campaigners and practitioners. Yet many of these experts believe CSR is at a turning point and may be facing a quiet death.

Worldwide practices have long been shaped, in good and bad ways, by the experiences of UK companies, non-governmental organizations and governments. The exploits of the East India Company, for instance, still negatively colour Indian attitudes to foreign investment. In contrast, the Lever soap factory at Port Sunlight, opened in 1884, was widely emulated as an alternative model of industrial development.

The launch of the Body Shop in 1976 showed there were market rewards for good CSR through consumerism with a conscience. Meanwhile, incidents such as the standoff between Greenpeace and Shell over the Brent Spar oil platform disposal in 1995 triggered fresh concerns about the accountability of both companies and campaign groups.

Pressure has steadily built for responsible business practices, be they in the sourcing of clothes or the provision of essential medicines. Kim Howells' appointment in 2000 as the world's first CSR minister seemed to herald a new era. Yet, for all its success, CSR has become a troublesome term that is actively avoided by many companies and campaigners. This is because there is little consensus on what CSR is; what its long-term outcomes should be (from 'ending global poverty' or 'sustainable development' to 'better financial performance'); or who should do what to achieve those ends. CSR has become discredited among its disciples.

There are signs of a deep malaise. In companies, CSR all too often sits in the corporate ghetto of public affairs, estranged from the heart of a business. Privately, specialists within leading companies complain of slow progress because of customer apathy.

The wobble extends to government. Margaret Hodge was recently appointed as the sixth UK CSR minister in as many years. Governments in the United Kingdom and overseas still focus on making companies realize that socially responsible business is profitable. But many campaign groups, such as the Core Coalition, want to see worthy words backed by hard laws on corporate accountability and the duties of directors.

CSR is at a crossroads. The way it heads is partly dependent on external events: the growing importance of China and India; the implications of outsourcing workforces to middle- or low-income countries; or the global security environment. But fundamentally, its future depends on the interaction of two factors. First, what business believes it 'ought' to do, which is set by both the profitability and moral acceptability of certain practices. And second, by what government says business 'must' do.

Governments, in theory, prefer a 'light touch'. Ideally, minimal market intervention would be coupled with a big commitment to sustainable development from business and consumers.

Such a scenario seems unlikely for now. Examples of bad practice – the Bhopal tragedy, failures of oil majors in the Niger Delta and corporate inaction on climate change – show that the pure business case is still too weak. But consumers and governments seem unwilling to do more and campaign groups acting alone cannot create anything more than islands of 'good practice'.

Many business leaders and non-governmental organizations are looking to the government to break this double bind by offering a clear policy framework. This inevitably means more intervention and more regulation. Trade associations, such as the CBI employers group, should pay heed and reform their lowest common denominator approach to issues ranging from mandatory company reporting on social issues to environmental regulation. Failure to do so will invite protests from members.

Leading businesses, in turn, need to raise their voices and act. Rather than passively wait for a socially responsible business case to emerge, they need to build one that tries to address challenges such as climate change and sustainable development. CSR is a term in flux that may wither in time. But its spirit – understanding business as part of society – will survive. And we can be sure that 'business as usual' will be no answer to the pressing issues of our time. CSR is dead . . . long live CSR!

NOTE

1. Originally published by the *Financial Times* 2006. © N. Craig Smith and Halina Ward.

PART TWO

STRATEGY

CHAPTER THREE

Corporate Responsibility in Strategy

Andrew M. Pettigrew, Saïd Business School, University of Oxford, UK

Corporate social responsibility (CSR) is a familiar phrase in management discourse that means different things to different people. CSR is a rallying cry and value crusade for optimists seeking to correct the business and environmental excesses of some corporations, as well as being used as a tactical ploy to protect and enhance the reputations of firms. *The Economist* has also famously dismissed CSR as 'completely stupid rhetoric' (Crook, 2005). Thankfully, CSR is also emerging as a legitimate area of scholarly and policy interest that warrants sustained attention.

In a recent academic review of the strategic implications of CSR, McWilliams, Siegal and Wright (2006) note the numerous definitions and dimensions of CSR and argue that the resultant ambiguities and complexities are making theoretical development and measurement difficult: 'we define CSR as situations where the firm goes beyond compliance and engages in actions that appear to further some social good, beyond the interests of the firm and that which is required by law' (McWilliams, Siegal and Wright, 2006, p. 1).

These same authors also note the multi-dimensional character of CSR, referring to activities ranging from the incorporation of social characteristics into firm products and processes, through the adoption of progressive human resource management practices, to achieving higher levels of environmental performance. Husted and De Jesus Salazar (2006) approach CSR from an explicitly cost benefit analysis under three scenarios concerning the firm's desire to engage in CSR: altruism, coerced egoism and the strategic use of CSR. They define altruism as firms sincerely wishing to be socially responsible without regard to the bottom line, where coerced egoism is defined as firms acting in a socially responsible manner only when compelled by regulation. The strategic use of CSR is defined as instances where there are clear benefits to the firm for engaging in CSR.

Lenssen *et al.* (2009) describe CSR as a 'contested term', and in a much quoted article in *The Economist*, Davis (2005) laments the tactical and defensive use of CSR. But whatever the definitional and motivational uncertainties, can the terrain that appears to underline CSR be construed as a strategic concern of firms? Here Lenssen *et al.* (2007) make a solid case in the affirmative. Building on the earlier stakeholder theory of Freeman (1984) and Donaldson and Preston (1995), Lenssen *et al.* (2007) argue that strategy is the link between the company and the entire market and non-market (social, environmental, political and cultural) environment, in which the firm is in dynamic interaction with a diverse set of stakeholders ranging from customers, employers, suppliers, government and NGOs, and competitors as competitors and collaborators. Lenssen *et al.* (2007) argue that these stakeholder linkages are an essential part of the assets that firms need to compete and collaborate in the modern world. Through these relationships, trust and legitimacy are built such that firms can strategically manage the choices and changes that occur at the nexus of market and non-market contexts. This portrayal of the strategically engaged firm in its business, economic, social and political contexts warrants a more inclusive object and descriptor than the term CSR. CSR now has a legacy of partiality, value contamination and exclusivity that makes it a poor base on which to build the intellectual structure of business and society relationships.

The phrase 'business and society' has a number of scholarly and practical benefits over CSR. First, it captures the meta-level concerns of how businesses impact on societies and vice versa. Second, compared to CSR, it is value neutral. Third, it is not only more intellectually inclusive, but also reaches out to the complete range of Social Sciences that will be necessary to truly develop the interdisciplinary domain of business and society.

But what are the elements of the new analytical vocabulary that can help to uncover key features of business and society relationships? My suggestion is that we need to move out from the 'R' word of responsibility to include some other key words, themes and questions that will open up the limited domain of CSR and provide a better analytical platform to understand and act upon the strategic management of business and society relationships. In navigating the landscape of business and society we can advance the field through a concern with five key words and issues:

- The POWER of the modern corporation
- The LEGITIMACY of the modern corporation
- The RESPONSIBILITY of the modern corporation
- The GOVERNANCE of the modern corporation
- The REGULATION of the modern corporation

POWER OF AND IN THE MODERN CORPORATION

Acquiring and using power is one of the central engines of human existence and yet the empirical study of power relationships of and in organizations is one of the most neglected areas of management inquiry. Sociologists of class and elites have, of course, long been interested in the domination of institutions in society by political, business and military elites (Mills, 1956; Scott, 1997). This tradition has also spun off a connectable literature on business elites and networks of interlocking directors (Mizruchi, 1992; Useem, 1984), but little of this literature has penetrated managerial thought and action. And yet senior executives are constantly taking actions that have powerful consequences. Firms make explicit choices to win and maintain power in certain product markets and geographical locations. In common parlance we think of firms having market power, financial power and even in some more limited spheres socio-political power. Some large corporations have equivalent or even greater economic assets than some nation states. For example, when BP acquired Amoco in 2000, they moved from fifth to being the second largest oil and gas company, and their move precipitated similar acquisition behaviour by their competitors. When the CEO of BP goes to China, he is likely to meet very senior political figures up to and including the President of China. When BP enters Angola, which is a notoriously weak performing country, it may be obliged to take on some of the social responsibilities of the state. In these ways, BP may have the potential to exercise some power even if it chooses not to do so.

Power is, of course, a relational and thereby a social concept (Pettigrew, 1973; Pettigrew and McNulty, 1995; 1998). One can have power only over something, whether an organization or a set of people. This relational view of power is a natural line of inquiry in addressing the relationships between business organizations and the multiple societies in which they ply their trade. Prior to the pervasive effects of globalization, it might have seemed possible to conduct such a power analysis in some relatively simple dyadic form with questions being asked, for example, about the relative power of multinationals and states in different contexts. However, contemporary theorizing about power in the globalized world (Beck, 2005; 2008) suggests a more complex view of contemporary society. In this view new features include:

> interrelatedness and interdependence of people across the globe, growing inequalities in a global space, emergence of supranational organizations in the area of the economy (multinational corporations), politics (non-state actors such as the International Monetary Fund, World Bank and World Trade Organization), Civil Society, advocacy social movements of global scope such as Amnesty International and Greenpeace . . . and new types and profiles of global risk, new forms of warfare, globalized crime and terrorism.
>
> Beck, 2008, p. 794

The effect of such developments is to erode clear borders separating markets, states, cultures, corporations and people leading to more permeable flows of information, capital and risk. In this world, the powerlessness of states is as evident as their power and multinationals may exercise power not only in investing, but also in threatening to withdraw their investments. As Lenssen *et al.* (2007) rightly argued, current strategic management theory is poorly equipped to sense and analyse such developments with or without the explicit use of power as a mobilizing intellectual concept.

Meanwhile current thinking in the more limited domain of CSR is quite silent about the power dynamics between large corporations, states, supranational organizations, NGOs and national institutional bodies.

Power *within* organizations has a stronger legacy than the power *of* large organizations. For a recent treatment of this topic, see Clegg and Hardy (2006). The within-organization treatment of power is, of course, central to the executive capacity to build coalitions around the key strategic choices and changes necessary to form and execute strategies for business and society relations, and I will return to this issue later.

THE LEGITIMACY OF THE MODERN CORPORATION

Legitimacy is the second core social science concept that may be profitably brought into the analysis of business and society relationships. Here again one finds a similar pattern of neglect and missed opportunities evident in the treatment of power. A recent review of elements of the literature on legitimacy in organizations by Deephouse and Suchman (2008), notes that the theoretical literature is a good deal more extensive than empirical studies of legitimacy. It is also currently rare to find studies of the legitimization and delegitimization processes of corporations in the literature on CSR and business and society relationships. This is surprising given the range of contemporary examples of highly visible corporations such as BP, Shell, Exxon and Niki who have all received well publicized challenges to their legitimacy.

Suchman (1995, p. 574) has offered the following broad definition: 'legitimacy is a generalized perception or assumption that the actions of an entity are desirable, proper or appropriate within some socially constructed system of norms, values, beliefs and definitions'. The possession of legitimacy may insulate a firm from certain kinds of external pressures. The loss of legitimacy may mean that a firm's licence to operate in certain domains of action is impaired, or in extreme situations lost altogether. Thus the consequences of legitimacy and illegitimacy are real and can impact survival, access to resources and stakeholder support. The fact that legitimacy is eminently connectable to prestige and reputation should make it a concern in the strategic management of any enterprise. Ansoff (1979) was an early advocate of bringing legitimacy into strategic management discourse arguing that one of his dimensions of strategy concerns the societal legitimacy of the firm. More recently Freeman (1984), Davis (2005) and Lenssen *et al.* (2007) have either implicitly or explicitly attempted to bring legitimacy into the perspective of business and society relationships, but the potential of this concept in strategic analysis is still underplayed.

Legitimacy is, of course, more readily known when it is absent than present. This makes the study of processes of delegitimization of corporations by regulatory bodies of the state, or by supranational bodies, or even by trade unions, advocacy bodies and NGOs, particularly interesting and valuable. Regrettably few such studies exist in the CSR and business and society literatures and the language of delegitimization is rarely to be found in the strategic management literature. Given that large corporations now have to make combined economic, political and social strategies and decisions, and in the relational and global world of stakeholder management they are heavily dependent on negotiation and trust, they are also dependent on legitimization. Although firms may admit to having public relations and reputational strategies, do they also make strategic choices and changes in the wider and deeper domain of legitimation? Many may not admit so, feeling that their mere presence and market power, and legal protection, guarantees legitimacy. But we do not know. The detailed comparative analysis of the legitimation strategies of globalizing firms awaits the analysis of the field of strategic management.

THE RESPONSIBILITY OF THE MODERN CORPORATION

Language can be an analytical prison and a liberating force. The thesis of this chapter is that by complementing the 'R' word of responsibility with power, legitimacy, governance and regulation, we will open up new lines of inquiry in the field of business and society. However, there is still a place for firm responsibilities in the strategic management of business and society relations. Given the developed treatment of firm responsibilities in the CSR and related literature, it is hardly appropriate for me to dwell on this theme.

In a recent treatment of the strategic implications of CSR, McWilliams, Siegal and Wright (2006) offer an insightful statement of a responsibility related research agenda. In summary they assert that an appropriate research agenda should include more work on

> defining CSR, identifying institutional differences in CSR across countries, determining the motivations for CSR, describing CSR strategies, modelling the effects of CSR on the firm and stakeholder groups, determining the effects of leadership and corporate culture on CSR on the firm and stakeholder groups, measuring the demand for CSR, measuring the costs of CSR and assessing the current knowledge base.
>
> McWilliams, Siegal and Wright, 2006, p. 8

Many studies focusing on responsibility issues have attempted to answer the question 'do firms do well by doing good'? McWilliam, Siegal and Wright (2006) confirm that the results of these studies so far show a very inconsistent picture. Such inconsistencies they contend may be a product of inconsistency in defining CSR, inconsistency in defining and measuring firm performance, imprecision in samples and research design and failing to study the performance effects of CSR investment over sufficient time. A further weakness of the research tradition in CSR is the scope of such work. So far there are few studies of large samples of firms of different sizes within and across industry sectors. Such 'mapping studies' are badly needed to map the terrain of the emergence of 'responsible behaviour' and to counterbalance existing work, which is often of exceptional firms in exceptional industries. Given that the strategic management of many firms is now played out on the international if not a globalizing stage, and that business norms and standards, legal and regulatory frameworks and stakeholder demands for CSR do vary substantially across nations and regions, it is equally crucial that such mapping studies are carried out in an international comparative mode. Finally, an interest in the strategic management of CSR must go way beyond the senior executive corridors of firms. Responsibility aspirations echoed in glossy documents from the top and centre of firms may not be so easily executed at operational levels. If management practice is to be influenced by future CSR research agendas, that research must capture the strategic and the operational execution of responsibility initiatives at firm and related levels.

THE GOVERNANCE OF THE MODERN CORPORATION

Issues to do with the purpose, values, control and strategic leadership of firms are also intimately connectable to the wider concern with businesses and society relations, and therefore firm governance matters are a legitimate part of the strategic management of business and society relations.

This is not the place to effect even a cursory treatment of the now vast literature on corporate governance matters. Instead, I simply justify the inclusion of governance in our business and society agenda by pointing to some of the strategic choices made in governance matters that can affect the quality of business and society relationships. One might argue that the central governance question for the firm is who controls its destiny? This is most often portrayed as the agency problem of maintaining shareholder power and influence over the executive agents of the firm. We know that this question is central and that it is played out quite differently in the varying institutional, legal and business contexts of different nations (Charkham, 1994). We also know that strategic choices about the purpose and values of the firm can be fateful for a firm's business success and societal legitimacy. There is ample evidence to show that shareholder value maximization as a corporate value had a profound impact on business cultures in North America and parts of Europe in the 1990s. This value choice was buttressed in turn by executive compensation and share option packages, which distorted firm performance requirements and directly or indirectly led to some of the corporate excesses now all too visible in parts of North American and European business life.

Lenssen (2007) and others have juxtaposed the value choice of shareholder value maximization against the stakeholder model of corporate relations. Lenssen also argues for some of the virtues of firms seeking to maximize two outcomes: competitiveness and social cohesion. He concludes that the relationship between these two values is complex, that there are likely to be real tradeoffs and that social cohesion does not always enhance competitiveness, but it can do so. Behind this view is a further crucial choice about the purpose of the modern corporation. Is the purpose of the firm to combine social and economic development, or is it there to maximize profit?

Beyond our concern with the purpose and values of corporations, our interest in governance also takes us into the board as an instrument of both control and strategic leadership. Here there is also a long-standing fascination with the agency problems of boards most often wrapped up in choices about the structure and composition of those boards. This established agenda now needs complementing with a wider discussion about the purpose, conduct and effectiveness of boards (Pettigrew and McNulty, 1995; 1998). Is the board in agency terms a protector of shareholder interests alone, or does it have a wider remit and set of responsibilities? The plethora of company legislation and codes of conduct mean it is now rare in the Anglo Saxon business context for the boards of large corporations to be merely 'decorations on the organizational Christmas tree'. But are boards capable of moving beyond their control function to exercise real corporate direction and value enhancement? Available evidence of this aspect of board conduct and performance is still sparse, but work completed a few years ago in a large sample of the top 500 plcs in the UK indicated that there was considerable variation in board capacity for strategizing (McNulty and Pettigrew, 1998).

THE REGULATION OF THE MODERN CORPORATION

The fifth and final domain concept to frame the conceptual and executive space referred to as business and society gives attention to the regulation of the modern corporation. Regulation is normally seen as a legislative concern of the state. This responsibility can be approached proactively to shape corporate behaviour on matters of governance, business practices and environmental care, but often states are reactive in regulatory matters responding only after manifest corporate excesses. A notable recent example of this is the Sarbanes Oxley governance legislation, which of course does not only impact US based and owned corporations but also foreign multinationals investing in the United States. Legislative regulation is highly societally embedded. Although well aware of the moral lapses in Enron and World Com that precipitated the Sarbanes Oxley legislation, the UK has persisted with its cultural predisposition to shape the governance patterns of firms more by codes of practice than formal legal requirements.

The research and executive agenda in the sphere of regulation as it relates to our inclusive definition of business and society relations is immense. Executive action here is, of course, well practised. Firms throughout the world employ political lobbyists and internal regulatory specialists to limit, thwart and shape the legislative actions of states. They also employ executive and staff officers to engage directly with regulators once they are empowered by legislation. This whole domain of business, political and legal action by corporations is a crucial area of strategic management that warrants greater understanding. Under what circumstances and in what dimensions of business society relations do states act proactively and reactively? What role do other stakeholders such as advocacy movements play in such processes and what are some of the conditions that are receptive to advocacy strategies? How are these power mobilization strategies played out in different nation states and regions? And what are the performance and reputational consequences for firms of different regulatory regimes in different domains of business and society matters? These are fundamental questions of academic and executive concern, which should be at the heart of the strategic management of business in contemporary society.

So far I have portrayed an inclusive agenda of business and society around the apparently separable elements of power, legitimacy, responsibility, governance and regulation. The reality of life, however, is that these five elements are not played out in isolation. Excesses of corporate power may impair hard won legitimacy and reputation and attract the delegitimization strategies of indignant stakeholders. Fuelled by an informed and sceptical media, citizenry may incite passive politicians to legislate and regulate firms who claimed their own ethical standards were sufficient curbs on their otherwise benign behaviour. Firms may use impression management to contain attempts to regulate and these actions suggest that the politics of strategic management represent a core area of academic concern and executive action in business and society relations. If this entirely new domain of scholarly inquiry in strategy appears, it will complement the existing concerns with the competitive advantage and resource-based theories of the firm.

ORGANIZING AND CHANGING THE FIRM FOR BUSINESS AND SOCIAL IMPACT

In a range of carefully argued papers, Abrahamson (1991; 1996) uses the language of fads, trends and band wagons to characterize management techniques as fashion commodities. Unlike many aesthetic and cultural forms, Abrahamson argues that management techniques emerge and are justified through a combination of rational efficiency (sound means to achieve important ends) and progressive (new as well as improved relative to older management) techniques. Crucially, Abrahamson also argues that management fashions are not cosmetic and trivial. They have shaped and continue to shape the behaviour of managers all over the world and can have massive – sometimes helpful, but also questionable – impacts on organizations and people.

Over the past 30 or 40 years we have seen the rise and fall of many management issues that have sought to become integral to the strategic management concerns of corporations. Few of these have made it on to the strategic agenda and stayed there. Not even the addition of the word 'strategy' and its implications for 'generalship' and significance has empowered information systems strategy and human resources strategy into the bloodstream of many firms. Human resource matters perennially appear on the strategy agenda after the fact of business strategy change when the human resource consequences are manifestly obvious to the sceptical senior executive. The fact that the rise of human resource issues is often associated with the value crusades of particular CEOs is sufficient warning for embryonic fields such as CSR and business and society relations. CEOs come and go: the average tenure in post of a CEO in the top 350 corporations in the UK is currently 4.3 years. CEO support is little guarantee of sustained strategic attention.

Of course, the perennial bureaucratic response by organizations to a new management phenomenon is to create a new core unit of specialists to own it. Thus we have seen the rise and fall of cadres of messianic specialists associated with organization development, quality improvement, process engineering and latterly knowledge management. Exclusive specialists often end up being powerless and politically isolated. If they choose to own the new language and the issues associated with them, they may in turn inhibit others from owning the issues and both the specialists and their issues fall off the organizational stage. Paradoxically, the activity of human resource management is often most strategic and within the organizational bloodstream when it is owned by senior and middle executive management with human resource specialists confined to roles as expert helpers, facilitators and problem solvers. The lesson here is that the activity supersedes the function. The function is at the service of the activity. The activity has become business-legitimate and the function merely business-credible.

But what are some of the lessons from the above political analysis for the fate of business and society as a rising corporate issue? The first lesson is that context matters (Pettigrew, 1985; 1992; 1998; 2002). There are bound to be receptive and non-receptive business contexts for the rise of business and society matters. It is no accident that early corporate movers in this field were the big energy, metal extractive and pharmaceutical firms. But receptive contexts still have to be mobilized and this requires corporate leadership to sense the issue and place it on and up the organizational agenda. But integrated and affirmative action at the top requires value debate and some level of senior executive consensus. This is likely to require focusing and persistence from senior executives and a commitment 'to walk the talk'. Early executive action needs to be sensitive to receptive context for change within the firm. Early failures can be negative and regressive and take firms back beyond their starting point, and at speed. Early successes, on the other hand, can be proclaimed and aid in the turning of cynics and sceptics.

Crucially, the issue of business and society has to be propelled out of the boardroom and executive salon and into the operating behaviour and managers of the firm. This is easier said than done as the advocates of many cultural change programmes in firms will testify. One approach to taking a rising issue such as business and society into the firm is to adopt a diffusion model of change with receptive contexts for change in the firms chosen as first generation sites. With high resources committed there and the possibilities of early successes to proclaim, the second generation sites can then be built up for subsequent penetration of the new ideas. Incentives and disincentives are also crucial mechanisms to embed new ideas in the hearts, minds and actions of operating managers. This may require the explicit change of performance management systems to reward managers for business successful initiatives in the business and society area.

Novel ventures also have to be labelled in some culturally appropriate manner for the firm. Thus CSR may work in some contexts and business and society in others. Here again there may be virtues in the more inclusive and value neutral phrase of business and society. Certainly the sheer scope of the present definition of business and society with the five themes of power, legitimacy, responsibility, governance and regulation can provide many more points of contact with the strategic concerns of the firm than the more limited agenda implicit in CSR.

REFERENCES

Abrahamson, E. (1991) Managerial fads and fashions, *Academy of Management Review*, **16**, 586–612.

Abrahamson, E. (1996) Management fashion, *Academy of Management Review*, **21** (1), 254–285.

Ansoff, H.I. (1979) The changing shape of strategic problem, *Journal of General Management*, **4** (4), 42–58.

Beck, U. (2005) *Power in the Global Age*, Policy Press, Cambridge, MA.

Beck, U. (2008) Reframing power in the globalised world, *Organizational Studies*, **5**, 793–804.

Charkham, J. (1994) *Keeping Good Company: A Study of Corporate Governance in Five Countries*, Clarendon Press, Oxford.

Clegg, S.R. and Hardy, C. (2006) Some dare call it power, in *The Sage Handbook of Organization Studies*, (eds S.R. Clegg, C. Hardy, T.B. Lawrence and W.R. Nord), Sage, London, pp. 754–75.

Crook, C. (2005) The good company, *The Economist*, 22 January.

Davis, I. (2005) The biggest contract, *The Economist*, 28 May.

Deephouse, D.L. and Suchman, M. (2008) Legitimacy in organizational institutionalism, in *The Sage Handbook of Organizational Institutionalism*, (eds R. Greenwood, C. Oliver, K. Sahlin and R. Suddaby), Sage, London, pp. 49–77.

Donaldson, T. and Preston, L.E. (1995) The stakeholder theory of the corporation: Concepts, evidence and implications, *Academy of Management Review*, **20** (1), 65–91.

Freeman, R.E. (1984) *Strategic Management: A Stakeholder Approach*, Pitman, Boston, MA.

Husted, B.W. and De Jesus Salazar, J. (2006) Taking Friedman seriously: maximising profits and social performance, *Journal of Management Studies*, **43** (1), 75–91.

Lenssen, G. (2007) Towards a strategic approach to business in society, Presentation to *European Academy of Business in Society*, St Petersburg, 2 July 2007.

Lenssen, G., Perrin, F., Tencati, A. and Lacy, P. (2007) Corporate responsibility, strategic management and the stakeholder view of the firm, *Corporate Governance: The International Journal of Business in Society*, **7** (4), 344–54.

McNulty, T. and Pettigrew, A.M. (1998) Strategists on the board, *Organization Studies*, **20** (1), 47–74.

McWilliams, A., Siegal, D.S. and Wright, P.M. (2006) Guest editors' introduction, Corporate social responsibility, strategic implications, *Journal of Management Studies*, **43** (1), 1–18.

Mills, C.W. (1956) *The Power Elite*, Oxford University Press, New York.

Mizruchi, M.S. (1992) *The Structure of Corporate Political Action: Interfirm Relations and their Consequences*, Harvard University Press, Cambridge, MA.

Pettigrew, A.M. (1973) *The Politics of Organizational Decision Making*, Tavistock, London. Republished in 2001 by Routledge.

Pettigrew, A.M. (1985) *The Awakening Giant: Continuity and Change in ICI*, Blackwell, Oxford.

Pettigrew, A.M. (1992) Receptive and non-receptive contexts for change, in *Shaping Strategic Change: The Case of the NHS*, (eds A.M. Pettigrew, E. Ferlie and L. McKee), Sage, London, pp. 268–99.

Pettigrew, A.M. (1998) Success and failure in corporate transformation initiatives, in *Information Technology and Organizational Transformation*, (eds R.D. Galliers and W.R.J. Baets), John Wiley & Sons, Ltd, Chichester, pp. 271–89.

Pettigrew, A.M. (2002) Invited report for the Prime Minister's Office, 10 Downing Street, London. Available from Saïd Business School, University of Oxford.

Pettigrew, A.M. and McNulty, T. (1995) Power and influence in and around the boardroom, *Human Relation*, **48** (8), 845–73.

Pettigrew, A.M. and McNulty, T. (1998) Sources and uses of power in the boardroom, *European Journal of Works and Organizational Psychology*, **7** (2), 197–214.

Scott, J. (1997) *Corporate Business and Capitalist Classes*, Oxford University Press, Oxford.

Suchman, M.C. (1995) Managing legitimacy: Strategic and institutional approaches, *Academy of Management Review*, **20**, 571–610.

Useem, M. (1984*) The Inner Circle*, Oxford University Press, New York.

CHAPTER FOUR

Microsoft: Bringing Technology to the Aging Population[1]

Maurizio Zollo, Bocconi University and Robert J. Crawford, INSEAD

INTRODUCTION

In the autumn of 2001, Rob Sinclair and Bonnie Kearney were waiting outside the office of Bill Gates, the Chairman and founder of Microsoft. They were there to make a 'Bill G' presentation – that is, to pitch an idea that could perhaps set the corporation in a new direction, specifically targeting people with disabilities and the elderly. It could be, they knew, a make or break moment in their Microsoft careers: if Gates liked what he heard, they would gain the authority to embed 'accessibility' tools into the new Windows software platform (Windows XP 2003) currently under development, which would facilitate the use of personal computers (PC) by customers with certain disabilities as well as encourage the further development of an embryonic ecosystem of specialized software vendors to develop tailored assistive technology solutions on the XP Platform. This was a mission that they passionately felt was both the right thing to do and made eminent business sense in view of the rapidly aging populations in the industrialized world. However, if Gates didn't like what they had to say, or found holes in the logic of their business plan, his dismissal promised to be blunt and brutal. It was probably their only shot to present their case.

They had had very little time to prepare their presentation. Sinclair, an engineer and user-interface designer who was newly installed as Program Manager for Accessibility in the Windows business unit, had sent a query e-mail to Gates only three weeks before. To their surprise, Gates responded immediately, asking Sinclair and Kearney to schedule a meeting for that month. 'We had expected him,' Sinclair said, 'to ask us to come in about six months, when we would have our data together. But he called our bluff.' Although happy that Gates was receptive to their idea, Kearney, an MBA graduate in business development with significant marketing experience, knew that they would have to scramble to come up with a presentation that was provocative, yet convincing and defensible under tough questioning. 'We were in our offices until midnight for the next three weeks sweating bullets,' she recalled, 'massaging data that everyone knew was incomplete.' She took a deep breath as they were ushered into Gates' office. They had one hour.

BACKGROUND

While a student at Harvard in December, 1974, Bill Gates telephoned Ed Roberts, the President of MITS in Albuquerque, New Mexico. He and a friend, Gates informed Roberts, had invented a BASIC computer language for the MITS Altair 8080, which was the first 'personal computer' kit for hobbyists. Could they license it along with each Altair kit, Gates asked, to customers for a royalty fee? It was an audacious proposal, because not only had Gates and his friend Paul Allen invented no such thing, but also they neither owned an Altair kit nor did they even know the technical specifications for its Intel 8080 chip. Sceptical of their claim, Roberts replied that whoever demonstrated a working BASIC language would win the account: Gates and Allen were in competition, he told them, with 50 other computer whizzes who had already made the same claim. Once Gates and Allen obtained the 8080 specifications manual, which they used to create a simulation of the chip on a Harvard mainframe computer, the two of them hunkered down for eight weeks to write the first BASIC for a microcomputer. The resulting 'software', which immediately won over Roberts, was the first application of what would become Microsoft BASIC. Gates was 19 years old and Allen 21 (Wallace and Erickson, 1992, pp. 67, 74–80, 110).

THE EARLY MICROSOFT

Paul Allen went to work for MITS as software director and Gates began to establish a business, which they named *Microsoft* from 'microcomputer software', to serve an entirely new market – personal computer languages. As the company founders, Gates and Allen shared a vision that virtually every home and office would eventually have a PC, all operating with their software. To run Microsoft full time, Gates dropped out of Harvard in January, 1977, and moved to Albuquerque; Allen later quit MITS and joined him as a partner and co-owner. Their business quickly expanded beyond the Altair as competing brands of personal computers emerged, including the Tandy from Radio Shack and the Apple II computer; they were also called upon to program BASIC into a number of other electronic devices. All along, Gates' goal was to gain market share, in effect setting the software standard for most, if not all, PC users. As a true believer who intimately knew the product, Gates was the principal salesman. Allen concentrated on technical development (Wallace and Erickson, 1992, pp. 109–110, 119–120, 153).

Perhaps as a result of hiring many of his programmers straight out of university, Microsoft's offices (and later the campus in Redmond, WA) took on the look and feel of a college campus; that is, an informal and a freewheeling intellectual atmosphere with 'late hours, loud music, walls full of junk, anything goes dress, Coke, adrenaline, unbuttoned behaviour' (Manes and Andrews, 1993, cited p. 103). Employees tended to be very young with a programmer or engineering mentality; they designed their products for tech-savvy customers – predominantly males in their early 20s – like themselves, a kind of fellowship for computer adepts. As the then Microsoft General Manager Sherri Bealkowski put it: 'Microsoft employees think "we're typical, so if we can do it, anyone can". That can be a problem because they keep adding features.'

Microsoft hired the brightest programmers with demonstrated practical abilities. Employees were also expected to work extremely long hours as a team toward a common goal, not as individualists. Gates encouraged them to develop their entrepreneurial passions, forcefully advancing their own ideas of useful products for new markets. Gates oversaw everything, gaining the reputation of a harsh and challenging critic with a relentless drive for excellence, whether to beat the competition or out of fear of falling behind in such a fast-changing industry. As the sole remaining founder after

Allen's departure in 1983, Gates remained deeply involved in both technical and business details as well as the general direction of company strategy. Nonetheless, as the principal revenue generators, Microsoft's product groups increasingly became the seats of decision-making power (Wallace and Erickson, 1992, pp. 125–129).[2]

By the early 1990s, Microsoft was perceived to have become the dominant player in the software industry, both in the disk operating system (called 'Windows', which contained the base code) and 'applications', such as Word or PowerPoint. Competitors, who had to share portions of their code with Microsoft to ensure compatibility with Windows, quickly brought this to the attention of anti-trust officials. Although Gates insisted that he had erected a 'Chinese Wall' between Microsoft's applications division and its Operating System's Group, it was not enough to deter the Federal Trade Commission (FTC) from opening a probe into the company for anti-competitive practices that purportedly hurt consumers. There was speculation about the imminent breakup of Microsoft into separate companies for the operating system and applications markets, similar to the dismantling of AT&T (Wallace and Erickson, 1992, pp. 305, 397–398). For their part, defenders of Microsoft argued that it was winning because it was better and smarter, presenting its customers with superior products at bargain prices (Stross, 1997, pp. 37, 176–192). The FTC probe led to a five-year anti-trust lawsuit, brought by the US Department of Justice and nine states; it ended in 2002 in Microsoft's favour in exchange for certain concessions (*The Economist*, 2002, p. 77).[3] In a similar anti-trust action led by the European Commission, Microsoft was found guilty in 2004 of breaking competition rules in the EU, resulting in a record-breaking fine of 497 million Euros (Buck, 2008, p. 15).

In 1995, a related concern was a lawsuit on behalf of disabled users of Microsoft products. Because of certain changes in US laws,[4] advocates for people with disabilities accused Microsoft of neglecting to include accessibility technologies in its latest products, which were on the verge of converting to a graphic-user interface. This change would thereby introduce a series of potential accessibility issues into everyday computer use, in effect, replacing the keyboard-based code entries with visual cues activated by the mouse clicks; disabled users feared they would be unable to read or physically operate the new system. If successful, their lawsuit would have halted or delayed the release of the Windows 95 Operating System. Once Microsoft promised to address these issues, the lawsuits were dropped. However, because the solutions were only partially successful, the issue of accessibility remained a concern for the leadership of Microsoft, which many felt should be attacked proactively.

THE MICROSOFT SENIOR INITIATIVE

In 1996, Craig Spiezle, a Microsoft marketing manager in the original equipment manufacturers (OEM) department, was investigating the markets in which computer hardware sales were low; they included Hispanics, blue collar workers and seniors. What really caught his attention was the third category, seniors, because their reluctance to use PCs, he said, 'was not because of income or educational levels. It was a generational thing, an attitude towards new technologies.' He had witnessed this from a personal perspective: his father, an architect, had recently passed his practice on to Spiezle's brother, in large part because he did not want to learn how to use PCs for his designs. 'At first,' Spiezle recalled, 'I thought it was just my dad, but then I realized that millions of older people worldwide were intimidated by computers.' With a little more research, Spiezle concluded that this represented a huge potential market, not only in view of the growth of the aging population, but also in the requirements of employers who increasingly needed to hire computer-literate seniors as their employees retired. After describing his findings, Spiezle was appointed director of emerging markets in 1997 with a mandate to create and run the Microsoft Senior Initiative; its purpose was to bridge the 'digital and generational divide'.

Essentially a one-man shop, Spiezle's operation was moved to the COO's office, where he was given a budget and almost complete freedom. Spiezle set himself two goals: he would begin by reaching out to seniors and the stakeholders concerned about their welfare, and then work to raise awareness within Microsoft regarding the opportunities emerging in the seniors market. For the outreach, he hired Joe Dobler, a marketer like himself, and they began to meet with representatives of non-governmental organizations, first with local representatives and then nationally.

They also sponsored partnership programmes with local authorities, including grants in cooperation with local governments. For example, in 1999, Spiezle made an in-kind donation of over US$125 000 to the government of West Virginia in the form of 40 multi-media computers with colour monitors, Microsoft software and curriculum and consulting support; the grant contributed to the creation of a 'technology training initiative for older adults', in which seniors would be instructed in the use of a number of Microsoft products. Spiezle and Dobler eventually helped to set up over 150 similar centres, prepared a number of training materials and continued their research into the potential markets for products geared specifically to seniors. It was the beginning of a sustained community investment effort by the Legal and Corporate Affairs Division of Microsoft (LA), that is, Microsoft's first corporate social responsibility (CSR) programme for the elderly.

Spiezle also approached Microsoft product groups, with whom he discussed a number of potential projects designed specifically for seniors, including web TV, Internet appliances and the like. Although many Microsoft managers expressed interest, Spiezle found it hard to get traction. 'There were so many competing priorities,' he explained. 'We knew it was the right thing to do, but it never entered the mainstream of what Microsoft was doing.' Eventually, around 2000, children's education emerged as the strategic priority area of the Microsoft product groups. When he saw that this would be the direction in which many of the product groups were heading, Spiezle decided to leave Microsoft to found his own business, the Age-Light Marketing Consultancy. 'It was clear to me that it was moving in a different direction, towards new products in education,' he explained. 'I was spending my time giving talks to outside groups instead of developing products.' After several years of running AgeLight, which informed companies about the seniors' market segment, Spiezle returned to Microsoft and joined its Technology Care and Safety Group with strategy development responsibilities (see Exhibit 4.1).

EMBEDDING ACCESSIBILITY TOOLS

In 1997, Rob Sinclair joined Microsoft's Human Resources Department as a member of the accessibility group. Having been trained in computer science and human factors design, Sinclair was attuned to the needs of the disabled. PCs, he believed, could provide enormous aid regarding the challenges they faced in their lives – particularly those with poor eyesight, hearing impairments and other communication or motor disorders. Customers with disabilities tended to be older, less technology-oriented than the typical Microsoft customer and in need of highly specialized products. Developing such products, either internally or with outside vendors, was not something Microsoft was accustomed to doing. In particular, it seemed to cut against the youthful culture of the company.

EXHIBIT 4.1 CRAIG SPIEZLE'S PRESS RELEASE EXAMPLE

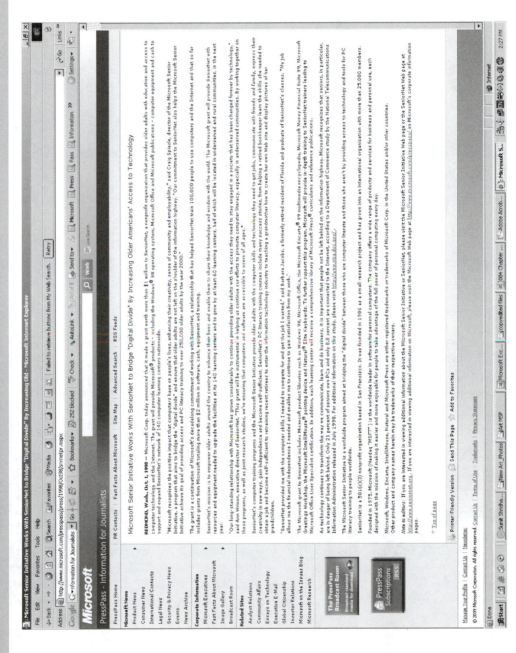

(Continued)

EXHIBIT 4.1 (Continued)

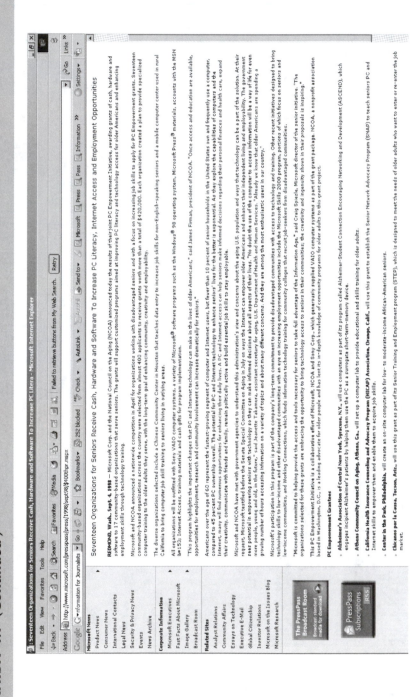

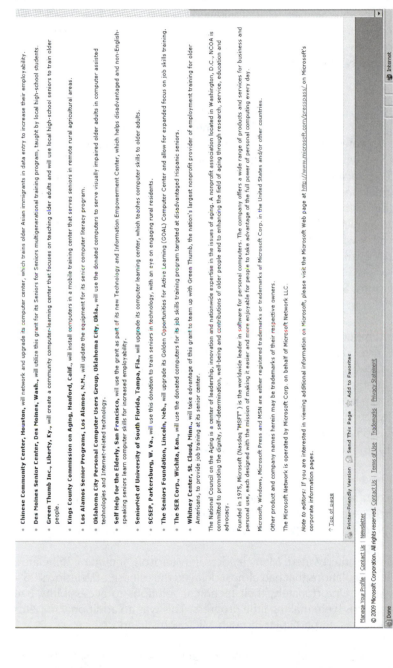

- **Chinese Community Center, Houston,** will network and upgrade its computer center, which trains older Asian immigrants in data entry to increase their employability.

- **Des Moines Senior Center, Des Moines, Wash.,** will utilize this grant for its Seniors for Seniors multigenerational training program, taught by local high-school students.

- **Green Thumb Inc., Liberty, Ky.,** will create a community computer-learning center that focuses on teaching older adults and will use local high-school seniors to train older people.

- **Kings County Commission on Aging, Hanford, Calif.,** will install computers in a mobile training center that serves seniors in remote rural agricultural areas.

- **Los Alamos Senior Programs, Los Alamos, N.M.,** will update the equipment for its senior computer literacy program.

- **Oklahoma City Personal Computer Users Group, Oklahoma City, Okla.,** will use the donated computers to serve visually impaired older adults in computer-assisted technologies and Internet-related technology.

- **Self Help for the Elderly, San Francisco,** will use the grant as part of its new Technology and Information Empowerment Center, which helps disadvantaged and non-English-speaking seniors learn computer skills for increased employability.

- **SeniorNet of University of South Florida, Tampa, Fla.,** will upgrade its computer learning center, which teaches computer skills to older adults.

- **SCSEP, Parkersburg, W. Va.,** will use this donation to train seniors in technology, with an eye on engaging rural residents.

- **The Seniors Foundation, Lincoln, Neb.,** will upgrade its Golden Opportunities for Active Learning (GOAL) Computer Center and allow for expanded focus on job skills training.

- **The SER Corp., Wichita, Kan.,** will use the donated computers for its job skills training program targeted at disadvantaged Hispanic seniors.

- **Whitney Center, St. Cloud, Minn.,** will take advantage of this grant to team up with Green Thumb, the nation's largest nonprofit provider of employment training for older Americans, to provide job training at its senior center.

The National Council on the Aging is a center of leadership, innovation and nationwide expertise in the issues of aging. A nonprofit association located in Washington, D.C., NCOA is committed to promoting the dignity, self-determination, well-being and contributions of older people and to enhancing the field of aging through research, service, education and advocacy.

Founded in 1975, Microsoft (Nasdaq "MSFT") is the worldwide leader in software for personal computers. The company offers a wide range of products and services for business and personal use, each designed with the mission of making it easier and more enjoyable for people to take advantage of the full power of personal computing every day.

Microsoft, Windows, Microsoft Press and MSN are either registered trademarks or trademarks of Microsoft Corp. in the United States and/or other countries.

Other product and company names herein may be trademarks of their respective owners.

The Microsoft Network is operated by Microsoft Corp. on behalf of Microsoft Network LLC.

Note to editors: If you are interested in viewing additional information on Microsoft, please visit the Microsoft Web page at http://www.microsoft.com/presspass/ on Microsoft's corporate information pages.

↑ Top of page

Printer-Friendly Version Send This Page Add to Favorites

Manage Your Profile | Contact Us | Newsletter

'When I started,' Sinclair explained, Microsoft 'designers and engineers made things for people like themselves. They rarely talked to marketing, except once they had finished what they were developing, so there was little customer input. Many of us felt there were huge gaps between our products and customers' needs.' It would, he knew, take an unusual skill set to get these groups to collaborate in any area. Nonetheless, Sinclair felt encouraged by a keynote address that Bill Gates gave in 1998 to a meeting of disability advocates and stakeholders on the Microsoft campus: Gates promised to invest in accessibility technologies for them. The issue of accessibility was, Sinclair concluded, a great opportunity to do good *and* well.

The Issues

Many in Microsoft were arguing that the company should become more consumer-oriented, rather than cater to the preferences of IT professionals. In current practice, most Microsoft products were sold to PC manufacturers (or OEMs), which embedded them as generic features into their PCs – they tended not to be designed in accordance with individual needs, with the exception of certain applications, but according to the expectations of engineers. Not surprisingly, when Sinclair approached Microsoft's business groups, he found it virtually impossible to get their commitment to invest in accessibility products. According to Sinclair, 'I kept hearing "what is Human Resources doing trying to affect my code?".' Though very busy with half a dozen other projects, Sinclair took it as a personal mission to effect a cultural change within the company regarding accessibility. 'It was viewed as a feel good thing,' he said, 'and I wanted to get it mainstreamed into the business.' In order to bolster his credibility with the product groups, Sinclair began to request a post within Windows, from which accessibility had been moved.

As Sinclair saw it, there were a number of problems to overcome. First, Microsoft product groups viewed the accessibility market as 'too limited', perhaps at 10% of the adult population. Moreover, they were not the typical tech-savvy customer, but a group that did not naturally 'take' to PCs. This would require not only an internal sales job for top executives, who had to be convinced that this market was both large and expanding as the population aged, but also a cultural change in the design/engineering mentality of Microsoft. Done correctly, Sinclair believed, it promised to broaden the base of Microsoft customers in time to catch the 'aging boomer' wave, those demanding consumers born between 1946 and 1966, who 'wanted their computers to work as reliably and easily as toasters'.

Second, there was little reliable data available: in the view of Sinclair and others, many advocates for the disabled undermined their case with wildly inflated claims. Somehow, much better data had to be generated on market potential, perhaps even redefining the target population.

Third, legal and technical issues were intertwined. Many leaders in Microsoft, including Bill Gates, were concerned with the disability regulations that had almost delayed the release of Windows 95 – another lawsuit was always possible. Unfortunately, their technical solutions to accessibility had proven wanting and the product groups were making little progress. This was an additional impetus to investing in accessibility technologies, in particular through Microsoft's vendors.

Finally, Microsoft vendors had to provide a wider variety of products in a way that made sense to them economically. As it stood, vendors of accessibility software products were both suspicious of Microsoft's intentions and, as predominantly boutique-style programming houses, found the continuous development of products slow and relatively unprofitable. A more efficient process would have to be developed.

The Business Development Plan

Early in 2000, Sinclair met Bonnie Kearney, a marketing specialist with solid business development experience. Kearney had been hired in 1999 as a product planner, with a mandate to help Microsoft product groups and vendors get their goods to market faster. She too was committed to enhancing the accessibility of PCs, in part because she had studied the trends regarding the aging populations in the industrialized nations. But she also had a personal motive: shortly after she began her job, her mother suffered an aneurism, which severely hindered her ability to speak. 'There had to be some way,' she concluded, 'that we could use technology to make life easier for her.' With this interest in common, Kearney and Sinclair discovered that they had complementary skills: he on the technical side – the mastery of engineering details that was the basis of getting things done with Microsoft's major product groups – and she with marketing and external relations with vendors.

Kearney and Sinclair went over the basics of the business case for 'accessibility', which included the needs of elderly users. Although their numbers were rough estimates taken from US Census data, a strong case could be made that the aging market was one that Microsoft should enter. First, the majority of working-age adults were likely to benefit from the use of accessible technology. Up to 60% (101.4 million) of working-age adults in the US were likely or very likely to benefit from the use of accessible technology. Second, the degree of severity of a difficulty or impairment was an important factor that influenced computer use, that is, usage declined as severity increased. Hence, by creating technology more accessible to these individuals, it was reasonable to assume that their computer use would rise. Third, the level of 'technology optimism' declined in accordance with the severity of the impairment. As such, this too represented a huge potential market: only 51% of computer users who were likely or very likely to benefit from the use of accessible technology were technology optimists, compared to 58% of computer users who were not likely to benefit from the use of accessible technology.

Regarding the projected evolution of the US population, the trends offered further evidence that Microsoft might build an entire business strategy around accessibility and the aging population. Because the US population was aging, the labour force would shift in favour of older workers: by 2020, one in five workers would be 55 years and older, nearly a 50% increase over the 2000 figure of 13%. This shift would place greater pressure on businesses to retain their aging employees both for longer periods and in as productive a way as possible, that is, with specialized computer capabilities.

Furthermore, in a population in which the age profile was shifting rapidly towards those most likely to have difficulties and impairments, the total number of people with difficulties and impairments would increase. Thus, Kearney and Sinclair agreed that there was an increasing need for accessible technology to allow individuals to customize their computers to help overcome physical and cognitive difficulties. Add to these trends the growing use of computers for work, information and communication, and it appeared clear that future computer users would demand and expect greater accessibility in computers regardless of their abilities.

Together, Kearney and Sinclair envisioned the expansion of the 'Microsoft accessibility vendor program', an informal group that was seeking to reduce the time it took vendors to develop software for the Microsoft platform from 18–30 months to six. It was similar to what Kearney was working on for Windows XP. If the programme were realized, it would be the first step in the development of a far wider array of accessible technologies for computers, which represented a strategic business opportunity for IT companies to improve technology optimism and perhaps customer satisfaction.

To accomplish this, Kearney began to investigate how to better reconcile the business models of the vendors and Microsoft. According to Kearney, because Microsoft made its money in large part by subscription fees, the company wanted to ship code updates every year. However, for vendors this created software compatibility issues, which were very expensive for them to fix (as measured in programming time). 'Most [accessibility] vendors are mom and pop shops,' she explained, 'really small operators. For them, de-bugging their products every year [to conform to a new code] was too expensive and time-consuming. They wanted updates every 10 years.' Not only did the difference in business models limit the range and quality of accessibility products available, but it threatened the financial viability of the vendors.

The solution, Kearney and Sinclair agreed, was to integrate certain accessibility technology features deeper into the operating system, which would make them available to support all Windows programs that ran them. Rather than spend time on basic questions of compatibility with the Windows operating system, Sinclair and Kearney knew they could turn their attention to improving the user experience. One possible method for doing so was the development of user-interface (UI) automation capability, which automatically tested the compatibility of the vendors' code with the operating system in question.

'This way,' Kearney said, 'we could reduce the time to market and keep the vendors in business, even increase their profits: they could co-market with us and their products would be better and more differentiated.' Moreover, they were confident that Sinclair would present their ideas to his fellow engineers in a manner that would appeal to them.

With this plan in mind, Kearney turned to the information gap: she would fund a major study by Forrester Research of the communities that would benefit from computer accessibility. In the meantime, she and Sinclair e-mailed a sketch of their business plan to Bill Gates, who quickly set up an appointment with them.

The 'Bill G' Presentation

Just prior to their appointment with Gates, Sinclair was officially transferred to the Windows business group as Program Manager of the Accessibility Framework. This position would be part of the group that was working on display technology for Windows Vista, which would operate within the Windows platform group on the client side. From this position, Sinclair reported to the Senior VP for Windows, who worked under the Group VP. The Group VP functioned with direct access to Microsoft CEO Steve Ballmer.

According to Kearney, Sinclair's new position changed the prospect of their accessibility plan 'from hugging trees to a genuine business case'. Kearney had also engaged Forrester Research, but they were years away from any results that they might use for the presentation. As such, she had to use data from the US census on the aging population and how their needs for accessibility tools would grow – not necessarily as 'disabilities', but as normal aids for accessibility. Kearney was able to make the case that, as baby boomers aged, they would need three key technology tools for accessibility:

- A mouse-controlled screen magnifier, which could highlight text and images that the user selected.
- A screen-based keyboard that could be used with a light pointer.
- A visual aid to render images and text easier to read via colour contrast and other methods for the visually impaired.

As the population aged, she argued, the need for accessibility technologies would increase. If current trends continued, she said, by 2010 the majority of the population in the US would be 45 or older; by 2020, 20% of the population would be older than 64. These were the age groups whose difficulties and impairments – in terms of eye sight, hearing, motor skills, and so on – were rapidly worsening.

In addition to Kearney's demographic data, Sinclair added a few touches to interest Gates. First, he said, once embedded in the platform, these tools might also function as UI automated testing tools for vendors of specialized accessibility software. In effect, the test capability would be built-in free of charge. This excited Gates, who had been thinking along the same lines. Second, knowing that Gates loved to play with new hardware, Sinclair brought in a Pac Mate mobile platform, by Freedom Scientific; it was one of a number of new devices to help individuals with disabilities. Gates handled the object during the entire presentation, which was extended by half an hour. They left with Gates' approval – in addition to UI automation, he had seen their idea as an 'important business driver'. 'There is no question,' Kearney related, 'that he got it.'

The Platform

With the mandate from Gates, Sinclair and his team set about covering the technical aspects of embedding the tools into the Windows XP Platform. (The Vista operating system under development would also benefit from this at a later date.) This was a highly technical task that would occupy him and his team from 2001 to 2006. First, he had to contact Windows teams in related areas to develop the basic architecture within the code. Then he had to engage Microsoft programmers to develop the tools themselves, which could be integrated into the Windows operating system. Because these were applications for highly specific consumer-related purposes, this was an unusually early stage to bring these considerations to the designer/engineers. 'We were at milestone zero,' Sinclair explained, 'at the brainstorming stage where the basic features were discussed. At that time, they didn't yet think of details like accessibility, features for elderly users, privacy or security. By getting in so early, we were really changing the engineering process, getting them to think of users and human factors way before they were accustomed to worrying about them.' Not surprisingly, this required continual consultation with top Windows executives in their area of responsibility, repeatedly re-selling them on the idea.

Beyond writing the code of the operating system itself, Sinclair's team had to create an 'ecosystem' of accessibility-technology vendors, of which there were approximately 125 in 2001. Each vendor had to be contacted for their expertise regarding their customers' needs, to discuss 'the what, where, when, why, how'. In effect, Sinclair's team had to listen to them and then convince them to invest in the new operating system as partners under Microsoft's direction. To do so, Sinclair turned to Gary Moulton, who had been working on accessibility technologies at Microsoft for some years and had been hired from Apple.

It was, Moulton explained, an intimate style of collaboration in three steps. First, he provided Microsoft operating-system code to each company (the 'base code'), giving technical support for up to five years for them to learn to operate within it. Second, Moulton consulted with the companies regarding what could be built into the code that would make it easier to develop specific products. This was extremely meticulous de-bugging work, but also a time to exchange fundamental ideas about the operating system's capabilities and potential. 'I design what we will do with them,' Moulton said. Third, there was the work at the alpha level of the software, preparing it for the customers' requirements. Most of this was accomplished in cooperation with Microsoft's software laboratories on campus, which strengthened the 'trust' that they were building into the relationship.

'It's a lot of grunt work to get the code locked down on both sides,' Moulton observed. 'We tie up all the loose ends so the customer has an elegant experience.' Although there was nothing unusual in this process, he emphasized, everyone involved was genuinely passionate about the technology, so he didn't need to build incentives into the process. 'As it moves up the system,' he said, 'parts of it get used or discarded. Everything gets sorted out and sticks together.'

The Research

Meanwhile, Kearney had become deeply involved in the data collection project with Forrester. After a review of available resources, Kearney was convinced that an extremely detailed study needed to be undertaken, both to confirm their conclusions and refine them. 'The state of available data was truly appalling,' she said. 'Even people who were supposed to be experts wanted to do things like Internet surveys, when we were trying to find out about who *didn't* use computers.' She wanted a study of such high quality that it would set a new standard and be of use even to scholars.

The first study consisted of a nationwide survey conducted by phone and mail, asking a range of questions designed to assess five types of difficulties and impairments that would most likely impact computer use: vision, dexterity, hearing, speech and cognitive function. Pollsters queried individuals on difficulties with daily tasks; assessed the proportion of the population who identified themselves as having an impairment or difficulty; gauged the impact on employment; and asked a range of lifestyle and demographic questions.

The results confirmed the original vision of Sinclair and Kearney. In the United States, 60% (101.4 million) of working-age adults who ranged in age from 18 to 64 years were likely or very likely to benefit from the use of accessible technology due to difficulties and impairments that could impact computer use. Among current US computer users who ranged from 18 to 64 years old, 57% (74.2 million) were likely or very likely to benefit. Maintaining productivity among US workers – regardless of abilities, difficulties and impairments – would become an increasingly vital economic issue and a concern to all managers. The development of more accessible technology for computers, they concluded, represented a strategic business opportunity for IT companies to improve technology optimism, and perhaps customer satisfaction.

Finally, Kearney and Sinclair reasoned that their group needed to finesse the definition of the mission. To address the growing need for accessible technology, they believed, the concept of 'disability' limited the understanding of the need for accessible technology. Rather than assume that it was useful only to a distinct group of people with *disabilities* (10% of the population), the IT industry needed to consider a wider range of people who could benefit from using *accessible technology*: the approximately 57% of the working age population who, in the years to come, could enhance their lives with the use of technologies currently aimed at people with severe difficulties and impairments.

Moreover, it was here that they recognized the need to include software for the aging population, which was rapidly growing in the industrialized West and would benefit from the same technologies. A large and growing potential market for accessible technology existed to serve individuals who had some degree of difficulty or impairment that impacts their ability to use a computer. In this light, their initiative represented an enormous opportunity for Microsoft.

The second report, issued in 2004, offered a glimpse of the strategy they were beginning to develop. They wrote:

> . . . the majority of people who are currently using accessible technology, and those who are likely to use accessible technology in the future, do not use this technology because they do not consider themselves as having an impairment or disability but rather look for ways to make computing easier. There is an opportunity for the IT industry to realize growth in the accessible technology market and improve computers by making accessible technology easier to find and use by all computer users. Specifically, presenting accessibility options and assistive technology products as part of a computer's functionality rather than as an aid for people with disabilities will reach more computer users and will increase the reach of accessible technology.

Next Steps

By late 2004, Sinclair's team had accomplished a number of their objectives. First, with Gates' green light, they had embedded the accessibility tools into the base code of the Windows XP operating system. Unfortunately, they discovered, the features were so difficult to find that few in the potential user pool knew of their existence. Nonetheless, the ecosystem of vendors was up and running, improving not only the speed of development, but also the user experience. Kearney had also begun to 'launch' the data from the Forrester reports, discussing the results in various fora; she was even engaged as an adjunct professor on aging and the work force by Sloan School of Business at the Massachusetts Institute of Technology (MIT). To incorporate systematically the views of outside stakeholders and monitor regulatory compliance, Sinclair regularly consulted a governmental affairs officer, Laura Ruby, who travelled often to Washington, DC, to meet policymakers and representatives from non-governmental organizations concerned with disabilities and aging. In particular, as regulations evolved, Ruby carefully monitored the potential for a law suit alleging discrimination against the elderly or disabled.

As they expanded the accessibility tools that would be available for Vista, the operating system under development, Sinclair and his team paused to reassess their progress. Whereas the industry was increasingly recognizing that the market was not 10% of the population but more like 57%, they wondered whether they might formulate some new strategy. 'Within Microsoft,' Kearney noted, 'the name "accessibility" just wasn't resonating. After a little brainstorming, we realized that "aging" is far better – it is the sexy bubblegum word.' Fortunately for Sinclair's team, many others within Microsoft were thinking along the same lines.

CORPORATE CITIZENSHIP AND STRATEGY

In 2002, Dan Bross was hired into Microsoft's Legal and Community Affairs (LCA), under the leadership of Corporate Vice President Pamela Passman, to create a Corporate Citizenship strategy. His mission was to develop programmes through which Microsoft would be recognized as a technological leader at the forefront of societal issues. During the next few years, he and others at the company explored a wide array of issues related to accessibility and the needs of elderly users. Operating in parallel to the many initiatives that Sinclair's team were pursuing, including new accessibility features for the Vista operating system under development, these CSR-related initiatives were exploring the accessibility market from the standpoint of the aging population. These were signs of grassroots support, which added crucial impetus to Sinclair's efforts.

Developments in EMEA

Elena Bonfiglioli was hired in February, 2003, as Director of Corporate Social Responsibility in Microsoft Europe, Middle East and Africa (EMEA). Over the next two years, the LCA team established a network of 50 managers throughout the company; drawn principally from LCA, communications and public relations, these managers developed the framework and structure of the Corporate Citizenship Initiative within the company. From the start, accessibility was one of the core elements of this programme. In cooperation with her counterparts at Corporate headquarters and with the support of EMEA Senior Chairman Umberto Paolucci – the champion of accessibility in Europe, along with Jean-Philippe Courtois, then President of Microsoft EMEA – Bonfiglioli began to develop an accessibility programme with a US$7 million budget, similar to that managed by Craig Spiezle a few years earlier. She also monitored the policy and regulatory developments in Europe, which had recently become concerned with issues of accessibility; aligned some of the community social investments to fund the training needs of NGOs serving people with disabilities and the elderly; and started a long-term process of engagement with stakeholder and user groups.

Think Tank

In 2003, Nelle Steele joined a group in a Microsoft think tank for a project entitled, What's Next? They were mandated to look 10 years into the future to foresee what features and products should be in the next operating system, beyond Vista. A design researcher, Steele was trained as an ethnographer: she observed how people used computers and conducted in-depth interviews on how technology fit into people's lives. 'I tell their stories,' she explained. Although many of her projects were for the very specific needs of product groups, she was particularly excited by the open-endedness of this one. The group split their work into a number of population segments, one of which was the 'boomer' generation. She led a literature review and then interviewed 10 'boomers', who indicated that accessibility technologies would enhance their living standards as they grew older. Steele wrote her observations into a report and presented it to her superiors. The reaction was positive. 'Many of them got very excited,' she recalled. 'The idea struck some deep emotional chord and a lot of people asked what it would take to carry it forward. I felt very passionately that it was the right way to go and said so.'

White Paper to Aging Alias

Across campus in mid-2004, Adrian Hall had begun to write a white paper, *The Avalanche of Aging and Microsoft*. Hall was a Senior Director of the Trustworthy Computing Strategy group, which monitored security issues for the Microsoft operating system and applications. Hall's interest in aging had been sparked by the difficulties that her parents were having while attempting to manage their finances on-line. 'They found all sorts of things that didn't make sense to them,' she observed, 'like the need to use "save as" when you first wanted to save a file . . . That made me think about the experience I had with my sons: they were far more skilled at computer games than I ever could be because they grew up with them. I am a tech person, too, so I figured the gap between me and my parents was even greater.' She began to ask herself what size the market was for the aging population and what kind of products might be developed, not only as accessibility aides, but perhaps also as cognitive exercises for Alzheimer's patients.

Hall's paper was one of approximately 200 papers in a competition entitled 'think week'. About 20 papers would be selected for Bill Gates' briefcase, which he would take on a retreat to read. Each paper was on an area that Microsoft employees believed were important opportunities or issues; they did not have to fall into the area of their regular job responsibilities, but instead could be about anything, so long as they believed in it passionately. Although it didn't make the Gates briefcase, the arbiters encouraged Hall to try again the following year. As an aid to her undertaking, Hall put the paper on the Microsoft intra-company site, where it generated great interest. 'For five or six months, I was receiving continual comments,' she recalled, 'and it kept me going. I was devoting [a quarter of my] time to it. People were telling me it was the right thing to do and also sharing stories from their own families that were like mine. The traffic got so overwhelming that I created an Alias about aging, where people put suggestions and personal vignettes.'

Among her conclusions, Hall singled out the following:

- the sensory attributes – visual, auditory and tactile – of the population over 50, which were 'radically different from those of 20-year-olds';
- the content matter that would appeal to these age groups was also on a divergent course;
- rather than video games and the applications that young professionals required, seniors faced different 'compelling triggers', e.g., issues of 'health and wellness, safety and security, intergenerational bonding, finance, travel, tourism and leisure, legacy work, second or new careering, life-long learning and staying connected'.

To become a second-half friendly software company, Hall argued, Microsoft needed to adopt a holistic approach as well as the targeted development of age-specific products and services. According to Moulton, Hall's efforts were key in raising awareness of the issue throughout the organization in the United States (see Exhibit 4.2).

Synergies

According to Sinclair, 'the interest of these groups came at just the right time for us . . . We had built a lot of good plumbing and now we needed to push it to a new level.' Nonetheless, Sinclair found that building his base of support at the high executive levels was slow going. Many top managers of Microsoft's product groups remained sceptical that the accessibility market and even the aging workforce question could ever become something profitable. According to one executive, 'it might be the right thing to do, but it will never drive the revenues of the company.' They continued to see the market, according to Sinclair, as 'that 10% for the disabled and not the 57%' of those who could use customized accessibility tools. The question was, how to move forward (see Table 4.1)?

EXHIBIT 4.2 ADRIAN HALL'S CHART ON AGING DEMOGRAPHIC CHALLENGE

The challenge: No software company is addressing the shift in the global population - will Microsoft?

- By 2009, 1/3 of the world's population will be 50+
- 60+ persons in 2005 (672M) will triple to 1.9B by 2050
- Top subs will see significant shifts: currently 48% of the U.S. workforce is 40+, 25% of Japan's population is 65+
- Increased longevity and lower birth rates is inverting the population pyramid of workforce to people in the second-half of life (50+) to retirees
- Largest generational wealth transfer underway: from WWII/Silent generation (b. 1943)
- Public policy priorities: extend the retirement age, reduce healthcare costs
- Individual priorities: Vary by generation, by more developed/less developed regions

World Population Aged 60+ *

Year	in thousands	% of pop.
1995	543,484	9.5
2005	672,386	10.4
2015	893,031	12.4
2025	1,192,603	15.1
2035	1,530,050	18.1
2045	1,810,680	20.3
2050	1,968,153	21.7

* United Nations Population Division, Feb 2005

Top Countries Accounting for 75% of World Population (1950, 2005, 2050)*

Lines reflect population trending over 100 year period

Impact on Microsoft Business: Under-represented segment can bring revenue growth through new products/services

Global Population Aged 65+ (1950 - 2030)

Top Activities: Communication & Connection, PC Games, Finance

Age	18-24	25-34	35-44	45-54	55-64	65+
Email/instant messaging	98.2	97.9	95.9	94.1	95.9	96.5
Game playing (PC and online games)	74.5	77.2	70.9	72.7	59.4	56.5
Surfing the Web	67.3	66.9	61.6	63.1	62.4	44.2
Shopping	58.2	57.2	51.7	49.7	45.9	29.8
Personal finances	4.0	46.9	38.4	36.9	38.2	23.5

IDC's 2005 Consumer Survey

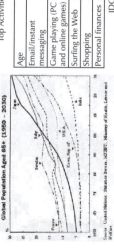

Top PC Activities Performed by % or total time — 50+ Online Use 2002 – 2010

- IBM's recent investments: WebAdapt2Me, IBM Easy Web Browsing, Anti-tremor mouse technology, 'older' messaging campaigns highlighting accessibility
- IBM, Mozilla, Yahoo and Macromedia collaborating to develop new DHTML Accessibility browser guidelines
- *BusinessWeek*: "IBM is leading the charge for seniors" ... is "bringing great products to market."

What is being done at Microsoft: Progress to date

- Additional accessibility features focus – Vista
  - "Accessibility" nomenclature in Vista changing to "Ease of Access"
  - Lightweight aging-related research and data on ms.com/enable/aging
- Informal "Aging Design Discussion" alias, interested BG personnel
- 50+ age-group personas developed for Longhorn wave; later all cut
- Isolated BG marketing studies on aging often funded, but not applied to prod strategy
- Concept exploration (thinkweek paper, Jan 2005)
- Age-related hardware scenarios review (Sept-Oct 2005, Japan sub)
- Cross-company project team created Oct 2005 ("Horizon"), to aggregate knowledge and build clearer recommendations
  - Combined HQ and Field projects
  - Included a review of the company's prior approach under Bob Herbold
  - Compilation of SME List (U.S. and EMEA)
  - Prioritization of new products/services ideas
- Proposed expansion of Accessibility team charter; to Lifestyle Products
- Policy leaders discussion: Businesses in Society Roundtable (EMEA)
- eGovernment Strategy paper (transforming operations) – red tape, aging population
- Consultant participation at White House Conference on Aging (occurs once/decade)
- Summary: No coordinated, cross-company center of gravity to capitalize

New investments or changes in our approach

- Drive company wide strategic focus on aging workforce
  - Create L67+ position to plan and drive the company's 50+ initiatives
  - Develop "One Microsoft" strategy to maximize technology, product and marketing investments
- Provide technology and thought leadership for aging workforce transformation
  - *Vista Ease of Access* awareness campaign to reach people with disabilities & 50+ customers
  - Educate Field on aging and accessibility; provide competitive talking pts for gov't and Ed sales
  - Anchor Lifestyle Products team resources in region (PanAsia and EMEA) to identify solutions, influence standards, policy and legislative matters related to accessibility and aging
  - Key campaigns to include messaging for seniors and people with disabilities
  - Restructure (and rename?) www.microsoft.com/enable/aging as mainstream portal for 50+ customers
- Innovate in products, technologies and services to attract 50+ customers
  - Repackage current MS accessibility offerings to be relevant for 50+ customers
  - Drive prioritized product offerings (from business plan)
  - Develop and execute mobile device GTMs for 50+ segment
  - Develop Windows Live "Lifestyle" service offering for key 50+ scenarios
  - Deepen MSR Research focus on 50+ opportunities
- Strategic Alliances
  - Partner with civil society organizations (i.e. AARP/Help the Aged) to develop custom Windows User Experience (built on our CAPE toolkit) for 50+ segment
  - Create Country Manager playbook and guidance for subsidiary level policy engagements
  - Drive global partnership with relevant multilateral agencies and influential policy bodies
  - Develop proof of concept medical service scenarios in three lead subsidiaries

Table 4.1 Sample list of Microsoft Initiatives

Proponent	Interest/Project	Notes
AnnuskaP	Corp. Accessibility – Product Planning	Product planner who was working for BonnieK who was responsible for EOA
BCrounse	• Healthcare • WW Public Sector	MD who is a major support of accessibility and is working within his group on aging related activities
BobbyC	Employee network for boomers/ mature workers	Started an internal Alias for employees 50+
BrannonZ	Xbox – Test	Arranged for Xbox's AARP 07 participation
CDouglas	MSN Managing Editor	MSN Lifestyles – Boomers Channel
CEales	PTA-EMEA and Vista 'Skin' project with UK's Age Concern	UK – Education/Digital Inclusion
CKwon	Community Affairs – Korea	Coordinated SteveB's announcement of training sites for seniors in Korea
DavidS	MSN Senior Channel Manager	MSN Lifestyles – Boomers
DianaP	PTA	Her group is working on the sale of PCs to seniors in Argentina
EllenK	Corp. Accessibility	Coordinated Microsoft's involvement in the City of Miami senior project
FloraGo	Consumer Prototyping	Responsible for senior scenarios in Microsoft Home of the Future
FTorres	• AARP interest • Govt. Affairs	Microsoft's liaison to AARP
JDavison	UX Research	Longitudinal study on Vista/Live that will include 20% 55+
KTolle	MSR – Stanford Ageing	www.assistedcognition.org
LaDeanaH	Corp. Accessibility	Responsible for Forrester study and aging-related marketing materials
Meagan	Employee network for boomers/ mature workers	Coordinating Alias for employees 50+
NanaB	SeniorPC offering – Denmark	DaneAge Association (Danish elderly organization)
NormanHo	WEX	
PNeupert	Health Solutions Mgmt	Consumer oriented technology that will have a major impact on seniors
ScottEdw	• Make History • Standards	ThinkWeek paper author who detailed the importance of legacy for seniors
TiraC	WEX UX	Worked closely with AnnuskaP on EOA
v-DonnF	Thinkweek paper collaboration	Worked with Adrienne on follow-up to her ThinkWeek paper
JPincus	• MLR • Strategy Development	Coordinated internal market scoping work as a follow-up to Hall's ThinkWeek paper
MikeWic	• FlexGo • Starter	Low-cost PCs that have potential in senior market

CONVERGENCE

In summer, 2005, aware of Hall's paper, Sinclair called her to ask if they should talk. 'It was a "well, duh" moment,' Sinclair said. 'What she was doing was so well aligned with my work that we decided immediately to amalgamate everything we had done.' With input from LCA, Hall and Sinclair began to develop a solid business case around aging that also incorporated corporate citizenship concerns. 'We had to start thinking about the issue differently,' Hall explained, 'and looked at things like the on-line experience of the elderly in banking or the uses of the Internet as a way to monitor healthcare biometrics. Who would use it? How would you make a profit with services like that? It appeared to be a great opportunity, and so what needed to be done?' As an engineer and Program Manager, they proposed, Sinclair should be designated as a kind of aging tsar, a person to oversee all aspects of the programme from technical questions to the marketing. However, because Sinclair was not in the top level of Microsoft managers, they reasoned, a senior level position should also be created, someone with 'rock star credibility' to strategically position an aging initiative within the company; in particular, once the technological issues were resolved, this leadership position should bring focus to the accessibility issue across the entire company. Although Hall's white paper never made it into Gates' 'think week' briefcase, it had had an impact.

At the same time, Elena Bonfiglioli contacted Adrian Hall. She was interested in Hall's work for the Business and Society Roundtable (BiS R). Championed by Jean-Philippe Courtois, the BiS R was a high-level stakeholder engagement effort of the company to discuss emerging societal topics that would impact the company; the topics were extensively researched, both within the company and in consultation with stakeholders. Gathering twice a year for a full day, the theme for the November 2005 Roundtable was: 'Where the Growth Is: Second-Half Demographics and the Future of Microsoft's Business'. The meeting would bring a number of international aging specialists together to make a number of recommendations (see Exhibit 4.3).

As a preparation for the Roundtable, Courtois asked Bonfiglioli to join forces with the WW Technology Officer Jonathan Murray and Adrian Hall and do an internal review of all activities already in place in the various divisions and countries on the topic of technology for the aging society. With the rapidly aging population in Europe, there was growing interest in some kind of related initiative, focusing on R&D and product development for the elderly, strategic community investments, targeted communications and marketing and re-training as a competitive priority. 'Their interest prompted me to re-think everything I had done,' Hall said. 'It was the start of an international network on the subject.'

By early 2006, Microsoft partner Sherri Bealkowski began to think about the aging issue. 'I saw it as an important market segment that we were not addressing,' she said. Up to that point, Microsoft had not segmented its operating-system market, but had instead treated its 800 million customers as a single group. Bealkowski, as a partner also a member of Microsoft's top 1% elite of 600 executives, served as a board member of United Way as well as volunteering at a NGO, Atwork! Having witnessed her father's computer-phobic behaviour, she had developed a personal interest in treatment of the elderly. She, like many others, believed that the aging market could serve as a new strategic direction for the company and perhaps a crucial engine of its growth. With a few phone calls, she found Rob Sinclair. He was delighted that a partner – the highest level executive to date – was interested in a hands-on role in the project.

EXHIBIT 4.3 NOVEMBER 2005'S ROUNDTABLE: 'WHERE THE GROWTH IS: SECOND-HALF DEMOGRAPHICS AND THE FUTURE OF MICROSOFT'S BUSINESS'

Business in Society Roundtable, Nov 7, 2005 (Europe)

Recommendations

- Products & Innovation – BY DESIGN and BY DEFAULT, MAKE ASSISTIVE TECHNOLOGIES MORE VISIBLE!
  - Short term - Package existing assistive technology features to make them much more visible, make them known to people, inform users more proactively and communicate on them.
  - Market assistive technology not only for people with disabilities but also for everyone getting ready for aging - as "readiness" features
  - Make products EASIER to use for the elderly
  - Integrate accessibility features across the new "Live Software" services
  - Longer term - work on different devices (mobile, TV, cars…) to make e-gov services more accessible and available

- Communication – HELP CHANGE MINDSETS
  - Advertising to encompass older people too
  - Use communications and advertising to convey the idea that older workers and creativity/productivity can go together

- Leadership and communication – TIPPING THE POINT, TAKING THE LEAD
  - Support the full development of the business case internally to substantiate the elements that are already emerging from initial data and discussions
  - Benchmark what other companies are doing
  - Take executive decision for Microsoft (and the ICT sector) to lead on the topic
  - Microsoft to work with a few companies on the topic via a reference platform organisation that can provide support and visibility (WBCSD/EU cooperation….)

- Policy
  - Work with other industry groups to push on the same policy issues
  - Work with countries to understand how to help them shape productivity programs and strategy

- Better understand orthogonal implications
  - Immigration
  - Transport
  - Finance/Tourism

CONCLUSIONS

While Bealkowski, Hall and Sinclair's team worked to sell the idea to Microsoft's product groups over the next six months, they also began to discuss options for a business strategy. 'I saw it as a trend that we had spotted,' Bealkowski explained. 'To get ahead of it, we had to figure out some way to bring it to market first, or do it with the greatest quality, or be the first to make money at it.' She argued for customized products, such as a 'seniors' edition' for Vista and/or Microsoft Office; they might also be supported by on-line subscription services, tutoring and so on. For a global market, she believed, they could go where it made sense to market these tools and then sell them in the right way. 'There were,' she emphasized, 'many different ways to do things. For example, our advertising wasn't reaching seniors, so why not partner with the AARP [the American Association of Retired Persons] and governmental organizations to disseminate information?' She was bursting with enthusiasm and believed in what they wanted to accomplish.

By spring, 2006, Sinclair had been appointed tsar for the aging initiative. Bealkowski had committed to join the effort, in effect as Sinclair's employee. However, Bealkowski's boss changed his mind one day before her appointment to Sinclair's team was to be announced. Soon thereafter, she took early retirement. This setback notwithstanding, managers all over Microsoft continued to work on their accessibility and aging initiatives.

Sinclair and his team supported the development of the Vista operating system, to which they were adding a number of improvements. First, to enhance the 'discoverability' of their accessibility tools, they included questions regarding user needs in the registration survey that had to be filled out during the first log-on to Vista. In other words, if symptoms were signalled early on, the user would be directed to certain tools or offered recommendations. Second, they were careful to develop a user vocabulary that would attract customers rather than repel them. In place of 'accessibility' or 'disability aid', they substituted *ease of access*. A similar notion was developed for an *ease of access* icon, replacing a wheelchair image. Finally, a voice recognition capability was added, which accustomed itself to the voice of the user to both transcribe what they said and also act to trigger certain commands, like an aural mouse. In the opinion of Sinclair's team, these represented significant improvements to their tool offerings.

Sinclair's team worked hard on other fronts as well. Gary Moulton's vendor ecosystem continued to grow and diversify. With 150 vendors with projects for 2007, according to Moulton, 'the sheer number of new products was the most ever.' Laura Ruby and others also continued to reach out to seniors' groups and governmental officials. Finally, Sinclair's team was developing a number of pilot projects, including:

- subscription services for seniors, such as ongoing training and support;
- various niche products, such as a seniors edition of Microsoft Office;
- cognitive stimulation games designed to keep the minds of Alzheimer's patients active.

Moulton also contacted both Hewlett-Packard (HP) and Best Buy (a US electrical retailer) regarding the development and marketing of a computer designed specifically for the elderly. At HP, the Director of Accessibility, Michael Takemura, had been seeking accessibility solutions for the aging workforce for a number of years. He saw potential synergies with the Microsoft programme. 'I knew of Gary [Moulton's] work,' he said, 'and we realized that people with disabilities have almost the same issues as those who are aging. We talked more, and agreed that we could build a lot of specialized hardware to run the accessibility software they had developed.' The accessibility computer was, he recalled, build from off-the-shelf components that HP had invented for other products; its attributes included larger keyboards, some of which were light-activated for those with motor disabilities, a dual tint display for the visually impaired, and so on.

In addition, Moulton convinced Jon Danger, Best Buy's then-Director of services and partnerships, that the retailer's 'Geek Squad' should sell the new HP computer in a pilot project. In effect, Geek Squad representatives would go into the homes of elderly or disabled users to both set up and teach them how to use the PC as well as promise to answer their questions in the future. To simplify the setup, which involved multiple services, such as the pricing schemes of telephone and cable companies, Moulton also gained valuable advice on how to configure the capabilities offered.

The LCA in the EMEA region of Microsoft continued to develop its own pilot products and initiatives. These included computer courses for the elderly and R&D at Microsoft centres on seniors-related issues and products. It also continued its engagement with seniors' groups and governmental bodies regarding issues of compliance and to gauge future needs. Finally, the 'Collage' project was created at Microsoft headquarters, which linked the compensation of country managers to the achievement of objectives and the enactment of initiatives aimed at improving the company's social footprint in their country or region. At the beginning of each year, each country manager has to declare the objectives to reach in the level of satisfaction of a whole list of stakeholders, and commit to a given set of initiatives to attain those goals. Among those metrics are also the degree of satisfaction of elder and disadvantaged users, evaluated with frequent surveys.

For EMEA, under Courtois' leadership, Bonfiglioli worked on a number of larger projects, including:

- A number of 'employability initiatives', for example, in which older workers laid off from the textile sector were re-trained to master personal computers, thereby enhancing their labour skills for new employment prospects; call centres in Portugal; a collaboration with UK-based AGE Concern, for which Her Majesty the Queen made an award as 'best elderly programme'; training programmes for retired people in Milano's Centro Stelline with AIM, a conference organizer in Italy; and support to an extensive network of millions of elderly citizens in Sweden.
- R&D investments and early pilot programmes in health and e-government services, such as the facilitation of data processing capabilities for social security benefits in the Czech Republic and Bulgaria.
- The development of multiple innovative products, including:
  - a device to aid the release of certain drugs (SensePill in the UK);
  - a camera designed to be worn by memory-impaired individuals (SenseCam);
  - various devices in Japan, such as a sensor to indicate when elderly residents used hot kitchen implements and a robot to provide eating assistance.

By spring, 2007, amid all these separate initiatives, Sinclair and his colleagues continued to discuss a more unified strategy for aging populations. They knew that all those projects did not add up to a real strategy for this specific market. They also understood that their real ambition – to gain a space in the minds of all Microsoft professionals regarding the social impact of their products – remained unfulfilled.

They needed to take a moment to re-group and consider the next steps in the ambitious project to diffuse a corporate citizenship mentality throughout the whole organization. What should their strategy become now, they wondered? How could they move ahead? To answer these questions, Moulton, Sinclair, Bonfiglioli and others planned a meeting to discuss their accomplishments and agree on next steps in order to align their agendas.

NOTES

1. The case is intended to be used as a basis for class discussion rather than to illustrate either effective or ineffective handling of an administrative situation.
2. Also based on conversations with Bonnie Kearney and Rob Sinclair.
3. Microsoft concessions included the licensing of certain communications protocols to competitors and the formation of a compliance committee at the board level.
4. These included 1) Section 508 of the Federal Code that restricted government procurement of electronics products to those that were accessible to the handicapped; 2) paragraph 205 of the Telecom Act that added accessibility requirements to communications technology, particularly those that are used in the workplace.

REFERENCES

Buck, T. (2006) Forcing Windows open: How Brussels and Microsoft squared up for an epochal battle, *The Financial Times*, 20 April.

Manes, S. and Andrews, P. (1993) *Gates*, Touchstone.

Stross, R.E. (1997) *The Microsoft Way*, Perseus Books.

The Economist (2002) The long shadow of big blue; Microsoft, 9 November.

Wallace, J. and Erickson, J. (1992) Hard drive: Bill Gates and the making of the Microsoft empire, *Harper Business*.

CHAPTER FIVE

IBM in China: Responding to a Government's Social Initiatives[1]

Steven White, CEIBS

In China, you're pushing water uphill if you decide to have a strategy that is against the government agenda. Information technology can enable large parts of that agenda. Of course, some areas won't be open to a foreign company. But there is no lack of opportunities to support that agenda. But you have to prioritize them, and decide where you can add value and make money. We're not a charitable institution; we're here to make money, and do make money, and grow.

Michael Cannon-Brookes, Vice President
Strategy and Business Development, Emerging Markets, IBM Asia Pacific Headquarters

CASE STUDY

15 January 2007

To: Executive Management Committee
From: Henry Chow, Chairman, IBM Greater China Group
Re: CSR strategy review for China

Since China first opened up to foreign companies in the 1980s, IBM Greater China has been able to align its activities closely with the Chinese government's major policy priorities. Over the years, we have made decisions that have supported those priorities and also benefited IBM's business, including increasing direct investment, local manufacturing and exports, supplying and transferring technology, and localizing R&D. Moreover, the extent of our philanthropic activities supporting education and IT-related human capital development in China clearly shows that we have a long-term commitment to China's development. We can be proud that we have led most if not all multinationals in this regard. (See Exhibit 5.1 and (Figure 5.1 within it) for a synopsis of our current organization and operations in China, and Exhibit 5.2 for our main philanthropic activities.)

Recently, as you should be aware from the extensive coverage in the Chinese media since early 2006, the Chinese leadership has been pushing two broad policy initiatives very hard: what they call *Modern Socialist Countryside* and *Harmonious Society*. Exhibit 5.3 summarizes these two initiatives and some of the specific programmes and policies that have been announced so far.

The timing and nature of these two initiatives provide a good opportunity for us to review several issues related to how IBM China positions itself in China and how to integrate our

EXHIBIT 5.1   SYNOPSIS OF IBM'S CURRENT ORGANIZATION AND OPERATIONS IN CHINA[2]

Presence

Some figures for IBM's presence in China are as follows:

- 10 000+ employees; 5000+ sales and technical force covering 320 cities;
- headquarters and 23 branch offices by end 2006;
- 9000 business partners (suppliers, development partners, resellers) in 300 cities.

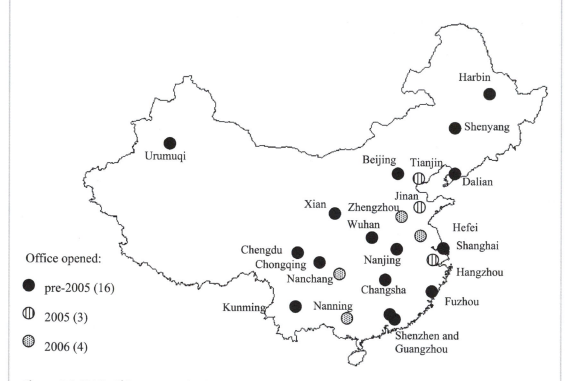

Figure 5.1 IBM's Chinese organization

Operations

Performance

Some performance data from recent years are:

- 2006 revenues US$1.7 billion, 16% annual growth year-on-year (excluding PC revenues):
  - market leader in servers and storage, middleware and services
  - 20% growth; first in consulting and systems integration

- 21% regional growth
- 24% growth in small-medium business segment
- Most Admired Company in China (*Fortune*, 2004);
- Most Admired Employer (2004, 2005, 2006).

Business

IBM delivers business solutions to its clients in the form of information technology hardware, software, systems and services. Operations in China serve both domestic and international clients, and include global hubs for specific products, services and corporate functions.

Hardware sales represent approximately 75% of revenues in China, compared to 43% for IBM globally. Although IBM has been profitable in China since 1993 (*China Business Weekly*, 2004), one goal of IBM's China strategy is to increase the proportion of revenues from software and services to 50% by 2010. One way to do this is to win more contracts that provide integrated hardware, software and services, usually combining resources from IBM with those from its business partners. One focus is to increase revenues from IBM's 'services oriented architecture' (SOA) solutions, which are industry-specific software solutions that are developed, managed and delivered from IBM's SOA Solutions Center in Beijing. These solutions enable companies to create new business services across their existing IT infrastructure; for example, a business service that can track inventory through the design, manufacturing, supply and payment processes that were previously disconnected. IBM also offers IT services (application development, maintenance and testing on its own or package-solution software such as SAP, Oracle and others) to domestic and international clients from its services delivery centres in Shenzhen, Shanghai and Dalian.

In terms of client industry, financial services account for more than half of IBM's China revenues. Major customers include China's 'big four' state-owned banks (for example, Bank of Communications and Agricultural Bank of China) and private banks (such as China Minsheng Banking) (*International Herald Tribune*, 2006). Government agencies are also a major group of customers, such as China's State Administration of Taxation for which it supplied Unix-based servers. It also serves major clients in the telecom and energy sectors. In December 2006, for example, IBM announced that it would join with Intel to establish an Energy Competency Center in Beijing to provide Chinese and other oil and gas companies in the Asia Pacific region with new data analysis and business process integration capabilities to help them find and extract hydrocarbon deposits more quickly and efficiently and at lower cost and risk.[3]

IBM's Global Procurement Center was moved to Shenzhen in October 2006, based on the local procurement centre that had been established there in 1996. It currently oversees US$36 billion in sales globally. Although this is currently hardware-focused, an increasing proportion of its activities will focus on sourcing software and services.[4]

(*Continued*)

EXHIBIT 5.1 (*Continued*)

Organization

In addition to its supporting functions (HR, Communications, Legal and so on), IBM Greater China is organized by functions for research and development (R&D) and manufacturing, and by channel, client type and industry for sales and marketing.

R&D

Research and development functions are organized as follows:

- China Research Lab (1995; 200+ computer experts, one of eight IBM corporate research labs);
- China Software and System Lab (1999; 3000+ software engineers);
- China System Center (2005);
- Global Services Oriented Architecture Solution Center (2006).

Manufacturing and Service Operations

Global Delivery Hubs (supporting IBM's operations worldwide) are organized as follows:

- Server Manufacturing (2002)
- Global Delivery Centers (Shenzhen 2002, Shanghai 2003, Dalian 2003)
- Global Procurement (2006)

Sales and Marketing

Sales and marketing teams are organized by product and industry sector. Products and services, sold stand-alone or as integrated solutions, are organized as follows:

- hardware (servers, workstations, storage, printers, POS, microelectronics);
- software (development management, data management, process management, system management, storage management, etc.);
- services (application development, integration and management; business processes; maintenance and technical support; site, server, storage and data management; IT strategy and architecture; networking; ITSM and SOA; end-user services; strategic outsourcing; etc.).

Industry sector teams deliver IT solutions meeting the specific needs of organizations in:

- financial services (banking, financial markets, insurance);
- public sector (education, government, healthcare);
- industry (aerospace, automotive, defense, chemical and petroleum, electronics);
- distribution (consumer products, retail, travel, transportation);
- communications (telecommunications, media and entertainment, energy and utilities);
- small and medium-size business (with less than 1000 employees).

EXHIBIT 5.2 IBM'S MAIN PHILANTHROPIC ACTIVITIES IN CHINA

The programmes that CCCA and UR develop and support, alone or in cooperation with the Chinese government, are chosen for the long-term benefits they generate for Chinese society. They are not justified internally by a business case, nor are they designed to generate near or even mid-term business for IBM. Some of these programmes are local implementations of IBM's global programmes, whereas others are China-specific. Below is a synopsis of major programmes that CCCA and UR currently oversee in China.

Cooperative Activities with the Ministry of Education (MoE)

IBM's education-related activities have become formalized through a series of Memoranda of Understanding between IBM and the MoE, the first signed in 1995 and revised in 2000, and a second Memorandum of Understanding signed in 2005. The overall objective is to cultivate talent and education related to information technology.

Universities

Starting with donations of computer equipment, hardware and software to Chinese colleges and universities in 1984, IBM has expanded its cooperative activities to include over 50 universities. Over 570 000 students have attended lectures and training related to IBM technology, 58 000 have been awarded IBM professional certifications and 4000 teachers have participated in teacher training programmes. Most of these programmes are heavily subsidized by IBM, with steep discounts on courses, programmes and certification examinations for university students. Most recently, IBM collaborated with the Chinese MoE to design the curriculum and establish a new multidisciplinary major in Services Science, Management and Engineering (SSME) in Chinese universities.

R&D IBM's research organizations work directly with groups in over 50 Chinese universities on development projects. Recent examples include the BlueSky Open Platform for Basic Education, developed jointly with Xian Jiaotong University, or projects with Beijing University's School of Software and Microelectronics related to accessibility. Collaborative projects involving more than one other college are also supported under the Shared University Research Project (see next section), with examples in the life sciences, supply chain management and other R&D targets.

Shared University Research (SUR) programme IBM is working as a facilitator to collaborative research activities with 24 member colleges and universities. Under this programme, IBM provides guidance, project management assistance and funding in the form of software and hardware for cross-institution joint research projects, of which 67 are currently underway. The programme also supports researcher exchanges among IBM labs, member institutions and other partners, such as Hong Kong University.

Internships and Career Support IBM has hosted over 1000 university student interns at the undergraduate and graduate levels in its China Research Center and China Development Center and in its major branches throughout China. Under its Blue Route programme, IBM is now hosting over 400 interns for summer positions. To further support individuals' career development, IBM has opened its Pioneer Tribe system to students, teachers and IT technical

(Continued)

EXHIBIT 5.2 (*Continued*)

personnel. Biographical information on the individual's IT expertise is placed in a database that IBM makes available worldwide to the rest of the IBM organization, its business partners and its users. This system is linked to IBM's training and certification system so that individual data are updated in real time as the individual gains more skills. At the individual level, IBM employees participate in the MentorPlace programme that brings together IBM employees and university students.

Continuing Education   Primarily working with Chinese universities and colleges, IBM offers a range of resources to improve and support IT-related teaching through the IBM Institute of Education. Some of these resources are on-line tutorials for self-guided study. Others are available to partner institutions to provide in turn to their teachers and students, with courses ranging from training for specific IBM software (e.g., Lotus Tivoli, DB2, WebSphere, etc.) to broader technical training and IT-related problem solving. IBM also collaborates with 13 institutions to offer IBM certification courses and examinations, and with the University of Science and Technology's School of Continuing Education to develop curricula for professional and vocational training.

Primary Education

Over 7000 primary school teachers have received free training in the following two programmes, thereby reaching over 100 000 children.[5]

KidSmart   Launched in 2001, IBM has donated 2350 KidSmart computer learning centres in 430 pre-schools in 45 cities across China, as well as in community computer centres in remote areas. These workstations, designed to fit the stature and preferences of children aged 3–7 years old, are loaded with educational software focusing on math, science and ecology. Teachers are trained how to incorporate KidSmart into their curricula (www.kidsmartearlylearning.org).

Reinventing Education   Launched in 2003 in 20 primary schools in Beijing, Shanghai, Guangzhou and Chengdu, this project brings experiences and resources to schools to improve the teaching effectiveness with IT.

Other China-Based Activities

Open Source and BLUESKY

Beginning in 2005, IBM collaborated with the Chinese government and academic institutions to develop an open source basic education community centred on K-12 education. Based on easy, reliable and low-cost Linux and network computer technology, the resulting education platform called BlueSky has been made available to a group of pilot schools and is scheduled to be expanded to benefit over 1 million students.

The Forbidden City: Beyond Space and Time

IBM teamed with The Palace Museum to develop an interactive programme presenting the history of China's Forbidden City to a worldwide audience, as part of the preparations for the 2008 Olympic Games in China.

Engineers Week

Held for the first time in China in 2006, over 100 volunteers from IBM's China Research Lab and China Development Lab shared their experiences with 4800 elementary and middle-school students from Shanghai and Beijing, helping them visualize how the future may develop.

Local Implementation of IBM'S Worldwide Programmes

On Demand Community

Launched in 2003 in Greater China, the On Demand Community programme encourages IBM employees to volunteer in community work and provides access to a common pool of IT solutions that they can use in these activities. These solutions include education modules, IT tools and other web resources, and are also used to support other IBM programmes (EX.I.T.E. Camps, World Community Grid, Kidsmart). IBM employees who volunteer above a certain level receive recognition certificates, and those who work with a school or not-for-profit organization for 40 hours over five months may request grants in the form of cash or equipment for the place where they volunteer.

TryScience Around the World

IBM has so far donated 40 TryScience kiosks to 11 science halls and museums in 10 Chinese cities. These multimedia computer terminals are connected to a high-speed network and servers globally, presenting visitors with content in such diverse areas as biology, space exploration, extreme sports and marine organisms.

EX.I.T.E. (Exploring Interest in Technology and Engineering)

In 2004, IBM began to roll out this programme for middle-school girls, and currently runs the one-week camps in Beijing, Shanghai and Guangzhou in the mainland, as well as in Hong Kong, Taipei and Tainan in Greater China. The campers learn to engineer robots, visiting universities and research labs, interact with IBM female engineers and scientists, and present in groups their innovations and robot designs. At the end of the programme, the girls are paired with IBM employees who will be available to them through the MentorPlace programme to give on-line academic assistance and career advice.

World Community Grid

Launched in 2004, IBM provides the technology and platform to create a virtual computer grid that combines the idle computing power of personal and business computers worldwide to enable complex computations on projects in the life sciences, environment and healthcare. Individuals download and install a free agent that links it to the grid to supply unused computing time to the collective projects. So far, over 36% of IBM employees in Greater China have participated, and we encourage our business partners, clients and not-for-profit organizations to participate. Any scientific programmes from volunteer groups, academic or research organizations may apply for support from the World Community Grid's computing resources (see www.worldcommunitygrid.org).

EXHIBIT 5.3 SUMMARY OF *MODERN SOCIALIST COUNTRYSIDE* AND *HARMONIOUS SOCIETY* POLICIES

In 2006, the Chinese government and Chinese Communist Party (CCP) under Hu Jintao have launched a comprehensive campaign to raise awareness and support for a series of specific policies and programmes under the two labels *Modern Socialist Countryside* and *Harmonious Society*. In some respects, these resemble the Go West initiative of 2000–2005 promoted by Jiang Zemin, the former Chinese President and Chairman of the CCP. That policy attempted to lure foreign and domestic companies to invest in operations in the western regions; that is, the 12 non-coastal provinces that are home to 25% of China's population but lagging further and further behind the economic powerhouses of the coastal provinces. That initiative is generally seen as unsuccessful. Urban-rural income gaps have continued to widen. In terms of investment, although the government claims that more than US$48 billion has flowed into the region, the vast majority was central government funding for various programmes, and at most US$2 billion was in new foreign direct investment.[6] Of that relatively small amount, most is focused on just two cities, Chongqing and Chengdu, where Motorola, Microsoft, Nokia and Siemens have set up R&D centres and Intel, Ford, Carrefour and Ikea, among other multinationals, have established regional operating bases. That initiative will not be officially assessed a failure, but we see it as being politely ignored by the new leadership as they push their own development policies, which share some ultimate goals with the Go West initiative, but are much broader and ambitious in both their means and ends.

Modern Socialist Countryside

The issues concerning agriculture, rural areas and farmers are fundamental ones that have a bearing on China's overall modernization drive. Building the New Socialist Countryside refers to putting agriculture and rural areas more prominently on the agenda of China's modernization drive. We must implement a policy of getting industry to support agriculture, cities to support the countryside and strengthen support for agriculture, rural areas and farmers.[7]

We will effectively shift the focus of state infrastructure development and development of social programmes to the countryside.

Premier Wen Jiabao
Speech at 10th National People's Congress
March 2006

Up to now, government development policies have essentially been an 'agriculture-supports-industry' approach. In macroeconomic terms, these policies have been largely successful as reflected in the dramatic rise in China's manufacturing and export performance and the doubling of its gross domestic product, national fiscal income and fixed asset investment over the last five years.

The benefits, however, have not been spread evenly. Urban residents have benefited disproportionately compared to the 65% of the population (800 million people) living in rural areas. Cities now have dramatically better infrastructure in health care and education, and urban resident incomes are 3.22 times those in the countryside. More than 300 million farmers have difficulty accessing safe drinking water. In recent years, over 200 000 hectares of farmland have been turned into factory or residential sites annually, often with local government officials colluding with developers and companies to improperly seize land from farmers.[8]

The Modern Socialist Countryside represents an attempt to narrow the rural-urban gap. During 2006, the Chinese government announced a set of broad set of activities and targets as part of this initiative:[9]

1. Plan economic and social development in urban and rural areas as a whole, and firmly promote construction of the new countryside.
2. Boost modern agriculture to consolidate industrial support for the new countryside construction.
3. Ensure sustained increases in farmers' incomes to lay a solid rural economic foundation.
4. Increase infrastructure construction in rural areas to improve rural material conditions.
5. Accelerate development of public services in the countryside and encourage new farmers.
6. Deepen comprehensive rural reform to guarantee systematic protection for rural people.
7. Improve democracy in rural areas and perfect rural management.
8. Enhance leadership and motivate all party members and the entire society to care, support and participate in the construction of a new countryside.

The central government has announced specific programmes and funding of US$45 billion to be invested over the coming years in education, healthcare, agriculture technology, environment and local government support. So far, these include:

- *Education:* Elimination of tuition and fees for compulsory education (up to age 12).
- *Healthcare:*
  - speed up the roll-out of the rural cooperative medical care system;
  - increase individual allowance for cooperative medical care system participation from RMB20 to RMB40 (US$3 to US$6);
  - US$ 2.6 billion to renovate hospitals and upgrade equipment.
- *Agriculture:*
  - eliminating the agricultural tax and various local fees and charges paid by farmers;
  - US$9 billion in agriculture science and technology.
- *Infrastructure and environment:*
  - investments in transportation network, including airports, railways and roadways;
  - US$ 500 million to improve rural drinking water supplies for half of the 300 million people who have unstable access to safe drinking water;
  - improve waste water treatment infrastructure.
- *Local government:* US$14 billion to support local government operations (including school operations).

(Continued)

EXHIBIT 5.3 (*Continued*)

Harmonious Society

Hu's predecessor, Jiang Zemin, was seen as promoting economic growth at nearly any cost. Although economic growth has certainly benefited China, it also ignored significant social costs that are just now being recognized as critical for China's further development. One often cited example is that 20 of the world's 30 worst polluted cities are Chinese.

Particularly worrying for Chinese leaders is the significant increase in social unrest. China officially recognized 74 000 incidents of 'internal unrest' during 2004, much of these occurring in the countryside. Their response has been to announce a set of social objectives and some specific policies to create what the CCP is calling a Harmonious Society (*Washington Post*, 2006). Like the Modern Socialist Countryside initiative, it is focused on the need to broaden the benefits of economic development. However, it draws particular attention to the need to address the sources of anger, fear and uncertainty that underlie recent social unrest. Those feelings have swelled as farmers have seen their incomes and opportunities fall further behind those in urban areas, and as local officials illegally assess taxes and fees or seize their land for commercial development for both personal gain and to meet revenue gaps as central government support declined in recent years. Other causes affect those in both rural and urban areas: an inadequate social welfare system to support pensioners, the unemployed and ill; endemic corruption; pollution and other environmental problems; and escalating crime and divorce rates.

Although some people see this as simply more propaganda, we see this policy as further evidence that President Hu Jintao is trying to make a real shift in national priorities. It is a pragmatic move to address worsening social tensions that could undermine China's long-term development.

---

responsibilities as a corporate citizen with our strategy and operations as a business. Our fundamental philosophy will not change. Namely, as a corporation, we will continue to do more than simply abide by the minimum legal requirements for doing business in China or in any country in which we operate. Furthermore, in keeping with IBM's global mission and identity, we want to be able to say that we are helping to shape China's development and support its growth into the future.

We do have alternatives, however, in how we pursue this corporate mission and achieve our business objectives. We have set for ourselves the goals of growing 1.5 times the market and doubling our emerging market revenues by 2010. For China, this means increasing revenues to US$3 billion (3% of IBM's global revenues) from US$1.5 billion. This is in light of China's current US$16 billion IT market that has been growing at an average of 14% in recent years and will likely become the 6th largest market by 2010. It is already a major hardware market, and there is a shift towards more spending on solutions, software and services.[10]

Our China Strategy, recently approved by the IBM leadership, calls for the following:

- build balanced and consistent growth:
  - rapid expansion of coverage and offerings
  - capture rapid growth in the small-medium business segment
  - grow high-value software and services from 25 to 50% of revenues[11]
  - partner to build world class clients
- deepen our relationship with the government;
- explore and build innovative new business models;
- leverage China skills and resources for global delivery of hardware and services.

We now must think concretely of how we can pursue our corporate mission and business objectives while aligning with the Chinese government leadership's new, broader social and developmental priorities. Therefore, at our coming meeting, I have set the following topics for our discussion:

1. We have a goal of China contributing significantly to IBM's growth in three ways: as a market, as a source of innovation and as a base for delivering products and services globally. What can we do that simultaneously satisfies our growth objectives and aligns with the priorities of the *Modern Socialist Countryside* and *Harmonious Society* initiatives? Considering the wide range of areas that are being targeted by the government – agriculture, healthcare, education, infrastructure, environment, local government – what are some possibilities for new business development? Are there some areas we should avoid?

2. We currently have a clear separation between activities under our philanthropic programmes (managed by CCCA and UR[12]), and activities in government-related business development (managed by Government Programs[13]) and sales and marketing. Should we increase the emphasis on social development policy considerations in our operations – procurement, manufacturing, marketing and sales? If so, how? Or, should our philanthropic programmes be our primary means of satisfying the government's expectations regarding IBM China's responsibility as a corporate citizen? Alternatively, should we shift our philanthropic programmes to be more directly linked to our business growth objectives?

3. For both our strategic objectives and corporate mission, it is necessary that the Chinese government and domestic stakeholders see IBM as a 'trusted advisor' so that we have a role in contributing to policy development, rather than as a self-interested lobbyist simply pursuing commercial profit. What can we do to create that perception?

4. Should we seek greater cooperation with other corporations, or continue to act relatively independently? In what areas does it make sense for us to cooperate? What would be the objective of such cooperation?

I look forward to your ideas on these issues.

NOTES

1. The case is intended to be used as a basis for class discussion rather than to illustrate either effective or ineffective handling of an administrative situation.
2. Data for this exhibit come from the presentation *IBM Investors Briefing, May 2007*, available on the IBM website, internal documents and published sources.
3. IBM Press Release, 13 December 2006, Beijing.
4. 'IBM shifts Global Procurement Center to Shenzhen', IBM Press Release, 12 October 2006.
5. China has 456 900 primary schools and 5.8 million primary school teachers for 122 million students. At the secondary level, there are 81 000 junior and senior high schools, 84 million students and 4.5 million teachers.
6. Reuters, 24 November 2006.
7. Xinhua News Agency, 14 March 2006.
8. Xinhua News Agency, 23 February 2006.
9. Xinhua News Agency, 21 February 2006.
10. IBM Investor Briefing, May 2007.
11. Although hardware currently represents 75% of IBM's revenues in China, globally it accounts for only 40%.
12. Corporate Citizenship and Corporate Affairs, and University Relations.
13. The Government Programs group is the primary liaison with policy makers in various government ministries and agencies. They hold both formal and informal discussions with government officials regarding policy and other developments. They not only gather information and views from these officials, but also offer them information and ideas that could be useful in developing and implementing policies.

REFERENCES

China Business Weekly (2004) IBM eyes 50% market share, 24 September.

International Herald Tribune (2006) IBM plans to join bid for Guangdong bank, 13 November.

Washington Post (2006) China's Party leadership declares new priority: 'Harmonions Society', 11 October.

CHAPTER SIX

IBERDROLA: A Utility's Approach to Sustainability and Stakeholder Management[1]

Tanguy Jacopin, IESE Business School, Serge Poisson-de Haro, HEC Montréal and Joan Fontrodona, IESE Business School

INTRODUCTION

In July 2004, José Ignacio Sánchez Galán, the CEO of IBERDROLA, was enjoying a few days in his native Aragon, as he did every summer. Looking at the birds flying around his beloved landscape and sipping his morning cup of *café con leche*, he was reflecting on his first three years as CEO of IBERDROLA, the second largest Spanish utility by size, and all that the company had achieved under his leadership. He was particularly proud that IBERDROLA was the top-ranking utility company in the Dow Jones Sustainability Index, demonstrating the timeliness of his decision to put sustainability at the core of IBERDROLA's strategy.

Sustainable development had become a priority of both governments and companies alike. Spain was under pressure from the European Union to introduce new directives on the energy sector and cleaner technologies into its legislation. A major issue was climate change, with the likely ratification of the Kyoto Protocol prompting increased calls for legislation in European countries. The Spanish utility sector was a large producer of greenhouse gas emissions at a time when green energy was being promoted and the energy sector itself was being liberalized, and Galán had seen this as a window of opportunity, the chance to make IBERDROLA a world-leading green utility company.

Sustainability was placed at the heart of the decision-making processes in IBERDROLA. The company sold off its most polluting facilities and all non-core activities, such as investments in non-related businesses. Investment was instead focused on the aim of becoming one of the largest green players in the world. Two years after implementation of its new strategic plan, IBERDROLA could already see the impact of renewable energies and combined cycle plants on its bottom line. The new strategy was directly responsible for a total increase of over 10% in EBITDA (Earnings Before Interest, Taxes, Depreciation and Amortization), more than compensating for the decrease in hydroelectric output, which the company ascribed to climate change.

One challenge of the new strategy was making sure that financial analysts and consumers understood the logic behind IBERDROLA's aim to become the greenest player on the market. A strong stakeholder dialogue policy was implemented, and Galán put specific effort into communicating with the financial sector on a regular basis. He also encouraged the team in charge of greening the company's production portfolio, in particular those involved in the implementation of wind energy strategies, to dialogue on a regular basis with environmental stakeholders.

IBERDROLA established contacts with several leading environmental non-governmental organizations (NGOs). The company's strategic objective of becoming the leading Spanish utility with the cleanest facilities formed the basis of a stakeholder engagement programme with these organizations. But being a sustainability innovator meant that the process was difficult at times, and the sustainability model needed constant fine-tuning as IBERDROLA's relationships with its stakeholders changed. The company was under the microscope.

Now Galán was worried. He had just read in the *Aragon Herald*, a regional newspaper, that two rare royal eagles (*Aguila Reale*) had been lethally injured after hitting IBERDROLA electricity pylons. NGO activists were complaining about the attitude of the utility company. Although IBERDROLA was an industry front-runner in terms of its sustainability policy, in particular in its greening of production facilities and engagement with stakeholders such as environmental NGOs, it was not enough to be a good corporate citizen – the company had to be irreproachable. Something that might have been considered a minor incident for other companies was different for IBERDROLA. The reputation of the company – one of the best-recognized brands in Spain – and the viability of the new business model were at stake. Incidents such as this could damage the image of the company, and the trust of investors and other stakeholders.

The week after he read about the eagles, Galán called an extraordinary meeting at the IBERDROLA headquarters in Bilbao to review the sustainability business model and to come up with a way of dealing with the bird issue. It was the third time in just a few months that IBERDROLA had found itself the subject of recriminations from NGOs. There had been criticisms of IBERDROLA's inability to develop a green certification process with one NGO, and negative comments from the third sector following IBERDROLA's media campaign to boost renewable energies. These events were at the forefront of Galán's mind as the meeting began.

IBERDROLA

IBERDROLA was formed in 1991 from the merger of two companies, Hidroeléctrica Española and Iberduero. Hidroeléctrica Española had been established in 1907 to supply electricity to Madrid and Valencia by exploiting inland rivers. Iberduero had its origins in Hidroeléctrica Ibérica, founded in 1901, and a 1944 merger with Saltos del Duero, and also had its core business in hydroelectricity, in the northern rivers of Spain. In the 1970s, both companies widened their scope of activity from hydroelectricity and coal plants to include nuclear power plants.

The merging of two of Spain's oldest power suppliers was agreed on 1 November 1992, and the next decade saw IBERDROLA going through the difficulties of creating a new and unique corporate culture. Nevertheless, the company managed to keep its leadership position in the generation, transmission, distribution and retailing of electricity in the Spanish utility sector, and was even able to initiate an expansion programme in Latin America and Europe. An environmental policy was established in 1992 (Figure 6.1) and this was recognized officially when an environmental unit and a renewable energy division were created as part of the structure of IBERDROLA in 1995.

1.	Fully INTEGRATE considerations of the environment into company strategy.
2.	Constantly ENSURE that financial gain and protection of the environment are compatible by means of innovation and eco-efficiency.
3.	INCORPORATE the environmental dimension when making decisions concerning investments and planning, as well as when carrying out activities, and encourage its inclusion in cost-benefit analyses.
4.	ESTABLISH suitable management systems that help to reduce environmental risk, including: a. Compliance with environment legislation, with international commitments and with internal rules applicable to IBERDROLA's activities, facilities, products and services, also bearing in mind legislative trends and the most advanced international practices, and establishing procedures that provide knowledge and help to monitor compliance with these commitments. b. An ongoing effort to identify, evaluate and reduce the negative environmental effects of the company's activities, facilities, products and services. c. Information and training for employees on the effects of carrying out and developing the company's processes and products in order to minimise the negative effects of these activities on health and the environment. Development of plans and programmes establishing objectives and targets, updating emergency plans and performing internal audits in order to reduce risk, minimise negative environmental risk and regularly monitor the advances and efficiency of the measures applied, thereby encouraging ongoing improvement in the company's processes and practices.
5.	RESPECT nature, biodiversity and the historic and artistic wealth of the natural settings in which the company's facilities are located.
6.	PROMOTE research into and development of new technologies that help to face key environmental challenges with a preventive focus, enabling a more efficient use of natural resources and allowing us to advance towards a more sustainable energy model.
7.	ENCOURAGE behaviour in accordance with the principles of this commitment among the company's main stakeholders, valuing alignment with this commitment particularly when recruiting business partners and suppliers.
8.	ESTABLISH a constructive dialogue with public administrations, non-governmental organizations, shareholders, clients, local communities and other stakeholders, with the aim of working together to search for solutions to environmental problems and helping to develop a public policy that is useful from an environmental point of view and efficient in economic terms.
9.	PROVIDE INFORMATION on environmental results and actions, maintaining proper channels that further communication with key stakeholders.

Figure 6.1 IBERDROLA's basic principles of conduct

In 2001, Galán was appointed CEO of IBERDROLA. He decided to unify the strengths of the two former companies under a project that required staff cooperation and strong leadership. Following a shareholder meeting, Galán set the agenda for a strategy based on sustainability, stating:

> The environment is a conditioning factor for the whole of human activity, as well as a competitive element for companies. Aware of the importance of this factor in fulfilling the company's mission, IBERDROLA is committed to promoting environmental innovation and eco-efficiency, to progressively reducing the environmental impact of its activities, facilities, products and services, and to harmonizing the performance of its activities with the legitimate right of future generations to enjoy a healthy environment.

Sustainable development was now at the core of the company's strategic thinking and actions.

INDUSTRY OVERVIEW

Global Challenges

In 1987, the World Commission on Environment and Development Report (known as the Brundtland Report) stated that business could play a positive role in furthering the cause of environmental protection, by integrating environmental protection with economic performance. The report defined sustainable development as 'development that meets the needs of the present without compromising the ability of future generations to meet their own needs'.

This led to important development targets being established in the 1990s, based on economic efficiency, energy security and environmental requirements. The EU Green Paper on Energy Security (2001) highlighted that the EU imported more than 50% of its energy and that a new energy model based on renewable energies was required.

December 1997 saw the introduction of the Kyoto Protocol at the United Nations Framework Convention on Climate Change, whereby signatories were committed to reducing emissions of CO_2 and other greenhouse gases. A system of emissions trading was established for countries unable to meet reduction targets. Spain signed the Protocol simultaneously with the European Union and other member countries in 1998, with ratification following in 2002. However, the Kyoto Protocol would only come into force when at least 55 countries responsible for at least 55% of all polluting emissions worldwide had signed, and in July 2004, Russia and the United States were yet to do so. (Russia ratified the Kyoto Protocol in November 2004, initiating the further application of the main measures to limit climate change.)

Although ratification of the Kyoto Protocol committed industrialized countries to reducing overall carbon emissions to 5.2% below 1990 levels by 2008, Spain was one of the countries given special conditions in recognition of its rapid economic development during the 1990s. Spanish companies were allowed to increase their gas emissions by 15% compared to 1990 levels, allowing for the fact that emissions had risen by more than 40% between 1990 and 2004 (*El Mundo*, 2005).

At the same time that climate change was moving up the international agenda, the importance of sustainability was also being recognised. The tremendous economic, environmental and social impact of electricity had placed it at the core of social development, making it a prime mover for productivity, wages and jobs throughout the world. The World Business Council for Sustainable Development stated that: 'Looking at the future, electricity will play an even greater transformative role in the twenty-first century [. . .] Electricity will act as a catalyst for business development in a number of sectors' (WBCSD Report, 2002). Regarding the challenges faced by the industry, the report added:

> In supplying power in the coming century, electrical utilities face growing expectations to decouple economic growth from natural resource consumption and environmental footprints. Demand for electricity is escalating against a backdrop of an unprecedented call to action to safeguard broad environmental and social interests. Electricity utilities have many stakeholders. They interact with governments, customers, communities, non-governmental organizations and many others, and must frequently manage diverse and conflicting expectations. One of the challenges of the industry is changing stakeholder expectations with current long-term technology choices, which may have a life cycle of 25 to 100 years.

WBCSD Report, 2002

The environmental impact of energy-related activities and issues of access to lasting, dependable and affordable primary energy sources, particularly for the one-third of humankind still without access to electricity, all contributed to a growing concern over the sustainability of current and projected trends in world-wide energy production and consumption.

Local Challenges

The Spanish government began taking action in 1997 with the Spanish Power Act, which established a target of 29.4% of gross electricity consumption to be supplied from renewable sources by 2010. Signing up to the Kyoto Protocol meant that Spain was legally mandated to reduce emissions (for more details of Spanish and EU activities regarding Kyoto, see Exhibit 6.1). One of the consequences of signing was that Spain had to introduce a system for allocating CO_2 emission rights to industry

---

EXHIBIT 6.1 THE KYOTO PROTOCOL

In the environmental sector, the main initiative was the launch within the European Union of trade in the right to emit greenhouse gases, which came into effect on 1 January, 2005 and which has significant repercussions for the energy industry. In January 2004, the European Commission published guidelines for the development of National Allocation Plans (NAPs), and in February 2004 it made public two decisions on the monitoring and reporting of greenhouse gases. In July and December 2004, the NAPs of 21 member states were approved, some of them subject to conditions, and in November 2004, a directive was published that permitted the incorporation of clean development mechanisms (CDMs) and joint applications (JAs) to be included in the trading of emission rights.

The official ratification of the Kyoto Protocol by Russia in November 2004 enabled compliance with the minimum requirements for its entry to come into force, providing legal support for EU initiatives in the fight against climate change, including community-wide trading of emission rights. Also within this framework, it is important to mention the publication of the directive on environmental responsibility in April 2004.

(Continued)

EXHIBIT 6.1 (*Continued*)

From a Spanish regulatory standpoint, the approval of the National Allocation Plan (NAP) by the Spanish government was a significant event, and during 2004, the following initiatives were launched:

- the Spanish strategy for compliance with the Kyoto Protocol was approved in February;
- Royal Decree Law 5/2004, which transposes the directive on the trading of emission rights, and Royal Decree 1866/2004, which approves the NAP for emission rights for the 2005–2007 period, were published in the autumn;
- the proposal for the allocation of emission rights by facility was presented in late November and, after minor adjustments, was approved by the Cabinet of Ministers on January 21, 2005;
- the NAP was submitted to the European Commission in December, and was conditionally approved by the Commission.

The NAP will contribute to attaining the goals established in the Kyoto Protocol and will encourage the replacement of Spanish generating facilities with clean technologies, mainly gas combined-cycle plants and renewable energy. Another important environmental regulation for the energy industry that became effective during 2004 was Royal Decree 430/2004, which adopted the directive on the limitation of polluting emissions into the air from large combustion facilities.

Following approval of the European emission trading directive regarding carbon dioxide in October 2003, Royal Decree Law 5/2004, incorporating this directive into Spanish legislation, was published on 27 August, 2004. The programme implemented is based on one of the market instruments provided for in the Kyoto Protocol, namely, emission trading. In conjunction with the instruments based on projected investments in clean technology in third-party countries (i.e., clean development and joint application), this programme is one of the so-called flexibility mechanisms of the Kyoto Protocol. Royal Decree 1866/2004, published on 6 September, 2004, approved the NAP for emission rights for the period 2005–2007. This plan specifies the emission rights total allocated to each industry in each period, as well as the procedures for their allocation, which are based on objective and transparent criteria.

The electrical power industry was assigned 86.4 Mt of CO_2 per year for 2005–2007, including rights for new entrants into the sector. The allocation also included 1.6 Mt derived from the manufacture of iron and steel, which was to be conveyed through electrical-power generation facilities, giving a total assigned to the sector of 88 Mt. Accordingly, over this period, the electrical power industry will receive 10% fewer rights than for its emissions in 2002, as opposed to the 11% increase for the other industries addressed in the directive.

According to the proposal presented by the Spanish government, coverage of estimated domestic demand would be satisfied in a manner that complied with the environmental objective, through the generation of electrical power using currently available technology and fuels. The rights allocated to power-generation facilities would represent the sum total of the actual emissions produced in order to achieve this goal.

The Spanish government has recognized that the electrical power industry needs to make the greatest effort toward reducing emissions, mainly through the renovation of generating plants, the gradual replacement of coal-based power generation by more efficient technologies, such as natural gas combined-cycle plants, and the use of renewable energy sources. Through the distribution of facility-based emission rights, finally approved on 21 January, 2005, technological change in the Spanish electrical power sector would be aimed at ensuring a reduction in CO_2 emissions in Spain.

sectors and to companies within a sector. This system penalized industrial sectors that had a high impact on the environment in terms of greenhouse effects. As the utility market was the most polluting sector (leaving aside the transport sector), utility companies came under pressure, particularly from NGO activists, to establish new policies. Utility companies had to begin greening their businesses by promoting eco-efficiency and developing cleaner production facilities.[2]

The Spanish Government adopted several methods to promote compliance with the Kyoto Protocol on limiting greenhouse gas emissions. Subsidies for renewable energies were introduced to encourage utility companies to invest more in this type of technology. Other technologies, such as combined-cycle plants, which were more efficient than oil- or gas-powered plants, were also promoted. In response, the utility companies embarked on significant investment programmes to build new generating facilities.

Market liberalization was another tool the Spanish Government tried to use to further Kyoto compliance. The European market was already going through a liberalization process to create a competitive energy sector in Europe. Spain was one of the first countries to implement the EU directive encouraging competition among domestic players in the electricity market (Expansión, 2007). Spanish consumers were thus able to switch utility provider, and could base their choice on how much a company was doing to reduce emissions – although few people did, due to a lack of awareness of this right.

A third option for managing Kyoto Protocol targets open to the Spanish Government was to acquire emissions rights to other countries or companies in the European market.

As well as the Kyoto Protocol and the liberalization of energy markets, a number of institutions have published guidelines and frameworks that outline further reasons and incentives for the utility sector to rethink its strategies for sustainable development. These include the EU Green Book, Norm UNE-EN-ISO 14001, the environmental principles of the OECD Guidelines for MNCs, the EU strategy for sustainable development, the Global Compact environmental principles, the guidelines of the 6th EU Program of Action for Sustainable Development, EU environmental directives, EURELECTRIC guidelines, the 2003/87/CE greenhouse gas directive, the 2001–2011 National Energy Plan and the Intelligent Energy Program for Europe.

Thus the Spanish utility market was being acted on by a combination of international and local legislative and competitive forces. Companies that could adopt and demonstrate a commitment to

Table 6.1 Endesa Production Mix 2002–2004 (% of Total Capacity)

	Year	Coal	Hydroelectric	Nuclear	Oil/Gas	Combined Cycle, Renewable and Co-Generation
Installed	2002	29.9	25.6	17.3	27.2	inc. oil/gas
capacity	2003	29	25	17	24	5
	2004	28.6	24.6	16.6	21.3	8.9
Produced	2001	45.2	15.4	34.4	5	—
power	2002	46	9.8	35.2	3.8	5.3
	2003	42.7	14	33.4	2.3	7.7
	2004	43.5	12	32.2	9	10.4

reducing greenhouse gas emissions and sustainable development would differentiate themselves and gain a competitive advantage.

Spanish Utilities and their Production Mixes

Historically, Spanish utility companies had developed their production facilities according to geographical location and state directives implemented when the government took over energy policy. In 2004, there were three main players in the Spanish utility sector, market leader Endesa, IBERDROLA and Unión Fenosa. Endesa was a former state-owned player with a diverse production mix whose size and former ownership meant that it endorsed both nuclear- and coal-powered energy (see Table 6.1).

In 2004, Endesa had a total installed capacity of 46 439 MW worldwide, generating some 184 951 GWh of electricity and supplying 192 519 GWh to a total of 22.2 million customers in the countries in which it operated. By the end of 2004, Endesa's generating facilities in Spain totalled an installed capacity of 23 092 MW.

IBERDROLA was the second largest utility company, and production was heavily biased towards hydroelectric facilities (on the basis of its proximity to the Pyrenees) and nuclear power (due to its size and government requirements) (see Table 6.2).

Table 6.2 IBERDROLA Production Mix 2002–2005 (% of Total Capacity)

	Year	Coal	Renewable and Hydroelectric	Nuclear	Oil/Gas	Combined Cycle and Co-Generation
Installed	2002	6.6	52.5	17.6	15.4	7.8
capacity	2003	6	54	15	14	10
	2004	6	53	13	13	13
	2005 (est.)	4.5	46.5	12.1	10.4	26.5
Produced	2002	14.1	21.5	46	14.3	4
power	2003	9	38	35	4	10
	2004	11	29	33	4	16
	2005 (est.)	8.6	18.6	28.3	4.2	40.3

Table 6.3 Unión Fenosa Production Mix 2002–2004 (% of Total Capacity)

	Year	Coal	Hydroelectric	Nuclear	Oil/Gas	Renewable and Co-Generation
Installed capacity	2002	36	32	13	14	5
	2003	35	31	13	13	8
	2004	35	31	13	13	7
Produced power	2002	57	11	23	6	4
	2003	52	17	22	4	5
	2004	56	11	24	4	5

In 2004, IBERDROLA had headquarters in both Bilbao and Madrid, and employed about 17 000 people in 28 countries. The company had around 18 million clients all over the world (almost 10 million in Spain), and a share of over 40% of the mainland market. IBERDROLA was one of the world's leading wind-energy producers (with over 3400 MW installed) and one of the largest operators of combined-cycle plants (with over 8000 MW under management).

IBERDROLA relied on a wide range of production methods based on renewable energies, coal, oil/gas, nuclear and combined cycles. In accordance with its strategic plan, IBERDROLA had invested considerably in renewable energy facilities (wind) and in combined-cycle and co-generation plants. Production using the latter increased tenfold in 2005 compared to 2002.

The third company, Unión Fenosa, was located mainly in the coal-mining regions of the northwest of the Spanish peninsula, and relied primarily on coal-powered facilities (see Table 6.3).

Unión Fenosa generates electrical power using hydroelectric, thermal and nuclear power plants. In 2004, it generated over 25 000 million kWh in Spain, representing a market share of 12.3% of the mainland Spanish electricity supply. In December 2003, Unión Fenosa sold 80% of its renewable and co-generation business to ENEL. These assets were integrated into a new company, ENEL-UF Renovables (EUFER), which is managed 50:50 by both companies.

In 2004, the main energy sources for all three companies were coal, oil, gas, water, wind, sea, biomass and solar. Looking at the production mixes for the three leading utility companies, it is clear that none of them could rely on a single technology to supply their end users. Each technology had advantages and drawbacks. Focusing only on renewable energies was problematic due to their dependency on weather conditions and cost of production,[3] although the situation was likely to improve as technology became more efficient and costs decreased (for solar and wind energy in particular). Concentrating only on fossil energy was not feasible due to the limited availability of resources and future generation needs. Nuclear energy was highly efficient in terms of the amount of energy generated, but waste disposal was a major societal issue because of the environmental risks.

The Spanish government established a regulatory framework within a grid system (see Figure 6.2) to address the fact that utility companies operated a portfolio of electricity generating technologies, to encourage further development of renewable energy sources and to provide a mechanism for emissions allocation. In 2004, Spain was second only to Germany in terms of installed wind energy

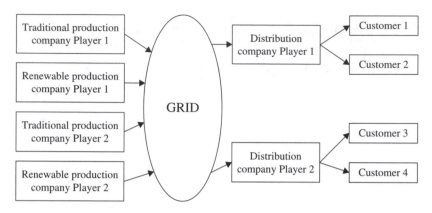

Figure 6.2 The grid system

capacity, but although there was an increasing demand for cleaner electricity among end users, the fact that all energy producers were connected to a grid made it difficult to say 'the energy I am using has been produced by the wind farm next door'.

The grid system obliged each utility to be split into at least three companies – a generating subsidiary, a renewable energy company (special energy subsidiaries) and a distribution subsidiary. On one side of the grid were the generating and renewable energy companies, and on the other side were the distributors. Producers sent their production to the grid, and the distributors supplied electricity from the grid to their customers. It was not possible to identify the origin of the electricity bought by any given customer, given that all electricity, no matter where it came from, reverted to the grid. The only way for companies to market the energy produced by their renewable facilities was to commit to not selling more electricity than that generated by those renewable facilities. The intention was to have each company match what it produced and what it sold.

In the event of insufficient output from renewable production facilities – for instance, due to low wind levels during a given year – a company could find itself in a situation where it was selling more than it had produced and sent to the grid, and so would have to buy power from other players. If the company had a buffer of traditional generation facilities, it could use this to bridge the gap between supply from its renewable energy sources and customer demand. If it had no buffer sufficient to cover the demand, it would have to buy from the grid and so indirectly oblige one of its competitors to produce the necessary energy, because the whole system is committed to providing electricity in a secure manner. This competitor might need to use a fossil energy-powered facility, which could increase gas emissions. A compensation mechanism was established to attribute the emissions for this shortage of green energy to the company for which the electricity was produced. The grid system made all players interdependent, with each player free, however, to select the technologies used to generate the power that it supplied to the grid.

SUSTAINABILITY AS A CORE IBERDROLA STRATEGY

José Ignacio Sánchez Galán left a fast-moving mobile phone company to join IBERDROLA as Vice-Chairman and CEO in 2001. Recognizing the increasing importance of environmental issues to society at large and to the utility industry in particular, he felt that he should commit IBERDROLA to greener energies. Galán singled out wind power, realizing that the first mover in that sector would obtain the best locations for their turbines. IBERDROLA had a historical commitment to hydroelectric power, so Galán reasoned that it already had a green ethos at the core of its culture. In 2003, in an introduction to a public document entitled *IBERDROLA's Business and Sustainable Development*, Galán stated:

> The hydroelectric vocation [of IBERDROLA] favored the emergence of a culture of knowledge and of identification with nature, which is – together with the company's current commitment to the development of wind energy – behind the significant participation of the company in renewable energies, which represent 55% of its installed capacity.

IBERDROLA developed a strategic plan for the period 2002–2006 that aimed to double production capacity by 2007 through new energy technologies and, above all, to develop a competitive advantage in sustainability. IBERDROLA's strategic focus in terms of technology was on renewable energies and combined-cycle plants – technologies that would enable IBERDROLA to position itself as a green energy player. The strategy drove rapid international expansion to secure the best locations for wind turbines and hydroelectric generation, and operations were quickly initiated in the European Union (Greece, Poland, Germany, Italy, France and Portugal), the United States, Canada, Mexico and Brazil.

Implementation

Galán was not proposing a complete upheaval in strategy and organizational structure for IBERDROLA. A unit had been created in 1995 to deal with all environmental aspects, although it did not report directly to the managing director (Figure 6.3). There were already 100 people with environmental functions working within the organization.

The first organizational change occurred in 2001, when the environmental unit was put under the leadership of the institutional relationships manager. The next move was in 2004, when Galán constituted a new management team integrating the environmental unit into the strategy division. The renewable energy unit kept its vertical organization but two policy-creating transversal departments, the corporate reputation department and the reputation committee, were created. Internal relationships with stakeholders were dealt with directly by the relevant department and cross-departmental initiatives were developed to provide a global picture of

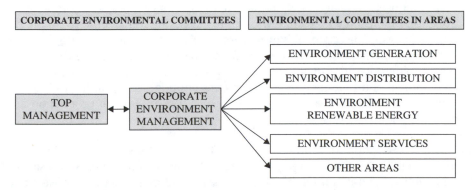

Figure 6.3 The environmental function at IBERDROLA

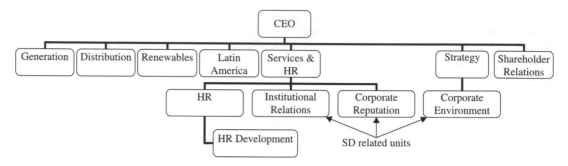

Figure 6.4 IBERDROLA organizational chart

stakeholder management (Figure 6.4). The corporate reputation department was an initiative of the CEO, set up to manage intangible assets. The reputation committee was chaired by the head of human resources and communication. All the company's departments are represented on the reputation committee[4] (communications, corporate reputation, investor relations, customer relations, providers, institutional relations, general secretary, regulation and the CEO's office), and its mission was defined by José Sarrio (corporate relations) as 'linking the actual actions or initiatives of the company with the perception of stakeholders about the company'.

Although IBERDROLA had always been sensitive to its stakeholders, and had an existing, if little known, commitment to the environment, the new strategy recognized the growing importance of sustainability to all its interest groups. Shareholders, users, suppliers, regulatory bodies, the media and employees were all recognised stakeholders; now society at large had become a new but informal interest group. To meet the communication needs implicit in the new strategy, the company initiated open contacts with environmental groups to discuss its proposals for large hydroelectric plants.

Impact

The results of IBERDROLA's 2002 strategic plan are evident in two main areas: the evolution of the company's production mix and its impact on the environment, and the financial results.

Energy efficiency, conservation and new products and services were the key components in tackling the production mix. Energy efficiency was improved during the electricity supply phase and electricity end-use phase. The company's most significant contribution in the supply phase was its commitment to a production structure in which renewable energy sources and natural gas combined-cycle technology played a major role. Initiatives were launched to improve the efficiency of auxiliary equipment and to reduce their power consumption. Electrical losses, due essentially to cable heating and representing a significant economic cost in terms of production and facility overcapacity, were addressed.

IBERDROLA also took action to improve energy efficiency and reduce electricity consumption by end users. Around 40% of the power consumed by public lighting fixtures was saved through a reduction in lighting intensity during off-peak hours. A night rate structure for users of accumulation heating systems was introduced, and consultation services aimed at saving energy were offered, including diagnostic testing of facilities on-site, suggestions for improvement and the implementation of proposed solutions. (For further details on products and services, see Exhibits 6.2 and 6.3).

EXHIBIT 6.2 SUSTAINABLE PRODUCTS AND SERVICES

Among IBERDROLA's initiatives to support more environmentally efficient and friendly energies, a major investment in clean and efficient energy will lead to lower consumption of primary energy, an effective reduction in emissions and an increase in guaranteed supply. Therefore, IBERDROLA has developed a range of environmental products and services in the following areas:

- *Green energy.* This initiative consisted of the sale of electricity obtained from 100% renewable sources, i.e., free of CO_2 and greenhouse gases. In 2004, the company consolidated its leadership in the sale of green energy in Spain, with 52 900 contracts with domestic consumers and 1100 with businesses and official agencies.

- *Photovoltaic solar energy installations.* IBERDROLA offers integrated services for the installation of this type of energy source, ranging from a feasibility analysis to installation and maintenance of the facility, and including the negotiation of subsidies and financing.

- *Customer awareness, information and management of PCBs.* Mailings have been sent to around 8000 customers who own transformers that may be contaminated with PCB (polychlorinated biphenyls), explaining the environmentally harmful nature of this compound and describing the regulations governing its elimination. Diagnostic tests have also been conducted and proposals for removal and replacement have been offered to interested customers.

- *Energy consultation.* IBERDROLA offers services related to energy efficiency and energy conservation in its environmental audit service.

- *Assessment of the environmental impact of the projects.* The focus of IBERDROLA environmental management is oriented toward minimizing the negative effects of its activities and associated risks, through environmental impact studies prior to the creation of production, transformation and distribution facilities and through the automation of its environmental management activities (environmental management systems complying with the UNE-EN-ISO 14001 standard), bearing in mind the principle of prevention.

In accordance with the regulations in force in Spain, almost all projects involving the infrastructure for the production, distribution and transformation of electricity are subject to environmental impact assessment (including, for large projects, a social assessment analysis). Only a few small low-voltage distribution systems are exempt from this overall requirement. The environmental impact assessment had a preventive focus, in terms of minimizing the impact of the infrastructures on the natural environment.

The environmental impact procedure begins with the preparation of a study that contains a diagnosis of the natural environment affected by the project and that analyses the effect of various alternatives on the natural environment, taking into consideration the technology and preventive and corrective measures.

EXHIBIT 6.3   PRINCIPAL ACTIONS FOR REDUCING THE ENVIRONMENTAL IMPACT OF ACTIVITIES

The principal activities conducted over the last few years to palliate the environmental impact of the production, transmission and distribution of electricity by IBERDROLA have been resource consumption, atmosphere, water, waste, land use and biodiversity, noise and electrical and magnetic fields, and emergency plans.

Resource consumption. The principal activities aimed at reducing fuel consumption have been oriented towards improved use of heat energy and residual heat, the use of more efficient fuels and the use of renewable resources. Regarding energy consumption, programmes have been implemented to reduce consumption by auxiliary equipment. With regard to water, plans have been implemented to minimize consumption and increase reuse in thermal power plants.

Atmosphere. Emissions of carbon dioxide (CO_2), sulphur dioxide (SO_2), nitrogen oxides (NOx) and other particulates are inspected and recorded in accordance with the applicable regulatory provisions. To reduce these emissions, more environmentally-efficient fuels are being used, such as low-sulphur (BIA) fuels (which make it possible to achieve a significant reduction in the concentration of sulphur oxide emissions) and additives that neutralize certain acids. Improvements have been obtained in the performance of existing power plants, and new systems have been installed, including low-level NOx burners, electrofilters and precipitators. Monitoring and inspection equipment has been installed to optimize the combustion process within power plants. In addition to these measures, the company has also invested in natural gas combined-cycle units, which will enable a significant reduction in emissions per kilowatt-hour produced by thermal power plants.

Water. In recent years, the company's activities in its thermal power plants have focused on the installation of new cooling towers to reduce the thermal effect of the effluent on the receiving bodies of water. Power plant waste treatment facilities have also been renovated, with the resulting improvement in quality, and recycling systems and programmes have been implemented.

Waste. In recent years, the company's efforts in this area have focused on the development of plans for the reduction of medium- and low-activity radioactive waste, waste-minimization plans and the elimination of dangerous pollutants. The company has also implemented activities for the reuse of slag and ashes generated by the combustion of coal in thermal power plants. These wastes were now being used in the production of cement and as filler materials in civil engineering infrastructure projects.

Land use and biodiversity. The amount of land occupied by each substation is gradually being reduced as a result of the downsizing plan that the company is implementing in Spain. To reduce the effects of electrical power lines on birds, research studies are being conducted in collaboration with wildlife organizations and institutions, and actions are being developed for their preservation, especially in areas of particular environmental value. Action has also been taken in the past to reduce the repercussions on forests and other plant life.

As a result, environmental guidelines have been developed for administrative procedures and for the implementation of infrastructures in the natural environment. The company is also currently implementing the MASVERDE (Greater Green) Project, which includes a range of innovative actions aimed at improving the management of the company's distribution activities in the natural environment.

Noise, electrical and magnetic fields. In 2004, the distribution division developed a plan for the measurement, recording and representation of electrical power substations, which because of their location could be considered high-risk. In the generation area, noise measurement campaigns have been conducted at several facilities, and in the renewable energy area, noise measurements have been made at all the sites covered by the environmental management system.

With regard to electrical and magnetic fields, the work done in 2004 was essentially in the area of occupational risk prevention, in preparation for the forthcoming incorporation of the European directive into Spanish legislation. Activities were not only aimed at the characterization of occupational environments in which higher levels are expected, but also at negotiations with equipment manufacturers and designers so that future products comply more fully with safety requirements.

Emergency plans. To minimize the consequences of a possible accident (caused by fire, waste, etc.), the environmental management systems currently in force require the implementation of the corresponding emergency plans in force at the different facilities. At least one emergency plan simulation is conducted annually at each of the thermal and combined-cycle power plants.

Sustainability and Visibility

IBERDROLA was able to implement a model based on sustainability because the timing was right. The company not only took advantage of government incentives for wind energy, but also managed to sell off non-strategic businesses to finance its investment in renewable energies while competitors were preoccupied with financial difficulties. The sustainability initiatives have gradually improved the company's visibility in the environmental arena. Since 2000, IBERDROLA has maintained constant contact with the major analyst companies focused on social responsibility, such as Sustainable Asset Management (which reviewed the companies eligible for entry to the Dow Jones Sustainability Index), SiRi and Vigeo. Moreover, the company's publication of a sustainability report following the Global Reporting Initiative (GRI) guidelines, and its commitment to Global Compact (a UN initiative to foster sustainable development among other principles) illustrated how IBERDROLA was 'walking the talk', focusing on sustainability at all levels in the company.

In less than two years – leaving aside executive office involvement in the strategy shift – IBERDROLA's environmental policy under the leadership of Galán was recognized worldwide and had received several awards, including best brand in the utility sector, the Interbrand-Expansión award for one of the top five brands in Spain (2003) and the World Business Research award for respect for the environment (2004).[5]

Financial Results

Two years after implementing its strategic plan, the development of additional organizational and knowledge competencies had enabled IBERDROLA to achieve its target. The financial results for the first half of 2004 showed that revenues had increased by 9.1% compared to the first half of 2003 – thanks to growth in all its businesses and despite lower hydroelectric production in Spain of –31%) – and net profits rose by 13.1%. The strong evolution of renewable energies and combined cycles were a clear signal that the new additional capacity had offset the lower hydroelectric capacity. But underlying this was the risk that climate change might affect IBERDROLA more than its competitors, given its historic dependence on hydroelectricity.

A mere two years after the new strategic plan was introduced, evidence from the EBITDA showed that it was possible to create a competitive advantage based on sustainability. However, management of stakeholders – and, in particular, NGOs – did not seem to be completely under control.

IBERDROLA AND THE NGOs

Historically, the Franco dictatorship kept Spanish NGOs distanced from global campaigns and worldwide concerns until the end of the 1970s. Their subsequent evolution showed a strong focus on developmental issues, but also on social and environmental concerns. In 2000, Spanish NGOs had around 500 000 full-time employees and one million volunteers (BBV Fundación, 2000). NGO operations represented 4 or 5% of Spanish GDP according to the BBV Fundación (2000) and the Confederación Empresarial Española para la Economía Social (2003)[6], respectively. As IBERDROLA was in the utility sector, environmental NGOs were a priority.

Organizing Relationships with NGOs

Until early 2000, most IBERDROLA executives were opposed to any collaboration with NGOs, while a minority considered negotiation with NGOs necessary because they were possible future allies. The growing weight of social opinion, however, demonstrated that those supporting negotiation were correct, and IBERDROLA began to promote dialogue with NGOs wherever possible. Although IBERDROLA recognized that environmental groups needed to remain independent from companies in the public eye, this did not rule out dialogue between them.

Discussing potential problems before they became a source of protest was considered the best option. Gonzalo Saenz de Miera, director of the renewable energy unit, adopted the motto: 'The more transparent and democratic the process/bidding is, the better.' In a transparent process, environmental groups could contribute their vision, support projects that matched their criteria and contribute valuable ideas. In many cases, the causes defended by environmentalists reflected societal concerns or expectations that would later develop in the mind of the average consumer, and their early input could keep IBERDROLA one step ahead of public opinion.

Renewable energies created difficulties with some local groups; in Gonzalo Saenz de Miera's words: 'In 2004, one of the barriers to the development of renewable energies was the environmental impact on bio-fauna, and in some cases another issue was visual impact.'

NGOs set up renewable energy rankings that detailed the worldwide situation and encompassed all existing information. IBERDROLA's renewable energy activities were so successful that it topped the Worldwide Energy WWF/Adena[7] ranking with a score of 4.3 out of 10. Two-thirds of the electricity companies ranked received a score of less than 1 for their response to climatic change, and 90% were graded below 3 (see Figure 6.5). IBERDROLA's early and in-depth adoption of a sustainability policy had paid off.

Ranking	Company	Country	Points
1	**IBERDROLA**	**SPAIN**	**4.3**
2	FLP GROUP	USA	4.1
3	SCOTTISH POWER	UK	3.7
4	HYDRO QUEBEC	CANADA	3.1
5	RAQ UES	RUSSIA	3.1
6	ESSENT	HOLLAND	3.0
7	TARONG ENERGY	AUSTRALIA	2.9
8	WESTERN POWER	AUSTRALIA	2.9
9	HOKKAIDO EPCO	JAPAN	2.9
10	ELECTRABEL	BELGIUM	2.7
14	**ENDESA**	**SPAIN**	**2.1**
51	**UNION FENOSA**	**SPAIN**	**0.4**

HOW THE SCORING WAS DONE

■ The study scores the performance of 72 large power companies that together produce 65% of all electricity generated in the OECD and Russia.

■ The companies are ranked in terms of their production, sale and investment in renewable energy and gas-CHP (combined heat and power, supplying both heat and electricity to consumers). For WWF, sustainable renewable energy excludes waste incineration, large hydro and peat.

■ Ranking occurred on scores between 0 (worst) and 10 (best).

■ WWF has chosen natural gas-CHP as the second-best choice after renewable energy, but WWF believes it should only be a bridging technology for the next couple of decades.

■ WWF solicited information directly from companies and relied on company reports when companies were unresponsive. These contained adequate information about a company's current energy generation, but generally did not reveal future investment plans, about which many companies remain secretive.

■ Many countries and states within the US have passed laws that mandate a minimum percentage of energy coming from renewable sources. We assume that the companies in these countries and states, assessed in this report, will comply with these laws. However, their plans for how to do so are in many cases unavailable and are therefore not included in the ranking.

Figure 6.5 Worldwide Energy WWF – Adena Ranking

Source: WWF/Adena (2004)

Despite these successes, IBERDROLA had yet to establish a formal basis for establishing and maintaining successful partnerships with NGOs. Variables such as defining the mission with an NGO, choice of partner and the procedure for dialogue, whether collaborative or belligerent, were still responded to in an ad hoc way.

Early Difficulties

WWF/Adena was the world's most important independent organization dedicated to nature conservation. Since its creation in 1961 (1968 in Spain), its mission had been to reverse the degradation of the environment. Apart from climate change, WWF/Adena had five main areas of expertise: forests, rivers, oceans, rare species and threats from chemical and toxic substances. In 2004, WWF had 3800 members and five million supporters in 90 countries. Despite having fewer than 20 full-time staff in Spain, WWF/Adena was the most prominent NGO among the climate change lobby in the country. The group advocated 'a strong, effective climate change bill', in which the government would deliver real benefits for people and nature. Given WWF/Adena's significance and mandate, it was strongly in IBERDROLA's interests to develop a good relationship with this group.

Initially, WWF/Adena was pleased with IBERDROLA's decision to implement a policy based on renewable energies and become a leader in this area. WWF/Adena invited IBERDROLA to become part of the European Green Electricity Network (EUGENE), set up to study the viability of promoting green energy certification. This initiative had already been launched in several other European countries, and IBERDROLA became a pioneer in Spain.[8]

The EUGENE network is a typical example of a multi-stakeholder dialogue involving environmental NGOs, consumer associations, energy experts and electricity companies. WWF/Adena was in charge of auditing companies in Spain and listed a number of conditions that companies had to fulfil, including finding an effective way to promote green energy production and consumption, and guaranteeing that the initial move towards renewable energies would be maintained in the long term.

At the end of 2002, IBERDROLA and WWF/Adena reached agreement on a six-month pilot test to develop green tag certification to track green energies in the same way that it had been developed in the European Union. But a difference of opinion soon emerged: the NGO wanted IBERDROLA to reinvest its profits in the renewable energy sector, to ensure the long-term success of renewable energy. Moreover, although the utility wanted to maintain interconnectivity between all the energy sources it used, the NGO wanted a specific distribution channel that would provide exclusively green energy to consumers. WWF/Adena wanted a dedicated distribution channel because it would be a unique way of providing transparency and supporting consumers who wanted a genuinely green product. IBERDROLA, however, favoured keeping the distribution channels as they were, due to the prohibitive cost of setting up a separate channel for renewable energy distribution. Not surprisingly, cooperation between the two entities came to an end. However, it was decided to maintain friendly relations, keeping the door open to potentially valuable initiatives in the future.

In 2003, IBERDROLA launched a mass campaign to promote its new green energy product, one that met the criteria established by the Spanish national regulatory institution, the National Energy

Commission (CNE). Among the Spanish utilities, IBERDROLA, Endesa and a smaller company ElectraNorte, had pushed for the product; Unión Fenosa and Viesgo Enel, on the other hand, rejected the initiative.[9] Surprisingly, the three companies promoting the new product selected different messages for their media campaigns.

Endesa decided to offer renewable energies through hydroelectric power plants benefiting from the Renewable Energy Certificate System of the Spanish Electrical Network, and planting a tree in areas of specific environmental interest for each new contract signed. Subscribers had to pay an extra 2.45% above their normal electricity contract. Interconnectivity with other distribution channels was the same as for IBERDROLA. IBERDROLA consumers could receive renewable energy directly if they paid an extra fee for the service.

Although there was a willingness to exploit this emerging business niche, consumer associations and NGOs such as WWF/Adena and Greenpeace claimed that not all the conditions suitable for launching such products were being met. In its report on green energy advertising campaigns (2004), the CNE[10] itself acknowledged that all three utility companies went too far in their advertising.

The issue was that the definition of green energy used by the CNE did not match that of the NGOs and consumer associations. Both sides tried to close their positions but failed to reach agreement. The electricity companies argued that establishing a separate distribution channel for renewable energy would be too expensive, due to the cost of interconnectivity between the different energy sources, and this was the reason why consumer access to renewable energy could only be achieved in terms of sales. The NGOs and consumer associations wanted the creation of a specific green energy distribution channel that ensured the development of a steady energy source. IBERDROLA's decision was to stop negotiations to sell green energy to the Spanish market according to CNE conditions. This situation provoked some turmoil in the relationship with WWF/Adena, and IBERDROLA had to pay off a patent conflict with the NGO.

At the time Galán called his meeting, IBERDROLA was selling only as many green energy contracts to the end consumers as it had installed capacity to fulfil. Consumers with green contracts, however, received their power from a mix of various sources via the grid system discussed earlier. Although this situation was not perfect, IBERDROLA defended it as the best possible solution under existing market conditions.

The failure of negotiations generated concern and apprehension on both sides: WWF/Adena could not ignore the world leader in renewable energies, and IBERDROLA had to face its responsibility towards the NGO; a stalemate could be highly detrimental to both parties.[11] Although a later reconciliation with WWF/Adena suggested that the relationship between the two partners was maturing, in the summer of 2004 Galán knew that collaborations with other NGOs were also causing problems.

IBERDROLA and SEO/Birdlife

Founded in 1954, SEO/Birdlife (the Spanish ornithology society) is the oldest Spanish NGO dedicated to the environment, and has a mission to study and conserve birds and their environment. Over the years, SEO/Birdlife environmental education and public awareness activities have

Figure 6.6 Organizational chart at SEO/Birdlife

Source: SEO/Birdlife (2006)

gained in importance. Working with schools, local communities and the general public are key aspects of the organization's success. The NGO was declared of public interest and awarded, among others, the National Environmental Prize in 1994 and the BBVA Prize for Biodiversity Conservation in 2004.

In 2004, the SEO/Birdlife affiliate had 40 employees, hundreds of volunteers and 8000 members in six delegations and three technical areas (Doñana, Delta del Ebro and Extremadura). SEO/Birdlife cooperates with various entities from the private sector, including banking (Fundación La Caixa, Fundación Santander Central Hispano, Caja Madrid, Caja de Ahorros del Mediterraneo, Hispamer and Triodos Bank), utilities (Red Eléctrica de España) and optical companies (Swarovsky Optik, Óptica Roma and Zeiss). Figure 6.6 shows the SEO/Birdlife organizational chart.

One of SEO/Birdlife's aims is to protect birds, their habitats and global biodiversity from utility installations. IBERDROLA, on the other hand, was not only interested in limiting the environmental impact of its activities, but also in limiting the damage that birds could do to its infrastructure (for example, by causing electrical blackouts). Birds are electrocuted on contact with electrical wires, and in 2004 SEO/Birdlife estimated that the 25 000 utility company pylons in Spain represented a serious risk. In June 2004, the NGO decided to launch a long-term campaign to raise public, institutional and utility company awareness, and obtain a greater commitment from these institutions towards bird safety.

IBERDROLA had long been keen to develop contacts with environmental groups. The company had been engaging in informal collaborations with SEO/Birdlife since 1993 (see Table 6.4). Cooperation had been facilitated by a common willingness to enhance sustainability through innovative partnership and a common scientific background, a fact that had been recognized by both sides. Fernando Barrio, Marketing Director of SEO/Birdlife stated: 'The dialogue with IBERDROLA is quite open. This is not only because the company is committed to renewable energies but also because there is good personal contact with people at IBERDROLA.' Francisco Olarreaga of IBERDROLA's corporate environment unit pointed out: 'It is easy to dialogue with SEO/Birdlife because we have similar views overall on renewable energies and also because we have good personal contacts.'

Table 6.4 Activities Breakdown between IBERDROLA and SEO, 1993–2004

Project	Year	Venue	Nature of the Project	Funder	Results for SEO/Birdlife	Results for IBERDROLA
Not registered as such	1993–1998	Misc.	Sporadic relationships based on occasional incidents	None	Solving short-term needs	Solving short-term needs
Publication of the book *Áreas Importantes para las Aves* (*Important Areas for Birds*)	1998		First publication in Spain on the main bird species with maps of each Spanish region	IBERDROLA	Dissemination of information on birds	Sponsorship
Spanish Ornithology Congress	1998			Sponsored (among others) by IBERDROLA	Enhanced academic knowledge of birds	Sponsorship
Blueprint Project. Birds normally return to the same place during migration	2004		Reproductive pairs usually breed in the same location each year			Project (still incomplete) with satisfactory results
Design of specific artefacts in order to eliminate accident risks for specific birds implemented with a preventive option	2004		Participation of the Extremadura government and IBERDROLA suppliers		Reduction in bird fatalities	Project (still incomplete) with satisfactory results
17th Spanish Ornithology Congress	2004	Madrid, Spain		Sponsored (among others) by IBERDROLA	Enhanced academic knowledge of birds	Sponsorship
Official complaint against IBERDROLA from SEO/Birdlife due to the death of a threatened bird	2004	Spain				SEO/Birdlife formal commitment to avoid negative public comment
Specific exit routes for birds in Maranchón eolic park (Spain)		Spain		IBERDROLA	SEO/Birdlife wishes to place an official complaint to the EU Commission for failing to complete the habitat law case concerning protected bird sanctuaries	No trial. Compensatory measures for nature losses in environmentally specific areas due to infrastructure works

The *Aragon Herald* article on the death of the royal eagles and the risk of a third scandal with an NGO in less than one year were forcing Galán to act. IBERDROLA's relationship with SEO/Birdlife was the longest running of all its relationships with NGOs, and the company did not want to lose the group's often valuable input. The ad hoc way that IBERDROLA had dealt with NGO problems up to now was inefficient and potentially damaging, but creating a more formal approach to these relationships raised a number of questions. How important were the NGOs to IBERDROLA's business model? Were events such as the death of two rare birds permanently damaging, or just a flash in the pan? If NGO relationships affected the core business, how should the company put them on a more formal footing? Galán was hoping that the meeting would identify innovative solutions that would help the company manage its relationships with NGOs better, particularly any conflicts that arose. He knew that the right solutions would also strengthen the company's sustainability policy.

NOTES

1. The case is intended to be used as a basis for class discussion rather than to illustrate either effective or ineffective handling of an administrative situation.

2. Some evidence of this phenomenon can be found in the example of Greenpeace pressuring oil companies, for instance their attack on the Shell Brent Spar platform in 1995, and in the recurrent demonstrations against nuclear energy initiated in the 1970s. In contrast, consumers were and still are passive on this issue. Despite the fact that the Spanish utility market has been liberalized, the vast majority of consumers still do not know they have the option to switch provider.

3. For windmills with a life expectancy of 25 years, the break-even point is reached after four years in use, on average.

4. The same committee determines the vision and values of the company: 'We want to be the preferred company for its commitment to value creation, quality of life and taking care of the environment.'

5. Other distinctions included a fourth consecutive top position in the Dow Jones Sustainability Index and a nomination in the renewable energy and efficiency category of the Prince Felipe Awards for Business Excellence.

6. On a global scale, the Civil Society Institute Center of the John Hopkins Institute estimated that NGOs spent US$1.1 billion in 1995, an amount similar to the UK budget in the same year. This sector employed 19 million people and had 29 million volunteers.

7. 72 companies were rated in this ranking. WWF/Adena requested information directly from companies, and took into consideration corporate reports when the companies did not respond. The available information was sufficient to grade the different companies according to their current energy production, but the reports did not mention future investment plans. The companies were ranked according to production, sales and investment in renewable energy and gas co-generation (heat and electricity combined-cycle). WWF/Adena did not take into consideration re-treatment incineration or turbine/hydroelectric central energies.

8. The European countries where the initiative had been already launched by the end of 2002 were Finland, Germany, Norway, Switzerland and the United Kingdom.

9. Unión Fenosa did not supply a green energy product to its consumers because it considered that the legal framework did not provide sufficient guarantees. The Viesgo Enel Group had not contemplated this issue in December 2003 but may do so in the future.

10. The CNE was critical of all the utility companies. For instance, if Endesa showed customers moderate support for green energy, the CNE wondered whether 'customers would purchase

green energy if they knew that the sole effective measure that was supposed to justify a 2% price increase was to plant a single tree costing €2.50.'

11. It was interesting to note that the CNE was even harsher in its official comments about the green energy campaign than WWF/Adena, suggesting that the NGO was rather moderate. The most virulent campaign against IBERDROLA came from the main Spanish consumer association, the OCU.

REFERENCES

BBV Fundación, 2000

El Mundo (2005)

Expansión, 2007

WBCSD (World Business Council for Sustainable Development), WBCSD Report, 2002.

PART THREE

ACCOUNTING

CHAPTER SEVEN

Corporate Responsibility in Accounting

Dennis Oswald
University of Michigan

INTRODUCTION

Corporate responsibility is extremely important to both the financial accountant and the management accountant. Generally, the financial accountant focuses on the communication of accounting information to external stakeholders, typically dealing with the rules that have been developed to guide how accountants measure an organization's financial position (e.g., Generally Accepted Accounting Principles in the United States (US GAAP), International Financial Reporting Standards (IFRS)). On the other hand, the management accountant generally focuses on the use of internally generated information for decision-making, planning, control and evaluation.

Traditionally, the arena of financial accounting has only focused on the presentation of the financial results of an organization, with the focus on ensuring that the annual report fairly presents the financial position of the organization. With the onset of corporate responsibility, accountants have become increasingly involved in both the measurement of performance relative to corporate responsibility metrics and the assurance of the data being communicated to all stakeholders. The role of the financial accountant is explored further in the following section.

Whereas the focus in financial accounting is on external users of accounting information, the focus in managerial accounting is on generating data to be used inside the organization. Traditionally, management accountants have two discrete (yet intertwined) functions: the determination of the cost of a firm's products and services in order to undertake product, product line, divisional and customer profitability analysis; and the creation, implementation and maintenance of the firm's management control systems (those tools used by the firm to ensure that all employees take actions consistent with achieving the firm's objectives). As a number of companies have updated their corporate objective(s) from focusing on maximizing firm value to including environmental and social objectives, the primary job for the management accountant is to ensure that the company's management control systems promote behaviour that ensures that the company excels not only from a financial perspective but also from a corporate responsibility perspective.

THE ROLE OF THE FINANCIAL ACCOUNTANT

Traditional Financial Reporting

In the last decade financial accounting has been in the spotlight numerous times, often for the wrong reasons. A number of egregious corporate scandals (e.g., Enron[1] and Worldcom in the United States, Parmalat in Italy, Royal Ahold in The Netherlands) resulted in concerns that there were problems with the preparation and assurance of corporate financial reports. It must be stressed that the number of these cases is extremely small in comparison to the total number of firms that are publicly traded worldwide, and in some instances it can be questioned as to whether the firms themselves or the public auditors followed best practice in the preparation and/or the auditing of the financial statements. In most (if not all) countries, the rules for financial reporting are dictated by the relevant authorities. Generally, the overall theme of these rules is that the company must present its financial results 'fairly'. For example, US GAAP, dictates that two primary qualities of accounting information are *relevance* and *reliability*. Relevance refers to the fact that information must be timely and must have predictive value and/or feedback value. Reliability refers to the fact that information must have representational faithfulness, which is defined as 'correspondence or agreement between a measure or description and the phenomenon that it purports to represent' (FASB, 1980, p. 6).[2] The International Accounting Standards Board (IASB) also states that information in the financial statements must be reliable, which they define as '. . . free from material error and bias and can be depended upon by users to represent events and transactions faithfully. Information is not reliable when it is purposely designed to influence users' decisions in a particular direction' (IASB, 2001, paragraphs 31–32). As the scrutiny of firms' annual reports increases, it is important that both the firm's senior management (including the financial accountant) and the firm's auditor ensure that any financial information disclosed to external parties adheres to the financial reporting requirements in their particular country. This requirement is exacerbated for those global companies that are listed and/or have subsidiaries (set up as legal entities) in multiple countries; in these instances senior management must be aware of multiple sets of financial reporting requirements.

In the United States, in addition to the GAAP rules governing the preparation and dissemination of the annual report, two further regulations are noteworthy. First, in October 2000 the Securities and Exchange Commission (SEC) issued 'Selective Disclosure: Regulation FD' to address concerns that managers of firms were disclosing material information to selected individuals (e.g., investment professionals) thereby giving them a trading advantage. Rule 100 of Regulation FD sets forth the basic rule pertaining to disclosure that states that whenever a person of an SEC registrant (or someone acting on its behalf) discloses material nonpublic information the information must be publicly disclosed simultaneously (for intentional disclosures) or promptly (for non-intentional disclosures).

The second significant regulation was the enactment of the Sarbanes-Oxley Act of 2002 (SOX) in July 2002, which was intended to enhance both corporate responsibility and financial disclosures, and also created the Public Company Accounting Oversight Board to oversee the activities of the auditing profession. Specifically, SOX contains 11 titles, each dealing with specific elements of public accounting reform and investor protection. As shown in Figure 7.1, SOX is quite extensive in the breadth of regulatory issues that it addresses. Regarding the role of the financial accountant, basically SOX re-iterates and makes more explicit the requirement to ensure that financial statements are 'correct'. Specifically, one requirement in Title III mandates that the principal executive officer or officers and the principal financial officer or officers certify in each annual or quarterly report that 'the financial statements and other financial information included in the report fairly present in all material respects the financial condition and results of operations' (Section 302 (a) (4)). Additionally, Title IV Section 404 (a) requires that management

Title I – Public Company Accounting Oversight Board
Title II – Auditor Independence
Title III – Corporate Responsibility
Title IV – Enhanced Financial Disclosures
Title V – Analyst Conflicts of Interest
Title VI – Commission Resources and Authority
Title VII – Studies and Report
Title VIII – Corporate and Criminal Fraud Accountability
Title IX – White-Collar Crime Penalty Enhancements
Title X – Corporate Tax Returns
Title XI – Corporate Fraud and Accountability

Figure 7.1 Sections of the Sarbanes-Oxley Act of 2002 (public law 107-204, statutes at large 745)

is responsible for 'establishing and maintaining an adequate internal control structure and proce-dures for financial reporting'. SOX also directly addresses the role of the auditor, as detailed in Title II – Auditor Independence. Most noteworthy is that the firm providing the audit is prohibited from contemporaneously providing a number of other services (Section 201 (a)). Examples of prohibited services include bookkeeping, financial information system design and implementa-tion, actuarial services, internal audit outsourcing services, investment banking services and legal services.

As with GAAP, all managers, financial accountants and auditors in the United States must ensure that they are in full compliance with all regulations (including Reg. FD and SOX) overseeing the preparation and disclosure of financial information. This requirement also extends to managers, financial accountants and auditors outside the United States if they are working for any organiza-tion that is listed on a securities exchange in the United States.

Outside of the United States, numerous other countries have developed codes of conduct, rules and/or regulations to deal with financial reporting. Exhibit 7.1 presents a partial list of regulations in other countries.

New Areas of Involvement for the Financial Accountant

A recent publication by the Institute of Chartered Accountants in England and Wales (ICAEW) provides a detailed discussion of a number of ways in which the financial accountant can become more involved in the corporate responsibility activities of the firm (ICAEW, 2004). However, it should be noted that this report is only providing suggestions for increased (voluntary) involve-ment because there have been no (at least in the United Kingdom) mandatory requirements that accountants become involved in corporate responsibility (over and above the financial reporting requirements detailed in the preceding section). Two of the areas discussed by the ICAEW in-clude engagement with stakeholders and the adherence to voluntary codes of practice. The ICAEW stresses that stakeholder engagement is useful in reducing reputation risk primarily through resolving

EXHIBIT 7.1   EXAMPLES OF FINANCIAL REPORTING REGULATIONS FROM AROUND THE WORLD

United Kingdom

The Combined Code on Corporate Governance (The Code), first developed in 1998 and updated on a regular basis since (the most recent was issued in June 2008). The Code details standards and best practices in such areas as board composition and development, remuneration, accountability and audit, and relations with shareholders. Although not mandatory, all companies incorporated in the United Kingdom and listed on the Main Market of the London Stock Exchange must describe in their annual report how they adhere to the main points of The Code and specifically any points of non-compliance (Financial Reporting Council, 2008).

Canada

Multilateral Instrument 52-109 (MI 52-109), which requires that the CEO and CFO personally certify that, among other things, the annual and interim filings do not contain any misrepresentations and fairly present the financial condition and results of operations and cash flows, and have designed disclosure controls and procedures and internal control over financial reporting. MI 52-109 was first issued in January 2004; an amended version (National Instrument 52-109) is to come into effect on 15 December, 2008 (Ontario Securities Commission, 2004).

Japan

Financial Instruments and Exchange Law of June 2006 (commonly referred to as J-Sox). Compliance with J-Sox requirements became effective for fiscal years beginning on or after 1 April, 2008. J-Sox basically requires that senior management undertakes an assessment and audit of internal control over financial reporting. (For a more detailed discussion of the requirements of J-Sox, refer to 'J-Sox Newsletter' by Deloitte Touche Tohmatsu, March 2007.)

Australia

Corporate Law Economic Reform Programme (Audit Reform and Corporate Disclosure) Act 2004 (also known as CLERP 9) (Australian Government, 2004), which became law on 1 July, 2004. CLERP 9 has 12 schedules dealing with topics such as audit reform, financial reporting, remuneration of directors and executives, disclosure rules and shareholder participation and information. CLERP 9 requires that the directors declare that the financial statements and notes comply with accounting standards and that they give a true and fair view (Schedule 2(2)).

South Africa

King Report on Corporate Governance for South Africa – 2002 (King II Report). This report addresses the following six areas of corporate governance: (1) board and directors; (2) risk management; (3) internal audit; (4) integrated sustainability reporting; (5) accounting and

(Continued)

EXHIBIT 7.1   (*Continued*)

auditing; and (6) compliance and enforcement. Most noteworthy is that in addition to the requirements for financial reporting, there is a separate section specifically addressing sustainability reporting, which discusses stakeholder relations, ethical practices and organizational integrity, safety, health and the environment, social and transformation issues, and human capital.

Germany

Deutscher Corporate Governance Kodex, first issued in 2002 and recently amended in June 2008. This code provides essential statutory regulations to promote the trust of international and national investors, customers, employees and the general public in the overall management and supervision of German listed companies (Government Commission on the German Corporate Governance Code, 2006).

France

Loi sur la Sécurité Financière (LSF) was enacted by the French parliament in August 2003 (Official Journal of the French Republic, 2003). The LSF focuses on three main areas: (1) modernization of the Financial Markets Control Authorities; (2) increased security for people with savings and insurance policies; and (3) reporting of financial accounts and corporate governance. Regarding financial reporting, the chairman of the board must report to shareholders annually on both corporate governance and the internal control procedures implemented by the company.

and avoiding conflicts. It provides a detailed process by which to implement a stakeholder engagement programme (ICAEW, 2004, pp. 29–36):

1. Identification of stakeholder groups (e.g., shareholders, employees, customers, the media, neighbors and local communities, environmental organizations etc.);
2. Obtain commitment throughout the organization;
3. Review existing dialogues with stakeholders;
4. Create a list ranking the stakeholders by priority, and create a list of the main issues likely to be of concern to each group;
5. Establish a strategy for engagement (decide what techniques to use and assemble the information required for effective dialogue);
6. Initiate any action deemed to be required as a result of the engagement.

Obviously one of the most difficult and controversial tasks in this list is the ranking of stakeholder groups (step 3). The ICAEW does not propose a generic ranking of stakeholder groups; however, the article does reference Hibbitt (2004) who reports the rankings of stakeholder groups made by managers of 32 Benelux and German firms. Hibbitt's results indicate the following ranking (Hibbitt, 2004, Table 9.8, p. 372):

1. Shareholders
2. Employees
3. Customers and consumers
4. Public authorities
5. The media
6. Trade creditors and suppliers
7. Neighbours and local communities
8. Industry and trade associations
9. Science and education
10. Environmental organizations
11. Non-participatory owners and lenders
12. Other pressure groups and NGOs.

The ICAEW report also discusses the importance of following voluntary codes that have been developed to encourage companies to adhere to common views on corporate responsibility. The report provides a detailed list of a number of voluntary codes, including the following examples: codes addressing more than one aspect of sustainability (e.g., AccountAbility 1000 Framework); environmental codes (e.g., EU Eco-Management and Audit Scheme); social codes (e.g., UN Norms on Human Rights Responsibilities of Companies); corporate governance codes (e.g., OECD Principles of Corporate Governance (UN, 2003)); and investment codes (e.g., The London Principles (Forum of the Future/Department for Environment, Food and Rural Affairs, 2002; ICAEW, 2004, p. 38)). Key to adhering to these voluntary codes is that accountants use their accounting expertise, and in particular their skills and knowledge to assist in the measurement of performance relative to corporate responsibility, economic, environmental, social, corporate governance and investment performance metrics.

Although a number of voluntary codes have been developed, one in particular deserves specific mention: the Global Reporting Initiative Reporting Framework for reporting on sustainability. The Global Reporting Initiative (GRI) was formed in 1997 as a joint project between the Coalition for Environmentally Responsible Economies (CERES), the Tellus Institute and the United Nations Environment Programme, but is now an independent organization (headquartered in Amsterdam). In 2000, the GRI released its first 'Sustainability Reporting Guidelines', and in 2006 it issued the third version known as G3). In these guidelines the GRI has made the following case for sustainability reporting:

> New knowledge and innovations in technology, management, and public policy are challenging organizations to make new choices in the way their operations, products, services, and activities impact the earth, people, and economies. The urgency and magnitude of the risks and threats to our collective sustainability, alongside increasing choice and opportunities, will make transparency about economic, environmental, and social impacts a fundamental component in effective stakeholder relations, investment decisions, and other market relations.
>
> GRI, 2003, p. 2

The GRI has developed a 'Reporting Framework', which provides guidance on how organizations can disclose their sustainability performance. Included in the framework are guidelines, protocols and sector supplements. The sustainability reporting guidelines provide the case for sustainability reporting, and a detailed list of standard disclosures that include a number of performance metrics and other disclosure items. Specifically, there are three types of standard disclosures: strategy and profile – intended to provide the high-level strategic view of the organization's approach to sustainability; management approach – intended to provide concise disclosures on the organization's specific approach to its economic, environmental and social performance; and performance indicators – 79 specific indicators measuring the organization's sustainability performance. Figure 7.2 provides further detail on the number of indicators by performance aspect. Although the reporting framework does not provide a 'title' for each performance indicator, it does provide specific details as to what is intended to be measured. Examples of performance indicators include the following:[3]

- *Economic:* Direct economic value generated and distributed, including:
  - revenues
  - operating costs
  - employee compensation
  - donations and other community investments
  - retained earnings
  - payments to capital providers and governments (EC1).
- *Environmental:* Percentage of materials used that are recycled input materials (EN2).
- *Labour Practices:* Composition of governance bodies and breakdown of employees per category according to gender, age group, minority group membership and other indicators of diversity (LA13).
- *Human Rights:* Total hours of employee training on policies and procedures concerning aspects of human rights that are relevant to operations, including the percentage of employees trained (HR3).
- *Society:* Percentage and total number of business units analysed for risks related to corruption (SO2).
- *Product Responsibility:* Programmes for adherence to laws, standards and voluntary codes related to marketing communications, including advertising, promotion and sponsorship (PR6).

The Reporting Framework also includes a number of indicator protocols and technical protocols. The indicator protocols provide definitions, compliance guidance and other information to assist preparers in their calculation of specific metrics, primarily to ensure consistency. The technical protocols exist to provide more general guidance in reporting (e.g., setting of the report boundary). The Reporting Framework also includes sector supplements that address the unique needs of specific sectors. Supplements are provided for the following sectors: airports, apparel and footwear, automotive, electric utilities, financial services, food processing, logistics and transportation, mining and metals, NGOs, public agency, telecommunications and tour operators. Finally, the GRI is currently involved in the development of national annexes that will address specific country or regional sustainability issues. However, so far no national annexes have been developed; on the GRI's website they are currently inviting all interested parties to share their views on the scope and form of the national annexes.[4]

Economic Performance Indicators
  1. Economic Performance: 4 indicators
  2. Market Presence: 3 indicators
  3. Indirect Economic Impacts: 2 indicators

Environmental Performance Indicators
  1. Materials: 2 indicators
  2. Energy: 5 indicators
  3. Water: 3 indicators
  4. Biodiversity: 5 indicators
  5. Emissions, Effluents and Waste: 10 indicators
  6. Products and Services: 2 indicators
  7. Compliance   1 indicator
  8. Transport: 1 indicator
  9. Overall: 1 indicator

Social Performance Indicators:

  A. Labour Practices and Decent Work Performance Indicators
    1. Employment: 3 indicators
    2. Labour/Management Relations   2 indicators
    3. Occupational Health and Safety: 4 indicators
    4. Training and Education: 3 indicators
    5. Diversity and Equal Opportunity: 2 indicators

  B. Human Rights Performance Indicators
    1. Investment and Procurement Practices: 3 indicators
    2. Non-Discrimination: 1 indicator
    3. Freedom of Association and Collective Bargaining: 1 indicator
    4. Child Labour: 1 indicator
    5. Forced and Compulsory Labour: 1 indicator
    6. Security Practices: 1 indicator
    7. Indigenous Rights: 1 indicator

  C. Society Performance Indicators
    1. Community: 1 indicator
    2. Corruption: 3 indicators
    3. Public Policy: 2 indicators
    4. Anti-Competitive Behaviour   1 indicator
    5. Compliance: 1 indicator

  D. Product Responsibility Performance Indicators
    1. Customer Health and Safety: 2 indicators
    2. Product and Service Labelling: 3 indicators
    3. Marketing Communications: 2 indicators
    4. Customer Privacy: 1 indicator
    5. Compliance: 1 indicator

Figure 7.2 List of performance indicators by category

Source: Global Reporting Initiative, 2006, *Sustainability Reporting Guidelines*

To date there have been very few published articles that critically evaluate the strengths and weaknesses of the GRI Reporting Framework. Nevertheless, Goel (2005) reports that three main strengths of the GRI are: it facilitates comparisons between companies and across time; it involves a multi-stakeholder process; and it allows for flexibility in that it can facilitate an incremental approach to sustainability reporting. However, he also notes the following four weaknesses: it is not a management tool; it is overly general; there are many indicators; and the business case for implementing the GRI guidelines is not yet clear.[5] Others have also criticized the GRI: 'This may be a useful starting point, but critics say it often amounts to little more than box-ticking; worse, it can provide a cover for poor performers' (*The Economist*, 2008). More outspoken critics include Milne, Ball and Gray (2008) who state: 'We argue that the TBL [triple bottom line] and GRI [Global Reporting Initiative] are insufficient conditions for organizations contributing to the sustaining of the Earth's ecology. Paradoxically, they may reinforce business-as-usual and greater levels of un-sustainability.'

Notwithstanding these views of the GRI's Reporting Framework, one question that still remains is whether it will become widely adopted and used by a majority of the world's organizations. Currently, very few organizations appear to be using it. Reed and Reed (2008) report that only a small minority of the over 400 participating firms report in accordance with the GRI Guidelines, and Gilbert and Rasche (2008) state that only about 200 firms work in accordance with the GRI (based on data available in October 2007). Finally, as of 14 September, 2008 the GRI website lists only 417 firms on their GRI 2008 Reports List.[6]

The final area in which financial accountants are becoming involved as regards corporate responsibility is that of providing assurance services. However, currently the verification of sustainability reports has been somewhat limited in terms of the number of reports that have been verified, although the numbers are on the rise. Specifically, in their 2008 international survey on corporate responsibility reporting, KPMG report that in the Global Fortune 250 companies, 40% of corporate responsibility reports had external assurance statements. Additionally, they report that in the top 100 companies in 22 countries, 39% of reports had external assurance statements (up from 30% and 33%, respectively, in 2005).[7] From these data it is clear that the role of the auditor is becoming increasingly important. To assist in the auditing of sustainability reports, two international standards have recently been issued: 'AA1000 Assurance Standard' by AccountAbility in 2003 and 'International Standard on Assurance Engagements (IASE) 3000: Assurance Engagements Other than Audits or Reviews of Historical Financial Information' by the International Auditing and Assurance Standards Board (IAASB) in 2005.[8]

The specific role of the auditor has also been addressed in a number of recent publications. For example, Wallage (2000) provides an interesting discussion of the initial experiences of auditors with respect to verifying sustainability reports. In 2004, the Association of Chartered Certified Accountants (ACCA) and AccountAbility issued 'The Future of Sustainability Assurance – ACCA Research Report No. 86', which provides a thorough discussion of sustainability and the process by which sustainability information disclosed by organizations can be verified. Additionally, O'Dwyer and Owen (2005) provide an analysis of the extent to which assurance practices enhance transparency and accountability to organizational stakeholders. Finally, KMPG and SustainAbility issued a report in 2008 titled 'Count Me In – The Readers Take on Sustainability Reporting', which found that not only is assurance of the sustainability report important but also the assurance must be undertaken by an expert. In summary, it seems that going forward there will be substantial demand for auditors to apply their expertise of assurance services in verifying information contained in corporate responsibility reports.

THE ROLE OF THE MANAGEMENT ACCOUNTANT

One of the main roles of the management accountant is in the design, implementation and maintenance of the firm's management control systems (MCS), which can be defined as those tools used to ensure that all employees take actions consistent with achieving the firm's objectives. If the objective is corporate responsibility, the MCS must ensure that they not only motivate and inspire employees to perform organizational activities that will further corporate responsibility, but also detect and correct unintentional performance errors and intentional irregularities (i.e., the MCS must assist in getting the organization back on track when corporate responsibility is not being fully achieved).

The starting point in the design and use of MCS is the definition of the organization's objective(s). This is not the responsibility of the management accountant, but rather the board of directors. Increasingly, a number of organizations are now defining their objectives to include not only maximizing firm value, but also ensuring superior environmental and social performance (also often referred to as 'sustainability' or 'corporate responsibility'). As corporate responsibility becomes the more prominent corporate objective, the management accountant must consider how to design, implement and maintain the organization's MCS with respect to this (relatively) new corporate objective, as opposed to (historically) focusing only on firm value.

This section of the chapter will focus on common mechanisms of control with specific reference to corporate responsibility issues that arise. My specific approach to considering the different mechanisms of control is to categorize them into the following four areas:

- market mechanisms;
- bureaucratic mechanisms;
- socialization;
- performance measurement and compensation.

These categories are not mutually exclusive, and are not appropriate in every situation. Instead, they should be viewed in terms of their appropriateness for assisting in the planning, execution and control, and evaluation of the specific organizational context.

Market Mechanisms

One fairly prominent view in microeconomics for the efficient allocation of resources is to create 'markets'. The same view can be applied internally in the organization; for example, when looking at the employment options of the senior management. It has been argued that both the internal and external labour market for managerial talent will act as a deterrent to managers undertaking actions that maximize their own well-being at the expense of the organization (Fama, 1980; Lazear and Rosen, 1981). Specifically, there may be competition among managers for more senior positions. Managers who are in this 'competition' or 'tournament' should focus their efforts/actions on tasks that provide outputs signalling that they are the 'best' manager. Additionally, these resulting outputs will also act as a signal of managerial talent to the external labour market. If the manager undertakes actions that result in a decrease to the organizational objectives (and this decrease is observable), it is argued that the manager will be penalized when seeking a promotion or when looking for alternate outside employment. Regarding corporate responsibility, the focus is on ensuring that managers who take actions that are consistent with corporate responsibility are appropriately rewarded for those actions (through promotion or by securing other employment). However, the question that remains is whether those employees who disregard corporate responsibility or only pay lip-service to it will be punished in the labour market in the years to come.

Bureaucratic Mechanisms

The bureaucratic mechanisms used in management control systems include all the formal rules, regulations and procedures used by the organization. From a planning perspective, the typical bureaucratic mechanism is the formal budget and detailed outline for how the budgeting process is to be completed. From an operational point of view, all the standard operating procedures, training manuals, guides for manufacturing products or actions to be completed for the provision of services can be considered as bureaucratic mechanisms. For control purposes, one common bureaucratic mechanism is the variance reports explaining the difference(s) between planned and actual results. Finally, from an evaluation point of view, many organizations have a very formal and detailed performance evaluation process, which often includes specific details pertaining to the appraisals to be completed, the time frame for completion and the awarding of bonus compensation. In terms of corporate responsibility, one example of a bureaucratic mechanism is any guidelines specifying how the organization engages with its stakeholders (e.g., see the discussion of the qualitative and quantitative survey of corporate responsibility by Enel in Chapter 8); another example is the adoption of ISO 14001 for effective environmental management.[9]

Socialization

The concept of socialization is that all employees have been 'socialized' to have similar values to each other and to the owners. If the primary objective of the firm is corporate responsibility, it is important to ensure that all employees also value corporate responsibility. There are a few ways to achieve such 'socialization' in the firm. The first is through the recruitment policies of the firm. For example, some organizations only employ individuals with specific academic qualifications or work experience. The reason for this is often twofold. First, these qualifications or experience may be necessary in order to complete the tasks required by the organization. Second, through the process of obtaining specific qualifications or getting specific work experience, individuals will often develop a particular way of thinking, which in turn may ensure that the action they take is consistent with the firm's objectives. In addition to relying on the qualifications and work experience detailed on an individual's CV, recruitment personnel may directly enquire as to an individual's particular value system (e.g., applicants may be questioned to ensure that they also value corporate responsibility). A second source of socialization is through formal training (internally or externally – for example, through a trade association or business school executive education programme). Finally, many organizations use informal tools to influence employee behaviour, such as the belief and boundary systems set out in Simons (1995).

Simons (1995, p. 82) defines 'Belief Systems' as:

> . . . concise, value-laden and inspirational. They draw employees' attention to key tenets of the business: how the organization creates value ('Best Customer Service in the World'); the level of performance the organization strives for ('Pursuit of Excellence'); and how individuals are expected to manage both internal and external relationships.

That is, belief systems are used to communicate to all employees what the organization stands for and what type of behaviour is expected in all business dealings. Common examples of belief systems include organizations' mission statements and core values. An interesting example of belief systems is Novo Nordisk's 'Vision and Values', which is part of the Novo Nordisk Way of Management (see Chapter 9).

Simons (1995, p. 84) defines 'Boundary Systems' as:

> . . . boundary systems are stated in negative terms or as minimum standards. The boundaries in modern organizations, embedded in standards of ethical behaviour and codes of conduct, are invariably written in terms of activities that are off-limits. They are an organization's brakes.

In many organizations the boundary systems are formalized statements of the type of behaviour that is not allowed. With respect to corporate responsibility, many organizations make explicit statements as to the type of business activities that they will not engage in, or types of clients with whom they refuse to do business. For example, in the United Kingdom, the Co-operative Bank's ethical policy (launched in 1992) has specific guidelines concerning human rights, the arms trade, corporate responsibility and global trade, genetic modification, social enterprise, ecological impact and animal welfare.[10]

Performance Measurement and Compensation

One very popular and common control mechanism is to select an array of performance metrics that provide information about the effort levels (i.e., work undertaken) by a specific employee or group of employees. Generally, to ensure that employees 'care about' the metrics, some (or all) of their compensation is tied to the realized value of the metrics. However, the use of performance measurement and compensation can have severe consequences. It is commonly viewed that 'you get what you measure'; therefore, if you compensate the CEO on accounting earnings, you are likely to see the CEO taking whatever actions he or she can to maximize accounting earnings. Certainly, a problem arises when the CEO goes beyond accepted practice to increase reported earnings.

With respect to corporate responsibility, the focus in performance measurement has been on the adoption of metrics that not only measure economic performance but also environmental and social impacts. One common tool that has been used is the Balanced Scorecard (Kaplan and Norton, 1992; 2001a; 2001b). The main aspect of a balanced scorecard is the fact that it allows managers to evaluate the business from four key perspectives (see also Figure 7.3):

- *Financial:* It is necessary to ensure that the implementation of the firm's strategy leads to improved economic success.

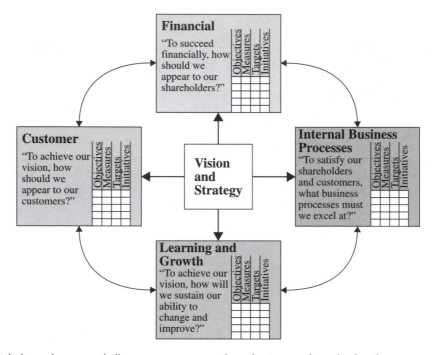

Figure 7.3 A balanced scorecard allows managers to evaluate businesses from the four key perspectives shown

Source: http://www.balancedscorecard.org/BSCResources/AbouttheBalancedScorecard/tabid/55/Default.aspx

- *Customer:* It is necessary to first define the customer and market segments in which the business competes. It is then essential to ensure that the internal processes and products/services offered are consistent with the expectations of the customers and market segments.

- *Internal Business:* It is necessary to ensure that the internal value-driving processes are in place to meet the expectations of the customers and the shareholders.

- *Learning and Growth:* It is necessary to ensure that the appropriate infrastructure exists to achieve the objectives in the other three perspectives. Specifically, the most important areas are the development and qualification of employees and the development and implementation of information systems.

The starting point for designing the Balanced Scorecard (as with any control mechanism) is the definition of the organizational objective(s). Once defined, specific objectives are then developed for each of the four perspectives. In order to ensure that objectives are achieved, both leading and lagging indicators are chosen to measure progress towards the objective. Lagging indicators are those indicators that measure what has been achieved (i.e., they are backwards looking). In contrast, the leading indicators are meant to provide information as to the direction that is being taken, and to provide some expectations as to what will actually be achieved (i.e., the results on the lagging indicators). One of the key elements of the Balanced Scorecard is that it provides an over-all framework that is meant to ensure consistency among all of the objectives and the indicators.

That is, achievement on one objective should lead into achievement on other objectives (e.g., increased customer satisfaction should lead to increased sales (through repeat business) which should lead to increased profitability). It is also important to note that Kaplan and Norton believe that the Balanced Scorecard should be adopted at all levels of the organization; that is, it should be 'cascaded' throughout the organization. They also suggest that the balanced scorecard should be linked with compensation.

Regarding the use of the Balanced Scorecard in assisting with corporate responsibility, Figge *et al.* (2002) suggest that there are three possibilities for integrating environmental and social aspects into the Balanced Scorecard. First, they suggest, that environmental and social aspects can be integrated into the existing standard four perspectives. For example, Novo Nordisk's Balanced Scorecard (see Chapter 9) has only the standard four perspectives (which they define as Finance, Business Processes, People and Organization and Customers and Society), and all the corporate responsibility objectives are included within these four perspectives. As a specific example, Novo Nordisk has an objective to 'ensure environmental, social and ethical performance', which is placed in their Customers and Society perspective.

Second, Figge *et al.* (2002) suggest that an additional (fifth) perspective can be added to account for environmental and social aspects. One example of this approach is detailed in the Harvard Business School Case by Kaplan and de Pinho (2008) titled 'Amanco: Developing the Sustainability Scorecard'. Specifically, Exhibit 11 of Kaplan and de Pinho (2008) shows that in addition to the four standard perspectives, Amanco has a fifth perspective titled 'Social and Environmental Perspective'. Included in this perspective are the following four objectives: assume leadership in transparency within sector; manage social impact in areas of influence; be a protagonist on water issues; and manage eco-efficiency, occupational health and prevent accidents.

Finally, Figge *et al.* (2002) suggest that a specific environmental and/or social scorecard can be developed. Their article provides a detailed discussion of how it might be possible to develop a specific sustainability scorecard.

Summary of Mechanisms of Control

As discussed above there are no direct linkages between corporate responsibility and the role of the management accountant. Rather, it is important that management accountants consider how they design, implement and maintain the organization's management control systems in line with any of the corporate responsibility objectives that have been adopted. One key question that the management accountant must ask him- or herself is: 'If there are cases where actions undertaken by employees impact the economic, environmental or social objectives differently, how do the management control systems help the employee make his or her decision?' For example, if a company is building a new factory, consider these two options: Option A – adhere to the current environmental legislation on pollution and only adopt this level of pollution reducing equipment; or Option B – adopt much more expensive pollution reducing equipment. Obviously Option A dominates from an economic perspective whereas Option B dominates from an environmental perspective. The question is which option should be chosen given the organizational objectives and the current management control systems?[11]

NOTES

1. See Chapter 10 – From Grace to Disgrace: The Rise and Fall of Arthur Andersen, for further discussion of the accounting issues at both Enron Corp. and Arthur Andersen LLP.
2. For further information on the qualitative characteristics of accounting information under US GAAP, refer to 'Statement of Financial Accounting Concepts No. 2: Qualitative Characteristics of Accounting Information', Financial Accounting Standards Board, 1980.
3. *Source:* Global Reporting Initiative, 2006, *Sustainability Reporting Guidelines.*
4. For further information on the Global Reporting Initiative see their website at www. globalreporting.org.
5. It should be noted that Goel's (2005) assessment of the GRI was prior to the release of G3.
6. See: http://www.globalreporting.org/GRIReports/.
7. See *KPMG International Survey of Corporate Responsibility Reporting 2008*, p. 56.
8. For a critical analysis of these two standards, see Oelschlagel (2005). For a discussion of how effectively these standards have been applied, see Manetti and Becatti (2008).
9. ISO 14001 was developed by the International Organization for Standardization in 1996 (amended in 2004) to assist organizations in ensuring that their environmental management systems help them to manage their environmental impacts and comply with all relevant legislation. ISO 14001 certification confirms that the respective organization adheres to international standards on environmental management. According to ISO International Standards (2008) up to the end of December 2006, more than 129 000 ISO 14001 certificates of conformity had been issued to private and public sector organizations in 140 countries and economies. For further information, see www.iso.org.
10. For example, regarding the arms trade, the Co-operative bank will not invest in any business involved in the manufacture or transfer of armaments to oppressive regimes or the manufacture of torture equipment or other equipment that is used in the violation of human rights. (*Source:* Co-operative Bank (2008).) For more information see www.co-operativebank.co.uk/ethics.
11. Although this is a hypothetical question, I do believe that in practice there are often many decisions that need to be made, or actions that need to be taken, that result in a tradeoff between the economic, environmental and social objectives of the organization. Unfortunately, many organizations are not forthcoming with providing details of these situations.

REFERENCES

AccountAbility (2003) *AA1000 Assurance Standard.*

Association of Chartered Certified Accountants and AccountAbility (2004) *The Future of Sustainability Assurance – ACCA Research Report No. 86.*

Australian Government, Attorney-General's Department (2004) *Corporate Law Economic Reform Programme (Audit Reform and Corporate Disclosure) Act 2004 No. 103, 2004.*

Co-operative Bank (2008) *Our Ethical Policy Statements in Brief,* Manchester.

Deloitte Touche Tohmatsu (2007) J-Sox Newsletter.

Fama, E.F. (1980) Agency problems and the theory of the firm, *The Journal of Political Economy,* **88**, 288–307.

FASB (Financial Accounting Standards Board) (1980) *Statement of Financial Accounting Concepts No. 2: Qualitative Characteristics of Accounting Information.*

Figge, F., Hahn, T., Schaltegger, S. and Wagner, M. (2002) The sustainability balanced scorecard – Linking sustainability management to business strategy, *Business Strategy and the Environment,* **11**, 269–84.

Financial Reporting Council (2008) The Combined Code on Corporate Governance, June.

Forum of the Future/Department for Environment, Food and Rural Affairs (2002) *Financing the Future – The London Principles – The Role of UK Financial Services in Sustainable Development.*

Gilbert, D.U. and Rasche, A. (2008) Opportunities and problems of standardized ethics initiatives – A stakeholder theory perspective, *Journal of Business Ethics*, **82**, 755–73.

Goel, R. (2005) *Guide to Instruments of Corporate Responsibility: An Overview of 16 Key Tools for Labour Fund Trustees*, Schulich Business School, York University, Toronto, Canada.

Government Commission on the German Corporate Governance Code (2006) *Deutscher Corporate Governance Kodex.*

GRI (Global Reporting Initiative) (2006) *Sustainability Reporting Guidelines Version 3.0.*

Hibbitt, C. (2004) External environmental disclosure and reporting developments in Europe: An economic, social and political analysis of managerial behaviour, Limperg Instituut, Amsterdam.

IASE (International Auditing and Assurance Standards Board) (2005) *International Standard on Assurance Engagements (IASE) 3000: Assurance Engagements Other than Audits or Reviews of Historical Financial Information.*

ICAEW (Institute of Chartered Accountants in England and Wales) (2004) *Sustainability: The Role of Accountants.*

International Accounting Standards Board (2001) *Framework for the Preparation and Presentation of Financial Statements.*

ISO International Standards (2008) *Practical Tools for Addressing Climate Change*, Geneva.

Kaplan, R.S. and Norton, D.P. (1992) The balanced scorecard: Measures that drive performance, *Harvard Business Review*, **70**, 71–9.

Kaplan, R.S. and Norton, D.P. (2001a) Transforming the balance scorecard from performance measurement to strategic management: Part 1, *Accounting Horizons*, **15** (1), 87–104.

Kaplan, R.S. and Norton, D.P. (2001b) Transforming the balanced scorecard from performance measurement to strategic management: Part 2, *Accounting Horizons*, **15** (2), 147–60.

Kaplan, R.S. and De Pinho, R.R. (2008) Amanco: Developing the sustainability scorecard, *Harvard Business School Case* #9-107-038.

KPMG (2008) *KPMG International Survey on Corporate Responsibility Reporting 2008.*

KPMG and SustainAbility (2008) *Count Me In – The Readers Take on Sustainability Reporting.*

Lazear, E.P. and Rosen, S. (1981) Rank order tournaments as an optimum labor contract, *Journal of Political Economy*, **89**, 841–64.

Manetti, G. and Becatti, L. (2008) Assurance services for sustainability reports: Standards and empirical evidence, *Journal of Business Ethics*, available at http://www.springerlink.com/content/t854x416508r5131 (accessed 2 March 2009).

Milne, M.J., Ball, A. and Gray, R. (2008) Wither ecology? The triple bottom line, the global reporting initiative, and the institutionalization of corporate sustainability reporting, working paper, University of St Andrews.

O'Dwyer, B. and Owen, D. L. (2005) Assurance statement practice in environmental, social and sustainability reporting: A critical evaluation, *The British Accounting Review*, **37**, 205–29.

Oelschlagel, J. (2005) Comparing sustainability reporting assurance standards, *Business and the Environment*, **16**, 1–3.

Official Journal of the European Communities (2001) *Regulation (EC) No 761/2001 of the European Parliament and of the Council of 19 March 2001 Allowing Voluntary Participation by Organizations in a Community Eco-Management and Audit Scheme (EMAS)*, Volume 44.

Official Journal of the French Republic (2003) *Loi sur la Sécurité Financière.*

Ontario Securities Commission (2004) Multilateral Instrument 52–109 – Certification of Disclosure in Issuers' Annual and Interim Filings.

Ontario Securities Commission (2008) Notice of National Instrument 52–109 – Certification of Disclosure in Issuers' Annual and Interim Filings and Repeal of Multilateral Instrument 52-109 – Certification of Disclosure in Issuers' Annual and Interim Filings.

Organization for Economic Co-operation and Development (OECD) (2004) *OECD Principles of Corporate Governance*.

Reed, A.M. and Reed, D. (2008) Partnerships for development: Four models of business involvement, *Journal of Business Ethics*, available at http://www.springerlink.com/content/f6081u1652515927/?p=547f2e2dc1ca49c3b9e20cc3104af4a4&pi=0 (accessed 2 March 2009).

Sarbanes Oxley Act of 2002 (Public Company Accounting Reform and Investor Protection Act of 2002), Public Law 107-204, Statutes at Large 745, enacted 30 July, 2002.

Securities and Exchange Commission (2000) *Selective Disclosure and Insider Trading*.

Simons, R. (1995) Control in an age of empowerment, *Harvard Business Review*, **73**, 80–8.

The Economist (2008) Corporate Social Responsibility – The Next Question, **386** (17) January, special section, pp. 8–10.

The King Committee on Corporate Governance (2002) *King Report on Corporate Governance for South Africa – 2002 (King II Report)*.

United Nations (2003) *Norms on the Responsibilities of Transnational Corporations and other Business Enterprises with Regard to Human Rights*, U.N. Doc. E/CN.4/Sub.2/2003/12/Rev.2.

Wallage, P. (2000) Assurance on sustainability reporting: An auditor's view, *Auditing*, **19**, 53–65.

CHAPTER EIGHT

Enel: CSR and Performance Measurement[1]

Anna Pistoni and Lucrezia Songini, Bocconi University

CSR IN ENEL

Introduction

Since 2003, Enel has had an on-going dialogue with its stakeholders, informing them of the concrete actions that demonstrate the company's commitment to fulfilling its economic, social and environmental responsibility. We have consequently adopted the most stringent international criteria when collecting data, commenting on them and making them available to the public. In the process, completeness and transparency have been our priorities. During the past five years, this commitment has gained international recognition in a number of ways. We have been admitted to the most important indexes that measure corporate social responsibility and growth sustainability and, over time, have improved our position in the ranking of companies that are most engaged with this issue (e.g., AccountAbility's worldwide ranking for Fortune magazine places us sixth). Socially responsible and ethical mutual funds are increasingly interested in Enel shares.

> Piero Gnudi, Chairman, and Fulvio Conti, CEO,
> Letter to our Stakeholders, the Enel 2006 Sustainability Report

In 2007, Enel was Italy's largest power company and Europe's second largest listed utility in terms of installed capacity. Listed on the Milan and New York stock exchanges since 1999, it had some 1.7 million shareholders, the largest number of any Italian company. Enel also had a significant presence in Spain, France, Slovakia, Romania, Bulgaria, Russia, and North and Latin America. However:

> As 2007 began, Enel seemed a fading national champion, reliant on a domestic market where it faced the steady erosion of its position under the challenge of its smaller and more dynamic rival, Edison, backed by EDF of France. Its efforts to break out of that trap, such as its overture to the Franco-Belgian utility Suez, had been rebuffed. While the European energy industry was restructuring under pressure from a new push from the European Union to liberalize markets and strengthen competition, Enel seemed to have been left behind. By his dramatic intervention in the long-running takeover battle for Endesa, Spain's biggest electricity company, Mr Conti (Enel's CEO) changed all that. The deal leaves several questions unanswered. But it has made the point that Enel has a role to play in reshaping Europe's energy industry, in the most dramatic way possible.
>
> Crooks, 2007

As a consequence of the acquisition of Endesa, the partnership with Acciona and the acquisition of OGK-5 in Russia in 2007, Enel would operate in 22 countries, had 75 000 MW of generating capacity and more than 50 million electricity customers. In 2007, the company had 73 500 employees and posted revenues of more than €43.7 billion and a group net income of €4 billion. With 30 000 MW in plants using renewable energy resources (hydro, geothermal, wind, solar and biomass) across the world, Enel was a world leader in the sector. Its electricity came mainly from fossil fuels (73%), while 21% was produced from renewable energy sources or from natural inputs (plus 6% from hydro sources from pumped inputs). In March 2007, the Ministry of the Economy and Finance owned 21.12% of the share capital of Enel SpA and the Cassa Depositi e Prestiti (a corporation controlled by this Ministry) owned 10.15%, leaving free-floating shares of some 68.80% to the market (32.90% held by institutional investors and 35.70% by retail investors). Shareholders included leading international investment funds, insurance companies, pension funds and ethical funds, along with Italian retail investors.[2]

The Company History

The electricity industry has played a key role in Italy's economic and social growth, reflecting key events in the country's history. After a long parliamentary debate, the Italian Chamber of Deputies adopted legislation to nationalize the country's electricity system on 27 November, 1962. The law gave Enel the sole right to generate, import, export, transport, transform, distribute and sell electricity. Enel started operations in 1963 by gradually absorbing the existing power companies. Under the National Energy Plan, presented in July 1975 by the Minister of Industry, Enel was summoned to 'call for tenders for the construction of eight nuclear power plants of the 1000 MW type'. However, on 8 November, 1987, a large majority of Italians rejected nuclear energy in a national referendum. In the 1990s, the power industry embarked on a process of liberalization that reduced the scope of Enel's core business, prompting the company to pursue a diversification strategy and develop new lines of business.

There was a radical change in the legal-institutional structure of Italy's national electricity sector via Legislative Decree no. 333 of 11 July, 1992, which was converted into Law no. 359 on 8 August; it made Enel a joint stock company – the first step towards privatization. On 19 February, 1999, the Council of Ministers approved a bill to liberalize Italy's electricity market. Known as the 'Bersani Decree', this legislation, which came into effect on 1 April, 1999, required Enel to be broken up into separate units for the generation, transmission, distribution and sales of electricity to 'eligible' customers. Enel was also required to reduce its generating capacity by hiving off 'not less than 15 000 MW' by the end of 2002.

As such, in 1999, Enel was privatized, by placing more than 3.8 billion shares (which became 1.9 after the reverse stock split of 9 July, 2001), which accounted for 31.74% of the share capital, for a counter value of €16.55 billion. It was the biggest quotation in Europe and the second largest worldwide, both in terms of the value and the number of underwriters. Consequently, Enel shares have been quoted on both the New York Stock Exchange and the Italian Stock Exchange since 2 November, 1999. From 20 December, 1999, Enel shares have formed part of the MIB30 index. In November 2002, following a diversification phase during which it developed new businesses, the company initiated a process of refocusing on the energy sector: it aimed to become the leading producer and distributor of electricity and gas. Enel has actively sought international expansion in the power and gas market since 2006.

The CSR Project

The adoption of corporate social responsibility (CSR) and its implementation in all activities and functions were directly sponsored by the CEO. In 2002, the CSR project was launched. The Identity and Image Unit within the Corporate Communication Department was in charge of CSR compliance. The task force operated between September 2002 and April 2004, when a Corporate Social Responsibility department was established. Internal communication played an important role in informing the employees and making the sustainability approach visible within the company. The top management's commitment and support played a significant role in the data gathering and CSR reporting at different organizational levels. The manager in charge of the Corporate Social Responsibility Unit described the context that favoured the adoption of CSR at Enel as follows:

It is important to point out that the CSR adoption was a final step in a process, which began with the adoption of the ethical code and of other self-discipline codes.[3] The ethical code was approved and adopted in March 2001, just before the Chairman (Chicco Testa) and CEO (Franco Tatò), who had managed the process of Enel's privatization and quotation, came to the end of their terms in office. At the end of May 2002, a new Board of Directors was appointed, as well as a new Chairman, Piero Gnudi, and a new CEO, Paolo Scaroni. During one of the first meetings aimed at verifying and understanding the company's situation, the new CEO and the new manager in charge of the Corporate Communication Department pointed out the need to launch a CSR policy. A first check of the project feasibility showed that Enel was prepared to embed CSR into its strategy, organization and managerial mechanisms.

Embedding CSR and the Impacts on Organization and Managerial Systems

The values and principles of the Enel organizational culture, the communication policy, the managerial systems, particularly the planning and control ones, the organizational structure and roles (Figure 8.1) allowed CSR to spread throughout the company.

In 1996, the first Environmental Report was published; in 1999, it summarized the principles and objectives of the Enel environmental policy for the first time. The focus was on the improvement of the plants' environmental performance; consequently, environmental Key Performance Indicators (KPIs) were developed. In addition, Enel established its Environmental Policy Unit, which is part of the Parent Company's Department of Institutional and Regulatory Affairs. There were about 200 full-time employees exclusively dedicated to examining and implementing the company's environmental plans.

In 2001, the Enel Board of Directors decided to initiate a process of reflection on the system of values that characterized and governed its business activities. Enel thus gradually adopted a plan of action in support of CSR. This plan provided for the elaboration and implementation of the Code of Ethics and for making it known inside and outside the company. Adopted in 2002 and then revised in 2004, the ethical code represented an essential component of the Enel corporate governance system. In order to foster the integration of respect for the environment and society into its business activities, Enel ensured that its Board of Directors assumed responsibility for environmental and social sustainability and for the integration of planning and audit processes with sustainability objectives and indicators.

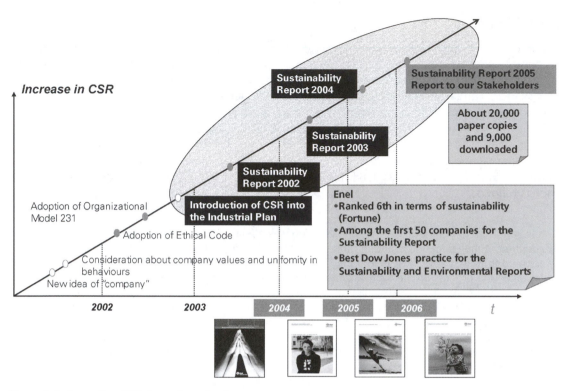

Figure 8.1 Spreading CSR throughout Enel

In 2002, two new organizational departments were established: the Corporate Social Responsibility Unit, within the Corporate Communication Department, and the EnelDATA Unit, within the Corporate Administration, Finance and Control Department. The Corporate Social Responsibility unit was in charge of CSR implementation and stakeholder engagement, as well as the communication and coordination of CSR initiatives. It communicated Enel's commitment to sustainability, organized the Sustainability Report, managed its relationship with rating agencies and assisted with the definition of CSR objectives.

EnelDATA was in charge of the CSR planning and control process, participated in defining CSR objectives, evaluated CSR projects and compiled managerial reports for top management. Within the Corporate Administration, Finance and Control Department, a new role was established: the CSR controller. The controller was in charge of CSR reporting and fell under the Planning and Control Unit, as well as the CSR Unit. Furthermore, approximately 50 'data owners' were identified to be in charge of and manage KPIs for the Sustainability Report and rating agencies' questionnaires.

In May 2003, the 2002 Sustainability Report was approved as a means through which the company would publicize its efforts; the report highlighted the content and quality of the relations it had built with each stakeholder in the three areas of responsibility: economic, environmental and social.

In July 2003, social and environmental questions arising from business activities and relations with stakeholders were translated into a set of CSR objectives and incorporated as an integral part of the Company Business Plan, as well as the budgeting and reporting systems. Among the initiatives undertaken by Enel in terms of corporate social responsibility, was its participation in the United Nations Global Compact initiative, which was formalized in February 2004.

In October 2004, the Domestic Infrastructure and Networks Division's distribution network obtained an ISO 14001 environmental certification. One hundred and thirty plants (approximately 43% of Enel's net production installed capacity) obtained an EMAS registration. By 2009, Enel plans to have an ISO 14001 environmental certification and an EMAS registration for all Italian hydro plants.

In parallel, the company also developed its internal MBO system, which identified personal CSR goals that were in line with the CSR KPIs of the Sustainability Scorecard. In 2005, out of a sample of 25% of employees involved in the MBO system, 100% listed performance as linked to environmental responsibility and social responsibility.

On 14 March 2006, the Enel Internal Audit Committee formally approved a specific provision specifying the anti-corruption measures adopted by the company: the Zero Tolerance against Corruption Plan (ZTC Plan). It gave substance to Enel's membership of the Global Compact in addition to fulfilling the commitment undertaken at the Davos Forum (in January 2005), when – together with more than 60 multinational companies – Enel signed the Pact Against Corruption Initiative (PACI).

In 2005 and 2006, training activities were developed specifically for people involved in data gathering and CSR reporting. In 2005, the CSR Unit, together with the Personnel and Organization Department, promoted a course for supervisors (about 4000 people) with the objective of explaining the value of CSR. The CSR principles and practices involved the Safety Department at both the corporate and divisional levels.

In addition, work started on the development of a policy on *Human Rights and Equal Opportunity*, which was completed at the end of 2006. This policy applied to all Enel activities throughout the world and was developed in cooperation with the Prince of Wales International Business Leaders Forum (IBLF). With regard to *diversity* during the last 15 years, the number of women employed by Enel had significantly increased and the ethnic range of its employees became more diverse. Moreover, employment at Enel was distinguished by the institution of a system of 'internal welfare' based on activities, initiatives and services ranging from complementary pensions and supplementary healthcare to cultural and sports activities, loans to personnel at special interest rates and special maternity benefits.

Since 2002, therefore, Enel had specifically focused on gaining international and national acknowledgment for CSR and sustainability. In November 2002, the company passed the ethical screening process of E. Capital Partners and was admitted to its Socially Responsible Indexes: Ethical Index EURO and Ethical Index GLOBAL®. On 21 March 2003, before publishing its first sustainability report, Enel was admitted to the sustainability indexes of the Financial Times Stock

Exchange (FTSE4Good) in London. The company was the first utility admitted to the FTSE4Good 100 and the FTSE4GOOD EUROPE 50. In September 2003, Enel was also admitted to the Advanced Sustainable Performance Index on the basis of evaluations made by Vigeo. In 2003, it was successfully screened for the Dow Jones Sustainability Index (DJSI), Enel stock being added to the DJSI in September 2004.

In September 2005, Enel was re-confirmed in DJSI World and admitted to DJSI STOXX. In the same month, and despite an EIRIS alert that a Colombian company owned by Enel did not meet human rights criteria, it was confirmed for the third year running in the FTSE4Good Index Series, the FTSE4GOOD GLOBAL 100 and the FTSE4GOOD EUROPE 50. The warning was, in fact, a mix-up of the name of the enterprise owned by Enel, Carbones Colombianos del Cerrejon, with another. Although Enel had nothing to do with this second firm, it had to sell the company it owned to be re-confirmed in the FTSE4GOOD. In October 2006, Enel was admitted to the 'Top Ten' of the Accountability Global 50+; it was placed sixth in the industry ranking and third in the utilities ranking. It was the only Italian company in this ranking and improved on its previous position.

In September 2006, Enel was removed from the FTSE4GOOD Index Series, as a result of its acquisition of 66% of Slovenske Elektrarne, which operated nuclear power stations. The CEO commented on Enel's deletion:

> We have the major ethical funds of the world investing in our company, as a result of Enel's listing on the major sustainability indexes. While we are happy about this, we simultaneously feel that some of the standards that define CSR will have to be readjusted. This definitely applies to our investments in nuclear power, which some of the indexes have used to lower our rating. I do not think that this is currently appropriate: when a company follows a policy of investing in different energy sources, this does not mean that it is abandoning its code of conduct and sustainability, but is a guarantee that it is a viable and environmentally friendly energy provider that is not dependent on other countries for raw materials.

Enel Stakeholders

Since 1963, when the Italian energy companies were nationalized, and Enel became a monopoly, it has developed a consolidated relationship with its stakeholders. In the 60s and 70s, Enel pursued a mission to electrify the whole country, especially Southern Italy, and support Italian industrial development. In this period, it had to cope with relationships with local institutions, mainly in those areas where new power plants had to be built. The relationship with local communities was based more on dialogue than on conflict. Enel also devoted its attention to the environment to cope with the impact that its power plants had on local areas. The relationship with stakeholders was based on an exchange of economic returns for local communities, which received a part of the plant power revenues for renewable energies and social investments. At the end of the 70s, a new phase in the stakeholder dialogue opened. It was based on the confrontation and negotiation between Enel and its stakeholders, mainly local institutions that represented the community's interests. Enel coped with these stakeholder engagements by lobbying them. A 'one-way communication' was thus developed between the company and its stakeholders. By mainly paying attention to local institutions, Enel was able to influence its stakeholders and to ensure that their expectations would be aligned with the company's objectives. In the 1990s, a new category of stakeholders emerged: associations representing interests. Enel reacted to these new stakeholders' pressures by partially changing its communication. An 'asymmetrical, two-way communication' was developed, based on communicating something to the stakeholders, listening to them, but not giving them channels and instruments to dialogue with the company at the same level.

Roberto Zangrandi, Enel CSR Manager, 2006

In the Letter from the Chairman, which introduced Enel's first Sustainability Report in 2002, Piero Gnudi presented the Enel definition of CSR and stakeholders for the first time:

> Enel intends to base its business strategy not only on economic considerations, but also on environmental and social ones, because we are convinced this will help make us competitive and boost our reputation. Our fundamental objective remains that of ensuring the long-term creation of value for our shareholders. Given its size and the kind of business in which it is engaged, Enel interacts intensely with society and consequently aspires to maintain and develop a solid relationship of trust with its stakeholders. With its shareholders first of all, because, with two and a half million of them, Enel has far more investors than any other Italian company, but also with its 30 million customers, its employees and others who work for it, its suppliers, associations, and local communities.

In the 2003 Sustainability Report, Piero Gnudi pointed out:

> The objective remains the same: to improve our shareholders' return, carry out the fundamental points of our mission and lower the company's risk profile in order to make it an attractive investment with steady growth and low volatility. At the beginning of this path, there were about 20 socially responsible specialized investment funds present among our shareholders. Now there are 32 of them, controlling more than 16% of the shares held by institutional investors, and we are committed to attracting an increasing number of this kind of investment.

The 2004 Sustainability Report specifically highlighted that:

Corporate social responsibility or CSR comprises:

- *economic responsibility:* all the activities that have an economic or financial origin or impact;
- *environmental responsibility:* the degree to which a company is able to govern the environmental variables and impact of its activities;
- *social responsibility:* the company's actions with regard to individuals and communities, interest groups and the people who work for it.

These three components and the company's ability to balance them efficiently and honourably create the sustainability concept.

The report also presented, for the first time, a list of major reasons – based on socio-demographic and market surveys – for Enel stakeholders to invest in the company:

- *Shareholders:*
  1. positive performance of Enel shares on the stock market;
  2. fiduciary relationship and transparent communication;

3. control of economic, environmental and social risks;

4. effective corporate governance;

5. long-term investment in sustainability.

- *Lenders:*

  1. debt volume, use and quality;

  2. confidence of the financial and final markets;

  3. short- and long-term perspectives.

- *Human resources:*

  1. management according to ethical principles and observance of the Code of Ethics;

  2. equal opportunity for professional development;

  3. job satisfaction;

  4. pay in line with role;

  5. on-the-job training, health and safety;

  6. fair industrial relations;

  7. widespread, effective and transparent internal communication.

- *Customers:*

  1. awareness of needs;

  2. quality and modernity of service;

  3. service continuity;

  4. fair and transparent rates;

  5. transparent, clear and widespread communication;

  6. new services.

- *Suppliers:*

  1. increased orders;

  2. quality of relationship;

  3. punctual payments;

  4. fast, clear and transparent procedures.

- *Institutions:*

  1. fairness and transparency in carrying out activities;

  2. participatory and concrete dialogue.

- *Future generations:*

  1. social and environmental sustainability of development strategies;

  2. effective environmental governance;

  3. environmental education;

  4. reduction of all emissions;

  5. waste recovery;

  6. reduction of internal consumption of energy and water;

7. reduction of raw material use;
8. development of research;
9. increased energy efficiency;
10. development of renewable energy sources;
11. respect for biodiversity.

- *Communities:*
    1. transparency and punctuality of communication;
    2. social and environmental sustainability of industrial installations;
    3. availability of channels for direct dialogue with the company;
    4. relations with interest groups;
    5. initiatives in favour of communities;
    6. redistribution of income to social projects and corporate philanthropy;
    7. relations with local, national, and international institutions;
    8. media relations.

During February and March 2006, when preparing the 2005 Sustainability Report, the company launched a large-scale qualitative and quantitative survey of its CSR activities. The objective was to explore how the different Enel stakeholders perceived the company's corporate social responsibility by showing the quality of their relationship with Enel and the possible areas of improvement for each specific target investigated. The results of this survey are summarized in Figure 8.2, which lists the stakeholders and compares them in respect of the 38 areas of interest that they consider to be of prime importance. According to CSR Manager, Roberto Zangrandi:

> In the near future, this system could be useful to define strategic planning targets by basing them on the stakeholders' expectations and perceptions.

In 2006, Enel continued to develop a relationship of trust with its stakeholders. In the view of CEO Fulvio Conti:

> Stakeholders are those who make investments tied to Enel activities, meaning, first and foremost, the shareholders, followed by the staff members, clients, suppliers and business partners. In a broader sense, the term refers to all those individuals or groups, whose interests are directly or indirectly affected by Enel activities: this encompasses the local and national communities in which Enel operates, as well as environmentalist associations, future generations, etc. Over the years, Enel has consolidated its ability to listen to associations that represent interests, which include consumers, environmental organizations, the world of small and medium-sized firms, and public bodies. However, Enel cannot overlook the fact that in the company's day-to-day operations there is a privileged relationship between the management and shareholders, and that managers have different and more compelling obligations to shareholders than to other stakeholders, who also represent legitimate interests.

In order to promote a symmetrical, two-way and transparent communication with its stakeholders, Enel revised the structure and contents of its homepage in the spring of 2007. In the Letter to

STAKEHOLDER INTERESTS (Level of interest: ● high; ○ medium; ▲ nil)

	Shareholders ▽ Financial analysts	Lenders ▽ Financial analysts Rating agencies	Human Resources ▽ Union organizations	Customers ▽ Consumer associations	Suppliers ▽ Business associations	Institutions ▽ Governments (foreign, national, local)	Future Generations ▽ Environmental associations	Communities ▽ Local interest groups
Share performance on stock market	●	●	●	○	●	●	●	○
Fiduciary relationship and widespread, clear, and transparent communication	●	●	●	●	●	●	●	●
Control of economic, environmental, and social risk	●	●	●	●	●	●	●	●
Effective corporate governance	●	●	●	●	●	●	●	●
Long-term sustainability of stock investment	●	●	●	○	○	●	●	○
Volume, use, and quality of debt	●	●	●	○	○	●	●	○
Management according to ethical principles and observance of Ethical Code	●	●	●	●	●	●	●	●
Equal opportunity for professional development of employees	○	○	●	●	▲	●	●	●
Employee job satisfaction	○	○	●	○	▲	●	○	●
Pay raise for employees	▲	▲	●	○	▲	●	○	●
Training	○	○	●	○	▲	●	●	●
Safety and health protection	●	●	●	●	○	●	●	●
Social institutions for employees	○	○	●	○	▲	●	○	●
Fair industrial relations	○	○	●	○	▲	●	○	●
Transparent, effective, and widespread internal communication	○	○	●	●	▲	○	○	○
Service quality and modernity	●	●	●	●	○	●	●	●
Fair (low) and transparent rates	▲	▲	●	●	▲	●	●	●
Proposals for new services for customers	●	●	●	●	○	●	●	●
Increase in orders for suppliers	▲	▲	▲	▲	●	○	▲	●
Punctuality in paying suppliers	▲	▲	▲	▲	●	●	▲	●
Rapidity, clarity, and transparency of procurement procedures	○	○	●	○	●	●	▲	●
Environmental and social sustainability of growth strategies	●	●	●	●	○	●	●	●
Effective environmental governance	●	●	●	●	○	●	●	●
Reduction of all emissions	●	●	●	●	○	●	●	●
Waste recovery	●	●	●	●	○	●	●	●
Reduction of internal consumption of energy and water	●	●	●	●	○	●	●	●
Reduction of use of raw materials	●	●	●	●	○	●	●	●
Development of research	●	●	●	●	●	●	●	●
Increased energy efficiency	●	●	●	●	●	●	●	●
Development of renewable energy sources	○	○	●	●	●	●	●	●
Respect for biodiversity	○	○	●	●	○	●	●	●
Social and environmental sustainability of industrial installations	●	●	●	●	○	●	●	●
Availability of channels for direct dialogue with Company	●	●	●	●	●	●	●	●
Relations with associations representing interest groups	●	●	●	●	●	●	○	●
Initiatives in favour of communities	○	○	●	●	○	●	●	●
Charity	○	○	●	○	○	●	●	●
Relations with international, national, and local institutions	●	●	●	○	○	●	●	●
Relations with the media	●	●	●	○	▲	●	○	●

Figure 8.2 The stakeholder interests map

our Stakeholders, which introduced the Enel 2006 Sustainability Report, the Chairman and CEO stated that:

> We have decided to change the way we tell you about our commitment to sustainability and social responsibility, in order to improve the channels of communication with you. We have consequently created a website (http://www.enel.it/azienda_en/sostenibilita/) that will present even more information on our social responsibility policy. This site is an instrument with which everyone can directly evaluate and analyse our actions, thus contributing to the interactive communication of our sustainability plans.

The new homepage put more emphasis on the stakeholder dialogue and allowed a more direct engagement of stakeholders. Stakeholders could participate in a survey that was directly linked to the Enel homepage and could offer their opinion on 24 'hot' CSR issues (the Sustainability Meter tool can be accessed at http://csrmeter.palomarlab.net/). Based on their answers, stakeholders were positioned according to the emphasis that they allocated to the different CSR dimensions: economic, social and environmental responsibility. From this survey, it was possible to map stakeholders' priorities. By comparing these priorities with the Enel top management's emphasis of the various dimensions, the gap between the stakeholder priorities and Enel's expectations could be derived and the way to reduce this gap identified.

Suggested Questions for Discussion

1. What are the particular features of the CSR concept and definition of stakeholders adopted by Enel and why?
2. What CSR implementation changes have been introduced into Enel's organizational structure and managerial mechanisms?
3. Considering Enel's approach to CSR, how would you design the structure of a performance measurement system both for external reporting and for managerial reporting (e.g., performance areas, KPIs, etc.)?
4. What are the strategic benefits to Enel in developing a comprehensive CSR framework, and how does this help the company to mitigate traditional risks in its industry?

CSR PERFORMANCE MEASUREMENT AND EVALUATION

Introduction

> The objective to compile the Sustainability Report (ready for issuing with the Consolidated Financial Statement at the General Shareholders Assembly in 2003) led to the debate on the key driver for CSR – whether it would be an instrument to improve company image or a strategic and managerial philosophy – going out of the window. The 2003 Sustainability Report reached an important conclusion: Enel publicly stated its commitment to CSR.
>
> Roberto Zangrandi, CSR Manager, Enel

In 2002, a team under the Corporate Communication Unit carried out a feasibility analysis of CSR disclosure. Enel, they concluded, was better equipped to produce a comprehensive sustainability report than most other big companies.

Publication of the Sustainability Report, they argued, would signal Enel's involvement in and commitment to a CSR strategy and was designed to communicate it both externally and internally. The report had three objectives: to provide a complete picture of the company's financial, environmental and social performance; to highlight the results achieved; and to support dialogue with Enel's main stakeholders.

Adopting a top-down approach, the entire company became engaged in the reporting process. The Sustainability Report was prepared in accordance with the AccountAbility 1000 (AA1000) principles, which included information of:

- *significance:* of interest to stakeholders;
- *response:* on the ways in which the firm intended to satisfy stakeholders' legitimate requests;
- *completeness:* on all the company's significant activities and performance.

Methodological sources taken into consideration were the principles of the Global Reporting Initiative (GRI), which were recognized as the principal basis of the Sustainability Report. In addition, Enel managers analysed approaches suggested by OCSE, ILO, Business in the Community, the UN Global Compact and by the CSR-SC project of the Italian Work and Social Policies Ministry. Moreover, the questionnaires of rating agencies and socially responsible investment funds analysts played a fundamental role in the process.

Future Sustainability Reports, to appear each year, were to be delivered by the Corporate Social Responsibility Unit, situated in the Corporate Communication Unit. The data would come primarily from the departmental units and business divisions. The Report was to be submitted to the Board of Directors as well as the Internal Audit Committee for appraisal and to the Internal Audit Unit for control. Its procedural conformity would then be certified by an external auditing firm. It was to be published together with the Consolidated Financial Statement.

Stakeholder Engagement

Until 2004, stakeholder engagement was limited to a few focus groups, which severely narrowed the range of stakeholders consulted. To remedy this, in support of the 2005 Sustainability Report the company launched a large-scale qualitative and quantitative survey of its CSR activities. The objective was to explore stakeholder perceptions of Enel as a 'responsible' firm, highlighting both current CSR performance and indicating possible areas of improvement.

The qualitative study was based on interviews with 18 suppliers, lenders and institutions as well as three focus groups. The study was conducted by Enel supervisors in close collaboration with external researchers and psychologists. Its questions aimed to evaluate the quality of each stakeholder's relationship with Enel, their attitudes and opinions on corporate social responsibility within the company and their expectations and evaluation of the Enel 2004 Sustainability Report. The quantitative survey was carried out through interviews with 4040 Enel customers,

728 'future generation' representatives aged between 14 and 25 years, and 99 retail investors (Figure 8.2).

Efforts to enhance the participation of stakeholders in CSR performance measurement continued. In order to promote two-way, transparent communication with its stakeholders, Enel revised the structure and contents of its website homepage in the spring of 2007. The new homepage put more emphasis on dialogue, enabling stakeholders to participate in a survey as well as offer their opinions on 24 'hot' CSR issues (access the tool at http://csrmeter.palomar-lab.net/). From this survey, it became possible to create the map of stakeholders' priorities shown in Figure 8.2. By comparing these with senior management's own emphasis on the various issues, the gap between stakeholder priorities and Enel's internal expectations could be delineated.

The Sustainability Report Framework

The Enel Sustainability Report was organized in descriptive and quantitative sections. The descriptive section offered extensive documentation of Enel's goals, initiatives, results, projects and targets for corporate social responsibility. The quantitative section covered the CSR Key Performance Indicators (KPIs).

With reference to the descriptive section, the *stakeholder interests map* outlined the expectations and priorities of the various stakeholder groups (shareholders, investors, employees, customers, suppliers, institutions, future generations, local communities).

This map showed stakeholders' views on the 38 areas that they considered most important, according to a social and demographic survey carried out in 2005. Each stakeholder category's greater or lesser concern with each of the areas was presented graphically, and the resulting table also clearly portrayed the stakeholders' conflict of interests. The most important questions that concerned all categories of stakeholders can be summarized in four areas:

- communication, ethics and fiduciary relations;
- professional competence and good governance;
- development of research and energy efficiency;
- responsibility regarding economic, social and (especially) environmental risks.

In the second section, the sustainability KPIs represented the priority measures of Enel's sustainability strategy. The process of selecting the relevant KPIs was developed over a number of years. During the start-up phase, approximately 700 KPIs were selected from those featured in widely recognized frameworks, such as the GRI, SA 8000 and AA 1000. In 2002, approximately 130 of these, which were immediately available and easy to calculate, were published. By 2003, the number of reported KPIs grew to approximately 200, a growth that reflected information requirements from sustainability rating agencies. Soon after 2004, the number of core KPIs reached 314. Finally, each group had a comment added to facilitate its interpretation. Although there were other Italian firms that compiled large numbers of KPIs, Enel became a benchmark company in the CSR field and its example encouraged other companies to increase their KPI disclosures.

The KPIs were grouped into categories that reflected the stakeholder concerns and critical performance areas. Each KPI was also classified according to its adherence to the CSR and social commitment principles developed by the Italian Ministry of Labour and Social Policies, as well as to the requirements of the SAM (Zurich) and EIRIS research institutes, which evaluated companies on behalf of the Dow Jones (DJSI) and Financial Times (FTSE4GOOD) international sustainability indexes, respectively.

The metrics aggregated performance across all business units, with the exception of indicators related to customers, which reported separately in each business division and for each market segment. Exhibit 8.1 provides the entire list of KPIs from the Enel Sustainability Report 2003.

In 2006, to improve the communication of the Sustainability Report, its results were displayed on part of the official company website (http://www.enel.it/azienda_en/sostenibilita/). It presented both more information and facilitated access to it in an interactive format. In addition, the website included detailed information regarding the methodology behind the KPIs, in accordance with the Sustainability Reporting Guidelines in the Global Reporting Initiative (GRI-G3). Where applicable, it also followed the GRI Boundary Protocol and the Indicator Protocols. Although the data for 2006 were not always comparable with those of previous years, they were calculated on the basis of the entries in Enel's financial accounting system and other information systems.[4] The GRI's additional performance indicators were also adopted.

According to the GRI-G3 standard, the KPIs are representative of the aspects shown in Table 8.1.

Under the area of economic performance, there were nine quantitative and qualitative indicators. Of these, the principal metric was the *value-added per stakeholder*, which indicated the economic value generated from the operations and its distributions among the different stakeholder categories.

Environmental performance was measured by 30 indicators, most of which were disaggregated for plant or other relevant dimensions, such as the type of waste water, emissions into the atmosphere or materials used.

Forty social performance metrics were used, of which 14 evaluated Enel's treatment of its employees, nine monitored human rights, eight covered the relationship with the society and nine assessed product responsibility.

A final section of the Sustainability Report 2006, entitled 'These are the numbers', compared the data of the same KPIs with those of previous years.

Internal Performance Measurement and Evaluation: CSR Planning and Control Mechanisms

To ensure that sustainability became part of everyday business decisions, CSR managerial control at Enel was integrated into not only the managerial level, but also – more importantly perhaps – the operational one.

EXHIBIT 8.1 SUSTAINABILITY KPIS 2003

Who we are

Corporate governance

Presence of socially responsible investors (SRI) in Enel's share capital

Number, percent

	2003
SRI* funds with Enel shares	33
Enelshares held by SRI funds out of total institutional shareholders	16.2%

In barely 12 months the CSR strategy has increased interest in Enel on the part of the institutional investors called socially responsible

*socially responsible investment

Geographical distribution of socially responsible investors that hold Enel shares

Percent

	2003
USA	9.9
UK	30.4
Rest of Europe	21.4
Italy	20.3
Benelux	18.0

Enel's socially responsible investors are mainly European. The United Kingdom and Italy stand out with respect to the USA component.

Shareholders

Performance of Enel shares with respect to those of comparable European companies (Jan. 2, 2003 – Jan. 2, 2004)

- Enel
- EDP
- RWE
- Endesa
- Centrica
- Scottish Power
- Iberdrola
- E. ON

Economic responsibility

Gross operating margin

Percent

	2002	2003
■ Generation and Energy Management	31.63	37.11
■ Market, Infrastructure and Networks	44.98	36.85
■ International	3.29	2.81
■ Terna	6.82	6.00
■ Telecommunications	7.98	10.26
■ Business Services and Diversified Activities	2.83	4.37
■ Parent Company	2.47	2.60

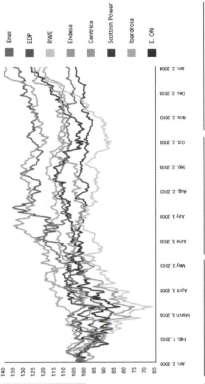

The gross operating margin (the difference between the revenues and the operating costs of the Enel Group in 2003 shows an increase of about 28% with respect to 2002 (restated on a pro forma basis). The Generation and Energy Management Division made a decisive contribution to this increase thanks to a rise in production and the related revenues, achieved in the presence of a containment of operating costs. The Market, Infrastructure and Network Divisions record an overall increase of the gross operating margin deriving almost entirely from the business expansion of the Gas area, given the fall in the volume of electricity sold following the liberalization of the market initiated by the Bersani Decree in 2001. The Telecommunications Division shows a substantial increase in the gross operating margin with respect to the previous year due to the rise in revenue from mobile telephony in the presence of practically stable operating costs. Also significant is the contribution of the Business Services and Diversified Activities Division, deriving from the increase in margins achieved in the engineering and construction business.

Shareholders

Weight of Enel shares in the main stock-market indices

Number, Percent

	2001	2002	2003
FTSE Eurotop 100	0.373	0.434	0.411
MIBTEL	6.821	6.614	6.766
MIB 30	8.781	8.346	8.578
Milan Index His.	6.858	6.614	6.766
Milan Public Utilities	21.345	22.779	27.807
Bloomberg Europe	0.569	0.640	0.637
BE500 Electric	17.978	19.941	17.056
DJ Euro STOXX 50	0.679	0.849	0.928
DJ Euro STOXX	0.463	0.545	0.597
DJ Euro Utilities	7.838	8.817	9.209

Structural evolution of the respective baskets.

Comparative analysis of dividends

Percent, Yield

	2002	2003
Enel	7.3%	6.7%
Acea	4.3%	no div
AEM MI	3.3%	2.8%
Enl	5.0%	5.0%
Endesa	6.1%	4.5%
Iberdrola	4.3%	3.9%
E. On	4.2%	3.4%
RWE	4.0%	3.5%
Scottish Power	5.8%	6.4%
Centrica	1.9%	2.0%
Electrabel	6.1%	5.8%

The decrease in Enel's yield is directly connected with the increasing price of its shares at an equal dividend per share. The yield was calculated comparing the dividend per share for year x (paid in year x + 1) with the price.

Evolution of the shareholding base

2001	2002	2003
10.8%	10.3%	17.2%
21.6%	22.1%	21.8%
67.6%	67.6%	61.0%

- Institutional investors
- Retail shareholders
- Ministry of the Economy

The percentage owned by the Ministry of the Economy decreases with respect to 2002 following the placement of the second tranche, while the percentage owned by the institutional investors increases, thanks in part to the action of the Department of Investor Relations.

Evolution of the geographical distribution of the institutional investors

2001	2002	2003
3.7%	3.7%	2.1%
17.5%	24.9%	25.8%
18.0%	16.8%	20.3%
12.5%	13.7%	29.2%
47.4%	40.9%	22.5%

- Italy
- North America
- UK
- Rest of Europe
- Rest of the world

In 2003 the percentage owned by the Italian institutional investors falls with respect to the other components. The UK and the rest of Europe increase in particular, in part thanks to the ad hoc initiatives carried out by the Department of Investor Relations.

(Continued)

EXHIBIT 8.1 (Continued)

Shareholders

Distribution of institutional investors by investment style

Percent

	2001	2002	2003
GARP	34.7%	37.4%	16.0%
Growth	7.6%	15.5%	25.6%
Index	38.4%	26.5%	16.6%
Value	18.2%	19.3%	20.8%
Hedge	n.a.	n.a.	19.1%
Other	1.1%	1.4%	1.9%

Ad hoc initiatives carried out by the Department of Investor Relations with regard to the most important institutional shareholders.

Encounters of the top management/ Department of Investor Relations with institutional investors

Number

	2002	2003
Encounters with investors	9	93
Number of which dedicated space to CSR issues	n.a.	n.a.

The encounters (conference calls, collective and individual encounters) in 2002 regard those that took place during the last quarter. In 2003 there were no encounters with investors in which CSR issues were discussed. The integration of CSR initiatives with the policies of the Department of Investor Relations took place in early 2004.

Lenders

Evolution of debt

Millions of euros

	2001	2002	2003
Net financial debt	21,930	24,467	24,174
Ratio net financial debt/shareholders' equity	1.04	1.17	1.13

In 2003 net financial debt decreased by about 290 million euros because of the combined effect of an increase of about 2,200 million euros in net long-term financial debt and a reduction of about 2,490 million euros in net short-term financial debt. The debt/equity ratio consequently fell from 1.17 to 1.13. The main financial transactions carried out during 2003 were characterized by: bond issues, the establishment of revolving credit lines, loans granted by the EIB, and the refinancing of a loan granted in 2001.

Customers – Gas market

Breakdown of customers in the gas* market

Thousands

	2002	2003
Business customers	1.2	1.6
Household customers	1,720.3	1,794.0
Total	1,721.4	1,795.7
Transport	0.5	2.2

The expansion of both the business and household markets is the result of the acquisition of both single customers and groups of customers.

*Data regarding Enel Gas.

Volumes sold on the gas market

Millions of m³

	2002	2003
Business customers	1,501.9	1,780.5
Household customers	2,355.1	2,655.0
Total	3,856.9	4,445.4
Transport	49.0	88.9

Gas distribution and sales improve substantially in 2003. In order to reinforce its market position Enel signed an agreement with British Gas for a 50-50 joint venture regarding the construction and operation of a plant (with an annual capacity of 8 billion m³ of gas) for the regasification of liquid natural gas located in Brindisi.

Customers - Electricity market

Breakdown of customers in the electricity market

Thousands

	2002	2003
Customers regulated market		
> private	22,653.8	22,513.5
> other uses	6,475.5	6,400.9
Total	29,129.3	28,914.4
Customers free market	5.3	4.1

The downward trend in the number of customers is a consequence of the Bersani Decree on the liberalization of Italian electricity market. In 2003 the process of selling distribution networks to local public utilities interested in their acquisition continued. A distribution network serving 46 municipalities and about 96,200 customers was sold to Asm Brescia.

Volumes sold on the electricity market

TWh

	2002	2003*
Customers regulated market		
> private	51.3	51.7
> other uses	99.2	89.4
Total	150.5	141.1
Customers free market	30.4	10.7

Among the causes that determined the considerable reduction in the volumes of electricity sold on the free market mention should be made of the repositioning of Enel in this area through selective focusing on large and medium-sized eligible customers with the most value added.

*Net of Deval.

Telecommunications

Total duration of interruptions per customer in the regulated market

Minutes

1996	2001	2002	2003*
239	125	103	88

The substantial improvement in the technical quality of the service in the regulated market was achieved thanks to the investment made in the electricity distribution networks and to better management of the material used in plant construction.

*Figure that must be validated by Electricity and Gas Authority.

Volume sold in the telephony market

Millions of minutes

	2002	2003
Mobile	7,771.8	9,492.5
Fixed-line	17,711.8	15,035.1
Total	25,483.6	24,527.6

The decrease in voice traffic in fixed-line telephony is connected mainly with the process of replacing fixed-line traffic with mobile and the consolidation of the leadership of the dominant company. Mobile telephony grew by 22%, with an increase of 36.5% in SMS volume with respect to 2002. Finally, profitability per customer also increased, with monthly ARPU (average revenue per user) amounting to 22.2 euros, against 19.6 euros the previous year.

Suppliers

Breakdown of the fuels purchased

Millions or euros

	2002	2003
Gas	754	1,183
Oil	1,475	1,014
Coal	488	412
Services	688	575
Total	3,405	3,184

There was a slight decrease (-6%) with respect to 2002; determined by a reduction of the consumption of oil, a large increase in gas due to the aggregation in the last quarter of 2003 of an annual supply contract, and the general effect of the euro/dollar exchange rate.

Specific atmospheric emissions of SO₂ and NOₓ from thermal production

net g/kWh - plants in Italy

	1999	2000	2001	2002	2003
SO_2	2.9	2.5	2.4	1.9	0.9
NO_x	1.1	0.9	0.8	0.7	0.6

Sulfur dioxide (SO_2) and nitrogen oxides (NO_x) are created by combustion in thermal plants. The quantities indicated show a substantial reduction, thanks mainly to the use of advanced combustion systems, the improvement of abatement systems, and the use of superior fuels.

Specific atmospheric emissions of particulates from thermal production

net g/kWh - plants in Italy

	1999	2000	2001	2002	2003
Particulates	0.11	0.10	0.09	0.06	0.03

Particulates show an appreciable reduction thanks to the adoption of abatement systems.

Fuel consumption

Millions of toe - plants in Italy

	2002	2003
Natural gas	7.6	9.4
Fuel oil	8.1	6.4
Orimulsion	1.1	1.0
Coal	7.0	6.4
Total	**23.8**	**23.2**

The breakdown of fuel consumption in toe (tons of oil equivalent) shows the large use of natural gas and to a lesser extent of coal and fuel oil. Specifically, there is an appreciable reduction in the use of high- and medium-sulfur oil in favor of low-sulfur and sulfur-free oil, in accordance with EU directives regarding air quality and pollution produced by industrial plants.

Millions of toe - plants abroad 2003

	2003
Natural gas	0.08
Fuel oil	0.07
Orimulsion	0
Coal	1.15
Total	**1.30**

In addition to the extensive use of coal for plants abroad, a significant amount of electricity is generated from renewable sources such as water, wind and biomass.

Emissions of carbon dioxide from thermal production

Plants in Italy

	1999	2000	2001	2002	2003
CO_2 specific emissions (net g/kWh)	696	692	707	720	670
CO_2 absolute emissions (millions of tons)	95	98	84	75	71.5

The specific and absolute emissions of carbon dioxide (CO_2), typical of combustion, show an appreciable reduction in 2003, thanks mainly to the sharp decrease in the use of fuel oil and the process of making production plants more efficient.

Waste produced

Thousands of tons - plants in Italy

1999	2000	2001	2002	2003
1,440	1,577	1,605	2,090	1,808

The residues of industrial activities show a reduction in 2003 due mainly to the use of superior fuels (less ash produced) and the generalized application of advanced technologies for abating particulates (more light ash trapped).

The share of waste reclaimed expresses the percentage of the quantity to be reclaimed (delivered to an authorized company) and the quantity produced.

Electricity production (net)

Millions of kWh - plants in Italy

	2002*	2003
Thermal	104,735	106,670
Hydro (from natural flows)	27,942	26,012
Geothermal	4,382	5,036
Other sources	53	77
Total	**137,112**	**137,795**

Net production is up by 0.5% with respect to 2002, with the largest increase in the summer months. The significant increase in geothermal production is due to new plants. With respect to 2002, thermal production was characterized by a substantial reduction of the use of fuel oil and by considerable use of natural gas.
* Production regarding Enel plant as of 12.31.2002.

Millions of kWh - plants abroad and before EUFR

	2003
Thermal	7,427
Hydro (from natural flows)	2,881
Other sources	235
Total	**10,543**

The increase in the net production of electricity abroad stems from the increase recorded by the American companies (+25%) and the good performance of Maritza East III Power Company AD, the Bulgarian operating company acquired by Enel in March 2003.

Non-hazardous special waste

Percentage of the quantity produced by plants in Italy 2003

	1999	2000	2001	2002	2003
Coal ash	106	101	93	94	99
Gypsum from desulfuration	99	102	91	94	97
Other non-hazardous special waste	n.a.	n.a.	n.a.	55	57

Waste produced

Tons - plants abroad 2003

	Non-hazardous	Hazardous special
Enel North America	4,326	0
Maritza East III	1,261,820	
Viesgo	845,163.5	406.1
Total	**2,111,309.5**	**406.1**

Data estimated on the basis of calculation made at the end of 2003.

Percentage of production from renewable sources other than hydro

Percentage of electricity produced in Italy

1999	2000	2001	2002	2003
2.3	2.4	2.7	3.2	3.8

The increase over these years in production from renewable resources is due to the gradual growth of the geothermal (+15% with respect to 2002), wind (5 new plants in 2003) and solar contributions.

(Continued)

EXHIBIT 8.1 (Continued)

Social responsibility

People who work at Enel

	as of Dec. 31, 2003		as of Dec. 31, 2002		Change
Parent Company	522	0.8%	527	0.7%	-5
Generation and Energy Management - Italy	10,318	15.9%	12,077	17.0%	-1,759
Market, Infrastructure and Networks - Italy	36,424	56.2%	39,489	55.5%	-3,065
Terna	2,821	4.4%	3,106	4.4%	-285
Telecommunications	8,769	13.5%	8,602	12.1%	167
Business Services and Diversified Activities	4,206	6.5%	5,765	8.1%	-1,559
Abroad	1,710	2.6%	1,638	2.3%	72
Total	**64,770**	**100%**	**71,204**	**100%**	**-6,434**

Number of injuries to Enel human resources per million hours worked from 1998 to 2003 (rate of frequency)

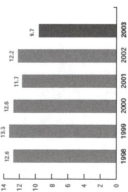

1998	1999	2000	2001	2002	2003
12.6	13.3	12.6	11.7	12.2	9.7

Job status (as of Dec. 31)

	2002	2003
Executives	891	785
Supervisors	5,402	4,979
White-collar worker	42,380	39,409
Blue-collar worker	22,531	19,597
Total	**71,204**	**64,770**

All the projects developed in 2003 aimed at bringing out more and more of the potential of internal resources and consolidating professional and managerial capabilities. During the year the process of management review was initiated and the new system of capability assessment was designed and implemented.

Education

	2002	2003
University degree	7,263	7,008
High school diploma	29,051	26,691
Other	34,890	31,071
Total	**71,204**	**64,770**

Considering that fewer people are now working at Enel, there is a slight increase in the percentage of university and high school graduates among Enel's human resources.

Hours of training per person

Number

	2002	2003
Generation and Energy Management	17	21
Market, Infrastructure and Networks	18.4	25
Terna	34.3	30.9
Business Services	19.1	24
Parent Company	14.7	22
Average*	19	25

The number of hours of training per person increased with respect to 2002, thanks to the 75% increase in distance training (+ 54,000 hours) and the 20% one in traditional training (+ 214,000 hours). Distance training provided courses to many people on the subjects of safety and sustainability, while traditionally provided courses in institutional training were perfected. As far as telecommunications are concerned, mention should be made of the substantial increase in the number of hours provided.

* Weighted.

Sustainability training

	2002	2003
Total cost of sustainability training (euros)	574,870	574,286
Cost per person of sustainability training (euros)	9.56	10.01

Expenditure on sustainability training was stable even though the average number of human resources fell by about 4.6%. This fact translates into an increase in expenditure per person, from 9.56 euros in 2002 to 10.01 euros in 2003.

(The data do not include Wind and foreign companies).

Share of distance training

Percent

	2002	2003
Generation and Energy Management	7	3
Market, Infrastructure and Networks	4.3	10.3
Terna	10.5	9.3
Business Services	14.9	8.7
Parent Company	8	6.6
Average*	6.2	8.9

2003 should be considered an exceptional year as far as the use of distance training is concerned. Important distance-training projects were initiated: for example, Ethical Code and Information Classification. Access from home to the corporate distance-training channel (EDSL, Enel Distance Learning System) is gradually increasing and can be improved thanks to the development of broadband. The areas of managerial, personal and professional development, as well as foreign languages and safety, were particularly emphasized.

* Weighted.

Source: Sustainability Report 2003

Table 8.1 Aspects Represented by KPIs

Area	Aspect
Economic performance indicators	Economic performance Market presence Indirect economic impacts
Environmental performance indicators	Materials Energy Water Biodiversity Emissions, effluents and wastes Products and services Transport Overall
Social performance indicators	
Labour practices and decent work performance indicators	Employment Labour/management relations Occupational health and safety Training and education Diversity and equal opportunity
Human rights performance indicators	Investment and procurement practices Non-discrimination Freedom of association and collective bargaining Child labour Forced and compulsory labour Security practices Indigenous rights
Society performance	Community Corruption Public policy Anti-competitive behaviour Compliance
Product responsibility performance indicators	Customer health and safety Product and service labelling Marketing communication Customer privacy Compliance

First, CSR policy formed an integral part of the Enel Business Plan, which charted the path of Enel's economic growth within a strategic framework of environmental protection and social development. Second, Enel set up a planning and control process that combined economic, environmental and social results based on a system of KPI data collection at quarterly intervals[5]; it was designed to:

- illustrate the main actions being undertaken for improvement, in effect guaranteeing information flow to stakeholders;
- indicate, in the case of shortcomings, where corrective action should be taken.

Figure 8.3 The five criteria of the sustainability database in order of priority

The gathering and processing of financial and non-financial data required the involvement of both the Corporate area and of Divisions/Companies; the former addressed broad cross-cutting concerns, whereas the latter covered specific business issues. The various corporate and professional bodies employed CSR reporters and data managers, who gathered, verified and processed data in their respective areas every three months. In cooperation with the CSR Unit, the Enel S.p.A. Planning and Control Unit consolidated the results, coordinated the reporting process and provided commentary.

In addition, an environmental accounting system, linked to the cost accounting system, enabled the Corporate Environmental Policy Unit to monitor related expenses. A new unit, called Business Planning and CSR Control (which was situated within the Accounting, Planning and Control Department) developed the sustainability reporting model. This unit cooperated with EnelDATA with a mandate to coordinate the CSR planning and control process; it also ensured the full integration of the sustainability targets into the strategic plan.

Figure 8.3 shows how the sustainability database was specifically designed according to five criteria in order of priority.

Sustainability Data and Platforms for Measurement

Data represented the centrepiece of the sustainability planning and control system, which contained the entire year's guidelines for the CSR planning and control activities, such as the timing, contents and people involved in the process. It also presented the appropriate formats for data collection and the list of sustainability KPIs.

In 2006, of the total 314 KPIs developed, 156 were related to the firm's financial perform-ance, 67 to the environmental perspective and 91 to the social goals. From the stakeholder perspective, 24% of KPIs concerned the employees, 22% the future generations, 16% the shareholders, 26% the customers, 5% the suppliers, 3% the lenders and the remaining 4% the wider community.

The current structure was defined in 2005. Between 2004 and 2005 the financial KPIs had grown from 90 to 156, expanding in the following areas:

- *Shareholders*:
  - risk exposure
  - operating performance (efficiency)
  - investment.
- *Telecommunications (TLC), electricity and gas market:*
  - customer satisfaction
  - service quality
  - service level
  - call centre.

The environment area had increased from 60 to 67 KPIs, largely due to additional measurements regarding a thermoelectric park. Social responsibility KPIs grew from 68 to 91, with increases in the following areas:

- *Personal development and satisfaction:*
  - knowledge management
  - internal communication.
- *Safety:*
  - accidents at work.
- *Relationship with the associations, institutions and media:*
  - company image
  - legal questions regarding institutions and the community.

Among stakeholders, the customer portion became the primary area of focus, with its weight growing from 11% in 2004 to 26% in 2005.

Categorizing Key Performance Indicators

KPIs were classified into three categories: *Strategic KPIs*, which represented specific CSR objectives as defined by the Enel Divisions; *Non-strategic KPIs*, which were subordinate to strategic KPIs; and *Financial KPIs*, which referred to the corporation's overall business responsibilities. Each KPI was compiled by both the owner and EnelDATA.

For each KPI, Sustainability Data provided:

- its code;
- its unit of measurement;
- a brief description;
- its GRI code;
- the area involved;
- its related critical success factor for the company;
- the weight of its critical success factor;
- its weight in the Sustainability Scorecard.

The Enel CSR Plan

The CSR Plan formalized the objectives and action plans required for the development and implementation of the sustainability strategy during the specific budget period as well as the following three years. It also included a set of 99 selected KPIs linked to the strategic CSR objectives. The finalized objective schedule defined the action plan and targets for the following five years. (See Exhibit 8.4 for an extract from the Sustainability Report 2006, including a synthesis of the CSR Plan 2006–2010.)

The Quarterly Scorecard

The most important CSR reporting document was the Quarterly Scorecard (April, July, October and February), first published in 2006 and addressed to the Chief Executive Officer. It was divided into a qualitative and quantitative section, the former containing highlights of the most relevant CSR facts of the quarter and the latter reporting on those KPIs that had not reached their target value or were experiencing delays in doing so. The document also indicated corrective actions to be taken or revised KPI targets.

The Business Review

The Business Review was prepared every six months, also addressed to the CEO and the Board of Directors. It was an information kit on the progress of all sustainability projects regarding the current CSR situation, describing the initiatives planned over the next 12 months. It also contained a wider set of KPIs than the Quarterly Scorecard.

The Sustainability Scorecard

Unlike the deadline-driven Quarterly Scorecard and the Business Review, the *Sustainability Scorecard* monitored CSR results on a continuous basis (see Exhibit 8.3). First produced in 2006, it highlighted the gaps between expected results and the actual performance of approximately 100 KPIs (out of the 314 total KPIs being monitored within the company) in accordance with the triple bottom line approach; that is, those taken into consideration in the CSR Plan. These KPIs reflected the 11 critical CSR success factors as identified in Enel's strategic map – each KPI was linked to a specific critical success factor.[6]

EXHIBIT 8.2 SUSTAINABILITY KPIS 2005

THESE ARE THE NUMBERS

The following tables show the magnitudes that Enel considers essential for its sustainability auditing and reporting.

The tables contain:
> the description of the magnitude recorded;
> the unit of measurement in which it is expressed;
> the datum for 2005;
> the datum for 2004;
> the percentage change between 2005 and 2004;
> the company/companies to which the datum refers;
> the number of the data or magnitude family used by the Global Reporting Initiative (GRI) with which the magnitudes measured by Enel are compatible and homogeneous;
> the number of the data or magnitude family included in the set of indicators developed by the Italian Ministry of Labor and Social Policies in preparing its Corporate Social Responsibility-Social Commitment Project (CSR-SC) with which the magnitudes measured by Enel are compatible and homogeneous;
> the direct or indirect correspondence or the uniformity of the magnitudes recorded by Enel with the requisites required by the SAM and ERIS sustainability analysis firms, which use special questionnaires to evaluate the companies to be included in the sustainability indices of, respectively, Dow Jones (Dow Jones Sustainability Index) and the Financial Times (FTSE4GOOD).

Criteria used for the Key Performance Indicators (KPI):
> by "Enel" is meant the whole Group, i.e. all the companies consolidated with the integral method;
> the Enel data for 2005 do not include Terna and Wind;
> the data regarding 2004 are those already recorded in the 2004 Sustainability Report, with the exception of the environmental data, which do not include Wind and Terna;
> the economic data regarding the item "Economic performance" regarding 2004 and 2005 are taken from the Consolidated Financial Statements, which was prepared according to the IAS/IFRS international accounting standards. Consequently, Terna and Wind are treated as discontinued operations.

ACRONYMS

ACR	Abandoned Call Rate
BOD	Board of Directors/Biochemical Oxygen Demand
CCGT	Combined Cycle Gas Turbine
COD	Chemical Oxygen Demand
DPS	Dividend per Share
DT	Distance Training
EBITDA	Earnings Before Interest, Tax, Depreciation and Amortization
EBT	Earnings Before Tax
EDLS	Enel Distance Learning System
EIB	European Investment Bank
EPS	Earnings per Share
GARP	Growth at Reasonable Price
GEM	Generation and Energy Management
IPO	Initial Public Offering
IRAP	Imposta Regionale sulle Attivita Produttive (regional tax on firms)
IRES	Imposta sul Reddito delle Societa (corporate income tax)
IVR	Integrated Voice Response
KM	Knowledge Management
LBG	London Benchmarking Group
LV	Low Voltage
MIR	Networks, Infrastructure, and Sales
MV	Medium Voltage
N.A.	Not Available
ORIM	Orimulsion
PCB	Polychlorinated Biphenyls
R&D	Research & Development
ROACE	Return on Average Capital Employed
S&P	Standard & Poor's
SRI	Socially Responsible Investment
TLC	Telecommunications (Wind)
TSR	Total Shareholder Return

LEGEND Units of measurement

,000	thousands	h/emp	hours per employee
,000 €	thousands of euro	index	rating
,000 h	thousands of hours	index n.	index number
#	number	km	kilometers
#/month	number per month	kW	kilowatts
%	per cent	l/kWh	liters per kilowatt-hour
,000 kg	thousands of kilograms	mil	million
,000 tons	thousands of tons	mil €	million euro
cm/emp	cubic meters per employee	mil cm	million cubic meters
d	days	mil min	million minutes
€	euro	min	minutes
€/month	euro per month	mtoe	million tons of oil equivalent
€/MWh	euro per megawatt-hour	MW	megawatts
€/s	grams per	sec	seconds
g/kWh	kilowatt-hour	t	tons
GWh	gigawatt-hours	TW	terawatts
h	hours	TWh	terawatt-hours

Useful links

> Global Reporting Initiative: www.globalreporting.org
> Ministero del Lavoro e delle Politiche Sociali: www.welfare.gov.it
> SAM: www.sam-group.com
> Dow Jones Sustainability Index (DJSI): www.sustainability-index.com
> EIRIS: www.eiris.org
> FTSE4GOOD: www.ftse.com

ETHICAL AUDITING

Magnitude recorded	UM	2005	2004	2005-2004	Companies	GRI	CSR-SC	SAM	EIRIS
Ethical auditing								•	•
Implementation of Ethical Code						HR1–HR8	7.6		
Total reports received	(#)	28	43	-35%	Enel	HR9			•
> Customers	(#)	13	21	-38%	Enel				
> Employees	(#)	8	15	-47%	Enel				
> Communities	(#)	3	2	50%	Enel				
> Suppliers	(#)	4	5	-20%	Enel				
Total violations of Ethical Code	(#)	2	13	-85%	Enel	HR10		•	•

Total reports received: the decrease of 15 in the total number of reports received with respect to the previous year is due to both the exit of Wind Telecomunicazioni from the Enel Group (finalized in the third quarter of 2005) and the fact that a major information campaign on the introduction of the Ethical Code had been carried out in 2004, the effects of which were gradually attenuated during 2005.

Total violations of the Ethical Code: the lower number of violations was due mainly to the decrease in the reports received during the year, especially from customers, the category in which violations are most frequent.

CORPORATE GOVERNANCE

Magnitude recorded	UM	2005	2004	2005-2004	Companies	GRI	CSR-SC	SAM	EIRIS
Corporate governance						LA11	2.5	•	•
Board of Directors						LA11	2.5	•	•
Total Board members	(#)	9	7	29%	Enel SpA	LA11	-	•	•
Independent Directors on the Board	(#)	8	6	33%	Enel SpA	LA11	2.5.1	•	•
Directors nominated by minority shareholders	(#)	3	2	50%	Enel SpA	-	2.5.2		-
Women on the Board	(#)	0	0	n.a.	Enel SpA	LA11	2.5.4	•	•
Board meetings	(#)	21	21	n.a.	Enel SpA	-	2.5.3	•	•
Internal dealing						-	6.3	•	•
Shares controlled by "important persons"	(,000)	330.8	244.6	35%	Enel SpA	-	6.3.1–6.3.2	•	•

Total members of BoD: the Shareholders' Meeting of May 26, 2005 raised the number of the members of the BoD from 7 to 9, as proposed by the majority shareholder (the Ministry of the Economy and Finance), in order to increase from 2 to 3 Board members designated by the minority shareholders.

Presence of independent Directors on the BoD: of the 9 members of the BoD, 8 quality as non-executive and independent according to what they declared at the time of their appointment.

Shares controlled by the BoD and important persons: the 35% increase in the number of shares controlled by important persons is due to the latter's participation in the Public Offering of July 2005. It should be observed that the number of stock options exercised by the important persons in the second half of 2005 did not entail a significant increase in share ownership, because almost all of those concerned chose to sell the shares subscribed.

(Continued)

EXHIBIT 8.2 (Continued)

LENDERS

Magnitude recorded	UM	2005	2004	2005-2004	Companies	GRI	CSR-SC	SAM	EIRIS
Lenders									
Debt						EC6	5; 5.1–5.3	-	-
Total debt	(mil €)	12,312	24,296	-49%	Enel	EC6	5	-	-
Debt to equity ratio	(#)	0.63	1.16	-45%	Enel	EC6	5	-	-
Rating									
S&P:	(Index)	A+	A+	-	Enel		2.4	-	-
> Outlook	(Index)	Stable	Stable	-	Enel		-	-	-
Moody's:	(Index)	Aa3	A1	-	Enel		2.4	-	-
> Outlook	(Index)	Stable	Stable	-	Enel		-	-	-
Grants									
Total grants during the year	(mil €)	25.5	32.7	-22%	Enel	EC9	6.4	-	-
> Energy networks	(%)	60.1	59.7	1%	Enel		-	-	-
> R&D	(%)	5.8	7.0	-17%	Enel		-	-	-
> Renewable energy	(%)	28.8	32.8	-12%	Enel		-	-	-
> Other	(%)	5.3	0.5	958%	Enel		-	-	-
Total number of projects receiving grants	(#)	76	69	10%	Enel	EC9	6.4	-	-
Loans granted by the EIB and others						EC9	6.4	-	-
Remaining debt regarding EIB and other loans	(mil €)	2,422	3,574	-32%	Enel	EC9	6.4	-	-
> Energy networks	(%)	64.0	68.5	-7%	Enel		-	-	-
> R&D	(%)	0.7	0.6	11%	Enel		-	-	-
> Renewable energy	(%)	14.6	12.0	22%	Enel		-	-	-
> Other	(%)	20.7	18.9	9%	Enel		-	-	-
Approved projects in progress with EIB loans	(#)	18	24	-25%	Enel	EC9	6.4	-	-

Grants obtained during the year: of the 76 projects that received funding in 2005, 17 did so for the first time. The change shown by the indexes of total debt is connected mainly with the change in the composition of the Group that took place in 2005.

Remaining debt regarding BEI and other loans: the 32% decrease in the amounted owed the BEI is due to the repayment of loans by Enel Distribuzione in the amount of about 63 million euro and Enel Produzione in the amount of about 37 million euro.

SHAREHOLDERS

Magnitude recorded	UM	2005	2004	2005-2004	Companies	GRI	CSR-SC	SAM	EIRIS
Shareholders						-	-	•	•
Composition of shareholder base*							2	-	-
Ministry of the Economy	(%)	21.4	31.5	-32%	Enel SpA		2.1	-	-
Cassa Depositi e Prestiti	(%)	10.2	10.3	-1%	Enel SpA		-	-	-
Retail shareholders	(%)	38.9	28.5	37%	Enel SpA		-	-	-
Institutional investors	(%)	29.5	29.7	-1%	Enel SpA		2.1	-	•
Location of institutional investors							2.1.2	-	-
> Italy	(%)	22.8	31.5	-28%	Enel SpA		2.1.2	-	-
> UK	(%)	24.7	26.0	-5%	Enel SpA		2.1.2	-	-
> Rest of Europe	(%)	26.6	19.9	34%	Enel SpA		2.1.2	-	-
> North America	(%)	24.4	22.1	10%	Enel SpA		2.1.2	-	-
> Rest of the world	(%)	1.6	0.5	220%	Enel SpA		2.1.2	-	-
Concentration index (Top 50)	(%)	30.8	34.2	-10%	Enel SpA		2.1.1	-	-
Investment style of institutional investors									
> GARP	(%)	21.7	19.7	10%	Enel SpA				
> Growth	(%)	33.0	32.4	2%	Enel SpA				
> Index	(%)	16.4	15.9	3%	Enel SpA				
> Value	(%)	15.9	19.0	-16%	Enel SpA				
> Hedge	(%)	4.0	11.8	-66%	Enel SpA				
> Other	(%)	9.0	1.2	650%	Enel SpA				
Socially Responsible Investors (SRI)*									
Presence of SRI funds	(#)	45	47	-4%	Enel SpA		-	-	-
Enel shares held by SRI funds	(mil)	409.4	360.1	14%	Enel SpA		-	-	-
Weight of SRI in institutional funds	(%)	22.6	19.9	13%	Enel SpA		-	-	-
Geographical breakdown of SRI									
> Italy	(%)	18.9	32.1	-41%	Enel SpA		-	-	-
> UK	(%)	43.5	35.0	24%	Enel SpA		-	-	-
> Rest of Europe	(%)	27.9	25.3	10%	Enel SpA		-	-	-
> North America	(%)	9.7	7.6	28%	Enel SpA		-	-	-
Presence of SRI in the top 10	(#)	2.0	2.0	n.a.	Enel SpA		-	-	-

*Data processed by external firm from market surveys carried out in September 2005.

Institutional investors: the percentages of the Treasury Ministry and Cassa Depositi e Prestiti and the number of floating shares are as of December 28, 2005. All the other percentages refer to the third quarter of 2005. No later figures are available. For this reason, the total of the shares in circulation is not 100%. N.B. The retail percentage has been increased by 0.51% as the computation the bonus shares.

Location of institutional investors: the data refer to the third quarter of 2005. No later data are available at the moment.

Magnitude recorded	UM	2005	2004	2005-2004	Companies	GRI	CSR-SC	SAM	EIRIS
Share performance									
Financial performance of shares	(%)	-5.7	40.7	-114%		-	2.3	-	-
Dividend Yield	(%)	8.3	9.8	-15%		-	2.3	-	-
Enel in the MIB30 (and other world stock indexes)									
>E100	(%)	0.7	1.0	-23%		-	2.2.1	-	-
>MIBTEL	(%)	6.3	7.9	-21%		-		-	-
>MIB30	(%)	8.8	10.5	-16%		-		-	-
>MIBHIS	(%)	6.3	7.9	-21%		-		-	-
>MIBPUBLH	(%)	37.4	28.5	31%		-		-	-
>BE500	(%)	0.6	0.8	-21%		-		-	-
>BEELECT	(%)	14.7	18.6	-21%		-		-	-
>SX5E	(%)	1.5	1.7	-9%		-		-	-
>SXXE	(%)	0.9	1.1	-11%		-		-	-
>SX6E	(%)	11.4	14.4	-21%		-		-	-
Enel in the FTSE4GOOD sustainability index	(index)	SI	SI			-		-	-
Enel's position in the DJSI	(index)	B	B			-		-	-
Shareholder return									
EPS	(€€)	63.3	43.1	47%		-	2.2.3	-	-
DPS	(€€)	55.0	69.0	-20%		-	2.2.3	-	-
TSR since the IPO	(%)	2.5	3.2	-21%		-	2.2.1	-	-
TSR in the last 2 years	(%)	21.3	31.0	-31%		-		-	-
Communication with shareholders						-	2.7	-	•
Meetings with investors	(#)	260	257	1%		-	2.71–2.7.6	-	•
Information about CSR	(#)	31	29	7%		-		-	•
Retail shareholder requests for information	(#)	683	623	10%		-	2.7.1	-	•
Economic performance									
Revenue	(mil €)	34,059	31,011	10%	Enel	EC1; EC7	-	-	•
EBITDA	(mil €)	7,745	8,071	-4%	Enel	EC1	-	-	•
> EBITDA GEM	(%)	47.8	46.8	2%	Enel	EC7	-	-	-
> EBITDA MIR	(%)	48.3	43.7	10%	Enel	-	-	-	-
> EBITDA other	(%)	3.9	9.4	-58%	Enel	-	-	-	-
EBIT	(mil €)	5,538	5,870	-6%	Enel	EC7	-	-	-
EBT	(mil €)	4,794	5,018	-4%	Enel	EC7	-	-	-
Group net income	(mil €)	3,895	2,631	48%	Enel	EC7	-	-	-
ROACE	(%)	17.7	19.1	-7%	Enel	EC7	-	-	-
> Revenue	(mil €)	34,059	31,011	10%	Enel	-	-	-	-
> External costs	(mil €)	23,034	19,222	20%	Enel	-	-	-	-
> Gross value added of continuing operations	(mil €)	11,025	11,789	-6%	Enel	-	-	-	-
> Gross value added of discontinued operations	(mil €)	2,952	3,482	-15%	Enel	-	-	-	-
> Total gross value added	(mil €)	13,977	15,271	-8%	Enel	-	-	-	-
> Shareholders	(mil €)	3,472	4,256	-18%	Enel	-	-	-	-
> Lenders	(mil €)	984	1,297	-24%	Enel	-	-	-	-
> Employees	(mil €)	3,100	3,793	-18%	Enel	-	-	-	-
> Government	(mil €)	2,480	1,828	36%	Enel	-	-	-	-
> Enterprise system	(mil €)	3,941	4,097	-4%	Enel	-	-	-	-

SHAREHOLDERS

Magnitude recorded	UM	2005	2004	2005-2004	Companies	GRI	CSR-SC	SAM	EIRIS
Investment									
Investment	(mil €)	2,829.0	3,834.0	-26%	Enel	-	-	-	-
> Valle d' Aosta	(mil €)	6.5	10.0	-36%	Enel	-	-	-	-
> Piedmont	(mil €)	156.2	257.0	-39%	Enel	-	-	-	-
> Lombardy	(mil €)	285.9	434.0	-34%	Enel	-	-	-	-
> Trentino Alto Adige	(mil €)	23.5	42.0	-44%	Enel	-	-	-	-
> Veneto	(mil €)	227.4	320.0	-29%	Enel	-	-	-	-
>Friuli Venezia Giulia	(mil €)	27.1	41.0	-34%	Enel	-	-	-	-
> Liguria	(mil €)	58.0	104.0	-44%	Enel	-	-	-	-
> Emilia Romagna	(mil €)	156.2	235.0	-34%	Enel	-	-	-	-
> Tuscany	(mil €)	266.1	259.0	3%	Enel	-	-	-	-
> Marches	(mil €)	52.5	69.0	-24%	Enel	-	-	-	-
> Umbria	(mil €)	26.3	40.0	-34%	Enel	-	-	-	-
>Latium	(mil €)	454.3	764.0	-41%	Enel	-	-	-	-
>Abruzzo	(mil €)	52.6	73.0	-28%	Enel	-	-	-	-
>Molise	(mil €)	14.6	30.0	-51%	Enel	-	-	-	-
> Campania	(mil €)	131.4	210.0	-37%	Enel	-	-	-	-
> Apulia	(mil €)	115.1	198.0	-42%	Enel	-	-	-	-
> Basilicata	(mil €)	20.9	30.0	-30%	Enel	-	-	-	-
> Calabria	(mil €)	123.4	154.0	-20%	Enel	-	-	-	-
> Sicily	(mil €)	148.9	266.0	-44%	Enel	-	-	-	-
> Sardinia	(mil €)	125.2	218.0	-43%	Enel	-	-	-	-
Total Italy	(mil €)	2,471.9	3,754.0	-34%	Enel	-	-	-	-
> Spain	(mil €)	222.4	130.2	71%	Enel	-	-	-	-
> Eastern Europe	(mil €)	58.3	114.7	-49%	Enel	-	-	-	-
> North America	(mil €)	5.5	3.1	76%	Enel	-	-	-	-
> South America	(mil €)	13.1	26.1	-50%	Enel	-	-	-	-
Total foreign	(mil €)	299.2	274.1	9%	Enel	-	-	-	-
Other	(mil €)	57.9	-194	-	Enel	-	-	-	-

Requests for information by retail shareholders: it is evident that there was a significant increase in the number of questions asked by retail shareholders in the second half, and especially in the third quarter, of 2005. However, the overall figures are in line with those of the previous year. The breakdown of the requests for all of 2005 – keeping in mind that these refer only to written requests, to which about 380 phone calls must be added – is as follows:

a) performance of Enel shares: 43
b) requests for accounting documents: 55
c) information on dividends, shares, and bonds: 168
d) information on activities of the Enel Group: 7
e) information on Shareholders' Meetings: 13
f) information on CSR: 0
g) other: 397 (especially: the Public Offering)
Requests from Italy: 616
Requests from abroad: 67

Investment: the 26% decrease in investment is mainly connected with the change in the composition of the Group.

(Continued)

EXHIBIT 8.2 (Continued)

SUPPLIERS

Magnitude recorded	UM	2005	2004	2005-2004	Companies	GRI	CSR-SC	SAM	EIRIS
Suppliers						EC3	4	-	•
Number of suppliers									
Number of suppliers	(#)	17,707	19,723	-10%	Enel	-	4.1.1	-	-
Concentration of suppliers (%) (top 15)	(%)	22.8	32.0	-29%	Enel	-	4.1.2	-	•
Procurement and fuels									
Purchases of materials and service	(mil €)	3,014	5,086	-41%	Enel	EC3	-	-	•
> Supplies	(mil €)	1,284	2,861	-55%	Enel				
> Contract work	(mil €)	919	717	28%	Enel				
> Services	(mil €)	811	1,508	-46%	Enel	EC3	-	-	-
Fuel purchases	(mil €)	2,694	3,454	-22%	Enel	EC3	-	-	-
> Gas	(mil €)	720	1,054	-32%	Enel				
> Oil	(mil €)	851	1,116	-24%	Enel				
> Coal	(mil €)	549	560	-2%	Enel				
> Services	(mil €)	574	724	-21%	Enel				
Management instruments						EC3	-	-	•
Active qualifications	(#)	2,960	2,663	11%	Enel	EC3	-	-	•
Online tenders	(%)	92	32	188%	Enel	EC3	-	-	•
Online purchases	(%)	98	84	17%	Enel	EC3	-	-	•
Litigation with suppliers									
Total proceedings	(#)	590	629	-6%	Enel	-	-	-	•
Incidence of proceedings as defendant	(%)	81.7	72.8	12%	Enel	-	-	-	-

Suppliers: the decrease in the number of suppliers and the procurement portfolio with respect to the previous year is due to the change in the composition of the Group that took place in 2005. If Terna and Wind are excluded in 2004 as well, the decrease in purchases of materials and services amounts to 3%.

The procurement data regard relations based on contracts (the value of the commitments assumed by Enel according to binding contracts, including those with terms of more than one year) and do not include intra-Group contracts.

Number of suppliers with contracts: the total number of suppliers who were awarded orders decreased by 10% with respect to 2004. The analysis regards networks and generation, and thus excludes telecommunications (Wind), fuels (Enel Trade), and contracts for the transportation and purchase of energy. The 2005 data do not include suppliers of Terna.

Concentration of Suppliers (top 15): the numbers shown refer to the percentage of contract sums out of the total, obtained by aggregating the top fifteen suppliers. The analysis regards networks and generation, and thus excludes telecommunications (Wind), fuels, (Enel Trade), and contracts for the transportation and purchase of energy. The 2005 data do not include suppliers of Terna.

Purchases of materials and services: the data refer to sums based on contracts (the value of the commitments assumed by Enel according to binding contracts, including those with terms of more than one year) and do not include intra-Group contracts. The decrease in the procurement portfolio (-41%) with respect to the previous year is due to the change in the composition of the Group that took place during 2005. In effect, the 2005 data do not contain the sum of the Terna and Wind contracts. A comparison of the data regarding the same composition of the Group shows a decrease of 3% (3,014 billion euro against 3,096 billion euro).

Fuel purchases: with respect to 2004, the sum of contracts for fuels shows a total reduction of 22%, with marked decreases for gas (-32%) and oil (-24%).

ELECTRICITY MARKET ITALY

Magnitude recorded	UM	2005	2004	2005-2004	Companies	GRI	CSR-SC	SAM	EIRIS
Electricity market Italy						EC1	3.1-13.1.2	•	•
Customer portfolio									
Electricity sales	(mil €)	16,994.4	16,576.6	3%	Enel	EC1	-	-	-
Volume of electricity sold	(TWh)	148.2	157.0	-6%	Enel	EC1	-	-	-
> Regulated market	(TWh)	129.6	136.1	-5%	Enel				
> Regulated market – consumers	(TWh)	52.1	53.8	-3%	Enel				
> Regulated market – other uses	(TWh)	77.5	82.3	-6%	Enel				
> Free market	(TWh)	18.5	20.9	-11%	Enel				
> Free market – business	(TWh)	8.5	7.5	13%	Enel				
> Free market – top	(TWh)	10.1	13.4	-25%	Enel				
Electricity customers	(,000)	30,029.6	29,654.3	1%	Enel	EC1	3.2	-	-
> Business customers	(,000)	6,456.0	6,429.5	0%	Enel				
> Consumer customers	(,000)	23,573.3	23,224.4	2%	Enel				
Market share	(%)	48.0	52.3	-7%	Enel	EC1	3	•	•
Customer value									
Sales revenue per customer [1]	(€/month)	47.5	47.2	1%	Enel	EC1	3.4-13.6	•	•
Sales network									
Regulated market						EC2	-	-	-
Contact points	(#)	1,005	1,089	-8%	Enel	EC2	-	-	-
> Qui Enel in Enel.si	(#)	325	527	-38%	Enel				
> Qui Enel in Wind	(#)	289	353	-18%	Enel				
> Qui Enel in city halls	(#)	170	104	63%	Enel				
> Qui Enel in post offices	(#)	193	105	84%	Enel				
> Other indirect	(#)	28	0	-	Enel				
Free market									
> Sales outlets – indirect channel	(,000)	58	15	287%	Enel	EC1	-	-	-
Outbound network	(#)	70	0		Enel				
Average training indirect network	(d)	70	6	1067%	Enel				
Supply activation									
Execution of simple jobs	(d)	8.6	8.9	-3%	Enel				
Supply activation	(d)	1.5	1.9	-21%	Enel				
Service management									
Productivity of indirect channel	(,000)	2,491	1,377	81%	Enel	EC1	-	-	-
Productivity of portal	(,000)	2,372	984	141%	Enel				
Call Center – regulated market									
Service level	(%)	90	84	7%	Enel				
IVR effectiveness (calls automatically answered)	(%)	50	68	-26%	Enel				
Average waiting time	(sec)	139	180	-23%	Enel				
Effectiveness	(%)	84	92	-10%	Enel				
Average training of operators	(h per emp)	25	31	-21%	Enel				
Calls answered	(,000)	16,753	13,305	26%	Enel				

(1) The value regarding 2004 published last year was not calculated on a monthly basis.

ELECTRICITY MARKET ITALY

Magnitude recorded	UM	2005	2004	2005-2004	Companies	GRI	CSR-SC	SAM	EIRIS
Technical quality									
Service continuity index	(min)	57	60	-7%	Enel	-	-	•	•
Investment in quality	(mil €)	222	333	-33%	Enel	-	-	•	-
Awards/penalties for service	(mil €)	63	203	-69%	Enel	-	-	•	-
Customer satisfaction and customer loyalty – regulated market						EC1	3.3.1-3.3.2	•	
Complaints and written requests for information – electricity	(,000)	93.2	268.8	-65%	Enel	EC1	3.3.1	•	-
Written complaint answering time	(d)	21.6	14.0	54%	Enel	EC1	3.3.1	•	-
Litigation with electricity customers									
Total proceedings	(#)	59,753	23,378	156%	-	-	-	-	-
Incidence of litigation as defendant	(%)	84.2	59.3	42%	Enel	-	-	-	-

Execution of simple jobs: the increase in the average time for supply activation is due to the fact that, as from August 2005, the Authority's reporting excludes services performed without the involvement of a technician.

Productivity of indirect channel: the growth in transactions at QuiEnels continued during 2005, in part thanks to the rationalization of the QuiEnel network and the partner expansion.

IVR effectiveness: the data refer to requests for readings, payments declared, and domiciliation successfully handled by the Enel Distribuzione Call Center's automatic services.

Call center effectiveness: the data refer to the requests via telephone satisfied without intermediary stages (openings – closings) and without having to leave the matter in the back office to wait for further handling.

Technical quality: the index of service continuity shows the average number of minutes wasted per low-voltage customer because of long and unannounced interruptions. If the data regarding interruptions due to external causes are added, the index amounts to 62 minutes in 2005 and 73 minutes in 2004.

As far as the bonuses regarding service continuity awarded by the Ministry are concerned, the data shown are based on when the bonuses were collected. The decrease is due to the Electricity and Gas Authority's reformulation of the parameters and objectives in 2005.

Answering time for written complaints: the average answering time for written complaints and requests for information increased, partly because of the effect of the handling of matters dating to before 2005.

Litigation with customers in the Italian electricity market: Litigation with customers increased by 156% with respect to 2004 because of the requests made during the year for damages regarding the blackout of 2003.

GAS MARKET

Magnitude recorded	UM	2005	2004	2005-2004	Companies	GRI	CSR-SC	SAM	EIRIS
Gas market								•	•
Customer portfolio									
Revenue from natural gas sales to end customers	(mil €)	1,556	1,390	12%	Enel	EC1	3.1-3.1.2	•	-
Volume sold	(mil cm)	5,089	5,186	-2%	Enel	EC1	-	•	-
> Consumer customers	(mil cm)	3,021	2,782	9%	Enel	EC1	-	•	-
> Business customers	(mil cm)	2,067	2,404	-14%	Enel	-	-	•	-
> Resellers	(mil cm)	1,617	1,667	-3%	Enel	-	-	•	-
Total customers	(,000)	2,143	1,966	9%	Enel	EC1	3.2	•	•
> Consumer customers	(,000)	2,141	1,964	9%	Enel	-	-	•	•
> Business customers	(,000)	2.1	2.0	6%	Enel	-	-	•	•
Dual fuel customers	(#)	1,993	0		Enel	-	3.2.2	•	-
Growth of customer base	(#)	15,942	15,093	6%	Enel	EC1	3.2.2	•	-
Switching rate	(%)	8.0	8.4	-5%	Enel	-	3	•	-
Market share	(%)	9.7	10.2	-5%	Enel	EC1; PR1;PR2	3.4-3.6	•	•
Customer value									
Revenue per customer[1]	(€/month)	63.1	61.6	2%	Enel	EC1	-	•	-
Sales network									
Contact points	(#)	88	75	17%	Enel	EC2	-	•	-
Average training indirect network[2]	(h)	141	52	171%	Enel	EC2	-	•	-
Outbound network[3]	(#)	71	38	87%	Enel	EC2	-	•	-
Effectiveness outbound network[4]	(,000)	137.1	45.0	204%	Enel	EC2	-	•	-
Supply activation									
Execution of simple jobs	(d)	9.5	7.1	34%	Enel	-	-	•	-
Supply activation	(d)	2.5	2.6	-4%	Enel	-	-	•	-
Service management									
Productivity of indirect channel	(,000)	19.8	14.2	40%	Enel	EC1	-	•	-
Productivity of portal	(,000)	292	90	225%	Enel	-	-	•	-
Call Center									
Service level	(%)	83	84	-1%	Enel	-	-	•	-
IVR effectiveness	(%)	40	32	24%	Enel	-	-	•	-
Average waiting time[5]	(sec)	137	65	111%	Enel	-	-	•	-
Effectiveness	(%)	98	99	-1%	Enel	-	-	•	-
Average training of operators	(h per emp)	30	270	-89%	Enel	-	-	•	-
Calls answered	(,000)	1,465	1,447	1%	Enel	-	-	•	-
Customer satisfaction and customer loyalty									
Customer satisfaction index[6]	(index)	7.7	7.7	-	Enel	EC2	3.3.1-3.3.2	•	•
Written complaints	(,000)	2,448	896	173%	Enel	EC2	3.3.1	•	•
Written complaint average answering time	(d)	17.7	9.4	88%	Enel	EC2	3.3.1	•	-
Litigation with gas customers									
Total proceedings	(#)	1,264	1,938	-35%	Enel	-	-	-	-

(1) The value regarding 2004 published last year was not calculated on a monthly basis.

(2) The hours of indirect training increased in connection with the growth of the sales agency network that took place in 2005.

(3) Number of teleselling and door-to-door sales agencies.

(4) New customers acquired per month by door-to-door network.

(5) This value recorded a physiological increase in consequence of the introduction of the IVR (automatic answer).

(6) This indicator, which expresses from 1 to 10 the degree of customer satisfaction, did not change with respect to 2004 inspite of the increase in written complaints caused by the introduction of the Electricity and Gas Authority's resolution 40/04, because the 2005 survey ended in June, before the impact of the resolution was felt.

Contact points: In addition to its QuiGas shops inside the Enel.Si stores, Enel Gas is present throughout Italy with its Customer Assistance Centers. Of the 88 Centers, 51 are for management, 35 are for acquisitions, and 2 are for both.

(Continued)

EXHIBIT 8.2 (Continued)

ENVIRONMENTAL MANAGEMENT SYSTEMS

Magnitude recorded	UM	2005	2004	2005-2004	Companies	GRI	CSR-SC	SAM	EIRIS
Environmental Management System									
Environmental certification									
ISO 14001 certifications[1]	(#)	26	20	30%	Italy	-	8.2	•	•
EMAS certifications[1]	(#)	14	10	40%	Italy	-	8.2	•	•
% installed power ISO 14001 certified	(%)	77	70	11%	Italy	-	8.2	•	•
% installed power EMAS certified	(%)	43	28	54%	Italy	-	8.2	•	•
Research and innovation									
Research expenditure	(mil€)	20	20	-3%	Italy	EN35	8.2	•	-
Research personnel	(#)	155	161	-3%	Italy	EN35	8.2	-	-
Environmental expenditure									
Environmental expenditure	(mil €)	444	587	-24%	Italy	EN35	8.2	•	-
> Total current expense[2][3]	(mil €)	344	495	-31%	Italy	EN35; EN27; EN29	8.2	-	-
> Total environmental investment	(mil €)	100	92	9%	Italy	EN35	8.2	-	-
Personnel dedicated to environmental issues[4]	(#)	197	216	-9%	Italy	-	8.2	•	-
Safety systems									
Inspections on ships transporting oil products					Italy	EN34	8.2	-	-
> Oil products	(%)	100	100	-	Italy	EN34	-	-	-
> Coal[6]	(%)	100	100	-	Italy	EN34	-	-	-

(1) The increase in the ISO 14001/EMAS certified organizations is due to the continuation of Enel's environmental certification program.

(2) The value regarding 2005, reclassified according to the ISTAT criteria, does not included taxes and the minimum vital flow, amounting to 106 million euro. The value regarding 2004, on the other hand, was stated according to the guidelines of the FEEM (Enrico Mattei Foundation).

(3) Included is an estimate (amounting to 263 million euro) of the additional cost of purchasing the sulfur-free and low-sulfur fuels used instead of more polluting fuels (with average sulfur content), calculated on the consumption of all oil and gas plants in the period January-December 2005. The decrease in the value with respect to 2004 is mainly due to the reduction in the expense of personnel dedicated to environmental tasks following a change in the criterion for calculating such expenses and the merger of Enel Green Power into Enel Produzione, which allowed the use of personnel dedicated to environmental aspects to be rationalized.

(4) The decrease in personnel used is due mainly to the rationalization of the personnel dedicated to the environment following the merger of Enel Green Power into Enel Produzione.

(5) The value regarding 2004 published last year included only inspections carried out by Enel (10%). This value now also includes the inspections performed by third parties and acquired by Enel.

ENERGY EFFICIENCY OF GENERATING PLANTS

Magnitude recorded	UM	2005	2004	2005-2004	Companies	GRI	CSR-SC	SAM	EIRIS
Energy efficiency of generating plants									
Generating plants									
Total net efficient power	(MW)	42,216	42,047	0%	Italy	EN14	8.1.1	•	-
Total net production	(TWh)	112.1	125.9	-11%	Italy	-	8.1.1	•	•
Net thermal production	(TWh)	81.8	91.9	-11%	Italy	-	8.1.1	•	•
> Coal	(TWh)	30.0	31.5	-5%	Italy	-	-	-	-
> CCGT	(TWh)	22.2	32.1	-31%	Italy	-	-	-	-
> Oil/gas	(TWh)	29.3	28.1	4%	Italy	-	-	-	-
> Other	(TWh)	0.3	0.1	167%	Italy	-	-	-	-
Net renewable production	(TWh)	30.3	34.0	-11%	Italy	-	8.1.1	•	-
> Hydro	(TWh)	24.9	28.7	-13%	Italy	-	-	-	-
> Wind and other	(TWh)	0.4	0.2	86%	Italy	-	-	-	-
> Geothermal	(TWh)	5.0	5.1	-2%	Italy	-	-	-	-
Number of thermal plants	(#)	161	159	1%	Italy	-	-	•	-
> Coal units	(#)	18	17	6%	Italy	-	-	-	-
> CCGT units	(#)	14	14	-	Italy	-	-	-	-
> Oil/gas units	(#)	49	51	-4%	Italy	-	-	-	-
> Turbogas units	(#)	28	28	-	Italy	-	-	-	-
> Diesel units	(#)	52	49	6%	Italy	-	-	-	-
Number of plants using renewable energy	(#)	554	549	1%	Italy	-	-	•	-
> Hydro plants	(#)	500	495	1%	Italy	-	-	-	-
> Wind plants	(#)	17	18	-6%	Italy	-	-	-	-
> Photovoltaic plants	(#)	4	5	-20%	Italy	-	-	-	-
> Geothermal plants	(#)	32	31	3%	Italy	-	-	-	-
> Biomass plants	(#)	1	0	-	Italy	-	-	-	-
Thermal plants									
Net efficient thermal power	(MW)	26,902	26,837	0%	Italy	-	8.1.1	•	-
> Coal	(MW)	4,939	4,616	7%	Italy	-	-	-	-
> CCGT	(MW)	5,005	5,005	-	Italy	-	-	-	-
> Oil/gas	(MW)	14,826	15,086	-2%	Italy	-	-	-	-
> Other	(MW)	2,132	2,130	-	Italy	-	-	-	-
CCGT incidence (power)	(%)	18.6	18.6	0%	Italy	-	-	-	•
CCGT plant yield	(%)	53.0	52.4	1%	Italy	-	-	-	-
Unavailability for call into service - coal plants	(%)	3.6	4.8	-25%	Italy	-	-	-	-
Investment in efficiency	(mil €)	232	214	8%	Italy	EN19	8.1.1	-	-
Environmental investment	(mil €)	52	37	43%	Italy	EN19	8.1.1	•	•
Green Energy									
Net efficient power from renewable energy	(MW)	15,314	15,210	1%	Italy	-	-	•	•
> Hydro	(MW)	14,363	14,318	-	Italy	-	-	-	-
> Wind	(MW)	277	247	12%	Italy	-	-	-	-
> Geothermal	(MW)	671	642	4%	Italy	-	-	-	-
> Other	(MW)	4	4	-2%	Italy	-	-	-	-
Development of renewable energy (net of divestments)[6]	(MW)	104	83	25%	Italy	-	-	-	-
Green-certificate production	(TWh)	1.3	1.4	-4%	Italy	-	-	-	-
Green-certificate coverage requirements	(%)	60.9	64.6	-6%	Italy	-	-	-	-
"Green Energy" sales	(GWh)	216.2	67.2	222%	Italy	-	-	-	-
Investment in renewable energy	(mil €)	262	335	-22%	Italy	EN17	-	-	•

(6) The value regarding 2004 published last year did not take into account divested capacity, amounting for 2004 to 42.5 MW.

NETWORK ENERGY EFFICIENCY

Magnitude recorded	UM	2005	2004	2005-2004	Companies	GRI	CSR-SC	SAM	EIRIS
Network energy efficiency							8.1	•	-
Electricity distribution									
Energy transported	(TWh)	251.0	250.7	-	Italy	•	-	•	-
Municipalities served	(#)	8,010	7,933	1%	Italy	•	-	•	-
Extension of power lines	(,000 km)	1,090.1	1,089.8	0%	Italy	•	-	•	-
Total LV lines	(,000 km)	736.0	734.9	0%	Italy	•	-	•	-
Total MV lines	(,000 km)	335.2	335.8	0%	Italy	•	-	•	-
Total HV lines	(,000 km)	19.0	19.1	-1%	Italy	•	-	•	-
% lines in underground cables	(%)	69.6	69.0	1%	Italy	•	-	•	-
% LV lines in underground cables	(%)	83.2	82.8	1%	Italy	•	-	•	-
% MV lines in underground cables	(%)	39.7	39.0	2%	Italy	•	-	•	-
Equipment and transformers with PCB/total[7]	(%)	7.1	8.7	-19%	Italy	-	-	•	-
Gas distribution									
Gas leaks[8]	(#)	433	498	-13%	Italy	EN13	8.1.1	•	•
Kilometers of network	(,000 km)	29.4	29.4	0%	Italy	-	-	•	•
Network inspected	(%)	53.4	50	7%	Italy	-	8.1.1	•	•
Remote-controlled substations[9]	(#)	800	199	302%	Italy	-	-	•	•

(7) The decrease in equipment containing PCB is consistent with the process of PCB disposal in accordance with the requirements of the environmental regulations in force.

(8) This is the number of leaks detected during the planned inspection campaigns carried out during the year.

(9) The increase of remote-controlled substations is the result of the substation installation project initiated in 2004 and carried out mainly in 2005.

RATIONAL USE OF ENERGY

Magnitude recorded	UM	2005	2004	2005-2004	Companies	GRI	CSR-SC	SAM	EIRIS
Rational use of energy						EN17	8.1		•
Promotion of energy efficiency						EN17	8.1.1		
Titles of energy efficiency[10]	(#)	51,408	0	-	Italy	EN17	8.1.1	-	-
Micro-generation	(kW)	1,890	1,890	-	Italy	EN17	-	-	-
Digital meters installed	(,000)	26,954	20,801	30%	Italy	EN17	-	-	•
Customers with differentiated rates	(,000)	540	18	2986%	Italy	-	-	-	-

(10) Certificates representing the units of primary energy saved (1 title = 1 toe of certified energy saving). These certificates, which are valid for ascertaining the attainment of the energy saving objectives set by the ministerial decrees for obligatory parties, are negotiable.

ENVIRONMENTAL PERFORMANCE

Magnitude recorded	UM	2005	2004	2005-2004	Companies	GRI	CSR-SC	SAM	EIRIS
Environmental performance						-	8.1	•	•
Resources used in productive process									
Fuels									
Consumption of fossil fuels	(Mtoe)	18.0	20.1	-11%					
Coal	(%)	39.6	37.6	5%	Italy	EN3	8.1	•	•
Oil	(%)	20.6	24.3	-15%	Italy	EN3	-	•	•
Gas	(%)	39.8	38.1	4%	Italy	EN3	-	•	•
Geothermal fluid									
Geothermal fluid	(mil t)	45.8	45.8	-	Italy	EN3	-	-	-
Water									
Specific requirements for thermal production	(l/kWh)	0.54	0.52	2%	Italy	EN5	8.1.2	-	•
Materials consumed									
Materials consumed	(,000 t)	219.4	263.8	-17%	Italy	-	8.1	-	•
> Limestone	(,000 t)	162.4	211.8	-23%	Italy	-	8.1	-	•
> Ammonia	(,000 t)	19.7	22.3	-12%	Italy	-	8.1	-	•
> Caustic soda	(,000 t)	9.2	9.9	-7%	Italy	-	8.1	-	•
> Lime	(,000 t)	8.4	9.2	-8%	Italy	-	8.1	-	•
> Sulfuric/hydrochloric acid	(,000 t)	6.5	5.8	13%	Italy	-	8.1	-	•
> Other	(,000 t)	13.2	4.9	170%	Italy	-	8.1	-	•
Polluting emissions									
Atmospheric emissions									
Net specific emissions of SO_2[11]	(g/kWh)	0.89	1.02	-12%	Italy	EN10	8.1.4	•	•
Net specific emissions of NO_x	(g/kWh)	0.60	0.61	-2%	Italy	EN10	8.1.4	•	•
Net specific emissions of H_2S	(g/kWh)	4.61	4.59	1%	Italy	EN10	8.1.4	•	•
Emissions of particulate	(g/kWh)	0.032	0.037	-14%	Italy	EN10	8.1.4	•	•
Emissions of greenhouse gases (CO_2)	(g/kWh)	687.1	691.1	-1%	Italy	EN10	8.1.4	•	•
Emission of greenhouse gases (CO_2)[12]	(mil t)	56.2	63.4	-11%	Italy	-	-	•	•
Emissions avoided[13]	(mil t)	16.2	18.3	-12%	Italy	-	8.1.4	•	•
Emissions of other greenhouse gases (SF_6)	(,000 kg)	4.2	4.2	1%	Italy	EN30	8.1.4	•	•
Other productive cycles (CH_4)	(,000 t)	13.0	6.6	99%	Italy	EN30	8.1.4	•	•
Other productive cycles (CO_2)	(,000 t)	24.4	30.0	-19%	Italy	-	-	-	-
Asbestos disposal	(t)	3,376.0	2,047.5	65%	Italy	-	-	-	•
Emissions into water						EN12	8.1.5		-
> COD	(t)	390.6	430.0	-9%	Italy	EN12	8.1.5	•	-
> BOD	(t)	76.6	71.2	8%	Italy	EN12	8.1.5	-	-
> Nitrogen	(t)	105.7	60.6	74%	Italy	EN12	8.1.5	-	-
> Metals	(t)	3.2	5.4	-40%	Italy	EN12	8.1.5	-	-
Waste management									
Waste produced	(,000 t)	1,801	1,906	-5%	Italy	EN2	8.1.6	•	•
> Total hazardous waste	(,000 t)	45.4	36.1	26%	Italy	EN2	8.1.6	-	-
Waste recovery	(%)	90.4	95.1	-5%	Italy	EN31	8.1.6	-	•
Environmental litigation in Italy						EN16	-	-	-
Environmental proceedings as defendant[14]	(#)	275	274	-	Italy				

(11) The reduction in this value with respect to 2004 is due mainly to the decrease in production with coal and fuel oil.

(12) Value calculated with regard to specific plant factors of emission and certified pursuant to the emission trading regulations, while in the 2005 Consolidated Financial Statements the recorded value, amounting to 56.8 million tons, is an estimate based on standard factors of emission.

(13) The decrease in the value with respect to 2004 is due to the reduction in the total net production of electricity.

(14) The environmental proceedings are described on page 120 of the present Sustainability Report.

(Continued)

EXHIBIT 8.2 (*Continued*)

PERSONNEL NUMBER AND COMPOSITION

Magnitude recorded	UM	2005	2004	2005-2004	Companies	GRI	CSR-SC	SAM	EIRIS
Personnel number and composition									
Number									
Employees	(#)	51,778	61,898	-16%	Enel	LA1	1.1	•	•
Hours worked	(mil h)	87.8	103.9	-16%	Enel	LA1	1.1	•	
Breakdown by geographical area									
Italy	(%)	90.1	97.1	-7%	Enel	LA1	1.1.4		
Rest of Europe	(%)	9.2	2.1	345%	Enel	LA1	1.1.4		
North America	(%)	0.4	0.3	33%	Enel	LA1	1.1.4		
South America	(%)	0.3	0.4	-20%	Enel	LA1	1.1.4		
Africa	(%)	0.0	0.2	-	Enel	LA1	1.1.4		
Asia	(%)	0.1	0.0	-	Enel	LA1	1.1.4		
Oceania	(%)	0.0	0.0	-	Enel	LA1	1.1.4	•	
Composition									
Breakdown by professional status									
> Executives	(%)	1.1	1.1	-5%	Enel	LA1			
> Supervisors	(%)	7.9	7.8	1%	Enel	LA1			
> White-collar	(%)	55.0	61.4	-10%	Enel	LA1			
> Blue-collar	(%)	36.0	29.6	22%	Enel	LA1			
Education									
> University graduate	(%)	11.3	11.3	-	Enel	LA1			
> High school graduate	(%)	41.9	43.3	-3%	Enel	LA1			
> Other	(%)	46.8	45.4	3%	Enel	LA1			
Average age	(years)	45.2	44.1	2%	Enel	LA1	1.1.2	•	
> Under 35	(%)	13.2	19.5	-32%	Enel				
> From 35 to 44	(%)	27.0	26.7	1%	Enel				
> From 45 to 54	(%)	48.5	44.7	8%	Enel				
> From 55 to 59	(%)	10.6	8.5	25%	Enel				
> Over 60	(%)	0.8	0.6	29%	Enel				
Average number of years at Company	(years)	20.7	19.2	8%	Enel	LA1	1.1.3	•	
> Less than 10	(%)	17.6	25.8	-32%	Enel				
> From 10 to 19	(%)	26.4	23.0	15%	Enel				
> From 20 to 29	(%)	32.2	35.2	-9%	Enel				
> From 30 to 34	(%)	21.4	14.0	53%	Enel				
> More than 35	(%)	2.4	2.0	19%	Enel				
Flexible labor: relations and modes									
Fixed-term contracts	(#)	0.2	0.1	112%	Enel	LA1	1.1.6	•	
Utilization of part-time	(%)	2.1	3.5	-41%	Enel	LA1	1.1.6	•	
Utilization of overtime	(%)	5.9	5.0	18%	Enel	LA1	1.1.6;1.1.5	•	
Interns at Enel	(#)	96	159	-40	Italy	LA1	1.4.3	•	•
Changes in number									
New hires	(#)	839	1,256	-33%	Enel	LA2	1.2	•	•
Terminations	(#)	3,316	3,214	3%	Enel	LA2	1.2.3	•	•
Personnel turnover	(%)	5.4	5.0	8%	Enel	LA2	1.2.1	•	•
Utilization of internal mobility	(#)	7,201	1,364	428%	Italy	LA2	1.2.1	•	•

Personnel number and composition: the 10,120-unit change in the number of employees with respect to 2004 is accounted for by -3,508 net terminations (mainly due to consensual early retirements with incentives), -7,633 former employees who worked for companies that are no longer part of the Group, and +979 new hires.

PROFESSIONAL SATISFACTION

Magnitude recorded	UM	2005	2004	2005-2004	Companies	GRI	CSR-SC	SAM	EIRIS
Professional satisfaction									
Pay									
Cost per employee	(,000€)	51.8	53.3	-3%	Enel	EC5	1.6.1	•	
Incidence of variable pay	(%)	5.2	4.5	15%	Italy	EC12	1.6.1	•	•
Executives with stock options	(%)	85	90	-6%	Enel	LA12	1.6.3	•	
Development									
Evaluations	(#)	632	4,256	-85%	Italy				
Diffusion of evaluations [1]	(%)	1.3	6.8	-81%	Italy				
Internal development	(%)	79.0	68.4	15%	Italy				
Status changes	(%)	12.9	12.6	3%	Italy				•
Training									
Hours of training per employee [2]	(h)	17.3	25.0	-32%	Italy	LA9	1.4	•	•
Evaluation of DT course quality	(#)	4.5	4.5	-	Italy	LA12	1.4.2	•	
Accessibility of EDLS	(%)	75.4	61.1	24%	Italy	LA9	1.4	•	
Accesses from home	(#)	5,493	5,446	1%	Italy	LA17	1.4	•	
Incidence of DT	(%)	9.5	3.4	179%	Italy	LA17	1.4	•	
Courses available on line	(#)	5,192	4,872	7%	Enel	LA17	1.4	•	
Productivity of EDLS channel	(%)	57.2	84.1	-32%	Enel	LA17	1.4	•	
Knowledge Management and Internal Communication									
Corporate intranet: employees with access	(%)	90.4	71.0	27%	Enel	LA17	1.10	•	•
Expenditure on KM systems	(mil€)	5.8	5.7	2%	Enel	LA17	1.10	•	
Intranet accesses per day	(#)	8,487	6,200	37%	Enel	LA17	1.10	•	
Enel TV accesses per day	(#)	2,671	1,000	167%	Enel				
Hard copies of *Enel Insieme*	(#)	54,000	22,000	145%	Enel				
Dissemination of sustainability									
Training on the environment and safety per employee [3]	(h per emp)	9.7	6.5	50%	Italy	HR8	1.4	•	
Corporate atmosphere									
Spontaneous supervisor and executive resignations	(#)	37	68	-46%	Enel		1.12		
Absences per employee	(h)	433	413	5%	Italy excl. executives				
Fringe benefits per employee	(€)	2,293	2,279	1%	Electr. workers Italy	EC12	1.12	•	
Litigation with employees									
Total proceedings	(#)	3,091	3,560	-13%	Enel				
Incidence of proceedings as defendant	(%)	80.3	82.0	-2%	Enel				

(1) The value for 2004 published last year (amounting to 93.4%) regarded only supervisors and executives, while the figure for 2005 regards all Enel employees.

(2) The value for 2004, excluding Terna and Wind, amounts to 16 hours per employee.

(3) Regards only GEM and MIR personnel.

Professional development: the number of expertise and performance evaluations decreased by 85% with respect to 2004, because they last two years and in 2005 were performed only for supervisors and executives.

Litigation with employees: labor litigation in which Enel is the defendant includes 1,763 lawsuits regarding economic matters and 61 regarding disciplinary matters and firings, while there are 25 proceedings in which Enel is the plaintiff.

EQUAL OPPORTUNITY

Magnitude recorded	UM	2005	2004	2005-2004	Companies	GRI	CSR-SC	SAM	EIRIS
Equal Opportunity						LA10	1.3	•	•
Equal Opportunity									
Female employees	(#)	7,959	11,463	-31%	Enel	LA11	1.3.1	•	•
> Executives	(#)	59	67	-12%	Enel	LA11	1.3.1	•	•
> Supervisors	(#)	723	798	-9%	Enel	LA11	1.3.1	•	•
> White-collar	(#)	6,829	10,567	-35%	Enel	-	-	•	•
> Blue-collar	(#)	348	31	1,023%	Enel	-	-	•	•
Incidence of female employees	(%)	15.4	18.5	-17%	Enel	LA11	1.3.1	•	•
Female supervisors and executives	(%)	16.8	15.6	8%	Enel	LA11	1.3.1	•	•
Pay of female employees	(%)	86.0	89.5	-4%	Italy	LA11	1.3.2	•	•
The disabled						LA10	1.3.3	•	-
Disabled employees / protected categories	(#)	2,900	3,484	-17%	Italy	LA11	1.3.3	•	-

Equal Opportunity: the reduction in female personnel is in line with the decrease in total GEM personnel, which is due to both retirements and employee transfers to the Parent Company.

The decrease of female personnel, amounting to 3,504 employees, is mainly due to transfers.

SAFETY

Magnitude recorded	UM	2005	2004	2005-2004	Companies	GRI	CSR-SC	SAM	EIRIS
Safety						LA5;LA7	1.11.1	•	•
Serious and fatal employee on-the-job accidents						LA7	1.11.1	•	•
Employee on-the-job accidents	(#)	15	13	15%	Enel	LA7	1.11.1	•	•
> Fatal accidents	(#)	4	3	33%	Enel	-	1.11.1	•	-
> Serious accidents	(#)	11	10	10%	Enel	-	1.11.1	•	-
Index of accident frequency	(#)	8.2	9.5	-14%	Enel	LA7	1.11.1	•	•
Index of accident seriousness	(#)	0.27	0.30	-11%	Enel excl. executives	LA7	1.11.1	•	•
Expenditure on safety per employee	(€)	842	796	6%	Enel	LA5; LA7	1.11.1	•	•
Medical checks	(#)	23,760	22,058	8%	Enel	LA5;LA7	1.11.1	•	•
On-the-job accidents of contractor workers						LA7	1.11.1	•	•
Total on-the-job accidents of contractor firms	(#)	19	38	-50%	Enel	LA7	1.11.1	•	•
Accidents involving third parties	(#)	76	56	36%	Enel	LA7	1.11.1	•	•
Certifications						LA6; LA14;LA15	1.11.1	•	-
OHSAS 18001 certified sites	(#)	70.2	83.0	15%	Enel	-	1.11.1	•	-

Employee on-the-job-accidents: the seriousness and frequency indexes for all accidents are decreasing.

RELATIONS WITH TRADE UNIONS

Magnitude recorded	UM	2005	2004	2005-2004	Companies	GRI	CSR-SC	SAM	EIRIS
Relations with Trade Unions						LA3	1.9	•	•
Relations with Trade Unions						LA3; LA4; LA13	1.9.2;1.9.3	•	•
Rate of union membership among electricity workers	(%)	74.2	73.9	-	Electr. workers Italy				

ASSOCIATIONS, INSTITUTIONS, AND MEDIA

Magnitude recorded	UM	2005	2004	2005-2004	Companies	GRI	CSR-SC	SAM	EIRIS
Extent of phenomenon									
Meetings with associations	(#)	461	197	134%	Enel	SO1	7.3;7.4	•	•
Subjects discussed with associations	(#)	31	38	-18%	Enel	-	-	•	-
Relations with institutions									
Taxes paid	(mil €)	2,480	1,828	36%	Enel	EC8	-	-	-
> IRES, IRAP, and other taxes	(mil €)	2,104	1,476	43%	Enel	EC8	-	-	-
> Foreign taxes	(mil €)	43	22	95%	Enel	EC8	-	-	-
> Other taxes and duties	(mil €)	184	195	-6%	Enel	EC8	-	-	-
> Fees net of contributions received	(mil €)	149	135	10%	Enel	EC8	-	-	-
Corporate image									
Presence index	(#)	3,372	4,495	-25%	Enel	PR9	-	-	-
Global visibility index	(,000)	1,330	1,486	-11%	Enel	PR9	7.4	-	-
Qualitative index of visibility (from -1 to +1)	(index)	0.9	0.8	11%	Enel	PR9	7.4	-	-
Image profile (from 1 to 5)	(index)	3.7	3.4	11%	Enel	PR9	-	-	-

INITIATIVES IN FAVOR OF COMMUNITIES

Magnitude recorded	UM	2005	2004	2005-2004	Companies	GRI	CSR-SC	SAM	EIRIS
Initiatives in favor of communities						EC10	7	•	•
LBG approach									
% of EBT donated to social initiatives	(%)	0.50	0.45	11%	Enel	EC10;SO1	7.2	•	•
Largesse	(mil €)	8.6	8.1	6%	Enel	SO1	7	•	•
Investment in communities	(mil €)	12.4	10.5	18%	Enel	SO1	7	•	•
Business initiatives with social impact	(mil €)	2.1	2.2	-5%	Enel	SO1	7	•	•
Socially sustainable business initiatives	(mil €)	0.8	1.8	-57%	Enel	SO1	7	•	•

Initiatives in favor of communities: for the projects carried out in 2005 and those for 2006 approved by the Board of Enel Cuore Onlus, see the related Report published on the website: www.enelcuore.org.

(Continued)

EXHIBIT 8.2 (*Continued*)

ENERGY EFFICIENCY OF PLANTS ABROAD

Magnitude recorded	UM	2005	2004	2005-2004	Companies	GRI	CSR-SC	SAM	EIRIS
Generating plants						-	-	-	-
Total net efficient power	(MW)	3,786	3,688	3%	Enel	-	8.1.1	-	-
> Spain	(%)	69.6	69.8	0%	Enel	-	-	-	-
> Eastern Europe	(%)	14.5	14.9	-2%	Enel	-	-	-	-
> Latin America	(%)	5.2	5.2	0.7%	Enel	-	-	-	-
> North America	(%)	10.6	10.1	5%	Enel	-	-	-	-
Total net production	(TWh)	13.6	12.3	11%	Enel	-	8.1.1	-	-
> Spain	(%)	62.0	56.1	10%	Enel	-	-	-	-
> Eastern Europe	(%)	22.1	26.1	-15%	Enel	-	-	-	-
> Latin America	(%)	6.5	7.5	-14%	Enel	-	-	-	-
> North America	(%)	9.4	10.3	-8%	Enel	-	-	-	-
Net thermal production [1]	(TWh)	9.6	8.4	15%	Enel	-	8.1.1	-	•
> Coal	(TWh)	8.3	7.5	11%	Enel	-	-	-	-
> Oil/gas	(TWh)	1.0	0.7	57%	Enel	-	-	-	-
> Other (co-generation, etc.)	(TWh)	0.3	0.2	50%	Enel	-	-	-	-
Net renewable production (including biomass) [1]	(TWh)	4.0	3.9	2%	Enel	-	8.1.1	•	-
> Hydro	(TWh)	2.9	2.9	-	Enel	-	-	-	-
> Wind	(TWh)	0.9	0.8	22%	Enel	-	-	-	-
> Biomass	(TWh)	0.2	0.2	-5%	Enel	-	-	-	-
Thermal generating plants									
Net efficient thermal production	(MW)	2,215	2,214	-	Enel	-	8.1.1	•	-
> Coal	(MW)	1,410	1,410	-	Enel	-	-	-	-
> Oil/gas	(MW)	731	731	-	Enel	-	-	-	-
> Other (co-generation, biomass, etc.)	(MW)	74	73	2%	Enel	-	-	-	-
Coal plant yield	(%)	31.1	31.3	-	Enel	-	-	•	•
Green Energy						-	-	•	•
Net efficient renewable power	(MW)	1,571	1,474	7%	Enel	-	-	•	•
>Hydro	(MW)	1,159	1,128	3%	Enel	-	-	•	•
>Wind	(MW)	412	346	19%	Enel	-	-	•	•

(1) The value regarding 2004 published last year classified production from biomass as thermal, while this year it has been classified as renewable.

FOREIGN PLANT CERTIFICATION

Magnitude recorded	UM	2005	2004	2005-2004	Companies	GRI	CSR-SC	SAM	EIRIS
Environmental certification						-	8.2	•	•
ISO-certified organizations	(#)	15	6	150%	Enel	-	8.2	•	•
% installed power ISO14001-certified	(%)	20.4	3.4	499%	Enel	-	8.2	•	•

EFFICIENCY OF NETWORKS ABROAD

Magnitude recorded	UM	2005	2004	2005-2004	Companies	GRI	CSR-SC	SAM	EIRIS
Electricity distribution									
% of network cabled						-	-	-	-
> Spain	(%)	67.3	67.2	-	Enel	-	-	-	-
> Romania	(%)	37.6	n.a.	-	Enel	-	-	-	-

ENVIRONMENTAL PERFORMANCE OF PLANTS ABROAD

Magnitude recorded	UM	2005	2004	2005-2004	Companies	GRI	CSR-SC	SAM	EIRIS
Fuels									
Consumption of fossil fuels	(Mtoe)	2.7	2.4	14%	Enel	EN1	-	•	•
> Coal	(%)	84.3	86.7	-3%	Enel	EN1	-	•	•
> Oil	(%)	10.2	9.0	14%	Enel	-	-	-	-
> Gas	(%)	5.5	4.3	27%	Enel	-	-	-	-
Atmospheric emissions [2]									
Emissions of SO_2	(,000 t)	284	286	-1%	Enel	EN10	8.1.4	•	•
Emissions of NO_x	(,000 t)	28	27	1%	Enel	EN10	8.1.4	•	•
Emission of CO_2	(mil t)	10.5	10.0	5%	Enel	EN30	8.1.4	•	•
Emissions of particulates	(,000 t)	8	8	2%	Enel	EN10	8.1.4	•	•
Waste management									
Waste produced	(,000 t)	1,799	1,961	-8%	Enel	EN2	8.1.6	•	•
> Total hazardous waste	(,000 t)	13.3	3.6	270%	Enel	EN2	8.1.6	•	•
Waste recovery	(%)	37.1	47.9	-23%	Enel	EN31	8.1.6	•	•

(2) The unit of measurement of this index has been changed from gr/kWh (used for 2004) to absolute values.

FOREIGN ELECTRICITY MARKET

Magnitude recorded	UM	2005	2004	2005-2004	Companies	GRI	CSR-SC	SAM	EIRIS
Customer portfolio						EC1	3.1;3.1.2	•	-
Volume sold abroad	(TWh)	11.4	4.5	155%	Enel	EC1	-	-	-
Customers abroad	(,000)	2,065.9	611.0	238%	Enel	EC1	3.1	•	-

Source: Sustainability Report 2005

EXHIBIT 8.3 SUSTAINABILITY SCORECARD

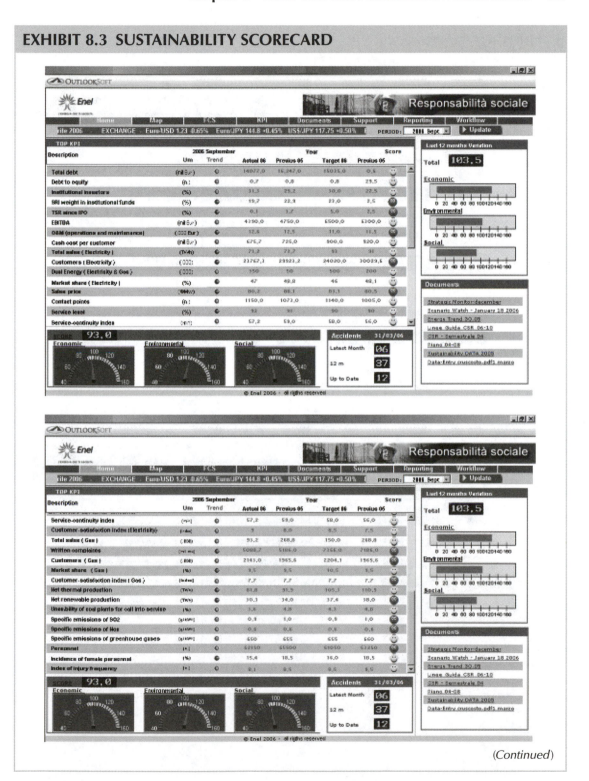

(Continued)

EXHIBIT 8.3 (*Continued*)

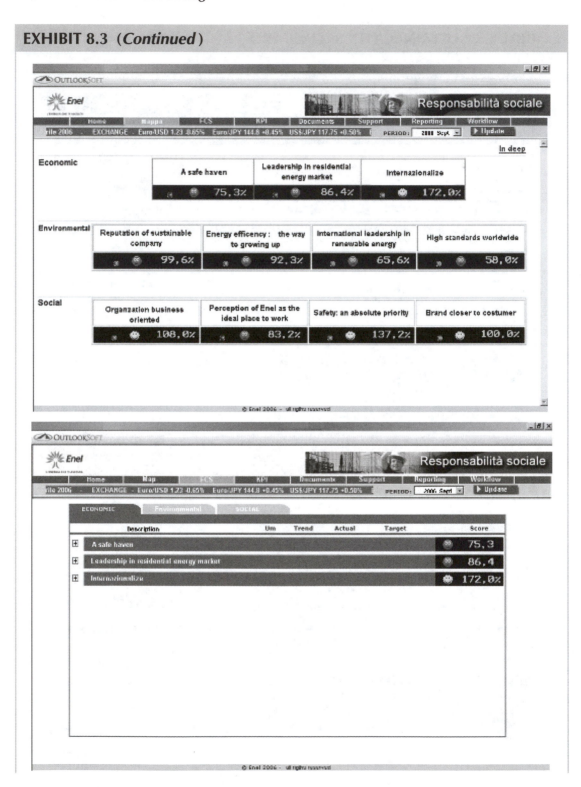

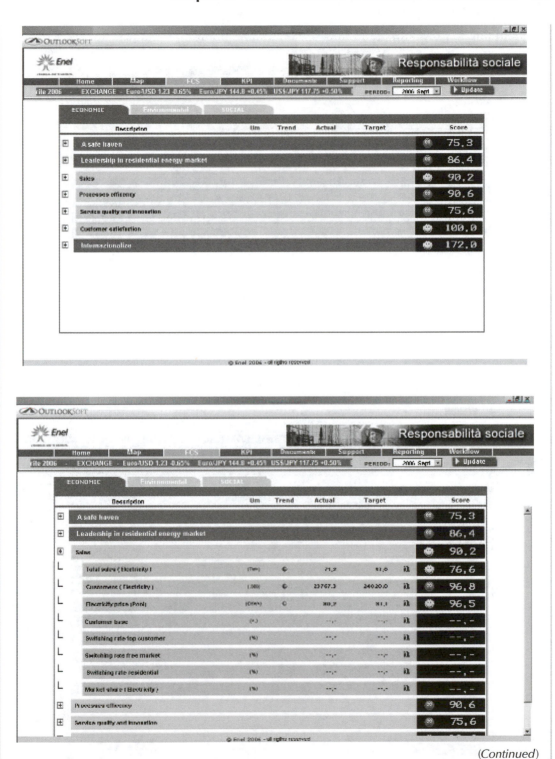

(*Continued*)

EXHIBIT 8.3 (*Continued*)

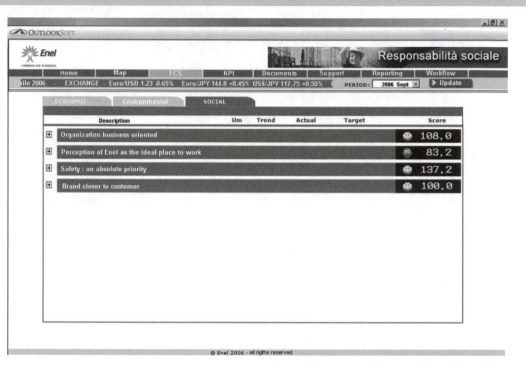

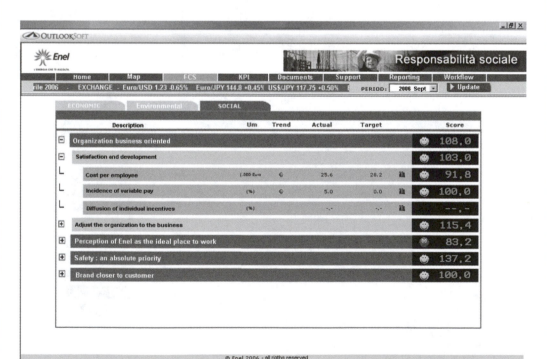

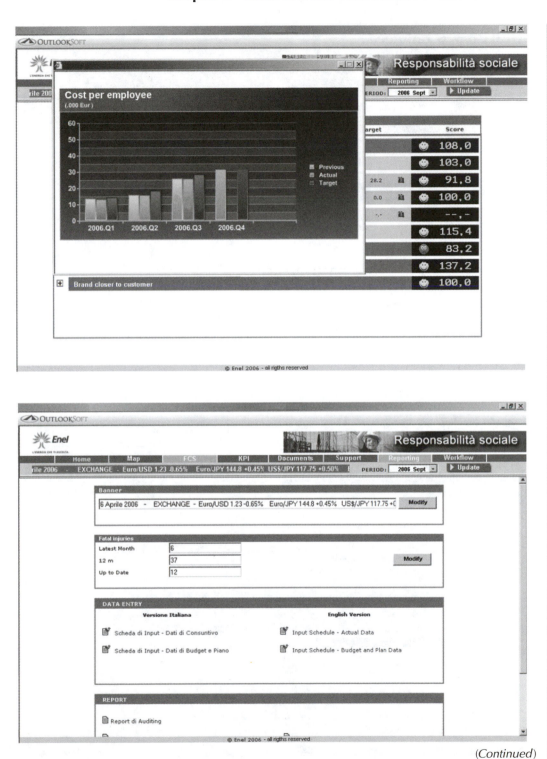

(Continued)

EXHIBIT 8.3 (*Continued*)

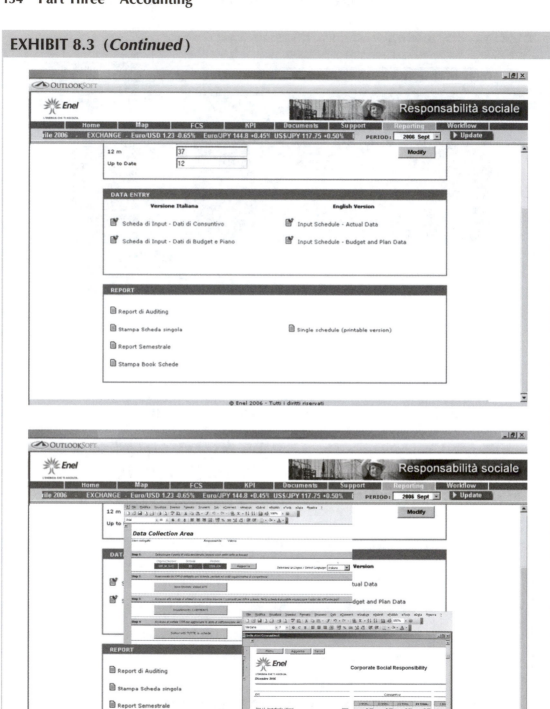

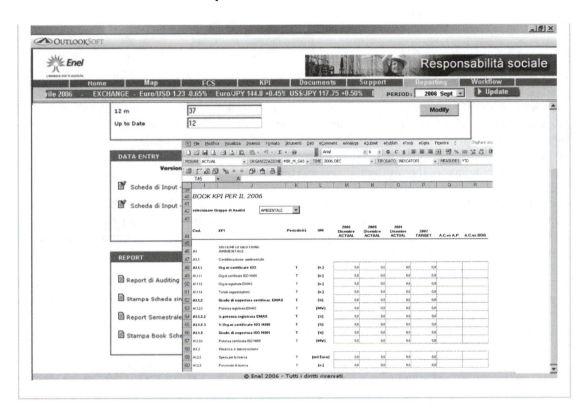

The critical CSR success factors and associated weights were identified as follows:

- *Financial perspective* (60% weight):
  - shareholder value (30% weight)
  - leadership position in the domestic energy market (40% weight)
  - development of overseas and gas markets (30% weight).
- *Environmental perspective* (25% weight):
  - image as a sustainable firm (15% weight)
  - growth through energy efficiency (35% weight)
  - worldwide leadership in respect of renewable power sources (35% weight)
  - guaranteed high standard of all assets (15% weight).
- *Social perspective* (15% weight):
  - organization's adaptation to the business (30% weight)
  - organization as an ideal place for the development of expertise (25% weight)
  - total work safety: towards zero injuries (40% weight)
  - well-known and familiar brand (5% weight).

A set of objectives, ranging from a minimum of two to a maximum of eight, was associated with each critical success factor.

In the economic area, for example, objectives for success regarding 'shareholder value' included: shareholder return, profitability growth, fit between growth and sustainability, and growth of the shareholder base. For 'leadership position in the domestic energy market', success factors included: sales, processes efficiency, service quality, innovation, and customer satisfaction. To gauge the meeting of the company's sales goal, eight KPIs were monitored: total sales, number of customers, electricity price, customer base, switching rate of the top customers, switching rate of the free market, switching rate of the residential and market share.

Success in the environmental domain – its 'image as a sustainable firm' – included six specific objectives: environmental governance, decrease in emissions, waste and water consumption, improved performance in respect of the Kyoto standard, impact on the landscape and attention to energy saving, and research and innovation.

Finally, regarding the social scale, success in 'the organization's adaptation to the business' included two related objectives: satisfaction and development as well as adjustment of the organization to the business. With reference to the first item, the associated metrics were: cost per employee, incidence of variable pay and diffusion of individual incentives.

With each goal assigned to a group of KPIs, the total number of KPIs was approximately 100. The actual value, target and trend of each KPI were measured by a score that reflected the degree of variance between their targets and the actual values realized. A red, yellow or green signal indicated the degree of success. (See Exhibit 8.3 for an example of the links between the critical success factors, objectives and KPIs.)

The Business Planning and CSR Control manager, both of the financial department, developed the Sustainability Scorecard, with the help of IT resources. The Scorecard was available on-line, based on an internal database and with an Excel front-end user platform. The data owner was responsible for the input.

The Business Planning and Control Unit was mandated to facilitate the diffusion and the use of the Sustainability Scorecard to support target setting and to ensure coherence between the monitored KPIs and the company's priorities.

Functional KPIs

In addition to the changes introduced to the managerial reporting system, the CSR approach also had a direct impact upon the reporting mechanisms managed by the company's functional units, including:

- *Human Resources.* The CSR approach enhanced the relevance of KPIs as applied to employees. Previously only publicized on an ad-hoc basis, by 2006 employee-related KPIs were compiled in a single report, which enabled managers to analyse their performance in this area, first by the identification of gaps and then the development of a corrective action plan.

EXHIBIT 8.4 SUSTAINABILITY PLAN 2006–2010

Guidelines by Division	Generation and Energy Management	Market	Infrastructure and Networks	International	Common Guidelines	Corporate Atmosphere	The Individual	Health and Safety
Objectives	> Attain positions of international leadership in energy efficiency > Optimize thermal power plants > Leadership in renewable energy > Minimize environmental and litigation risks	> Strengthen customer trust and loyalty > Continue the promotion of informed consumption > Personalization of service and direct communication with customers > Complete and accurate information > Further improvement of service standards and their assessment > Become a European reference model > Development of socially responsible products	> Ensure satisfaction of the demand for electricity > Minimize network leakage > Further reduction of supply interruptions > Rationalize network, including in cooperation with local governments > Continue adapting plants to preserve/ enhance the environment and landscape	> Search for new opportunities for growth in renewable energy > Bring the performance of the foreign subsidiaries up to the general Group standards > Develop the environmental management system and complete the process of environmental certification of plants > Bring the standards of environmental safety up to the general Group level	Objectives	> Motivation and welfare > Attraction and retention of the most talented human resources > Equal opportunity	> Make the most of individual capabilities > Perception of Enel as the ideal place to work	> Maintain high standards of on-the-job health and safety > Continue promoting safety for contracting companies and third parties
Action areas	> Optimization of technology and fuel mix > Continual research and development for adoption of clean technologies (clean coal and hydrogen) > Development of renewable energy > Environmental certification > Protection of tangible and intangible corporate assets > Further reduction of emissions	> Expand call center activity to assist linguistic minorities in Italy > Dissemination of high-efficiency products for civil and industrial use > Promotion of differentiated rates and related savings	> Improve level of service quality > Promote energy efficiency in final uses > Extend to the gas network the certification systems that already exist for the electricity network	> Promote the dissemination of the Ethical Code and the culture of sustainability > Develop training plans and disseminate the instruments of knowledge management > Ensure the safeguard of the rights of all employees > Make the improvement of environmental safety and health standards a priority > Implement measures of risk prevention through a system of inspections at contracting companies	Action areas	> Create a corporate atmosphere based on shared values > Implement a policy on human rights > Plan internal communication on the Company's values and objectives aimed at the entire Group > Continually promote a policy of equal opportunity > Develop systems for assessing the corporate atmosphere	> Improve and intensify training > Disseminate systems of knowledge management > Extend evaluation processes > 'Personalized' professional development paths > Instill the culture of sustainability	> Expand measures for the prevention of and protection from risk > Focus on training activities > Certification > Bring offices and industrial installations up to standard > Intensify inspections > Actions aimed at the protection of contracting firms and third parties
Commitments	> Broaden dialogue with institutions and communities in areas subject to extensive industrial conversions and restructurings	> Upgrade level of offer and services to customers in the distribution companies acquired abroad	> Maximize the synergy deriving from the integrated management of the gas and electricity networks > Ensure constant recourse to innovation and development in the areas of efficiency recovery	> Be an engine of development in the countries in which Enel operates by contributing to the dissemination of a corporate culture respectful of the relation with stakeholders	Commitments	> Extend to all levels policies to make the most of professional expertise, respect differences, and ensure equal opportunity	> Disseminate corporate responsibility as a daily business practice and continue to include CSR goals in management by objectives	> Continue pursuing the objective of 'zero accidents'
Challenges	> Put Enel's strategic decisions in appropriate perspective, sharing them with stakeholders and obtaining the necessary operating legitimization	> Transform 'customer value' into 'value for the customer'		> Make the industrial and commercial practices in the different affiliates uniform, while respecting local specificities and observing the best practices at the Group level	Challenges	> Achieve equal quality in industrial relations in all the foreign affiliates of the Group	> Complete the preparation of the policy on human rights and equal opportunity valid for Group companies both in Italy and abroad	> Align policies regarding on-the-job health and safety for employees, whether direct or not, in all foreign affiliates

Also for 2006, the operating heads of the Enel Divisions received the Chief Executive Officer's 'Plan Letter', which contains the guidelines for developing the sustainability plan. The Letter contains the objectives that the Divisions must set for themselves individually and specifies the areas of general action. Similarly, it specifies several common assumptions that must be followed. The Letter is the basis for the specific action plans for sustainability drawn up by the operating units. The latter are then included in Enel's sustainability auditing system. This table contains a summary of the goals for 2006. They do not differ essentially from those for 2005, because the plan is a five-year one; that is, every year the five subsequent ones are taken into consideration. The duration of the action plans varies from a few months to the entire five-year period.

Source: Sustainability Report 2006

- *Market Divisions.* The CSR approach renewed company focus on the measurement of customer satisfaction. KPIs in this area included: the number of switches from constrained to free markets, the number and the type of commercial channels and selling points, telemarketing, the number of days devoted to the development of business and consumer customers, the ratio between calls answered and received by the call centre, and the level of service supplied.

- *Safety.* Always considered to be a key area for measurement and control, safety data were not only requested by the stakeholders, but also by officially recognized companies, mostly for purposes of international certification. The principal safety-related KPIs covered: accidents at work, particularly the frequency and gravity of these, but also labour-hours lost and training expenditures. Since 2005, a specific section on safety has been incorporated into the Environmental Report, compiled on a quarterly and, by 2007, a monthly basis rather than the previous annual survey.

- *Environment.* The emphasis on the environmental impact of Enel's plants and related KPIs had not substantially changed over time. A new project would be undertaken to develop an environmental accounting system, with industrial accounting as a starting point that distinguished environmental costs (such as plant adaptation, new plant installation, and so on) from other costs.

The CSR Planning and Control Process: Key Actors and Phases

As coordinator of the entire CSR planning and control process, EnelDATA, produced sustainability data annually at the end of December.

Actors

There were three important categories of actors involved in the CSR planning and control process: the Area Coordinators, the Line Coordinators and the Data Owner.

The *Area Coordinators* were the CSR representatives inside the divisions. They reported to the planning and control unit of every Business Area in order to:

- ensure integration of CSR into the divisional industrial plans;
- coordinate the entire process of data collecting;
- determine, with the support of the line coordinator, the objectives and define the contents of the Business Review;
- guarantee compliance with the schedule as well as the reliability and completeness of the information provided.

Soon, Area Coordinators would take over the preparation of the CSR reports from EnelDATA.

The *Line Coordinators* were the CSR representatives inside functional departments. They were mandated to:

- ensure coherence between CSR and business objectives relative to the process managed in their specific area;
- collaborate with the Area Coordinators in the preparation of the objectives as determined in the Business Review.

The *Data Owners*, of whom there were approximately 50, were responsible for information availability and reliability in their data domains. They supplied KPI data to the Area Coordinators on deadline and maintained quality standards. Each Data Owner managed three or four employee data specialists as well.

Key Phases

To begin the CSR planning and control process, the CEO proposed guideline definitions; that is, the critical success factors and objectives for each business area. Next, the Planning and Control Unit (under the Corporate Administration, Finance and Control Department) and CSR (under the Corporate Communication Department) helped the CEO to refine his proposals. The result was then sent to the directors of the business divisions.

Each division director, with assistants responsible for the functional areas, processed the preliminary data, converting the guidelines and the objectives into specific actions, key variables and indicators. With the aid of the Line and the Area Coordinators' contributions, EnelDATA collected the information, which it checked to guarantee the coherence between the business and CSR objectives. The objectives were merged into the next CSR three-year Plan. The divisions then submitted their CSR Plan proposals, together with the industrial plan, to the CEO.

After approval of the plan proposals, the Area Coordinators confirmed the time schedule and the modes defined in the Sustainability Data to EnelDATA. The Line Coordinators simultaneously submitted their plans, which had already been approved at the Corporate level. EnelDATA consolidated and prepared the final CSR Plan, with the support of the Line and Area Coordinators and, if required, the Data Owners. The CSR Plan preparation was carried out between August and September of each year.

The last step was the presentation of the CSR Plan for approval, first to the Corporate Administration, Finance and Control, and Communication department managers, as well as the CEO. In addition, the CSR Plan was submitted for approval to the Audit Committee and to the Management Committee. Following those consultations, it was then submitted to the Board of Directors.

CSR reporting represented a standardized process to achieve the strategic objectives, closely related to the industrial plan, which were systematically formalized in documents. The feedback process was carried out by an analysis of the Quarterly Scorecard, which identified missed targets and also noted the corrective actions taken in consequence.

The Business Review was then prepared and sent to EnelDATA by the Corporate departments and divisions. It was finalized to highlight the progress of open projects and to describe the initiatives scheduled for the following 12 months.

Conclusion: Benefits Obtained and Problems Incurred

On the positive side, Enel's CSR planning and control system succeeded in standardizing KPIs across the business divisions and corporate units. The process increased the visibility of Enel's CSR mission to top management, engendering sponsorship and greater collaboration. Moreover, because each KPI had a specific 'owner', who became committed to the process, which, many argued, enhanced the system's capacity to represent Enel's CSR impact in great detail.

On the other hand, it was difficult to involve business units that were not accustomed to reporting CSR-specific indicators. There was also great resistance to fulfilling the new requirements. Furthermore, standardizing the data from various units and departments was both methodologically complex and extremely time-consuming. Finally, information was often difficult to acquire in a timely manner.

In order to overcome these obstacles, the CSR team focused first on data reliability and on the effectiveness of the collection, processing and communication of the data. Thereafter their attention shifted to the control activity. Another important step was the appointment of Area and Line Coordinators as well as a CSR representative for each area (business divisions and corporate departments). They were chosen from inside the control department. To support their work, a new IT platform devoted to CSR monitoring was put in place that was designed to reduce structural strain and reduce errors and data collection time. Finally, an extensive training project was launched, which included all 5000 middle managers and all other employees involved in the CSR process.

Suggested Questions for Discussion

1. What were the motives for Enel engaging in a CSR measurement and reporting process?
2. What principles do you apply to the development of a set of KPIs and why?
3. Are the contents and structure of the Sustainability Report aligned with the CSR approach adopted by Enel and with the stakeholders' information needs?
4. Do you consider the CSR planning and control system to be effective enough to support the CSR implementation?

NOTES

1. The case is intended to be used as a basis for class discussion rather than to illustrate either effective or ineffective handling of an administrative situation.
2. At the end of 2007, socially responsible investors owned 388 millions of shares, equivalent to 18.3% of the stocks held by investment funds, and there were 45 socially responsible investors (33 in 2003).
3. These codes were the Management and Organization Model provided for by Legislative Decree no. 231 and the 'Codice Preda', the self-discipline code for companies quoted on the Italian Stock Exchange.
4. The financial data in respect of the economic performance area were taken from the Consolidated Financial Statement, which was prepared according to the IAS/IFRS principles.

5. The planning and control mechanisms consisted of: 1) the Sustainability Data; 2) the CSR Plan; 3) the Quarterly Scorecard; 4) the Business Review; 5) the Sustainability Scorecard.

6. All 314 KPIs monitored and described in the Sustainability Data are associated with a specific critical success factor.

REFERENCE

Crooks, E. (2007) CEO interview: Triumph for a fading national champion, 19 June. Available at www.ft.com: http://search.ft.com/ftArticle?queryText=Triumph+for+a+fading+national+champion&aje=true&id=070619000979&ct=0&nclick_check=1 (accessed 4 March 2009).

CHAPTER NINE

Novo Nordisk A/S – Integrating Sustainability into Business Practice[1]

Mette Morsing, Copenhagen Business School and Dennis Oswald, University of Michigan

INTRODUCTION

> We all have a vision of how we'd like the world to be. For a company like Novo Nordisk committed to sustainable development, that vision is one of trust, openness, shared values and partnerships. We translate that as the Triple Bottom Line – social and environmental responsibility and economic viability. In an age where companies are scrutinized and transparency is the only way to gain trust, social responsibility is vital to maintain a business advantage.[2]

Novo Nordisk is an excellent example of an organization that attempts to consider sustainability as an integrated part of its strategy and in all of its business decisions. To meet this goal, the company has adopted a management philosophy, which they call the 'Novo Nordisk Way of Management', to ensure that all actions taken by employees meet corporate objectives. Within this management tool are three pillars that are used as control mechanisms to integrate sustainability into Novo Nordisk's business practices: Facilitators, Sustainability Report and the Balanced Scorecard. However, it is not certain to what extent each of these pillars is effective in influencing behaviour at the operational level.

Novo Nordisk defines sustainable development as being about preserving the planet while improving the quality of life for its current and future inhabitants. From a business perspective this involves the inclusion of economic, social and environmental considerations in the business strategy. During the 1990s many companies experienced an enormous pressure from critical stakeholders, governments, media, NGOs and international organizations to demonstrate that they had adopted sustainable business practices:

> The days when Aristotle Onassis could tuck his whalers out of sight behind convenient icebergs are almost gone. New technologies and open borders render most forms of economic, environmental, and social abuse increasingly visible. Indeed, far from being drowned in a floodtide of useless information, many of the world's citizens – thanks in large part to the public interest groups a number of them support – are becoming increasingly adept at keeping track of the activities of corporations and governments.
>
> Elkington, 1999, p. 161

The concept of 'sustainability' is often traced back to the World Commission on Environment and Development (the Brundtland Commission) report, which coined the following definition: 'Sustainable

Development is development that meets the needs of the present without compromising the ability of future generations to meet their own needs' (World Commission on Environment and Development, 1987). As the number of organizations that claim to adhere to sustainable business practices increases, so does the number of pieces of information that are prepared and disseminated about these practices. In a recent publication, the ACCA (Association of Chartered Certified Accountants) and CorporateRegister.com reported that in 1993 there were fewer than 100 cases of corporate non-financial reporting worldwide, but by 2003 there were over 1500 reports produced worldwide on an annual basis.[3] As these practices become more common among corporations, there has been criticism as to whether these same firms are purely 'window dressing', with no ambitions to embed sustainability in their business practices. A recent survey on corporate social responsibility in *The Economist* stated:

> Under pressure, big multinationals ask their critics to judge them by CSR criteria, and then, as the critics charge, mostly fail to follow through. Their efforts may be enough to convince the public that what they see is pretty, and in many cases this may be all they ever intended to achieve. But by and large CSR is at best a gloss on capitalism, not the deep systematic reform that its champions deem desirable.
>
> Crook, 2005, p. 2

This case raises the question of how managers can adopt appropriate management control systems to communicate to employees and other stakeholders what behaviour is desired, and to ensure that their corporate sustainability claims are implemented at the operational level. That is, how can organizations demonstrate that their sustainability declarations are not just 'good looks'? Specifically, this chapter unfolds Novo Nordisk's long-term commitment to sustainable business practices and the company's validations of these practices by focusing on how issues of sustainability are integrated and cascaded throughout the entire organization via the company's 'Way of Management'. The Novo Nordisk business unit – Diabetes Finished Products – is used as an example.

INTRODUCTION TO NOVO NORDISK A/S

Novo Nordisk A/S was founded by August Krogh in the 1922, a Danish Nobel laureate in physiology. He was inspired by two Canadian researchers, Frederick Banting and Charles Best, who had begun extracting insulin from the pancreas of cows in the previous year. August Krogh's wife, Marie, had type 2 diabetes; therefore, he established Nordisk Insulinlaboratorium to produce insulin for the treatment of diabetes. In 1925, two former employees, Harald and Thorvald Pedersen, established a competing insulin company, Novo Terapeutisk Laboratorium. In 1989, the two companies merged and became Novo Nordisk A/S.

Today, Novo Nordisk is a world leader in diabetes care; the company also holds a leading position in haemostasis management, growth hormone therapy and hormone replacement therapy. Novo Nordisk previously was involved in the production of enzymes. However, a demerger in 2000 saw the establishment of Novozymes, which took over the enzymes production, leaving Novo Nordisk to focus entirely on healthcare. Novo Nordisk headquarters is located in Denmark, on the outskirts of Copenhagen, and employs approximately 20 000 employees in 78 countries. Novo Nordisk markets its products in 179 countries.

Figure 9.1 contains Novo Nordisk's current organizational structure. In 2002, Corporate Stakeholder Relations became part of the executive management team along with R&D, Quality, Regulatory & Business Development, Finance and Operations.

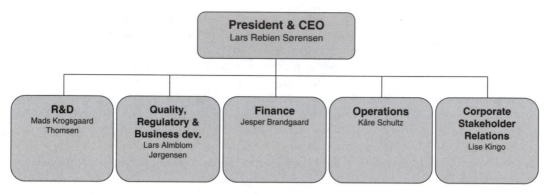

Figure 9.1 Novo Nordisk A/S organizational structure

Source: Internal document provided by Susanne Stormer

Novo Nordisk is a company based on research. R&D expenditure equalled 43.2% of the total wage costs in 2004 and was in the range of 15.0–16.6% of total turnover over the period 2000–2004. During this same period, Novo Nordisk had between 526 and 778 active patent families, with 85–45 new patent families per year.[4]

Financially, Novo Nordisk has performed well, with strong growth in turnover combined with continued high profitability; the market value of Novo Nordisk followed the booming American pharmaceutical sector and recently outperformed the European pharmaceutical index. In 2004, Novo Nordisk reported an operating profit of 6980 million Danish kroner (DKK), turnover of DKK 29 031 million and a diluted earnings per share of DKK 14.83. Additionally, Novo Nordisk reported a return on invested capital of 21% in 2004. Over the period 1 May, 2004, to 30 April, 2005, Novo Nordisk had a negative share return of 1.55%; however, over the five years 1 May, 2000, to 30 April, 2005, Novo Nordisk's share return equalled 44.17%.[5] Exhibit 9.1 provides key financial data for the last five years, and return data for Novo Nordisk, the Danish market and other large European pharmaceutical companies over the same period.

The share ownership of Novo Nordisk ensures that the organization has a high degree of freedom, because it is not open for takeovers, for example, from larger pharmaceutical companies. Specifically, total share capital is divided into A-shares and B-shares (each B-share carries 1/10 of the votes of an A-share). The A-shares are non-listed and held by Novo A/S (a private limited Danish company that is 100% owned by the Novo Nordisk Foundation, which was established with the merger in 1989). The B-shares are publicly traded on the Copenhagen, London and New York stock exchanges. As reported in the 2004 Annual Report, Novo A/S controls 26.1% of the B-shares, giving it 70.6 % of the total number of votes. Large block-holdings of the remaining B-shares include large institutional investors such as the Danish ATP Pension Fund (4.3%), the Capital Group Companies (10%) and Fidelity Investments (4.4%). Additionally, the company itself holds 6.4% of the shares. 'Other' investors hold the remaining 48.8%, which includes employees.[6] Novo Nordisk's board of directors consists of 10 members: seven elected by the shareholders and three by the employees.[7] Novo Nordisk's six executive directors as well as the directors of the Novo Nordisk Foundation are not represented in the Novo Nordisk board, which is in accordance with the general guidelines of corporate governance at the Copenhagen, London and New York

EXHIBIT 9.1 SELECTED FINANCIAL INFORMATION

Panel A: Financial Statement Information (in DKK million)[1]

	2000	2001	2002	2003	2004
Sales	20485	23385	24866	26158	29031
Operating Profit	4703	5410	5927	6422	6980
Net Profit	3154	3620	4116	4833	5013
Total Assets	24597	28662	31612	34564	37433
Total Current Liabilities	5860	6138	6152	7032	7280
Total Long-Term Liabilities	2117	2824	2983	2756	3649
Equity	16620	19700	22477	24776	26504
R&D/Sales	16.6%	16.6%	15.9%	15.5%	15.0%
Net Profit Margin	15.4%	15.5%	16.6%	18.5%	17.3%
Return on Invested Capital	22.3%	22.7%	20.5%	19.5%	20.6%

Panel B: Share Return Information[2]

Company	Country	Current	5 Year
Astrazeneca	UK	–11.47%	–3.99%
Glaxosmithkline	UK	16.48%	–22.78%
Novartis 'R'	Switzerland	2.16%	9.08%
Novo Nordisk 'B'	**Denmark**	**–1.55%**	**44.17%**
Roche Holdings 'B'	Switzerland	–11.29%	–11.82%
Sanofie-Aventis	France	32.65%	80.82%
Schering	Germany	18.89%	7.08%
Shire Pharmaceuticals	UK	5.87%	–39.68%
UCB	Belgium	13.74%	9.71%
Danish Market (KFX)		23.14%	17.77%

[1] *Source:* Novo Nordisk A/S – Annual Report 2004; Net profit margin equals net profit as a percentage of sales; Return on invested capital equals operating profit after tax (using the effective tax rate) as a percentage of average inventories, receivables, property, plant and equipment and as well as intangible assets less non-interest bearing liabilities including provisions (the sum of above assets and liabilities at the beginning of the year and at year-end divided by two).
[2] *Source:* Thompson Financial Datastream; the current return is calculated over the period 1 May, 2004 - 30 April, 2005, and the 5 Year return is calculated over the period 1 May, 2000 - 30 April, 2005

stock exchanges. It has become an increasingly important issue to demonstrate that Novo Nordisk is doing business according to these guidelines. However, the former CEO of Novo Nordisk from 1981 until 2000, Mads Øvlisen, had a chair of the same company from 2000 until he retired in April 2006.

SUSTAINABILITY AS PART OF NOVO NORDISK'S BUSINESS STRATEGY

Novo Nordisk has worked strategically with environmental and social responsibility for more than a decade, and today sustainability is an integrated part of the business strategy. Engagement in stakeholder dialogue and CSR is extremely important to Novo Nordisk, and the company believes that trust is imperative:

> 'Public authorities and NGOs have sharpened their tone, and we must take them seriously,' says President and CEO of Novo Nordisk, Lars Rebien Sørensen. 'It is important to be open and honest about our stand and our actions. Trust has to be earned'.[8]

Executive management at Novo Nordisk has made corporate values and sustainability an integrated part of the company's corporate brand. Mads Øvlisen often expressed strong views in the business press, on a number of occasions on the front page, on issues of sustainability. Additionally, many Danish business managers agree that he is the embodiment of corporate sustainability.[9] He participated in a number of government and business initiatives in this area, as well as contributing to the foundation of the European Academy of Business in Society. He is also an adjunct professor of corporate social responsibility at Copenhagen Business School.

Novo Nordisk's annual financial report of 2003 demarcates top management's dedication to sustainability, because it carries the same title as the sustainability report 2003: 'What does being there mean to you?' In their welcome letter, Lars Rebien Sørensen and Mads Øvlisen explain why stakeholders matter to core business:

> Whom do corporations serve? Not so many years ago, we would have said 'shareholders', without hesitation. But increasingly business enterprises are recognizing commitments to serve other stakeholders – such as customers, employees, societies at large – in addition to shareholders. In order to serve the long term interest of stakeholders, companies must regard it as a core part of their business to assume a wider responsibility and consider broadly the wide range of factors which may impact its ability to generate returns over long periods of time.[10]

The conspicuous commitment to sustainability is reinforced in the 2004 Annual Report, which was the company's first integrated triple bottom line report combining economic, environmental and social results. The commitment is stated clearly by Lars Rebien Sørensen and Mads Øvlisen on page 1:

> Novo Nordisk takes a multi-pronged approach to providing better access to health through capacity building, a preferential pricing policy for the poorest nations and funding through the World Diabetes Foundation, which is now reaching out to many millions of people with diabetes. In terms of sustainability, Novo Nordisk demonstrates its determination to play a leading role by setting a target for an absolute reduction of CO_2 emissions over the next decade. When people can overcome the challenges of diabetes, we must as a company tackle the global challenges of social and sustainable stewardship.

In 2002, the inclusion of Stakeholder Relations as part of the executive management team demarcated a strengthening of Novo Nordisk's sustainability focus. In 2004, the Stakeholder Relations area was expanded and Lise Kingo (Executive Vice President) became responsible for corporate communications, human resources and occupational health service in what is now referred to as 'People, reputation and relations'; currently there are approximately 200 employees working in this group. Ms. Kingo believes that her group is responsible for the two most important assets in Novo Nordisk: the people and the brand. This department drives, challenges and monitors Triple Bottom Line strategies and helps the business units to implement new activities in relation to sustainability by:[11]

- monitoring issues and spotting trends that may affect future business;
- engaging with stakeholders to reconcile dilemmas and find common ground for more sustainable solutions;
- building relationships with key stakeholders in the global, international and local communities of which Novo Nordisk is a part;
- driving and embedding long-term thinking and the Triple Bottom Line mindset throughout the company;
- accounting for the company's performance and conveying Novo Nordisk's positions, objectives and goals to audiences with an interest in the company;
- translating and integrating the Triple Bottom Line approach into all business processes to obtain sustainable competitive advantages in the marketplace.

HISTORY OF SUSTAINABILITY AT NOVO NORDISK

The focus on sustainability is not new for Novo Nordisk. In the late 1960s, the company was confronted with severe stakeholder criticisms for the first time, and close interaction with a broad variety of stakeholders has been part of the company's strategy since then. Novo Nordisk's first encounter with stakeholder criticism surrounded new production methods that introduced genetically engineered micro-organisms, resulting in the development of a new product line of enzymes. These enzymes were important ingredients in many products (e.g., detergent). Environmentally-oriented NGOs, as well as scientific articles, initially raised awareness that the use of detergents with enzymes could lead to those coming into contact with the product developing allergies, and then that the dust from the production process could have implications for the health of employees. Novo Nordisk's sales fell dramatically, and the company reacted with a strong, quick response by developing dust-free enzymes presenting no risk for employees and consumers.[12] Sales rose again and enzyme production became an important part of Novo Nordisk's production in Denmark, the United States and Japan.

In 2001, Novo Nordisk was once again confronted with criticism from NGOs. A consortium of medical companies, including Novo Nordisk, raised the issue of protecting intellectual property rights with the South African government. This led to major public criticism of the consortium members, who were accused of prioritizing profits at the expense of the health of less-advantaged people. Again, Novo Nordisk reacted quickly. By engaging in dialogue with the NGOs, the company defined a new policy to strengthen the company's presence and development of medicines to combat diabetes in developing countries. A new pricing policy and the establishment of the World Diabetes Foundation in late 2001 can be seen as a strategic result of Novo Nordisk's response to the criticism.

Issues of importance for sustainability in Novo Nordisk have changed from a predominantly environmental focus to one that includes health, safety and bioethics issues, as well as a focus on how

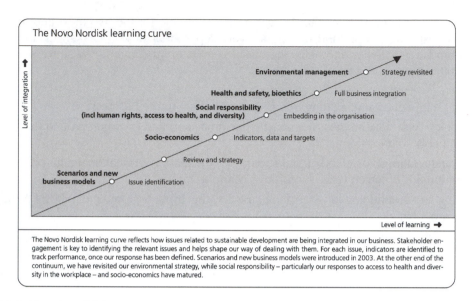

The Novo Nordisk learning curve reflects how issues related to sustainable development are being integrated in our business. Stakeholder engagement is key to identifying the relevant issues and helps shape our way of dealing with them. For each issue, indicators are identified to track performance, once our response has been defined. Scenarios and new business models were introduced in 2003. At the other end of the continuum, we have revisited our environmental strategy, while social responsibility – particularly our responses to access to health and diversity in the workplace – and socio-economics have matured.

FIGURE 9.2 Novo Nordisk learning curve

Source: Corporate Stakeholder Relations' Strategic Plan 2004–05, March 2004, p. 15

to integrate issues of social responsibility. To illustrate this concurrent broadening of the scope, Novo Nordisk developed a learning curve, as shown in Figure 9.2.

The learning curve shows that Novo Nordisk perceives sustainability as a continuous learning process, in which the company needs to be able to take in new issues and integrate these concurrently in the business strategy towards 'full business integration'.

HOW DOES NOVO NORDISK MEET ITS OBJECTIVES OF BEING SUSTAINABLE?

In 1997, the Novo Nordisk Way of Management (see Figure 9.3) was introduced as an overall guideline to ensure that Novo Nordisk's strategic goals were reached at the operational level. A central part of the strategic goal is the integration and implementation of sustainable business practices:

> The Novo Nordisk Way of Management serves as the solid footing from which innovative ideas can take off. Its immediate strengths lie in its consistency, coherence and systematic follow-up methods. It is the way we do things.[13]

The Novo Nordisk Way of Management was designed and introduced to strike a balance between corporate control and decentralized decision-making. It was implemented as a reaction to the situation in 1996 where company systems, procedures and routines were standardized and centralized at headquarters in Bagsværd in Denmark; this led to dissatisfaction among managers in the foreign subsidiaries who found that the systems did not always fit with the local situation and needs. As an illustration of this balance, Henrik Gürtler, CEO of Novo A/S, saw the Novo Nordisk Way of

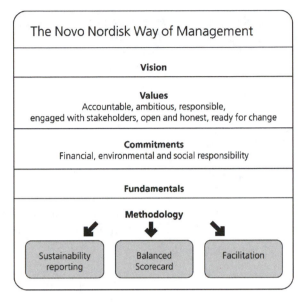

The Novo Nordisk Way of Management serves as the solid footing from which innovative ideas can take off. Its immediate strengths lie in its consistency, coherence and systematic follow-up methods. To people working at Novo Nordisk, it simply is the way we do things.

FIGURE 9.3 Novo Nordisk Way of Management

Source: Corporate Stakeholder Relations' Strategic Plan 2004–05, March 2004, p. 15

Management as an opportunity to develop new and motivating control systems throughout the entire organization:

> New initiatives and management programmes were introduced regularly, but they had no effect across borders. They were encapsulated and never seemed to make much difference outside corporate headquarters. It annoyed me, and when the Novo Nordisk Way of Management was designed as a new and overall guideline, I decided to do something about it. [14]

The then CEO, Mads Øvlisen, explained the Novo Nordisk Way of Management for all managers and employees in a letter in January 1997:

> The Novo Nordisk Way of Management is a comprehensive and easy-to-use guide which should allow you to use your insight and judgement in complying also with the 'local' management and quality systems derived from this corporate basis for use in functions and departments throughout Novo Nordisk.[15]

The Novo Nordisk Way of Management extends beyond products and manufacturing operations to include all activities, and as such it is a broad frame that describes the rationale that should set the tone and the standards amongst managers and employees in the entire organization. Additionally, Novo Nordisk has also developed a vision, values, commitments and fundamentals in order to inspire and guide its employees to achieve superior performance (see Exhibit 9.2).

EXHIBIT 9.2 NOVO NORDISK'S VISION, VALUES, COMMITMENTS AND FUNDAMENTALS

The Vision

We want to be the world's leader in diabetes treatment
We offer products and services in other areas where we can make a difference
We deliver competitive business results
A job with us is more than 'just a job'
Our values are reflected in our actions
Our history shows that it can be done

The Values are six corporate values to guide decision-making and action: account-able, ambitious, responsible, engaged with stakeholders, open and honest, ready for change

The Commitments are a reflection of the commitment to sustainability and to integrating the Triple Bottom Line thinking in organizational practices.

The Fundamentals consist of 10 behavioural guidelines on how to organize and behave in everyday organizational life in all units at all levels in Novo Nordisk:

1. Each unit must share and use better practices.
2. Each unit must have a clear definition of where accountabilities and decision powers reside.
3. Each unit must have an action plan to ensure improvement of its business and performance and working climate.
4. Every team and employee must have updated business and competency targets and receive timely feedback on performance against these targets.
5. Each unit must have an action plan to ensure the development of teams and individuals based on business requirements and employee input.
6. Every manager must establish and maintain procedures in the unit for living up to relevant laws, regulations and Novo Nordisk policies.
7. Each unit and employee must know how they create value for its customers.
8. Every manager requiring reporting from others must explain the actual use of the report and the added value.
9. Every manager must continuously make it easier for the employees to liberate energy for customer related issues.
10. Every manager and unit must actively support cross-unit projects and working relationships of relevance to the business.

Source: http://www.novonordisk.com/about_us/about_novo_nordisk/the_charter.asp

To ensure that the entire organization understands and adheres to the Novo Nordisk Way of Management, the company developed a methodology consisting of three elements: facilitators, sustainability reporting and the Balanced Scorecard. Each of these elements is discussed in the following sections.

Facilitators

The facilitators are a team of around 16 high-profile professionals at the holding company, Novo A/S. Each of them has a professional background from senior specialist or managerial positions in Novo Nordisk or Novozymes. They travel in pairs to visit all business units and levels of the entire organization every three years. The first team of facilitators was recruited internally in 1996; the facilitator team has a blend of ages, sex, professions and nationalities. They serve to assess, assist and facilitate units and projects to perform better. Their tasks are as follows:[16]

- Through on-site auditing/facilitating of departments, factories and affiliates, assess whether or not the company-wide minimum standard requirements or 'ground rules' as specified in the Novo Nordisk Way of Management are met.
- Through on-site advice and help, assist the unit in question in correcting identified non-compliance with these requirements.
- Through on-site identification of 'best practices' applied, facilitate communication and sharing of these across the organization.

A facilitation is a structured, planned assessment of the status of the Novo Nordisk Way of Management within the unit or project, with the aim of developing agreed actions for improvement. In conducting the facilitation, the facilitators will carry out the following:[17]

- Obtain objective evidence through a fact-finding process.
- Provide objective, validated assessments and conclusion.
- Include recommendations for improvements where appropriate.
- Agree on action plans with unit or process managers.
- Follow up on the implementation of the action plan.
- Fulfil their responsibilities in a manner demonstrating integrity, objectivity and professional behaviour.

The facilitation process consists of three stages:

1. The pre-facilitation, in which the scope of the facilitation is identified and material to support the process is developed.
2. The facilitation itself, in which facilitators meet with the individual unit or project members, and an agreement is made on how to improve.
3. A post-facilitation process, in which the facilitator is responsible for following up and reporting to executive management on the achievements with respect to the action points agreed upon in stage two.

Exhibit 9.3 provides excerpts from a recent facilitation at the Diabetes Pharmaceutical Site Hillerød.

EXHIBIT 9.3 EXAMPLE OF A RECENT FACILITATION

Following are excerpts from a recent facilitation at Diabetes Pharmaceutical Site Hillerød:

Facilitation Start Date: 15 November 2004
Facilitation End Date: 22 December 2004

Purpose and Scope of Facilitation

The purpose and scope of the facilitation is to assess the state of compliance, within Pharmaceutical Diabetes Site Hillerød, with the Novo Nordisk Way of Management, excluding Financial Commitments, and to agree and follow up on actions resulting from the facilitation and to report the results.

At the time of the facilitation the organization is influenced by a number of changes. The unit VP and the QA (quality assurance) VP were appointed in the Q4 2004 and several department managers have been appointed to their current position within 2004.

Executive Summary

The facilitation of DPSH in Site Hillerød has shown a unit dedicated to live up to the targets and challenges set by Diabetes Finished Products (DFP). All interviewees were aware of Novo Nordisk Way of Management and feel that the unit and management are living up to the values of Novo Nordisk. Facilitations show that there are different levels of compliance amongst the departments with respect to the implementation of Fundamentals.

The unit is highly focused on achieving its business targets, sometimes at the expense of overlooking the quality of some of the management processes such as APIS and development planning.

DPSH is currently developing its own strategy in alignment with DFP strategy and business plans. There is a clear understanding by all in the unit that focus must be on supporting the needs defined in the production agreements. Roll out of cLEAN™ is at variable stages within the different functions within DPSH.

Target setting based on the DPSH Balanced Scorecard and follow up needs to be improved for both teams and individuals. The lack of specific targets in some teams also influences the frequency and quality of feedback given in the organization and needs to be enhanced.

DPSH is an organization in close daily contact with its key stakeholders within Novo Nordisk and interviewees are aware of their customers' needs.

Source: internal document provided by Eric Drapé, SVP Diabetes Finished Products

Sustainability Reporting

Sustainability reporting is used to ensure that sustainability thinking becomes part of everyday business practice at Novo Nordisk. In 1989, Novo Nordisk produced its first environmental management review as part of its proactive stakeholder strategy – long before environmental reporting became compulsory for companies like Novo Nordisk. In 1994, Novo Nordisk produced its first environmental report including resource consumption, emissions and use of experimental animals. Later, in 1998, a social report was issued, and since 1999 Novo Nordisk has published annual reports on sustainability integrating environmental, social and economic concerns.[18] For the first time in 2004, Novo Nordisk integrated this information with its financial results, and now reports a combined social, environmental and economic report – The Annual Report 2004. These reports address issues recommended by United Nation's Global Compact, the Global Reporting Initiative's 2002 Sustainability Reporting Guidelines, and follow the approach laid out in the AA1000 Framework; the reports deliver a comprehensive documentation of Novo Nordisk's ambitions, goals, initiatives, results and new targets for environmental and social responsibility.

Novo Nordisk is renowned nationally and internationally for its dedication to corporate sustainability and for pioneering new agendas and concurrent development of stakeholder relations. Recent recognition includes being ranked by Corporate Knights Inc. in February 2005 among the top 100 sustainable companies in the world, and being ranked second in the world by SustainAbility and the United Nations Environment Programme in November 2004 for its ability to identify and manage social and environmental issues as accounted for in its sustainability report. Additionally, their Sustainability Report 2003 won 1st prize (for the sixth time) of the European Sustainability Awards (sponsored by the Association of Chartered Certified Accountants), and in Denmark, Novo Nordisk has won six prizes for the best annual social report awarded by the Association of Danish Accountants and the Danish business newspaper Børsen.[19] In the annual image analysis reported in Børsen, Novo Nordisk has in 1992, 2001, 2002, 2003 and 2005 ranked either first or second, with a high score on the CSR element. In 2004, Novo Nordisk was second to A.P. Møller (*Berlingske Nyhedsmagasin*, 2005, p. 28).

In order to measure its progress towards sustainability, Novo Nordisk uses a Triple Bottom Line approach, which links a set of key targets to sustainability goals. Figure 9.4 provides details from Novo Nordisk's Annual Report 2004 on the specific indicators used, and the reason for using them (impact). As shown in this figure, there are six strategic areas for Novo Nordisk's triple bottom line performance:

- *Living our values*, which aims to measure whether business actions are consistent with corporate values. Three performance metrics are used to gauge how well the company performs in this area; two are taken from an annual employee survey (eVoice[20]) and one is directly related to the use of facilitators (discussed in the preceding section).

- *Access to health*, which is a means to ensure that the company as a pharmaceutical is involved in promoting improvements in global health standards. Two measures are used to gauge Novo Nordisk's presence in less developed countries.

- *Our employees*, which ensures that Novo Nordisk maintains high standards in relation to its workforce. Four performance measures are used to gauge Novo Nordisk's treatment of their employees; two of these measures are taken from the eVoice employee survey.

STRATEGIC AREA	INDICATORS	IMPACT
Living our values Two indicators show how we live up to the company's values, as perceived by employees. This is measured as part of the climate survey, eVoice, conducted annually. One indicator shows follow-up on the facilitation process.	Average of respondents' answers as to whether social and environmental issues are important for the future of the company. Average of respondents' answers as to whether management demonstrates in words and action that they live up to our Values. Percent of fulfilment of action points planned arising from facilitations of the Novo Nordisk Way of Management and Values.	Organizational support for and understanding of responsible business practices. Integration of corporate values in all decisions. Corrective actions on values following facilitations.
Access to health Two indicators measure progress on one of the programmes for global access to health, the best possible pricing scheme in Least Developed Countries (LDCs). In 2004 there were 50 LDCs.	Number of LDCs where Novo Nordisk operates. Number of LDCs which have chosen to buy insulin under the best possible pricing scheme.	Access to essential medicines. Affordability of essential medicines.
Our employees Four indicators measure standards of health and safety in the workplace, employee development and equal opportunities.	Frequency of occupational injuries. Employee turnover rate. Average of respondents' answers as to whether their work gives them an opportunity to use and develop their competences/skills. Average of respondents' answers as to whether people from diverse backgrounds have equal opportunities (for example in terms of hiring, promotion and training) at Novo Nordisk, regardless of gender, race, ways of thinking etc.	Increased quality of life for employees, improved work flow and productivity, and less absence due to illness. Influx and outflux of knowledge. Increased competence level for employees and increased competence capital in the company. Increased diversity in the workplace.
Our use of animals Two indicators track efforts to reduce the number of experimental animals and improve their welfare.	Percent of animal test types removed from external and internal specification. Housing conditions for experimental animals, considering the needs of the animals.	Reduction and replacement of experimental animals. Improved welfare of experimental animals.

(Continued)

Eco-efficiency and compliance		
Two environmental indicators, eco-productivity indices (EPIs), are based on eco-efficiency thinking and reflect internationally adopted views. Full compliance with local laws and regulations is a company policy. Certification of production facilities is instrumental to that end.	Annual improvement in water efficiency.	Water use efficiency.
	Annual improvement in energy efficiency.	Energy use efficiency.
	Compliance.	Compliance with regulatory requirements. Accidental releases.
	ISO 14001 implementation.	Pollution prevention through decreased use of raw materials, water and energy and decreased environmental impact per produced unit.
Economic contribution		
Five financial measures for reporting to shareholders and the financial markets serve as indicators for economic contribution.	Operating profit margin.	Contribution to company efficiency, growth and investors' economic capacity.
	Growth in operating profit.	Contribution to company growth and investors' economic capacity.
	Total corporate tax as share of sales.	Contribution to national economic capacity.
	Return on invested capital.	Efficiency of invested capital, contribution to asset base, and investors' economic capacity.
	Cash to earnings (three-year average).	Contribution to the company's degree of freedom in terms of available cash funds (resources).

Figure 9.4 Indicators of Triple Bottom Line performance

Source: Novo Nordisk A/S Annual Report 2004

- *Our use of animals*, which ensures that Novo Nordisk, as a pharmaceutical, is in good standing with a key stakeholder group – animal welfare groups (in particular, the Danish Animal Welfare Society). Two metrics are used to ensure the ethical treatment of all animals used in research.
- *Eco-efficiency and compliance*, which measures Novo Nordisk's impact on the environment. Four performance measures are included to measure the organization's use of water and energy, their compliance with regulations and the implementation of ISO 14001.[21]
- *Economic contribution*, which is more than the traditional area of financial performance – it also covers the company's socio-economic impacts. Five metrics are used, including traditional measures such as operating profit margin and return on invested capital, but also one metric that measures how much the company contributes to the national economic capacity (total taxes as a percentage of turnover).

The Triple Bottom Line is used as a firm-wide tool to ensure Novo Nordisk takes actions that are consistent with operating as a sustainable company. All metrics used in the Triple Bottom Line report aggregate performance across all business units to present the full picture. Novo Nordisk does not report Triple Bottom Line performance at a disaggregated level (that is, for each business unit), but does provide specific and detailed data for eight major production sites.

> Transparent reporting is a vital instrument for us in accounting for our performance on the Triple Bottom Line. This is where we can account for our approach to doing business in a single document and cohesively present performance, progress, positions and strategic initiatives as well as the dilemmas and key issues we face as a pharmaceutical company. Most importantly, what we present in the report is the result of our interactions and engagements with stakeholders.
>
> Susanne Stormer, manager in Corporate Stakeholder Relations and responsible for Novo Nordisk's sustainability reporting[22]

Balanced Scorecard

Rather than assessing each division with a Triple Bottom Line performance report, Novo Nordisk relies on the Balanced Scorecard:

> The Balanced Scorecard is the management tool for embedding and cascading the Triple Bottom Line approach throughout the organization. The Scorecard is a vital element of the corporate governance set-up in Novo Nordisk and thus a very powerful tool to ensure integration of the sustainability approach into all business processes.[23]

Novo Nordisk has been using Balanced Scorecards since 1996, and they were introduced primarily as a finance initiative. The administration of the scorecards rests with the Finance, Legal and IT department, which has a mandate to use the best management methods, of which the Balanced Scorecard is viewed as an effective tool. The involvement of finance personnel with respect to Balanced Scorecards is to facilitate workshops (that is, supporting management teams), assist in setting of targets, review Balanced Scorecards and changes to/improvements in financial management (that is, integrating the Balanced Scorecard with processes).

Novo Nordisk cascades its Balanced Scorecard down to the business unit level, from where it translates into individual employees' personal targets, which are set and reviewed on a biannual basis. Specifically, a Balanced Scorecard is prepared for the organization as a whole; this scorecard is then cascaded down to the executive VP level (currently there are five executive VPs, each with their own scorecard). From this level, each of the twenty Senior VPs also has a Balanced Scorecard (that is, the business unit level). From this level there is no formal mandate that the scorecards are further cascaded; however, in some business units, scorecards may be prepared for each individual sub-unit (for example, a particular factory). In general, the sub-unit typically is evaluated on a collection of Key Performance Indicators (KPIs), rather than having objectives in each of the four traditional sections of a Balanced Scorecard.

Novo Nordisk currently has a total of 24 objectives in its Balanced Scorecard under the following four headings:

- Customers and Society
- Finance
- Business Processes
- People and Organization.

To facilitate the operation of the Balanced Scorecard, each objective is 'owned' by one of the five executive areas at Novo Nordisk. Corporate Stakeholder Relations is responsible for the following seven of the 24 objectives:

- Increase internationalization
- Support diversity
- Ensure talent development
- Ensure performance management
- Ensure superior company reputation
- Ensure environmental, social and ethical performance
- Improve collaboration with key stakeholders in diabetes care worldwide.

USE OF THE BALANCED SCORECARD AT DIABETES FINISHED PRODUCTS

One of the key business units at Novo Nordisk is Diabetes Finished Products (DFP). This group is responsible for the production and distribution of all products related to the treatment of diabetes. In 2004, the group produced 807 million units of its four key products (Penfill® 3 ml filling, Prefilled 3 ml total, Penfill® 3 ml blister and Insulin vials).[24] There are approximately 3100 employees, spread across eight sites and DFP headquarters. Figure 9.5 provides the organizational chart for DFP. Specifically, there are five production sites (three in Denmark, one in the United

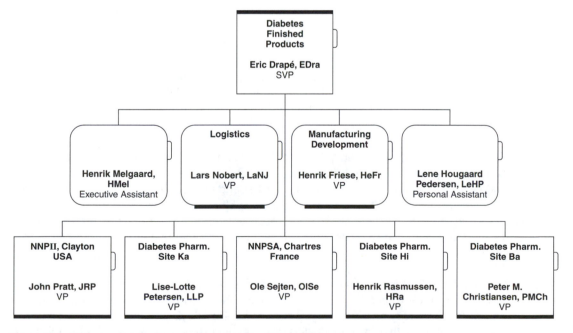

Figure 9.5 Diabetes finished products – organizational chart

Source: Internal document provided by Eric Drapé, SVP Diabetes Finished Products

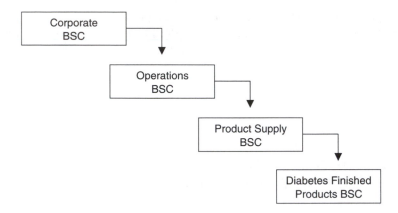

Figure 9.6 Cascading of the Balanced Scorecard (BSC)

States and one in France); Novo Nordisk is currently expanding another production facility in Brazil. Additionally, there is a logistics unit, and a manufacturing development unit that works to take new products to mass production. Eric Drapé is the Senior Vice President (SVP) of DFP. Eric is a pharmacist by training, and has been with Novo Nordisk since 1990. He has been in his current role since January 2004; his previous position was as a site manager (VP) at the French production facility.

Figure 9.6 shows how the Balanced Scorecard is cascaded from Corporate to DFP. However, in our more detailed illustrations in Figures 9.7, 9.8 and 9.9, we do not include information for Corporate, because the objectives we have chosen are 'owned' by Corporate Stakeholder Relations, not Operations. However, all objectives are cascaded from Corporate.

To illustrate how specific critical success factors (CSF) are cascaded through the organization, Figures 9.7, 9.8 and 9.9 describe the KPI, the KPI definition and the 2005 target for three CSFs for Operations, Product Supply and DFP. The three CSFs illustrated are those that are most closely aligned with the social and environmental issues in Novo Nordisk's Triple Bottom Line.

The first CSF (Figure 9.7) is to ensure environmental, social and ethical performance. With respect to DFP only one KPI is included – EPI performance – which is intended to measure the relationship between total yield of product and consumption of water and energy. Further up the organization, the emission of carbon dioxide (CO_2) is also measured. Noticeably missing from the corporate Balanced Scorecards are any KPIs that measure social and ethical performance – most likely a reflection of the general difficulty of defining meaningful and quantifiable social indicators at a corporate level.

The second CSF (Figure 9.8) is a focus on supporting diversity and social responsibility. Throughout the organization, three KPIs are used. The first is intended to ensure that each level of the organization supports diversity and ensures equal opportunities to its employees. The second KPI is the number of employees that have evaluated progress according to the OA. The final KPI is a metric that focuses on the functioning and value of the Job Transfer Centre, which is a centre that has been established in connection with the company's global sourcing strategy, according to

	Operations	Product Supply	Diabetes Finished Products
KPI	1. EPI performance. 2. CO_2 emission reduction target.	1. EPI performance. 2. CO_2 emissions reduction strategy and action plan. 3. CO_2 emission reduction target.	1. EPI performance.
KPI Definition	1. EPI is calculated as the relation between the total yield of product and the respective consumption of water and energy. Performance is tracked annually against previous year. 2. CO_2 emission reduction target to be approved by Environment & Bioethics Committee and communicated to relevant stakeholders.	1. EPI is calculated as the relation between the total yield of product and the respective consumption of water and energy. 2. A CO_2-compliance plan for Bagsvaerd and Hillerød to be drafted and implemented. 3. Establish an implementation plan for the CO_2 strategy with base year 2004.	1. EPI is calculated as the relation between the total yield of product and the respective consumption of water and energy. Performance is tracked quarterly against previous year. Simple average of the two indexes is the target.
Target 2005	1. Increase the eco-productivity index for water in the period 2001–2005 by an annual average of 5% corresponding to a total increase in EPI of 30% end of 2005. Increase the eco-productivity index for energy in the period 2001–2005 by an annual average of 4% corresponding to a total increase in EPI of 25% end 2005. 2. S&R to set target.	1. Increase the eco-productivity index for water in the period 2001–2005 by an annual average of 5% corresponding to a total increase in EPI of 30% end of 2005. Increase the eco-productivity index for energy in the period 2001–2005 by an annual average of 4% corresponding to a total increase in EPI of 25% end 2005. 2. CO_2-compliance plan approved by PS management. Information seminar for key internal stake-holders to ensure effective implementation of the CO_2 strategy. 3. Include the CO reduction target in PS BSC06.	1. 2005: Water: 101 Energy: 99

Figure 9.7 Cascading of Balanced Scorecard 2005 – Ensure environmental, social and ethical performance

Source: Internal documents provided by Eric Drapé, SVP Diabetes Finished Products

	Operations	Product Supply	Diabetes Finished Products
KPI	1. Equal opportunity implementation. 2. Number of EVPs/ SVPs that have evaluated progress achieved according to plan as part of the OA process.	1. Equal opportunity implementation. 2. Number of employees that have evaluated progress achieved according to plan as part of the OA process. 3. JTC (Job Transfer Centre) process is running smoothly.	1. Equal opportunity implementation. 2. Number of employees that have evaluated progress achieved according to plan as part of the OA process. 3. JTC process is running smoothly.
KPI Definition	1. Action plans for 2005 achieved. 2. EVPs/SVPs have evaluated progress.	1. % of targets in the action plans for 2005 achieved. 2. % of EVPs/SVPs that have evaluated progress. 3. The KPI measures: A) JTC's ability to send the right people to the right job; B) The interviewers' acceptance of these candidates.	1. % of targets in the action plans for 2005 achieved. 2. Progress evaluated. 3. The KPI measures: A) JTC's ability to send the right people to the right job; B) The interviewers' acceptance of these candidates.
Target 2005	1. % of targets in the action plans for 2005 achieved; Red < 80%, Yellow 80%, Green > 80%. 2. % of EVPs/SVPs have evaluated progress according to plan from OA (combined SVPs); Red <95%, Yellow 95–99%; Green 100%.	1. 80% 2. 100% 3. When JTC has relevant candidates for vacant positions, 90% of those vacant positions must be filled by a JTC candidate.	1. Target >= 80% 2. Target = 100%; Evaluation done according to templates from Corporate Responsibility Management. 3. When JTC has relevant candidates for vacant positions, 90% of those vacant positions must be filled by a JTC candidate.

Figure 9.8 Cascading of Balanced Scorecard 2005 – Support diversity

Source: Internal documents provided by Eric Drapé, SVP Diabetes Finished Products

which new jobs are created abroad, not in Denmark. The Job Transfer Centre assists Novo Nordisk employees in those units that are facing staffing changes to find a new job within, or outside, Novo Nordisk.

The third CSF (Figure 9.9) is to ensure talent development. Similar to the previous CSF, the use and number of KPIs is consistently applied throughout the organization. Specifically, two KPIs are used. The first is the utilization of talent pools with respect to the filling of new or vacant VP positions.

	Operations	**Product Supply**	**Diabetes Finished Products**
KPI	1. Utilization of talent pools – % of VP positions filled from talent pools. 2. Employee perception of development based on eVoice survey (development theme).	1. Utilization of talent pools – % of VP positions filled from talent pools. 2. Employee perception of development based on eVoice.	1. Utilization of talent pools – % of VP positions filled from talent pools. 2. Employee perception of development based on eVoice.
KPI Definition	1. VP positions (new or vacant) filled from talent pools. 2. Percentage of units score.	1. VP positions (new or vacant) filled from talent pools. 2. Units to score an average of >= 3.0 on the mandatory eVoice theme 'development of people'.	1. VP positions (new or vacant) filled from talent pools. 2. Percentage of units score 3.0 or above on the mandatory eVoice theme 'development of people'.
Target 2005	1. % VPs filled from talent pools. Red <55%, Yellow 55–60%, Green >60%.	1. 60% 2. 85%	1. Target >= 60% 2. Target = 85%

Figure 9.9 Cascading of Balanced Scorecard 2005 – Ensure talent development

Source: Internal documents provided by Eric Drapé, SVP Diabetes Finished Products

The second KPI is the result of the section of questions on an annual employee survey (eVoice), which aims to gauge perceptions of employee development.

As a SVP, Eric is responsible for the Balanced Scorecard for his business unit, and he believes that it is an effective management tool:

> The primary benefit [of the Balanced Scorecard] is to secure that people are aligned to the strategic goals of the company, and that they are not working for something which is not necessary to work for. We have full alignment, and that's very convenient and comfortable.[25]

Eric is responsible for the 2005 DFP Balanced Scorecard, which has 23 KPIs: three in Finance, eight in Business Processes, eight in People and Organizations, and four in Customers and Society (Figure 9.10 illustrates the CSFs, CSF rationale and KPIs for DFP's 2005 Balanced Scorecard). There is no formal cascading of this Balanced Scorecard to the seven VPs. Nevertheless, each site is responsible for, and evaluated on, the majority of KPIs that are in the DFP Balanced Scorecard (each site is evaluated on approximately 20 KPIs).

The formal monitoring of the sites is done on a monthly basis. Specifically, data on all KPIs are calculated and updated into Novo Nordisk's IT system (PEIS), and each site manager must prepare a monthly report that explains any deviations from targets. Additionally, any deviation that is significantly large (gaining a red designation in the system) must be answered with a specific action plan. Eric also has informal discussions with his VPs every one to two months. The purpose of these

FINANCE		
CSF	**CSF – Rationale**	**KPI**
Realise growth in operating profit	Secure industry competitive growth	Operating Profit
Ensure competitive ROIC – Working Capital and Investments	Ensure industry competitive return on invested capital	Inventory
Investments	Ensure investment management	Investments

BUSINESS PROCESSES		
CSF	**CSF – Rationale**	**KPI**
Improve productivity in DFP	Secure cost efficiency in production	Output vs. cost (unit costs) Approval of batch records Reduction in number of NCs
Timely and efficient execution of investment portfolio	Critical to increase production capacity in future demand and to improve productivity	Progress on major investments projects
Ensure successful implementation of IT projects	Successful implementation and use of IT	IT project milestones
Improve quality management focus in all business processes	Quality issues and documentation will be subject to increasing attention from both customers and authorities	% of non-conformity reports approved Audit NC timeliness Inspection readiness

PEOPLE AND ORGANIZATION		
CSF	**CSF – Rationale**	**KPI**
Increase internationalization	Support the globalization of Novo Nordisk	Internationalization initiatives carried out
Support diversity/social responsibility	Enhance and promote innovation, attraction and reputation	Equal opportunity implementation Evaluated progress achieved JTC process is running smoothly
Ensure talent development	To ensure specialist and leadership capabilities that will support and drive growth	Utilization of talent pools Employee perception of development
Ensure performance management	Improve individual performance and alignment with overall business goals All units with absence due to illness >5% have to decrease this absence	Implement uniform global performance management system Absence due to illness

(*Continued*)

CUSTOMERS AND SOCIETY		
CSF	CSF – Rationale	KPI
Ensure superior customer satisfaction – Improve production quality	Product Quality is a critical parameter for achieving customer satisfaction	Customer complaint
Ensure environmental, social and ethical performance	Help the organization to ensure social, environmental, and bioethical performance	EPI Performance
Ensure timely and efficient delivery to market	In order to be the world's leading diabetes care company we have to have products ready to meet customer demands Launch of Levemir®	Affiliate inventory level Levemir® finished product production

Figure 9.10 Diabetes Finished Products – 2005 Balanced Scorecard

Source: Internal document provided by Eric Drapé, SVP Diabetes Finished Products

meetings is to gauge how performance is proceeding. In addition to the monthly monitoring and informal discussions, Eric meets each of his site managers twice a year as part of a formal Business Review. The purpose of these meetings is to discuss the monthly action plans and the overall site's Balanced Scorecard.

In addition to being evaluated on the Balanced Scorecard, Eric's (and his VPs') bonus compensation is also tied to the Balanced Scorecard performance. Figure 9.11 provides Eric's Performance Index for 2005. As shown, Eric is compensated based on 13 KPIs (two in Finance, three in Customers, six in Processes and two in People and Organization). The weighting scheme works as follows: if Eric achieves each target, he receives a score for that KPI of 100. If he exceeds the target, the score for the particular KPI is greater than 100; if he does not achieve the target, the score for the particular KPI is less than 100. Each KPI score is multiplied by its respective percentage weight (e.g., 15% for Investments). The achieved index score is equal to the sum of the weighted scores across all KPIs. For Eric, the amount of bonus he receives is 50% dependent on his achieved index score and 50% dependent on the achieved index score of Product Supply. For each VP in DFP, their bonus calculation is similar, except each VP only has 10 KPIs influencing their bonus calculation. Of these 10, some are mandatory (across all sites) and some are voluntary (agreed between Eric and each VP). The voluntary KPIs tend to be related more to social objectives, because they are geared towards addressing issues that reflect the local environment. The payment of the bonus to each VP is 50% dependent on their achieved index score and 50% dependent on the achieved index for DFP. Finally, Novo Nordisk uses stretch targets so that to receive a full bonus Eric (and his VPs) need an achieved index score of 105 (that is, if targets are only hit (i.e., not exceeded), only a 50% bonus is paid).

CONCLUSION

As illustrated, Novo Nordisk is prime example of one organization that includes sustainability as an integrated part of its strategy, and attempts to consider sustainability in all its business decisions. To help achieve this aim, the company has adopted the Novo Nordisk Way of Management

Diabetes Finished Products						
		YTD Dec 2005 Results			Weighted	
	Weights	**Target**	**Expected**	Index	perf.	Perf. +/-
Finance	40.0				40.0	0.0
Investments	15.0	1,762	1,762	100	15.0	-
Operating costs*	25.0	2,539	2,539	100	25.0	-
Customers	30.0				30.0	0.0
Stock outs	5.0	10	10	100	5.0	-
EPI performance	5.0	100	100	100	5.0	-
Production output **						
- 3ml Penfill, fill	10.0	345	345	100	10.0	-
- disposables pack (NL,FP,IL)	5.0	164	164	100	5.0	-
- vials pack	5.0	102	102	100	5.0	-
Processes	20.0				20.0	0.0
NN248 timeliness ***	2.5	100	100	100	2.5	
Unit cost	2.5	100	100	100	2.5	-
Number of actual recalls	5.0	4	4	100	5.0	-
FDA Inspection readiness	2.5	100	100	100	2.5	
QAP	2.5	80%	80%	100	2.5	-
COGS20, volume/fte	5.0	100	100	100	5.0	-
People & Organisation	10.0				10.0	0.0
Decrease in absence	5.0	10	10	100	5.0	-
JTC	5.0	90	90	100	5.0	-
Total	100.0				100.0	0.0

* Operating profit target is AB05 plus logbooks and approved target corrections.
** Target to be corrected downwards if reduced demand in local markets create excess capacity
*** Final product specification. Target is August. If target is reached in September = index 66.6,
October = index 33.3, November or later = index 0. If target is reached in July = index 133.3,
June = index 166.6, and May or sooner index 200.

Figure 9.11 Eric Drapé's Performance Index 2005

Source: Internal document provided by Eric Drapé, SVP Diabetes Finished Products

as one of its primary operating tools. Included in the Novo Nordisk Way of Management are three pillars that should help to operationalize Novo Nordisk's corporate objectives: the facilitators, the annual (sustainability) reporting and the Balanced Scorecard. The significant question that remains, however, is to what extent each of these pillars is effective in influencing behaviour at the operational level.

ACKNOWLEDGEMENTS

We sincerely want to thank manager Susanne Stormer for her generous invitation into Novo Nordisk A/S and for helping us collecting data and checking facts and figures for this case study. From Novo Nordisk we also want to thank Lito Valencia, business analyst in Finance and Business Integration, Hanne Schou-Rode, VP of Knowledge, IT and Quality in Corporate Stakeholder Relations, and Eric Drapé, SVP in Diabetes Finished Products for their time and constructive reflections. And we appreciate the valuable input from Professor Niels Mygind, Copenhagen Business School, Stephanie Robertson, Lene Hougaard Pedersen, Henrik Nielsen, research assistant at Copenhagen Business School, and Henrik Melgaard. This case study builds on a paper that was published by Palgrave Macmillan (Kakabadse and Morsing (eds)) in 2006 and we thank Palgrave Macmillan for support to publish this revised version. Finally, we gratefully acknowledge financial support from Copenhagen Business School, London Business School and the European Academy of Business in Society (EABIS).

NOTES

1. The case is intended to be used as a basis for class discussion rather than to illustrate either effective or ineffective handling of an administrative situation.
2. Lars Rebien Sørensen, CEO, Novo Nordisk, Take action: Make the triple bottom line your business, May 2003, p. 2, www.novonordisk.com.
3. ACCA and CorporateRegister.com (2004) Towards transparency: progress on global sustainability reporting, p. 8, www.corporateregister.com.
4. Novo Nordisk A/S, Annual Report 2004, pp. 49, 60, 98, http://www.novonordisk.com/sustainability/sustainability.
5. Novo Nordisk A/S, Annual Report 2004. p. 38, http://www.novonordisk.com/sustainability/sustainability; and Thompson Financial Datastream.
6. Novo Nordisk A/S, Annual Report 2004, p. 108, http://www.novonordisk.com/sustainability/sustainability.
7. For more than 30 years it has been mandatory to have employees represented at the board of directors in Danish companies, see for example, Rose, 2004, pp. 21–32.
8. Novo Nordisk A/S, Annual Report 2004. p. 18, http://www.novonordisk.com/sustainability/sustainability.
9. For example: 'This is Mads Øvlisen, the former CEO of Novo Nordisk and one of the most admired individuals in Danish business. As he retired in 2000 after 19 years as chief executive officer in Novo Nordisk, he had increased the number of employees from 4000 to 15 000. He has won prizes for his management style of trustworthiness, and he has made Novo Nordisk synonymous with corporate social responsibility. But he has remained the approachable Mads with tucked-up sleeves. Øvlisen is a success, a living legend, a walking lump of gold' (*Euroman*, 2005, p. 46).
10. Novo Nordisk, Annual Report 2003, p. 2.
11. Novo Nordisk, Corporate Stakeholder Relations' Strategic Plan, 2004, slide 2.
12. See Novo Nordisk History, p. 15; available at: http://www.novonordisk.com/about_us/history/milestones_in_nn_history.asp.
13. Novo Nordisk, Corporate Stakeholder Relations' Strategic Plan, 2004, p. 13.
14. Quote from CEO Henrik Gürtler, Novo A/S, 2 June, 2005.
15. Novo Nordisk Way of Management: a short interpretation guide to the fundamentals, preface, 1997.
16. Novo Nordisk (1998) The facilitation process: charter of standards, procedures and guidelines, www.novonordisk.com.
17. Novo Nordisk (1998) The facilitation process: charter of standards, procedures and guidelines, www.novonordisk.com.
18. These reports are available at http://www.novonordisk.com/sustainability/sustainability.
19. For further accolades, refer to http://www.novonordisk.com/sustainability.

20. eVoice is an annual survey that asks a minimum of 48 questions around eight mandatory themes (Vision and values, Development of employees, Employee engagement, Equal opportunity, Stress and workload, Quality mindset, Performance orientation and Internationalization). In addition, each unit and project group can include up to an additional 72 questions from 12 themes (Customer orientations, Winning culture, Working climate, Empowerment, Cooperation across functions, Communication, Innovation, Planning and execution, Working conditions, Novo Nordisk policies, Best practice and Reporting).

21. ISO 14001 is an environmental management standard with auditing tools and procedures.

22. Quote from Susanne Stormer, 19 June, 2005.

23. Novo Nordisk, Corporate Stakeholder Relations' Strategic Plan, 2004, p. 13.

24. Information supplied by Eric Drapé.

25. Interview with Eric Drapé on 26 October, 2004.

REFERENCES

Berlingske Nyhedsmagasin (*Danish Business Week*) (2005), **13**, 29 April–13 June.

Crook, C. (2005) A survey of corporate social responsibility, *The Economist*, 22 January.

Elkington, J. (1999) *Cannibals With Forks. The Triple Bottom Line of 21st Century Business*, Capstone Publishing, Oxford.

Euroman, March 2005, *Euroman*, Copenhagen, www.euroman.dk.

Rose, C. (2004) Medarbejderrepræsentation i danske bestyrelser. Center for Kreditret- og Kapitalmarkedsret, Copenhagen Business School Press.

World Commission on Environment and Development (1987) *Our Common Future*. Oxford University Press, Oxford.

CHAPTER TEN

From Grace to Disgrace: The Rise and Fall of Arthur Andersen[1]

N. Craig Smith, INSEAD and Michelle Quirk, London Business School

INTRODUCTION

On 15 June, 2002, Arthur Andersen LLP ('Andersen') made history by becoming the first accounting firm to be convicted of a felony, when a US district court jury found the firm guilty of obstruction of justice. The conviction related to events that had taken place between October and November 2001, both prior to and immediately following notice of an impending Securities & Exchange Commission ('SEC') investigation into Andersen's former star client Enron. These events included the following:

- The large-scale destruction of Enron-related documents that Andersen publicly announced had taken place (the original subject of the indictment).[2]
- An internal e-mail sent by an Andersen lawyer suggesting that specific alterations be made to a memo relating to earnings advice given to Enron (see Exhibit 10.1). This memo was a key determinant of Andersen's ultimate conviction.

It was not the first time that Andersen had found itself in legal trouble. Indeed, over the preceding years, each of the Big Five accounting firms had been ordered to pay out millions of dollars to settle shareholder lawsuits filed as a result of lost value from accounting restatements (see Figure 10.1 for a summary of the largest such settlements). However, it soon became apparent that the SEC regarded Andersen as a 'serial offender' and, in the face of public (and political) outcry following Enron's collapse, was determined to make an example out of Andersen.

Enron's own problems had become evident on 16 October, 2001, when the company announced it was taking a US$544 million after-tax charge against earnings related to one of its off-balance sheet partnerships (a partnership created and managed by Enron's CFO, Andrew Fastow) and was reducing shareholders' equity by US$1.2 billion (Enron's reported total assets in 2000 were US$66 billion). On 22 October, the SEC opened an inquiry into possible conflicts of interest related to dealings between Enron and its subsidiary partnerships. This inquiry was upgraded to a formal investigation on 31 October. In November, Enron further announced that it was restating its accounts for the period 1997–2001 due to accounting errors relating to transactions with other off-balance sheet entities. Enron's downward spiral continued and on 2 December, 2001, Enron filed for protection from creditors and became the largest corporate bankruptcy in US history.

EXHIBIT 10.1   E-MAIL FROM ANDERSEN LAWYER (NANCY TEMPLE) TO DAVID DUNCAN

To: David B. Duncan
CC: Michael C. Odom@ANDERSEN WO: Richard Corgci@ANDERSEN WO
BCC:
Date: 10/16/2001 08:39 PM
From: Nancy A. Temple
Subject: Re: Press Release draft
Attachment: ATT&ICIQ: 3rd qtr press release memo.doc

Dave - Here are a few suggested comments for consideration.

I recommend deleting reference to consultation with the legal group and deleting my name on the memo. Reference to the legal group consultation arguably is a waiver of attorney-client privileged advice and if my name is mentioned it increases the chances that I might be a witness, which I prefer to avoid.

I suggested deleting some language that might suggest we have concluded the release is misleading.

In light of the 'non-recurring' characterization, the lack of any suggestion that this characterization is not in accordance with GAAP, and the lack of income statements in accordance with GAAP, I will consult further within the legal group as to whether we should do anything more to protect ourselves from potential Section 10A issues.

Nancy

Source: www.HoustonChronicle.com

The impact of Enron's collapse was both profound and widespread: Enron's share price plunged from a 52-week high of US$43 on 13 August, to less than US$1 by the end of 2001 (see http://bigcharts.marketwatch.com); thousands of Enron employees were left facing retirement without retirement funds; questions were raised about Enron's political connections with the Bush administration and the Blair UK government; and global banks, investment analysts and industry 'experts' found their reputations seriously tarnished as their involvement in the affair was discovered.

In turn, Andersen's indictment and subsequent conviction in the wake of Enron's collapse effectively rang the death knell for one of the largest and most well respected accounting firms in the world. Even before the verdict in June 2002, Andersen in the United States was a shadow of its former self, having lost 690 of its 2311 public company clients and 17 000 of its 27 000 employees since January of the same year (*The Accountant*, 2002). Soon after the verdict was read, Andersen stated that it would stop auditing publicly-held companies by 31 August. Although promising to appeal the conviction, it was nonetheless a sad end to an audit business that Arthur Andersen had started with such good intentions almost 90 years earlier.

Firm	Client	Settlement* ($US million)	Settlement Date
Ernst & Young	Cendant	335.0	12/99
	Informix	34.0	6/99
Arthur Andersen	Sunbeam	110.0	5/01
	Waste Management	95.0	6/01
	Colonial Realty	90.0	7/97
	DeLorean Motor	63.0**	5/99
PwC	MicroStrategy	55.0	5/01
KPMG	Piper Jaffray***	13.9	4/00

Figure 10.1 The biggest settlements of shareholder lawsuits

* The largest settlements paid by accounting firms to settle shareholder lawsuits filed as a result of lost value from accounting restatements
** Includes US$35 million settlement reached in 1998 with the British Government
*** Institutional Government Income Portfolio

Source: Public Accounting Report, Atlanta: David Ward and Loren Steffy *'How Andersen Went Wrong',* Bloomberg, May 2002

ANDERSEN

In 1913, a young certified public accountant named Arthur Andersen, together with fellow accountant Clarence DeLany, set up a small auditing firm in downtown Chicago. When DeLany left the firm in 1918, the firm was renamed Andersen & Company.

Andersen hired top university graduates and taught them to 'think straight and talk straight'. This became a mantra within Andersen and the firm demanded the same behaviour from its clients. After the Wall Street crash of 1929 and the ensuing depression, Andersen led the way in rebuilding Americans' faith in business as he continued to insist on honest accounting and eliminating conflicts of interest (Babington and Rigby, 2002a). Public accountants should be answerable to the investing public, Andersen argued in his many writings, not to the companies they audit (Babington and Rigby, 2002b).

When Andersen died in 1947, his 'think straight and talk straight' culture was deeply infused throughout the firm and continued under the leadership of Leonard Spacek. Business continued to grow and through the 1970s Andersen expanded its international reach and became the world's largest professional services firm in 1979.[3]

Andersen was perceived as a market leader, a firm that set the standard for honest and law-abiding accounting – 'people thought there was the Andersen way – and the wrong way'(Babington and Rigby, 2002b). Inside the firm, the culture was both a proud and a cohesive one. Andersen fostered a 'one-firm philosophy' – even as the firm expanded globally, employees were bound into the firm through the many team building and morale raising exercises as well as the reported 135 hours

Firm	Worldwide Revenues ($US billion)	US Revenue ($US billion)	Auditing	Tax Compliance*	General Consulting Services**
Deloitte & Touche	12.4	6.1	33%	21%	35%
Pricewaterhouse Coopers	19.8	8.1	35%	20%	31%
Ernst & Young	9.9	4.5	58%	39%	–
KPMG	11.7	3.2	62%	38%	–
Arthur Andersen	9.3	4.3	43%	31%	26%

Figure 10.2 The money trail – revenues of The Big Five, 2001

For the fiscal year ended 31 August 2001. Percentages are based on US revenues and do not include M&A advising, valuation or other sources of revenue
* Includes some tax consulting services
** Includes computer systems, business management and financing

Source: Public Accounting Report, Atlanta: David Ward and Loren Steffy *'How Andersen Went Wrong',* Bloomberg, May 2002

a year training that each employee received (Arnold, 2002). This trend towards conformity (and particularly the training component) gave rise to the company moniker 'the Marine Corps of Accounting' and led many outsiders to label Andersen employees 'Androids' (*BBC Money Programme,* 2002a).

The merger and acquisitions boom of the 1980s represented a crucial change in the way that accounting firms operated, with the realization that the fees generated by the largely 'bread and butter' audit work paled in comparison to the potential fees to be earned from management consulting. The Big Five firms (Andersen, Deloitte, KPMG, PwC and Ernst & Young) started aggressively undercutting each other on price for auditing services, treating them as a springboard for the more lucrative consulting contracts (see Figure 10.2).

By 1988, Andersen Consulting (Andersen's consulting arm) was generating around 40% of the combined company profits and a rift developed between the consulting and accounting arms of the firm.[4] This situation was not helped when the accountants themselves formed a consultancy arm aimed at small businesses.[5] A bitter court battle ensued and the International Chamber of Commerce ordered Andersen Consulting to either pay US$15 billion in compensation for withholding fees or pay US$1 billion in compensation and discontinue using the Andersen name. In 2000, Andersen Consulting opted for the latter and spent US$175 million re-inventing itself as Accenture. This 'divorce' pitched Andersen down from the top to the fifth largest among the Big Five accounting firms.

By 2001 Andersen had grown from a small one-office firm in downtown Chicago, to a leading professional services firm with 85 000 staff spread throughout 390 offices in 84 countries, together bringing in US$9.3 billion in revenues (Arnold, 2002).

ENRON[6]

> Enron has accomplished more in its 15-year history than many of the world's best-known companies have in a century. Why? Because Enron employees have an insatiable drive for trying the unexpected, thinking the unthinkable, and accomplishing the unattainable. We have set a new course for energy and communications in the new millennium.[7]

In 1985, Houston Natural Gas and InterNorth, a natural gas company based in Omaha, Nebraska, merged to form Enron Corp. ('Enron'), an interstate and intrastate natural gas pipeline company with 37 000 miles of pipe. Soon after the merger, Kenneth Lay, an energy economist who had previously held both academic and government positions, became Enron's chairman and chief executive.

Over the next 15 years, Enron was to grow from a small regional natural gas company to a global energy-trading giant, the seventh largest corporation in the United States by reported revenues. The company became the darling of Wall St and investors and analysts piled praise, bullish appraisals and money on Enron and its dynamic management for its consistent innovation and growth.

Deregulation (for which Enron had been a prominent proponent), the Gulf War and the Internet boom all played their part in Enron's spectacular rise to prominence, a rise that saw Enron's share price reach a high of over US$90 in August 2000. Much of Enron's success was attributed to the decisions of Enron's senior management, particularly Lay and Jeff Skilling, who was brought onboard in 1990 from his position as head of McKinsey & Company's energy practice.

Skilling believed that Enron could profit from trading futures in gas contracts – effectively betting against future movements in the price of gas-generated energy. Although deregulation had arguably opened the industry to competition, it had also brought price volatility to the market, and when Enron offered to buy and sell tomorrow's gas at a fixed price today, many suppliers and consumers seized the opportunity. Buoyed by its initial success, Enron expanded its trading operations into a myriad of other energy-related (and some non-energy related) products including oil, coal, emissions and even weather.

A further string to Enron's bow was EnronOnline, an on-line trading platform that was officially launched in November 1999. EnronOnline simplified the trade of Enron's standardized contracts so that all a customer had to do was log on and 'point and click'. By July 2001, on-line trade had increased to over 5000 transactions (worth US$3 billion) a day. EnronOnline was a public relations coup and a clear example of why *Fortune* magazine consistently selected Enron as the most innovative company in the United States from 1996 to 2001 (Fusaro and Miller, 2002).

Internally, Skilling championed what became known as the 'rank or yank' appraisal policy for employees. During Enron's six-monthly performance reviews, each employee was ranked on a scale of 1–5. Those in the upper ranks (4–5) enjoyed bonuses and promotion, while those in the bottom 15% (category 1) could lose their jobs. Employees were given until the next review to improve their performance, however, most chose to accept severance packages rather than risk the chance of being 'yanked' at a later date. In addition, employees in categories 2 and 3 were put on notice that they were at risk of being yanked in the future – this effectively meant that 50% of Enron's staff were at serious risk of losing their jobs at any given time (Fusaro and Miller, 2002, p. 51).

According to former Enron employees, this rating system led to a 'super-charged' competitive culture, a culture that incentivized employees to make as much money as possible for the company (*BBC Money Programme*, 2002b). Indeed, it was Lay himself who best described Enron's view of its employees, when in a statement to shareholders in the 1999 Enron Annual Report, he stated that 'individuals are empowered to do what they think is best . . . we do, however, keep a keen eye on how prudent they are . . . we insist on results' (Fusaro and Miller, 2002).

With annual reported global revenues of US$100 billion and earnings up 40% over three years, 2000 was a great year for Enron and for Enron executives and directors, whose compensation and bonuses allowed them a life of undreamed of luxury. However, this was not to continue indefinitely. On 14 August, 2001, Skilling resigned as CEO, citing personal reasons. His departure came as a shock to investors, who began to worry that all was not as it seemed.

On 16 October, an accounting oversight relating to an off-balance sheet partnership forced Enron to disclose a US$544 million third-quarter after-tax loss and a US$1.2 billion reduction in shareholder equity. The SEC announced an inquiry into a possible conflict of interest relating to transactions between Enron and its subsidiary partnerships (Enron's CFO Andrew Fastow was also managing a number of these companies), and on 31 October, the SEC inquiry was upgraded to a formal investigation.

Enron admitted that it had overstated earnings by almost US$600 million since 1997 and was forced to restate profits for that period. Concerns about the company's financial problems continued to drive Enron's share price down. At the same time, Enron employees, whose retirement plan (401(k)) accounts were filled with Enron stock, were unable to cash out due to a lock out period imposed after Enron had changed its 401(k) administrator. By the time the ban was lifted, Enron's share price had fallen to less than US$10 and thousands of Enron employees had watched their retirement funds virtually disappear.

On 8 November, Enron reached agreement to enter into a merger with rival energy company Dynergy. However, on 28 November, Dynergy pulled out of the deal, claiming that Enron had breached a number of warranties and covenants in the merger agreement (*Platts Energy Economist*, 2002). Standard & Poors downgraded Enron to a B-minus status, causing a liquidity crisis for Enron as its access to some US$3 billion in cheap short-term money was lost (*Platts Energy Economist*, 2002). Less than a week later Enron was forced to file for protection from creditors in a Chapter 11 bankruptcy application. The New York Stock Exchange suspended trading of Enron shares on 15 January 2002, and moved to delist the stock.

BACK TO BASICS: WHAT ACTUALLY HAPPENED?

> Oh what tangled webs we weave, when first we practice to deceive.
>
> Sir Walter Scott, *Marmion*

The roots of the legal case against Andersen were to be found in the growing financial problems within Enron during 2001, problems largely tied up in the web of off-balance sheet partnerships created by Enron CFO Andrew Fastow. Prior to Enron's bankruptcy in December 2001, approximately

3500 of these partnerships were responsible for keeping between US$15–20 billion of debt off Enron's books (Cornwell, 2002).

However, Enron had long been pushing the interpretation of accounting rules to its limits and as Enron's auditor for over 16 years, Andersen found itself increasingly caught up in the emerging scandal.

Enron: A History of Creative Interpretation?

> Enron is a company that deals with everyone with absolute integrity. We play by all the rules; we stand by our word. We want people to leave a transaction with Enron thinking that they've been dealt with in the highest possible way as far as integrity and truthfulness.
> in extract from Enron promotional video (BBC Money Programme 2002b) Lay, Kenneth

During 1990, fuelled by the energy shortages created by the Gulf War, Enron's earnings soared. As growth slowed through 1991, Enron bosses had to find new ways to meet aggressive growth targets. Using ambiguous accounting rules in increasingly creative ways was to become the tool for achieving Enron's earnings objectives.

The problem of how to value assets and when to realize associated gains and losses was not a new one. The traditional approach was conservative accounting; recognizing a decrease in value when it occurred and an increase in value once the asset was sold. In contrast, under the mark-to-market ('MTM') approach (known as 'Current Cost Accounting' in the United Kingdom), assets were regularly revalued, with any increase or decrease in value recorded in the income statement and balance sheet for the relevant financial year.

The problem with MTM accounting was that in the absence of a price-setting market for the asset, values were ambiguous (US GAAP required such assets to be accounted for on a 'fair value' basis). This ambiguity certainly existed with Enron, where there was no objective way to price the various (and often 'first to market') commodity trades that made up much of Enron's business. In response to this ambiguity, Enron created a range of complex forward pricing models based on internally generated assumptions in order to value the thousands of (largely intangible) assets on its books (Fusaro and Miller, 2002). Enron was thus creating a potential monster: the ability to manufacture seemingly solid (albeit mostly non-cash) profits, which Wall Street was willing to capitalize with dot.com growth multiples of 40 times expected earnings (*Platts Energy Economist*, 2002).

The standard to which company auditors were required to measure the application of MTM accounting in any particular case was that of 'reasonableness', a term that clearly left significant scope for interpretation. As Enron's auditors, Andersen was effectively the primary judge of what was to be considered 'reasonable' and what was not.

One of Enron's first deals involving MTM accounting occurred in 1991 when Enron brokered a 20-year deal to supply a power station in New York State. Rather than reporting profits on a year-by-year basis, Enron booked all 20 years' worth of *estimated* profits in one financial year. As one commentator observed, this was equivalent to Enron 'placing a huge bet and telling the world they'd already won' (*BBC Money Programme*, 2002b).

Apart from the fact that the use of MTM accounting was intended for much shorter term application, Enron's interpretation was all the more aggressive because it used its own estimates about expected revenues and profits, estimates that were often arbitrary or made up. Enron also failed to disclose to the SEC that its use of MTM accounting had a material impact on annual earnings (in fact, the New York power deal had contributed almost 50% of Enron's profit growth for the year) (*BBC Money Programme*, 2002b). Nonetheless, Andersen signed off on the accounts, analysts recommended the stock and Enron's share price and bonus pool continued to rise.

As Enron executives became addicted to rapid growth, their eyes turned to new sources of revenue. Trading in energy commodities was an attractive option. Although industry regulators considered introducing controls over these new and largely speculative markets, they ultimately decided not to interfere, leaving the market players to police themselves.

In the meantime, Enron bosses in the United Kingdom were starting to feel the pressure from their US bosses to 'tweak the knob' (*BBC Money Programme*, 2002b). By changing various accounting assumptions, Enron was able to show sustained earnings and profit growth, earning Enron executives tens of millions of dollars in bonuses and share sales.

By the late 1990s, the situation was getting more precarious. Despite appearances, Enron was facing ballooning debts and the fear that the facade might crumble was very real (it was only the presumption of credit-worthiness that allowed Enron to act as counterparty in its many derivatives trades (*Platts Energy Economist*, 2002)). Persuading the ratings agencies that the huge debts being incurred were really 'non-recourse' to Enron was critical and became a single-minded preoccupation for Lay and Skilling (*Platts Energy Economist*, 2002). Rather than face reality, Andrew Fastow suggested an extremely aggressive alternative: by creating a series of off-balance sheet partnerships, Enron's debts could effectively be concealed from the world at large. These partnerships were approved by both Fastow's bosses and by Enron's Board of Directors, who had to waive Enron's code of conduct to get around the potential conflict of interest caused by putting Fastow in charge of the subsidiary partnerships (see Exhibit 10.2 for extract from Enron's Code of Ethics) (*New York Times*, 2002).

EXHIBIT 10.2 EXTRACTS FROM ENRON'S CODE OF ETHICS

Foreword

As officers and employees of Enron Corp., its subsidiaries, and its affiliated companies, we are responsible for conducting the business affairs of the companies in accordance with all applicable laws and in a moral and honest manner.

To be sure that we understand what is expected of us, Enron has adopted certain policies, with the approval of the Board of Directors, which are set forth in this booklet. . . .

We want to be proud of Enron and to know that it enjoys a reputation for fairness and honesty and that it is respected. Gaining such respect is one aim of our advertising and public relations activities, but no matter how effective they may be, Enron's reputation finally depends on its people, on you and me. Let's keep that reputation high.

July 1, 2000

Kenneth L. Lay
Chairman and Chief
Executive Officer

Conflicts of Interests, Investments, and
Outside Business Interests of Officers and Employees

Employees of the Company have inquired from time to time as to the propriety of their association with, or the investment of their personal funds in, business enterprises similar in character to certain activities of the Company. In response, the Company has established certain principles for the guidance of officers and employees with respect to personal business and investment interests.

The primary consideration of each full-time (regular as well as temporary) officer and employee should be the fact that the employer is entitled to expect of such person complete loyalty to the best interests of the Company and the maximum application of skill, talent, education, etc., to the discharge of his or her job responsibilities, without any reservations. Therefore, it follows that no full-time officer or employee should:

a. Engage in any outside activity or enterprise which could interfere in any way with job performance;

b. Make investments or perform services for his or her own or related interest in any enterprise under any circumstances where, by reason of the nature of the business conducted by such enterprise, there is, or could be, a disparity or conflict of interest between the officer or employee and the Company; or

c. Own an interest in or participate, directly or indirectly, in the profits of any other entity which does business with or is a competitor of the Company, unless such ownership or participation has been previously disclosed in writing to the Chairman of the Board and Chief Executive Officer of Enron Corp. and such officer has determined that such interest or participation does not adversely affect the best interests of the Company.

Notwithstanding any provision to the contrary in this Policy on Investments, securities of publicly owned corporations which are regularly traded on the open market may be owned without disclosure if they are not purchased as a result of confidential knowledge about the Company's operations, relations, business, or negotiations with such corporations.

If an investment of personal funds by an officer or employee in a venture or enterprise will not entail personal services or managerial attention, and if there appears to be no conflict or disparity of interest involved, the following procedure nevertheless shall be followed if all

(*Continued*)

EXHIBIT 10.2 (*Continued*)

or any part of the business of the venture or enterprise is identical with, or similar or directly related to, that conducted by the Company, or if such business consists of the furnishing of goods or services of a type utilized to a material extent by the Company:

a. The officer or employee desiring to make such investment shall submit in writing to the Chairman of the Board and Chief Executive Officer of Enron Corp. a brief summary of relevant facts; and

b. The Chairman of the Board and Chief Executive Officer of Enron Corp. shall consider carefully the summary of relevant facts, and if he concludes that there appears to be no probability of any conflict of interest arising out of the proposed investment, the officer or employee shall be so notified and may then make the proposed investment in full reliance upon the findings of the Chairman of the Board and Chief Executive Officer of Enron Corp.

In the event the Chairman of the Board and Chief Executive Officer of Enron Corp. should desire to make such an investment, he may do so only upon approval of the majority of a quorum of the Executive Committee of the Board of Directors of Enron Corp., other than himself at any regular or special meeting of such a Committee.

Every officer and employee shall be under a continuing duty to report, in the manner set forth above, any situation where by reason of economic or other interest in an enterprise there is then present the possibility of a conflict or disparity of interest between the officer or employee and the Company. This obligation includes but is not limited to (1) any existing personal investment at the date of promulgation of this policy, (2) any existing personal investment at the time of employment of any officer or employee by the Company, and (3) any existing personal investment, whether or not previously approved, which may become in conflict with the provisions of this policy because of changes in the business of the Company or changes in the business of the outside enterprise in which investment has been made.

In the event of a finding by the Chairman of the Board and Chief Executive Officer of Enron Corp. (or by the Executive Committee of the Board of Directors of Enron Corp., if applicable) that a material conflict or disparity of interest does exist with respect to any existing personal investment or an officer or employee, then, upon being so notified, the officer or employee involved shall immediately divest himself or herself of such interest and shall notify the Chairman and Chief Executive Officer of Enron Corp. (or the Executive Committee, if applicable) in writing that he or she has done so.

Source: www.thesmokinggun.com

Special Purpose Entities

The use of Special Purpose Entities (SPEs) (sometimes known as Special Purpose Vehicles (SPVs)) was by no means a new development and had been a common mechanism for securitizing various asset portfolios for years. Asset securitization typically involved the transfer of on-balance sheet assets (such as mortgages) to a third party or a trust, who would create securities out of those assets and issue certificates or notes to investors. The cash flows from the assets (for example, mortgage repayments) were used to fund repayments to investors. Among other benefits, securitization allowed institutions such as banks the ability to transfer risk, improve financial performance ratios and access alternative funding sources.[8]

The transfer of financial assets through an SPE enabled an originator to remove assets (or a portion thereof) from its balance sheet if 'control' over those assets was surrendered. Financial Accounting Standard 140 (previously FAS125) required three tests to be satisfied to meet this 'control' threshold:[9]

- that the transferred assets (or liabilities) had been put out of reach of the transferor and its creditors (even in bankruptcy or other receivership);
- that each transferee had the right to pledge or exchange the transferred assets;
- that the transferor did not maintain effective control over the transferred assets (e.g., through an agreement allowing the transferor to repurchase or redeem the assets).

Enron's increased use of SPEs was due to its unique position in the newly deregulated energy markets – unlike a stock exchange where most trades are made directly between a buyer and a seller and the exchange merely acts as an intermediary, Enron served as the counterparty to each trade that passed through its 'market'. By Wall Street standards, however, Enron's lack of hard assets and its large debts made its position as counterparty vulnerable because of the risk that it might default on its obligations – any downgrade of its credit rating could therefore have put Enron out of business as a market maker (Fusaro and Miller, 2002, pp. 63–4).

SPEs provided the vehicle by which Enron could hedge its exposure as counterparty, entering into numerous derivative transactions with these subsidiary partnerships (most notably LJM, LJM2 and Raptors I, II and III) (Fusaro and Miller, 2002, pp. 63–4). In an interview with *CFO* magazine in mid-1999, Fastow described how almost US$1 billion in debt was kept off Enron's balance sheet through this complex and innovative arrangement – 'what we did . . . is we set up a trust, issued Enron Corp. shares into the trust and then the trust went to the capital markets and raised debt against the shares in the trust, using the shares in the trust as collateral' (Fink, 2002). Enron's use of SPEs (and MTM accounting) was disclosed in the notes to its consolidated financial statements (see Figure 10.3 for more on Enron SPEs).

The problem was that these types of transactions carried a high level of risk (that Enron's stock price and asset value could both fall – which they ultimately did). Although risk alone was not the problem, it appeared that certain loan guarantees supplied by Enron to its SPEs were triggered when Enron's stock price fell below a pre-specified level.[10] Thus, the deals were not really non-recourse to Enron at all.

In the latter stages of 2001, it was discovered that (a) two Raptor partnerships had insufficient credit to pay Enron on its hedges and (b) another SPE (Chewco) had failed to meet the 3% ownership threshold required to keep its accounts off Enron's consolidated accounts, and Enron was forced to consolidate – the complex web began to unravel. In the meantime, transactions between Enron and Fastow's partnerships had boosted Enron's reported financial results by more than US$1 billion, enriching Fastow and other managers by millions of dollars in the process (Fusaro and Miller, 2002, p. 171).

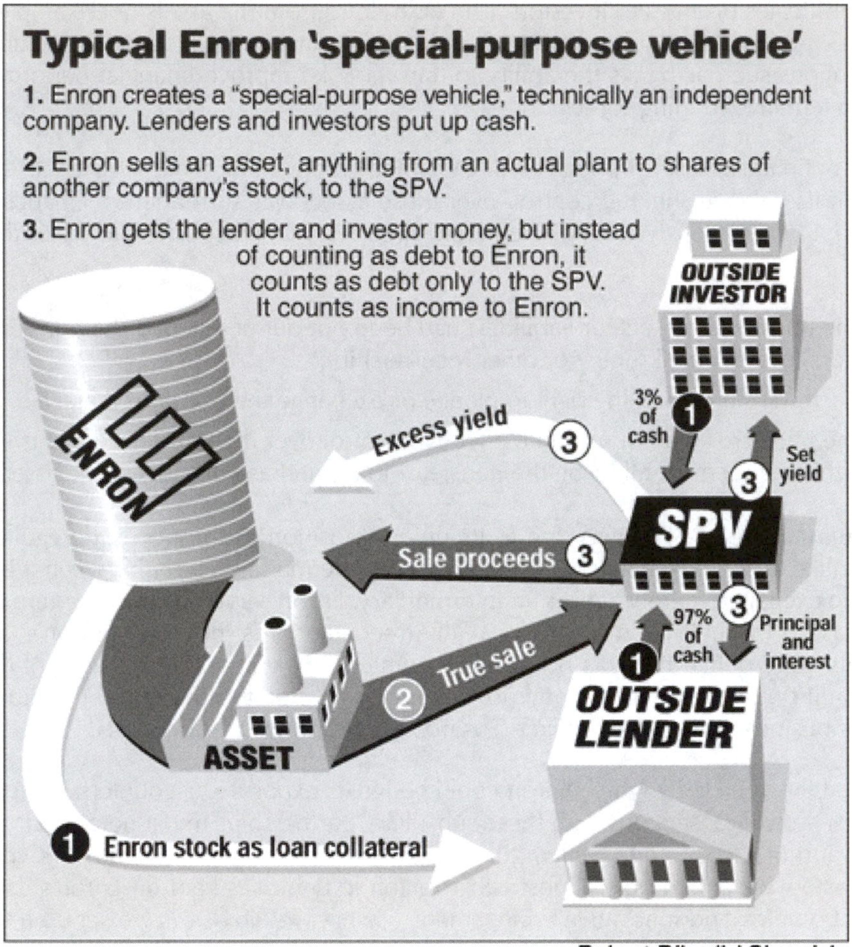

Typical Enron 'special-purpose vehicle'

1. Enron creates a "special-purpose vehicle," technically an independent company. Lenders and investors put up cash.

2. Enron sells an asset, anything from an actual plant to shares of another company's stock, to the SPV.

3. Enron gets the lender and investor money, but instead of counting as debt to Enron, it counts as debt only to the SPV. It counts as income to Enron.

OUTSIDE INVESTOR

Excess yield

SPV

Sale proceeds

3% of cash

Set yield

97% of cash

Principal and interest

True sale

ASSET

OUTSIDE LENDER

1 Enron stock as loan collateral

Robert Dibrell / Chronicle

Figure 10.3 Enron Special Purpose Entities (or Vehicles)

Source: HoustonChronicle.com

The Role of the Auditor in the Prevention and Detection of Business Fraud

When fraud is alleged or discovered within a business, the initial response is generally 'how could it have happened?' If audited financial statements were issued, the question becomes 'why didn't the auditors notice?'. The question of whose responsibility it is to prevent and detect crime has been brought sharply into focus following Enron's collapse and has sparked significant debate concerning the differences between the role of the external auditor and the public's perception of that role (sometimes referred to as the 'expectations gap').

The Auditing Standard Board issues Statements on Auditing Standards ('SAS'). One of the most important provisions governing auditors is found in Section 110 of SAS No. 1, 'Responsibilities and Functions of the Independent Auditor':

The auditor has a responsibility to plan and perform the audit to obtain reasonable assurance about whether the financial statements are free of material misstatement, whether caused by error or fraud. Because of the nature of audit evidence, and the characteristics of fraud, the auditor is able to obtain reasonable, but not absolute, assurance that material misstatements are detected. The auditor has no responsibility to plan and perform the audit to obtain reasonable assurance that misstatements, whether caused by error or fraud, that are not material to the financial statements are detected.

SAS No. 82, 'Consideration of Fraud in a Financial Statement Audit', provides auditors with operational guidance on the consideration of fraud when a financial statement audit is conducted. SAS No. 82 requires the assessment of the risk of material misstatement and consideration of around 40 specific fraud risk factors. These include management, industry and operational characteristics. Specifically, auditors are required to make inquiries of management concerning the possible risk of fraud and to document in the workpapers any identified risk factors as well as their response for these risk factors (see Exhibit 10.3 for an extract from Practitioner's Guide to Generally Accepted Auditing Standards ('GAAS')). Exhibit 10.4 shows Andersen's statement to Enron's shareholders and Board of Directors (from Enron's Annual Report).

EXHIBIT 10.3 EXTRACT FROM PRACTITIONER'S GUIDE TO GENERALLY ACCEPTED AUDITING STANDARDS (GAAS)

100-230 THE AUDITOR'S RESPONSIBILITIES AND FUNCTIONS, INTRODUCTION TO GAAS, AND THE GENERAL STANDARDS[11]

NOTE: All sections apply whether the financial statements are presented in conformity with GAAP or OCBOA unless otherwise noted.

EFFECTIVE DATE AND APPLICABILITY

Original Pronouncements	Statement of Auditing Standards (SAS). 1, November 1972; SAS 5, July 1975; SAS 25, November 1979; SAS 41, April 1982; SAS 43, August 1982; SAS 78, December 1995; SAS 82, February 1997.
Effective Date	When issued, November 1972, except for amendments on quality control (November 1979), services other than audits of financial statements (August 31, 1982), and consideration of fraud (February 1979).
Applicability	All audits in accordance with generally accepted auditing standards and other services covered by SASs.

FUNDAMENTAL REQUIREMENTS

Objective of Ordinary Audit

To express an opinion on the fairness, in all material aspects, with which the financial statements present financial position, results of operations, and cash flows in conformity with generally accepted accounting principles or another comprehensive basis of accounting.

2. 100-230 Auditor's Responsibilities; Intro to GAAS

Auditor's Responsibilities

In every audit, the author has to obtain reasonable assurance about whether the financial statements are free of material misstatement. Material misstatement includes

1. Material error. (See Section 312)

(Continued)

EXHIBIT 10.3 (*Continued*)

2. Material fraud. (See Section 316)

3. Certain illegal acts. (See Section 317)

Management Responsibilities

The fairness of the representations made through financial statements is an implicit and integral part of management's responsibility. Management is responsible for

1. Adopting sound accounting policies.

2. Establishing and maintaining internal control that will, among other things, record, process, summarize, and report financial data that are consistent with management's assertions embodied in the financial statement.

The auditor's participation in preparing financial statements does not change the character of the statements as representations of management. In brief, management is responsible for the financial statements; the auditor is responsible for expressing an opinion on those financial statements.

Generally Accepted Auditing Standards

The generally accepted auditing standards (GAAS) approved by the American Institute of Certified Public Accountants (AICPA) membership are

A. General Standards

  1. Training and proficiency. The audit is to be performed by a person or persons having adequate technical training and proficiency as an auditor.

  2. Independence. In all matters relating to the assignment, an independence in mental attitude is to be maintained by the auditor or auditors.

  3. Due Care. Due professional care is to be exercised in the planning and performance of the audit and the preparation of the report.

B. Fieldwork Standards

  4. Planning and supervising. The work is to be adequately planned, and assistants, if any, are to be properly supervised.

  5. Internal control. A sufficient understanding of internal control is to be obtained to plan the audit and determine the nature, timing, and extent of tests to be performed.

  6. Evidential matter. Sufficient competent evidential matter is to be obtained through inspection, observation, inquiries, and confirmations to afford a reasonable basis for an opinion regarding the financial statements under audit.

C. Reporting Standards

  7. GAAP. The report shall state whether the financial statements are presented in accordance with generally accounting principles.

  8. Consistency. The report shall identify those circumstances in which such principles have not been consistently observed in the current period in relation to the preceding period.

  9. Disclosure. Informative disclosures in the financial statements are to be regarded as reasonably adequate unless otherwise stated in the report.

  10. Reporting obligation. The report shall contain either an expression of opinion regarding the financial statements taken as a whole or an assertion to the effect that an opinion cannot be expressed. When an overall opinion cannot be expressed, the reasons should be stated. In all cases where an auditor's name is associated with financial statements, the reports should contain

  a. A clear-cut indication of the character of the auditor's work, if any.

  b. The degree of responsibility the auditor is taking.

NOTE: Materiality and audit risk underlie the application of all standards (see Section 312).

Other Services

The preceding 10 formal standards apply to all other services covered by SASs unless they are clearly not relevant or the SAS specifies that they do not apply.

Source: Practitioner's Guide to GAAS

Quality Control Standards

A firm of certified public accountants (CPAs) should establish quality control policies and procedures to provide it with reasonable assurance of conforming with GAAS in its audit engagements.

Training and Proficiency

The auditor holds out himself as one who is proficient in accounting and auditing. Attaining proficiency begins with formal education and extends through later experience. The auditor must be aware of and understand new authoritative pronouncements on accounting and auditing.

Independence

To **be** independent, the auditor must be intellectually honest; to be **recognized** as independent, he or she must be free from any obligation to or interest in the client, its management, or its owners. For specific guidance, the auditor should look to AICPA and the state society rules of conduct and, if relevant, the requirements of the Securities and Exchange Commission (SEC) and the Independence Standards Board.

Due Care

The auditor should observe the standards of fieldwork and reporting, possess the degree of skill commonly possessed by other auditors, and should exercise that skill with reasonable care and diligence. The auditor should also exercise professional scepticism, that is, an attitude that includes a questioning mind and a critical assessment of audit evidence. However, the auditor is not an insurer and the audit report does not constitute a guarantee because it is based on reasonable assurance.

Interpretations

There are no interpretations for this section.

EXHIBIT 10.4 ANDERSEN'S STATEMENT TO ENRON'S SHAREHOLDERS AND BOARD OF DIRECTORS (FROM ENRON'S ANNUAL REPORT)

REPORTS OF INDEPENDENT PUBLIC ACCOUNTANTS

To the Shareholders and Board of Directors of Enron Corp.:

We have examined management's assertion that the system of internal control of Enron Corp. (an Oregon corporation) and subsidiaries as of December 31, 1999, 1998 and 1997 was adequate to provide reasonable assurance as to the reliability of financial statements and the protection of assets from unauthorized acquisition, use or disposition included in the accompanying report on Management's Responsibility for Financial Reporting.

Management is responsible for maintaining effective control over the reliability of financial statements and the protection of assets against unauthorized acquisition, use or disposition. Our responsibility is to express an opinion on management's assertion based on our examination.

Our examinations were made in accordance with attestation standards established by the American Institute of Certified Public Accountants and, accordingly, included obtaining an understanding of the system of internal control, testing and

(*Continued*)

EXHIBIT 10.4 (*Continued*)

evaluating the design and operating effectiveness of the system of internal control and such other procedures as we considered necessary in the circumstances. We believe that our examinations provide a reasonable basis for our opinion.

Because of inherent limitations in any system of internal control, errors or fraud may occur and not be detected. Also, projections of any evaluation of the system of internal control to future periods are subject to the risk that the system of internal control may be become inadequate because of changes in conditions, or that the degree of compliance with the policies or procedures may deteriorate.

In our opinion, management's assertion that the system of internal control of Enron Corp. and its subsidiaries as of December 31, 1999, 1998 and 1997 was adequate to provide reasonable assurance as to the reliability of financial statements and the protection of assets from unauthorized acquisition, use or disposition is fairly stated, in all material respects, based upon current standards of control criteria.

Arthur Andersen LLP

Houston, Texas
March 13, 2000

To the Shareholders and Board of Directors of Enron Corp.:

We have audited the accompanying consolidated balance sheet of Enron Corp. (an Oregon Corporation) and subsidiaries as of December 31, 1999 and 1998 and the related consolidated statements of income, comprehensive income, cash flows and changes in shareholders' equity for each of the three years in the period ended December 31, 1999. These financial statements are the responsibility of Enron Corp.'s management. Our responsibility is to express an opinion on these financial statements based on our audits.

We conducted our audits in accordance with auditing standards generally accepted in the United States. Those standards require that we plan and perform the audit to obtain reasonable assurance about whether the financial statements are free of material misstatement. An audit includes examining, on a test basis, evidence supporting the amounts and disclosures in the financial statements. An audit also includes assessing the accounting principles used and significant estimates made by management, as well as evaluating the overall financial statement presentation. We believe that our audits provide a reasonable basis for our opinion.

In our opinion, the financial statements referred to above present fairly, in all material respects, the financial position of Enron Corp. and subsidiaries as of December 31, 1999 and 1998, and the results of their operations, cash flows and changes in shareholders' equity for each of the three years in the period ended December 31, 1999, in conformity with accounting principles generally accepted in the United States.

As discussed in Note 18 to the consolidated financial statements, Enron Corp. and subsidiaries changed its method of accounting for costs of start-up activities and its method of accounting for certain contracts involved in energy trading and risk management activities in the first quarter of 1999.

Arthur Andersen LLP

Houston, Texas
March 13, 2000

The Andersen Indictment

'Enron robbed the bank, Arthur Andersen provided the getaway car, and they say you were at the wheel.'

Congress questioning of David Duncan, the Andersen partner in charge of the Enron audits
BBC Money Programme, 2002a

Andersen was Enron's auditor for 16 years, bringing in US$52 million in fees from the Enron account in 2000 alone. Approximately 50% of those fees came from Andersen's audit role; the remaining 50% was derived from other consulting (such as taxation) services (*Platts Energy Economist*, 2002). The nature of the relationship between auditor and audited appeared close, illustrated by the fact that David Duncan (the Andersen partner in charge of Enron's account) and his 100-strong team worked out of Enron's Houston offices. In addition, around 300 middle and senior managers at Enron were ex-Andersen employees (Cohen, 2002).

Given the public outcry following Enron's spectacular collapse, few were surprised that investigators knocked on Andersen's door. Although questions and intense interest surrounded Andersen's audits of Enron's financial statements and possible conflicts of interest that may have led Andersen to 'turn a blind eye' to some of Enron's dealings, those audits were *not* the subject of Andersen's indictment. Issues surrounding that auditing role did, however, generate debate on the role and responsibilities of auditors more generally.

As Enron's financial problems intensified in 2001, a number of discussions between Enron and its auditors took place. During one such discussion, Andersen disagreed with Enron's characterization of a US$1 billion loss as 'non-recurring'. Following that discussion, Andersen lawyer Nancy Temple sent an e-mail to Duncan recommending that her name and reference to legal consultation be deleted from the earlier memo recording the events (see earlier Exhibit 10.1).

Another earlier e-mail, sent by Temple on 12 October (before the SEC had started its inquiry into Enron), also contributed to the indictment. That e-mail was sent to Michael Odum, Andersen's risk management partner for the Houston office, and stated that 'it would be helpful' if members of the Enron audit team made sure that they were in compliance with a document-retention policy that required destruction of records other than audit-related work papers, consistent with industry practice (see Exhibit 10.5). Those two e-mails later served as a red flag for the Department of Justice, who saw them as a clear attempt to tamper with documents during an SEC investigation (Thomas and Fowler, 2002, p. 66).

EXHIBIT 10.5 NANCY TEMPLE'S E-MAIL ON DOCUMENT RETENTION, 12 OCTOBER 2001

To: David B. Duncan@ANDERSEN.COM WO
CC:
BCC:
Date: 10/12/2001 08:56 AM
From: Michael C. Odom
Subject: Document retention policy
Attachments:

More help.

------------- Forwarded by Michael C. Odom on 10/12/2001 10:55 AM

(*Continued*)

EXHIBIT 10.5 (*Continued*)

To: Michael C. Odom@ANDERSEN.COM WO
CC:
Date: 10/12/2001 10:53 AM
From: Nancy A. Temple, Chicago 33 W. Monroe, 50/11234
Subject: Document retention policy

Mike –

It might be useful to consider reminding the engagement team of our documentation and retention policy. It will be helpful to make sure that we have complied with the policy. Let me know if you have any questions.

Nancy

Source: HoustonChronicle.com

According to the official indictment, on 22 October Andersen partners assigned to the Enron engagement team (including Duncan) ordered the wholesale destruction of Enron-related documents. Over the next few weeks, tonnes of physical files were shredded and computer files deleted. It was only on 8 November, when Andersen was served with official notice of the SEC investigation, that the shredding stopped (refer to Exhibit 10.6 for Temple's memo to the Enron engagement team following this notice). Andersen was subsequently charged with obstruction of justice.

EXHIBIT 10.6 NANCY TEMPLE'S MEMO ON DOCUMENT RETENTION, 10 NOVEMBER 2001

To: David B. Duncan; D. Stephen Goddard Jr; Thomas H. Bauer; Debra A. Cash; Roger D. Willard; Timothy K. McCann
CC: Caroline K. Cheng; Michelle A. Molay, Anne C. O'Loughlin
BCC:
Date: 11/10/2001 08:40AM
From: Nancy A Temple
Subject: Enron – Procedures for Responding to Subpoenas and Litigation
Attachments:

Please forward this message to the European engagement team which confirms the voicemail message that was forwarded to the team yesterday regarding instructions for responding to subpoenas and litigation relating to Enron.
Thank you.

Nancy Temple.

MEMORANDUM TO ALL U.S. ENRON ENGAGEMENT PERSONNEL

The press stories relating to Enron have led to an increasing number of lawsuits in recent days. Although the initial lawsuits that were filed did not name Andersen as a defendant, we have learned of one new lawsuit that does name Andersen and there have been reports of a second suit. The SEC has recently opened a formal investigation relating to Enron and as mentioned in the voicemail previously sent to you on Thursday afternoon, we received our first communication from the SEC in the form of a subpoena for the production of documents. We have also received a second subpoena in a lawsuit in which Andersen is not a defendant.

One of the first things we must do in preparing to respond to these subpoenas and lawsuits is to take all necessary steps to preserve all of the documents and other materials that we may have relating to the claims that are being filed. To do this, we must first ensure that all documents and materials already in existence are preserved and that nothing is done to destroy or discard any of the information and materials now in your possession. The second step is to ensure that going forward any documents or other materials that are created as part of Andersen's continuing work relating to Enron and related to the claims being filed in the lawsuits are also preserved. This second step may go beyond what the law requires us to do under these circumstances, but we want to take this step so that no one in the future can falsely accuse Andersen of trying to hide any information relating to these matters and so that the lawyers representing Andersen in these matters will have all of the information necessary to represent us.

We are in the process of setting up a system to collect all of the documents and materials relating to the litigation and for copying and storage in one central location. We hope to create a system that causes all of you as little inconvenience as possible and that will not interfere unduly with your ongoing work on Enron-related matters. In advance of our physically collecting these materials, however it is important that you take steps to preserve all of them. We are therefore instructing that you take the following immediate steps relating to documents and other materials relating to Enron engagements:

1. Existing Documents. Effective immediately, all existing Enron-related documents and materials must be preserved and nothing should be destroyed or discarded. This includes all copies and all originals of work papers, all drafts, and all informal files, desk files, e-mails, Lotus Notes, handwritten notes, faxes, memos, forms, calendar entries, lists and so forth, whether in electronic or hard copy and whether on the Firm's shared drive or on the hard drive of your firm-issued computer or any location where you commonly store business information, including your home computer and any hand held computing device. You should not, for example, delete from your computer any e-mails relating to Enron, or any computer work files relating to Enron, or any documents relating to Enron, even if those documents are only in the form that it now exists.

2. Continuing Work. With respect to work in progress and new documents and materials that are created in the course of ongoing work in the future, you are not required to

(*Continued*)

EXHIBIT 10.6 (*Continued*)

preserve materials on new Enron work that is not related to legal claims about Enron's prior financials and public statements. You should however take steps to preserve any new materials that are generated related to prior financial or public statements issues. This would include, for example, new materials that may relate to any restatements of prior transactions, as well as any off-balance sheet transactions involving Enron. The simplest way to do this going forward is to create a box in your office and a separate file on a computer where you can collect new materials in these categories that might not otherwise be kept, such as drafts, notes, e-mails, superseded memos, etc. We will provide a label for your box and will periodically collect materials from these boxes as our work continues.

We understand that the document preservation steps described above are a burden, but it is important that we do everything we can in these areas for the reasons explained above, and the lawyers handling these matters are available to answer any questions you may have to help streamline the process.

Finally, it is very important that you not discuss Enron and the lawsuits with anyone, whether inside or outside of the Firm. This specifically includes any individuals at the client and former employees of Andersen. If anyone attempts to discuss any lawsuit-related matters with you, please ask the individual to call Caroline Cheng, an attorney in our legal group. Nancy Temple will be the attorney primarily responsible for Enron-related litigation. Caroline Cheng and paralegals Michelle Molay and Anne O'Loughlin will be assisting her. If you have any further questions, please contact one of them.

Thank you for your cooperation.

Source: FindLaw at www.findlaw.com

Andersen had volunteered in a statement in January 2002 that its Houston office had disposed of a 'significant but undetermined number of Enron-related documents' during the SEC investigation. This release of information was consistent with a policy of openness followed by Joe Berardino, Andersen's CEO, during investigations of Andersen's role in Enron's collapse. In an article in the *Wall Street Journal* in December 2001, he had pledged: 'We are cooperating fully with investigations into Enron. If we have made mistakes, we will acknowledge them. If we need to make changes, we will.' Later that month, Berardino told a Congressional hearing that his firm had erred in the audit of one of the off-balance sheet partnerships at the centre of the accounting controversy.

In order to convict Andersen of the charge of obstruction of justice, the jury had to find that someone within Andersen 'corruptly persuaded' someone else to destroy documents or alter documents with the purpose of impeding the SEC's investigation. The government argued there were several such persuaders; the defence argued there were none. The jury found that Temple, by dictating the edits in the memo, was the 'corrupt persuader' and Andersen as a firm was convicted of the charge.[12] (See Figure 10.4 for timeline, October 2001 to June 2002.)

22 October 2001

The SEC announces an investigation into collapsed energy giant Enron, one of Andersen's biggest clients. Andersen partners on the Enron engagement team order wholesale destruction of Enron-related documents.

8 November 2001

Enron is forced to revise its financial statements for the past five years, statements that Andersen had previously approved, to account for US$586 million in losses. Andersen officially notified of the SEC investigation and orders preservation of all Enron-related documents.

2 December 2001

Enron files for Chapter 11 bankruptcy, the largest corporate failure in US history.

13 December 2001

Andersen executives tell US Congress that they had warned Enron about 'possible illegal acts' after Enron withheld crucial data about its finances from Andersen.

9 January 2002

The US Justice Dept announces it has opened a criminal investigation into Andersen.

10 January 2002

Andersen admits that its partners and staff shredded thousands of Enron-related documents.

15 January 2002

Andersen fires David Duncan, the partner in charge of Enron's audits.

17 January 2002

Enron fires Andersen, blaming the firm for destroying documents needed by government investigators.

4 February 2002

Former Federal Reserve chairman Paul Volcker hired to introduce reforms at Andersen in an effort to restore its reputation.

14 March 2002

The US Justice Department charges Andersen with obstruction of justice, for deliberately destroying evidence relating to its audit of Enron while an investigation was underway.

8 April 2002

7000 employees laid off, around 25% of the firm's US workforce.

7 May 2002

The trial begins, after settlement talks between Andersen and the Justice Dept break down.

12 June 2002

The jury is deadlocked. The judge grants permission to deliver a guilty verdict against Andersen even if jury members fail to agree which individual was responsible for the alleged actions.

15 June 2002

Andersen (US arm) is found guilty of obstruction of justice. The firm agrees to cease auditing public companies by 31 August.

Figure 10.4 Timeline of Andersen's fall from grace

Source: BBC News *'Andersen's Fall From Grace',* 17 June 2002, at www.news.bbc.co.uk

WHO WAS INVOLVED?

At Andersen

> The wonderful thing about Andersen is that it could do so much wrong without ever knowing it. It could certify Enron's books for years, and even after Enron admitted its numbers were false, Andersen didn't know it had done wrong. It could shred and delete thousands of Enron-related documents without knowing that was wrong either. Maybe that was Andersen's problem: It seems so much better at not knowing than it was at knowing.
>
> Ackman, 2002

This was not the first time Andersen or the other Big Five firms had found themselves in trouble following accounting restatements by their audit clients. Indeed, Ernst & Young, PwC and KPMG had, like Andersen, paid out millions of dollars to settle shareholder lawsuits following such restatements (see Figure 10.1 earlier in this chapter).

However, on this occasion, it appeared that the SEC considered Andersen a 'serial offender' and even though the case was not strictly to do with any alleged negligence by Andersen in its audits of Enron financial statements, Andersen's actions in relation to Enron-related documents and the culpability that those actions implied (in terms of interfering with the SEC investigation) proved to be the final straw.

Although Andersen was convicted as a firm, there had been several attempts within Andersen to bring Enron back into line in its use of accounting standards. Internal Andersen documents released by a US house committee (mostly comprising e-mails between Andersen technical experts in Chicago and members of the Enron engagement team in Houston), indicate that Carl Bass, an Andersen partner in the Professional Standards Group, had argued against Enron's interpretation of accounting rules for up to two years before Enron's problems were made public. Bass had expressed a number of concerns about deals between Enron and its SPEs and had argued that various transactions fell outside the rules and should be consolidated into Enron's statements (see Exhibit 10.7). Enron demanded Bass's removal from the engagement team – Bass told congressional investigators that he was removed from the Enron account in March 2001 because he had refused to 'rubber stamp' many of Enron's most aggressive accounting manoeuvres (*Forbes*, 2002).

EXHIBIT 10.7 MEMO FROM ANDERSEN'S CARL BASS ON ENRON ACCOUNT

ARTHUR ANDERSEN   **PROFESSIONAL STANDARDS GROUP**

To: John E. Stewart@ANDERSEN WO
Date: 03/04/2001 06:46 PM
From: Carl E. Bass, Houston, 237 / 2314
Subject: Enron

I know you did not ask for this but I believe you should be [sic] at least have a version of what I know about this Enron 'thing' from me. You may share this with anyone you deem appropriate – we are after all partners in this Firm and should be able to have an open dialogue about issues, especially those that affect partners. In addition, it appears that I have been the subject of some conversation and no one has discussed this with me directly. So treat this as my own New York Times OpEd piece, expect [sic] we are not discussing Presidential pardons.

The Enron 'thing' with me

With regard to this 'thing', I believe that several points need to be made. There appears to be some sort of assertion that I have a 'problem' with Rick Causey or someone at Enron that results in me having some caustic and inappropriate slant in dealing with their questions. You may recall that when I joined the PSG on December 1, 1999, Dave Duncan had requested 500-750 hours of my time on Enron specific consultation. At the time, I/we was/were told that this was cleared with the client. If in fact I had some sort of 'problem', one would have thought that would have surfaced at that time. The client would have vetoed such an arrangement. In fact, I was told this was sold to them. Logic would also seem to dictate that if there was some sort of 'problem' I would have been removed as one of the engagement partners, much less been placed on it to begin with. Believe me, if I had some 'problem' I would have never requested to have been put on the engagement given the complexity and challenges that that engagement entails. So any notion that there is some sort of long, deep seated animosity needs to be dispelled as it simply is not true – nor do the facts warrant it. I should also note that I have gone to great lengths to get Causey in front of standard setters. For example, I was able to get Causey to be a guest at the EITF meeting when tolling agreements were discussed because they had a vested interest in the accounting for those transactions. If I had some sort of ax to grind, I would not have even orchestrated that.

With regard to the yearend issues that apparently triggered this 'thing with me', let's go through them one by one. Again, there was dialogue on process here that I was not party to but apparently I have some sort of 'problem' here.

1. Blockbuster transaction – Roger Willard and Clint Carlin approached me for about 15 minutes one afternoon to discuss two things. One, whether an interest in a joint venture could be securitized and two, what are the requirements to be a joint venture. With respect to the first question, I said yes as long as it is accounted for on the equity method. We then discussed the requirements of a joint venture, including the fact that it had to be a business. The original Blockbuster transaction was simply one where Enron was going to contribute this contract and the other party was going to contribute systems and expertise to deliver this product to households. I received one other question from Clint Carlin, dealing with some puts and calls. About two months later Roger Willard asked whether the equity needed to be 3% of fair value or book value. At that time I was told that they were going to have some $50 million gain on the sale of this venture interest immediately after the contract was signed and the venture was entered into. Furthermore, the other venture partner was not contributing anything. At that time, both you and I had expressed some concern about this deal. It should be noted that despite all of the turmoil over this, we (PSG) did not object to this transaction as it appeared to meet the technical requirements of Statement 125. We relied on the engagement team to address both the definition of a business and the valuation issues of immediate gain. The

(Continued)

EXHIBIT 10.7 (*Continued*)

client's proposed accounting nonetheless was sustained. At that time, I was aware of another securitization in which the client had provided a side agreement to guarantee the 3% residual equity at risk with the same counterparty in this transaction. Although it is not my job (which I acknowledged to the engagement team), I did suggest confirmation as an audit procedure. I believe knowledge of this did prompt us over a weekend to have the engagement team involve various levels of practice directors in this decision. In effect, this was a very risky transaction and we did not believe that the PSG should solely be in on this without others.

With respect to the infamous 4:1 test, they did not follow our advice on this. I did acknowledge several times with the engagement team that although our test is grounded in GAAP, we did make it up and it is no where to be found in the accounting literature.

2. Networks transaction – Tom Bauer involved me on this transaction. It was similar to the one above but did involve the sale of an existing Enron business through a securitization transaction. This was probably the nth step of a series of permutations of this transaction that I had been involved in since November. The only late issue on this came after the deal had been signed. This was one of those deals where Enron contributed a business worth $100. A bank contributed cash totalling $100. The bank did this through an SPE whereby the residential equity holder contributed $3 and the debt holder contributed $97. I was asked after the deal had been signed whether that was OK. We discussed this issue a lot within the PSG and had in fact had a client issue with the SEC along these lines. In addition, we had discussed this issue with the Enron engagement team last summer in which they documented the conclusion that the equity person would have had to contribute $6. I understand now that the gain on that transaction was $100 million. In addition, other Enron transactions had been capitalized as we have suggested.

The engagement team went back and had the equity holder contribute additional equity. The equity holder in this case was the LJM entity, a related party because the CFO is the managing equity member.

3. 'Raptor' derivative transactions – Enron has entered into a series of complicated derivatives with a related party (the CFO) in which this related party CFO writes options to Enron to protect Enron's investments in various internet businesses. The capital for the SPE is derived from Enron cash settled derivatives that are European in that they cash settle at the end of the derivative life. I will honestly admit that I have a jaded view of these transactions and 'dragged my feet' initially. This was in part due to an impairment test that Deb Cash had devised to keep these transactions honest. The yearend issues dealt with the impairment test. The engagement team had asked whether these various SPEs could be cross collateralized so that losses in one entity could offset losses in another. I told them that as long as they were truly cross collateralized that seemed OK. The problem I was told was that the CFO had no reason to inject a loss on one vehicle. The client's proposal was that the vehicles be cross collateralized but if there was a loss in one vehicle, the CFO had the option to remove the cross collateralization any time he chose to. Based on how the impairment test was devised, I did not see any way that this worked. In effect, it was heads I win, tails you lose. The engagement team appeared to be split on this – two partners had a problem with the client's proposed accounting and one did not. In the end, however, the engagement team agreed with me as did the Practice Director. It was decided by them to 'fix' this feature before the release of the financial statements. One thing to note was I was told that the client never agreed to the impairment test to begin with. So the real issue that I thought had been addressed and resolved had never been resolved with the client.

One problem I had with Raptor was that the original structure was one in which the PSG was not consulted on. In that transaction, the SPE had at risk only a nominal amount of equity (less than the 3% residual at risk of the notional value of an internet investment). Furthermore the SPE was in a bankrupt entity so any loss on the derivative could not be funded by the SPE. I understood that there was a $100 million loss on an internet investment that otherwise should have been reported absent the derivative. At no time was PSG consulted on the original structure – we did attempt to make sure the subsequent structures were adequately capitalized.

Those are the yearend issues. In total they represent about $150 million plus of income or avoided losses at yearend – and all involved the Practice Director. At no time did I ever have communication with the client on these issues. All of my communications were solely with the engagement team. You can understand then as to how I am perplexed as to how the client even knows I was consulted on with respect to these issues and how they believe I am too caustic and cynical with respect to their transactions (see below).

The only other issue that came up post yearend but affected 2000 was the Azurix impairment. I was consulted on an impairment issue at the Azurix level. I told the engagement team that their facts were a little shaky but if they could prove them then they had a position. It was not, however, without risk. At the time, Azurix was going through a 'going private' transaction. The client wanted to record an impairment in the fourth quarter. I was also consulted on the impairment issue at the Enron level of its investment in Azurix. You had told them about 6-9 months ago that 6-9 months was a good indicator of whether an impairment was permanent with respect to that investment. I had repeated that advice post yearend but by then the investment was under water for about 18 months. I told the engagement partner that it was judgment – not really PSG's call. I was told by him that 'he had never communicated the original advice to the client and therefore he could not go in and do so now.' I was led to believe that he went to his Practice Director. Again, not really our call.

Process

Apparently, part of the process issue stems from the client knowing all that goes on within our walls on our discussions with respect to their issues. I believe that when we are either having discussions or have reached a decision, the FIRM has done so. The PSG only gives advice. The engagement partners and practice directors then reach a decision based on that advice as well as other considerations, but it is the FIRM that does so. We should not be communicating with the client that so and so said this and I could not get this past so and so in the PSG. I learned that lesson the hard way when I was senior working for Gary Goolsby about 17 years ago. I have first hand experience on this because at a recent EITF meeting some lower level Enron employee who was with someone else from Enron introduced herself

(Continued)

EXHIBIT 10.7 (*Continued*)

to me by saying she had heard my name a lot – 'so you are the one that will not let us do something'. I have been on calls where the EA has interrupted the call saying that so and so was waiting for an answer from me on this that or the other. In fact, the client called during a meeting on the Raptor derivative transactions between me, the Practice Director, and the engagement team. One of the partners told the EA that interrupted us that 'they were still meeting with Carl'.

I have also noted a trend on this engagement that the question is usually couched along the lines 'will the PSG support this?' When a call starts out that way, it is my experience that the partner is struggling with the question and what the client wants to do. But lately managers have been posing their questions that way.

Let me propose an alternative. The engagement team should prepare a memo documenting all aspects of the transaction as well as the research that supports a conclusion or the conflicting research that leads to grayness. All too often (in fact, without exception), it has lately been a call from a manager with a flowchart and we then have to slug through it to find the real issues. For example, within the past week the client proposed placing a contract into a 'joint venture'. An interest in the joint venture would then be sold for a $20–40 million gain. The parties to the joint venture were the same parties to the contract. There were no customers (the customer was the other 'venturer'), no process, no business. In fact the press release was clear that a contract had been entered into. There is no mention of a joint venture. In effect, nothing was accomplished in this transaction except a sale of future revenues. The engagement partner agreed with my view and in fact had the same view. She was seeking concurrence. I was told they booked the transaction any way and that we will propose a PAJE.

Once we conclude on something, or render some advice, the engagement team should deliver that advice or conclusion as if it was their own. It is after all the engagement team's responsibility to sign the opinion – not ours.

Source: http://energycommerce.house/gov/107/pubs/EnronDocumentsApril2.pdf

At Enron

From the start, Enron's top management surrounded themselves with other smart and driven people, many of whom had advanced degrees in business, economics and finance. A fiercely competitive culture in which the rewards of success were potentially huge, helped create the environment of 'innovation and aggression' that Lay and Skilling believed was necessary to grow Enron into the powerhouse they wanted it to be.

As Enron's reported earnings and share price boomed, Enron executives reaped hundreds of millions of dollars in salary, cash bonuses and share options. Even as Enron headed into bankruptcy in the latter stages of 2001, senior Enron employees received US$100 million in cash bonuses for the year. And as Enron employees found themselves unable to sell their own shares (in their retirement fund accounts), senior executives, in particular Lay and Skilling, continued to sell off their own holdings for millions of dollars. Between 1999–2001 alone, Lay was estimated to have grossed US$247 million in salary and share sales (Cheng, 2002).

What became apparent after Enron's collapse was the serious breakdown in corporate governance that had occurred at Enron. Paid as much as US$350 000 per year (more than twice the average remuneration for directors on the boards of the 200 largest US companies (Cornwell, 2002)), Enron's non-executive directors appeared to turn a blind eye to many of the questionable activities undertaken by management.

An example of this occurred in February 1999, when David Duncan described Enron's accounting practices to the audit committee of Enron's Board of Directors ('the Audit Committee') as 'high risk' and 'pushing limits'. Despite similar warnings through 1999–2001, not one director on the committee (including a former Stanford accounting professor) objected to the use of these procedures, asked for a second opinion or demanded a more prudent approach (Byrne, 2002, p. 50).

A six-month Senate investigation also discovered other events that further illustrated the apparent failure of Enron's Board of Directors ('the Board') and its various oversight committees to fulfil its duty of care to investors (Byrne, 2002, p. 50):

- During 2000, the Board's compensation committee approved US$750 million in cash bonuses to Enron executives. This was in a year where total reported net income amounted to US$975 million – apparently no one added up the numbers.
- The Board approved a credit line of US$7.5 million for CEO Lay that allowed him not only to borrow shareholder funds for his personal use, but also repay those loans with Enron stock. It was later revealed that in the 12 months preceding Enron's collapse, Lay drew down US$77 million in cash from the facility and repaid it with Enron shares.
- The Board waived Enron's code of ethics to accommodate Fastow's SPE partnerships – an event that even the directors belatedly agreed was 'a red flag the size of Alaska' (Charan, Useem and Harrington, 2002, p. 36).
- In August 2001, Sherron Watkins (a corporate development executive at Enron) sent a letter to Lay expressing concern over accounting irregularities that she believed could pose a threat to Enron. However, when Enron's lawyers first mentioned the letter to the Board, the actual document was not shown to the Board and no one asked for either her name or for a copy of the letter.

Wall Street

No one likes a good growth story better than Wall Street.

Charan et al., 2002, p. 36

Through the 1990s Enron gave Wall Street exactly what it wanted and in return Wall Street turned Enron into a star, in the process helping to make its executives rich beyond their wildest dreams. Enron's collapse soon stirred up debate over Wall Street's involvement, particularly over the dual role played by the large investment banks – as Enron's banker on the one hand and 'as stock analysts whipping up enthusiasm' for Enron's stock on the other (Puscas, 2002).

Enron's top management had made it clear to the banks from the start that their analysts *had* to recommend its shares in order to get the deals (at least one analyst was fired for not doing this). Those favoured banks (including Merrill Lynch, Citigroup and JP Morgan) went on to reap millions of dollars in fees for making and syndicating loans to Enron's many SPEs (*Platts Energy Economist*, 2002). As *Platts Energy Economist* put it:

> If Enron and Andersen created the monster, the banks force-fed it with billions of dollars of credit, mustering money from other banks all over the world.

Politicians

Another story to emerge from the scandal surrounding Enron's collapse was the extent of Andersen and Enron's political connections in the United States and United Kingdom. As well as being one of President Bush's top financial backers (donating US$212 825 to Bush between 1998 and 2002), Andersen also spent US$6 million lobbying the US government on such issues as electricity de-regulation and self-regulation for the accounting profession. Andersen lobbied particularly strongly against former SEC Chairman Arthur Levitt's proposal to restrict the amount of non-audit-related work that firms such as Andersen could do for clients, though it was not the only accounting firm to lobby against this initiative (Dunbar and Heller, 2002).

Enron also had extensive political access, particularly in the United States, where Enron had sub-stantial influence on Vice President Dick Cheney's energy policy, having met with Cheney or his aides at least six times in 2001 alone. It was Enron's use of this political influence that was heav-ily criticized by many commentators – one example occurred in 2001 when it was revealed that Cheney and others tried to use their political muscle to help Enron sell its interest in the Dabhol Power Plant in India for US$2.3 billion. Enron was facing non-payment by the Indian government, which was disputing Enron over power prices. In addition, when local villagers protested about the construction of a power plant because of its threat to the environment and their livelihood, Enron paid state forces to quash the dissent, with many villagers being severely beaten. Events like these led to Enron becoming the only company in history to be the subject of a full Amnesty Interna-tional Report (Puscas, 2002).

POSTSCRIPT

In 2002, WorldCom replaced Enron as the biggest ever US corporate bankruptcy following rev-elations of an estimated US$11 billion fraud. Operating expenses had been booked as capital expenditures, inflating reported income and putting WorldCom in profit for at least two years when it was in fact losing money. WorldCom's auditor was Arthur Andersen.

NOTES

1. Michelle Quirk, MBA (Dist.) prepared this case from public sources under the supervision of N. Craig Smith, Associate Professor of Marketing & Ethics at London Business School, as a basis for class discussion rather than to illustrate either effective or ineffective handling of a management situation. The authors gratefully acknowledge the guidance provided on accounting standards by Ronnie Barnes, Assistant Professor of Accounting at London Business School.

2. Grand Jury Indictment CRH 02 121: *U.S.A. v Arthur Andersen LLP.*

3. Associated Press, Analysts: It's the end of Andersen, 15 June 2002, www.chron.com.

4. Basic background: Arthur Andersen at www.justpeople.com, September 2001.

5. Basic background: Arthur Andersen at www.justpeople.com, September 2001.

6. Unless separately referenced, the dates and events in this section reflect information from 'Enron Timeline', www.news.bbc.co.uk; and www.CBSNews.com, 31 July 2002.

7. The press room at www.enron.com (2002).

8. '*Interagency Guidance on Asset Securitization Activities*' http://www.federalreserve.gov/boarddocs/SRLETTERS/1999/sr9937a1.pdf.

9. Financial Accounting Standards Board Statement No. 140 (replaced Statement No. 125) relating to accounting for transfers and servicing of financial assets and extinguishments of liabilities. Refer to www.fasb.org for the FASB summary of Statements 125 and 140.

10. Prof. Steven Schwarcz, Lessons from Enron: The use and abuse of special purpose entities in corporate structures, talk delivered at Duke University, 8 Feb 2002.

11. In May 2001, the Auditing Standards Board issued an Exposure Draft of a proposed SAS titled Generally Accepted Auditing Standards. This SAS would supersede SAS 1. Codification of Auditing Standards and Procedures. AU Section 150, Generally Accepted Auditing Standards, to identify auditing publications that auditors should follow in conducting an audit and clarify the authority of such publications.

12. *Online News Hour* (2002) Arthur Andersen: Called to account, http:/ww.pbs.org/newshour, 17 June.

REFERENCES

Ackman, D. (2002) Andersen guilty; Enron still unindicted, *Forbes.com*, 17 June.

Arnold, J. (2002) Tough times for the 'Androids', *BBC News*, 15 June, www.news.bbc.co.uk.

Babington, D. and Rigby, B. (2002a) Recalling Andersen's Glory Days, News24.com, 16 June.

Babington, D. and Rigby, B. (2002b) In glory days, Andersen led from the front, *Houston Chronicle*, 16 June, www.chron.com.

BBC Money Programme (2002a) The Andersen files, 23 July.

BBC Money Programme (2002b) Inside the Enron scandal, 4 April.

Byrne, J. (2002) No excuses for Enron's board, Special Report: The Angry Market, *Business Week*, 29 July.

Charan, R., Useem, J. and Harrington, A. (2002) Why companies fail, *Fortune (Asia)*, **145** (11), 36–45.

Cheng, I. (2002) Executives in top US collapses made $3.3 billion, 30 July, www.ft.com.

Cohen, N. (2002) Without prejudice: Half-baked bean counters: US accountancy scams could never happen in Britain, they say: Don't believe it for a moment, *The Observer*, 7 July.

Cornwell, R. (2002) Pressure builds for reforms after Senate finds Enron directors knew of crisis, *The Independent*, 8 July.

Dunbar, J. and Heller, N. (2002) Administration ties to Arthur Andersen nearly as tight as those to Enron: The Center for Public Integrity at www.public-i.org, 16 January.

Fink, R. (2002) What Andrew Fastow knew, *CFO Magazine*, 1 January, www.cfo.com.

Forbes (2002) Enron documents indicate possible cover-up, *Forbes.com*, 3 April.

Fusaro, P. and Miller, R. (2002) *What Went Wrong at Enron*, John Wiley & Sons, Inc., New York.

New York Times (2002) Report links Enron directors to questionable key decisions, 18 January.

Platts Energy Economist (2002) Why Enron crashed, April, www.platts.com.

Puscas, D. (2002) A few points for clearer understanding, Polaris Institute, 4 February, www.polarisinstitute.org.

The Accountant (2002) Arthur Andersen is found guilty of obstructing justice, 21 June.

Thomas, C. and Fowler, D. (2002) Called to account, *Time South Pacific*, 24 June.

CHAPTER ELEVEN

Corporate Social Responsibility in Finance

John Becker-Blease, Washington State University

Considerable interest has emerged recently concerning the objective function of the public corporation. Spurred on by the corporate scandals plaguing the United States over the past decade, many have questioned whether the focus on shareholders' interests, long the primary model of most business schools, is in part, or entirely, to blame. Financial economists have typically responded that the failures are the result of governance limitations rather than a misdirected objective function. In addition, they note that models that focus on constituencies other than shareholders, frequently known as the *stakeholder models*, are impractical because they are *ad hoc* and lack a widely applicable measure of success. Despite these short-comings, there remains a growing acceptance that the current 'shareholder-first' model is sufficiently incomplete, or flawed, to validate a concerted search for a better functioning alternative.

In this chapter, I examine this controversy and highlight the sources of the apparent tension between the two models. I argue that if one assumes that the underlying goal of the corporate objective function is maximizing overall economic welfare, the guidance offered by the shareholder-model and the stakeholder model are, essentially, identical. However, while reaching the same conclusion, the nuances of each model can provide important new insights into the value-creation process. In addition, neither model is free from limitations due to market frictions.

Before delving into a description of the model, it is important to highlight the distinction between positive and normative economics. Milton Friedman described positive economics as limited to the description of what is, whereas normative economics is what ought to be. In general, positive economics is objective in that it is based on testable descriptions and normative economics is subjective in that it contains elements of moral and ethical choice. For example, one might argue that all stakeholders should have an equal vote in the direction of a firm since all have made an investment of one degree or another. This is a normative assertion based, for instance, on beliefs of equality. In contrast, a positive assertion can be that the financial value of a firm in which all stakeholders' interests are explicitly incorporated into decision-making is less than one in which only shareholders' interests are considered. This assertion represents a testable hypothesis that can be rejected through standard scientific inquiry.

The current dominant model taught in most business schools comes primarily from financial economics, which is the science of managing real and financial assets. This model is frequently known as the *shareholder primacy* or *shareholder-centric* view of the firm, so-called because of its apparent exclusive focus on shareholders' interests. The model, in short, argues that the managers of a firm should pursue the single objective of maximizing the wealth of current shareholders, captured by the current stock price. As stated by Jensen (2002), this theory owes its roots to over 200 years of work in economics and is construed as positive rather than normative in nature. Specifically, most financial economists assert that focusing on the interests of shareholders results in optimizing a particular outcome, rather than claiming that shareholders are somehow deserving of the greatest consideration on ethical or moral grounds.[1]

The traditional rationalization of the shareholder model starts with the widely assumed economic principle of utility maximization. If more utility is preferred to less, actions that result in the greatest increase in utility are the most desirable. This concept is applicable at both the macro- and micro-level, which is important because at its root, shareholder wealth maximization is about maximizing aggregate macro-economic wealth, even though its application occurs at the micro-level.

Although utility maximization is a widely accepted principle among economists, it is a complex process that takes place as each market participant attempts to locate the basket of goods that best satisfies his or her preferences, subject to his or her wealth constraint. Since higher wealth leads to higher consumption, the owners of firms have a clear self-interest in maximizing the profitability of their operations. Furthermore, financial economists have frequently taken a neoclassical view of the world in which individuals seeking market exchanges that advance their own well-being serve to maximize the surplus of society as a whole through the guidance of the invisible hand. Because the market value of firms is maximized when the difference between their revenues and resource costs is as high as possible, the optimization of financial wealth not only benefits firm owners, but also signifies that all potential surplus-enhancing trades in the economy have taken place. As such, aggregate social welfare is maximized.

Within the context of a publicly-held firm, what actions lead to the greatest enhancement of aggregate financial wealth? Here again, assumptions can be important. A firm is, in essence, a collection of implicit and explicit contracts that exist among the universe of interested parties (Alchian and Demsetz, 1972; Jensen and Meckling, 1976). In a world where markets are perfect in the sense that information is costless (i.e., no one has an information advantage), the average participant is rational, there are no externalities, no monopolies or monopsonies, and all goods and services are accurately priced, then all contracts are, in effect, perfect. Each stakeholder is adequately represented and enters into an optimal contract based on the competitive environment in which they operate. In this situation, given that shareholders are the residual claimants, optimizing the overall value of the firm represented by all its contracts on the left-hand-side of the balance sheet is equivalent to optimizing the plug-value on the right-hand-side, that is, shareholder value. The underlying directive from the shareholder model then is to maximize the total value of the firm, and it is the outcome of this exercise that results in optimizing shareholders' wealth. Indeed, one could argue that a more accurate label for this model is 'firm value maximization' rather than 'shareholder wealth maximization'.

Firm-value theorists are not unaware of the limitations of the assumptions of this model. Information asymmetries are wide-spread, monopolies not only exist but can also be a critical component of innovation, externalities are common, not all goods are priced, and governments can be ill-equipped or ill-motivated to properly regulate. These limitations can lead not only to a divergence between shareholder wealth maximization and total firm value maximization, but also a schism between firm value maximization and optimal societal welfare.

The most common alternative model to the firm-value primacy model is the so-called stakeholder model. In general, the stakeholder model suggests that all stakeholders, not just shareholders, should be the focus of managers' attention. The stakeholder theory of the firm can perhaps draw its roots back to at least the early part of the 20th century and especially in the post-Crash legislation of the early 1930s. Many legal scholars consulted and testifying for the legislation that was to become the Securities Act of 1933 and the Securities Exchange Act of 1934 were of the opinion that the purpose of the corporation was to benefit the public good. For instance, Merrick Dodd argues that legally, managers are 'fiduciaries for [the firm] and not merely for its individual members'. Even Adolph Berle and Gardiner Means, sometimes viewed as the original proponents of a shareholder-centric view of the firm, state in their 1932 book *The Modern Corporation and Private Property* that the officers and directors of corporations should 'accept responsibility for the well-being of those who are subject to the organization, whether workers, investors, or consumers' (Berle and Means, 1932, p. 310).[2]

Among business academics, the R. Edward Freeman book *Strategic Management: A Stakeholder Approach* is often cited as the landmark source of stakeholder theory. Freeman defines stakeholders as 'all of those groups and individuals that can affect, or are affected by, the accomplishment of the business enterprise' (p. 25).[3] The basic idea behind the stakeholder model is that good managers must explicitly incorporate the interests of the firm's diverse stakeholders, however they are defined, into their decision-making rather than focusing exclusively on the interests of a single group, that is, shareholders, in order to achieve superior performance. As described by Donaldson and Preston (1995) and later by Laplume, Sonpar and Litz (2008), stakeholder theory has attracted an enormous amount of attention in both the academic and practitioner fields, despite the fact that the theory itself remains in its relative infancy.

Most financial economists remain unconvinced of the merits of the stakeholder model although they may acknowledge, as does Jensen (2002), that 'stakeholder theory taps into the deep emotional commitment of most individuals to the family and tribe' (p. 243). He describes the primary weakness of the model as being that requiring managers to show allegiance to multiple parties with differing interests allows these managers to have no allegiance other than to themselves. That is, many stakeholders have competing interests and stakeholder theory, at least in its current form, does not provide a coherent method for determining the necessary tradeoffs among stakeholders in any purposeful manner; there is no underlying 'objective function' on which to base the decisions. As a result, economists argue that if stakeholder-based management is implemented in its current form it would enable managers to pursue self-interest under the guise of concern for a particular stakeholder.[4] Recent corporate scandals provide strong evidence that some managers at least have this self-serving predisposition.

A second closely related question is how, under the stakeholder model, would control rights be vested? In the shareholder model, control rights purportedly rest with the shareholders, through their control of the board of directors. Shareholders are also the sole residual claimants of the firm.[5] As the residual claimants, it is in shareholders' interests to assure that firm value is maximized (or at least the stock price on their expected liquidation date), and since managers' tenure is linked exclusively to shareholders' satisfaction, managers have a single objective to pursue. However, the allocation of control rights is less clear under the stakeholder model. Identifying stakeholders becomes critical at this stage as well as whether all stakeholders should receive equal control rights or whether these rights should be distributed based on a more complex algorithm.

One such idea is forwarded by Mitchell, Agle and Wood (1997), who advocate relevance based on *power, legitimacy* and *urgency*. However, even this more refined method, which offers both a limitation on the number of stakeholders and a potential ranking of their relative merit to possess control rights, remains incomplete as power, legitimacy and urgency can vary with changing business conditions.

Despite the problems of the stakeholder model, it helps to draw attention to several of the unresolved limitations of the shareholder-first paradigm. For instance, shareholders are a diverse group with many different time horizons, and as such, actions that might enhance stock price at the end of one year, five years and 30 years can be very different. Similarly, what is the role of ethics and morality in business decisions? In theory, the government is responsible for protecting the commons and codifying morality. However, as pointed out by Alchian and Demsetz (1972), the government is not exempt from self-interested, incomplete and irrational actions, leaving potentially important discretion to managers. Consider the situation of an automotive manufacturer that has purchased and installed defective fuel tanks into a large number of vehicles. From a value-maximizing perspective, the company should only undertake the recall if the expected cost of not doing so, in the form of penalties, legal judgments and reputational loss exceeds the expected cost of making the recall. From a social-desirability perspective, one might hope that penalties and reputational costs are 'priced' accurately to ensure a recall. However, inefficient regulation and information distribution can impede the efficient functioning of this market. Further, if managerial actions can impede the market's operation, through the dissemination of misinformation and the active lobbying against regulation, does a shareholder-centric focus encourage this interference? History suggests that simply relying on managers to behave 'ethically' is insufficient to lead to the likely, socially-desired business behaviour in this situation.

Stakeholder theory offers a potentially useful, though admittedly incomplete, avenue towards devising a more complete vision of the firm. Indeed, Jensen (2002) and Freeman in Agle *et al.* (2008) have offered separate, but in essence potentially similar reconciliations of the two models, while acknowledging that more work is needed. If the goal of the corporate form is to maximize aggregate economic wealth, then Jensen's *Enlightened Wealth Maximization* and *Enlightened Stakeholder* models dictate similar actions by managers. That is, maximizing the aggregate value of all implicit and explicit contracts among stakeholders is accomplished by maximizing the value of the firm. In order to achieve this goal, managers must pay serious attention to the interests of stakeholders and not simply treat them as an input to be managed. This is similar in spirit to Freeman's suggestions that instead of there existing a so-called *Freeman-Friedman* debate, that Jensen, Friedman and others are actually stakeholder theorists. That is, Freeman suggests that the tension between stakeholder and shareholder theorists is more accurately described as a miscommunication. Economists are particularly interested in how markets work under particular circumstances, whereas *stakeholderism*,[6] at least as envisioned by Freeman, is about how best to create value among all stakeholders. He concludes that maximizing firm value 'is an outcome of a well-managed company, and that stakeholder theory is an idea of what it means to be well-managed'.

Given the state of the debate between shareholder and stakeholder models, an open question is whether the traditional corporate finance, and indeed general business school curriculum, is improved by not only introducing students to the nature of the debate, but also by enhancing attention to stakeholders' interests throughout the curriculum. That is, are there discernible advantages for students, and ultimately businesses, to have an increased emphasis on stakeholders' interests clearly incorporated into financial training and decision-making, or is the 'shareholder wealth maximization' paradigm sufficient to incorporate any of these advantages? I believe that a more careful and inclusive treatment of a broader slate of stakeholders' interests is beneficial to students for several reasons.

First, attention to the stakeholder view helps to focus students' attention on the outcome that matters, namely long-term firm value and the left-hand side of the balance sheet. It helps to accomplish this by removing some of the illusions that may emerge from a 'resource' view of the firm. Students and the public frequently fall into the illusion of the firm as a single economic actor, materializing in statements such as 'the firm does'. However, in the mid-1970s, based largely on the work of Jensen and Meckling (1976), economists began to understand the firm as a nexus of contracts, both implicit and explicit, among and between stakeholders. The stakeholder vision of the firm helps to draw attention to the importance of all of the contracts rather than focusing too narrowly on the one between managers and shareholders. Indeed, good decision-making in areas such as capital budgeting or capital structure requires the identification and careful consideration of the response of other stakeholders. For example, from a shareholder-perspective, one might view an automation decision as a tradeoff between the investment and operating expense of the machinery versus the savings resulting from a smaller workforce, because these are the most obvious contracts. A stakeholder-perspective will more carefully identify and consider the impact of the decision on any implied contracts existing, or believed to exist, with the downsized and remaining workforce, customers, suppliers and the community. Thus, a stakeholder-focus will encourage managers to carefully consider the systemic effect of their decision.

Of course, stakeholders are not absent from the shareholder-centric view of the firm (Jensen, 2002), but stakeholder theory helps to highlight the importance to long-term firm value-maximization of managers carefully incorporating stakeholders' interests in and responses to important decisions. Maximizing aggregate firm value is, admittedly, an enormously complex task, and reducing this to a single-task statement such as 'maximize shareholder wealth' is a convenient simplification. However, the past several decades suggest that this simple statement leads to systematic misinterpretations. This sentiment is echoed by Jensen in Agle *et al.* (2008), who admonishes academics (and non-academics) to 'stop using stockholders as the whipping boy. Stockholder value maximization has been wrong from the social viewpoint from the start. There is nothing special about stockholders of the firm' (p. 12). Instead, only by focusing on firm-value-maximization, and the inconvenient myriad of stakeholder interests contained therein, can a student or manager hope to create additional firm value systematically.

The second reason why treatment of stakeholder interests is beneficial to students is that explicit inclusion of stakeholders' interests offers important pedagogical opportunities. Measuring stakeholders' interests can provide concrete examples of advanced valuation tools frequently taught in graduate corporate finance courses. For instance, real option analysis is useful not only for a better understanding of follow-on or expansion options but also for valuing potential tax-breaks, pollution credits and contracting opportunities with employees and suppliers. Similarly, adjusted-present value allows for the easy and transparent incorporation of stakeholder effects into capital budgeting. Finally, exposure to some of the creative methods economists have devised to price hard-to-value commodities, such as clean beaches or air, can provide students with interesting insights into other valuation problems. Identifying stakeholders' interests in other corporate finance decisions improves the depth of students' understanding as well. Indeed, since both models suffer practical limitations brought about by market imperfections, each model provides excellent teaching opportunities of the importance of these imperfections. The tradeoff theory of capital structure, for instance, explicitly incorporates stakeholders' interests in identifying the optimal level of debt. Students who can best identify and quantify stakeholders' interests will most accurately optimize the tradeoff. The recent debacle in US and world financial institutions offers a very compelling example. Similarly, the agency conflicts arising from incomplete contracting occur among many stakeholders and provide students with a more nuanced understanding of the nexus-of-contracts view of the firm. In fact, the existence of tensions within stakeholder classes, for instance shareholders with different time horizons, helps to solidify the difficulty of complete contracting. Thus, understanding the stakeholder perspective can improve the quality of managerial decisions, regardless of the underlying objective.

Third, a stakeholder perspective is also helpful to students in increasing their marketability. As discussed in Stout (2002), many firms appear to be adding increasingly explicit language in their prospectuses, annual reports and other communications with the public about the importance of stakeholders in their decision-making, and the corporate citizenship of the firm. The Social Investment Forum, for instance, finds that half of the S&P 100 firms published sustainability reports in 2007. In addition, there is emerging appreciation for the impact that Environmental, Social and Governance (ESG) considerations can have on risk profiles and valuation. Liroff (2005), for instance, describes Sony's 2001 experience in the Netherlands, in which sales of its popular gaming console were banned prior to the holiday season due to excessive levels of cadmium, leading to a dramatic shift in supply chain and internal management. Similarly, FAS 143, which required that liabilities for existing legal obligations associated with the future retirement of long-lived assets be recognized in financial statements when the asset is acquired or the legal duty is created, and FIN 47, which states that the fair value of a liability for a conditional asset retirement obligation should be recognized when incurred, have forced a wide range of firms to bring future environmental costs into the present. ESG considerations are not strictly about risk, but also can provide opportunities. For instance, the 'greening' of many healthcare providers (such as Kaiser Permanente and Premier Inc.), retailers (such as Wal-Mart's Smart Products Initiative) and manufacturers (such as General Electric's Ecomagination initiative) offer promising business-to-business opportunities in which stakeholder-oriented students can help to create value.

Financial service firms are taking note. The Goldman Sachs Group recently launched a *GS SUS-TAIN* list in June of 2007, which incorporates the group's proprietary ESG framework into analysing firms. They contend that their ESG framework 'is a good overall proxy for the management quality of companies relative to their peers and, as such, gives insight as to their ability to succeed on a sustainable basis'.[7]

Indeed, interest in a more stakeholder-centric view of the firm is also gaining momentum in other financial service sectors as well. Social responsible investing (SRI), for instance, though not new, has been growing in popularity. The Social Investment Forum reports that the number of mutual funds that incorporate social screening rose from 55 in 1995 (with US$12 billion in assets) to 260 in 2007 (with US$202 billion in assets). The Dow Jones launched its Sustainability Index in 1999 and the FTSE4Good was launched in 2001. The growing interest in stakeholders evidenced by these patterns suggests a dramatic shift in the perceived importance of these issues among investors. Again, the recent financial crisis is only likely to increase interest in a broader stakeholder perspective.

Considerable work remains in our evolving understanding of corporations and their role in society. Although stakeholder theory is undeniably under-developed, it does provide important clarifying insights into firm-value-maximization, and whereas it is almost certain that unprincipled pursuit of stakeholders' interests will and has been used to mask opportunistic managerial and directorial behaviour, one can also fairly note that current governance technology is not up to the task of aligning managers' interests with shareholders. A principled form of the theory, such as *Enlightened Stakeholder Theory* or *Enlightened Wealth Maximization*, offers a promising refinement, but additional work needs to be done.

NOTES

1. An interesting debate exists among legal scholars concerning the purpose of the corporation. Indeed, the debate between Adolph Berle, an advocate of shareholder primacy, and Merrick Dodd, an advocate of a stakeholder view, published in the *Harvard Law Review* in the early 1930s is frequently cited as one of the original debates on the topic (see Stout, 2002).

2. This opinion is contrary to Berle's interpretation of current law, which was the focus of his famous debate with Dodd in the pages of the *Harvard Business Review* in 1932 entitled 'For Whom Are Corporate Managers Trustees?'. Similarly, the opinion is counter to the then recent Michigan Supreme Court decision *Dodge v. Ford* (1919), which included the statement 'a business corporation is organized and carried on for the profit of the stockholders. The powers of the directors are to be employed for that end'. This case is frequently identified as the legal basis for shareholder primacy within most corporate legal texts (Stout, 2008).

3. Freeman also offered a narrower definition based on all those whom the corporation is dependent upon for survival. Mitchell, Agle and Wood (1997) offer a comprehensive examination of the various definitions used in the literature.

4. Under varying definitions, 'stakeholders' can include a dizzying array of interested parties. Phillips and Reichart (2000) go so far as to suggest that all living entities can fall under the umbrella of managerial interests.

5. These statements are not strictly true, as discussed by Stout (2002) and Black (2001). However, from a practical standpoint, shareholders can be thought of as possessing at least the control rights.

6. Freeman is reluctant to assign a label such as *theory, hypothesis or framework* to the term.

7. Available at http://www.unglobalcompact.org/docs/summit2007/gs_esg_embargoed_until030707pdf.pdf.

REFERENCES

Agle, B., Donaldson, T., Freeman, R.E., Jensen, M., Mitchell, R. and Wood, D. (2008) Dialogue: Toward superior stakeholder theory, *Business Ethics Quarterly*, **18** (2), 153–190.

Alchian, A. and Demsetz, H. (1972) Production, information costs, and economic organization, *American Economic Review*, **62**, 777–95.

Berle, A.A. (1931) Corporate powers as powers of trust, *Harvard Law Review*, **44**, 1049–74.

Berle, A.A. and Means, G.C. (1932) *The Modern Corporation and Private Property*, Harvest Books (this edition published 1968).

Black, B. (2001) Corporate Law and Residual Claimants, Working Paper, Columbia University.

Dodd, E.M. (1932) For whom are corporate managers trustees?, *Harvard Law Review*, **45**, 1145–63.

Donaldson, T. and Preston, L. (1995) The stakeholder theory of the corporation: Concepts, evidence, and implications, *Academy of Management Review*, **20** (1), 65–91.

Friedman, M. (1953) The methodology of positive economics, in *Essays in Positive Economics*, University of Chicago Press, Chicago.

Jensen, M. (2002) Value maximization, stakeholder theory, and the corporate objective function, *Business Ethics Quarterly*, **12** (2), 235–47.

Jensen, M. and Meckling, W. (1976) Agency costs and the theory of the firm, *Journal of Financial Economics*, **3**, 305–60.

Laplume, A.O., Sonpar, K. and Litz, R.A. (2008) Stakeholder theory: Reviewing a theory that moves us, Working Paper, University of Manitoba.

Liroff, R.A. (2005) Benchmarking corporate management of safer chemicals in consumer products – A tool for investors and senior executives, *Corporate Environmental Strategy: International Journal for Sustainable Business*, **12** (1), 25–36.

Mitchell, R.K., Agle, B.R and Wood, D.J. (1997) Toward a theory of stakeholder identification and salience: Defining the principle of who and what really counts, *Academy of Management Review*, **22** (4), 853–86.

Phillips, R.A. and Reichart, J. (2000) The environment as a stakeholder? A fairness-based approach, *Journal of Business Ethics*, **23**, 185–97.

Stout, L. (2002) Bad and not-so-bad arguments for shareholder primacy, *Southern California Law Review*, **75**, 1189–1209.

Stout, L. (2008) Why we should stop teaching *Dodge v. Ford*, *Virginia Law Review*, **3** (1), 163–76.

CHAPTER TWELVE

Maximizing Shareholder Value: An Ethical Responsibility?

Theo Vermaelen, Schroders Chaired Professor of Asset Management and International Finance, INSEAD

INTRODUCTION[1]

Finance professors and other proponents of shareholder value maximization have come under intense attack from corporate social responsibility (CSR) advocates and professors of business ethics, among others. For example, the 2007 business education report of the Ethical Corporation stated that in India ethics and success are not mixing, because 'the Indian elite business schools continue to focus on shareholder value'. It is also quite common to blame the focus on shareholder value maximization for the Enron, Tyco and other scandals of recent years.[2] Some even argue that the focus on shareholder value encourages MBA students to become less ethical.[3] Although I understand that some of the authors may be motivated by hostility to capitalism and free markets,[4] I believe that there are others who are simply confused or misinformed about what we teach in finance classes. Specifically, there seems to be a perception that maximizing shareholder value means manipulating stock prices through earnings per share manipulation. This chapter is aimed at the latter group because I have no illusions of convincing the first one. Once this confusion is cleared up, it will become clear that maximizing shareholder value may well be an ethical responsibility for many CEOs and that some well-intended CSR initiatives are unethical.

At the same time, I believe that it is necessary to develop ethical guidelines that are useful for business people but that are not associated with highly time-specific and person-specific 'values'. Leonardo Lessius, the 17th century Flemish Jesuit and theologist, is regarded by many as one of the first ethical thinkers in business (van Houdt, 1995). In his monumental tractate of 1605, *De iustitia et ure*, he argued about when it was ethical to charge interest. However, in the same book there is also a less well publicized chapter on when torture should be applied by the judiciary. Specifically, Lessius argues that torturing women is acceptable, but not when they are pregnant, because this would hurt the unborn child. The fact that someone at the same time can argue that torturing women is ethical, but charging interest is not, vividly illustrates how values can be highly subjective. As in the case of Lessius, these values are often based on religion, which raises the immediate issue of how to make decisions when decision makers have different religious beliefs.

I believe that, in order to have a code of business ethics, it has to less subjective, free of individual ideological biases, free from any values other than the respect for implicit contracts. By defining ethical responsibility as *the responsibility to respect implicit contracts*, I believe ethics education in business schools can be embraced by all, regardless of ideology, as a crucial tool to make managers into more effective and ethically responsible leaders. Indeed, I will argue that not respecting implicit contracts will be costly and threaten the long-run survival of the firm.

There seems to be some confusion about what shareholder value maximization means. To wit, the numerous articles that blame the Enron disaster on pre-occupation with shareholder value maximization.[5] Therefore, this chapter starts with explaining what shareholder value is and what it is not. I then provide some traditional macro-economic arguments for shareholder value maximization in the finance literature (Jensen, 2002). Next, starting from the agency theory view of the firm, which assumes that a firm is a nexus of contracts, I identify the conditions under which shareholder value maximization is an ethical responsibility. I conclude with some applications.

WHAT IS SHAREHOLDER VALUE MAXIMIZATION?

In order to answer this question, we have to first define what we mean by shareholder value: *the value of a company's shares is the present value of expected free cash flows from now until infinity.*

Present Value

We calculate the present value, because of the time value of money and because we want to adjust for risk: more risky cash flows are discounted at a higher rate. The discount rate is the rate of return investors require to hold assets of similar risk as the company we are trying to value. So when valuing a company, we are comparing the expected returns from investing in the company with expected returns that an investor can obtain in financial markets by investing in assets of similar risk. This discount rate is also called the cost of equity as opposed to the cost of debt, that is, the rate of return creditors demand for lending the firm money. The cost of equity is an opportunity cost, determined in competitive financial markets, and is therefore outside the control of the CEO, once he has determined the riskiness of the equity. The riskiness of the equity depends on the nature of the business as well as on the firm's capital structure, where leverage tends to increase risk. Because the cost of equity is an opportunity cost and ignored by accountants, accounting profits overstate the true economic profitability of the corporation.

Expected Free Cash Flow

Valuing a firm is a highly personal affair. It depends on the expectations of those who do the valuation. Market expectations, which by definition are reflected in stock prices, may well differ from the expectations of the decision maker, that is, the CEO. The fact that markets are not always perfectly efficient in the sense that they reflect all relevant information is well accepted in the finance literature. Generally, market prices do not reflect inside information. So, maximizing shareholder value, as perceived by the CEO, may be different from maximizing the current stock price. For example, in the case of Enron, the CEO may well have realized that the value of the shares was zero, but the market was misled by accounting manipulations of short-term profits. So, Enron is not an example of what happens when you focus too narrowly on maximizing shareholder value, as is alleged by numerous critics.[6] Eventually, all Enron shareholders lost their money. Enron is instead a case of fraud to manipulate stock prices for the benefit of a few stakeholders (i.e., the management) at the expense of shareholder value.

Note that we focus on free cash flows, not profits. Free cash flows to equity holders are defined as cash revenues minus cash expenses minus investments minus interest payments and repayments of debt minus cash taxes. Hence, shareholders are residual claimholders: they are paid after everyone else. If a shareholder receives money, it means that everyone else (employees, bondholders, the government) is paid. The fact that we focus on cash flows, not profits, means that 'focus on shareholder value' cannot be blamed for some of the famous scandals related to accounting fraud. For example, WorldCom was accused of capitalizing investments rather than expensing them. Although capitalizing investments produces higher short-term profits, it has no effect on the firm's cash flow. Therefore, as with Enron, the WorldCom scandal has nothing to do with a focus on shareholder value.

From Now Until Infinity

Valuing a firm requires an infinite horizon, because companies are expected to live forever.[7] In their seminal book on corporate valuation, Koller, Goedhart and Wessels (2005) calculate that, depending on the industry, between 56% and 125% of firm value is explained by the present value of cash flows after eight years.[8] So, in general, the market has a long-term view. Shareholder value maximization is *not* about maximizing short-term profits; quite the opposite. Because of its perpetual framework, shareholder value maximization *has the longest decision horizon of any objective function one can think of.*

Of course, occasionally, as in the Enron case, the market is misled by accounting manipulations of short-term earnings. Enron essentially sold assets at inflated prices to other firms, that is, entities set up by Enron's CEO, together with a promise to buy them back at an even higher price. The asset sales were recorded as revenue, while the promises to buy them back were hidden. Earnings manipulation may be encouraged by the fact that not everyone uses discounted cash flow to value companies. It is a fact that many financial analysts are focused on short-term earnings per share because they use simplistic valuation methods. These methods involve multiplying earnings per share with an earnings multiple based on 'comparable' companies. Such a simplistic approach may indeed lead to excessive pre-occupation with short-term profits. Practitioners such as investment bankers usually justify these methods on the basis that they are simple and that their clients are not sophisticated enough to understand DCF (Discounted Cash Flow). Another justification is that such multiple methods look more precise than DCF. Using multiples for valuation gives the impression that valuation is an exact science (which it is not) rather than a forecast about perpetual cash flows of the company (which it is). In order to value a business you have to understand the business and its value drivers. However, in finance courses, we teach that the value maximizing manager should keep his or her eyes on the ball and focus on value maximization, using the DCF method, because in the long run the true value of the firm will be reflected in security prices. In other words, we do not teach valuation with multiples. I believe that the use of valuation methods that focus on short-term profits is largely responsible for the bad name 'shareholder value maximization' has received in the press.

Occasionally markets can be inefficient, and therefore we care about long-term shareholders. In the long term the value of the firm, which may be different from the current stock price, will be reflected in equity prices.[9] Caring about short-term shareholders would mean caring about those investors that want to sell their shares in the short run. Occasionally we care about short-term shareholders, that is, for example when the market price of the stock is below its fair value. In that case, one could argue that companies should try to 'signal' the undervaluation through, for example, a share buyback (Vermaelen, 1981). But even in this case, the pre-occupation with the stock price in the short run may be motivated by concern for the long-term shareholders: if a company is undervalued, it may become a target for a takeover bid at a price below fair value. Note that a finance course that focused only on maximizing the stock price in the short run would justifiably be criticized as encouraging short-termism and manipulation.

WHY SHAREHOLDER VALUE MAXIMIZATION IS THE ONLY SUSTAINABLE OBJECTIVE: TRADITIONAL ECONOMIC ARGUMENTS

Shareholders are Residual Claimholders

Maximizing shareholder value is usually contrasted with maximizing stakeholder value. Maximizing stakeholder value as proposed by theorists such as Agle *et al.* (2008) means that 'the executive has to figure out how to make the tradeoffs between different stakeholders and figure out how to improve the tradeoffs for all sides'. This is easier said than done.[10] Because stakeholder value cannot be measured, it actually leaves managers unmonitored and unaccountable (Jensen, 2008), because practically every decision can be justified by an unobservable objective function. Moreover, as Jensen (2002) points out, one can only maximize over one dimension at a time. The reason for choosing shareholders above other stakeholders is that shareholders are the *residual claimholders*. This means they get paid only if everyone else is paid. There is no guarantee that this happens when you focus on maximizing the value of other stakeholders. For example, one could maximize customer value by lowering prices, providing generous payment terms and holding on to excessive inventories so that customers do not have to wait for delivery. One could try to maximize worker value by increasing salaries, agreeing not to fire workers. Some may want to even increase bondholder value by paying higher interest rates than necessary or by lowering the risk of the assets of the firm. Yet others may want to increase government value by paying more taxes than necessary. But the fact remains that focus on one stakeholder category other than the residual claimholder ignores the reality that in competitive product, labour and capital markets it will be impossible to keep the company alive with a strategy that does not guarantee that all the stakeholders involved in the company receive a competitive compensation. Through its residual nature, shareholder value encompasses the value of all stakeholders: customer value that generates revenues in competitive product markets, worker value in the form of wages paid in competitive labour markets, bondholder value in the form of interest payments charged by competitive debt markets and internal revenue value in the form of taxes.[11] Therefore, business really creates massive benefits to society by promoting consumer, worker, lender and government welfare, not simply shareholder value. As Jensen (2002) puts it:

> Since it is logically impossible to maximize in more than one dimension, purposeful behaviour requires a single valued objective function. Two hundred years of work in economics and finance implies that in the absence of externalities and monopoly, social welfare is maximized when each firm in an economy maximizes its total market value.[12]

Hence, although it *appears* that only shareholders are cared about, the indirect effect of this optimization is that general social welfare is maximized.

Note that, by definition, residual cash flows *incorporate* the interests of all stakeholders, that is, the interests are all represented in the DCF spreadsheet. However, I believe that it is meaningless to try to *balance* interests as is advocated by, for example, Agle *et al.* (2008). This balancing act assumes that the firm operates in a vacuum and ignores completely the competitive environment.

A perfectly competitive market leaves no room for balancing. In such a market increasing the compensation of one stakeholder (say workers) above the competitive level, requires lowering the compensation of other stakeholders (e.g., capital suppliers) below the competitive level, something that is not sustainable. When there is some room for redistribution because the firm makes 'abnormal' profits in the short run, the stakeholder approach does not explain how and why we should make this tradeoff (Jensen, 2002). How is an extra pound given to an employee at the expense of a shareholder making 'society' better off? Moreover, in order for shareholders to earn a return that compensates them for taking risk, short-term abnormal losses have to be offset by short-term abnormal profits. If workers want a larger share when the firm makes abnormal profits, they should also lower their salaries when the firm makes losses.

The Market for Corporate Control

An alternative policy to shareholder value maximization is not sustainable in the long run if the CEO wants to keep his or her job. The reason is simple. If a firm wants to pursue a strategy that does not maximize shareholder value (such as a CSR policy not consistent with a business case, that is, where the cost of the CSR policy is not compensated by an increase in shareholder value[13]), its shares will trade at a value V_{SR}. This creates an incentive for large investors, arbitrageurs or hedge funds to replace the management, either through activism or through takeovers, and make arbitrage profits by implementing a value maximizing strategy that results in shareholder value of $V_{Max} > V_{SR}$. Hence finance professors believe it is unethical to charge MBAs £50 000 and then tell them to follow policies that will make them lose their jobs as a result of a hostile takeover bid. Of course, if a company is well protected against hostile bids, as used to be the case in many continental European countries, it may well survive in the long run. But the global trend towards bringing down anti-takeover provisions and giving more power to active shareholders makes shareholder value-destroying strategies less and less sustainable.

WHY SHAREHOLDER VALUE MAXIMIZATION CAN BE AN ETHICAL IMPERATIVE

Ethical behaviour is important in business because a company is a nexus of contracts between various stakeholders: workers, management, bondholders, the government and shareholders (Jensen and Meckling, 1976). Each of these contracts has explicit and implicit characteristics. For example, labour contracts have a large explicit component: salary and incentive compensation, health and pension benefits and severance payments. But they also have large implicit features. For example, employees assume that they do not have to buy their own office furniture. If companies subsequently force employees to do so, this can be considered as unethical (a violation of an implicit contract). Employees will react to these violations by asking for higher salaries; refusing to work for companies that build up a reputation of not respecting implicit contracts; and insisting on a more explicit contract that specifies all obligations of the company. Considering that these alternatives could be very costly, it makes sense for corporations to be ethical and respect implicit contracts.

In contrast to the labour contract, the contract between shareholders and the company is largely an implicit contract. Shareholders cannot force the company to pay dividends or to repay their investment (e.g., via a share buyback). Although in cases of great misconduct shareholders can use the courts to obtain restitution, empirical evidence shows that the overwhelming majority of the payouts benefits lawyers and accountants, not stockholders (Sundaram and Inkpen, 2004). In contrast to employees who have *rented* their human capital to the firm, and can walk away at any time,[14] shareholders have *given* their money to the firm. The only explicit right shareholders have is the right to vote, which is relatively meaningless for small stockholders. So, the shareholder-corporation contract is largely based on implicit promises that managers make to shareholders.[15] When investors expect the firm to maximize shareholder value, deviating from this promise can be considered as a violation of an implicit contract. I believe that breaking this promise is unethical as it boils down to issuing overvalued stock to investors. Therefore, a firm that carries out a road show to get investors' money *with an implicit understanding* that the goal of the firm is to maximize shareholder value,[16] has an ethical responsibility to maximize shareholder value.[17] Violating this implicit contract would also be costly because it would make it difficult for firms to raise money in the future. So here again, the company has an incentive to pursue shareholder value maximization.

Note, therefore, that it is crucial for the firm to make the rules of the game clear in advance (i.e., the nature of the implicit contract). If it is clear from the start, when the firm raises equity from investors, that another objective than shareholder value maximization will be pursued, not maximizing shareholder value is not unethical. For example, if a company goes public and states it will give 50% of its profits to charity, it will have to go public at a 50% discount from the price that would prevail if it stated it will maximize shareholder value. In both cases, investors who buy shares in the initial public offering can expect the same risk-adjusted rate of return on their investment.[18] Of course with such a huge amount of shareholder value destruction, the non-value maximizing strategy will be unsustainable due to the arguments put forward in the previous paragraph (i.e., the company will become a takeover target). But in this case the company cannot be accused of unethical behaviour if it does not maximize shareholder value. The finance literature calls losses to shareholders resulting from non-shareholder value maximization 'agency costs' (Jensen and Meckling, 1976), that is, activities that destroy shareholder value. If these costs are reflected in security prices when firms are set up, agency costs do not imply unethical behaviour. For example, in 2004 Google went public and stated that it would donate 1% of the company's equity and 1% of its profit to philanthropic enterprises. Therefore, shareholders could not complain afterwards when in January 2007 the company announced it would spend US$25 million on good causes, such as monitoring climate change in ecosystems in Africa and the Amazon. Similarly, an investor in BP who was aware of the CEO's speech on climate change in 1997 and its implications for oil companies, should have realized that BP was committed to action on climate change, and Exxon was not. Hence, to the extent that these policies lowered shareholder value,[19] BP's policies cannot be considered as a violation of the implicit contract with shareholders, at least to those shareholders that became investors after 1997.

SOME IMPLICATIONS

The Ethics of Corporate Social Responsibility Initiatives

A corporation is a nexus of contracts and so the term 'Corporate Social Responsibility' is a meaningless concept because only people, not legal fictions, can have moral responsibilities. Therefore, we assume that CSR proponents are pre-occupied with the responsibilities of the CEO and other major decision makers. Note that even without 'doing good', business, by definition, is a positive force for good at the macro-economic level because it creates benefits to numerous members of society (customers, employees, shareholders, potentially everyone else through taxation). Note also that activities related to CSR are not necessarily inconsistent with shareholder value maximization. A corporation that uses an environmentally friendly technology may gain sympathy from customers, workers and the government, which translates into revenue increases, labour cost savings and tax reductions/subsidies that may well exceed the higher costs of the technology. It may well be that today customers and employees are more sensitive to environmental or social issues than 10 years ago, which means that, depending on the country, industry and company, CSR programmes can be consistent with shareholder value maximization. As Patrick Cescau, CEO of Unilever, recipient of the 2007 Botwinick Prize in Business Ethics, said when he described one of the company's CSR activities in India:

> The project is not a philanthropic activity. It is a serious and profitable commercial proposition.[20]

The business case for CSR policies was made by Milton Friedman (1970) in an article in the *New York Times Magazine*:

> To illustrate, it may well be in the long-run interest of a corporation who is a major employer in a small community to devote resources to providing amenities to that community or to improve its government . . . In each of these . . . cases, there is a strong temptation to rationalize these actions as an exercise of 'social responsibility'. In the present climate of opinion, with its widespread aversion to 'capitalism', 'profits', the 'soulless corporation' and so on, this is one way for the corporation to generate goodwill as its by-product of expenditures that are entirely justified by its own self-interest. It would be inconsistent of me to call on corporate executives to refrain from this hypocritical window dressing because it harms the foundations of a free society. If our institutions and the attitudes of the public make it in their self-interest to cloak their actions in this way, I cannot summon much indignation to denounce them.

Many CSR initiatives deal with firms getting involved with avoiding negative externalities such as pollution. Although dealing with externalities should be the role of the government (Jensen, 2002), it could be argued that many developing countries have very lax standards. One executive of a large European chemical firm once asked me whether, given these low standards, his company should pollute when producing in India, even though the company in Europe had always tried to be concerned about the environment. My answer was that, considering that his shareholders were well aware of the high environmental standards of his company, they may well expect that the firm would maintain these standards when going abroad. Giving up excess profits in India was therefore not unethical. Moreover, the company should make sure that other stakeholders such as customers and workers were aware of these high standards, making it less likely that this policy would be inconsistent with shareholder value maximization. Hence, although this policy may create smaller profits in the short run, it may well increase shareholder value created by gaining goodwill from other stakeholders.

Ideally, these principles and policies should be stated at the time of the Initial Public Offering (IPO), and they should be part of a well publicized, regularly repeated mission statement. If a subsequent change in policy would be negatively perceived by the stock market (i.e., the introduction of a CSR programme with no business case) this decision then can be considered as unethical to the existing stockholders. This is a strong argument for making sure that CSR initiatives following an IPO are justified by a strong business case.

On 26 May, 2008, the *Wall Street Journal* reported that the Rockefeller family wanted to change Exxon's investment policy and bring it in line with BP; that is, invest more in alternative energy sources and show more concern about global warming. Interestingly, at the time Exxon's stock price was trading at an all-time high. Exxon's CEO Rex Tillerson resisted this attempt by pointing out that his job was to protect shareholders' investments and focus on its core business of oil and natural gas and that he would not invest in potential new fuels simply because it was the politically correct thing to do. If he truly believed that the Rockefellers' policy would destroy shareholder value, he had an ethical responsibility to fight the Rockefeller family. Although some of the Rockefellers were trying to make a business case, others were obviously driven by other considerations. According to the *Wall Street Journal*, 'the new found activism appears to be another outburst of the unease about their oil-based fortune that periodically grips family members' and by challenging Exxon 'they are trying to remove the stain of oil from their family name. For them Exxon is not only an environmental malefactor, it's also original sin'. Note that during the previous two years Exxon's share price increased by 50%, while BP's stock price did not increase over the same time period. So the Rockefellers' desire to shift strategy was clearly not motivated by the relative performance of BP's and Exxon shares. It seems that other investors were quite happy with the current Exxon policy. If the Rockefeller family disagreed with this optimism, the logical step would be to sell its overvalued shares and use the cash to invest in firms that invest in alternative energy sources.

One could argue that CSR programmes that don't hurt shareholders are not really 'social', they are just public relations exercises.[21] The view in this chapter would suggest the opposite: unanticipated CSR initiatives that deliberately aim to hurt shareholders are unethical. Examples of such programmes are initiatives to counter global warming. Apart from a few major oil companies, no individual firm has a significant impact on the planet's temperature. If a car company deliberately cancelled the production of its high-end polluting cars, it would not affect global temperatures, but would make its customers, workers and shareholders worse off (unless, of course, out of sympathy, the increased demand for the other cars offset the losses from cancelling the high-end cars). As it is difficult to imagine that there are implicit contracts that expect managers to deliberately destroy shareholder value, without any offsetting benefits, such CSR programmes should be considered unethical. In a similar way, a firm that does not pursue all possibilities to minimize its taxes acts unethically unless it has clearly stated that the goal is to maximize *before* tax profits, not after tax. Note that the relationship with the tax authorities is governed by a massive amount of explicit rules and regulations, and so it is hard to argue that this relationship is governed by implicit contracts such as a contract to 'pay taxes in good faith'. As the Honorable Learned Hand, US Appeals Judge, concluded in *Hevering v. Gregory* in 1934:

> Anyone may arrange his affairs so that his taxes shall be as low as possible . . . he is not bound to choose that pattern which best pays the treasury. There is not even a patriotic duty to increase one's taxes. Over and over again the Courts have said that there is nothing sinister in so arranging affairs as to keep taxes as low as possible . . . To demand more in the name of morals is a mere cant.

Implicit Contracts with Other Stakeholders

James and Tang (1996) report that the CEOs of the 20 companies with the largest announced layoffs in 1995 saw their salaries and bonuses jump by 25%, and Chen and Tang (2006) consider this to be an example of unethical behaviour because 'the savings of labour costs go to

CEO's own pockets'. If this was simply a transfer from workers to the CEO, shareholders would not have benefited from the layoffs. Hence the decision was not motivated by shareholder value maximization, but by stakeholder value maximization: increasing the wealth of one stakeholder (the CEO) at the expense of another stakeholder (the employees). The authors do not estimate the gains to shareholders (present value of after tax cost savings from the layoffs), and so it is not obvious that this decision was unethical, if managers were expected to maximize shareholder value.

One could argue that employee contracts also have implicit features, and that breaking these implicit contracts is also unethical. I fully agree, but I believe that the shorter maturity of the employee contract means that an employee is better equipped to protect him- or herself against unethical behaviour. Take for example the case of privatization of public enterprises. Workers perceive a public enterprise as less risky than a private enterprise and therefore may be willing to accept lower salaries. If privatization only increases risk without increasing expected salaries, one could argue that this is a violation of the implicit contract between the company and the employees, and an unexpected windfall to the shareholders of the public company (i.e., the tax payers). However, to the extent that workers can find another job, they are protected against this risk increase. In other words, they can rent their human capital to another employer who will compensate them for the incurred risk. Note that in the case of privatizations, it is the government that breaks the contract, not the CEO.

Goshal (2005) challenges this view by claiming that employees carry more risks than shareholders. His logic is that 'the shareholders can sell their stock more easily than employees can find a job' (Goshal, 2005, p. 80). The problem with selling the shares is, of course, at what price? On 28 November, 2001, Enron's stock price fell by 85%. Some Enron shareholders who saw what was coming may have been able to pass the hot potato to others, but eventually shareholders as a group lost US$70 billion. The employees of Enron lost part of the value of their Enron-specific human capital, but some of them did not. The *New York Times* reported on 8 March, 2002, that there was 'a rush by investment banks and Enron competitors to hire Enron employees'. These were the employees with a lot of industry-specific human capital such as knowledge about energy trading. Employees also received US$85 million in severance payments and US$335 million in compensation for lost pension benefits.

The situation of employees is not unlike the situation of bondholders, who also are concerned about an increase in the riskiness of the firm's assets. However, besides asking for collateral, they can protect themselves by shortening the maturity of the debt. Shortening maturities means that debt has to be refinanced continuously. If firms unexpectedly increased the riskiness of the business, they would be forced to pay higher interest rates at the time of the refinancing or simply give the money back and search for other lenders.

The same can be said about implicit contracts with customers. Companies that behave unethically by misleading customers will be punished in the future by reduced sales, making unethical behaviour uneconomic. Of course, this reputation effect will play less when we are dealing with sales of durable goods or services that are used only rarely.[22] For example, investment bankers are often criticized that they behave unethically in mergers and acquisitions by artificially increasing valuations of takeover targets. As the value of a company is the present value of a stream of perpetual cash flows, one can easily increase transaction values by making excessively optimistic forecasts.

This incentive is a result of the practice of paying success fees in acquisitions, and bonuses paid to bankers following these fees. However, acquirers should know that investment bankers are supposed to maximize shareholder value of their bank, not the value of their customers. The CEO of the acquirers is also responsible for acquisition decisions, so that person should be able to understand company valuation methods and have an informed discussion about the valuation methods and assumptions used. In other words, the CEO should provide the inputs for the valuation spreadsheet, not the bank. The situation is not unlike that of the buyer of a car, who knows that private sellers have an incentive to sell the car at the highest price and that it is the duty of the buyer to collect independent information on the quality of the car, or to ask for guarantees.

THE BOTTOM LINE

In this chapter, I propose a code of ethics that is free from ideological bias, free from subjective values other than the respect for implicit contracts. This respect does not arise from a desire to 'do good' but from a desire to promote the function of a free market economy, where managers and shareholders are different people. This definition implies that, in order for corporations to survive, it is important to respect implicit contracts, especially when it is very costly or impossible to write explicit contracts. Respecting the implicit contracts with *all* its stakeholders is important,[23] however, I believe that the contract between the shareholder and the corporation is the most implicit of all contracts. Indeed a shareholder has an explicit right to vote, but not much else. Hence, if shareholders expect that a firm maximizes shareholder value, non-value maximizing strategies, such as unanticipated CSR initiatives without a business case, are unethical. Respecting this ethical commitment will create the trust that is necessary for the company's survival in competitive markets.

What is important, however, is to communicate clearly to all stakeholders the nature of the implicit features of their respective contracts. Therefore, a non-profit organization behaves ethically if shareholders get no compensation and all benefits accrue to the other stakeholders. But at the same time, a 'non-wage' organization that employs volunteer workers and pays out all profits to shareholders behaves no less ethically.

By focusing on the need to respect implicit contracts, and not on the 'values' of decision makers, it is my hope that relations between Ethics professors and Finance professors will become less antagonistic, to the greater benefit of the student population who will be less confused as a result. Future research then should be focused on how effective companies are in communicating the implicit contracts they have with each of their stakeholders. Agle *et al.* (2008) report that out of a random sample of 100 Fortune 500 companies, approximately one-third mention in their mission statements that their goal is to maximize shareholder value, whereas the rest aim at maximizing the well-being of all stakeholders. The problem with the latter type of general statements is that they can be interpreted in various ways. Stating that you care about all stakeholders can also be interpreted as maximizing shareholder value because shareholders are residual claimholders. If shareholders are paid, it means that your customers like your product and everyone else is paid as well.

Finance core courses should make it clear from the beginning that there is nothing unethical about the pursuit of shareholder value, quite the opposite. Students should also understand that when markets are not perfectly efficient, maximizing the current stock price is not the same as maximizing shareholder value. Through its focus on perpetual cash flow, shareholder value maximization implies being concerned about the long run and about cash flows, not accounting profits. The Enron and other notorious scandals driven by accounting fraud have *nothing to do* with the presumed focus on shareholder value. They are the result of a focus on the current stock price and the use of accounting tricks to manipulate earnings. This manipulation may be encouraged by the perception that company valuation involves multiplying short-term earnings with some earnings multiple and/or the fact that managers are compensated on the basis of short-term performance (such as earnings per share).

Managers should also be less timid in defending the pursuit of shareholder value as a policy that maximizes social welfare, as well as a policy that is ethically responsible. I understand that this is difficult, because defending capitalism is still as politically incorrect as 40 years ago when Milton Friedman complained about the widespread aversion to 'profits' and the 'soulless corporation'.

If the prices that customers pay and/or the salaries that workers are willing to accept are influenced by CSR policies, a business case for CSR can be made and these policies are not inconsistent with shareholder value maximization (as pointed out by Milton Friedman back in 1970). However, whether a business case for CSR policies can be made is ultimately an empirical question, and a case-specific question. CSR policies for which no business case can be made are not necessarily unethical, provided these policies were clearly communicated to investors at the time when they bought shares in the company. However, any policy that leads to large shareholder value destruction is not likely to survive the discipline imposed by the market for corporate control.

NOTES

1. I am grateful to Jake Cohen, Marcel Corsjens, Katrina Maxwell, Craig Smith and David Ronnegard for helpful comments. Of course all errors and opinions are mine.
2. See, for example, Goshal (2005).
3. In a 19 May, 2008, *Financial Times* article, written by Paul Broughton, entitled 'MBA students swap integrity for plagiarism', INSEAD ethics professor Craig Smith is quoted as saying 'the focus on maximizing shareholder value causes some students to minimize other important codes of behavior'. Recent evidence that MBA students cheat more on exams than other students is provided by McCabe, Butterfield and Trevino (2006).
4. Such hostility towards money and finance can be traced to ancient times when various religions opposed 'the usurer who is a sinner because he does not work and as such does not involve himself in time as God intended' (Van Houdt, 1995).
5. For example, Kochan (2002) claims that the root of corporate scandals is 'the overemphasis American corporations have been forced to give in recent years to maximize shareholder value without regard for effect of their actions on other stakeholders'. Deakin and Konzelman (2003) state that 'the narrowness of the focus on shareholder value is the major contributing factor to the present round of corporate scandals of which Enron is the most emblematic'. Bratton (2003) sees the scandals as an example of 'the dark side of shareholder value'. See also Goshal (2005).
6. See footnote 5, for examples.
7. Even if a company's life is shortened, for example, through a takeover, the value of the bid should again be based on the present value of expected future cash flows.
8. Koller, Goedhart and Wessels are all McKinsey consultants.

9. Note that in an efficient market, where stock prices reflect all available information, the distinction between short-term and long-term shareholders is irrelevant.

10. The authors also do not provide tools on how managers are supposed to accomplish this heroic task.

11. For example, The American Petroleum institute reported that in 2006 US oil companies paid US$135 billion in corporate taxes, roughly the same amount as the personal income taxes collected from the 100 million Americans who represent 75% of tax payers.

12. Note that Jensen (2002) talks about total market value (debt plus equity) not shareholder value. As long as the debt is risk-free, both decision frameworks are identical.

13. For a definition of the business case, see Smith (2003).

14. Of course, this assumes perfect mobility of labour. On the other hand, in contrast to workers, shareholders do not get severance payments or other forms of social assistance when they lose their invested capital. For example, Enron employees received US$ 70 million in severance payments plus US$ 335 million of compensation for the loss of pensions.

15. Arguable to all stakeholders, but as pointed out before, contracts with other stakeholder are far more explicit than contracts with shareholders.

16. Of course, investors realize that shareholder value maximization is always constrained by the law. Shareholders do not believe that engaging in criminal activity in order to maximize shareholder value is an ethical responsibility!

17. One way to reduce the importance of ethics is to tie managerial compensation to stock prices, e.g., via stock options etc. The problem with these remedies is that they are costly or inefficient solutions. Specifically, stock prices are to a large extent driven by factors out of control of the management, which makes the incentivizing effect of stock options questionable. Managers may also be induced to focus on short-term stock prices rather than long-term value. For example, the exercise prices in stock options can often be paid with the firm's common stock at the time when the options are exercised.

18. This means that one cannot test the profitability or costs of CSR programmes by calculating long-horizon stock returns (e.g., by comparing returns on ethical and non-ethical mutual funds). If market prices reflect the cost of these programmes at the time the CSR programme is announced, subsequent risk-adjusted returns should be independent of the CSR programme. The cost/benefit of CSR programmes should be reflected in the stock price, not in the subsequent returns. An alternative method is to do an event study that examines market responses around the announcement of a CSR initiative. One of the earlier examples of such an approach is Hall and Rieck (1998) who find no significant announcement returns around the announcement of 99 CSR events. One exception: donations generate significant positive announcement returns of 2.3%. However, the problem with this event study (as well as with event studies in general) is that this positive response could also be interpreted as an information signal: firms that give away goods and services are firms with good earnings prospects.

19. Personally, my choice of a petrol station is mainly driven by the fact that I happen to run out of fuel and stop at the nearest station. However, I may not be the representative consumer and appealing to green sensitivities may well be a profitable strategy.

20. Acceptance speech of Patrick Cescau, Columbia Business School, Social enterprise Conference, 26 October 2007.

21. See, for example, *The Economist* on 17 November, 2001: 'The new commitment to social responsibility is a sham, beginning where the search for profit carries on as before, leaving capitalism in good shape after all'.

22. Of course, word of mouth may have a major effect on reputation.

23. As pointed out by Donaldson (1982).

REFERENCES

Agle, R.B., Donaldson, T., Freeman, R.E., Jensen, M.C., Mitchell, R. K. and Wood, D. J. (2008) Dialogue: Toward superior stakeholder theory, *Business Ethics Quarterly*, **18** (2), 153–90.

Bratton, W. (2002) Enron and the dark side of shareholder value, *Tulane Law Review*, **76**, 1275–361.

Chen Y.-J. and Tang, T.L.-P. (2006) Attitude toward and propensity to engage in unethical behavior: Measurement invariance across major among university students, *Journal of Business Ethics*, **69**, 77–93.

Deakin, S. and Konzelmann, S.J (2003) After Enron: An age of enlightenment?, *Organisation*, **10** (3), 583–87.

Donaldson, T. (1982) *Corporations and Morality*, Prentice Hall, Englewood Cliffs, NJ.

Friedman, M. (1970) The social responsibility of business is to increase its profits, *New York Times Magazine*, 13 September, **33**, 122–6.

Goshal, S. (2005) Bad management theories are destroying good management practices, *Academy of Management Learning and Education*, **4** (1), 75–91.

Hall, P.L and Rieck, R. (1998) The effect of positive social actions on shareholder wealth, *Journal of Financial and Strategic Decisions*, **11** (2), 83–9.

James, T.A.W. and Tang, T.L.P. (1996) Downsizing and the impact on survivors – a matter of justice, *Employment Relations Today*, (Summer), 33–41.

Jensen, M. (2002) Value maximization, stakeholder theory and the corporate objective function, *Business Ethics Quarterly*, **12** (2), 235–47.

Jensen, M. and Meckling, W. (1976) Theory of the firm: managerial behaviour, agency costs and ownership structure, *Journal of Financial Economics*, **3**, 305–60.

Kochan, T.A. (2002) Addressing the crisis in confidence in corporations: Root causes, victims and strategies for reform, *Academy of Management Executive*, **17**, 139–41.

Koller, T., Goedhart, M. and Wessels, D. (2005) *Measuring and Managing the Value of Companies*, John Wiley & Sons, Inc., New York.

Lessius, L. (1605) *De Iustitia et Ure*, Library of the Department of Theology of the Catholic University of Leuven.

McCabe, D., Butterfield, K. and Trevino, L.K. (2006) Academic dishonesty in graduate business programs: prevalence, causes and proposed action, *Academy of Management Learning and Education*, **5** (3), 294–305.

Smith, C. (2003) Corporate social responsibility: Whether or how?, *California Management Review*, **45** (Summer), 52–76.

Sundaram, K.A. and Inkpen, A.C. (2004) The corporate objective revisited, *Organisation Science*, **14** (3), 350–63.

Van Houdt, T. (1995) Money, time and labour; Leonardo Lessius and the ethics of lending and interest taking, *Ethical Perspectives*, **2**, 11–27.

Vermaelen, T. (1981) Common stock repurchases and market signalling: an empirical study, *Journal of Financial Economics*, **9** (2), 138–83.

Wells, J.T. (2001) Why employees commit fraud, *Journal of Accountancy*, **191** (2), 89–92.

CHAPTER THIRTEEN

Veridian: Putting a Value on Values[1]

Rakesh Khurana, Joel Podolny and Jaan Elias, Harvard Business School

INTRODUCTION

David Langstaff, the CEO of Veridian, could be excused if he identified with those doomed fishermen in the film *The Perfect Storm*. An unexpected combination of factors had made his medium-sized defence and intelligence contractor, which focused on security and information systems, an extremely attractive takeover target. Now with an offer on the table, the first wave had broken over the bow and he wondered whether his company was about to be engulfed.

Although some CEOs might have welcomed the opportunity to sell their companies for a substantial premium, Langstaff had not built Veridian to be a high flier in the stock market. He had assembled it through the acquisition of small technical service and research companies with the purpose of undertaking critical information technology work for the US defence industry. As Veridian grew, Langstaff emphasized values-based leadership to build a corporate community that would serve the long-term interests of customers, employees and suppliers, as well as shareholders. Veridian had managed to attract some of the best technologists in the country and had built a solid reputation with US defence and intelligence clients.

But in the first half of 2003, Veridian's mix of capabilities had attracted takeover interest from the top tier of defence contractors. One of the 'primes' (as the top-tier defence contractors were known), Quiescent Systems,[2] had put an all-cash offer of US$28 a share on the table. Since the offer represented a 40% premium on Veridian's current stock price, Langstaff felt obligated to bring the offer to the attention of his board. Although the board had not been shopping the company and felt the US$28 offer was too low, they believed they had a fiduciary obligation to explore this and other credible offers.

Langstaff now faced some tough analysis. As the CEO, he had concerned himself with inculcating his organization with the values necessary for superior achievement over the long term. But as a fiduciary, he had to come up with a single value to monetize the reputation the company had built. Langstaff wondered what was best for the firm and its customers, and what other options he had. He was also concerned with how the prospect of selling the firm would square with Veridian's commitment to its constituencies and values-based leadership.

THE GENESIS OF VERIDIAN

From HBS to Space

Like many of his peers in the Harvard Business School class of 1981, David Langstaff took a job in finance upon graduation. Unlike his classmates, however, Langstaff soon traded the world of finance for the out-of-the-world business of space.

Langstaff's finance job was with The Inverness Group in Houston, Texas. Inverness made venture and small capital investments. One of the firm's projects soon after Langstaff arrived was providing 'angel capital' for an R&D partnership of former NASA engineers. After a year and a half during which the R&D partnership did some solid technical work but financially yielded little more than tax write-offs, Langstaff and his colleagues were faced with a decision about what to do with their investment. Impressed by the engineers and having a predilection for investing in up-and-coming industries, they decided that they would arrange for more financing if the engineers would commit to building a full-fledged company. And so, Space Industries was born.

Rather than watch Space Industries from the sidelines, Langstaff decided that he, too, would commit his time and energy to the young firm. He was drawn to the company by the reputation of its founders: 'I joined the company to work with some remarkable people; the people to whom President Kennedy turned in order to put a man on the moon – the great architects of the United States manned space program. When they asked me to join them and do something with the company, I realized I had to do it.'

Working with the NASA veterans shaped Langstaff's perspective on management. 'In talking with people like Max Faget, Bob Gilruth, Chris Kraft, and Alan Shephard, you got a sense of what human beings can accomplish when bound together by a common vision and commitment, working as a team,' Langstaff recalled. Beside the impressive technical achievement, he continued, 'people who were part of the early NASA years talk about that time as their most satisfying professional experience. Although the mission was bigger than any individual, each person's work had the clarity you get when you share a goal. You don't get that often in life.'[3]

Langstaff became the senior businessman in a company of rocket scientists. When he joined in 1984, he was made CFO, but soon found that his duties included everything from operations to marketing: 'My essential responsibility was to turn an engineering project into a business. And as one of the few non-technical employees, I had to deal with the entire business side of the company.'

The fledgling concern encountered numerous setbacks. However, President (and former astronaut) Joseph Allen observed, 'Despite the obstacles we faced at Space Industries, the people became increasingly confident of each other as members of a team. We clearly had a very good chemistry going.' In the early 1990s, NASA's priorities shifted; most discretionary dollars were focused on designing the International Space Station. In this new era, funding of new civilian initiatives would be limited, and Space Industries management decided it had to diversify its customer base in order to stay afloat.

Midcourse Correction

In 1993, Space Industries agreed to merge with Calspan, a division of Arvin Industries. Calspan was a well-known aeronautics testing and evaluation company with contracts primarily with the US Air

Force. The merger brought the diversification that the Space Industries leadership desired, but it also plunged the management team into a turnaround situation.

Calspan had been founded in the late 1940s. During the Second World War, the government had built an advanced wind tunnel in Buffalo, New York. Once the war ended, the government offered the facility to Cornell University. For the next decades, the Cornell Aeronautics Laboratory (the 'CAL' of Calspan) conducted tests and evaluations of just about every government-sponsored aircraft. When the space programme began, the laboratory also tested all US and European manned spacecraft. Langstaff noted: 'During this period, Calspan had a stellar reputation. If you were one of the top people in aeronautics engineering or a related field, regardless of where you were in the Western world, you owed it to yourself to see if there was a job opportunity at Calspan.'

When Cornell became the object of protesters against the Vietnam War, Calspan was spun off. Soon after its debut as a public company, Arvin, a company whose core business was in automobile parts, purchased Calspan.

In pursuing the merger with Space Industries, the Arvin management team was looking for help to reinvigorate Calspan. Arvin had been treating the division as a cash cow and had not reinvested in the business. Langstaff, who was appointed the CFO (and later COO) of the merged entity, noted: 'Arvin acquired us not so much for our contracts, but for our management team.'

The new management team recognized that some tough choices had to be made in order to cut expenses and refocus the entity. They reduced the number of divisions, made some layoffs, terminated the defined-benefit pension plan and began to focus the business on future growth. Despite the difficulty of these changes, Langstaff believed that the turnaround had gone quite smoothly.

When the combined company (now renamed Space Industries International, Inc., or 'SIII') decided to sell one of its product lines, Langstaff learned a lesson in building employee goodwill. The product line did not fit with SIII's service focus, and so Langstaff sold the business to another firm. However, it became clear that the acquiring firm would employ the SIII employees who worked on the product line only for the short time it took to integrate the product into the company's own offerings and then let them go with nominal severance. Some of these employees had been with the SIII predecessor company in excess of 20 years; so Langstaff decided to take 10% of the sale proceeds and set up a separate severance fund to augment the severance the employees would get from their new employer. Beside the goodwill this built with the directly affected employees, Langstaff noted:

> The story started to spread throughout the company. We didn't publicize it – word just got out. What I didn't realize was the impact that little action would have on the employees throughout the rest of the company. It earned more goodwill among the remaining 2000 or so employees of SIII than I could have ever imagined. It was a clear example of living our values.

Entering the 'Solutions Business'

Just as SIII was emerging from its two-year period of reorganization, Arvin's management changed. The new leadership decided to divest itself of SIII in order to concentrate on its core automotive business. Langstaff and Allen believed Arvin was making the right decision, and asked if they could arrange financing to purchase the business. Arvin agreed, and after obtaining the appropriate fairness opinions, sold the business for US$42.6 million – essentially book value. In the year before the sale, SIII had recorded sales of continuing operations of just under US$120 million.

Langstaff, who became the CEO of the private entity, decided the company had to diversify its customer base. In the mid-1990s, the defence industry was going through massive consolidation. Langstaff feared that the company was too dependent on just one part of the US Department of Defense (DoD). In 1997, the company merged with Veda International, a company that did aeronautics testing for the Navy. After the merger, the combined entity took the name 'Veridian' – a name whose root origin came from the Latin and Greek words for truth. In 1998, Veridian purchased the Rail Company, a small company that did aeronautics testing for the Army.

However, even as Veridian was broadening its client base, the management team knew that the company had to increase the scope of its offerings. The aeronautics testing market was stagnant and the company wanted to add capabilities in fields for which there was increasing demand. The management team therefore decided to focus in the areas of information technologies and intelligence. Board Chairman Allen saw this move as an extension of Veridian's testing work:

> Veridian was a service company in the business of providing the federal government with individuals who were trained in running tests. Test data had become increasingly computer intensive. We were developing clever and sophisticated application programs to glean information from the data that we were generating. Since we were dealing with secret data, we also developed expertise in computer security.

Langstaff believed that the new strategic focus continued the historic legacy of Veridian's predecessor companies:

> I believed that Veridian needed to continue to be active at the cutting edge of work that mattered. For nearly 50 years, Calspan and Veda had been at the forefront of research, test, and evaluation in the aeronautics industry. I knew that we couldn't turn our back on this heritage. In fact, it was a huge cultural asset on which to build.

In late 1998, Veridian started its diversification push by purchasing Pacific-Sierra Research Company, a small technology company that had the bulk of its contracts with intelligence agencies. In 1999, Veridian took a bold step in adding capabilities by acquiring three companies simultaneously: Environmental Research Institute of Michigan (ERIM) International, a leader in sensor technology; Trident Data Systems, a company that specialized in computer network security systems; and MRJ Technology Solutions, a company that designed and integrated technical operating systems. Each company had specialized in supplying highly technical services or products to defence and intelligence agencies. The companies had similar cultures and were entrepreneurial ventures with a high percentage of employee ownership. Bob Farrell, president of the Information Systems Division of MRJ Technology Solutions, recounted why his employee-owned company decided to join Veridian:

> MRJ was a group of people who really believed in what we were doing for the government and the country. In 10 years, the company had grown from UA$30 million to US$150 million in annual sales and we were excited about our prospects. MRJ was entirely owned by its employees through an ESOP (employee stock ownership plan), and by ERISA rules, it was necessary for us to cash out those employees who were retiring. Therefore, we were faced with the prospect of having to borrow money in order to retire some of our best talent . . . We started talking with David Langstaff about his vision

for expanding Veridian and decided that his vision made a lot of sense. For example, Trident Data Systems was a partner of ours in many government contracts and we knew we would be complementary. When the decision went to a vote, the employees decided that they liked Langstaff's approach to leadership, were excited by his plans to do something big in defence information and intelligence, and seemed to have sufficient financial backing to carry this vision forward.

The acquisitions doubled Veridian's revenues to over US$600 million a year and boosted its payroll to over 5000 employees. Langstaff then took on the important job of integrating the acquisitions. He recounted:

> After we made the acquisitions, we took three months and put all of Veridian on the whiteboard. We had seven heritage companies that we then cut and pasted into three operating divisions: Veridian Engineering, Veridian Systems, and Veridian Information Solutions. I believed this move was essential, in that we had 'sold' the companies and their employees on the vision of what Veridian could become. We had to show them that we were serious in pursuit of the vision. Taking this approach was an exciting and, at times, frightening exercise. But it helped break through the parochial loyalties and gave people a sense of the entire company. It got everyone focused on the future and how best to realize it.

With its new acquisitions, Veridian moved into the 'solutions business' of using its capabilities in information and intelligence to provide mission-critical systems for defence and intelligence agencies. (See Exhibit 13.1 for a detailed look at Veridian's capabilities.) The solutions and information technology business was a new niche among defence contractors. Most large defence contractors designed and manufactured large-scale weapons platforms, such as tanks, airplanes or artillery pieces. As Jerry Howe, Veridian's senior vice president, noted:

> Veridian differed from the primes in that their legacy is in industrial production, whereas our core identity is in professional services. We understood from the outset that what we were doing was developing a world-class professional services organization. We knew that the key was creating a virtuous cycle where you get good people, which in turn allows you to do interesting and important work, which allows you to get more good people, which in turn generates new ideas for even more work.

EXHIBIT 13.1 VERIDIAN'S CORE CAPABILITIES

NETWORK SECURITY AND ENTERPRISE PROTECTION

- *Intrusion Prevention, Detection and Response.* We provide solutions that protect networks on a 24/7 basis through a system of firewalls and security applications that monitor systems, detect intrusions and unauthorized activity, notify users of suspicious activity, identify and track intruders and provide repairs to restore security in the system.

- *Threat and Risk Assessment.* We provide services to test network and enterprise security status, specifically for vulnerability to potential threats, and provide consultation services regarding the required security upgrades and implementations.

- *Information Operations.* We develop and deploy a broad range of information tools to combat cyber aggression and other threats, including high-level planning, intelligence analysis, forensic analysis, attack signature identification and technical implementation.

(Continued)

EXHIBIT 13.1 (*Continued*)

- *Computer Forensics and Emergency Response.* We provide tools and techniques to determine the impact to digital systems of intrusions or unauthorized activity, as well as provide services for the rapid recovery of digital media to sustain business operations.
- *Multi-Level Secure Communications.* We provide technologies and systems that permit simultaneous access to data and applications involving different levels of security classification and authorization on a single protected system.
- *Security Policy and Administration.* We develop and implement policies to ensure the availability, safety and integrity of enterprise applications to include applications for both cyber and physical security.

INTELLIGENCE, SURVEILLANCE AND RECONNAISSANCE (ISR)

- *Remote Sensing Technology and Systems.* We research, develop and deploy leading-edge sensors which collect information about a target or a geographic region from remote aircraft and spacecraft to provide valuable, timely information to intelligence analysts or battlefield planners.
- *Sensor Processing and Exploitation.* We develop tools to extract useful information from remotely-sensed images or other data products, including techniques to enhance images and computer methods to automate target detection and identification.
- *Data Collection Management.* We develop and deploy tools and systems for the optimal scheduling of complex constellations of satellite-based data collection sensors in space.
- *Modeling and Simulation.* We develop models to predict sensor and total ISR system performance and their effectiveness in realistic operational scenarios.

KNOWLEDGE DISCOVERY AND DECISION SUPPORT

- *Data Mining and Event Correlation.* We develop, deploy and operate systems that allow customers to gather and analyze large volumes of data and detect unseen patterns or abnormalities through the application of sophisticated techniques such as customized data algorithms, neural networks and multiple regression models.
- *Data Warehousing.* We develop and deploy systems that combine separate databases and files into a single logical entity, primarily for databases and files that may not have been designed to work together, improving the effectiveness of a customer's mission-critical operations.
- *Multi-Source Data Fusion.* We provide capabilities to combine data from distinctly different sources, such as radar and optical sensors, into a common model for intelligence analysis and decision-making.
- *Detection Technology Research.* We develop sensor technologies that detect chemical and biological agents and nuclear contaminants, materials and weapons.

- *Monitoring Systems.* We design, develop and deploy nuclear detection systems to support counter-proliferation requirements and national security needs.

- *Incident Response Systems.* We design and develop systems that merge collection, analysis, assessment, and decision aids into a comprehensive system to support authorities in responding to natural and man-made disasters.

NETWORK AND ENTERPRISE MANAGEMENT

- *Network Design, Implementation and Operation.* We provide end-to-end network services including network design services, Local Area Network design, Wide Area Network design, total network support, network and telecommunications engineering, network operations, technology upgrades, security and system maintenance support.

- *Training and Simulation Systems.* We design, create and integrate large, network-based computer models that simulate the complex environment of military operations, providing a realistic training environment for senior battlefield commanders and their staffs.

- *Development and Management of Network and Enterprise Operations Centers.* We develop operations centers to improve network and enterprise efficiency by instrumenting and measuring network performance and by providing quantitative data to enable decision-making in support of the enterprise mission and its infrastructure. We manage these centers on a 24x7 basis for our customers.

- *Information Systems Integration.* We integrate new hardware and software platforms with existing computer networks, upgrade communication protocols and interfaces, ensure systems compatibility and migrate applications to new operating systems and platforms all to improve network system reliability, availability and security.

SYSTEMS ENGINEERING SERVICES

- *Spacecraft and Aircraft Research, Development, Testing and Evaluation.* We provide expert systems engineering analysis, tools, techniques and models to support the research, development, test and evaluation of the U.S. government's spacecraft, aircraft, and missile programs.

- *Systems Life Cycle Support.* We provide expert engineering support for all phases of design, development and operations of major national intelligence systems.

- *Modeling and Simulation for Systems Acquisition Support.* We develop models and simulations and perform engineering and operational analyses to support the Department of Defense's weapons systems acquisition processes from early concept development to full system production.

- *Intelligent Transportation Systems.* We develop vehicle-based technologies to make vehicles safer and to add 'smart' technologies to vehicles in order to provide more effective and efficient emergency responses.

Source: Company documents

VALUES-BASED LEADERSHIP

Employer of Choice

As Veridian was increasing its technical capabilities and establishing itself in its emerging market space, Langstaff was defining his company's strategic intent in terms of its employees and the kind of work they performed. He wanted to make Veridian the most attractive workplace so that the company could dominate its particular niche of the labour market. Langstaff told his top executives:

> The premier workers will be able to choose their employer. I believe that if a company cannot offer an exciting and inspiring vision – values that it doesn't just state, but acts on; and a stimulating work environment – then that company simply won't be able to attract the premier knowledge employees, much less retain the ones it has. Our goal is to become the employer of choice – the place where the best want to work.

Langstaff believed the employee focus fit with Veridian's overall strategy. The services Veridian offered demanded top-flight employees who not only had the relevant technical skills but also could be creative and exercise judgement. In addition, since gaining security clearances was essential for most of Veridian's work, employees had to be of exemplary character. There were constant shortages of technical professionals with security clearances and the process of gaining a security clearance could take over a year. The fact that 80% of Veridian's employees had a high-level security clearance was a major asset.

In order to become the employer of choice, Langstaff believed Veridian had to offer its employees the following:

- **The opportunity to participate in a compelling mission.** Although it is possible to do technically challenging work within any market area, the best technologists are motivated by taking on the most important problems of their day. Veridian's projects in the defence and security area carried great weight (especially in a post-9/11 world). The company was dealing with problems in areas such as cyber security, critical infrastructure protection, bio-terrorism, nuclear proliferation and threat identification that were on the front pages of the world's newspapers. Langstaff could tell his managers with no hyperbole, 'Our success or failure as a business matters – not only to our customers, but also to our society, our country and increasingly to our world.'

- **Sufficient size to attract resources and to play a leading role in projects.** Langstaff knew that scientists could become frustrated if they always played the role of a subcontractor on projects. Therefore, Langstaff wanted Veridian to attain the scale necessary to take the lead and serve as the prime contractor on most of the contracts it secured. Attaining this scale also would mean that Veridian employees would be directly serving the end customer, without other intermediaries.

- **A community built around values such as integrity, trust, responsibility and ethical behaviour.** Of the three components for making Veridian the employer of choice, Langstaff believed that this objective was the most critical. He noted:

> People are social animals. They are better, more productive, and more fulfilled when they see themselves as part of something bigger than themselves. What is a community but a group

held together through shared values? There's no reason why you can't think of a corporation in this way. These values must exist in the way we work with our customers, and in the way we work with ourselves.

Langstaff articulated Veridian's values in a vision statement and leadership model that was distributed to all of the employees (see Exhibit 13.2). Veridian's model of 'values-based leadership' was a series of statements of principle, urging employees to embrace cooperation, innovation, integrity and excellence in customer service. Leadership at Veridian, Langstaff maintained, was an attitude meant for everyone; it was not a function of title or position.

EXHIBIT 13.2   VERIDIAN VALUES-BASED LEADERSHIP MODEL

Vision

Applying technology to solve problems that matter for our customers; setting the standard of performance as a community of leaders and the employer of choice; making a difference in areas that make a difference.

Values

Do the right thing, consistently and over the long term, for our customers, our employees, our shareholders and our communities.

Leadership Model

Redefine Superior Customer Service

The Veridian leader has a deep understanding of customer needs and exceeds customer expectations in all respects, positioning the company to shape and subsequently address future customer needs. Leadership means taking customer service and support to continually higher levels and essentially redefining customer expectations of excellence. Delivering superior customer service means providing total solutions to the whole customer, i.e., all major participants in the delivery chain. Attention to detail, bursts of innovation, commitment to quality and, above all, unquestioned integrity are part of redefining superior customer service.

Leverage Total Resources

The Veridian leader moves beyond what the individual or the team can deliver and pulls resources from across the organization to meet current and emergent requirements and to create entirely new opportunities for the corporation. The Veridian leader is familiar with plans, capabilities and technologies throughout the organization and can connect customer needs with appropriate responses.

Drive for Results

The Veridian leader is passionately committed to meeting goals and performance levels critical to the long-term competitive position of the corporation, holding him/herself and others accountable. Follow-through, accountability and a willingness and ability to achieve closure

(Continued)

EXHIBIT 13.2 (*Continued*)

in a timely manner are characteristics of the Veridian leader. Actions and decision-making are tempered by the need to remain consistent with Veridian's core values and by an understanding of the potential long-term implications that day-to-day business decisions may have. Effort, passion and a sense of urgency for and about the business are critical. Outstanding effort that stays true to Veridian values in achieving success will be recognized and rewarded.

Create the Future

The Veridian leader creates the future by having a vision, understanding the ramifications of the vision, and possessing the ability to communicate and achieve the vision. He/she plans from the future, not forward from the present and understands the business environment and the trends impacting Veridian's future direction. The Veridian leader has the courage to chart a new course and the commitment to follow it through.

Champion Change

The Veridian leader demonstrates a willingness to accept change, to anticipate the need for change that is appropriate to our business, and then to act and embrace that change. The Veridian leader reflects an ongoing questioning of the status quo and promotes the concept of seeking continuous improvement in the conduct of our business.

Lead with Confidence

The Veridian leader leads by example; adheres to the highest levels of integrity and ethical standards of conduct; and deals with issues directly, openly and decisively. He/she takes action in the face of challenge, demonstrating wisdom, independent judgment and self-confidence in making decisions, even when consensus cannot be achieved. The Veridian leader possesses a thorough understanding of the business and has the courage to make difficult choices and to do the right thing.

Develop Capabilities

The Veridian leader chooses, develops and motivates individuals and teams to achieve exceptional levels of performance over extended periods of time; recruits and retains outstanding talent and nurtures that talent; and invests time and resources to enhance the long-term effectiveness of individuals and teams. Veridian leaders constantly strive to develop their own capabilities while nurturing and mentoring the talents and capabilities of others.

Communicate

The Veridian leader builds an environment where information is actively shared, sought and used, leading to empowerment, meaningful feedback and improved performance. Information sharing and communications are open, honest, reliable and unimpeded up, down and across the organization. Effective, honest communication knows no hierarchy or direction and must be accepted and natural characteristic of our corporate environment and culture.

Live the Values

The Veridian leader embodies and reinforces our corporate values, doing the right thing for customers, employees, shareholders and communities consistently and over the long term; contributes to and reinforces a work environment and culture of mutual respect and a recognition of the value of the individual; sets a strong personal example by sustained actions consistent with the corporate vision and values; and meets the highest levels of professional and personal integrity and ethical conduct.

Deliver the Veridian Vision

The Veridian leader creates a working environment where employees are excited to be part of Veridian. Employees are empowered to do their jobs in the best way possible; they are provided with state-of-the-art tools and resources; they are challenged to reach continually for higher standards of excellence; and they are encouraged to innovate and to continually expand the capabilities of the corporation. The entire workforce is proud of the corporation and is committed to building Veridian into a recognized leader in the industry. The Veridian leader builds an organization where employees truly have a passion for their work, where customers seek to do business, where competitors look with respect and admiration, where communities value our presence and involvement and where shareholders are proud to be owners.

Source: Company documents.

Langstaff lost no opportunity to reinforce the company's message about values. He spoke frequently on this topic, even framing issues such as acquisitions or marketing as expressions of the company's value system. Besides articulating the vision and the principles, Veridian's management team sought to reinforce Veridian's values by encouraging horizontal communication throughout the company. Veridian instituted newsletters and brought together employees in conferences to exchange ideas and gain an understanding of the scope of the work that the company could perform. The management team reinforced this emphasis on horizontal communication and values by tying employee compensation, in part, to how well an employee managed to support other business divisions and live up to the articulated values of the company. Part of an employee's incentive compensation was determined by an individual's financial output – the amount they contributed to Veridian's operating margins. However, a substantial element of the compensation depended on more subjective evaluations of cooperation and leadership.

Values-Based Leadership as 'Glueware'

Langstaff knew that there was some tension in articulating his corporate objectives in terms of values. Did the company believe these were inherently good principles, or was the senior management only behaving instrumentally? Langstaff noted:

> I went down the route at one point, trying to seize the high ground and say, you ought to do this because it's the right thing to do and that's all. Now, I find that gets you so far. To really get people's attention you also have to really bring it down and show some good business reasons why.

Besides making Veridian a meaningful and attractive place to work, Langstaff believed that values-based leadership was essential to the company's ability to confront its core management dilemma. On the one hand, Langstaff believed that Veridian 'must be aligned as one holistic, integrated operating system'. On the other hand, Langstaff wanted to have a loose decentralized decision-making structure. 'Smart people are used to being able to make decisions about their work,' he observed. 'If a customer calls, you want to be able to help that customer without going through a big bureaucracy.' Adding to this challenge was Veridian's growth and geographic spread. At the end of 2002, Veridian had over 7000 employees working in over 50 locations in 38 states on over 2000 contracts and task orders.

Langstaff described Veridian's vision of values-based leadership as the 'glueware' holding his company together. Without an emphasis on principles and internalized values, the company would have difficulty coordinating its workforce and satisfying its customers. Langstaff believed that the only alternative means for holding the company together would be the imposition of a thick set of rules and a heavier administrative structure, but this alternative would stifle creativity and cooperation and, in fact, drive the best people from the company. Bob Farrell noted that the principles appealed to his colleagues: 'As we got more familiar with values-based leadership, we really started to like this. The system allowed us to maintain the kind of entrepreneurial spirit that had attracted us to MRJ in the first place.'

The values also inspired Veridian to continue to pursue innovative projects. Phil Lacombe, a member of senior management, observed:

> The Veridian leadership model influenced the type of work we pursued. There were instances where we stopped doing certain kinds of work because the work had evolved so that it was no longer cutting-edge. There were other instances when we decided not to pursue work that would have been profitable but wasn't innovative enough to meet our values.

Ultimately, the values served to strengthen the relationship between the customer and the employee. Lacombe noted that the Veridian values were 'a compact between management and the employees on behalf of the customer.' Veridian management believed that nothing frustrated employees more than not being able to meet the needs of their customers. Whereas other defence companies would encourage employees to put corporate interests first, Veridian celebrated the employee's identification with the customer's mission. As Jerry Howe observed, this difference was felt most distinctly when problems occurred:

> Inevitably when you are running a company as large as ours, a problem arises. Because we had a very clear understanding from the senior management team all the way down to the program managers, there was very little debate as to what we would do. At our own initiative, we would propose a program to remedy the problem even if this program proved expensive to us. And then we would keep the customer completely informed about the progress of our program. The values hierarchy for dealing with these problems was clear: the interests of our customer was [sic] first, ramifications for our employees was second, and the financial consequences were third. Other defence companies do not approach this kind of problem with the same clarity. People at other companies would say, 'Do we really need to do this' or 'Can't we just fix it without letting the government know,' and so on.

Values-Based Leadership and Employee Recruitment

The dot-com boom represented a particular challenge to Veridian because it affected the labour market for specialists in information technology. In the late 1990s, the Silicon Valley start-up environment attracted many of the best and brightest with the promise of enormous financial gain in a short time. In a speech to his employees in March of 2000, Langstaff noted the difference between Veridian and Silicon Valley values:

> [Veridian] characteristics and the values underlying them would appear to be in real conflict with the values talked about today. Today, it seems there is no long-term . . . Silicon Valley venture capitalists and entrepreneurs are more focused on quick wealth now. They are focused on getting something started, taking it public, or being acquired and then getting out. Build to flip. Get out fast with your money. Lasting value? Not my problem.

Langstaff wondered if there was 'room for a Veridian in this world of new economic capitalism – a company built on values, seeking to make a lasting difference, committed to attracting and retaining outstanding employees and building sustainable long-term value for its financial shareholders and other constituents?'

Even in this environment, Veridian's values proved crucial to hiring and retaining employees. Phil Lacombe remembered when Langstaff came to recruit him:

> I had spent 20 years in the Air Force and eight years working with the White House and running a nonprofit foundation. When David described Veridian, it sounded to me like a rare opportunity to join a company where I would not have to change or subordinate my value system . . . The Veridian values were essential to my joining the firm and they proved essential to most of the people I hired over the next five or six years.

Empirically it would seem that Veridian won its bet on values. Even during the height of the boom, Veridian was making its hires. Langstaff reported:

> We were hiring people who had six other offers and would come to us at a lower salary because they really locked in on the vision of the company. Sixty percent of our new hires were employee referrals, which I viewed as a great indication of morale. There was just a buzz in the marketplace about Veridian being a different kind of place to work.

Values-Based Leadership in the Market for Companies

Not only did values-based leadership attract employees, but the commitment to values also served as a powerful inducement to firms that Veridian targeted for purchase. Acquisitions had spurred Veridian's growth, diversified its customer base and expanded its scope of capabilities. Veridian's acquisitions were all relatively small, private research or technology firms that liked Veridian's approach and vision. Langstaff explained:

> I believe values-based leadership is one of the secrets of doing mergers and acquisitions properly. When I presented Veridian to companies we were considering acquiring, I did not simply describe what we do today, but shared the vision of the company and how they, upon being acquired, not only

fit into it, but were essential to it. We focused people on what we could be rather than what we were. We were clear that in getting to the future, we were going to remain true to our values – how we treated employees and the customer. And then, of course, we had to follow through on the integration and fulfill our promises.

In 1999, Veridian's values and Langstaff's approach played a decisive role in allowing Veridian to acquire three firms simultaneously. For example, Trident, a network security firm, accepted Veridian's offer, despite receiving the promise of higher offers from other companies. The values approach also helped in identifying and integrating the companies. Joe Allen noted:

> We tended to look for businesses that had a value space that would match ours. So that while integration was never easy, we wouldn't have a clash in terms of personalities once the deal was concluded. We developed a reputation not just as the employer of choice but as the acquirer of choice. There were owners of businesses that would take a slightly lower price as they headed off into retirement, just so that they could place their employees in a company where they felt the management team had good values.

Again in 2002, Veridian's culture proved a draw. Signal Corp, a private company with annual revenues of US$227 million, approached Veridian about being acquired. Langstaff noted:

> They came to us and said we were their first choice. It came down to values and integrity. The kind of company we were building was the kind of company they wanted to be part of. I know that the owner of Signal and their investment bank got calls after the acquisition and were asked, 'Why didn't you let us have a shot at it? We would have paid more.'

VERIDIAN AND ITS INVESTORS

Serving an Expanded Set of Stakeholders

In addition to creating a corporate community that would attract the best employees, Langstaff stressed that Veridian would serve an extended set of constituencies, including employees, customers, business partners, communities and shareholders. No single group's interests would be given priority over the others – rather, the company would be managed with an eye towards creating the greatest long-term value.

Such a 'stakeholder' approach to management was in direct contrast with the perspective that maximizing shareholder value was the primary aim of any corporation. Langstaff viewed with disdain the manipulations that some CEOs engaged in to maximize the short-term value of their stock. He argued that Veridian's statement of values committed the company to 'do the right thing, consistently and over the long term', which implied a greater sense of responsibility. Langstaff told his senior managers:

> A legalistic interpretation of responsibility would obligate the company to seek to maximize shareholder value – period . . . While the law establishes a minimum level of responsibility that is acceptable to society, our commitment to excellence and service requires a higher level of responsibility. This higher standard is what sets Veridian apart.

Applying higher standards to managing the company's relationships with all its stakeholders meant making tradeoffs in the short term to benefit the longer-term value of the company. For example, Langstaff noted that Veridian was 'willing to "leave a nickel on the table" in our dealings with customers – that is, tradeoff the short-term goal of maximizing profitability in order to strengthen a customer relationship and thus better meet the long-term goal of shareholders and constituents.'

Langstaff warned that the company's work with its constituents did not represent a recipe, but instead identified components that would continually need realignment:

> The fact that Veridian explicitly recognizes five constituents introduces not only the possibility, but also the likelihood of needing to sort through conflicting loyalties, and therefore, conflicting responsibilities. In fact, I would suggest that it is the balancing of these conflicting responsibilities that is the art of leadership for any CEO.

From Private Equity to Public Company

Langstaff characterized Veridian's relationships with private investors as 'terrific'. From 1987 to 2002, Veridian had relied on three private equity funds to support the company (pre-Arvin), take the company private and fund growth: Rho Management, Texas Growth Fund and Monitor Clipper Partners. In lining up Veridian's private equity investors, Langstaff had been successful in aligning the investors' expectation with the company's strategy in terms of values and growth. Langstaff noted, 'Deal negotiations with Monitor Clipper Partners and Texas Growth Fund were not so much on price as on other issues that would impact how we would run the company.'

Both the Texas Growth Fund and Monitor Clipper Partners had seats on Veridian's board. However, Langstaff stressed, the representatives of the equity funds had not performed their roles any differently than any of the other board members. 'Watching the board deliberate,' Langstaff noted, 'you could not tell the equity investors apart from the other board members.'

In early 2002, Veridian's board made the decision to take the company public.[4] Langstaff noted:

> The business reasons for doing an IPO were clear. It would reduce our cost of capital by more than a thousand basis points.[5] The IPO enabled us to de-lever in a meaningful way. Furthermore, the IPO signaled that Veridian had reached maturity. For our investors, I knew that when we took private equity back in 1999, we would have to find a way to provide them liquidity. For our employees, the IPO made the stock options more real. For our customers, it gave us further stature because we were listed on the New York Stock Exchange . . . I never felt that going public was a goal, it was always a means to an end. We were dealing with an industry that was consolidating, and we felt that for future acquisitions, we would be more effective as a public company. The IPO positioned the company for greater growth since it gave us the ability to access greater capital resources.

However, Langstaff did have some concerns about Veridian's decision to go public:

> I knew that by going public, Veridian would be gaining a new partner: the public investor. I wondered if the interests of this new partner would force uncomfortable changes on the way the company had been run, particularly in terms of Veridian's core values. Could Veridian be successful as a public company?

After many deliberations between his executive team and the board, Langstaff concluded that Veridian could thrive as a public company as long as the company remained clear on its fundamental purpose: to build sustainable long-term value.

Road Show – Angling for GARPs

Having decided to go public, Veridian turned to Credit Suisse First Boston (CSFB) to be the lead manager on its offering. CSFB, Langstaff and Veridian CFO James Allen began preparations for a grueling, cross-country tour to introduce Veridian to potential investors across the United States, Canada and Europe. Besides 'building the book', Langstaff hoped to target a specific kind of investor:

> The issue of the 'right' kind of shareholders was important. We had pitched the company to be particularly attractive to value and GARP ('Growth At a Reasonable Price') investors, which I believed would be the right kind of shareholder for us over time. Obviously, you don't choose your investors . . . they choose you! We were going to tell the Veridian story in the most accurate way possible, not looking for a quick hit on the IPO price, but instead a successful relationship over the long term.

During the road-show presentations, Langstaff and Allen had the difficult assignment of not only describing Veridian in a 30-minute presentation but also the new product/service space that Veridian occupied.[6] At times, Langstaff did feel frustration during the discussions with some potential investors:

> I would talk about what we think we can deliver over the next five years and the kind of consistency the investor could expect. I wanted to develop an interest in the longer-term financial metrics. The problem is that most people either didn't hear or didn't care and were still waiting to hear our quarterly guidance.

Following their road show, CSFB told Langstaff that the interest in Veridian had been very strong. However, the market was skittish as it was still dealing with the fallout from the revelation of corporate corruption at Enron, Global Crossing and Tyco (Figure 13.1 for the Dow Jones Industrial Average). On the positive side, CFSB noted that investors viewed Veridian management as strong and were pleased that none of the existing shareholders were liquidating their positions. CSFB believed that a few days after the IPO, Veridian would be trading in the US$19 range. Longer term, analysts had Veridian in the US$20–24 range with one investor projecting a US$30 valuation. CSFB felt, however, that in such a nervous market, investors really needed to see how the overall market reacted to Veridian before they would be willing to add to their initial positions.

In discussing valuation, what counted against Veridian was its projection of 8–9% growth for the rest of 2002 and 10–12% sustainable long-term growth. These numbers stood in stark contrast to the optimistic projections offered by Veridian competitors Anteon (14% growth) and SRA (20% growth). In addition, the lack of details from Veridian about some of its contracts (due to its intelligence and classified customer base) led CSFB to suggest that Veridian might need to be priced at a modest discount to its peers. (See Exhibit 13.3 for Veridian's financials from its prospectus.) At a fully distributed price of US$19 a share, Veridian would be trading at approximately 10.6x 2003 EBITDA, with its peers trading at about 11.1x. The market remained volatile – the multiple for Veridian's peers, for example, had declined from 11.9x EBITDA in just a few days. Langstaff noted, 'We were pricing into a doubly weak market: from the overall market psychology and from the performance of our competitors.'

No Ticker Shock

On 5 June, 2002, Veridian went public at an initial offering price of US$16. The subscription book was oversubscribed by a factor of 10, and the market pushed the price per share to above US$19 within a week. (See Figure 13.2 for Veridian's stock history.) The *Financial Times* rated the IPO as one of the 10 best of the first half of the year (Earle, 2002, p. 27).

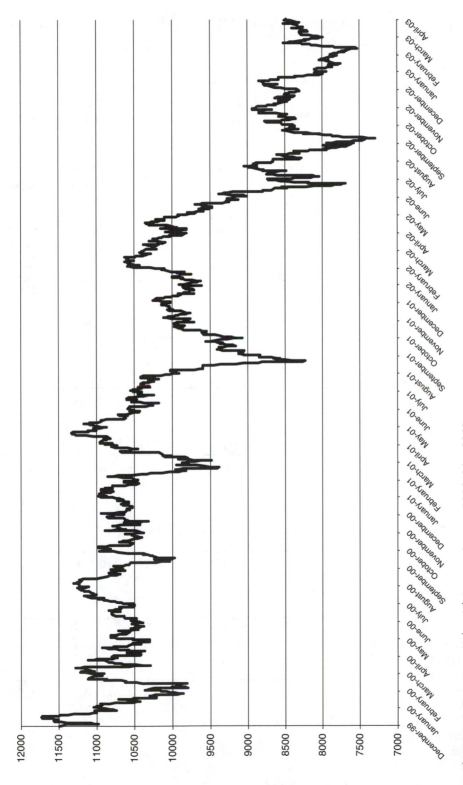

Figure 13.1 Dow Jones Industrial Average, January 2000–May 2003

Source: Thompson Datastream, accessed February 2006.

EXHIBIT 13.3 VERIDIAN INCOME STATEMENTS (ALL DOLLAR AMOUNTS IN THOUSANDS)

	Three Months Ended March 31		Year Ended December 31		
	2002	2001	2001	2000	1999
Revenues	176,602	162,723	690,225	632,270	399,814
Costs and expenses:					
Direct	115,434	105,002	446,719	415,927	275,777
Selling, general and administrative	46,477	44,313	187,090	164,801	94,435
Depreciation	2,579	2,818	10,606	9,947	6,232
Amortization	—	2,994	11,760	12,579	6,217
Acquisition and integration	—	199	2,067	4,637	6,271
(Gain) loss from pension plan settlement	—	—	1,119	—	(190)
Total costs and expenses	164,490	155,326	659,361	607,891	388,724
Income from operations	12,112	7,397	30,864	24,379	11,072
Other (income) expense:					
Interest income	(220)	(201)	(844)	(380)	(97)
Interest expense	6,150	7,219	29,076	34,658	18,541
Gain from sale of assets	—	—	—	(723)	—
Other expense, net	—	—	227	69	50
Other (income) expense	5,930	7,018	28,459	33,624	18,494
Income (loss) from continuing operations before income taxes and extraordinary items	6,182	379	2,405	(9,245)	(7,422)
Income tax expense	2,612	1,482	6,222	1,823	378
Income (loss) from continuing operations before extraordinary items	3,570	(1,103)	(3,817)	(11,068)	(7,800)
Loss from discontinued operations, net of taxes	—	(3,099)	(11,277)	(7,110)	(163)
Loss on disposal of discontinued operations, net of taxes	(1,103)	—	(6,355)	—	—
Income (loss) before extraordinary items	2,467	(4,202)	(21,449)	(18,178)	(7,963)
Extraordinary item — loss from early extinguishments of debt, net of taxes	—	—	—	(925)	(659)
Net income (loss)	2,467	(4,202)	(21,449)	(19,103)	(8,622)
Preferred stock dividends and accretion to preferred and Class A common stock redemption values	(2,253)	(1,938)	(8,208)	(6,635)	(1,880)
Net income (loss) attributable to common stockholders	214	(6,140)	(29,657)	(25,738)	(10,502)

Source: Veridian prospectus.

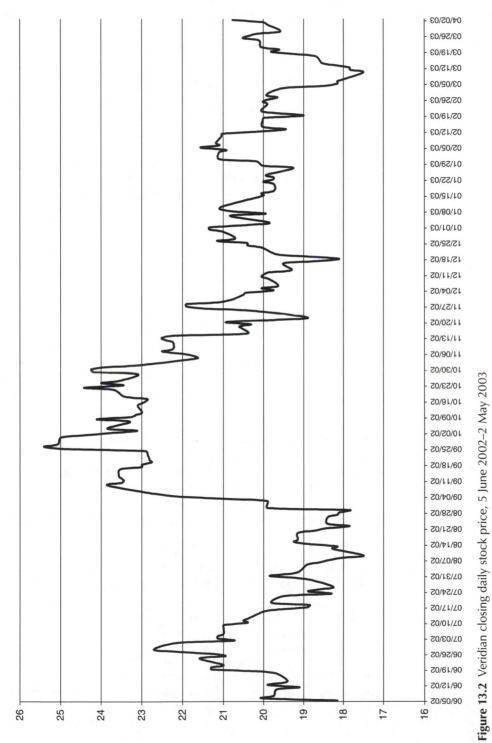

Figure 13.2 Veridian closing daily stock price, 5 June 2002–2 May 2003

Source: Thompson Datastream, accessed February 2006.

Langstaff had concerns that his employees would get infected with interest about the daily fluctuations of the stock price. He didn't allow employees to post the daily closing price of Veridian's stock on the company's website or anywhere else. Phil Lacombe noted that there was little change in the day-to-day activities of the company:

> I was concerned that the pull of the shareholders would get stronger after we went public. But I didn't see any evidence of that after the IPO. There was little or no discussion of being public or the share price among the employees or even among senior management. Being public was not what was making us successful.

Veridian's first two quarters as a public company proceeded extremely well. During the conference call releasing the results of the first quarter after the IPO (actually the third quarter of 2002), Veridian management announced the purchase of the Signal Corporation, a move that pleased analysts. The acquisition boosted Veridian's annual revenues to more than US$1 billion.

THE PERFECT STORM BUILDS

The Changing Defence Industry

From the end of the Cold War in 1991 to the war on terror in 2002, the changing needs of the DoD led to dramatic changes in the structure of the US defence industry.

When the Cold War ended, the DoD dramatically reduced its spending. From a peak in the mid-1980s, the DoD slashed its procurement budget by 70%, and in 1996, defence expenditures accounted for just 2.5% of the GNP (the smallest share since before the Second World War).

The budget cutbacks prompted concerns at the Pentagon about the structure of the defence industry. Since defence contracts were essentially priced off the industry cost base, the DoD worried about having to pay for unused capacity in the form of overhead. At a 1993 event dubbed 'the Last Supper', Defense Secretary William Perry urged defence contractors to consolidate the industry (Cole, 1996). Defence contractors responded: many companies sold their defence-related businesses, while others expanded their defence businesses by absorbing those that had decided to exit the industry.[7]

The defence giants that emerged (Lockheed Martin, Boeing, Raytheon and Northrop Grumman) believed their size was a necessary element to their future success. One study noted:

> The companies remaining in the US defence industry argue that they need to be large in order to remain flexible, win contracts, and have enough money to support the acquisition or development of technologies that will keep them competitive in the future. The Pentagon can cut budgets and programs faster than small companies can react, and the impact of specific cutbacks on a small firm's revenue can be sudden and severe. However, a large company can more easily adjust to change by reallocating its resources through a plan of diversification that can absorb a cutback or cancellation of a program.
>
> Advani *et al.* 1997

But there was a limit to the consolidation that the DoD would allow. In 1998, the DoD blocked the proposed merger of Lockheed Martin and Northrop Grumman because the merger would eliminate any competition in key product areas.[8]

As the defence industry was consolidating, the DoD was changing its view on how wars were to be fought. Starting in the last years of the Clinton administration and taking force in the Bush administration, top DoD officials began pushing for a 'revolution in military affairs' (RMA). RMA stood for using lighter, swifter, more precise armaments tied together with advanced information technology. *The Economist* observed:

> For the past 100 years, the main emphasis in military equipment has been on 'platforms,' i.e., the ships, aircraft, or tanks that carry weapons. Now the platform is becoming less important than the network – an electronic web tying all weapons together to make the whole greater than the sum of its parts . . . In the language of the Pentagon, 'transformation' means getting from traditional platform warfare to this network-centric way of fighting.
>
> *The Economist*, 2002

The wars in Afghanistan and Iraq proved to be a major boost to the RMA advocates. Defense Secretary Donald Rumsfeld employed RMA principles in drawing up war plans and the success of American forces seemed to confirm the new direction of the military.

The post-9/11 conflicts also brought substantial increases in defence spending. The defence giants benefited from this increase, and their stock prices began to rise in 2002. But the rising defence tide also lifted second-tier firms such as Veridian. A number of other second-tier and even third-tier firms went public during 2002. In the first two years of the Bush administration, the defence industry raised nearly US$5.6 billion in IPOs or follow-on placements (which was more than half of the capital raised by defence firms during all of the 1990s) (Bowe, 2002, p. 24).

Some analysts speculated that the only source for further consolidation in the defence industry was for the primes that had traditionally focused on large weapons platforms to pick up smaller firms that would provide them with RMA technologies (Speers, 2002). Since this type of vertical integration did not decrease the number of product lines, it was unlikely that the DoD would raise antitrust concerns.

However, some observers worried that if the defence industry's middle-sized companies were absorbed by the primes, creativity would be lost. A senior manager at Veridian who had experience at one of the primes observed:

> In order to be capable of designing and delivering huge systems for the government, a big prime had to stifle some of the creativity of its people and replace it with policy standards and process . . . Veridian was filling a great void between the primes, who are very good at what they do but couldn't adjust quickly to changing needs in the country's defence posture, and the very small research labs that were innovative but resource-constrained. With Veridian you had some muscle based on size, but with great agility. For example, Veridian heard about the military's challenges in Afghanistan to supply systems and capabilities to help integrate various units from different services. We quickly put together a team based on our wide range of capabilities and hammered out some solutions in a few months.

Veridian Gets Put into Play

As a system integrator and technology solutions provider recognized for having market-leading capabilities, Veridian had working relationships with most of the largest defence contractors. Besides the usual ticklishness of working with one's competitors, Veridian soon found themselves in the position of working with potential purchasers. Langstaff explained:

> We had a bull's-eye on us, because we were one of the biggest companies in the defence information area with over a billion dollars in revenue and world-class technology. We were different from all the other IT companies because we were exclusively high-end defence and security contracts. So we were 'pinged' constantly by companies looking to purchase us. I told them, we're not looking to sell the company. Thanks for your interest.

In late March 2003, Langstaff met with a representative of Quiescent Systems to discuss ways the two companies might collaborate on future contracts. During this meeting, Quiescent Systems asked Langstaff if Veridian might be for sale. Again, Langstaff responded that Veridian was not for sale, but inquired whether Quiescent would consider a sale of portions of its information technology businesses to Veridian (which Quiescent declined). Given the importance of the relationship between the two companies, Langstaff agreed to meet again with representatives of Quiescent so that each company could learn more of the other's capabilities. A confidentiality agreement was signed between Quiescent and Veridian to facilitate this review.

Two weeks later at the request of Quiescent, Langstaff met again with the company. This time, Quiescent presented him with a verbal all-cash offer for the company of US$28 a share. With Veridian shares trading at about US$20, the offer represented a 40% premium on Veridian's market valuation. Langstaff noted, 'With a 40% premium, I felt obligated to go to the board to tell them what had happened.'

The Veridian board's Audit and Finance Committee met soon after Langstaff's meeting with Quiescent, and Langstaff told the committee of the offer. In order to ensure that they were following proper procedure, the committee hired CSFB to provide financial advice and a law firm to provide legal guidance. The committee then arranged a special session of the full board to discuss the offer and confer with their advisors.

Even as Veridian was considering Quiescent's offer, other defence contractors were contacting Langstaff and expressing their interest in purchasing the company. None of them made a specific offer, and Langstaff continued to tell them that the company was not for sale.

On 1 May, 2003, Veridian released its earnings report for the first quarter of 2003, which included significant increases in revenue and earnings (see Exhibit 13.4). Sales increased to US$281.9 versus US$176.6 million over the same quarter of the previous year. Although most of the sales growth was due to the Signal acquisition, the heritage companies showed an outstanding 19% organic sales growth over the previous year. Earnings came in at US$10.2 million (29 cents a share), which was an increase over the 26 cents EPS in the previous quarter. During the conference call with investors, Veridian increased its guidance for the entire year from an EPS of US$1.09–1.14 to US$1.16–1.20. The next day, Veridian shares jumped nearly 10% to US$22 and analysts at SG Cowen upgraded the stock to a 'strong buy'.

EXHIBIT 13.4 VERIDIAN QUARTERLY RESULTS (ALL FIGURES EXCEPT PER SHARE IN THOUSANDS)

Income statement for quarter ending 31 March, 2003

Sales	281,919
Cost of Goods Sold	200,802
Gross Profit	81,117
Selling, General, & Administrative Expense	57,031
Operating Income Before Depreciation	24,086
Depreciation, Depletion, & Amortization	2,920
Operating Profit	21,166
Interest Expense	4,303
Non-Operating Income/Expense	223
Special Items	0
Pretax Income	17,086
Total Income Taxes	6,886
Minority Interest	0
Income Before Extraordinary Items & Discontinued Operations	10,200
Preferred Dividends	0
Available for Common	10,200
Extraordinary Items	0
Discontinued Operations	0
Adjusted Net Income	10,200
Earnings Per Share Basic Including Extraordinary Items	0.30
Earnings Per Share Diluted Including Extraordinary Items	0.29
EPS Basic from Operations	0.30
EPS Diluted from Operations	0.29
Dividends Per Share	0
Com Shares for Basic	34,153
Com Shares for Diluted	35,381

Balance Sheet as of 31 March, 2003

ASSETS

Cash & Equivalents	7,540
Net Receivables	256,208
Inventories	2,457
Other Current Assets	16,255
Total Current Assets	282,460
Gross Plant, Property & Equipment	95,359
Accumulated Depreciation	45,425
Net Plant, Property & Equipment	49,934
Other Assets	427,073
TOTAL ASSETS	759,467

(Continued)

EXHIBIT 13.4 (*Continued*)

LIABILITIES

Debt In Current Liabilities	11,637
Accounts Payable	42,365
Income Taxes Payable	6,009
Other Current Liabilities	90,697
Total Current Liabilities	150,708
Long Term Debt	279,786
Deferred Taxes and Investment Tax Credits	0
Minority Interest	0
Other Liabilities	8,429
TOTAL LIABILITIES	438,923

EQUITY

Preferred Stock	0
Common Stock	4
Capital Surplus	404,870
Retained Earnings	−84,330
Less: Treasury Stock	0
TOTAL EQUITY	320,544
TOTAL LIABILITIES & EQUITY	759,467

Source: Standard & Poor's Compustat® data via Research Insight^SM, accessed February 2006.

Also on 2 May, the full board of directors met along with senior management and their financial and legal advisors. At the meeting, Langstaff gave a presentation, concluding that staying independent would be more in the long-term interest of Veridian's stockholders than selling the company for US$28 per share. The board then met in executive session. Its consensus at the end of the meeting was that it was too early to decide whether a sale was in the best interests of shareholders and that Veridian management should continue to explore Quiescent's offer. In addition, the board requested that CSFB contact other defence companies to gauge their interest. The board asked all parties to conduct their inquiries in strict confidence, because the company was not for sale. Langstaff added that confidentiality was important because premature disclosure could have a negative impact on the employees and the customers. Langstaff later commented:

> I think the board did exactly what you'd want a board to do. They did not overreact or try to zero in on an answer right away. They just set up a process to consider the sale. Remember, the environment at the time was difficult for boards given the Enron and WorldCom scandals where the boards were seen to be AWOL. Because of the '*Revlon* rules', we were advised that no matter how we decided on a specific offer, we had to know what the market was for our company. We had an obligation to find out how attractive the offers were, assess what we thought we could do with the company, and then make a decision.

The 'Revlon rules' referred to the case in Delaware corporate law (where Veridian was incorporated) of *Revlon Inc v. MacAndrews & Forbes Holdings, Inc.* One view of *Revlon* was as follows:

> Under the *Revlon* test, once the Board has decided to sell control of a company, the directors' role changes 'from defenders of the corporate bastion to auctioneers charged with getting the best price for the stockholders at a sale of the company'. This involves, among other things, the Board's evaluation of any competing transaction in light of this obligation. Long-term strategic, business and other non-monetary considerations – which in other circumstances may form the basis of a Board's decision – become irrelevant in the context of the Board's duties under *Revlon*, except to the extent that they are reasonably related to the Board's objective of maximizing short-term value.
>
> Brownstein and Munoz, 2004

However, others did not believe *Revlon* to be controlling in such instances:

> This [*Revlon*] is a very limited context, however. Subsequent Delaware cases have dramatically reduced *Revlon's* significance by making it clear that if the directors of the firm decide not to sell, or if they prefer a stock-for-stock exchange with another public firm, *Revlon* is irrelevant. Accordingly, directors can avoid *Revlon* duties when they want to. All this suggests that *Revlon* may prove to be an evolutionary dead-end in corporate law, doctrinal deadwood that the courts have already pruned back and eventually, may remove entirely.
>
> Stout, 2002

Putting a Value on Values

After the board meeting, a number of board members approached Langstaff informally and asked, 'If US$28 is too low, what is the right price?' (See Table 13.1 for comparisons with Veridian's competitors.) Langstaff noted:

> I've always been pretty good at putting on one hat as the CEO and thinking things through from that perspective and then putting on my director's hat and thinking things through from that perspective. I was interested in the analytical challenge of figuring out a 'right' price. If someone offered US$50 a share, everyone would sell, but at US$20 no one would. So the challenge was where to draw the line.

In the market for corporate control, Langstaff would have to judge the prospects that his management team could produce a higher value for shareholders than those promised by competing offers:

> The challenge was in reconciling numbers that were based on different assumptions. The offers from prospective purchasers were all-cash, based almost entirely on our current profitability and stock price. We had been running the company to build long-term sustainable value, were making investments and therefore had not been looking to maximize current profitability. The question was, 'What could management deliver over time and what was the present value of that value?'

The 'perfect storm' of factors had made Veridian seem very valuable in the short term, but Langstaff felt that these values were not sustainable:

Table 13.1 Veridian Comparison

Companies (data in millions except for stock price and EPS)

Data for Year Ending		Market Value	Total Debt	Preferred Stock	EBITDA	EBIT	Stockholder Equity	EPS	Stock Price	Shares Outstanding
Jun 03	CACI Intl Inc	985.2	4.6	0.0	83.0	70.4	421.5	1.56	34.30	28.7
Dec 02	Anteon International Corp	823.6	105.7	0.0	68.7	64.4	128.8	0.90	24.00	34.4
Jun 03	SRA International Inc	514.3	0.4	0.0	51.0	42.0	283.0	0.69	16.00	50.1
Dec 02	Titan Corp	811.4	602.0	0.7	95.7	74.0	312.3	-0.11	10.40	78.1
Dec 02	Mantech Intl Corp	293.5	26.0	0.0	41.1	38.5	246.0	0.89	19.07	31.3
Dec 02	MTC Technologies Inc	325.5	0.0	0.0	14.2	13.7	49.8	0.67	25.30	12.9
Dec 02	Veridian Corp	704.2	292.7	0.0	71.7	60.6	309.6	-1.52	21.34	34.1

Source: Standard & Poor's Compustat® data via Research Insight[SM], accessed February 2006

In retrospect, where I believe I may have confused the market was when our current period performance and quarterly guidance were exceeding what I believed to be the long-term sustainable levels.
We were delivering organic growth of 17–19% at the end of 2002 and beginning of 2003, and yet my
message was that we could sustain 10–12% organic growth over the long term. What people didn't
hear was 'over the long term'. As a result, the market may have overly discounted our stock, thereby
setting off a series of events that ultimately put us in play.

Langstaff had concerns about his employees and national security, as well, and wondered how a
sale would square with Veridian's commitment to all of its constituents. Langstaff had vowed not
to be influenced by short-term shareholder interests in the stock market, but what principles should
guide him in the market for control of the company?

I was excited about the company we were building at Veridian. I felt that we were very much a work
in progress and that on our own we could do great things. I also knew that senior management and
employees felt the same way. Furthermore, doing what is right for the customer and the country was
very much a part of Veridian culture. When your business is national security, your mission goes well
beyond just serving shareholders. Veridian was playing a significant and unique role in contributing to
the security of the country and the world. Would we be able to make the same contribution as part of
an acquired company? How could we ignore these considerations in our deliberations? Were we right
to consider selling the company simply as a result of a net present value analysis? What, in fact, was
the right thing to do given the different aims of our constituents?

NOTES

1. Professors Rakesh Khurana and Joel Podolny and Research Associate Jaan Elias prepared this
   case with assistance from the Aspen Institute. Some information has been disguised. HBS
   cases are developed solely as the basis for class discussion. Cases are not intended to serve as
   endorsements, sources of primary data or illustrations of effective or ineffective management.
2. Quiescent Systems is a pseudonym for a top-tier defence contractor.
3. Faget, Kraft and Gilruth along with astronauts Neil Armstrong and Sally Ride were later directors
   of Space Industries/Veridian. Alan Shephard was one of the founding shareholders.
4. The IPO did not put all of Veridian on the market. After the IPO, insiders (including private equity
   firms and employees) would still control more than 40% of the stock of the company. Nearly all
   employees had Veridian stock in their 401K plans.
5. When Veridian had doubled its size during 1999, it had planned to tap the high-yield loan market
   to finance its acquisitions. However that market had fallen apart, leaving the company to rely on
   high-cost bank bridge financing.
6. There were only a few public companies in Veridian's sector and they did not offer the same kind
   of high-end technical services and solutions that differentiated Veridian.
7. It was in this environment that Arvin spun off Calspan.
8. Although it is the Department of Justice that actually files antitrust actions, the Department of
   Defense's opinions provide guidance on all antitrust matters related to defence contractors.

REFERENCES

Advani, J.R., Anderson, M., Bowling, S., Doane, D. and Roberts, E. (1997) Technology strategy
   in defense industry acquisitions: A comparative assessment of two giants, MIT Sloan School of
   Management working paper, August.

Bowe, C. (2002) U.S. Defense Sector Cashes in on Bush's War on Terrorism, *The Financial Times*, 18 July, p. 24.

Brownstein, A. and Munoz, L. (2004) The current state of deal protection, *International Financial Law Review*, March.

Cole, J. (1996) Defense Consolidation Rushes Toward Era of 3 or 4 Giants, *Wall Street Journal*, 6 December.

Earle, J. (2002) Morgan Stanley tops bookrunners for IPOs, *The Financial Times*, 26 June.

Speers, K. (2002) Limited options, *The Daily Deal*, 9 January.

Stout, L. (2002) Bad and not-so-bad arguments for shareholder primacy, *Southern California Law Review*, July, **75**, 185–1210.

The Economist (2002) Military revolutions, 20 July.

PART FIVE

ECONOMICS

CHAPTER FOURTEEN

Corporate Responsibility in Economics

H. Landis Gabel, INSEAD

INTRODUCTION

Those who have spent much time in the halls of a business school know that most economists are hostile to the ideas wrapped up in the term 'corporate social responsibility' (CSR). The objective of this chapter is to try to end that hostility; to try to find a solid economic basis for CSR. To succeed, however, requires that the presented case differ from the two cases that are most commonly expressed and that have created or exacerbated this hostility. One of those two cases is the 'business case for CSR', which, it is argued below, is simplistic, inconsistent with the way economists customarily think about how businesses are run and intellectually uninteresting. The second case, a model of competing stakeholder interests, is so radically at odds with the economist's model of the role of business firms in a market economy that it has drawn withering criticism and virtually universal rejection by economists.

This chapter starts by dismissing the two common views of CSR that have alienated economists and perhaps blinded them to thinking about CSR in their own terms, before attempting to make a case for CSR in a language familiar to economists: voluntary social codes of conduct represent an institutional alternative to compulsory government laws as a means to constrain potentially toxic corporate profit-seeking in conditions of market failure. The term 'institutions' is used in this chapter to mean 'humanly devised constraints that structure human interactions' (North, 1994, p. 360). From an institutional economics perspective (Commons, 1931; North, 1991), the paper compares voluntary and compulsory constraints according to criteria of cost, legitimacy, jurisdiction and flexibility. By these criteria, there are circumstances in which voluntary codes of conduct are the more efficient and effective institution, and thus are to be preferred to a lack of social constraints on profit-seeking on the one hand and compulsory laws and regulations on the other.

Corporate social responsibility is introduced into the model as a mechanism to improve the benefit-to-cost ratio of voluntarism relative to compulsion and thus to expand the domain in which voluntarism is the instrument of choice to mitigate problems of market failure.

The chapter concludes with some potentially testable hypotheses which derive from the arguments developed.

LOW-HANGING FRUIT AND THE BUSINESS CASE FOR CSR

The low-hanging fruit metaphor is widely used to deny a cost/benefit tradeoff; low-hanging fruit yields benefits for free. In the CSR context, it underlies what is called the 'business case for CSR', which promotes the view that there is no tradeoff between CSR and profits (Scott and Rothman,

1992). Not surprisingly, this is a popular view in business circles; as Vogel (2005, p. 19) puts it: 'Virtually all contemporary writing on CSR emphasizes its link to corporate profitability.'

The business case for CSR goes as follows. If firms treat their employees well, they will retain them (and perhaps be able to pay them lower salaries). If firms support their local communities, they will find recruiting easier. If firms reduce resource waste or energy consumption, they will save their own money. The stock market will favour firms that face low risk of environmental litigation. Firms that are attentive to their customers will earn a valuable reputation. In each example, enlightened management pay attention to environmental or stakeholders' interests and will, it is argued, serve shareholders' interests as well. That is, a firm can unilaterally and simultaneously contribute to social welfare and increase profit.

This argument makes the business case for CSR an all-too-easy sell to economists, yet a perplexing one as well. It is an easy sell because maximizing profit and serving social welfare are what economists always assumed businesses did, although they imagine the causality going from profit to social welfare rather than vice versa. And who could dare object if being a good citizen earns money? It is perplexing because economists might wonder why there would be low-hanging fruit in the first place, and if there were some, why a firm would need outsiders – advocates of CSR – to point to it. Do managers not have the incentive and the knowledge to run their firms as profitably as possible? Economists would likely argue that the low-hanging fruit metaphor is misleading; the correct metaphor is the £20 note lying untouched on a pavement.[1] Although seeming to imply low-hanging fruit, the £20 note metaphor has a subtly different meaning. It suggests an illusion; in this context that low-hanging CSR fruit is as illusory as is money lying ignored on a pavement.

What economists fail to appreciate, of course, is that although it is easy to make a theoretical assumption that firms are always run for maximum profit, it is difficult to run real firms that way. The thriving business of business schools should be sufficient evidence that running a firm well has to be learned. The business case for CSR is not the stuff of revolution, and it may be intellectually uninteresting to an economist, but it is not vacuous. It is analogous to other three-letter management tools such as MBO, TQM and CRM.[2] Each appears in business school curricula and in the portfolios of management consultancies to help managers increase their firms' profitability.

A few other remarks will end our discussion of CSR as low-hanging fruit. First, it is ironic that this interpretation of CSR is consistent with the views of oft-quoted real and fictitious bêtes noires of CSR such as Milton Friedman, Ivan Boesky and Gordon Gekko:

> The Social Responsibility of Business Is to Increase Its Profits.
>
> Friedman, 1970

> Greed is all right, by the way. I want you to know that. I think greed is healthy. You can be greedy and still feel good about yourself.
>
> Boesky, 1985

> Greed is . . . good. [3]

If CSR were a way to increase profits, all three would presumably be leading proponents of it.

Second, there is an obvious limit to how far the business case for CSR can be pushed. Firms that deny employees healthcare insurance or pensions will have trouble recruiting or will have to pay higher salaries, and profits may suffer for it. And yet, overly generous healthcare and pension plans have nearly bankrupted some large American companies in recent years. GM is a conspicuous example. The metaphor of low-hanging fruit hides the fact that at some point a tradeoff will appear, and it is not obvious where that point is or how to make the tradeoff when it is reached. Expressed another way, one cannot claim that in general CSR will increase a firm's profitability. It may or it may not. And this point provides a transition to the next model of CSR; one in which there is an explicit tradeoff between CSR and profits.

CSR: BALANCING COMPETING STAKEHOLDERS' INTERESTS

The second model of CSR – that of balancing competing stakeholders' interests (Elkington, 1994, 1997) – is as revolutionary to economists as low-hanging fruit is not. It is revolutionary because it fundamentally rejects the traditional role economists ascribe to the business corporation in a capitalist economy. That role is to get the greatest value out of society's limited resources. In the process, different stakeholders will get different shares of that value. Consumers will get consumer surplus, suppliers will get producer surplus and employees will be paid above their no-rent margins, but those shares are not consciously and arbitrarily decided by a firm's management. They are decided by the impersonal market.

The stakeholder interest model of CSR gives the firm's management a very different and inconsistent role. Management consciously, and essentially arbitrarily, allocates income to competing stakeholders: employees, customers, suppliers, the local community and the firm's shareholders. This imagined political role of balancing rival interests in a zero-sum game causes both positive and normative problems for the stakeholder interest model.

As to its predictive power as positive theory, the CSR case literature offers us few if any examples of business leaders who claim purposely, significantly and repeatedly to reduce the economic value of their firms for the sake of non-shareholding stakeholders, nor is there empirical evidence of any tradeoff between CSR and shareholder returns, as one would expect if CSR meant diverting those returns to others.[4]

In normative terms, this interpretation of CSR faces a major intellectual problem. By what principles of justice are the rival claims to be settled? Should one applaud GM's generous pension and healthcare plans or condemn them for reducing the size of the work-force and threatening to bankrupt the company? If employees are not to be paid the competitive wage (or the legal minimum if it is higher), what should they be paid? How far should a firm go in supporting community cultural activities? The business case for CSR would say in each instance, 'progressively more generously as long as there is a positive marginal net profit', but the stakeholder interest theory provides no answer at all.

Finally, such is the social acceptance of the traditional role of the business firm that we see multiple institutional safeguards preventing the diversion of wealth from shareholders to others. These include the fiduciary obligations of boards of directors,[5] the power of institutional investors, shareholder suits and the market for corporate control.[6] So it is not obvious that management could divert more than trivial revenue flows to non-shareholder stakeholders even if it wanted to.

If we want a perspective on CSR that would interest economists, we have to build an alternative model to these two.

OBJECTIVES AND CONSTRAINTS

Open any intermediate or advanced microeconomics text book and you will see the formalization of a model that originated with Adam Smith and has been elaborated upon – but not fundamentally changed – over the ensuing nearly two and a half centuries. It is a model of rational decision-makers – producers and consumers – pursuing their self-interest:

> It is not from the benevolence of the butcher, the brewer, or the baker, that we expect our dinner, but from their regard to their self-interest. We address ourselves, not to their humanity but to their self-love, and never talk to them of our own necessities but of their advantages.
>
> Smith, 1776, p. 20

No economic model purports to describe reality perfectly. All models are necessarily abstractions and simplifications. Regarding the assumption of rationality, clearly all the people are irrational some of the time, and some of the people are irrational all the time, but not all people are irrational all the time. Furthermore, no alternative behavioural assumption has the simplicity, tractability and versatility of self-interest. Although it may not characterize everything we do, purposeful pursuit of self-interest plays an important and perhaps even a dominant part in the decisions of our daily lives. As consumers, most of us try to satisfy our preferences in our daily spending decisions. This does not necessarily imply materialism. 'Consumption' decisions might better be thought of as income allocation decisions, which could include savings, spending on children's education and donation to charities. But however it is characterized, this consumption is usually purposeful. As producers, even those of us who enjoy our work might do something else if we were not paid.

The self-interest objective is one part of the economist's decision-making model. The other part is a set of constraints. In the simplest model, a consumer is assumed to maximize the utility of consumption subject to the constraints of income and the prices of goods and services. A producer is modelled as a business firm – a *persona ficta* – that seeks to maximize profit as a fiduciary for its self-interested shareholders, subject to the constraints of technology and the prices of inputs and outputs.

The importance of the constraints on producers' and consumers' self-interested choices cannot be overstated because they determine whether the result of millions of such choices is good or bad for the community that the producers and consumers constitute. When Adam Smith wrote in his *Wealth of Nations* that

> . . . every individual necessarily labors to render the annual revenue of the society as great as he can. He generally . . . neither intends to promote the public interest, nor knows how much he is promoting it . . . he intends only his own gain, and he is in this, as in many other cases, led by an invisible hand to promote an end which was no part of his intention.
>
> Smith, 1776, p. 351

he was making, but not stating, a host of assumptions about the constraints needed to link 'own gain' and 'public interest'. As a simple example, he was assuming a sufficiently large number of producers that no single one of them has the power to influence prices. That is, he was assuming a competitive market. Were there but a single producer, the result would be a monopoly price above the socially optimum. To emphasize the point of the example, a good outcome is not threatened by a decision-maker's self-interest; it is threatened by weak constraints on self-interest. Smith's 'invisible hand' must be firm.

So important and so burdened with responsibility are these constraints that economists are trained to pay more attention to them than to individuals' preferences, which are generally accepted as exogenous and beyond questioning. Whether a consumer's preferences include hybrid autos or sex with children may have moral significance, but it has no bearing on behaviour because the consumer is free to satisfy the first preference, whereas there are severe constraints that prohibit satisfying the second. That is, the constraint is crucial to determining what preferences can be realized, and reality – actual behaviour – is the economist's concern.

The precise nexus in economic theory between individual self-interest and collective – or social – welfare is complex, and it is not the subject of this chapter. Let us simply assert the obvious point that there must be constraints on self-interested behaviour if it is to serve the common good.

Constraints in the economist's model are of several types. Some are natural; for example, the state of technology, which limits what can be produced with a fixed quantity of inputs. Other constraints are endogenous to the economic system but exogenous to the individual producers and consumers. The set of market prices is an example. Still other constraints are 'rules of the game', or what are called 'institutions' in the vocabulary of institutional economics. They are defined and enforced by social processes. Rules of the game are the focus of this chapter.

These human-made constraints define what self-interested behaviour is socially acceptable and what is not. They are not technologically determined, although technology may influence how easily they are enforced.[7] They are not created by the economic system itself as are market prices. Instead, in the words of Garrett Hardin (1986, p. 1247), they are rules of 'mutual coercion, mutually agreed upon'. They are rules that members of the community define and then collectively bind themselves to because, paradoxically, they may all be better off if each is less free to further his or her own interest. So, for example, Smith's butcher, brewer and baker may compete with better meat, beer and bread, but society has a rule that they may not compete with guns.

Economics texts recognize these behavioural rules, and some of the rules are given considerable attention. One will find pages devoted to antitrust laws, environmental regulations, intellectual property laws and other laws and regulations that are necessary to ensure that the clockwork of the market system turns smoothly. Text books generally neglect other rules – rules against violence toward competitors, for example – because they are so obvious. I will argue, however, that neglecting some types of rules can blind one to their significance. More important for my argument, it can cause one to neglect to question the relative efficiency of different categories of behavioural rules, to which we now turn.

COMPULSORY AND VOLUNTARY SOCIAL CODES OF CONDUCT

Behavioural rules or codes of conduct can be put into two mutually exclusive categories. One consists of compulsory laws and regulations. These might be set democratically or dictatorially, but either way they are presumably formally codified, and enforcement is by the police power of the state. Eliminate a competitor with a gun and criminal laws will confront one with that power. Violate the environmental laws and there will be the same result. Break a contract, and civil law enforcement by a court can follow.

The second category of behavioural rules, and the one of particular interest here, is voluntary. Voluntary rules may not be formally codified, and the state does not enforce them. You will not go to jail or be fined for violating them, although violations may be punished in other ways, perhaps severely, as will be explained below.

What are examples of voluntary behavioural rules? Moral and ethical standards, social mores, manners and industry codes of advertising and of competition all fit the category. As another example, consider implicit employment agreements (Vermaelen, 2008). With only a little introspection, we can each quickly recognize that most elements of our relationship with our employer are not explicitly stated in our written contract. Are we expected to work overtime if there is a tight deadline for a project? If we do, will we be paid? If not, can we leave early when the pressure relaxes? Are we expected to travel and spend nights away from home? If so, how often is too often? How should we dress? These and many other implicit contract details complement those of the explicit contract and govern our behaviour and our expectations of others' behaviour.[8]

These voluntary codes of conduct are rarely discussed in economics, yet they serve exactly the same purpose as compulsory laws. They constrain self-interest and direct it toward the common interest. In terms many readers will be familiar with, they resolve the prisoners' dilemma; they protect against free-riding.

But where do these voluntary codes of conduct come from? Who defines them? How are they enforced? What role do they play vis-à-vis compulsory laws and regulations? If compulsory and voluntary constraints serve the same purpose, why do we have both? I now turn to these questions.

The origin of the most basic and powerful constraints on self-interest such as altruism and self-sacrifice may be biological. Theories of evolutionary psychology and sociobiology argue that altruistic behaviour is the result of the physical process of natural selection (Wilson, 1975). If it did not evolve biologically, altruism, or the willingness to contribute to the public good, evolved socially. Most of our elemental values appear in our earliest religions. The virtues expressed in the Hebrew Bible or the Ten Commandments are sufficiently ubiquitous that they are no longer confined to religion, and the invocation to 'do unto others . . .' is a virtually universal moral code.

Voluntary social codes of conduct, of course, go far beyond these basic moral values. As societies evolve and become more complex, as populations grow and as new technologies appear, new risks of the 'tragedy of the commons' genre appear, and more behavioural codes are needed and are created. A code of conduct governing the use of mobile telephones in public places is a recent example.

To the question of the relationship between these two complementary institutions, compulsory and voluntary behavioural codes, one can imagine that this is a comparative institutional choice. The two have different costs and benefits so that they differ in their adequacy to deal with specific collective problems.

In his critique of stakeholder theory, Jensen speaks of a distinction between what he terms the 'micro-cosmos' of the family or tribe and the 'macro-cosmos' of the larger community such as the nation. To Jensen, voluntary controls within the micro-cosmos such as loyalty and altruism,

> continue to retain some importance by assisting voluntary collaboration, even though they are incapable, by themselves, of creating a basis for the more extended order [of the macro-cosmos].
>
> Jensen, 2001, p. 15

Jensen correctly notes that different types of social control make sense in different contexts. Yet voluntary social codes should not be relegated only to the micro-cosmos. They have advantages that favour them over compulsory laws and regulations even in the larger community. What are those advantages?

VOLUNTARY OR COMPULSORY? COMPARATIVE INSTITUTIONAL STRENGTHS AND WEAKNESSES

If we face a comparative institutional choice, by what criteria can we compare voluntary and compulsory institutions for constraining self-interest? And given some criteria, which institution is preferred in what circumstances?

Let us consider four different criteria: cost, legitimacy, jurisdiction and flexibility in the following sections.

Cost

The principal strength of voluntary codes of conduct is that relative to compulsory laws, they are cheap to set and to enforce. Compulsory laws must be formalized, and formal laws and their state enforcement require legislatures, courts, lawyers and judges, police and prisons. By contrast, we learn manners, respect for others, honesty, loyalty, thrift, diligence, the duty of care and many other social codes at our mother's knee. The threat that, 'if you . . . , you will burn in Hell forever' can be inexpensive social enforcement.

This relative cost advantage only exists under limited circumstances. The relevant community must be sufficiently homogeneous, first to grant general legitimacy and acceptability to the codes and thus ensure a high rate of voluntary compliance, and second to provide a means to punish violators. By definition, the state, with monopoly power over physical force, will not do the enforcing; the community must do it in some more subtle way.

To illustrate the point, consider this summary of a judge adjudicating a property dispute involving one of the author's Mennonite ancestors more than a century ago:

> It is to be regretted that the members of this religious organization should have such differences which they cannot harmonize. The Mennonite Church is world-wide renowned for peace, brotherly love, and good will to all, and for the amicable settlement of all their difficulties among themselves in a Christian spirit. The court is the last place to which they should resort, and indeed never should until all other amicable modes at an honest method of adjustment have failed.
>
> Supreme Court of Pennsylvania, 1883

The judge is clearly shocked that such a particularly closed and homogeneous community, with a strong internal code of conduct, has, in this rare instance, brought its conflict into the legal domain where it will be settled by the state at high cost.

Consider next the matter of enforcement cost. Even informal and voluntary social constraints need collective enforcement (or 'mutual coercion') because they deny a decision-maker some gain. If the enforcement mechanism is not the state's power, what is it? Again, a Mennonite or Amish community suggests an answer: social stigma. In a Mennonite or Amish community, 'shunning', a well-developed code of social exclusion, is extraordinarily costly to an individual who breaks the community's rules. Similarly, excommunication is extraordinarily costly to faithful Catholics. In business circles just as in religious ones, those who acquire a reputation for failing to satisfying others' ethical standards will find they are shunned. And again, this mechanism is relatively cheap if there is a sufficient degree of homogeneity to the community. By contrast, social or business exclusion will not harm those who do not belong to the community or care about its values.

Although it might seem fanciful, as Jensen argued, to imagine that voluntary rules could really prove a basis for social control in the macro-cosmos, it is a conventional wisdom that business in much of Asia is transacted at relatively low cost within homogeneous social networks without the contractual formalization and litigation that is commonplace in the West.

Legitimacy

Ironically, voluntary behavioural codes may have a legitimacy that compulsory and formal laws lack. A 51% majority can generally pass laws that demand compliance by 100% of the community. Can this properly be called, 'mutually agreed upon'? Voluntary social rules, to be legitimate and thus effective against free-riding, necessitate much wider community support.

Garrett Hardin prompts our thinking about this when he discusses what he terms the 'double-bind':

> If we ask a man who is exploiting a commons to desist 'in the name of conscience', what are we saying to him? What does he hear? – not only at the moment but also in the wee small hours of the night when, half asleep, he remembers not merely the words we used but also the nonverbal communication cues we gave him unawares? Sooner or later, consciously or subconsciously, he senses that he has received two communications, and that they are contradictory: 1. (intended communication) 'If you don't do as we ask, we will openly condemn you for not acting like a responsible citizen'; 2. (the unintended communication) 'If you *do* behave as we ask, we will secretly condemn you for a simpleton who can be shamed into standing aside while the rest of us exploit the commons.'
>
> Hardin, 1986, p. 1246

Hardin does not seem to appreciate that widely accepted voluntary codes of conduct offer a way out of the double bind. I will not feel a simpleton for contributing to the commons if I see others doing so. On the contrary, that gives me even more incentive to contribute. There are two behavioural equilibria here, not one.

On the other hand, just as formal laws suffer from the potential tyranny of the 51% majority, informal rules may suffer their own kind of tyranny. Legal proceedings are conducted under precise rules of procedure intended to ensure justice. No protections against ignorance or prejudice exist in social codes, and there are unfortunately many examples of social codes that are objectionable to many people. Discrimination on the basis of race is an obvious example.[9] Another example of a voluntary code that many would find objectionable, even if not based on ignorance or prejudice, is the code against whistle-blowing that seems to be exceptionally strong in business and the military.

A less obvious problem of legitimacy derives from true moral ambiguity. Consider, for example, the case of low-skill jobs in France being off-shored to Pakistan. Displaced French workers suffer, but newly employed Pakistanis benefit. International trade theory tells us that this will raise total wealth. It will also cause wages to fall in labour-scarce France and to rise in labour-rich Pakistan. On the other hand, returns to capital should rise in France and fall in Pakistan. Where does the public good lie here? What positions are self-interested? What geographical boundary does 'the public' imply? What institutional mechanism is best prepared to deal with this situation: our government's laws, which generally favour free trade, or the pressure of unelected non-governmental organizations, which often try to shame companies that move their operations abroad?

This sort of moral ambiguity raises frequent conflicts between communities with different values, cultures and social codes. What intermediary transactions really constitute immorality versus 'grease' payments to under-paid agents that are a culturally established component of their fair compensation? What age and type of work constitutes immoral child labour, and might the answer to that question be sensitive to a country's level of development? When does job protection unfairly freeze out new labour force entrants? When are local environmental standards superior to remote but tighter ones? Is it right to expropriate pharmaceutical companies' patent rights for the sake of poor would-be consumers? All these examples raise complex questions of the public interest as well as of the most suitable institution – voluntary or compulsory – to answer the questions.

Jurisdiction

Voluntary rules can serve effectively in cases where formal legal institutions are weak or non-existent. This is particularly obvious in international affairs where governance organizations are notoriously weak. It may not be coincidental, as will be discussed below, that the CSR movement has waxed as globalization has shined light on the failings of international law and international institutions.

A good example of this is voluntary action on the part of some major multinational firms to police the practices of their suppliers in poor countries.[10] Laws in the West are generally inadequate to hold Western companies legally liable for the conduct of their foreign independent suppliers, and the enforcement of laws in poor countries, if laws do exist, is weak.

Even where international laws exist, they may be inadequately enforced. This is often attributed to the lack of an international police force, but a complementary explanation is that international law is not really law at all; it is rather a web of international treaties. If one signatory breaks a treaty, the only recourse the others have is to retaliate by breaking the same or other treaties themselves. This does not uniquely penalize the transgressor; it penalizes all parties, and this in turn undermines the force of the 'law'.

Flexibility

Voluntary behavioural codes have a flexibility that compulsory laws lack. This flexibility takes several forms. First, legal proceedings require a dichotomous ruling: the defendant is guilty or not guilty. There is no scaling of judgment if two-thirds of the jury votes guilty and one-third not guilty, or if all the jurors think the defendant is two-thirds likely to be guilty.[11]

With enforcement via social stigma and exclusion, adjudicated in the court of public opinion, scaling or other nuances of judgment are possible. For example, the segment of the community that feels that Wal-Mart Stores abuses employees' rights (while not being guilty of any crime under the law) shops elsewhere. Those who are not offended shop at Wal-Mart. Economic punishment is scaled to the intensity of public opinion in a way that is impossible in a court case.

Second, informal rules are relatively effective when it is difficult to define transgressions clearly.[12] We are all familiar with conflicts between the letter and the spirit of the law. Like it or not, laws should be enforced to the letter, so they should be letter-clear.[13] Although specific acts such as theft can be prohibited by law, one cannot easily legislate generosity or fair dealing. Informal social sanctions have the flexibility to enforce a spirit. The Enron case illustrates the difficulty of dealing in the courts with novel and complex business practices that lack the smoking gun that laws often look for, and one might still debate the extent to which Enron is a case of criminal fraud or of unethical, but not illegal, practices.[14]

Third, laws are inherently 'sticks'; they are not 'carrots'. By contrast, social relationships built via compliance with social codes can be rewarding as well as punishing. Reputation is one of the most cherished of corporate assets, and corporate behaviour can help as well as harm it.

Unfortunately, flexibility has some drawbacks, and one not commonly discussed is the following. Voluntary codes commonly rely on moral or ethical values for their legitimacy and to give the incentive of a clear conscience for self-enforcement. The proscription against polluting the environment would seem to be a universal morality. But this can confront a problem illustrated by carbon emissions and climate change, arguably the most serious environmental problem of our generation. Emitting carbon into the atmosphere is not immoral, per se. We do it when we breathe. The socially optimal carbon emission rate is obviously not zero, and determining it is not properly a moral problem but an economic one. Each one of us may be driven by conscience to reduce our demand for fossil fuel-based energy, but no single decentralized decision-maker has the knowledge to know where he or she should stop. It will certainly be at a level above zero. Instead of moral invocations, we need complex and formal environmental regulatory institutions to try to balance marginal social costs and benefits of emissions, to fix an optimal aggregate emission rate and then define a policy – for example, taxation or cap-and-trade – to constrain decentralized decision-makers.[15] What is true of carbon emissions is true of all cases of pollution short of those rare instances where zero emission is truly optimal.

In the field of development economics, 'rule of law' became a fashionable phrase in the 1990s as a solution to development problems in the former Soviet Union and elsewhere. It has been discredited since then for its failure to deliver on its promise, but I suggest an alternative critique of the 'rule of law' in this chapter. The phrase neglects the power of rule *without* law. Perhaps we should speak more of 'rule' and less of 'law'. To the extent that it is possible, a society governed by voluntary but widely accepted and observed social rules would be more economically efficient than one in which all transactions were governed by compulsory laws and police enforcement.

ENTER CSR

The low-hanging fruit model provides a role for CSR, although this is not the focus of this chapter. Firms can, and many surely do, use the imagery of CSR unilaterally as a public relations tool to burnish their reputations and enhance their profitability. Indeed, corporate critics often charge that CSR is commonly little more than public relations. Yet this may be unfairly cynical. Firms can, and some do, build their entire corporate strategies around the image of social responsibility. The Body Shop is the classic case example, albeit one that shows the vulnerability that such a strategy entails. This can be a profitable differentiator in the marketplace and can represent sincere and not just superficial social concern.

Without intending to diminish the virtue of such a strategy, CSR will come into the model developed in this chapter in a different way. Might it be possible to improve the relative advantages of voluntary behavioural codes? The argument to be developed now is that the CSR movement attempts to do just that. It attempts to reinforce the voluntary constraints that have been discussed, creating them where they are lacking and strengthening them where they are weak. In other words, its goal is to raise the benefit-to-cost ratio of voluntary constraints relative to compulsory ones and in so doing, improve the efficiency of the whole system of constraints on self-interest that are necessary to advance the public interest.

Although this model may superficially resemble the low-hanging fruit model presented earlier, it is not the same. The similarity is that in both models, CSR and profitability are consistent (or at least not in conflict), and in that sense, both views of CSR could be called 'business cases' for it. But the difference is nonetheless significant. In the low-hanging fruit model, the firm can *unilaterally* increase its profits by CSR activities. That is not possible here; unilateral action in this model will lower profits. A firm unilaterally undertaking CSR activities would internalize external costs and thus increase its private costs (albeit while lowering social costs). This will only make business sense – that is, it will only increase profits – if it induces other firms to follow. Those other firms could, of course, try to be free-riders, but they face two threats. One is pressure on their reputations that the non-governmental organizations (NGOs) in the CSR movement can provoke, and that pressure will increase as the number of free-riders declines. The other threat is compulsory government regulation.

There are many examples that could illustrate this model of CSR; let us take that of timber harvesting and the Forest Stewardship Council. The problem is as follows: unconstrained harvesting threatens the environment's flora and fauna. In a classic prisoners' dilemma game structure, all foresters would be better off with a sustainable harvesting schedule, but each individual has an incentive to exceed his or her share. If they all do, they condemn to ultimate destruction not only the forests but also their own livelihoods. Even if one forester feels the constraint of his own conscience, he may nonetheless distrust others and reason that he should cut all he can before the unconscionable free-riders destroy the forests.

The long-term interest of each individual forester and of the whole community would be served by a system of sustainable harvest quotas and their enforcement. But what kind of system? One possibility is a system of formal and compulsory national and international laws along with governmental enforcement institutions. Unfortunately, this had proven inadequate to reduce the rate of forest degradation and destruction.[16] So into the void came CSR. Of course, CSR is not an organization, per se; it is perhaps better called a multi-party movement, with campaigns typically launched by NGOs that then capture the involvement of affected businesses.

The Forest Stewardship Council (FSC) was the precipitating organization for the CSR campaign in this case. Established in 1993, it is an association of members including NGOs such as Greenpeace and WWF as well as timber companies and their customers down the supply chain. Its rules entail standards for sustainable harvesting and for air and water quality protection. Although the FSC is international and voluntary, it has means of weak but still adequate enforcement. The FSC maintains a system of certification and labelling through to retail sales. This not only gives consumers assurance of responsible production processes, but also affords a visible weapon to shame non-compliant companies, reduce the value of their reputations and sustain a consumer boycott.

This paradigmatic case illustrates how the CSR movement, working outside of government legislatures, can change the profit calculus of affected businesses and provide an incentive for them to comply with voluntary codes of conduct. It does not require that those businesses forsake profit maximization, but it is not simply showing them low-hanging fruit.

Prospective business targets of CSR campaigns often have an ambiguous attitude to CSR that comes from a natural tension that exists along a spectrum from no rules to voluntary rules to government enforced laws. No firm wants to be fingered publicly as an exploiter of the commons, and we can assume that each realizes that its long-term interest is served by protecting the commons. If a firm wants to protect the commons, it will want to be sure that there is no leakage of business to free-riders. That might suggest a desire for enforced laws. Laws, however, may be impractical due to the lack of formal organizations with an international jurisdiction and police power (as is the case with forest degradation) or they may be high-cost, privately and socially. So the option of cooperation with NGOs in the CSR movement can often be preferred. Businesses and NGOs can make natural bed-fellows in defining and enforcing voluntary codes of conduct.

This corporate preference for voluntarism can be virtuous, but it can also be corrupt. When some (but not all) US corporations lobbied US President George W. Bush to block formal and compulsory legal controls on carbon emissions, arguing in favour of voluntary industry action instead, one cannot help but suspect that they purposely and cynically favoured what they knew was an inadequate institution.

The current US financial crisis, originating in the sub-prime mortgage market, is an example of conflicting pressures for voluntarism versus legal compulsion. To summarize the story very briefly, some mortgage brokers' lending practices allegedly helped trigger large-scale defaults and foreclosures. Many critics of the industry, although granting that the lending practices were not illegal, felt that they were unethical and responsible for provoking the ensuing financial crisis. In short, a constraint on self-interest, which might have been sustained by informal codes of conduct within the financial sector, failed. What should be done now?

A bill before the US House of Representatives requires compulsory licensing of mortgage brokers as a first step, and then further compulsory legal controls. An alternative preferred by the finance sector relies on improved voluntary codes of lending practice. (The firms were surely aware of the cost of compliance with requirements of the Sarbanes-Oxley Act of 2002.) But will a new voluntary code work? Is this an arena where the CSR movement might help provide an effective incentive for compliance with a voluntary code of conduct? Or must we have formal laws that, for example, allow borrowers to sue brokers and firms that securitized the loans the borrowers had no chance of repaying? Although this chapter does not answer these questions, it does show how to think about them.

Finally, some of these examples and others the reader may think of suggest a generalization: that the growth and success of the CSR movement is a consequence of changes in the past several decades that diminished the extent or power of compulsory economic laws and regulations and thus created a vacuum for voluntarism to fill. Two such changes come immediately to mind. One is globalization. This has expanded the volume and value of transactions that fall into a netherworld where national laws and regulations cannot reach. At the same time, the spread of global businesses, the gradual harmonization of standards of business conduct internationally and the increasing ease of learning about and communicating to the public how firms behave when away from home, have made firms increasingly vulnerable to shaming and loss of reputation.

The second big change in the last decades has been market liberalization. Although this was undoubtedly socially constructive in many cases, the wave of deregulation and privatization just as surely led in some instances to unconstrained and abusive self-interest, which in turn prompted a CSR response.

SOME HYPOTHESES

The above discussion can be shaped into testable hypotheses about when CSR will be most observed and when it will be most effective. The following list is not intended to be exhaustive, is not expressed sufficiently concisely to constitute something immediately testable, and necessitates the compilation of data to perform empirical tests. Nevertheless, here are outlines of some hypotheses concerning what we should expect to observe about CSR:

- The success of CSR initiatives will increase with the homogeneity of the relevant communities. Initiatives that are local and small-scale might find this condition easy to satisfy. Large-scale and especially international initiatives would invariably be more difficult to execute and so would have to be based on more nearly universal moral codes. To give an example, the UN Global Charter's Ten Principles[17] represents a noble attempt to establish universal standards in the areas of human rights, labour, the environment and anti-corruption. If one believed that the moral basis of human rights was more nearly universal than that dealing with bribery, one would predict that CSR campaigns based on the Charter's human rights principles would prove the more successful.
- The CSR movement will pursue cases in the court of public opinion. We would not expect to see direct advocacy for legal reforms.[18] This follows from what has been presented in this chapter, even though a cynic might offer a complementary argument: it is in the self-interest of the various parties participating in CSR movements to prevent control from passing from their hands into those of the courts.

- CSR will target cases where, and be most effective when, formal laws and regulations are weak, untrustworthy, high cost or otherwise inadequate. So, for example, we can hypothesize that a significant fraction of CSR campaigns will concern international business affairs.

- We should expect to see CSR initiatives launched in areas that have been deregulated in the last decades. Presumably, these are areas where markets are flawed and where those flaws had, at some point in the past, led to compulsory behavioural constraints. Deregulation signifies a political realization that compulsion was flawed, too, but deregulation just swung the pendulum back toward its laissez faire starting point. It fixed nothing. That leaves the possibility of trying voluntarism.

- CSR will be most often observed and most effective where the flexibility of voluntary codes is of greatest value. As argued earlier, this will imply situations where the behaviour to be condemned is hard to specify, ex ante, and therefore would be too vague to sustain a legal challenge.

- CSR will be observed where the evolution of social values is most rapid because formal laws will have trouble keeping up with rapid social change.

- CSR initiatives must constrain behaviour by social pressure, and this suggests a number of hypotheses regarding the characteristics of the best prospective CSR campaign targets. For example, a target's behaviour must be visible to the community that must exert social pressure, which is very likely to be the community of customers. This would in most cases be the largest potentially aggressive community. This would make targets in consumer goods markets more attractive than those in producer goods markets. Obviously, large firms make more attractive targets than small firms, all other things equal.

- The cost of enforcing voluntary codes of conduct will fall on the community, just as does the cost of enforcing the law. There is a difference, however, in that individuals are obliged to pay for law enforcement because it is financed by compulsory taxes. By contrast, the cost of enforcing voluntary codes of conduct is borne voluntarily. One can hypothesize that the probability of success of a CSR campaign will be inversely related to the cost that individuals must voluntarily pay to sustain it. So, for example, a consumer boycott is likely to be more successful than a campaign launched and 'financed' by a much smaller number of employees.

- Oligopoly theory suggests some hypotheses about when voluntary industry codes of conduct will be most successful: for example, when there are relatively few firms, when they are symmetrically exposed to risk and when the actions of each are visible to the others.

CONCLUSION

The hostility that economists have shown for corporate social responsibility is a consequence of the two main CSR models that, for different reasons, economists cannot embrace. The intent of this chapter is to show that there is an alternative model of CSR that can be embraced without shame. There is nothing radical about the model; it fits naturally into institutional economics, a sub-field of economics pioneered more than 75 years ago (Commons, 1931). Furthermore, it presents economists interested in this topic with testable hypotheses.

ACKNOWLEDGEMENTS

The author would like to thank Gilbert Lenssen, Subi Rangan, Janet Sidaway, Craig Smith and David Vogel for useful comments on early drafts of the paper.

NOTES

1. The story goes as follows. An economist and a friend were walking together when the friend sees a £20 note on the pavement ahead. 'We're in luck,' she says. 'No,' the economist replies. 'If it really were a £20 note, someone would already have picked it up.'

2. 'Management By Objective', 'Total Quality Management' and 'Customer Relations Management' respectively.

3. Gordon Gekko, in the film, *Wall Street*, directed by Oliver Stone, 1987.

4. Of course, there are many examples of managerial decisions that destroyed shareholder value, some of which management might try to justify ex post as having socially redeeming virtues. And there are ambiguous cases where there was a possibility of a financial return which may have weighed into a 'social' decision. See, for example, Merck & Co. (1991). But proper evidence would be a clear ex ante expectation of a non-trivial loss of shareholder value for the sake of social gain.

5. The fiduciary responsibility of managers and boards of directors to maximize the value of the firm is not absolute, although the scope for other objectives is tightly limited. Section 2.01 of the American Law Institute's Principles of Corporate Governance states that 'even if corporate profit and shareholder gain are not thereby enhanced, the corporation, in the conduct of its business: (1) is obliged to the same extent as a natural person to act within the boundaries set by law; 2) may take into account ethical considerations that are reasonably regarded as appropriate to the responsible conduct of business; and (3) may devote a reasonable amount of resources to public welfare, humanitarian, educational and philanthropic purposes.'

6. This argument is not relevant for privately held firms whose owners may legitimately pursue objectives other than profit maximization.

7. As an example, the Internet poses a challenge to the constraint on unauthorized use of intellectual property. In fact, it has all but created a culture of free use of music under copyright.

8. 'Work-to-rule' strikes provide a nice example of what can happen when explicit and formal contractual work rules expand and displace flexible albeit informal work codes. More will be said of the advantage of flexibility later.

9. One should note, of course, that laws are not immune to these problems, and it was not long ago that they legitimized both racial and sexual discrimination.

10. Adidas is the definitive case; see 'Adidas: Human Rights and the Euro 2000', INSEAD case study, 2002.

11. Jurors do not vote between guilty or innocent. Rather, they vote between proven guilty or not proven guilty according to a standard of proof that differs with the severity of the case. So it is possible that all jurors could believe a defendant guilty but still vote for acquittal because the standard of proof was not met.

12. There is a parallel here with the point made previously concerning explicit and implicit elements of contracts. Just as complexity and bounded rationality may necessitate incomplete contracts, they may also necessitate incomplete and flexible voluntary codes rather than hard-to-enforce laws.

13. US Supreme Court Justice Potter Stewart allegedly said about pornography that, 'I can't define it, but I know it when I see it'. Given the frustration the Court has faced over pornography, and the point being made here, he should have reversed the phrases and said, 'I know it when I see it, but I can't define it.'

14. Christopher Stone (Stone, 1975) recognized this difficulty with the application of law to corporations, but his prescription was compulsory changes to corporate governance structures rather than to invoke social opprobrium as an instrument of social control.

15. One is reminded of President Jimmy Carter's claim during the 1979 energy crisis that conserving energy was 'the moral equivalent of war'. Yet morality had little to do with the crisis or its solution. Economics did, and consumption habits only began to change with higher prices. When prices later fell, consumption reverted to its earlier pattern, and as these words are being written, prices are again rising rapidly with serious consequences for the sales of fuel-inefficient vehicles.

16. One such disappointing attempt at a formal system was via CITES, the Convention on International Trade in Endangered Species of Wild Fauna and Flora.

17. United Nations, 'Global Compact', 2000.

18. There are, of course, NGOs that take their cases to the government legislatures or the courts. The Natural Resources Defense Council is one, the Core Coalition is another. Nonetheless, and at the risk of tautology, I still claim that the standard CSR model is one that eschews the courts in favour of public opinion.

REFERENCES

Boesky, I. (1985) University of California-Berkeley School of Business Administration, commencement address.

Commons, J.R. (1931) Institutional economics, *American Economic Review*, **21**, 648–57.

Elkington, J. (1994) Towards the sustainable corporation: Win-win-win business strategies for sustainable development, *California Management Review*, **36** (2), 90–100.

Elkington, J. (1997) *Cannibals with Forks: The Triple Bottom Line on the 21st Century Business*, Oxford University Press, Oxford.

Friedman, M. (1970) *New York Times Magazine*, 13 September, 32–3.

Hardin, G. (1986) The tragedy of the commons, *Science*, **162**, 1243–8.

Jensen, M.C. (2001) Value maximization, stakeholder theory, and the corporate objective function, *Journal of Applied Corporate Finance*, **14** (3), 8–21.

Merck & Co., Inc., Stanford Business School case study, 1991.

North, D.C. (1991) Institutions, *Journal of Economic Perspectives*, **5** (1), 97–112.

North, D.C. (1994) Economic performance through time, *American Economic Review* **84** (3), 359–68.

Scott, M. and Rothman, H. (1992) *Companies with a Conscience: An Intimate Portrait of Twelve Firms that Made a Difference*, Citadel.

Smith, A. (1776) *An Inquiry into the Nature and Causes of the Wealth of Nations*, Collier.

Stone, C.D. (1975) *Where the Law Ends: The Social Control of Corporate Behavior*, Harper & Row.

Supreme Court of Pennsylvania (1883) *Samuel H. Landis, et al. v. Henry S. Borneman, et al.*, Eastern District, January Term, Paper Book of Appellants, Reading, XLVIII, XLIX.

Vermaelen, T. (2008) Maximizing shareholder value: An ethical responsibility?, INSEAD working paper, February.

Vogel, D. (2005) *The Market for Virtue: The Potential and Limits of Corporate Social Responsibility*, Brookings Institution Press.

Wilson, E.O. (1975) *Sociobiology: The New Synthesis*, Harvard University Press.

CHAPTER FIFTEEN

Unilever and Oxfam: Understanding the Impacts of Business on Poverty

N. Craig Smith, INSEAD and Robert J. Crawford,
London Business School[1]

INTRODUCTION

> More than eight out of ten people in the world today live in developing and emerging markets, where Unilever already has a strong presence. Improving their economic prospects in a sustainable way is central to our future growth.
>
> Unilever Environmental and Social Report, 2005

> If we accept that MNCs exist and will continue to, we must ask ourselves how we should work toward best outcomes and what choices need to be made.
>
> Becky Buell, Head of Programme Policy,
Campaigns and Policy Division, Oxfam, GB

Attending a talk late in 2001 at Chatham House (a foreign policy research institute in the United Kingdom), Mandy Cormack, Vice President Corporate Responsibility at Unilever, was struck by an argument advanced by one of the speakers. 'Managed well, TNC [transnational corporation] investment can bring major development benefits,' claimed Sophia Tickell of the non-governmental organization (NGO) Oxfam. 'Managed badly, the same investment can exacerbate poverty and damage the environment.' She argued that corporate social responsibility (CSR) had taken off because governments had failed to regulate the international private sector effectively and she saw the burgeoning global civil society movement, including Oxfam, as an attempt to hold big corporations to account.

Cormack listened to Tickell's speech in the full knowledge that Oxfam was a campaigning NGO and that it was running a hard-hitting campaign in which the impact of multinational companies (MNCs) in developing countries was strongly criticized. Cormack was keen to avoid Unilever becoming the focus of such attention. She was also concerned that *how* MNCs contributed to wealth creation and to lifting people out of poverty was not well understood. Tickell's position potentially provided an opportunity to move the debate forward.

Cormack and Tickell shared an interest in dialogue that was more than intellectual. Developing countries were central to Unilever's corporate strategy and Oxfam was increasingly focusing on trade, not aid, as a key to alleviating poverty. Cormack believed that Tickell's argument carried an implicit threat. After all, as part of the *Make Trade Fair* campaign, Oxfam activists were attempting to raise consumer awareness by disseminating information and demonstrating against selected MNCs, which they attacked and portrayed as villains. Cormack was concerned that Unilever might become the next target of an Oxfam campaign. What could she do about that? How, if at all, might she initiate a dialogue with Sophia Tickell? As she explained, 'The prospect of seeking a relationship with one of the world's most important and aggressive NGOs was daunting, but it was better to try that than to wait to get attacked.'

UNILEVER

Unilever originated with William Hesketh Lever, who founded Lever Brothers. In addition to developing a profitable business, Lever had a personal mission to improve cleanliness and hygiene in Victorian Britain. The purposes of his Sunlight Soap, he wrote, were 'to make cleanliness commonplace; to lessen work for women; to foster health and contribute to personal attractiveness, that life may be more enjoyable and rewarding for the people who use our products.' This credo became rooted at the heart of the business, which pioneered the development of products with a 'positive social impact', in an attempt to balance profit with responsible behaviour.

Not only did Lever Brothers offer better housing to its employees in its 19th-century model industrial village, Port Sunlight, than typical employers of the day, but it was also one of the first companies in Britain to employ a full-time safety inspector and a company doctor, to have an eight-hour working day and generous pay, and from 1905, pensions for both male and female workers. Unilever employees were proud of its heritage as an ethical company, claiming to enjoy an unusually close relationship with its customers, whom the company sought to serve with high-quality, affordable products. Unilever was established in 1930 by the merger of the Lever Brothers soap company with Margarine Unie of the Netherlands, a company with many similar values, which produced vitamin-enriched margarine. Unilever was from its inception an international company with headquarters in London and Rotterdam.[2]

Over the next 70 years, Unilever grew into one of the world's largest companies, with operations in over 100 countries. It specialized in nutrition, home care and personal care products. Every day, approximately 150 million consumers worldwide purchased a Unilever product from among its approximately 400 brands, such as Surf washing detergent, Bertolli olive oil, Hellman's mayonnaise, Knorr soup, Lipton tea, Sunsilk shampoo and Dove soap. Eleven Unilever brands each had sales in excess of €1 billion while food accounted for more than 50% of total sales. By 2005, Unilever had a worldwide revenue of €39 672 million, an operating profit (before tax) of €5 314 million and 206 000 employees.

The 21st century started with the launch of *Unilever's Path to Growth* – a strategy to transform the business (e.g., by simplifying the brand portfolio and increasing margins and capital efficiency). Five years later, Unilever admitted that the company was 'not where we set out to be'. It launched another five-year strategy, *Unilever 2010*, and a new mission statement with an emphasis on adding vitality to life (see Exhibit 15.1). Unilever explained:

> Vitality is at the heart of everything we do. It's in our brands, our people and our values . . . Vitality defines what we stand for: our values, what makes us different, and how we contribute to society. It's the common thread that links our brands and it's central to the unique way we operate around the world.

Unilever management was keenly attuned to consumer trends reflecting this view of vitality – and to the opportunities in developing and emerging markets, which would account for 90% of the world's population by 2010.

EXHIBIT 15.1   UNILEVER AT A GLANCE, 2005

Mission

Unilever's mission is to add vitality to life. We meet everyday needs for nutrition, hygiene and personal care with brands that help people feel good, look good, and get more out of life.

Key Facts

In 2005 . . .

Our worldwide turnover was €40 billion.

We employed 206 000 people in around 100 countries worldwide.

Every day, 150 million people chose our brands to feed their families and to clean themselves and their homes.

Over half of our sales were generated by our eleven €1bn brands: Knorr, Flora/Becel, Hellmann's, Lipton, Omo, Surf, Lux, Dove, Blue Band/Rama, Sunsilk and our Heart ice cream brand.

We were the global market leader in all the food categories in which we operated: Savoury and Dressings, Spreads, Weight Management, Tea, and Ice Cream.

We were also global market leader in Skin and Deodorants, and have very strong positions in other Home and Personal Care categories.

We invested around €1 billion in research and development, for example at the Unilever Food and Health Research Institute, which has a worldwide reputation for scientific excellence.

We spent over €79 million on a wide range of community projects.

We had 337 manufacturing sites across six continents, all of which strived for improved performance on safety, efficiency, quality and environmental impacts, working to global Unilever standards and management systems.

We invested €5 billion in advertising and promotions.

Source: www.unilever.com/

Unilever characterized itself as a 'multi-local' MNC. Rather than a unified global system, the various Unilever companies sought to satisfy local demand with particular sensitivity paid to the local cultural context. This meant that, in addition to seeking profits through the sale of products tailored to local conditions, the company viewed itself as an active participant in efforts to improve the lives of those living in developing countries, where Unilever considered that its success 'depends on the economic health of the countries in which it operates'.[3] According to its *Environmental and Social Report*, 'Unilever generates wealth by meeting consumer needs: we add value to the raw material and other supplies we buy in as we process them into branded goods, market them to consumers and sell them through our retail customers.'[4]

In 2005, out of €39.7 billion in turnover (sales), over €27 billion was spent with suppliers, creating €12.2 billion in value added; this directly benefited employees, the company contended, but also diffused into the wider economy in a positive way. In Africa, for example, Unilever operated in 18 countries, with sales of €2 billion (5% of company total). The majority of the products it sold in Africa were manufactured and supplied locally. The company had a total of 40 000 employees there, with 90% of its managers of African origin. The company prided itself on the affordability and quality of its products, and its attention to environmental and health concerns in Africa.[5] In the new millennium, Unilever's leadership remained concerned with poverty in developing countries.

POVERTY AND MNCs

Although the nature and causes of poverty had long been debated, some agreement was emerging regarding how to define it. Three levels of poverty were identified. First, there was *extreme poverty*, where a household often lacked the most basic survival requirements, including nutrition, safe drinking water, sanitation and health care, and also education, shelter, stable employment and income. The World Bank estimated that this group was living on less than US$1 per person per day (more precisely US$1.08 in 1993 Purchasing Power Parity terms). This group comprised 1.1 billion people worldwide (2001 estimate). The overwhelming majority lived in Africa and Asia, with those in Asia declining in relative and absolute numbers, while those in Africa were increasing in both relative and absolute terms. Second, those people living in *moderate poverty* had many of the basic needs satisfied, but only at minimum levels. They were estimated by the World Bank scale to be living on between US$1 and US$2 per person per day (US$2.15 in 1993 Purchasing Power Parity terms). This group comprised 1.6 billion people worldwide (2001 estimate). Third, *relative poverty* referred to individuals whose living standards were below the national average, if higher than those in the first two categories. In spite of the accepted definitions of poverty, little agreement existed as to its causes and what the remedies should be (see http://go.worldbank.org and Sachs, 2005, pp. 20–22) (see Figure 15.1).

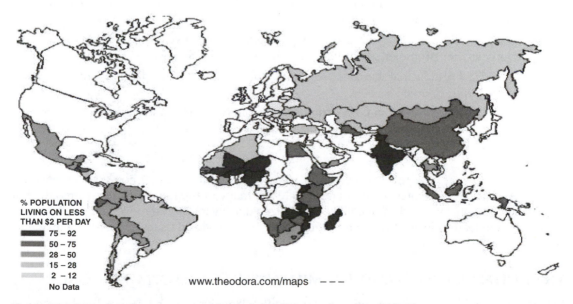

% POPULATION LIVING ON LESS THAN $2 PER DAY
- 75 – 92
- 50 – 75
- 28 – 50
- 15 – 28
- 2 – 12
- No Data

www.theodora.com/maps

Figure 15.1 Map showing percentage of population living on less than US$2/day

Source: Map courtesy of www.theodora.com/maps, used with permission

The impact of MNCs on poverty in developing countries had also long been a subject of debate. Proponents of globalization tended to argue that MNCs played a vital role in the continual improvement of the efficiency of the international economic regime: they created jobs, diffused wealth into the local economy via a multiplier effect, generated tax revenues, allocated resources efficiently in accordance with the comparative advantage of trading nations and implanted higher international environmental, safety and health standards in developing countries.

Critics in the anti-globalization movement, however, believed that MNCs caused (or exacerbated) poverty. Oxfam was somewhat unique among NGOs in that it acknowledged the potential contribution of MNCs to poverty reduction. Oxfam's stated position on the private sector was as follows:

> In theory, MNCs have the potential to offer valuable assets that developing countries need: capital; technology; a skills and knowledge base; managerial experience and access to markets. However, these same companies, while spurring growth, can also harm the poor. Oxfam's work at the local, national and international level questions the disproportionate price paid by the poor in the tradeoffs required when developing countries attempt to attract investment and trade on equal terms with the north.[6]

Oxfam levelled some heavy criticisms at MNCs for their potential to increase poverty:

- although jobs may have been created by MNCs, they were usually bad jobs in which the workers suffered abuse of their human rights;
- although MNC jobs brought poor workers into the value chain, they were unable to capture sufficient value from it;
- the provision of services to the poor by MNCs, though on the increase, were often unevenly distributed and hence compounded inequalities;
- MNCs have not always transferred technology, in effect locking the poor into low-value-added jobs that continue to pay poorly;
- with aggressive marketing and predatory pricing of goods, MNCs frequently increased poverty as they promoted goods for which the poor had little need;
- because of lax industrial standards, MNCs contributed to the degradation of the environment;
- although MNCs invested in poor countries, they often did so by forcing local governments to bargain away tax gains, environmental and other standards that in aggregate worsened poverty.[7]

As well as Oxfam, critics of globalization and MNCs included many other non-governmental organizations.[8] There were literally thousands of NGOs, many of them local, which were adept at forming international networks that could be mobilized quickly for protest movements, lobbying of politicians and leaders in MNCs, and reporting on highly specialized issues and far-flung incidents (see Yaziji, 2004).

THE UNITED NATIONS AND THE MILLENNIUM DEVELOPMENT GOALS

In September 2000, the United Nations convened the Millennium Assembly at its headquarters in New York City. With 147 heads of state in attendance, it was touted as the largest summit of leaders in history. The purpose of the meeting was to forge an agenda to end extreme poverty, eliminate

EXHIBIT 15.2 UN MILLENNIUM DEVELOPMENT GOALS

- Eradicate extreme poverty and hunger. By 2015, halve the proportion of people living on US$1 per day as well as those who suffer from hunger.
- Achieve universal primary education by 2015.
- Promote gender equality and empower women, in particular in all levels of education by 2015 (and hopefully in primary and secondary education by 2005).
- Reduce child mortality (under 5 years of age) by two-thirds by 2015.
- Improve maternal health. By 2015, the maternal mortality ratio should be reduced by three-quarters.
- Halt the advance and reverse the spread of HIV/AIDS, malaria, and other diseases by 2015.
- Ensure environmental sustainability. All countries should integrate sustainable development principles and programmes into their national policies as well as reverse the loss of environmental resources. Halve the proportion of people without access to safe drinking water and basic sanitation by 2015. Achieve a significant improvement in the lives of 100 million slum dwellers by 2020.
- Develop a global partnership for development.*

*The eighth goal represented a commitment to develop a global partnership that would implement goals 1–7. It called for: a) the development of good governance practices in an open, rule-based, predictable, non-discriminatory trading and financial system; b) special consideration for the needs of LDCs, including the reduction of tariffs and quotas on their exports and increased development assistance; c) addressing the special needs of landlocked countries and small islands; d) long-term debt relief via national and international means; e) development and implementation of strategies for decent and productive work for youth; f) pharmaceutical companies cooperating to provide access to affordable, essential drugs; g) in cooperation with the private sector, dissemination of the benefits of new technologies, in particular those of information and communication.

Source: http://www.undp.org/mdg/basics.shtml and Sachs, 2005, pp. 210–213.

treatable diseases and alleviate environmental degradation in the 21st century. After deliberation and discussion of a UN report, *We the Peoples: the Role of the United Nations in the 21st Century*, the leaders adopted the Millennium Declaration, which set concrete and quantifiable goals – the Millennium Development Goals (MDGs) – as well as specific deadlines to accomplish them (Sachs, 2005, pp. 210–213) (see Exhibit 15.2). One of the business leaders who followed these developments carefully was Unilever's CEO, Niall FitzGerald. He resolved that Unilever's contribution to international development should be more widely understood and appreciated.

THE RISE OF INTERNATIONAL ACTIVISM

In the late 1950s, consumers and activists began to play an increasingly direct role in questioning business, beginning with safety concerns at home and eventually moving to corporate ethics and global corporate citizenship. Activists such as Ralph Nader, for example, who founded Public Citizen in Washington, DC, in 1971, led lobbying and protest campaigns against powerful and entrenched economic interests for causes such as car safety and later against environmental pollution

(Croft, 1999). These pressure groups, as they were then known in Europe and the United States, tended to recruit young idealists and operated largely through the provision of investigative information and media campaigns. With the rise of the Internet in the 1990s, a new form of global activism arose. For the first time, independent agents and local observers had the means to find and publicize, instantaneously and at little cost, the incidents that concerned them. If an issue caught on, it could generate explosive interest worldwide, resulting in protests ranging from spontaneous outpourings to coordinated campaigns (Spar, 1998). Activists often used the following key criteria when formulating a campaign against companies:

- a clear problem or solution or villain;
- a reasonable chance of success;
- the opportunity to form alliances with other groups, in order to leverage their knowledge and local connections;
- the possibility of generating passion via enhanced understanding (Klein, Kapstein and Crawford, 2003, pp. 9–10).

Although the character of NGO–MNC interaction was predominantly adversarial, in the late 1990s a number of more cooperative relationships arose. The advantages they provided to MNCs reflected the inherent strengths of NGOs – their extensive networks, specialized expertise, heightened awareness of emerging social concerns and political legitimacy – and included the following:

- *Wider perspective.* NGOs could give MNCs a perspective on issues that they might not have access to on their own, for example, in understanding the reasons behind the anger of social movements against MNCs, seeing their impacts beyond their immediate operations and contextualizing their business within a wider socio-political environment.
- *Heading off trouble.* Interest shown in an issue by an NGO was an early warning that it could become a wider political concern with alarming rapidity. NGOs could often signal to MNC headquarters where operations on the ground might not be consistent with stated company policies and where there was potential risk.
- *Accelerating innovation.* Because NGOs often demanded improved product or environmental safety, MNCs that adopted their suggestions might gain a first-mover advantage in new markets, such as eliminating ozone-destroying chemical coolants from refrigerators.
- *Foreseeing shifts in demand.* Because NGOs tended to focus on a broader range of issues than MNCs, they often foresaw trends in consumer preferences earlier than businesses. One example in the 1990s was the unexpected opposition to genetically modified organisms (GMOs) that Monsanto experienced in Europe.
- *Shaping legislation.* With their growing legitimacy, NGOs enjoyed access to like-minded politicians, who took their concerns into consideration while formulating legislation. MNCs could learn from NGOs how public expectations were evolving and how this might play out in a legislative arena.
- *Setting industry standards.* NGOs were also increasingly influencing international practices in a wide array of areas and in a more global manner than national laws and regulations.

For example, the World Wildlife Fund for Nature (WWF) worked with Unilever to found the Marine Stewardship Council (MSC) in the mid-1990s, to establish mutually agreed standards for sustainable fishing to inform consumer purchasing. The MSC standard was subsequently adopted by major retailers, including Wal-Mart, as part of their environmental strategies.

Not only was the number of NGOs rapidly increasing – they were reported to have quadrupled in number over the previous decade – but the sophistication of their campaigners was on the rise, too. More NGOs were taking on campaign tactics as a key strategy for achieving wider, systemic change on issues about which they were concerned. Half of employees at larger NGOs had either masters' or law degrees and up to 20% had doctorates. This could only enhance their political savvy for protest campaigns as well as their ability to communicate new ideas in a language familiar to policymakers, corporate executives and the media (Spar, 1998, p. 12).

OXFAM'S APPROACH TO OVERCOMING POVERTY

Founded as a development charity in 1942, Oxfam had grown into one of the world's most prominent NGOs, with operations in over 100 countries addressing poverty, suffering and injustice. The name Oxfam came from the Oxford Committee for Famine Relief, which was established in Britain during the Second World War. This group of Oxford citizens campaigned for grain ships to be sent through the allied naval blockade to provide relief for women and children in enemy-occupied Greece.

Oxfam International was a confederation of 13 organizations, including Oxfam GB and Oxfam Novib in the Netherlands, working with over 3000 partners worldwide as 'a movement capable of global responses to global issues'. As a federation of relatively autonomous groups, Oxfam advised governments and other organizations on farming techniques and food distribution strategies, brought relief aid during local crises and consulted on similar issues. According to its statement of purpose, Oxfam GB worked 'with others to overcome poverty and suffering', by saving lives through emergency relief work, 'developing programmes and solutions that empower people to work their way out of poverty' and 'campaigning to achieve lasting change'.[9] Oxfam's expenditure on poverty alleviation through worldwide programmes was £213 million in 2006.

Campaigning

Oxfam's commitment to campaigning came from the belief that the scale and urgency of poverty and inequality must be addressed through changes in the policies and practices – of governments, institutions and the private sector – that exacerbate poverty. Oxfam had an activist organization to address issues related to globalization and poverty. Run by a group of passionate advocates for developing countries with increasing sophistication and reach, they had developed tools to campaign against the practices of MNCs and the World Trade Organization (WTO). Oxfam's campaign capabilities gathered momentum with the launch of the first global Oxfam International *Education Now* campaign. The goal of this campaign was to seek 'basic education for all' by 2015, consistent with the UN Millennium Development Goals. Oxfam was also attempting to improve the livelihood of the poor in campaigns such as the LDC (least developed countries) debt forgiveness initiative as well as seeking change in the procedures by which the WTO operated to better address the health needs and development requirements of developing countries.

A key moment of the anti-globalization movement came during a meeting of the WTO in Seattle in November 1999. Not only were there violent protests in the streets, but for the first time the split along the North–South divide of developed and developing nations appeared irreconcilable. Seattle was the beginning of a new wave of developing country assertiveness in multinational negotiations that would set the campaigning tone for NGOs over the following years. At this stage Oxfam moved from a general call for fairness and transparency in WTO negotiations to more focused campaigns on specific issues that were of utmost importance to poor people, although a major problem for the activist groups was how to translate the highly technical issues of the global trade regime into a vocabulary and a campaign that could mobilize consumers to some kind of action. The *Cut the Cost* campaign for access to essential medicines, and the *Mugged* campaign for fair prices for coffee producers, exemplified this shift and consumer-relevant campaigning.

Cut the Cost *and* Mugged *Campaigns*

Begun in 2001 by Oxfam with other NGOs, the *Cut the Cost* campaign targeted the pharmaceutical giant GlaxoSmithKline (GSK) in a call to leadership on access to medicines. Tickell, as head of the Private Sector team at Oxfam, was one its main architects. Although designed specifically to persuade GSK to take industry leadership on lowering the prices it charged for HIV/AIDS antiretroviral treatments, Oxfam's deeper concern was reform of TRIPS (Trade-Related aspects of Intellectual Property Rights), the intellectual property protection clauses of the WTO. The campaign message – that GSK and the WTO via its policymaking and standard practices were arrogantly ignoring a humanitarian crisis of unprecedented proportions – quickly became a major story in the international press (Klein, Kapstein and Crawford, 2003, pp. 16–17).

With *Cut the Cost* and related pressures taking their toll on its reputation, GSK backed down and created an industry-leading policy of offering preferential (not-for-profit) pricing of HIV/AIDS and other medicines in LDCs (Smith and Duncan, 2005). Nonetheless, some GSK managers suggested that Oxfam, with whom they had engaged in discussions prior to the launch of the campaign, had turned on the company when it was to its advantage, violating their trust. Oxfam insisted that although GSK may not have agreed with what Oxfam had said, it had been transparent with the company at each stage of the campaign. 'It was only when GSK refused to budge that we went public,' according to Tickell, 'and we told them we would do this.'

Although the official position of the WTO remained unchanged, it made a number of moves to open up its decision-making process about trade rules to representatives of developing countries, and indicated that the next round of trade negotiations (Doha) would seek to better represent the interests of developing countries. This was regarded by many in the anti-globalization movement as a major policy triumph and a hugely important change that would potentially save hundreds of thousands of lives.

The next major stage in Oxfam's Trade Campaign in 2002 was to examine how coffee was bought and sold within the international trade regime. This resulted in the report, *Mugged: Poverty in Your Coffee Cup*, co-authored by Tickell, which called for a 'coffee rescue plan', initiating a new campaign against a number of MNCs.[10] The coffee market, according to *Mugged*, was undermining the livelihood of 25 million farmers around the world. It claimed that while the price they received for coffee was falling to 30-year lows, the profit margins of the biggest food-processing companies in the world remained high:

The big four coffee roasters, Kraft, Nestlé, Procter & Gamble, and Sara Lee, each have coffee brands worth US$1 billion or more in annual sales. Together with German giant Tchibo, they buy almost half the world's coffee beans each year. Profit margins are high – Nestlé has made an estimated 26% profit margin on instant coffee . . . a very high figure compared with other food and drink brands. If everyone in the supply chain were benefiting this would not matter. As it is, with farmers getting a price that is below the costs of production, the companies' booming business is being paid for by some of the poorest people in the world.

The report argued that the reason for this was a shift from a managed market to a free market and 'market failure' – production was exceeding demand, leading to catastrophically low prices being paid to farmers in developing countries. As the report observed:

Until now, rich consumer countries and the huge companies based in them have responded to the crisis with inexcusable complacency. In the face of human misery, there have been many words yet little action. Existing market-based solutions – Fair Trade and the development of speciality coffees – are important, but only for some farmers. They can help poverty reduction and the environment. However, a systemic, not a niche solution, is needed . . . The challenge is to make the coffee market work for all . . . The low coffee price creates a buyers' market, leaving some of the poorest and most powerless people in the world to negotiate in an open market with some of the richest and most powerful. The result, unsurprisingly, is that the rich get richer and the poor get poorer.

Mugged called for a number of measures to raise prices as well as to provide alternative livelihoods, including 'roaster companies paying farmers a decent price (above their costs of production) so that they can send their children to school, afford medicines and have enough food', and 'increasing the price to farmers by reducing supply and stocks of coffee on the market'. Longer term, as part of a 'commodity management initiative', the report urged that companies pay 'a decent price' for all commodities. This was particularly germane to Unilever as one of the world's major tea processors.

This campaign helped to make coffee 'a big testing ground for what it means to be an ethical consumer' and sales of Fairtrade coffee increased dramatically (*The Economist*, 2006, p. 1).[11] If the coffee-processing companies refused to take certain measures – in effect 'managing' the trade in one of the world's most visible commodity products – they risked seeing their reputations tarnished in media campaigns similar to that against GSK. While Oxfam sought to negotiate with the coffee MNCs, the process remained far more adversarial than cooperative because of continuing mutual mistrust. In the end, according to Oxfam activist Phil Bloomer (Tickell's supervisor), the coffee MNCs made a number of potentially positive changes, including a voluntary code – agreed to by producers and coffee MNCs – to improve working conditions and environmental standards (Burns, 2005, p. 2).

Although Oxfam might have been better known by the public for its campaigning against MNCs, from 1999 its newly created Private Sector team, under the leadership of Tickell, began to engage in new ways of working with the private sector. Oxfam's new Director, Barbara Stocking, encouraged her staff to seek new kinds of relations with MNCs, through participation in events such as the talk at Chatham House. According to Becky Buell, then Oxfam's Head of Programme Policy, Campaigns and Policy Division: 'We were challenged to look at how we might work *with* certain MNCs and not *on* them,' in dialogue and engagement in addition to an on-going campaigning approach. The idea, Buell explained, was 'to see what we could achieve through networks and collaboration. We came from the standpoint that the problems were so big, there was no way we could resolve them on our own.' Buell recognized that there was internal resistance to this notion: 'we were used to challenging the private sector and had a sense of our own moral purity on the issues. People were worried that we would be selling out if we worked with [the MNCs].' Some worried that Oxfam might become too deeply involved with the MNCs, perhaps even becoming dependent on their financial contributions. It was seen as a potential slippery slope along the way to becoming co-opted, eroding the passion of Oxfam staff and ultimately undermining its mission by turning them into public relations adjuncts. The result was a vigorous debate within Oxfam on what form, if any, such collaboration should take.[12]

UNILEVER REACHES OUT

For Unilever the 1990s had seen a number of difficult corporate relations events. The company, which had traditionally relied on its ability to communicate via its brands, found itself in a sceptical and at time hostile public environment, managing a number of corporate communications challenges without the infrastructure, in-house capabilities or external networks to be able to manage communications effectively. The company's response was to start to build a professional corporate relations function, drawing in experts from around the business and recruiting from the company's outside advisors, including Cormack. This newly created team drew on the successful activities of their environmental colleagues, notably the work involved in the establishment of the Marine Stewardship Council and the effective outreach to GMO activists, and began to build a base from which to develop a proactive stakeholder engagement strategy.

Rather than wait for something to happen to Unilever, Cormack argued, the corporate relations team should attempt to *anticipate* contingencies or trends and begin to put policies in place to address them in advance. In particular, this meant that the company should cultivate relations with critics, such as the activist NGOs. 'There was a blinding recognition,' she said, 'that once something goes critical, it is too late to change the public perception of it. At that point you can only contain it, wait for the heat to die down, and then re-approach it. If you want a conversation *before* the heat, you need to be pro-active – because you know that eventually, if you are big, they will find something.'

A pro-active approach, Cormack believed, was entirely compatible with the company's identity and brand, and would take advantage of certain aspects of it. 'The Unilever culture respects differences of perspective,' Cormack said, 'so we wanted to gain a better understanding of how NGOs thought. We wanted to open a dialogue that would be mutually beneficial.' However, she acknowledged that there were some within the company who did not share this view, suspecting instead that certain NGOs were too adversarial to be relied on as constructive partners. They argued that opening up to NGOs might merely provide ammunition to be used against Unilever in some future campaign. Nonetheless, Cormack knew that many Unilever employees sincerely believed that the company was good and deserved recognition for its everyday good business practices. In this view, it had important stories to tell. To test this hypothesis, Cormack decided to investigate a number of them in depth. She enjoyed the support of Unilever's CEO, Niall FitzGerald, who in the late 1990s had been strongly supportive of the work Cormack had done on Unilever's approach to CSR. Unilever's first CSR report appeared in 2000.[13]

A LEARNING PROJECT

In February 2003, Barbara Stocking and Niall FitzGerald met at the World Economic Forum Conference in Davos, Switzerland. Although they came from very different backgrounds, the two leaders knew they shared common ground: both organizations were founder members of the UN Global Compact (UNGC) and both were supporters of the UN Millennium Development Goals. (The UNGC of 2000 advanced a set of core principles in the areas of human rights, labour standards, the environment and anti-corruption, to which companies were asked voluntarily to adhere; see Exhibit 15.3.) The UNGC committed its members to a willingness to learn from each other and to share good practice. After an informal conversation about the UN MDGs and what they might do to further them, Stocking and FitzGerald decided that Unilever and Oxfam should engage in a more in-depth discussion with a view to a collaborative project. However, their plans were no more specific than that; it would be up to their colleagues to negotiate a precise scope of work and a clear set of rules of operation.

EXHIBIT 15.3 THE 10 PRINCIPLES OF THE UN GLOBAL COMPACT

The Global Compact's ten principles in the areas of human rights, labour, the environment and anti-corruption enjoy universal consensus and are derived from:

The Universal Declaration of Human Rights;
The International Labour Organization's Declaration on Fundamental Principles and Rights at Work;
The Rio Declaration on Environment and Development;
The United Nations Convention Against Corruption.

The Global Compact asks companies to embrace, support and enact, within their sphere of influence, a set of core values in the areas of human rights, labour standards, the environment, and anti-corruption:[†]

Human Rights

Principle 1: Businesses should support and respect the protection of internationally proclaimed human rights; and

Principle 2: make sure that they are not complicit in human rights abuses.

Labour Standards

Principle 3: Businesses should uphold the freedom of association and the effective recognition of the right to collective bargaining;

Principle 4: the elimination of all forms of forced and compulsory labour;

Principle 5: the effective abolition of child labour; and

Principle 6: the elimination of discrimination in respect of employment and occupation.

(Continued)

EXHIBIT 15.3 (*Continued*)

Environment

Principle 7: Businesses should support a precautionary approach to environmental challenges;

Principle 8: undertake initiatives to promote greater environmental responsibility; and

Principle 9: encourage the development and diffusion of environmentally friendly technologies.

Anti-Corruption

Principle 10: Businesses should work against corruption in all its forms, including extortion and bribery.

[†] This adherence procedure involved: 1) a letter from the CEO, with board approval, to the UN General Secretary expressing support; 2) changes in business practices to incorporate the principles into the strategy, culture, and day-to-day operations of the company; 3) public advocacy of this process and its principles; 4) the production of an annual report on the company's progress in implementing them. If the company failed to produce the annual report and refused attempts by the UN Global Compact Office to discuss the reasons for this failure, its voluntary adherence could be annulled.

Source: http://www.unglobalcompact.org/AboutTheGC/TheTenPrinciples/index.html

---

On returning to their respective organizations, FitzGerald and Stocking sent follow-up requests to Cormack and Tickell. It would be their job to plan and then carry out the project as collaborators. On the one hand, Cormack and Tickell saw this as an opportunity to learn about each other and how their organizations operated, and for both organizations to fulfil their commitments to the UNGC and support the UN MDGs. On the other, both recognized the risks. From Cormack's point of view, in opening itself up Unilever might enable what many regarded as a highly adversarial NGO to turn round and attack her company, as some claimed had happened with GSK. Oxfam activists were equally worried; not only could this collaboration be misconstrued by the activist community, perhaps irrevocably damaging Oxfam's reputation, but it could be used by Unilever as a public relations tool. As they made an appointment to meet, Cormack and Tickell knew that they would have to negotiate carefully. If a project was initiated, they both knew it could become very costly in terms of the allocated resources.

Getting Started

In early 2003, with a mandate to investigate jointly the impact of Unilever's business operations on poverty, Cormack and Tickell agreed to meet for initial discussions. Their respective agendas appeared far apart.

First, whereas Oxfam sought an open-ended inquiry of Unilever's global supply chain, which Cormack felt could lead virtually anywhere, Unilever hoped to focus on the entire value chain of the company's activities in a chosen national economy. Second, Oxfam argued that contract workers should be included in the study, greatly expanding the scope of the research into areas over which the company lacked direct control, whereas Unilever preferred to focus on its own employees. Third, each proposed a different scope of work for the study, in particular what product line(s) the study should investigate and the geographical area to cover. Oxfam made the case that palm oil was a natural fit for the project, with the many issues surrounding it, including the destruction of rain forests and other environmentally sensitive areas to clear land for planting purposes. Unilever did not support this selection, because its palm oil operations were already engaged in dialogue with WWF and other environmental NGOs in the incipient Palm Oil Round Table. Fourth, there were also a number of semantic issues. Was the project a 'collaboration' (Oxfam) or a 'partnership' (Unilever)? Was the project an 'audit' by Oxfam, implying some kind of official approval or agenda for change? Or was it a 'joint study' for educational purposes? This was by no means an exhaustive list of the potential conflicts between the two parties' agendas.

The initial conversations were sketchy as each side sought to map out a brief that would be acceptable internally and to the other side. To facilitate relationship building, Cormack enlisted the support of her colleague Anne Weir, who had trained in managing cross-sector partnerships. Weir worked on sustainable development issues and had considerable experience, having managed Unilever's environmental stakeholder engagement. According to Weir, a large part of what she did was to get the participants to 'sit around the table and talk in the most open and transparent manner possible'. The goal, she explained, was to understand the other's perspective, acknowledge the legitimacy of that person's concerns and to treat each other equitably. Weir used ice-breaking techniques, such as asking each to 'introduce' the other, expressing what she believed the other was 'hoping to get out of the process'. According to Cormack, this exercise 'humanized the process right away and oriented our relations'.

Weir challenged both sides to question what they understood about the other. While Oxfam pushed to expand the scope of the research, Unilever resisted, insisting that the agenda would become unwieldy. In summer 2003, they finally agreed a Statement of Intent (SOI). The SOI performed a pivotal role (see Exhibit 15.4). As Cormack explained:

> Not only did it set the project in the context of the aims of the first MDG, it also provided a framework for the project that was active, that is to say, the research project was not a static, point-in-time critique of Unilever, but an attempt to answer the question: how do international companies interact with people living in poverty (for good or bad)? If we understand the impacts better, we know what international companies can do to play their part in poverty reduction strategies. Unilever can then tackle these tasks better and Oxfam can campaign more effectively to achieve the MDGs, in particular MDG 1 [to halve the number of people living in poverty by 2015]. This dynamic, results-oriented approach was very important and helped everyone to stop being precious when in close debate.

The outline of a Memorandum of Understanding (MOU) was also drafted, which would lay the ground rules for the process to follow. At this point, Weir left the negotiations to a facilitator, David Logan, CEO of the Corporate Citizenship Company (CCC), a consultancy retained by Unilever that specialized in the development of CSR policies. Logan, whose career had started in the trades union movement, had a deep understanding of the impact of MNCs and their role in international

EXHIBIT 15.4   STATEMENT OF INTENT

Statement of Intent

Unilever: Oxfam GB

The Challenges of Pro-Poor Investment in the Developing World

The Millennium and Johannesburg Declarations (2000, 2002) place poverty eradication at the centre of global strategies for sustainable development. Wealth creation, through the provision of goods and services, is vital for poverty reduction and business has a key role to play. But wealth creation alone is insufficient as a prerequisite for poverty reduction. It needs to be accompanied by public policies and incentives that enable poor people to participate successfully in markets.

Unilever, through its worldwide operations meeting everyday consumer needs for nutrition, personal and home hygiene, has extensive experience of working in developing economies with low-income consumers. This brings understanding and insight into the opportunities and barriers for business to extend the wealth creation benefits it offers to the poor.

Oxfam's work in more than 70 developing countries brings day-to-day contact with some of the poorest people in the world and a deep knowledge of the challenges they face. Through its support to local communities, advocacy and policy work, Oxfam is highly influential in shaping national and international poverty reduction strategies.

Unilever and Oxfam GB believe that the combination of their insight and expertise in business, participatory development and public policy can make a valuable contribution to addressing the challenge of sustainable poverty reduction.

Unilever and Oxfam GB intend to undertake, in partnership, an applied research project to explore the links between wealth creation and poverty reduction. The project will look at this through the experience of the local operations of a multinational company in a specific location. The findings and recommendations from this research will be published and shared with all stakeholder communities.

Unilever   Oxfam GB

August 2003

development, having worked for many years with Levi Strauss and the International Finance Corporation, as well as a number of other companies and institutions.

There was also a change of personnel representing Oxfam: Tickell left to work at the UK Social Investment Forum, and to found the Pharma Futures investor-led dialogue, aiming to achieve a better balance between shareholder and societal needs. Her colleague Heather Grady continued as Oxfam's project manager on the Unilever project, supported by Becky Buell, a long-standing Oxfam employee. Buell had joined Oxfam in Central America in 1992 and had previously worked at aid agencies specializing in economic development, including the Peace Corps.

The Scope of Work

During the autumn of 2003, Oxfam and Unilever arrived at agreement on a number of provisions. First, Oxfam agreed to limit the scope of the study to one country and to select for in-depth study one product line in the fast-moving consumer goods market with a clear agricultural supply chain that was typical of Unilever products. Unilever had argued that without this focus the project might expand indefinitely, which Buell acknowledged was a valid concern. This was a major compromise for Oxfam, and Unilever conceded that the study should include contract workers. Second, in assessing the company's positive or negative impacts on poverty, they agreed to four areas of research:

- the macroeconomic level, including employment generation, public-sector investment, productivity improvements and macro-level stability;
- the impact on employment in terms of worker treatment and poverty reduction, including not only direct employees, but also contractors hired by Unilever but not formally part of its workforce;
- the entire value chain, from supply (including small-scale producers) to manufacturing, distribution and retailing (including street vendors) and through to final consumers;
- the impact on low-income consumers in the marketplace, including an inquiry into Unilever's marketing and advertising practices.

Third, the project was designed as a 'learning' opportunity – to share best practices – rather than an 'audit' of Unilever by Oxfam, which might also be misconstrued as a search for endorsement or as a form of pressure to change Unilever's business practices. As Buell put it, 'There was no advocacy agenda, which was a first for us.' Both organizations hoped that it would lead to improvements that could benefit poor people, but knew they had to enter the project with an honest desire to learn on both sides. Finally, although Vietnam had been discussed as the subject country, both parties agreed that Indonesia offered better information resources as well as a longer history of Unilever involvement: the company had been operating in Indonesia since 1933.

UNILEVER INDONESIA

Indonesia was one of the countries hardest hit by the Asian currency crisis of 1997–8. As GDP shrunk below pre-boom levels and unemployment more than doubled to nearly 10 million, violence spread against foreigners and the local Chinese population, and civil strife threatened to turn into civil war. Half the population lived in either extreme or moderate poverty. It was in the midst of this crisis, in November 1998, that Nihal Kaviratne took over as CEO of Unilever Indonesia (UI), which then had approximately 2100 employees. Rather than cut back production in the face of falling sales and margins, Kaviratne decided to purchase, or invest in, struggling local companies, reasoning that once the crisis had passed, UI would be ready to cater to the pent-up demand of local consumers – UI mostly served the Indonesian market.

Kaviratne also changed the packaging and pricing policies of UI, introducing small sachets of many basic hygiene products (e.g., shampoo) to make them available to less affluent consumers. As

Indonesia's economic growth revived (going from −13.3% in 1998 and +0.79% in 1999 to +4.5% in 2003), UI's sales increased from a low of US$534 million in 1999 to US$948 million in 2003, and pre-tax profits doubled from US$100 million to US$212 million. Home and personal care items (soap powder, household cleaning products, hand soap and shampoos) made up 84% of sales, with food (tea, margarine and ice cream) comprising the balance. UI was ranked as the 13th largest company by sales in Indonesia and the fourth largest in the FMCG sector. According to Kaviratne, some UI brands, such as Pepsodent toothpaste and Blue Band margarine, enjoyed 70% market share in Indonesia, and Unilever products were found in 95% of Indonesian homes. Ninety per cent of poor people bought UI products in the course of a year. As well as global brands such as Sunsilk shampoo, Huggies nappies, Lux soap, Lipton tea and Wall's ice cream, UI marketed local brands such as Taro snack foods and Kecap Bango soy sauce. In 2003, UI had 5000 employees, 40% of whom were contract workers. Contract employees provided increased labour force flexibility to meet project objectives and generally received lower pay and fewer benefits than direct employees (see Exhibit 15.5 and Figure 15.2).

EXHIBIT 15.5 UNILEVER INDONESIA PURPOSE AND PRINCIPLES

Our corporate purpose states that to succeed requires 'the highest standards of corporate behaviour towards everyone we work with, the communities we touch, and the environment on which we have an impact'.

Always Working with Integrity

Conducting our operations with integrity and with respect for the many people, organizations and environments our business touches has always been at the heart of our corporate responsibility.

Positive Impact

We aim to make a positive impact in many ways: through our brands, our commercial operations and relationships, through voluntary contributions, and through the various other ways in which we engage with society.

Continuous Commitment

We're also committed to continuously improving the way we manage our environmental impacts and are working towards our longer-term goal of developing a sustainable business.

Setting out Our Aspirations

Our corporate purpose sets out our aspirations in running our business. It's underpinned by our Code of Business Principles, which describes the operational standards that everyone at Unilever follows, wherever they are in the world. The code also supports our approach to governance and corporate responsibility.

Working with Others

We want to work with suppliers who have values similar to our own and work to the same standards we do. Our Business Partner Code, aligned to our own Code of Business Principles, comprises ten principles covering business integrity and responsibilities relating to employees, consumers and the environment.

Environment and Society

We aim to manage our social and environmental impacts and play our part in sustainable development.

Science and Technology

Innovation enables us to meet people's needs and aspirations in ways that engage and appeal.

Nutrition, Hygiene and Personal Care

We're constantly striving to create more foods that make a positive contribution to health.

Our People

The Unilever community is shaped and led by its people, who operate creatively within a framework of shared values and business goals.

Source: http://www.unilever.co.id/ourvalues/

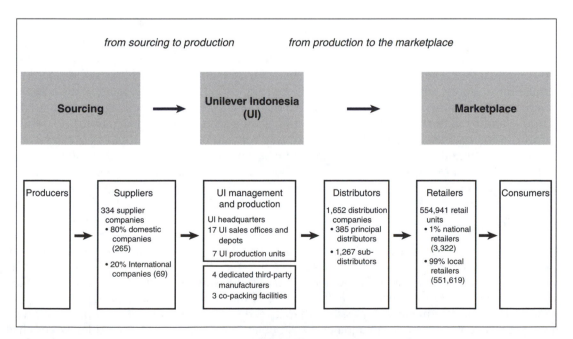

Figure 15.2 Unilever Indonesia structure of operations from sourcing to marketplace

Indonesia remained a poor country despite the economic recovery and abundant human and natural resources. Half the population of 213 million still lived on less than US$2 per day, with 7.4% on less than US$1 per day (2002); more than a quarter of children under five were moderately or severely underweight, with 8.6% severely underweight (2003); 21 million or 23% of the urban population lived in urban slums (2001).[14] Unemployment was 9.7% (2004) nearly double the pre-crisis rate of 4.9% (1996). Poor Indonesians faced insecure livelihoods, lack of access to basic services, limited opportunities for economic advancement and had little scope to change their situation.

In summer 2003, Kaviratne expressed misgivings about the risks he faced through involvement in the learning project. First, he was concerned that the participants would become mired in disagreements about definitions, particularly in view of the different rhetorical styles of Unilever and Oxfam. This threatened, he said, to 'signal an end to similar projects' that UI had undertaken. Second, he worried that UI had spent 70 years building its *bona fides* with Indonesians, through the usefulness of its products, as well as its CSR performance and its community programmes. For example, UI had developed its Supplier Quality Management Programme, which promoted sustainable manufacturing and other practices (UI certified contractors that did so successfully) and spent US$1 million on community activities in 2003. 'We have a very good reputation there with the press, consumers and politicians,' observed Kaviratne. 'So the report could damage us, particularly if it was full of anti-globalization talk. We didn't need that.' In particular, he knew his single-use packaging strategy already had come under criticism as 'exploitative' and 'frivolous'. Third, he argued, there were internal issues to UI. 'There was the winning spirit of the employees,' he explained, 'which the report might disrupt with doubts. It could shake our faith.' After the Asian financial crisis of the late 1990s, he said, UI 'had achieved a good recovery. Morale was high.'

Cormack telephoned Kaviratne to discuss his concerns. They knew and respected each other from previous work on CSR issues in Indonesia as well as the development of a self-assessment tool based on TQM (Total Quality Management) techniques and the CSR reporting work they had done together. Their shared experience helped to convince Kaviratne to ask his board for permission to do the report. 'I felt confident,' he said, 'that UI practices could withstand sustained outside scrutiny . . . I genuinely believed that we had a robust case that would stand the sharpest, and even the most prejudiced, scrutiny.' Indeed, he believed not only that UI would learn from the exercise, but also that the company's image and brand would be enhanced in the long run. Nonetheless, the project was the first time that UI – and indeed Unilever – had invited an NGO into the company to review documents and interview employees in such a sustained manner.

Rules of Engagement

As the dialogue progressed during the autumn of 2003, Unilever and Oxfam worked to establish a kind of safety net for themselves in the form of the rules they would follow to carry out the investigation, to be formalized in a Memorandum of Understanding (MOU) and Confidentiality Agreement. The MOU was signed early in 2004 (see Exhibit 15.6). To enable the parties to operate in as transparent a manner as possible, they agreed to keep the contents and results of their investigations confidential prior to a joint official publication. Furthermore, both sides agreed that as far as possible public documents (corporate as well as those from outside sources) would serve as the baseline for the research, to be supplemented by internal documents as required (internal assessments, memos and e-mail messages), interviews in Indonesia with local workers and managers, and survey work by local researchers, who would write background reports. That way, Cormack explained, they would 'have as consistent a database as possible, a basis from which to work back'.

EXHIBIT 15.6 MEMORANDUM OF UNDERSTANDING (KEY EXTRACTS)

17 January 2004

**Memorandum of Understanding
Oxfam and Unilever**

**The Challenges of Pro-Poor Investment
in the Developing World: an Applied Research Proposal**

1. **Statement of Intent**

   The Millennium and Johannesburg Declarations (2000, 2002) place poverty eradication at the centre of global strategies for sustainable development . . .

2. **Objectives of the Partnership**

   Unilever and Oxfam GB intend to undertake an Applied Research Project (the 'Project'). The research will seek to explore the links between wealth creation and poverty reduction through the experience of the local operations of Unilever Indonesia. The findings and recommendations from this research will be published in a report, and shared with all members of the Stakeholder Reference Group.

   The research will incorporate the following areas of investigation:

   - Value Chain Analysis;
   - Exploration of Unilever Indonesia's Policies and Practices (including commitment to labour standards);
   - Mapping macro-economic indicators of Unilever Indonesia; and
   - The Poor and the Marketplace.

3. **Composition of the Project Team and the Project Board . . .**

4. **Decision-Making Principles**

   1. The Project Board will manage the Project.
   2. The Project Leaders in Unilever and Oxfam, respectively, will be responsible for informing and managing the members of the Project Team.
   3. The Project Board will attempt to meet on a quarterly basis during the Project to make decisions about the aims, objectives, timeline, implementation of the Project and the Report and dissemination.

   (Continued)

EXHIBIT 15.6 (*Continued*)

4. The Project Board meetings will take place in Jakarta and London and consideration will be given to the possibility of undertaking meetings on conference call.

5. Notes of the meetings will be taken by the Research Coordinator, and circulated to the Project Board for agreement within two working days. The final version will be circulated to the extended Project Team.

6. Each Project Team member will work to agreed objectives and clear reporting requirements.

7. The Project Board will have joint editorial control over the Report.

8. The Project Board will be responsible for a joint strategy for the dissemination of (i) pre-report publication findings (ii) the final Report, including media coverage and external representation of its findings by the partner organizations.

9. In the event of a strong difference of opinion concerning the conclusions of the research, both parties will have recourse to the Grievance Mechanism (as per Section 9).

5. **Confidential Information**
The Partners recognise that some information concerning Unilever's business is by its nature confidential, and have executed the Confidentiality Agreement in Schedule 3. Unilever Project Leaders shall have the opportunity to review the final Report for such information, and request the removal of the information, if felt appropriate, in accordance with Section 9. As the Project is intended to be transparent, the parties shall endeavour to be as open as this Section and Section 9 permit.

6. **Timetable . . .**

7. **Joint Work plan . . .**

8. **Funding Arrangements . . .**

9. **Grievance Mechanism**

1. The Project Board shall endeavour to resolve any differences between Unilever and Oxfam.

2. In the case of a difference of opinion between Oxfam GB and Unilever, the issues shall be escalated to the Unilever Advisory Director, who chairs the External Affairs and Corporate Relations Committee, Baroness Chalker of Wallasey, and Norman Sanson, who is a Trustee of Oxfam GB, or failing him another Oxfam GB Trustee nominated by the Chair of Oxfam GB, who shall, as soon as reasonably practicable after a written request from either party to the other, meet in good faith to resolve such dispute or difference without recourse to legal proceedings.

3. Any subsequent dispute will be subject to English law and the exclusive jurisdiction of the English courts.

10. Procedures for Transparency and On-Going Communications Between Partners

1. The Project Board will agree written plans and notes from each meeting that will be shared with all members of the Project Team. These plans will form the basis of the research activities and can be shared with the Stakeholder Reference Group.

2. The Project Board will be responsible for interim communications concerning progress review and adjustments throughout the Project's life.

3. The first draft of the Report will be made available to the Project Board and, with the Project Board's agreement, will be circulated to all members of the Project Team. The draft Report will then be submitted to a review and a revised version will be sent to the Stakeholder Reference Group for comment. A final draft of the Report will be sent to the Project Leaders for sign-off. Timings on the above activities will be defined in the Project Brief.

4. The Project Board will be responsible for interim communications concerning progress review and adjustments throughout the Project's life, with each other and with others within the respective organizations.

11. Measures to Mitigate External Risks and Threats to the Partnership

1. The Memorandum Of Understanding will be available to the public (and announced publicly if deemed to be appropriate by both parties).

2. A reactive media line should be identified and agreed. It should be transparent and available for use by the Project Team.

3. The parties have executed the confidentiality agreement in Schedule 3 concerning rights of disclosure and dissemination.

4. The parties should endeavour to ensure the expectations of the members of the Stakeholder Reference Group are realistic, clear at the outset, and the Project should be managed to ensure that these expectations are met.

12. The Stakeholder Reference Group

1. Agreement of the Members of the Stakeholder Reference Group:

   The Project Board will agree a list of people, selected from the following groups, to be invited to participate as a member of the Stakeholder Reference Group:

   a. employees of Unilever and Oxfam and their representative organizations;

   b. suppliers of goods and services to Unilever;

   c. representatives of Indonesian civil society organizations with expertise in participatory development; and

   d. relevant academics and/or researchers involved in this research Project.

   Should it be deemed desirable to include additional members in the Stakeholder Reference Group at a later stage, then the Project Board will agree in writing who should receive an invitation to join prior to their being contacted.

(Continued)

EXHIBIT 15.6 (*Continued*)

    2. Functions of the Stakeholder Reference Group

        a. The Research Brief will be shared with the Stakeholder Reference Group, and their input will be invited at relevant stages of the Project's Implementation.

        b. The Stakeholder Reference Group will be invited to participate in discussions, where felt to be appropriate by the Project Board.

        c. The draft Report will be sent to the Stakeholder Reference Group for comment. Unilever shall review the draft in accordance with section 5 of this agreement with respect to confidential information before it is sent to the Stakeholder Reference Group.

13. End-of-Project Evaluation and Application of the Research Findings

    1. Unilever or Oxfam may use learnings from this Project for educational purposes, with the consent of the Project Board.

    2. The Project shall end on the date indicated in the Project Brief. Thereafter, Oxfam and Unilever may decide to host a concluding workshop to evaluate how the findings could be progressed (based on the agreement of both parties at that time).

14. Miscellaneous . . .

The parties also agreed to retain an independent report writer to write up the outcome of the research and their dialogue around the results. The report writer would be briefed to set out clearly where the two organizations agreed and disagreed, and what they learned about each other, and then, if necessary, they would draw their own lessons in separate sections.

Outside parties were also to participate. In the case of a serious disagreement, Unilever and Oxfam created a dispute-resolution mechanism: if Oxfam find something that Unilever refused to make public, two designated individuals were empowered to arbitrate the matter, one a Unilever Advisory Director and the other an Oxfam GB Trustee. For expertise and review, there would also be a reference group of independent advisors from Europe and Indonesia, drawn from business, academia and NGOs. Finally, Oxfam insisted that it should be able to hire local researchers who knew the Indonesian economy and society and who could function independently of UI. In the end, both sides felt, after each had made significant concessions to the other, that the safeguards would create an acceptable level of security for both organizations.

GETTING IT DONE

The participants believed the project would take about a year to complete, perhaps concluding with a public conference in late 2004 to discuss the report. Together, Oxfam and Unilever selected the members of four teams in Indonesia, one for each subject area (the participants split the costs of the research teams and the independent report writer). The external reference group was also assembled. In the meantime, UI aligned its internal resources to supply information as requested. In order to develop a detailed case study of an agricultural supply chain, the participants agreed to examine in depth a sweet soy sauce, Kecap Bango, important because of its two key ingredients, sugar cane and black soya bean. Other Unilever products of interest to Oxfam, such as tea and palm oil, were not included as they were already the subject of separate stakeholder dialogues through the Palm Oil Round Table and Tea Sourcing Partnership; further study was deemed potentially disruptive of these existing efforts. The researchers began to interview employees, contractors and suppliers.

The Research

To kick off the research portion of the project, UI invited participants from both Oxfam and Unilever headquarters to UI headquarters in Jakarta, 27–30 January 2004. The team met a number of UI managers and employees, who made themselves available for the project in a frank and open-ended way that surprised the Oxfam team. According to Cormack, 'the Oxfam team was allowed to approach whomever its members wanted. Kaviratne and his deputy chairman, Maurits Lalisang, gave them a great degree of freedom.' They also toured UI manufacturing sites as well as those of UI contractors, including soya bean farmers. At a detergent factory, Unilever employees introduced the Oxfam team to the TQM techniques that the company had developed. These had been used as the basis for a CSR review in which managers assessed their own performance in a number of areas, gradually involving their employees and then outside observers and critics. This project, Unilever managers stressed, was part of UI's efforts to expand their TQM criteria to assess the social impact of company practices. Although Oxfam remained suspicious of the ability of MNCs to evaluate their own performance on CSR issues, its team agreed that these data could be included in the project. Finally, the Oxfam team also visited a number of UI projects related to CSR, including the development of black soya seeds at the University of Yogyakarta.

From February to June 2004, the researchers conducted interviews and led surveys, while Oxfam employees concentrated on UI's internal documents. The research teams, taken from local universities and NGOs, prepared background papers on the four research areas, although it became apparent to the Unilever and Oxfam teams that the agenda was too open-ended to cover all the areas they had intended to include. The teams interviewed a total of over 400 individuals, including UI managers, UI joint venture partners, contractors, raw material providers, and distributors and retailers of Unilever products. They also reviewed dozens of internal documents, including CSR self-assessment documents, as well as secondary sources. The Corporate Citizenship Company supported the interpretation, analysis and evaluation of all the information gathered. It was an exhaustive process in which the Indonesian managers and employees researched and answered many questions and requests for data.

During this process, the original independent writer announced his resignation in order to pursue other career opportunities. Because of his intimate familiarity with the issues from the project's inception, his departure was deeply regretted. His replacement, Jason Clay, who worked for WWF, was hired as a freelance writer (outside his duties at the WWF). Clay was enthusiastic and supportive of the project, but it proved extremely difficult for him to reconcile some of the teams' positions and conflicting interpretations of the data, a responsibility that was inevitably relegated to the principals, Cormack and Buell.

Interpretations and Contention

In July 2004, Cormack and Buell held a workshop to interpret the research data that had been collected. There were many areas of agreement, such as the stabilizing impact that UI had had during the turbulent period that followed the financial crisis in the late 1990s, and the need to pay more attention to workers at the farther-removed ends of the value chain. Although they agreed that the data were not sufficient to provide a comprehensive picture of the overall economic impact of UI, they felt that the report would offer many valuable perspectives.

However, several areas of basic contention emerged. First, calculating figures to approximate the total employment generated, in particular downstream in the distribution and retail sectors, proved difficult. Much of this hinged on definitions; for example, a *contractor* ranged from companies in direct contract with Unilever, to subcontractors, to organizations or individuals who in some way added value in the provision of related services, such as retailing. The participants were aware that the solution they settled upon – full-time equivalents – was a flawed, if useful, aggregate. 'We realized,' Buell said, 'that it would have been better to do more survey work earlier on. We all knew that this just scratched the surface, but we felt in the end that it gave an indicative picture of Unilever's reach that could serve for exploring a range of poverty issues.'

Second, there were strong disagreements as to what 'fair prices' should be, especially for low-income consumers. This disagreement extended to such practices as the sale of micro-packets of staple goods, such as sachets of shampoo or clothing detergent. Unilever argued that these allowed Indonesians to purchase high-quality staple items for basic hygiene, whereas some in Oxfam believed that their higher unit cost and higher retail price by volume gouged poor consumers, *lowering* their standard of living as well as polluting the environment by increasing packaging. Kaviratne disagreed with this, arguing that poor consumers 'were very discerning and went for higher quality', which the smaller sachets enabled them to purchase, albeit less frequently than lower-quality, cheaper alternatives. In the end, he said, '95% of our washing powder was sold in small sachets and 90% of our shampoo in PET biodegradable packets. It sold like that because the brand is better.'

Finally, and perhaps most difficult, Oxfam disputed the utility of Unilever's marketing and advertising strategies, which the former regarded as wasteful and perhaps even misleading, whereas the latter argued that they provided useful information about product quality, personal hygiene and health. According to Buell, 'We at Oxfam reaffirmed our sense that the poor consumer is powerless in the face of advertising. In many cases, we didn't see much of a free-market choice or [we saw] even products of limited utility, such as skin-lightening cream', which was marketed to Indonesian women who wished to appear more like Europeans. 'It was hard to draw the line between where UI was meeting needs or creating them,' she concluded.

How would they resolve these differences? In Cormack's view, the research had 'forced both Oxfam and Unilever to look at issues and assumptions we hadn't wanted to talk about, like the contention that "advertising is bad". The discussions got the issue on the table. We expressed our view that [advertising] is part of the spectrum of communication, so the question became "how can you make it positive?".'

Doing his best to reconcile Oxfam and Unilever interpretations, Clay produced a draft report in September 2004. Cormack and Buell immediately realized that his draft would be unacceptable to both their organizations. 'It was an impossible task for Jason,' Buell said, 'patching together a text when there were so many institutional sensitivities on both sides.' According to Cormack, 'A lot of the discussion revolved around drop-dead phraseology and negotiating what we could both endorse and what would have to be put in separate sections.' Oxfam remained concerned that it would be viewed as an exercise in corporate public relations. 'Throughout the entire process,' Buell said – speaking for Cormack's team as well as her own – 'our harshest critics were internal.' Logan and Grady set to and line-by-line worked through the text, resolving questions where they could, deferring to others for broader discussion or reference to Buell and Cormack. It was a long slog.

At the beginning of 2005, Cormack and Buell consulted the reference group, circulating a provisional draft report to members. The pressure to finish the report curtailed the period available for review and dialogue with the group, but members returned a range of helpful comments and suggestions. Meanwhile, major changes at Unilever, including the appointment of a new CEO, meant that pressures on Cormack were mounting. Not only did she have 30 employees to manage, but also she was supposed to be focused on rolling out CSR as a major plank of corporate strategy for the next year and through to 2010. Buell also had other commitments to address. Both Cormack and Buell wondered if, for all their work and the vital importance of the poverty issue, a project report would ever see the light of day.

ACKNOWLEDGEMENTS

The development of this case and the overall project has been made possible due to the generous financial support of EABIS' founding corporate partners: IBM, Johnson & Johnson, Microsoft, Shell and Unilever. The involvement in the development of this case study of Mandy Cormack, formerly of Unilever and now an independent CSR Advisor, and Becky Buell of Oxfam, is also gratefully acknowledged.

NOTES

1. This case was written by Robert J. Crawford under the supervision of Professor N. Craig Smith. It is intended to be used as a basis for class discussion rather than to illustrate either effective or ineffective handling of an administrative situation.
2. See the Unilever website, www.unilever.com.
3. Unilever Annual Report, 2005.
4. Unilever, Environmental and Social Report 2005, p. 16.
5. Unilever, Environmental and Social Report 2005, pp. 17–18.
6. *Source:* Oxfam Council of Trustees – 'Oxfam GB's Private Sector Strategy: Update', 16 October 2000.
7. *Source:* http://www.oxfam.org.uk/what_we_do/issues/private_sector/introduction.htm.
8. Defined as groups that mobilized resources, provided information, and advocated for change. See Debra L. Spar and Lane T. LaMare, 'The Power of Activism: Assessing the Impact of NGOs on Global Business,' *California Management Review*, Spring 2003, p. 79.
9. http://www.oxfam.org.uk/about_us/mission.htm and http://www.oxfam.org/en/about/who/.
10. http://www.maketradefair.com/assets/english/CoffeeSummary.pdf.
11. Certified Fairtrade coffee sales in the UK doubled between 2002 and 2004 to £49 million. See: http://www.fairtrade.org.uk/about_sales.htm.

12. This debate over the merits of conflict versus collaboration with corporations was also taking place in other NGOs. See Halina Ward and N. Craig Smith, *Corporate Social Responsibility at a Crossroads: Futures for CSR in the UK to 2015*, London: International Institute for the Environment and Development, 2006.

13. http://www.unilever.com/Images/2000SocialReview1999Data_tcm181-5331.pdf

14. http://mdgs.un.org/unsd/mdg/Data.aspx?cr=360.

REFERENCES

Burns, J. (2005) Oxfam's deal with Starbucks comes to an end, *Financial Times*, 4 March.

Croft, K. (1999) *Citizen Nader*, Salon, Great Careers #11.

Klein, J., Kapstein, E. and Crawford, R.J. (2003) Oxfam and the campaign to bring affordable HIV treatment to South Africa, INSEAD Case Study, ECCH No. 703-018-1.

Sachs, J.D. (2005) *The End of Poverty: Economic Possibilities for Our Time*, Penguin, New York.

Smith, N.C. and Duncan, A. (2005) GlaxoSmithKline and developing country access to essential medicines (B), *Journal of Business Ethics Education*, **2** (1), 123–132.

Spar, D. (1998) The spotlight and the bottom line, *Foreign Affairs*, March/April, 7–12.

The Economist, 'Oxfam versus Starbucks', 7 November, 2006, 1.

Yaziji, M. (2004) Turning gadflies into allies, *Harvard Business Review*, February, 110–115.

CHAPTER SIXTEEN

Revenue Flow and Human Rights: A Paradox for Shell Nigeria[1]

Ulrich Steger and Aileen Ionescu-Somers, IMD

INTRODUCTION

September 2006: Alan Detheridge, British vice president of Shell's External Affairs, and Joshua Udofia, his senior Nigerian corporate advisor, had managed issues in the Niger Delta during some of Shell's most challenging years. Their careers with Shell had both been long: 29 and 35 years respectively. They had seen it all, from NGOs pointing the finger at the environmental and social impacts of oil spills and gas flaring, to extensive media coverage of human rights issues that had occurred after the much-publicized Ken Saro-Wiwa execution in 1995. But by the end of 2006, both men would be retiring. In the run-up to retirement, they often found themselves discussing what the future would hold for their successors, and whether Shell's current strategies were likely to lead to successful outcomes.

Both men agreed that poverty was at the root of the problems of both Nigeria and the oil-bearing Niger Delta region. Shell had made significant changes in its approach to its community development programme, including partnering with NGOs and development agencies. But NGOs remained generally unimpressed. Even if the programme delivered to its full potential, they knew that it alone could not improve the quality of life for most of the Niger Delta's 27 million inhabitants.

A fundamental problem was related to oil revenue flow. The corruption that was endemic to Nigeria was a serious impediment to desperately needed development. In addition, state politicians were enmeshed with war lords for the sake of political and personal gain and a new generation of more unpredictable militias had intensified hostage-taking involving oil company staff. The Nigerian president's anti-corruption support was encouraging but elections in 2007 might mean that efforts so far would be jeopardized. The paradox was that no matter what Shell did, no matter how much money it ploughed into community development and programmes, if revenue transparency was not sorted out, could attitudes change and life be improved for people in the Delta? Had Shell gone as far as it could in the last 10 years to alleviate the human rights crisis in the Delta? Many of the international NGOs did not think so.

SHELL

Royal Dutch was founded in 1890 in the Netherlands by Aeilko Jans Zijlker, who first discovered oil in the Dutch East Indies. The Shell Transport and Trading Company was a British company founded in 1897 by the Samuel brothers. In 1907 the two companies merged and it was agreed that Royal

Dutch would handle oil refining and production operations and Shell would deal with the transport, storage and marketing of the oil products. The two companies were separately traded holding companies owning 60% and 40% respectively of Royal Dutch/Shell Group's operating subsidiaries. In November 2004, the Shell Group moved to a single parent company, Royal Dutch Shell plc (Shell), with headquarters in the Netherlands. Unification was completed on 20 July 2005. Shell was an impressive success story. By 2005, its revenues reached US$306 billion with profits of US$25 billion, maintaining its position as one of the world's top three private oil companies. Shell was a veritable 'super major' with 112 000 employees operating in over 140 companies worldwide.

Shell and Nigeria

In 1937, Shell was authorized to prospect for oil in Nigeria during British colonial rule in equal partnership with British Petroleum (BP). Oil was discovered in the Niger Delta in 1958. On 1 October, 1960, Nigeria gained independence. Its leaders faced the daunting task of holding 250 ethnic groups together as a nation. They organized a loose federation of self-governing states, each one with a large degree of constitutional autonomy. In 1973, following a period of civil war, military coups and turbulence, the two-way partnership with Shell and BP gave way to a joint venture with the Nigerian government. The Shell Petroleum Development Company of Nigeria Limited (SPDC) held Shell's share. By 2006, SPDC was the principle operator of Nigeria's largest oil and gas joint venture (Nigerian National Petroleum Company 55%, SPDC 30%, Total 10% and Agip 5%), producing approximately 40% of Nigeria's oil from over 1000 wells in the Delta.

By the 1980s, Nigeria had become an African success story, with the 33rd highest per capita income in the world. However, subsequent undemocratic military regimes, corruption and governmental inefficiency took their toll, together with a 3% per annum population growth. By 1997, the country was ranked the world's 13th poorest country. With the dawn of the new millennium, despite being the world's sixth largest exporter of petroleum, 66% of its 131 million people lived on less than US$1 per day. In 2005, the NGO Transparency International classed Nigeria as the sixth most corrupt country in the world (Shell had more trouble with corrupt employees than in any other country, sacking several staff and delisting a certain number of contractors every year in line with its business principles). The UN ranked Nigeria among the world's top 20 'most unlivable countries', and per capita Gross National Income (GNI) was still only at a level of US$400.

In 1999, General Olusegun Obasanjo, a former military ruler of Nigeria, was democratically elected. Initially, Obasanjo was revered for his commitment to democracy and fighting corruption (before becoming president, he was the Chairman of Transparency International's International Advisory Group). The first legislation Obasanjo put forward as elected president was a corrupt practices bill. He led a drive to recuperate billions stolen during a previous military regime. In spite of these efforts, anti-corruption officials estimated in 2005 that 45% of Nigeria's oil revenues were being siphoned away each year.

In 2000, a Memorandum of Understanding (MOU) to stipulate a method for the sharing of oil revenues was signed between the government and the major oil companies working in the Delta. The MOU hedged the multinationals for risk when oil prices were low rather than enabling them to benefit when prices were high. Joint venture partners including SPDC would receive a fixed margin as long as the oil price ranged from US$15 to US$19 a barrel. At higher oil prices, the Government share of the profit would gradually increase to 95% (see Figure 16.1 for the split of the barrel between partners and government within a range of oil prices).

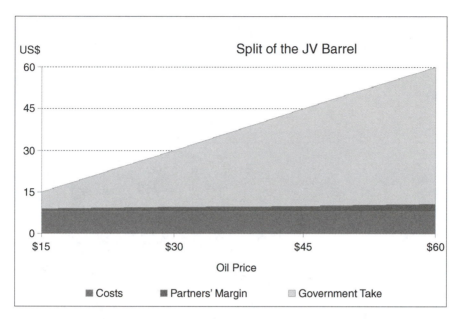

Figure 16.1 Split of the barrel between the Government and Joint Venture Partners

Source: Company information

By 2006, some 2.5 million barrels of Nigerian oil per day were being pumped, including on-shore and offshore operations (3% of global oil production). Crude oil prices on the world market reached an all-time high of US$72.35 a barrel in April 2006, giving the Nigerian government record revenues. SPDC paid US$4.3 billion in petroleum profit taxes and royalties to the federal government in 2005, representing a considerable increase on the US$2.2 billion paid in 2003. By 2006, petroleum accounted for more than 80% of government revenues, 90% of foreign exchange earnings, 95% of export receipts and 40% of gross domestic product.

HUMAN RIGHTS IN THE NIGER DELTA

Oil majors in Nigeria operated in an extremely difficult economic and political environment, both nationally and locally. Detheridge pointed to the complexity:

> The more I learn about Nigeria, the more I realize just how little I know. Some humility is not only sensible, but essential. As a Nigerian, my colleague Joshua Udofia knows more than we will ever know.

The Delta was a densely populated region that had been a major producer of palm oil in colonial times, ironically earning itself the name of 'oil rivers' because of this agricultural heritage. The area was an extensive network of swamps and creeks spread over some 70 000 kilometers (7.5% of Nigeria's total land mass). It included land from nine states (see Figure 16.2 for a map of the area), of which four – Akwa Ibom, Bayelsa, Delta and Rivers – were the major oil producers. Of the 131 million population of Nigeria, some 20 million people (from over 40 ethnic groups) lived in the Delta. The primary activities of local people were fishing and farming.

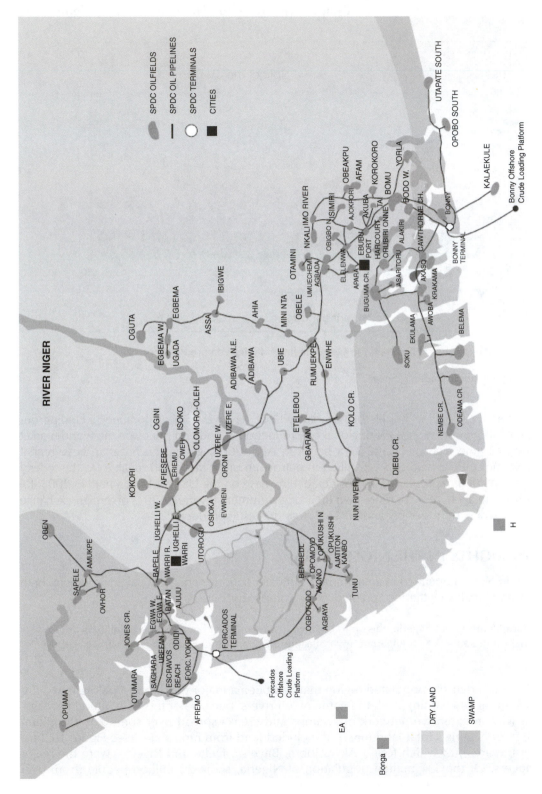

Figure 16.2 Map of the Shell facilities in the Niger Delta

Source: Company information

As required under the constitution, the Nigerian government returned a significant proportion of the federal revenues it received to state governments (31.1%) and local government areas (15.2%). In addition, 13% of its revenues from oil and gas was returned to the states where production took place. But over a prolonged period, human rights groups claimed that various governments had either misspent or siphoned off into foreign bank accounts the very funds that should have gone back to develop the communities of the oil producing areas.

> Politics has become an exercise in organized corruption . . . large commissions and percentage cuts of contracts have enabled individual soldiers and politicians to amass huge fortunes.
>
> Human Rights Watch, 1999

It was a constant battle for companies to get successive governments to fund their agreed contribution to the joint ventures. It was also self-evident that oil revenues received by the government were not reaching the people that needed them most:

> Though the government is a 55% to 60% shareholder in oil operations and earns billions in royalties each year, local infrastructure at the source of these billions is in shambles, food shortages abound, malnutrition is common among Niger Delta children, power blackouts regularly occur, and roads are usually in terrible condition.[2]

Rising community resentment at the lack of improvement to quality of life in spite of rich resources gradually gave way to active protests against oil company activities – since protests to government had proved unfruitful. Hostage-taking, closures of flow stations, intimidation of staff and even sabotage of oil installations became endemic in the Delta states as resentment increased.

During the 1990s, Shell came under immense pressure because of specific human rights issues. Confrontations between indigenous populations and Nigerian government security forces over human rights regularly occurred. In 1990, when an initially peaceful protest in Umuechem in Rivers State turned violent, Shell requested police protection. The police were attacked by the protestors, resulting in the death of a policeman, which in turn led to a large number of people being killed by the police and homes being destroyed. In 1994, the military sent security forces into Ogoniland in the southern part of the Delta where a movement for recognition of rights for the indigenous Ogoni people was growing. Ogoniland (with a population of 500 000) was home to the writer Ken Saro-Wiwa, a charismatic, outspoken human rights campaigner, who ultimately became leader of the Movement for the Survival of the Ogoni People (MOSOP).

In 1990, MOSOP issued a bill of rights that demanded political autonomy for the Ogoni people, a fair share of the proceeds of oil extraction and the right to protect the Ogoni environment and ecology from further degradation. Saro-Wiwa and eight other Ogonis were hanged in November 1995, accused of instigating riots leading to the killings of four Ogoni elders, former founders of MOSOP. NGOs perceived the prosecution as politically motivated and the trial as unfair, but the appeal that was lodged fell on deaf ears, to some extent because the group was being judged by a military tribunal. External calls for clemency from multiple heads of state, intergovernmental organizations and human rights groups worldwide were ignored, provoking widespread condemnation around the world and drawing international sanctions and suspension from the Commonwealth for Nigeria.

Human rights NGOs claimed that Shell, though not directly responsible, was heavily implicated by association with such incidents. Shell's business principles at the time of the Saro-Wiwa incident spelt out that Shell would abstain 'from participation in party politics and interference in political matters'. On advice from its lawyers, Shell limited its influence to pointing out to the government the negative implications of going ahead with the executions and petitioning for clemency. But this was to no avail. Mark Corner, deputy managing director of SPDC, said:

> It took us too long to recognize that our voice should be heard. We were engineers interested in clever engineering, more introverted and conservative than we should have been. We are clearer now and feel that it is legitimate to have a more assertive position on human rights.

NGOs continued to accuse Shell of not using a potentially powerful influence to bring about change in the Delta. A conflict expert group commissioned by Shell in 2004 produced a confidential report (later leaked to the press) that stated: 'If current conflict trends continue uninterrupted, it would be surprising if Shell could continue on-shore resource extraction in the Niger Delta whilst complying with Shell Business principles.' It also said that SPDC '. . . could not ignore Niger Delta conflicts or its role in exacerbating these.'

Because of Shell's close business relationship with the government, local communities perceived the company as working 'in cahoots' with the authorities. This perception was compounded by the fact that the government seconded the so-called 'supernumerary police' to Shell and other oil companies to protect staff and property. Like other oil companies, Shell was dependent on the Nigerian government for security arrangements that were critically important to protect their facilities.

Local communities in the Delta objected to the degradation of their environment resulting from oil spills, much of which, according to Shell, was due to sabotage. The company argued that such sabotage was usually motivated by the desire for economic gain on the part of some, but by no means all, individuals in its host communities. The prospect of compensation (if incidents could be disguised as the fault of the company), employment opportunities during the spill clean-up and the attempted charging of 'access fees' before staff and equipment were allowed on site, were all temptations for communities that felt cheated of the benefits of local oil production.

In 1999 and 2003, to compound problems, politicians financed local warlords to intimidate local people and help rig elections. Given his political stance on corruption, President Obasanjo and his state governors lost credibility. After the elections, some Delta state governors continued to engage warlords to deal with political rivals. The governors also turned a blind eye – and almost certainly profited from – warlords' involvement in the theft of crude oil from existing pipelines. At the peak of the crisis, some 10% of total annual production was stolen by ethnic militias in this way. The lucrative dividends from this rich booty led to inevitable rivalry between competing groups.

The proceeds from the stolen oil helped to build up the arsenals of local militias. Over time, arms entering the Delta paved the way for violent clashes between these groups and an increasing lack of security in the area. Militancy reached a new high, and even ordinary villagers tended to want to possess arms as a measure of self-defence. Levels of corruption deepened; in January 2005, two navy rear admirals were court-martialed and ousted, implicated in the disappearance of an impounded tanker carrying stolen crude oil. Lack of employment in the Delta facilitated the recruitment into militias of numerous disillusioned and bored young men only too willing to earn some money.

During 2005, some 50 Shell employees were kidnapped. Although hostage-taking of oil company staff had been commonplace since the early 1990s, the profile of these actions changed dramatically, with hostages being kept for two to three weeks rather than the same number of days, and increasingly difficult negotiations with kidnappers. In 2006, particularly violent militia group attacks in the Delta succeeded in cutting about 20% of Nigeria's 2.5 million barrels per day production. The main culprit was the Movement for the Emancipation of the Niger Delta (MEND), a loose coalition of guerrilla groups that were involved in crude oil theft and claimed to have local Ijaw support (the majority tribe in the Delta). MEND demanded the release of an imprisoned warlord and even a former state governor convicted for money laundering. Becoming more powerful in the Delta towards the end of 2005, MEND later demanded US$1.5 billion from Shell to compensate for environmental damage, and demanded increased access to oil revenues from the oil-producing states of Nigeria.

MEND transformed the security context of the Delta. It had well-armed units and trained supporters with the potential to destroy oil facilities more effectively than any group before them. Hostage-taking episodes were often followed by military attacks by the federal government on the guerrilla groups, who hid in villages in the area. Local resentment increased even further. It seemed that there would inevitably be more militancy, more unrest and more chaos in the run-up to new elections in 2007.

SUSTAINABILITY AND HUMAN RIGHTS AT SHELL

In 1996, after the Saro-Wiwa incident and also as a result of the Brent Spar debacle,[3] Shell had moved from a risk and reputation management focus to integrating sustainable development into its general business principles strategies and operations. It reviewed its community activities in Nigeria and made changes to its philanthropic Community Assistance Program, renaming it Community Development and placing more emphasis on capacity building and the empowerment of communities. It started to engage in more extensive stakeholder discussion. This was an eye-opener for the company, as Detheridge pointed out:

> We had discussions with international NGOs, Foundations and Government officials. Everyone, including Shell, sat in meetings pointing the finger elsewhere, effectively saying; 'If only you did what I am telling you to do, we wouldn't be in this situation.' Shell came at it from the angle of 'You just don't understand – get better informed.' Each party thought that others could solve the problem, not realizing that solutions were beyond the reach of a single actor. Not surprisingly, it took a while for these discussions to lead to anything positive happening on the ground in Nigeria.

Eventually, however, Shell began to set up partnership projects, first with local NGOs and later with international NGOs and development agencies such as UNDP and UNAIDS. Udofia commented:

> We moved from a stance of 'We want to do everything ourselves', which was impossible, to the idea that collaboration would be more effective.

In order to place more emphasis on transparency and social accountability, in 1996 the company started publishing an annual SPDC People and the Environment report and began a yearly stakeholder consultation workshop to review SPDC's environmental and community programmes.

Starting in 2001, the company asked a team of independent experts (from international NGOs, UN agencies and so on) to verify and grade the projects within its community development programme. The results of these reviews were published in the People and the Environment report, and in 2005 results indicated that 86% of the projects were functional and 64% were successful. Detheridge knew from discussions with developmental organizations (none of which published such figures openly) that this was a good track record, particularly in Nigeria. But there was considerable scope for improvement. Corner commented:

> In the past we tended to over promise and under deliver. The legacy of this approach is still around today – projects that we rushed into to get things done saying that we would worry about problems later. Also, the Niger Delta Development Commission, the body charged with doing development projects in the Delta is often under funded, increasing reliance on SPDC. This situation is gradually improving but slowly. We have now learned that you need to work with community leaders, prepare well and hand over efficiently. Regaining the confidence of the communities is important.

THE EXTRACTIVE INDUSTRIES TRANSPARENCY INITIATIVE (EITI)

The EITI was a voluntary partnership of companies, governments, investors and civil society organizations. It was launched by UK Prime Minister Tony Blair, at the World Summit for Sustainable Development in September 2002, to improve transparency and accountability related to the payments that oil, gas and mining companies (including those that were state-owned) made to governments and the revenues that governments received from these companies. Shell was an active participant in the EITI and one of its main instigators.

Detheridge and Udofia believed from the start that this was an important initiative, which was necessary though insufficient to improve the governance of oil revenue flows in Nigeria to ensure that they were put to good use. They realized that the US$30–40 million that Shell spent on community development could not, on its own, make a significant improvement to the lives of all the people in the Niger Delta, and that better use of the substantial funds available to the state and local governments was essential.

The two men worked on bringing EITI to the president's attention, and from 2002 onwards, Shell began to publish the revenues it paid to the Nigerian government, having first obtained the requisite authorization to do so from the government. Corner stated:

> In fact, there was nothing to stop Shell as an organization helping to make the case for transparent revenue flow. We should have started sooner, but we balked at appearing overly paternalistic. The question is, are we a foreign company in Nigeria or a Nigerian company in Nigeria? It is actually more helpful to think of ourselves as the latter.

The EITI worked toward improving transparency in government budget practices as well as empowering ordinary citizens to hold their governments to account for the use of the revenues (see Exhibit 16.1 for the EITI's principles and criteria). The main objective was to assure country ownership of the initiative. Given his political agenda of good governance and his keenness to secure relief for Nigeria's staggering US$30 billion external debt, President Obasanja was one of the first leaders to support the initiative. The Nigerians set up a country-specific, Nigerian Extractive Industries Transparency Initiative (NEITI) in February 2004.

EXHIBIT 16.1 THE EITI PRINCIPLES AND CRITERIA

The EITI Principles

1. We share a belief that the prudent use of natural resource wealth should be an important engine for sustainable economic growth that contributes to sustainable development and poverty reduction, but if not managed properly, can create negative economic and social impacts.

2. We affirm that management of natural resource wealth for the benefit of a country's citizens is in the domain of sovereign governments to be exercised in the interests of their national development.

3. We recognize that the benefits of resource extraction occur as revenue streams over many years and can be highly price dependent.

4. We recognize that a public understanding of government revenues and expenditure over time could help public debate and inform choice of appropriate and realistic options for sustainable development.

5. We underline the importance of transparency by governments and companies in the extractive industries and the need to enhance public financial management and accountability.

6. We recognize that achievement of greater transparency must be set in the context of respect for contracts and laws.

7. We recognize the enhanced environment for domestic and foreign direct investment that financial transparency may bring.

8. We believe in the principle and practice of accountability by government to all citizens for the stewardship of revenue streams and public expenditure.

9. We are committed to encouraging high standards of transparency and accountability in public life, government operations and in business.

10. We believe that a broadly consistent and workable approach to the disclosure of payments and revenues is required, which is simple to undertake and to use.

11. We believe that payments' disclosure in a given country should involve all extractive industry companies operating in that country.

12. In seeking solutions, we believe that all stakeholders have important and relevant contributions to make – including governments and their agencies, extractive industry companies, service companies, multilateral organizations, financial organizations, investors, and non-governmental organizations.

The EITI Criteria

1. Regular publication of all material oil, gas and mining payments by companies to governments ('payments') and all material revenues received by governments from oil, gas and mining companies ('revenues') to a wide audience in a publicly accessible, comprehensive and comprehensible manner.

(*Continued*)

> **EXHIBIT 16.1** (*Continued*)
>
> **2.** Where such audits do not already exist, payments and revenues are the subject of a credible, independent audit, applying international auditing standards.
>
> **3.** Payments and revenues are reconciled by a credible, independent administrator, applying international auditing standards and with publication of the administrator's opinion regarding that reconciliation including discrepancies, should any be identified.
>
> **4.** This approach is extended to all companies including state-owned enterprises.
>
> **5.** Civil society is actively engaged as a participant in the design, monitoring and evaluation of this process and contributes towards public debate.
>
> **6.** A public, financially sustainable work plan for all the above is developed by the host government, with assistance from the international financial institutions where required, including measurable targets, a timetable for implementation, and an assessment of potential capacity constraints.
>
> *Source:* http://eitransparency.myaiweb15.com/principlesandcriteria.htm

On 1 January, 2005, Basil Omiyl was the first Nigerian managing director appointed to SPDC. Up to then, the post had been filled by expatriate staff. Corner said:

> We gained a lot of credibility with this appointment amongst our senior stakeholders. Somehow a Nigerian managing director had more leeway to openly state that the federal and state government should be more accountable to communities.

Nigeria set up two statutory bodies with powers to investigate and prosecute corruption-related crimes. By 2006, the finance minister, Ngozi Okonjo-Iweala, a former World Bank vice president and corporate secretary, was making valiant efforts to model Nigerian practice on the World Bank's integrity unit. She pushed three new corruption-related laws and set up institutions for budget control, public procurement and oil and gas transparency. British government experts praised Nigeria for going further than any other country in terms of disaggregating payments and tracing production volumes and procurement practices. From the beginning of 2004, Okonjo-Iweala started researching and recording allocations of revenue paid since 1999 to the federal government, the 36 states of Nigeria and the national capital of Abuja, and to local government authorities in each state. SPDC assisted in the process. But Detheridge had a concern:

> In civil society in Nigeria, there is no track record of holding publicly elected officials accountable. It is good to publish the numbers, but government capacity building is needed to enable these to be presented in an understandable way to citizens. The same is true for civil society so that they can make use of the information that they receive.

When the figures were published, it was clear that the four main oil-producing states in the Delta received more revenues than other Nigerian states. In the first 10 months of 2005, for example, Lagos (not a Delta state but with a population of 10.6 million) received US$200 million in revenues from the federal government. In contrast, Delta states Rivers (pop. 5.7 million), Bayelsa (pop. 2 million) and Delta (pop. 4.2 million) received US$790 million, US$710 million and US$570 million

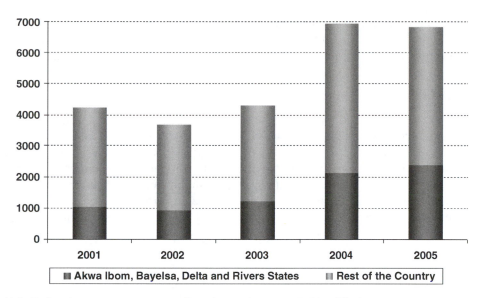

Figure 16.3 Federation account revenue allocation to the states (US$ million)

Source: Company information

respectively. In total, the federal government allocated US$6.8 billion to the 36 states in Nigeria. Nearly 35% of that amount went to the four major oil-producing states of the Delta (see Figure 16.3 for the federal government's revenue allocation to states).

Partly because of moves on the transparency initiative, Nigeria was granted US$18 billion debt relief by international creditors and, from being bottom of the rankings of Transparency International's corruption index in 2000, Nigeria improved marginally by 2005 to sixth among the eight worst countries (out of 159).

In 2005, a British company, Hart Nurse Group, was asked by the NEITI to audit the accounts of payments made by the oil companies against government-reported revenue for the period 1999–2004. A three-volume report was produced in April 2006 with breakdowns of payments made by each company. The audit was only partial in that the auditors did not have a mandate to look at the destination of funds once deposited in the Central Bank, and did not address the controversial issue of oil block licensing rounds and how contracts were awarded. A National Planning Commission survey of the state governments revealed significant shortcomings in accounts maintenance, controls against payroll fraud, fiscal management, service delivery and procurement procedures in general. Few States had any level of transparency. Moreover, the federal government was not in a position to insist on such transparency because the Nigerian constitution stipulated the autonomy of the states on matters such as revenue management. Olav Ljosne, regional external affairs manager for Africa (based in Nigeria), explained:

> The intention of the constitution is to prevent federal interference in state affairs. Only the state legislative, not the president, has power to call state governors to account for the moneys given to them.

Under the military dictatorships, control was centralized. Under civil rule, the states had considerably more power and autonomy. The Delta State's economic power was greatly strengthened by its 13% share of the federal government's revenues from oil. This did not stop its governors from campaigning at the July 2005 constitutional conference and elsewhere for an even greater percentage, while diverting attention from the accountability issue that was also on the agenda.

SHELL'S NEXT STEPS

Detheridge and Udofia realized that, given the complexity of Nigerian human rights challenges, a longer-than-usual series of briefing sessions with their successors would be necessary. They had to describe the learning process that Shell had gone through. Udofia's view was that Shell was at a 'make it or break it' point. Where did the role of a private company begin and end, and where did the government's role begin – how far could Shell go with the values it espoused without exceeding its remit? What else needed to be done on the governance and transparency agenda? And crucially, what other longer term partnership initiatives, like EITI, were needed? While discussing this, they wondered what their best advice might be for Shell's next steps. They prepared an agenda for the upcoming session.

NOTES

1. The case is intended to be used as a basis for class discussion rather than to illustrate either effective or ineffective handling of an administrative situation.
2. Essential Action report available at http:/www.essentialaction.org/shell/report.
3. When Shell attempted to dispose of the Brent Spar in the North Sea, the NGO Greenpeace organized a worldwide, high-profile media campaign against this plan, including calls for boycotts of Shell service stations. Under enormous public pressure, Shell abandoned its disposal plans although it later transpired that this would have been the safest option, both from an environmental and a health and safety perspective.

REFERENCE

Human Rights Watch, (1999) The Price of Oil. Available at http://www.hrw.org/en/reports/1999/02/23/price-oil (accessed 5 March 2009).

PART SIX

ENTREPRENEURSHIP

CHAPTER SEVENTEEN

Corporate Responsibility in Entrepreneurship

Filipe Santos, Assistant Professor of Entrepreneurship, INSEAD

INTRODUCTION

Entrepreneurship, broadly defined, is the pursuit of opportunities for value creation through a new business initiative. This business initiative can be a new venture (*new venture creation*) or a new business developed inside an established company (*corporate entrepreneurship*). I use the term 'value creation' because many entrepreneurs are not motivated by a narrow definition of profit. Rather, they seek to leave their mark in the world in a particular area of life and business about which they are passionate. Still, one distinction is important. Commercial entrepreneurs usually include value capture as one of their key goals and tend to associate to their business initiative other stakeholders who pursue financial returns as a goal, such as venture capitalists. In contrast, some entrepreneurs do not consider value capture as a central goal and, instead, measure their success in terms of the impact of their activities for society, often addressing deep problems where making profits is perceived as very unlikely. They are called social entrepreneurs. This chapter focuses on the issues of corporate responsibility that are specific to new venture creation, including both commercial and social entrepreneurship.

In a discussion of corporate responsibility in entrepreneurship it is also important to consider what entrepreneurship is not. Entrepreneurship is not small business management or creating your own job by selling professional services through a company shell. Entrepreneurship involves the ambition to build an organization to provide products or services in a systematic way, independent of the entrepreneur. It is also not a 'me too' business concept or doing resource arbitrage by buying low and selling high. Entrepreneurship should involve some element of innovation in a particular context, in the business model, market addressed, technologies used or organizational form in which resources are combined. It is this element of innovation that enables an entrepreneurial individual or team to create and appropriate value systematically, at least in the short and medium term, until market dynamics catch up with successful innovators.

This chapter starts by highlighting three key issues for corporate responsibility in entrepreneurship and then focuses on the specific corporate responsibility issues associated with the emerging field of social entrepreneurship.

ORGANIZATIONAL IMPRINTING AND THE RESPONSIBILITY OF THE ENTREPRENEUR

Most executives in large, established companies have limited ability to shape the culture of their organization. Entrepreneurship is the opposite of this, as the well established area of research on organizational imprinting makes clear.[1] The founding members of an organization start with a relatively clean slate on which to build an organizational identity and culture. The type of people they initially recruit and how they select and coordinate them are key elements in shaping this culture. The first employees will often refer to the founders as role models and as guides for the type of behaviours that are expected and approved in the organization. They will then adopt these cultural norms and behaviours and pass them on, as the venture grows, to the people they then recruit and manage, thus perpetuating the initial organizational identity (the central and enduring elements of the organization) and its culture (how it does business and what behaviours are accepted and expected). This ability to shape their organization creates a responsibility for founders to think about what kind of company they want to have and on what values it will be based. Founders also need to think carefully about the policies and systems that they want to establish to support those values.

The most interesting and often most successful new ventures are the ones that make very clear statements about what values they stand for and what their aims are. This will allow selected market audiences to connect and engage with the company, providing initial support and adoption for its products or services. Sometimes the resonance of the venture's identity with key stakeholders is so great that it creates a cult-like level of engagement with the organization. Think of eBay creating a fair marketplace for the communities of collectors across the world, Southwest Airlines generating fierce employee loyalty and Google's 'do no evil' mantra to create trust with users who provide the company with personal information. It is thus the corporate responsibility of the founders to create a venture identity that resonates with something meaningful that benefits society.[2]

It is also the founders' responsibility to be consistent with the venture's identity over time; that is what makes it an authentic identity versus mere marketing spin. The drinks company 'innocent', discussed in Chapter 18, is illustrative of this point. Its identity is reflected in its name and distinct attitude as a business: innocent stands for healthy, natural products. These central elements then became key drivers of the founder's product development efforts. The innocent brand also stands for a responsible way of doing business, translated into all its business practices – use of low emission fuels, sharing of profits with the community and hiring guidelines. Still, innocent is very clearly a commercial, profit-oriented company. And yet, as a value-led venture, it is likely to be a more responsible corporate actor than a company that tries narrowly to maximize profit.

THE CHALLENGES OF ENTREPRENEURIAL GROWTH

As ventures grow, new challenges arise – the level of discretion of the founders is usually reduced, tradeoffs become more complex and a broader set of stakeholders can influence policies and actions. In this context, maintaining a high standard of corporate responsibility becomes increasingly challenging, even for values-led businesses. One issue is that what seemed easy choices for a small company, soon become complex tradeoffs as they grow. For example, how should Google apply the 'do no evil' principle in the Chinese market? Should it abide by Chinese government censorship and information control demands or shut out 1 billion people from the benefit of using Google mail and search services?[3]

Another issue is that founders may have less discretion in running their organization because of increasing pressure from stakeholders, in particular if they conceded a majority of their firm's shares to outside investors. Becoming a public firm is particularly troubling because founders then become subject to the scrutiny of investors and analysts who demand increased profits every quarter and may have less consideration for issues of identity and responsible management. Which set of stakeholders does the entrepreneur satisfy? How to maintain responsible behaviours in the face of increasing pressure for short-term profitability growth? Partly the answer is how ingrained these core values are in the organizational fabric and how clearly they were communicated by the founders to all stakeholders. When corporate responsibility in a new venture is not an after-thought or marketing spin but is ingrained in the identity of the company from its foundation, embodied in shared values and regularly practised, it is more resilient and able to withstand pressures of the environment, pressures that, sometimes, may push organizations towards irresponsible behaviours.

EXITING THE BUSINESS IN A RESPONSIBLE WAY: WHEN AND TO WHOM?

A new challenge to corporate responsibility in entrepreneurship arises in the decision of when and how to concede leadership and management control of the business. Organizations require different styles of leadership at different growth stages and many entrepreneurial founders are not able to grow and develop their leadership skills at the pace and level that the business requires. If the new venture is addressing an important problem in the market and creating value for its stakeholders, it would be irresponsible for the founders to keep a tight rein in the business and constrain its growth. Unfortunately, tight control and micro-management is often the preferred management style of entrepreneurs, particularly those that view entrepreneurship as a lifestyle career option of self-employment and life balance. In the case of ventures that grow beyond the management ability of its founders, the founders themselves should organize the transition to professional managers or to new owners who have the skills and motivation to take the business to the next level of growth. Otherwise, the entrepreneur may stay too attached to the business and constrain its ability to grow and create value in the market, which would be irresponsible. Responsible entrepreneurs often seek mentorship from business leaders whom they trust and who are not invested in the business, to advise them on when to 'let go of their baby'.

However, particularly in the case of a trade sale of the venture, new issues may arise. Is it responsible to sell the venture to an owner who is not committed to respecting the core values of the business and may even decide to close down operations to reduce competition in the market? If the new venture is economically viable then the transfer of ownership from the founder's to new owners should involve credible commitments of the buying firm to maintain and grow the business while respecting and strengthening the core organizational values. This suggests that other entrepreneurs with shared values, complementary buyers or companies that are building a portfolio of brands are likely to be more responsible owners than competitors looking at consolidating the market or financial groups looking for value extraction opportunities, despite the fact that the latter may be able to pay a higher price for the business.

If executed properly, the sale of a venture to a corporate parent may even turn into a 'Trojan horse' strategy in which the values and business practices of the venture get adopted and disseminated by the corporate partner at a scale and impact that was unimaginable before. That was the hope of the founder of the Body Shop, Anita Roddick, when selling out her organization to L'Oréal: 'When you have the biggest cosmetics firm saying – we want you to teach us how to support small farms and women's cooperatives, it is a very exciting moment' (Elkington and Hartigan, 2008).

SOCIAL ENTREPRENEURSHIP AND CORPORATE RESPONSIBILITY

Although innocent has been a highly responsible company since its founding, clearly it is also a commercial enterprise with profit-oriented goals. Some entrepreneurs differ from the founders of innocent in that they do not have a profit-seeking motivation and instead focus on social impact as the key measure of their success and driver of organizational decisions. These are called social entrepreneurs and their approach is illustrated by the case of Waste Concern and its co-founders Iftekhar Enayetullah and Abu Hasnat (see Chapter 19).

Young and well educated, the founders of Waste Concern were faced with the pervasive problem of waste accumulation in the Bangladeshi cities and vowed to address it. They adopted an innovative approach of looking at waste as an economic resource and used their post-graduate studies to develop a novel solution for waste management in which solid waste is collected, composted and then sold as fertilizer to generate revenues that make the business model sustainable. Their solution worked well and is being replicated in many Bangladeshi cities. Any profit generated by these activities, as well as the founder's consulting activities income, is re-invested for business growth, with the goal of increasing the social impact of the organization. This is a good example of how social entrepreneurs are developing innovative business solutions to some of the world's most intractable problems.

Social entrepreneurship is a growing field of practice. The Schwab Foundation for Social Entrepreneurship, an organization founded in 2001 and connected to the World Economic Forum, has done much to raise global awareness and legitimate social entrepreneurship. Ashoka, a global organization founded more than 25 years ago with a mission of identifying, selecting and supporting high-impact social entrepreneurs throughout the world has close to 2000 social entrepreneurs in its network. This number is just the visible tip of the iceberg. For example, a recent entrepreneurship study from the United Kingdom suggests that up to 5% of economic activity in the country is done through social enterprises (Harding, 2006). As the field of social entrepreneurship gains momentum, many organizations have recently emerged to support social entrepreneurship at a national level. Social entrepreneurship is also receiving increasing interest from students and academics alike, particularly in business schools, becoming a recognized area of research and education.[4]

Social enterprises can operate with a profit or nonprofit status. They can rely on subsidies or develop earned-income models. They can use mostly volunteers or rely on regular employees to whom they pay living wages or even market wages. The distinguishing feature of social enterprises is that their objective function is the maximization of benefits for society using a sustainable business model. Social entrepreneurs, like commercial entrepreneurs, look at problems as opportunities for improving society. But they are different in that they tend to focus on social areas that are neglected by commercially-oriented firms due to their low prospect for profitability. Thus, they often deal with basic human needs, such as health, education and the environment, and focus on disadvantaged segments of the population who are usually unable to pay for the services they need and value. If they generate profits, social enterprises re-invest them in growing their activities and augmenting their social impact, not in remunerating their owners.

Social entrepreneurs thus have a responsibility mandate at the core of what they do. By addressing social problems in an economically viable way they not only have a direct positive impact in society but also show through their innovations how market-based mechanisms can be effectively deployed to alleviate social problems that either appeared invisible before or were very visible but appeared insurmountable to other economic agents. After proving that their innovation works, social entrepreneurs are responsible for scaling up their innovative solution to achieve greater social impact. This creates difficult challenges related to the degree of control chosen in the scaling up process, as illustrated by the Waste Concern case.

One such issue is the choice of growing in a way that ensures full control of the quality of the solution delivered (using direct branching or a tight franchise system) as opposed to giving more autonomy to local partners through a loose affiliation model or even allowing the free dissemination of the solution (Dees, Battle Anderson and Wei-skillern, 2004). An example is Unis-Cité, a French social enterprise founded in 1994 offering youth voluntary work to community organizations. After a successful pilot in the Paris region, the founders of Unis-Cité opted to grow the business across France using a loose affiliation model based on independent local organizations tied by a licence agreement. Later, given inefficiencies caused by model variations and lack of coordination, they decided to move to a tighter franchise model that involved a higher level codification of the values and processes of the organization. These were then systematically deployed by the regional affiliates. Interestingly, this type of franchise model is starting to be increasingly recognized by social entrepreneurs as an effective way to scale their social innovations (Elkington and Hartigan, 2008, pp. 73–75).

In general, in the early stages of their venture's development, social entrepreneurs should err on the side of control to make sure that their solution is replicated with sufficient quality so that the model gets legitimated and improves with scale. In later stages, once the core elements of the model are well understood, entrepreneurs should focus on more scalable growth mechanisms that accelerate adoption. At this stage, competition and imitation should actually be desired and supported by social entrepreneurs. This represents a clear distinction between social and commercial entrepreneurship – whereas commercial entrepreneurs will try to fight competition, true social entrepreneurs should invite it because competition will accelerate adoption and lead to higher social impact.

Once the social entrepreneur's innovation is validated in the market, developing scalable growth mechanisms usually involves leveraging the installed base of resources and competencies of established players, often commercial enterprises. This raises the issue of the governance of these partnerships so that economic and social objectives stay compatible as the social innovation grows. Recent tensions in Grameen Phone, the very successful joint-venture between Grameen Bank and Telenor to develop telecommunication services for rural populations in Bangladesh, illustrates the difficulty of finding a long-term basis for collaboration between commercial and social enterprises, given their very different goals and distinct stakeholder interests (Prasso, 2006). For these partnerships to be sustainable, the initial agreements should be very clear about the goals of each partner in the joint-venture, the goals and governance of the joint-venture itself, and the rule for allocation of the potential surplus generated by the partnership.

CAN SOCIAL ENTREPRENEURS BEHAVE IRRESPONSIBLY?

The above discussion may seem to suggest that social entrepreneurs have strong values and are thus less likely to engage in irresponsible behaviours such as bribery, causing pollution or committing fraud. Although this may be true, there is a dimension of corporate responsibility in which many social entrepreneurs are likely to struggle – the use of resources. Being economic actors to whom society entrusts resources, social enterprises have certain duties, namely the efficient management of resources, accountability and measurement of impact.

First, in a society characterized by scarcity of resources and given the scope of human problems that need addressing, social enterprises have the responsibility to use the resources that society provides in the most efficient way possible. This may involve using well-tested business methods and tools, such as cost accounting techniques, performance evaluations and management by objectives. These are business methods that, for a long time, the more traditional nonprofit sector organizations have eschewed. Second, social enterprises are accountable to society for the resources they are given, how they use them and the results they obtain so that there will be enough information for economic actors (social investors, employees, volunteers, donors, governments) to make informed decisions about future allocation of resources to social enterprises. Finally, social enterprises should be able to show they are focused on pursuing their mission and that their resources are being used effectively; that is, they are being applied in areas that generate an important social impact. Only by being efficient, accountable and measuring their impact, can social enterprises become responsible stewards of the resources with which they are entrusted and therefore fulfil the mission they set out to achieve.

CONCLUSION

Entrepreneurship, understood as launching innovations in the market through new ventures to create value, with either a social or commercial aim, raises distinct issues for corporate responsibility when compared to established firms. These issues pertain to the ability of founders to shape their organizations, imprinting them for good and bad behaviours, and also to the role of the founder as the organization grows, often requiring a different style of leadership over time. In the case of social enterprises, a host of issues are raised relating to the functioning of this new type of economic agent that gives primacy to the social mission but often operates through market-based mechanisms. Social enterprises thus straddle two worlds that are often seen at odds – the for-profit world and the social sector – but actually co-exist within the same organizational structure. Investigating how social entrepreneurs manage to take the best from these distinct institutional worlds, and turn their venture into a coherent organization that creates value for society, can provide novel insights for a new paradigm in corporate responsibility.

NOTES

1. For a recent academic perspective on organizational imprinting, see Johnson, V. (2007) What is Organizational Imprinting? Cultural Entrepreneurship in the Founding of the Paris Opera, *American Journal of Sociology*, **113** (1), 97–127. For a more applied perspective, see Baron, J. and Hannan, M. (2002) Organizational Blueprints for Success in High-tech Start-ups: Lessons Learned from the Stanford Project on Emerging Companies, *California Management Review*, **44**, 8–36.

2. By benefiting society I mean that the long-term impacts of the organizational activities are positive for society after accounting for known externalities.

3. In fact, Google decided to abide by the demands of the Chinese government, in a controversial decision on which executives spent over a year deliberating to come up with a viable moral and business solution. Yet this solution has been found to be unethical. For more details, see Dann, G. and Haddow, N. (2008) Just Doing Business or Doing Just Business: Google, Microsoft, Yahoo! and the Business of Censoring China's Internet, *Journal of Business Ethics,* May, **79** (3), 219–34.

4. For research, see Nichols, A. (ed.) (2006) *Social Entrepreneurship: New Models of Sustainable Social Change,* Oxford University Press. For education, see Tracey, P. and Phillips, N. (2007) The Distinctive Challenge of Educating Social Entrepreneurs: A Postscript and Rejoinder to the Special Issue on Entrepreneurship Education, *Academy of Management Learning & Education, June,* **6** (2).

REFERENCES

Dees, G., Battle Anderson, B. and Wei-skillern, J. (2004) Scaling social impact, *Social Innovation Review*, Spring, 24–32.

Elkington, J. and Hartigan, P. (2008) *The Power of Unreasonable People: How Social Entrepreneurs Create Markets that Change the World,* Harvard Business Press, Cambridge, MA.

Harding, R. (2006) *Global Entrepreneurship Monitor 2006 – UK Report,* Social Entrepreneurship Specialist Summary, London.

Prasso, S. (2006) Nobel Laureate Yunus says Telenor is taking from poor, *Fortune*/CNNMoney, 5 December. Available at http://money.cnn.com/2006/12/04/news/international/yunos_telenor.fortune/index.htm (accessed 5 March 2009).

CHAPTER EIGHTEEN

innocent: Values and Value[1]

David Grayson and Robert Brown, Cranfield School of Management

INTRODUCTION

In 2008, innocent's vision was to be 'Europe's favourite little smoothie company' by 2010. How far does a reputation for ethical business and sustainability help fuel the growth of what has become an iconic consumer brand in less than a decade? What are the potential pitfalls of such a strategy?

Three young friends who met at Cambridge University, Adam Balon, Richard Reed and Jonathan Wright, founded innocent in 1998 following six months of intense market research and testing on their pulped, pure fruit smoothie drinks. All three were in their mid-twenties and still bachelors. When their research efforts showed encouraging results, they agreed to take sabbaticals from their marketing and consulting jobs (see Figure 18.1 for the founders' CVs) to sell their pre-packaged smoothies and juices – a new fast-growing market – through grocers and independent stores in the United Kingdom. By year four of their business plan (2002) sales stood at £6 million, exceeding their original forecast, and then soared to over £100 million by 2007 (see Figure 18.2).

The new company benefited greatly from increased consumer concern for healthier eating and life-styles and the UK media's interest in the subject. In January 2005 the *Sunday Times* ran a full-page article entitled 'Smoothie Operators Think Big', which gave six experts' advice, at times contradictory, on how innocent should grow (see Exhibit 18.1). The three directors often reflected on these experts' comments at their weekly management meetings. In January 2008, faced with continued fast growth and success, they agreed that a major priority in their European expansion was how to maintain values and value. This was a particularly important question for markets and countries where media interest in the company was high and where the slightest error would immediately be publicized. Other prominent companies had suffered at the hands of the media. Perrier's bottled sparkling spring water had temporarily fallen from grace in the 1990s after traces of benzene were found in a single bottle sold in the United States. More recently, the TV presenter and journalist Janet Street-Porter had attacked the Prince of Wales, a prominent supporter of organic farming, alleging that the organic produce from his farms contained added sugar. Balon, Reed and Wright needed constantly to remember their simple beginnings and keep to their innocent values if they were to continue to add long-term value. But what was the best way to go about it?

Adam Balon, 26 *Commercial*	• Educated at St John's College, Cambridge, after Latymer Upper School, London. First class degree in economics, June 1994. • One year on the Arthur Andersen Scholarship Programme. • Two years at McKinsey & Company as a Business Analyst. Worked in a variety of sectors including financial services and grocery retailing. Spent seven months in South Africa running two client teams during the major restructuring of one of South Africa's big four banks. • Two years at Virgin Cola. Previous roles: Brand Manager, Logistics and Production Planning. Most recent role: Marketing Manager – ran UK marketing for Virgin Cola, developing the brand strategy, coordinating the 10-person department and controlling the £5 million budget. Had extensive experience of dealing with impulse and grocery multiples to drive listings. • Earned a place on the Harvard MBA course in 1998. • Responsible for west London's music festival, Jazz on the Green (with Richard Reed).
Richard Reed, 25 *Marketing*	• Educated at St John's College, Cambridge, after Batley Grammar School, Leeds. Upper second class degree in geography, June 1994. • Four years at advertising agency BMP DDB Needham. Previous roles: Business Director for BMP's interactive Marketing Consultancy; New Business Director for the agency. Most recent role: Account Director on the agency's Volkswagen business. Responsible for devising and implementing new marketing strategies to double VW's market share and to exploit new revenue streams for the agency by developing new services, including macro-planning and retail communications. Responsible for west London's music festival, Jazz on the Green (with Adam Balon).
Jonathan Wright, 26 *Operations*	• Educated at St John's College, Cambridge, after Winchester College, Hampshire. Masters degree in manufacturing engineering, June 1995. • ESSO Petroleum Bursary including 12 months in Plant Technical Services at Fawley refinery, Southampton • Three years at Bain & Company. Joined as Associate Consultant, promoted to Senior Associate in June 1997 and promoted to Consultant (post-MBA Level) in June 1998. Worked across a range of industries including manufacturing, financial services and media in the UK, the US and Asia. Projects have included developing start up plans for established companies setting up new ventures overseas, business cases for corporate parents to invest/dispose of their business units and negotiating strategies as part of subsequent disposals. Also heavily involved in internal operations including IT and recruiting.

Figure 18.1 Brief CVs at start-up in 1998

Source: London Business School (LBS-C505-016) and Harvard Business School (5-806-196)

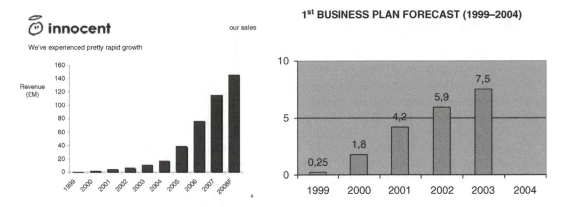

Figure 18.2 innocent actual revenue growth 1999–2006

Source: Company and *Ethical Corporation Magazine,* March 2007, London Business School (LBS-C505-016) and Harvard Business School (5-806-196)

EXHIBIT 18.1 WHAT THE EXPERTS SAY (EXTRACTS FROM THE *SUNDAY TIMES* ENTERPRISE NETWORK, JANUARY 2005)

Don't wait. Innovate
Bob Barbour, Chief Executive,
Northern Ireland Centre for Competitiveness

Richard Reed faces an innovator's dilemma. He is an aggressive and customer-focused entrepreneur who must protect this reputation to maintain his competitive edge. Smoothies are a profitable niche product with growing market opportunities but are vulnerable to attack by competitors with deep pockets.

Reed must develop new innocent-branded products that will appeal to his present customers and attract new ones. The firm has succeeded because of its brand leadership and enthusiastic workforce rather than because it has rights over a particular recipe of drink. This leaves it exposed to competition from the big players who produce high volumes and sell at lower prices.

Reed must not delay in creating new products to make competition more difficult for his rivals and maintain his advantage. If he waits too long, he will be forced to fight off attacks and lose his focus on growth.

Give customers a good experience
Beth Rogers, Research Director,
Institute of Sales and Marketing Management

Richard Reed is wise to start extending the innocent brand by competing in a closely related product category such as juice. Nevertheless, with so many established brands making health claims but also competing on price, the company needs a strong unique selling point.

(Continued)

EXHIBIT 18.1 (*Continued*)

innocent should research which large-pack juice buyers it wants to reach. What characterizes them? Is the psychological factor of 'pure juice from fresh fruit' enough to justify a premium price? Perhaps it will be necessary to convince new customers that the taste really is much better. innocent should encourage its customers to sample the Tetrapaks by promoting them on the bottled product.

Packaging and labelling design also plays a role. innocent could make its product stand out by loudly displaying differences in manufacturing process and taste on the packs. Each promotional method should be reviewed frequently.

Create goods for other markets
Judith Rutherford, Chief Executive
Business Link for London

innocent is an incredibly strong brand. However, competitors are hot on its heels and it might be risky if the company delays taking its brand into other areas. This market is moving quickly, and although concentrating on the existing brand is sensible, innocent must be careful not to miss opportunities in other markets.

The brand is recognisable and has loyal customers, so innocent should look at capitalizing on this by producing new products while maintaining core brand values. When developing new products, research is crucial and the innocent team must make sure the products meet customers' needs.

As the company is expanding it would be a good time to think about restructuring the business. The founder directors could concentrate on using their creativity to extend the brand, while employing new people, or using their loyal employee base, to look after the core drinks.

Focus on healthy nature of products
Paul Gostick, International Chairman
Chartered Institute of Marketing

A move into new product areas could give innocent an opportunity to boost its sales. But, by increasing exposure and adding weight to the innocent brand, it could also help the company to maintain the upper hand in the smoothies market as competition increases.

But the new products would need to be a perfect fit. Stamping a dull and unworthy product with the innocent logo would dilute the brand and blur the identity of the new product.

Richard Reed has a keen sense of his brand's personality, and he needs to make certain that the edgy and ethical stance that has underpinned its success can be mirrored in the new product area.

innocent should not move into territory occupied by another player with the same traits. It made its mark because it stood out from the crowd by focusing on healthy, ethical products. It should strive to achieve a similar individuality in any new area.

Form a joint venture
Karl Jefferman, Area Director
Allied Irish Bank

The company is at a crossroads. The business could be sold to a rival, continue to grow organically, or form a joint venture with a multinational competitor.

Disregarding outside investment will limit the rate of growth innocent can sustain otherwise funding will have to come from cashflow and reinvested profits. Given the small profit margins this may restrict innocent's ambition of expanding in Britain and on the continent, and leave the company vulnerable when a multinational gets the right product in the market. It could be better to form a joint venture with a multinational rival. This would enable innocent to enjoy the benefits of a larger business and at the same time retain control of the brand.

Have confidence to break the rules
John Timpson, Chairman
Timpsons

Richard Reed needn't worry too much about the competition. His priorities are to continue to produce the best product on the market and break the rules of professional management.

The innocent brand could be extended to related products, growth is not a problem, but Reed should beware of becoming impersonal like his competitors. innocent has a great product but a business is created by people, not packaging and, if Reed isn't careful, a bigger company could be destroyed by people.

innocent's success will continue as long as there is a weekly talk at Wonderwall.

Source: Sunday Times Enterprise Network, January 2005

THE FIRST BUSINESS PLAN, 1998

The three friends had met at St John's College, Cambridge, where they had collaborated in a number of ventures, including organizing college May balls, which later (1997–98) led them into organizing a music festival in west London called Jazz on the Green, attended by over 20 000 enthusiasts. They continued to take holidays together. Driving back from a skiing weekend in Val d'Isère in February 1998 they discussed the possibility of starting their own business, based on what they had learned in their marketing and consultancy roles.

Despite their good career starts, they felt that they were too young and did not have enough connections to start their own consultancy, and so the conversation soon switched to consumable products and their own lifestyles. They soon identified healthier food and drink intended for people like themselves, with too much work and too little time. All three were keen consumers of smoothies, the crushed and pulped fruit drinks. Wright had worked in the United States and knew that two smoothie manufactures, Odwalla and The Fresh Juice Company, were growing strongly. Although the overall fruit juice market in the United Kingdom was huge (£6 billion in 1998), per capita consumption was only one-third of the US market and the smoothie sector was only just developing. The biggest UK smoothie company was PJs, with a turnover of just under £3 million after three years. Jonathan Wright felt that PJs smoothies failed to taste as good as homemade smoothies or smoothies he had tasted in the United States, perhaps because PJs used concentrates rather than fresh fruit. However, PJs was doing well with a high priced product and growing very rapidly.

The three agreed that the young UK smoothie market looked promising and that they should undertake further research while continuing their jobs. Further investigation by Wright provided the real breakthrough: previously, they had assumed it would be necessary to invest in manufacturing facilities for a new company (as the New Covent Garden Soup Company had done in Reading for its high quality soups), which would set high investment barriers. But in June 1998, when Wright visited the facility near Nottingham where PJs bottling was done, he found a small factory run by a local farmer, which, in addition to bottling, also contained a small fruit processing plant. The farmer was able 'to harvest and process his carrots into fresh juice within five hours and it tasted great,' said Wright.

The three-man team refined their recipe ideas and worked with the farmer to produce test drinks in his processing plant. The results were highly encouraging. The plant pasteurised the juice lightly before bottling, without impacting on taste, extending the shelf life of the finished product to four weeks. The way was now open to market-test the juice made at the Nottingham factory and Balon, Reed and Wright agreed that there was enough potential in their project to justify taking sabbaticals from their jobs.

At Jazz on the Green in 1998, the team set up a smoothie stall, selling 250 ml bottles for £1.89 each. They branded the drinks Fast Tractor in honour of their farming collaborator. A large placard by the stall read 'Should we give up our own jobs to sell this juice?' and by it they put two bins labelled 'Yes' and 'No'. Customers were asked to put their empty bottles in one of the two receptacles. At the end of the day, the 'Yes' bin was full with nearly 800 bottles, whereas there was a negligible number of bottles in the 'No' bin.

The die was almost cast. Further consumer research was undertaken to test different ingredients. The favourite recipe emerged as 1½ freshly squeezed oranges, a crushed banana and ¼ pressed pineapple. Product freshness and quality were essential to tackle PJs, because the smoothies would be selling for the same price in a smaller bottle (250 ml versus 330 ml). Research into distribution costs led Balon, Reed and Wright to believe that the sales effort should focus on London-based independents and 'alternative' channels for the first 18 months, with a move to multiples later. Initial deliveries of bottled products from the Nottingham farmer could be made in their own chilled van, at an initial cost of £20 000 plus a similar amount in annual running costs.

Sales and financial forecasts then had to be made from their experiences to date. An implementation plan was developed (see Figure 18.3), including an estimate of outside finance required to cover costs and the first 18 months operating losses, revealed by their first draft financial forecasts (see Figure 18.4). They would need at least £235 000 to add to their own £45 000 for the first 12 months of the operation – but, if all went as planned, they could be making close to £1 million profit by year five.

Despite their enthusiasm, research and impressive CVs, raising the start-up capital in late 1998 proved extremely difficult. By outsourcing production the prospective company had no hard

Summary implementation plan

		Start–4 months	5–12 months	13–24 months	Year 3	Year 4	Year 5
		Stage I	Stage II	Stage III	Stage IV		
Production		Outsourced production			Dedicated facility		
Sales and Distribution [1]	Channel	Independents (sandwich shops/cafés; workplace restaurants, gyms, bars)	Independents plus multiple impulse	Independents plus multiple impulse and grocers			
	Region	London		Other key urban centres			
	Method	Own van sales and small delivered wholesalers		Large wholesalers and direct to RDC			
Headcount including founders [2]		3	5	11	16	19	23
Funding		Owners equity	1st round equity	2nd round equity + £100k overdraft	Loan for dedicated production facility		Trade sale
		£45 000	£235 000	£400 000			

Figure 18.3 Implementation plan (excerpt from business plan)

[1] Initial sales strategy was to establish a depth in a narrow base to gain impactful brand presence, while avoiding channels where PJ was already stocked.

[2] In Year 5, the three founders would co-run the organization of 23 people. Adam, as Commercial (sales) and Finance Director would manage 12 people, Richard as Marketing Director would manage three people and Jon as Operations Director would manage three people (unless the venture invested in its own production facility). There would be a shared PA and a receptionist.

Source: First Business Plan (and London Business School)

Summary profit and loss	Unit	5 months	Year 1	Year 2	Year 3	Year 4	Year 5
Outlets	#	60	100	560	1,340	2,020	2,690
Bottles/ outlet/ day	#	2	8	12	11	11	10
Customers	'000	1	5	50	115	160	200
Penetration of London target (c1m people)	%	0.1%	1%	6%			
Penetration of UK target of (5m people)	%				2%	3%	4%
Volume	'000 bottles	50	275	2,375	5,575	7,775	9,625
Litres	'000	10	100	800	1,850	2,550	3,150
Unit price	£	0.80	0.90	0.78	0.74	0.76	0.78
Revenue	£'000	40	250	1,845	4,180	5,940	7,450
Materials	£'000	15	80	575	1,330	1,845	2,280
Packing	£'000	5	40	310	720	1,000	1,240
Logistics	£'000	-	10	40	85	120	145
Distribution	£'000	5	40	235	495	700	895
Gross profit	£'000	15	80	685	1,550	2,275	2,890
Gross margin	%	38%	32%	37%	37%	38%	39%
Gross profit per bottle	£	0.30	0.29	0.29	0.28	0.29	0.30
Marketing	£'000	25	95	185	380	555	690
Sales	£'000	15	55	160	240	325	420
Head Office	£'000	60	175	350	540	695	840
Depreciation	£'000	-	5	15	40	65	70
Bad debt	£'000	-	5	10	20	35	55
Operating profit	£'000	(85)	(255)	(35)	330	600	815
Operating margin	%	(213%)	(102%)	(2%)	8%	10%	11%
Cumulative operating profit	£'000	(340)	(255)	(290)	40	640	1,455
Financial costs	£'000	-	-	15	20	195	260
Profit	£'000	(85)	(255)	(50)	310	405	555
Cumulative profit	£'000	(85)	(255)	(305)	5	410	965

Figure 18.4 Summary financials (excerpt from business plan).

Source: First Business Plan (and London Business School)

assets, and so no security for bank lending. On that basis, banks were unwilling to promote the UK government's Small Business Loan Guarantee Scheme, which helped small firms to raise capital. The sums required were too small to interest venture capital houses and business angels were deterred by the team's lack of experience in this market sector. However, by e-mailing all their friends and colleagues, they secured an introduction to Maurice Pinto, a successful entrepreneur.

Pinto liked the business plan and the research the team had undertaken but had never known a business that succeeded with three leaders. The team would not budge on this issue.

Although Pinto tried to interest other business angels in the investment, his usual trusted syndicate would not cooperate. By this time Pinto had commissioned two Harvard Business School students to investigate the proposal, been impressed by the management team and decided that the potential upside made it an attractive prospect. He also knew that his investment would qualify for tax relief under the UK's Enterprise Investment Scheme and would be capital gains free if the investment was held for over three years. Pinto received 20% shares for his £235 000 investment and the team listened politely to his suggestion that he could provide a non-executive chairman to help them and represent his interests.

The investment was made in January 1999 and three months later the first pallet of smoothies was delivered from Nottingham. The holding company was called Fresh Trading and the brand name was 'innocent', reflecting the founders' belief in the purity of their product, the main point of differentiation from all competitive offerings.

TEN BLOOD, SWEAT AND FRUIT JUICE YEARS LATER[2]

By 2008 innocent was on the verge of moving from a medium-sized to a large business; it had 240 employees worldwide, 50 of whom joined that summer, and was operating in nine countries. The financial statements showed that it was a major financial success story (see Figure 18.5). Thanks to strong cash flow, a second round of external financing had not been necessary, leaving the three founders firmly in control with 80% of company shares. The company's commitment to the product also remained unchanged even though the innocent family of smoothies had grown (see Exhibit 18.2), to include a one litre Tetrapak format priced at £2.99 for sale in supermarkets, and a range specially packaged to appeal to children.

Marketing

At the outset, marketing had not had a real budget and was very simple. Dan Germain, a school friend of the founders who joined the company in 1999 to deliver juice to retailers, had commented that the labels on the bottles were boring. The founders decided to liven them up with off-beat messages. One of the first was written by Reed:

> We're not saying that there's anything wrong with having a gym workout, it's just, you know, all a bit of an effort really, isn't it? If I were you, I'd just have an innocent smoothie instead. They're 100% pure fruit, they're made with fresh rather than concentrated juice and they contain no additives whatsoever. As a result they taste good and do you good. And you don't need to take a communal shower afterwards.

The fun messages on the labels became a regular feature of innocent's shoestring marketing, along with visually arresting delivery vehicles and the distribution of free samples in locations such as London's Covent Garden, where large numbers of potential customers congregated.

Like many small businesses, the majority of innocent's most successful promotional activities started as one-off, opportunistic events. These included putting woollen hats on the bottles in winter. Initially the hats were knitted by 40 grannies, recruited via the company's website, in return for 20 pence per bottle donated to their favourite charities. This soon became a

Turnover Ratios	31/12/2006 12 months (£'000)
Turnover	75,521
Profit (loss) before Taxation	6,464
Net Tangible Assets (Liab.)	8,107
Shareholders Funds	4,899
Profit Margin (%)	8.56
Return on S'holders Funds (%)	131.95
Return on Capital Employed	35.71
Liquidity Ratio	0.97
Gearing Ratio (%)	281.57
Number of Employees	18

Balance Sheet

Fixed Assets	10,783
Current Assets	23,469
Stock	(7,801)
Debtors	(9,943)
Total Assets	34,252
Current Liabilities	19,153
Creditors	(9,639)
Long-term Liabilities	13,200
Total Assets less Liabilities	4,899

Profitability Ratios	31/12/2006
Profit Margin (%)	8.56
Return on Shareholders'Funds (%)	131.95
Return on Capital Employed (%)	35.71
Return on Total Assets (%)	18.87
Interest Cover	n.s.
Stock Turnover	9.68
Debtors' Turnover	7.60
Debtor Collection (days)	48.06
Creditors' Payment (days)	46.59
Net Assets Turnover	4.17
Fixed Assets Turnover	7.00
Salaries/Turnover (%)	8.88
Gross Margin (%)	36.35
EBIT Margin (%)	8.57
EBITDA Margin (%)	9.03
Turnover per Employee (Unit)	640,008
Average Remun. per Employee (Unit)	56,839
Profit per Employee (unit)	54,780

Figure 18.5 innocent financial performance (2006)

Source: FAME Analysis of Company Accounts, published by Bureau van Dijk Electronic Publishing

fully-fledged, cause-related marketing campaign[3] called SuperGran, run with the charity Age Concern, generating £80 000 for the latter in 2005 and £115 000 a year later. The 2006 campaign was run simultaneously with Age Concern's Fight the Freeze campaign, which high-lighted the plight of older people in winter. For each woolly hat-wearing smoothie sold in Sainsbury's stores and Eat Cafés nationwide, innocent gave 50 pence to Age Concern to fund programmes providing hot meals, room thermometers, blankets, safety checking of electric

EXHIBIT 18.2 GROWTH OF innocent

 innocent

products

And innocent smoothies live up to that ideal

100% fruit

Never, ever from concentrate

Nothing added, nothing taken away

 innocent   our little family of juice

From those early days our little family of smoothies has grown

Smoothies	Super Smoothies	Thickies	Really Lovely Juices	Juicy Waters
Seasonal: Blackcurrants and gooseberries	Natural vitamin C	Yoghurt, vanilla bean and honey	Oranges, mangoes and limes	Blackcurrants
Cranberries and raspberries	Natural detox	Seasonal: Yoghurt, figs and honey	Nothing but oranges	Cranberries and limes
Oranges, bananas and pineapples	Fruit and veg			Lemons and limes
Mangoes and passion fruits				Mangoes and passion fruits
Pineapples, bananas and coconuts				
Strawberries and bananas				
Blackberries and blueberries				

blankets and advice on how to handle rising energy costs. The SuperGran campaign resulted in a record-breaking rise in sales for innocent smoothies and innocent's biggest ever week of unit sales in Sainsbury's. Furthermore, the campaign encouraged unprecedented involvement from innocent consumers with over 230 000 hats knitted and £300 000 of PR generated across the campaign (see Exhibit 18.3).

EXHIBIT 18.3 innocent's SUPERGRAN CAUSE-RELATED MARKETING CAMPAIGN

 innocent   in store

The hats get put on bottles and on shelf...

The 2006 campaign was run simultaneously to Age Concern's Fight the Freeze campaign which highlighted the plight of older people in winter. For each woolly hat-wearing smoothie sold in Sainsbury's stores and Eat Cafes nationwide, innocent gave 50p to Age Concern to fund programmes such as winter warmth measures providing hot meals, room thermometers, warm blankets, safety checking of electric blankets and advice on how to handle rising energy costs for their homes. The Supergran campaign leveraged the work and resources of four partners, innocent, Age Concern, J Sainsbury and Eat Cafés. The woolly hats were knitted by local Age Concern users, Sainsbury's employees, innocent staff and the general public. Age Concern recruited 90 local Age Concerns and over 2,300 knitters, who produced 160 000 hats, over 40 000 more than they had planned, whilst Sainsbury colleagues knitted 21 000. innocent organized knitting events for partners and consumers alike. Wool specialists, Rowan, provided all the wool for the knitting kits and in-store knitting activities.

Impact

- 230 000 little woolly hats were knitted.
- This raised £115k for Age Concern.
- There was a significant increase in sales over a six week period.
- Approximately 55 000 older people in Age Concern centres across the UK benefited from the money raised. Increased funds and resources enabled centres to provide extra services such as helping older people claim warm front grants and funding minibuses to take them shopping.
- The vibrant campaign generated positive internal team-building and increased interaction and engagement of consumers.
- The Supergran campaign resulted in a record-breaking uplift in sales for innocent smoothies, and innocent's biggest ever week of unit sales in Sainsbury's. Furthermore, the campaign encouraged unprecedented involvement from innocent consumers with over 230 000 hats knitted and £300k worth of PR generated across the campaign.
- The knitting groups that were established to meet the demand for bobble hats also encouraged older people to get involved and take advantage of support at Age Concern centres, and boosted numbers of younger Age Concern campaigners.

The campaign was awarded the prestigious Business in the Community Award for Excellence Cause-Related Marketing Award 2007

SuperGran illustrated innocent's strong brand equity and the team's ability to bring it to life through good story telling. It created awareness and distinctiveness, despite little absolute marketing investment at the outset. This brand equity helped define the brand's values in the beginning, and later on informed the sustainability strategy that the company adopted. Their good-natured brand character allowed them to bring this to life for consumers in a way that was entirely consistent with the brand. Overall, marketing skilfully interweaved an informal, irreverent, tongue-in-cheek 'conversation' with customers and an increasingly overt commitment to sustainability. The two aspects were integrated, emphasizing that commitment to responsible business did not have to be earnest and dull.

Company vans were designed to promote the company's pastoral image. Summer jazz festivals, called Fruitstock, were run for several years in London public parks, replaced in 2007 with the innocent Village Fête. All these low-cost activities created media interest in the company. As early as the autumn of 1999, the BBC Food and Drink programme called innocent 'the UK's best smoothie' and the company was referred to as 'more of a cult than a brand'. Fan mail from satisfied customers was plastered all over the reception area of the company headquarters, called Fruit Towers, in Hammersmith, West London. From 2001, the company ran a blog and in 2005 Reed began contributing a monthly column in a national British newspaper (*The Guardian*).

Sales took off significantly in 2003 as innocent moved into a wider range of retail outlets, reaching £37 million by 2005, and giving innocent a 60% market share in a fast-growing UK market for smoothies, estimated at £70 million that year. This placed innocent well ahead of PJs (£13 million sales) and private label brands (£20 million). Eleven other smoothie brands came and went during this period, including PJs, which was acquired by PepsiCo. Coca-Cola began strong support for its Minute Maid orange juice brand, resulting in even faster total smoothie market sector growth. innocent sales climbed to £80 million in 2006 and to over £100 million in 2007. By summer 2007, innocent was quoting a 72% share of the then £169 million UK smoothie market. At the beginning of 2008, innocent was selling two million smoothies per week. Further sector growth was coming from supermarket own-label smoothies.

Organization and Sustainability

Throughout this period of growth, innocent decided to extend its existing smoothie product range rather than develop completely new products such as ice cream, which at an earlier stage had been one option mooted. The company also expanded into Ireland and continental Europe, with offices in Dublin, Paris, Amsterdam, Copenhagen and Hamburg.

The three founders continued as joint managing directors, joined at formal board meetings by Jules Hydleman, as a non-executive director, representing Maurice Pinto, and at management meetings by Jamie Mitchell,[4] the UK managing director. Balon, Reed and Wright enjoyed debating with each other, often for hours on end: every new idea had to have a recommender, who argued for its implementation, and a decider, who made the final decision. Although this often slowed down decision-making, as the controlling owners, the three could freely promote environmental and social policies, which a publicly owned company, with accountability to shareholders, might find more difficult to introduce.

innocent increasingly emphasized the company's spirit of social responsibility and sustainability, gradually becoming more vocal and willing to address these issues publicly (see Exhibit 18.4).

Detailed company strategies were developed for procurement, packaging, emissions and even for the company's head office. Each was delegated to specific managers to champion. For example, all bananas were purchased from Rainforest Alliance certified suppliers (see www.rainforest-alliance.org); and the outsourced bottle manufacturer in the United Kingdom was encouraged to move from 50% to 100% recycled plastic. In 2007, innocent became the first company in the world to use bottles made from 100% recycled plastic. The company also experimented briefly with a fully compostable bottle made from polylactic acid. The vehicle fleet was converted to meet low engine emission targets, and Fruit Towers from the start was supplied with green (wind-powered) electricity. A full-time sustainability manager, Jessica Sansom, formerly with McDonalds, helped to shape and sharpen innocent's sustainability strategy and messages (see Exhibit 18.5).

Workplace practices also reflect innocent's commitment to sustainability and responsibility. A range of benefits, including a generous profit-sharing scheme, was developed for all staff. There was a conscious effort to make innocent a learning organization. Rather than import learning, innocent chose to codify its own learning through the innocent academy, an in-house training capacity, where five employees, each considered to model a core management skill, were designated to distil

EXHIBIT 18.4   RICHARD REED'S FOREWORD TO *BETTER BUSINESS JOURNEY*, A PUBLICATION AIMED AT SMALL FIRMS

" Responsible business practice should be a part of the culture of your business, however small, culture being 'the way we do things around here'."

RICHARD REED, CEO, INNOCENT

innocent
little tasty drinks

You know, it doesn't matter what size company or how limited your time or resources are, you can still do something towards being responsible. If every small company did even one thing, imagine what the impact would be. Start somewhere and you'll probably be surprised about the benefits you get for your business and realise like we did, that it's just good business sense.

In a way you have already started on the journey by reading this practical guide. In our own small way, innocent is getting the reputation for being one of the most ethical companies in the UK. That's a good image to have, but boy does it scare me. Hopefully, anyone that does look closely would find in innocent a company that does take its responsibilities seriously.

Firstly, we make things that actually are good for people. Secondly, we try to source responsibly. All our suppliers have to comply with International Labour Organisation standards before they even get to the table. Thirdly, we're moving towards eco-friendly packaging material. Fourthly, we're looking at the emissions from our entire business system. I get scared when I think about how many there are (the trucks delivering the juice, the boat bringing the fruit etc.). But our commitment is to take responsibility for these emissions, reduce them where possible and off-set them where not. And we're asking our suppliers to do the same, to make it a term of doing business with innocent. Finally, we think companies should share some of the wealth they create.

That's why 10% of our profits each year get paid into the innocent foundation, a separate registered charity that supports NGOs in the countries where our fruit comes from. So that's what we mean by being responsible. Will we ever get there and fully realise this vision? I've no idea, but for as long as we're called innocent we're going to keep trying.

Richard Reed, CEO, Innocent

DID YOU KNOW?

99%
of all businesses in the UK are small and medium sized (4.3 million of them)

13m
people are employed by smaller businesses

59%
of all employees work for smaller businesses

60%
of commercial waste is generated by smaller businesses

It all adds up –
the social impact that smaller businesses have is ENORMOUS

Better Business Journey   **01**

---

the innocent way of developing and applying their particular skill. In 2007, this was supplemented with an innocent people academy for developing senior managers. There were also plans for craft training, for each core business skill, developed by specific functions, for example, finance for the finance team. 'In time,' said UK managing director Jamie Mitchell, 'we will develop the innocent view of marketing.'

As well as developing a strong culture around learning and personal development, innocent provided competitive compensation packages, created a good working environment and encouraged staff to become personally involved in sustainability. Offers included gift vouchers for employees signing up for renewable energy in their own homes; an annual scholarship for an employee to work with an NGO partner of the innocent foundation (see Exhibit 18.6); and training in sustainability, customized to each part of the innocent business. As a result, the company won plaudits and accolades, collecting a string of business and consumer awards such as a listing in *The Times* 100 Best Companies to Work For (2006, ranked 16th). No wonder that Maurice Pinto was led to reflect:

> The co-managing director arrangement has worked brilliantly. In my 40+ years of operating and investing, this is the most effective management team I have come across. And it was almost unthinkable that after knowing each other for 13 years, and after building the company as equals, that one of them would step up and become 'the boss'.

EXHIBIT 18.5 innocent's SUSTAINABILITY STRATEGY

 it also makes good business sense

	Internal	External
Tomorrow	**Clean Technology** Realise major improvements through new clean technology. Stay competitive in resource-constrained future. = Innovation and repositioning	**Planning for the future** Focus purpose on the major global environmental and social issues. Meet unmet needs of emerging markets and future generations. = Growth and trajectory
Today	**Resource efficiency** Lower costs and risks by reducing resource use. Eliminating waste either at source or use as a useful input = Cost and risk reduction	**Product Stewardship** Assume responsibility for product's entire life cycle. Engage with stakeholders. = Reputation and legitimacy

Source: S. Hart 1997, Beyond Greening: Strategies for a sustainable world

 sustainability strategy

Our strategy has 5 key elements

| 100% natural drinks | ethical ingredients | sustainable packaging | resource-efficient business | sharing the proceeds |

EXHIBIT 18.6 THE innocent FOUNDATION

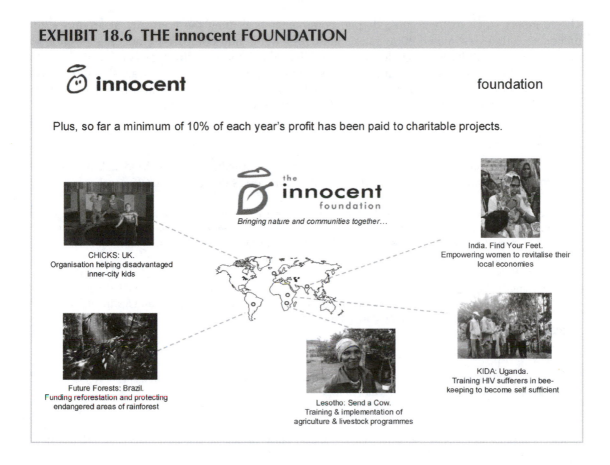

Plus, so far a minimum of 10% of each year's profit has been paid to charitable projects.

the innocent foundation
Bringing nature and communities together…

CHICKS: UK.
Organisation helping disadvantaged inner-city kids

India. Find Your Feet.
Empowering women to revitalise their local economies

Future Forests: Brazil.
Funding reforestation and protecting endangered areas of rainforest

Lesotho: Send a Cow.
Training & implementation of agriculture & livestock programmes

KIDA: Uganda.
Training HIV sufferers in bee-keeping to become self sufficient

Nonetheless, questions and strong competitive pressures remained. Would newer, often older, management recruits fit in with innocent's style? Would innocent's humorous marketing work in continental Europe? Would supermarket own-label smoothies cannibalize sales or help grow the category still further? Would bigger multinationals with deeper pockets try to muscle in on the market? In February 2008, for example, PepsiCo announced it was extending its Tropicana brand of fruit juices into the smoothies market, backed by an initial £4.5 million advertising campaign. At the same time, PepsiCo repositioned its existing smoothie unit, PJs, at a cheaper price point, to appeal to younger customers.

Several trade sale approaches were received and rejected, despite frequent warnings that 'if we don't buy you we will crush you'. Should innocent sell and pass the short-term growth problems to an established food group? Still the team remained committed. In 2006, the three founders made a legal agreement to continue together for at least four more years, although the agreement would not preclude the founders from collectively deciding to sell.

As Richard Reed said, 'Yes, we want to be financially independent . . . but we haven't proved anything yet. People would say it was easy to be ethical when small. I want to prove we can do it and grow.'

The founders stuck to their guns, despite commentators valuing the company at around £200 million (2.5 times estimated 2006 sales). Journalists frequently compared innocent's position to the sale of Ben and Jerry's to Unilever, Green & Black to Cadbury Schweppes and Body Shop to L'Oréal. In those cases, iconic brands, famous for their commitment to corporate social responsibility, had been acquired by large, multinational companies – with much accompanying debate about whether the core brand values could be preserved by the new owners.

Values

During innocent's rapid growth, the company had become something of a role model. A 2007 survey of young British entrepreneurs, who had started their businesses in the previous 25 years, concluded:

> [P]erhaps most revealing, the majority of later interviewees explicitly talked about one firm when they wanted to exemplify their entrepreneurial ideals: innocent. innocent clearly summed up for them the right balance of success, commitment to cool, having a worthy and good product, an ideal corporate culture, and an independence marked by staying true to their original personality:

> 'One thing that I appreciated very early on with them is that they just have this amazing culture . . . they managed to build this really strong brand through hiring really good people and having this really unique culture – you go through the doors there and everyone is working hard but they're friendly and it's chatty and it's fun . . .'.

> 'innocent – they have perhaps defined for this decade the more people-centric entrepreneurship, creating a culture and lifestyle and being in touch with your ethical values and that sort of thing. Even outside drinks people see them as a model for that.'

> Slater, 2007[5]

innocent had in fact developed a formal set of company values during 2005 (see Exhibit 18.7):

- be natural
- be entrepreneurial
- be commercial
- be generous
- be responsible.

These values were used in the initial assessment of job applicants. In the induction programme for all new staff, Richard Reed and Jamie Mitchell separately ran two sessions on their interpretation of the innocent values. The values were used in company decision-making and in staff appraisals. A crucial feature was that innocent encouraged all staff to contribute examples of where they had seen/lived the innocent values. This story telling became increasingly important as the company grew and staff had less face-time with the founders (there were five levels of staff in the company and more employees worked in overseas offices).

Values Put to the Test

In early summer 2007, innocent faced what Jamie Mitchell described as their 'most difficult decision so far', whether to trial the sale of innocent smoothies in 80 McDonalds restaurants in the

EXHIBIT 18.7 innocent's PRINCIPLES AND VALUES

 **innocent**

core principle

We have one core principle which we make all decisions

Create a business we can be proud of

a.k.a The Nursing Home Test

 **innocent**

company values

This breaks down into five simple values.
Each reflects something we currently are and increasingly want to be

Be natural	Be entrepreneurial	Be responsible	Be commercial	Be generous
Keep it warm, friendly and human, put people first	Chase opportunities and be responsive	Be true to our principles, and do what we believe is right	Create growth and profit for us and our customers	With feedback
Make 100% natural, delicious, healthy stuff, 100% of the time	Be creative and challenge the status quo	To be conscious of the consequences of our actions, in both the short and long term	Be tough, but fair	With our time for others
Treat others, especially our drinkers, as we want to be treated.	Do it better than anyone else, and have fun doing it	To leave things a little better than we find them, and to encourage others to join us too	Think clearly, act decisively and keep the main thing, the main thing	With rewards when people deliver
				With charitable support

northeast of England. The decision was debated in two open meetings where all innocent staff were asked to express their opinion. It aroused intense debate on the innocent blog and critics in the media asked: 'innocent guilty of sell-out?' (*Marketing Week*, 10 May 2007) and 'the end of innocence?' (*The Independent*, 11 June 2007). Both inside and outside the company, critics of the decision – which had been in favour of the trial – argued that it was wrong to associate the wholesome innocent brand with a multinational company that was widely blamed for unsustainable practices. Proponents of the tie-up argued that they were creating a healthy option for consumers and that it was better to offer McDonalds' customers the opportunity to have a fruit drink with no added sugar rather than the typical carbonated drink. Reed and other innocent leaders personally phoned many of the on-line critics to explain the rationale for the decision to distribute through McDonalds.[6] In 2008, the trial was extended to the southeast. There was further negative publicity in autumn 2007, with complaints to the UK Advertising Standards Authority (ASA) that innocent advertising was over-claiming the detoxifying properties of its smoothies. The advert was swiftly withdrawn.

Before the furore over the McDonalds trial and the ASA complaint, Richard Reed had told a journalist:

> I don't expect a single person to buy our smoothies for any other reason than that they taste better and are better quality. The second we think people will buy them because we give 10% of profits to charity or are carbon neutral is a mistake.[7]

He added, however*:*

> I think we are more innocent today than we ever have been but we're a thousand miles off being as good as we want to be.
>
> *Ethical Consumer Magazine*

Nevertheless, the ASA complaint and the McDonalds trials illustrated the risks and the opportunities contingent to innocent's strong social and environmental values.

The innocent team might be forgiven for daring to wonder if, in the long term, they could build a major company, like Cadbury and Rowntree, both of which had started with a small shop and a similar pure product idea ('introducing pure chocolate, unadulterated with starch or other additives' (Bradley, 2007, p. 4) in 19th century England. More immediately, the furore over the decision to trial smoothie sales in McDonalds showed that innocent was now a high profile company. With their European expansion they needed to ensure that the 'statement of innocent values' was fully embraced and lived throughout the organization, particularly as more employees were now working for overseas offices, where there was no day-to-day contact with the founders. How should the values be implemented and monitored? Would values continue to create value as the business became increasingly international? And values aside, what were the challenges innocent faced relative to European expansion and competitive pressure from PepsiCo and own-label supermarket brands? This will be ever more important after the Spring 2008 announcement that the innocent founders had sold a minority stake in the company to Coca Cola in order to finance future continental Europe expansion of the business.

NOTES

1. The case is intended to be used as a basis for class discussion rather than to illustrate either effective or ineffective handling of an administrative situation.

2. Allen, P. (2007) Your Ethical Business: How to Plan, Start and Succeed in a Company with a Conscience, p. 209 (ngo.media.org).

3. Cause marketing or cause-related marketing is 'a commercial activity by which business and charities or causes form a partnership with each other to market an image, product or service to mutual benefit' (Adkins, 1999).

4. Jamie Mitchell joined innocent after completing his MBA at London Business School, where he had led a student team that wrote a strategy case study on innocent.

5. See website at www.shell-livewire.org.

6. See http://innocentdrinks.typepad.com/innocent_drinks/2007/05/to_burger_or_no_1.html, where the blog provides an overview of the arguments.

7. Allen, P. (2007) Your Ethical Business: How to Plan, Start and Succeed in a Company with a Conscience, p. 21 (ngo.media.org).

REFERENCES

Adkins, S. (1999) *Cause-related Marketing: Who Cares Wins*, Butterworth-Heinemann.

Bradley, I. (2007) *Enlightened Entrepreneurs*, Lion.

Slater, D. (2007) The Changing Face of UK Entrepreneurism, A Shell Livewire – London School Of Economics Report, June.

CHAPTER NINETEEN

Waste Concern: Turning a Problem into a Resource[1]

Johanna Mair and Jordan Mitchell, IESE Business School

INTRODUCTION

> Waste is merely raw material in the wrong place.
>
> Frederick A. Talbot, Journalist, Millions from Waste, 1920

In late September 2005, co-founders of Waste Concern, Iftekhar Enayetullah and Abu Hasnat Md. Maqsood Sinha, were looking at a pile of waste at the Matuail landfill site on the outskirts of Dhaka, Bangladesh. For 10 years, Waste Concern had followed a decentralized composting model whereby each composting site was a small-scale operation processing three tons of organic waste per day. However, the Matuail site was different from past models because it would be a dual-purpose operation consisting of a gas recovery site and a 700-ton per day composting plant. Under the United Nations Clean Development Mechanism (CDM), the project would be eligible to earn tradable certificates for US$11 per ton of reduced methane gas, making it the first in the world to garner credits through composting waste (see www.wasteconcern.org, 2004).

Although Enayetullah and Sinha were elated at the recent approval from the United Nations to build the site, they still had to overcome one key hurdle – getting approval from the Dhaka City Corporation (DCC) for access to the land and waste. Enayetullah and Sinha believed there were three alternatives:

- follow through with the original plan whereby DCC would supply both the land and waste;
- purchase the land for the composting site and rely on the DCC for a waste supply;
- purchase the land and take on the responsibility of waste collection themselves.

Each option had its benefits and drawbacks, and Enayetullah and Sinha were weighing up the financial, social and environmental aspects. A number of questions were at the fore. How could they benefit from transferring their experience between small-scale and large-scale operations? How should they organize themselves to best support the new initiative? How could they manage the relationship with the DCC, their international partners and the citizens of Dhaka?

BANGLADESH

Located between India and Burma, at that time Bangladesh had a land area of 144 000 km^2 and a population of over 144 million people (*CIA World Factbook*, 2006). The country had the ninth largest population in the world with one of the highest population densities at 1000 people per km^2. Population in urban areas such as the nation's capital, Dhaka, exceeded 18 000 people per km^2 in some areas. The city was home to 11.3 million people, making it the 11th largest city in the world. Dhaka was expected to grow to 21.1 million people by 2015 (Country Paper Bangladesh, 2004, p. 3). It was estimated that approximately 25% of the country's population lived in an urban area. This was expected to increase to 40% within 20 years.

Total GDP was estimated at US$299.9 billion and GDP per capita was ranked 175th out of 232 countries (*CIA World Factbook*, 2006). Approximately half of the population lived below the poverty line. Observers cited the central impediments to growth as: extreme monsoons and cyclones creating climatic instability, poor transportation and communication infrastructure, insufficient energy sources and inefficient government. See Figure 19.1 for a map and more facts about the country.

Agriculture in Bangladesh

63% of the labour force was employed in the agricultural sector compared to 11% in industry and 26% in services. The primary agricultural products were rice, jute, tea, wheat, sugarcane, potatoes, tobacco, spices and fruit.

Only 17% of the country's soil was suitable for growing crops. Soil fertility was not only affected by improper waste management, but also through the use of 4 million tons of chemical fertilizer per year, which hardened the soil and dried the moisture from the earth. Soil fertility was critical to the government's plan to increase crop output to ensure foodstuffs for the country's growing population.

WASTE MANAGEMENT IN BANGLADESH'S CAPITAL DHAKA

The government-run Dhaka City Corporation (DCC) was responsible for all local governmental policy and management within the Dhaka metropolitan area, which covered 360 km^2 and included six million residents of Dhaka megacity's 11.3 million. Each day, these six million residents generated about 3,500 tons of waste (Waste Concern, 2004, slide 6). This compared to over 17 000 tons per day of waste generated throughout the country (Waste Concern, 2004, slide 5). In Dhaka, approximately 70–80% of the waste was organic and the remainder was paper, plastic, glass and other human-made materials.

Nationally, the country did not have a consistent waste recycling programme and waste was disposed of in nearly any area – on the streets, in pits, in front of people's homes or in the best case, in large cement containers. Large deposits of waste exposed the population to over 40 diseases (Waste Concern, 2004, slide 5). It created insufferable odour and seeped into the land affecting soil fertility and ground water. During the monsoon season, waste was carried by extreme floods into the city. Mosquitoes and flies reproduced in waste and carried diseases to humans and other animals. In addition to the extreme health hazards, the physical mass of waste caused traffic problems on roads. Large deposits of waste also emitted harmful greenhouse gases (GHG)[2] into the atmosphere. It was estimated that Dhaka had an emission potential of 0.76 million tons of CO_2 gas per year (Zurbrügg *et al.*, 2004). See Figure 19.2 for photos of Dhaka's waste challenges.

People

Population	144,319,628
Age structure	
0-14 years old	33.1%
15-64 years old	63.5%
+65 years old	3.4%
Median age	21.87
Population growth %	2.1%

Economic

GDP	299.9 billion
GDP growth rate	5.2%
GDP/capita	2100
GDP by sector	
Agriculture	20.5%
Industry	26.7%
Services	52.8%
Inflation	6.7%
Unemployment	2.5%
Public debt as % of GDP	46.1%

in US$ except where otherwise noted.

Industry

Agricultural products	Rice, jute, tea, wheat, sugarcane, potatoes, tobacco
Industries	Cotton textiles, jute, garments, tea processing, newsprint, cement, chemical fertilizer, light engineering, sugar
Industrial product growth rate	6.7%
Electricity production	17.42 billion kWh
Oil production	6,825 bbl/day
Oil consumption	84,000 bbl/day
Natural gas - production	9.9 billion cu m
Current account balance	-591 million
Exports	$9.372 billion
Exports partners	US 22.4%, Germany 14.5%, UK 11.2%, France 6.9%, Italy 4%, India 15.1%, China 12.5%, Singapore 7.5%, Kuwait 5.5%, Japan 5.3%, Hong Kong 4.5%
Imports partners	
Currency	Taka (BDT)
F/X rate to US$	64.26
F/X rate to euro	

Figure 19.1 Information about Bangladesh

Source: CIA World Fact Book, www.cia.gov, Accessed 1 February 2006.

Waste Collection

The DCC was responsible for collecting all solid waste. However, due to its human, technological and financial resources, the DCC collected only 37% of all solid waste, even though it spent 50% of its operating budget on solid waste management. All waste collected by the DCC was piled into trucks and disposed of in low-lying areas outside of the city district. Observers believed that the collection process was inefficient given that the waste was handled four to five times before being

Figure 19.2 Dhaka's waste problem

Source: Company documents

disposed of. The cost of collecting one ton of waste by the DCC was estimated at BDT670 (Bangladesh Taka) (equivalent to US$11.26 at that time). The cost of the entire waste management process (from collection through to landfill operation) by the DCC was estimated at BDT2045 (US$38) per ton. The price of collecting waste was exacerbated by the habit of many dwellers of leaving their waste in front of their homes instead of taking it to designated concrete containers for pickup.

In addition to the DCC, individuals known as Tokais or informal waste collectors, sought plastic, glass or paper and attempted to sell the waste to recycling factories for cash. Approximately 120 000 people were involved in informal waste collection and collected about 15% of the inorganic waste. Also, small companies had begun offering services for house-to-house collection in exchange for money, which was more prevalent in affluent areas of the city.

Waste Disposal

The Matuail landfill was the only official dumping site in the DCC district, which would be completely exhausted by the end of 2006. With strains on the land due to overpopulation, it was unlikely that another official dumping site would be opened. This led the DCC and other waste collectors to dump residuals in any available area.

HISTORY OF WASTE CONCERN

While conducting postgraduate research in early 1994, A.H. Md. Maqsood Sinha and Iftekhar Enayetullah had the idea of launching a non-governmental (NGO) research organization aimed at improving the environment by encouraging waste recycling in Bangladesh. Sinha, an architect and urban planner, met Enayetullah, a professional civil engineer and urban planner, while both were postgraduate students. As part of their postgraduate research, they set up a model of waste management whereby solid waste was collected and composted. The compost would then be used as a substitute for chemical fertilizer. The pair believed that the concept could be put into practice and sought support from different governmental agencies offering consultancy services for free. However, governmental officials did not support the project and Enayetullah and Sinha decided to establish their own NGO in 1995 in order to launch the first pilot project. The aim of the organization was to promote the idea of converting waste into a resource. The first project was directed at: 'developing a low-cost technique for [the] composting of municipal solid waste' (Zurbrügg et al., 2004). Enayetullah commented:

> In 1994, we tried hard to convince different government agencies to initiate the project by offering free consultancy services but they were all sceptical . . . We believe that waste should be considered as a resource, rather than just a problem and it can be managed in a decentralized manner with public-private-community partnership. That's why in 1995, we took the alternative course of demonstration of our model to convince different social groups. (Waste Concern, 2004, slides 13–14)

Besides the scepticism in the government, Sinha and Enayetullah faced other barriers. They did not have access to appropriate waste treatment technology nor did they have any land to launch their pilot project. The lack of knowledge of waste recycling combined with no official policy or framework further complicated their attempts to get the project off the ground. The pair sought seed money and financing, but for a year were unsuccessful in garnering support. Eventually, they convinced the Lion's Club Dhaka North to donate 1000 m² of land in the area of Mirpur for a three-month period. Sinha reflected, 'The Lion's Club was very hesitant to give us land, because they were very afraid of creating a lot of odour.'

After getting the project operational in less than three months, Sinha and Enayetullah demonstrated that the odour from the site was not problematic. The Lion's Club gave them permission to continue housing the project on Lion's Club land. They used the project as a demonstration site and showed it extensively to individuals from government, private companies and the community. Sinha and Enayetullah estimated that the Mirpur project alone reduced the cost of the DCC by US$15 085 annually (Zurbrügg *et al.*, 2004). This represented an 80% reduction in per ton management costs for waste for the DCC in the project area of Waste Concern.

In 2000, Sinha and Enayetullah set up a for-profit consultancy arm of Waste Concern, allowing them to generate revenues to fund Waste Concern's not-for-profit research and development division. As of the fall of 2005, this dual structure was still in place. See Figure 19.3 for the co-founders' CVs.

IFTEKHAR ENAYETULLAH
Date of Birth: August 18, 1967

Education

Masters Degree in Urban and Regional Planning with specialization in urban waste and environmental management from Bangladesh University of Engineering and Technology (BUET), Dhaka.

Experience

- Co-founder and Director of Waste Concern – conceptualized, designed and implemented the community-based decentralized composting model, using public-private-community partnerships approach
- Member of the Institution of Engineers Bangladesh (IEB), Bangladesh Institute of Planners (BIP) and Building Partnership Development for Water and Sanitation of United Kingdom
- Founding member of WasteNet in Bangladesh
- Editor of a quarterly newsletter on waste management and recycling in Bangladesh
- Served as a Member of the Expert Committee on Clinical Waste Management constituted by the Government of Bangladesh
- More than forty publications to his credit, including scientific papers, articles, fact sheets, manuals, reports, recycling and urban environmental management
- A professional civil engineer and urban planner by training

Awards and Recognition

- Outstanding Social Entrepreneur by the Schwab Foundation of Switzerland for the year 2003
- Tech Museum Awards 2003. Selected as Tech Laureate by the Tech Museum of USA for developing technology benefiting humanity
- Outstanding Engineers' Award 2003 from the Institution of Engineers, Bangladesh (IEB)
- Professional Excellence Award 2003 as an engineer from the Daily Star – a prominent newspaper of Bangladesh

---

Figure 19.3 CVs of co-founders

Source: Company documents

- United Nations Poverty Eradication Award 2002 from entire Asia and the Pacific region
- Fast Company magazine's first ever Fast 50 – fifty champions of innovation for the year 2002
- Elected as an Ashoka Fellow in Ashoka Innovators for the Public of USA in 2000

ABU HASNAT MD. MAQSOOD SINHA
Date of Birth: April 4, 1963

Education

Masters Degree in Urban and Regional Planning with specialization in environment, urban waste management and recycling from Asian Institute of Technology (AIT), Bangkok, Thailand

Experience

- Co-founder and Director of Waste Concern – conceptualized, designed and implemented the community-based decentralized composting model, using public-private-community partnerships approach
- Member of the Institution of Engineers Bangladesh (IEB), Bangladesh Institute of Planners (BIP) and Building Partnership Development for Water and Sanitation of United Kingdom
- Founding member of WasteNet in Bangladesh
- Editor of a quarterly newsletter on waste management and recycling in Bangladesh
- Member of the Local Consultative Group (LCG), an environmental subgroup in the field of waste and solid waste management and environment
- Served as a Member of the Expert Committee on Clinical Waste Management constituted by the Government of Bangladesh
- More than forty publications to his credit, including scientific papers, articles, fact sheets, manuals, reports, recycling and urban environmental management
- An urban planner and architect by profession

Awards and Recognition

- Outstanding Social Entrepreneur by the Schwab Foundation of Switzerland for the year 2003
- Tech Museum Awards 2003. Selected as Tech Laureate by the Tech Museum of USA for developing technology benefiting humanity
- Outstanding Engineers' Award 2003 from the Institution of Engineers, Bangladesh (IEB).
- Professional Excellence Award 2003 as an engineer from the Daily Star – a prominent newspaper of Bangladesh
- United Nations Poverty Eradication Award 2002 from entire Asia and the Pacific region
- Fast Company magazine's first ever Fast 50 – fifty champions of innovation for the year 2002
- Elected as an Ashoka Fellow in Ashoka Innovators for the Public of USA in 2000

Figure 19.3 (*Continued*)

THE WASTE CONCERN MODEL OF DECENTRALIZED COMPOSTING

Waste Concern's model integrated house-to-house waste collection, composting and marketing the compost as a fertilizer. The operation revolved around a small-scale, decentralized composting plant – each plant was set up to process three tons of waste per day.

Depending on the income level, households paid BDT 10–20 (US$0.17–0.34) to Waste Concern per month. Waste was collected by one, two or three Waste Concern employees who rode on rickshaws with 1.18 m³ capacity. Each rickshaw served 300–400 households and the revenue from households paid for the salaries of the collectors. For each three-ton plant, there were 20 workers: nine workers for house-to-house collection and 11 people at the plant, including the plant manager.

After the waste was collected, the rickshaw driver and collectors took the waste to the composting site. All waste was sorted and all recyclable products such as glass, plastic and metals were separated and stored in a separate area. Three tons of organic waste yielded 750 kg of compost per day. The process of converting organic waste to saleable compost took 55 days: 40 days to produce the compost and 15 days for the compost to mature.

Waste Concern used the Indonesian Composting Method – all waste was piled in large heaps on top of a wooden structure and was turned every four to five days. The waste piles were under a covered shed, which protected the compost workers from the sun and rain. In order to turn solid waste to compost, a temperature of between 55 and 65° C was optimum. Workers used long bamboo sticks to turn over the waste. Workers also watered the waste heaps, which gave the bacteria a new food source (Sinha and Enayetullah, 1999, pp. 8–9). Figure 19.4 shows the process and pictures of the operation.

Once the compost had matured, it was sold to MAP Agro for BDT 2.5 (US$0.04) per kg. MAP Agro then enriched the compost and sold it through its parent company's (ALPHA Agro) extensive distribution network at prices from BDT 6 (US$0.10) to BDT 12 (US$0.20).

Revenues were split at 30% from house-to-house collection and 70% through the sale of composted materials (Hiller, 2002, p. 12). Waste Concern's operating costs comprised raw materials used in composting, the salaries of the workers (both the waste collectors and the plant staff) and utilities. Each three-ton plant brought in total revenues of approximately BDT 741 000 (US$12 449) and spent approximately BDT 551 200 (US$9260) per year. All surpluses were used to fund compost testing at the government's laboratory (US$2500 per year). The remainder was invested back into the site to maintain the building and supply uniforms for the workers.

The fixed costs for establishing a new three-ton plant were BDT 1 008 000 (US$16 934). This included: the construction costs of the sorting platform, the composting shed with drainage, an office, a toilet and a storage area for the recovered recyclable products. Waste Concern relied solely on the donation of land from third parties and did not include the value of land in its fixed costs. Each plant offered a payback in 23 months. Figure 19.5 shows the key revenues and costs of a three-ton plant.

The Replication of the Decentralized Small-Scale Model

In 1997, the Regional Urban Development Office-South Asia agreed to offer support and further test the model by scaling up the activity of Waste Concern in Dhaka. A year later, the Ministry of Environment and Forest of the Government of Bangladesh under the Sustainable Environmental Management Program supported by the United Nations Development Program (UNDP) requested that Waste Concern roll out the model to five communities within Dhaka. The DCC and Public Works Department, however, did not come forth with land, which led Sinha and Enayetullah to

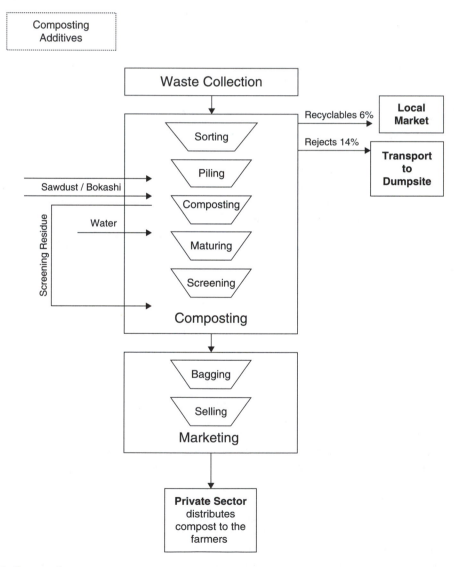

Figure 19.4 Composting process

Source: Company documents

Digital Representation of Decentralized Composting Site

Collection Sorting Piling

Composting Composting (Turning) Bagging

Figure 19.4 (*Continued*)

more demonstrations. Finally, the DCC and Public Works provided suitable land plots. Sinha talked about the obstacles:

> The single biggest obstacle for the model of community based decentralized composting project was availability of land in the city for such facilities. Public-private-community partnership and the concept of the 4 R's (reduce, reuse, recycle and recovery of waste) . . . were absent in Bangladesh before our intervention.

> Sinha and Enayetullah, 2002

Annual Financials of a Typical 3-ton Plant

	BDT	US$
F/X Rate		*59.524*
Revenue from House-to-House Collection	141,000	2,369
Revenue from Sale of Compost	600,000	10,080
Total Revenue	**741,000**	**12,449**
Total Costs		
Raw Materials	96,000	1,613
Salaries		
Waste Collectors' Salaries	141,000	2,369
Composting Plant Workers' Salaries	132,000	2,218
Plant Manager	78,000	1,310
Total Salaries	351,000	5,897
Electricity, Water and Maintenance	104,220	1,751
Total Costs	551,220	9,260
Total Surplus/(Deficit)	**189,780**	**3,188**

Major Assumptions for 3 ton/Day Plant

Land Required / Plant (Katha)	7	
Fixed Cost / Plant *	1,008,000	16,934
Operating Cost / Plant **	300,000	5,040
Total Labourers for Composting Only/Plant ***	4	
Total Labourers (Including Collectors)	20	
Compost Produced (Daily) (kg)	750	
Expected Revenue form Sale of Compost ****	600,000	10,080
Pay Back Period (Months)	23	

Figure 19.5 Revenues and costs of a composting plant

*Without Land Cost/Rent
**Operating Cost Excludes Cost-Neutral Collectors and Raw Material Costs.
***Labourers Required for Composting Purpose Only.
****From 1 Ton of Organic Waste 250 kg of Fine Compost Can Be Produced.

Source: Company documents

In 1999, Waste Concern began talking to the country's pre-eminent fertilizer supplier, MAP Agro (a sister concern of ALPHA Agro), to purchase the organic fertilizer being produced at Waste Concern's composting plants. Initially, MAP Agro was uncertain that local farmers would adopt organic fertilizer as part of their growing techniques. Waste Concern convinced MAP Agro by comparing the superior quality of crops grown with organic fertilizer in place of chemical fertilizer. Eventually,

MAP Agro agreed to purchase all Waste Concern's organic compost output and was the first in the country to begin marketing organic compost.

In 2000, Waste Concern successfully rolled out the decentralized model to five communities in Dhaka city. With greater visibility, representatives from other Bangladeshi cities approached Waste Concern to see if the same concept could be rolled out to more sites. Enayetullah stated:

> We thought originally that we would be able to roll out the decentralized model and replicate it our-selves to other sites. But, it was not possible to do from a manpower perspective. If we had tried to do it all ourselves, it would have resulted in major delays in implementing it. With these types of projects the major barrier is the financing. We realized that if we could get the financing then we could supply the technology.

In looking for financing, Waste Concern approached several international banks and other in-ternational organizations. However, Waste Concern was unable to secure funds. International banks were concerned that the organization in its not-for-profit structure would not be able to pay back the bank loan. Development organizations supported similar projects but for piloting purposes only. This led Waste Concern to look for other sources of funding. After several pres-entations from Waste Concern and multiple levels of approval, the Department of Public Health Engineering of the Government of Bangladesh secured funding from UNICEF and replicated the Waste Concern model in 14 locations in 2002 (Waste Concern, 2004, slide 70). In 2004, another 20 sites were approved to be implemented throughout Bangladesh. All projects were organized as a three-way partnership: Waste Concern supplied the technology and know-how; the Bang-ladeshi government, UNICEF, CIDA (Canadian International Development Agency) and SDC (Sustainable Development Commission) funded the initiative; and the private sector marketed the final composted fertilizer.

Sinha and Enayetullah dedicated 50% of their time to research and development activities under the not-for-profit arm of Waste Concern. The other 50% was directed at the for-profit waste con-sultancy. Enayetullah stated: 'We use the consultancy to generate revenues to fund the not-for-profit research and development arm.'

By 2005, the government of Bangladesh actively encouraged farmers to increase their utilization of organic compost. Compost was cheaper than chemical fertilizer and most agreed that it produced superior crops. The acceptance of organic fertilizer encouraged three other companies to include organic fertilizers as part of their product portfolios. As of 2005, MAP Agro was the market leader followed by Northern Agro, Faruk Fertilizer and Fuvid Agro Ltd. Enayetullah stated: 'The demand for organic fertilizer is growing and there's currently a problem with supply. Now, with four com-panies all offering organic fertilizers, this is good for fair competition.'

Waste Concern's model was recognized internationally as an efficient and cost-effective way of using waste. The model was being replicated in Vietnam and Sri Lanka. It was also lauded for providing employment for unskilled labourers. Sinha and Enayetullah were honoured by becoming Ashoka Fellows in 2000, and won numerous awards such as the United Nation's 'Poverty Eradica-tion Award' in 2002, the 'Fast Company Champions of Innovation' in 2002, the 'Technology for

Humanity' from the US Tech Museum in 2003 and 'Outstanding Social Entrepreneurs' from the Schwab Foundation of Switzerland in 2003.

CDM PROPOSAL FOR LANDFILL GAS EXTRACTION SITE AT MATUAIL, DHAKA

Throughout 2003, Sinha and Enayetullah had the idea of increasing the scale of the three-ton composting plant. As Enayetullah stated:

> Small is beautiful, but you need to have scale. The small-scale decentralized three-ton composting plant is great for small and medium sized cities. However, in Dhaka, it's probably best to have a larger centralized composting site. And, with a larger site, you have a real opportunity with tradable certificates. Without trading certificates, the opportunity of creating a centralized 700-ton per day composting site would not be feasible. Also, with large centralized sites, you can transfer the learning to smaller decentralized locations.

Waste Concern submitted a proposal to the United Nations, which would allow the organization to earn tradable certificates called Certified Emission Reductions (CERs). Under the programme known as the Clean Development Mechanism (CDM), nations were able to buy and sell CERs to hit their specific Kyoto Protocol emission reduction targets.[3] Sinha and Enayetullah's idea was to use the existing landfill site in Matuail – an area 7 km from Dhaka – to recover methane gas from the 5m high landfill pile. They also wanted to use the land to build a large-scale centralized composting plant.

In 2004, the Waste Concern team began conversations with the Dutch company World Wide Recycling BV (WWR) to develop jointly the landfill gas recovery site. WWR was a for-profit company that acted as an investor and operator by partnering with private and public enterprises in the creation of decentralized recycling centres (see Exhibit 19.1 for more information). In September 2004, WWR and Waste Concern signed a memorandum of understanding to form a special purpose company and put forward a proposal for consideration by the United Nations CDM Executive Board. WWR would provide all of the financing and Waste Concern would supply the local knowledge and technology and seek Bangladeshi government approval. Both parties would engineer the site and make the landfill site operational. The organizations would be able to sell the CERs for US$11 per ton of reduced methane gas.

During 2005, both organizations met extensively with United Nations representatives, foreign and local government officials, academics, engineers, waste experts, electricity operators and local residents. In making their presentations to various stakeholders, the team presented the following benefits:

- environmental – capture 50% of the landfill gas emitted from the Matuail waste disposal site, which would reduce greenhouse gases and reduce the risk of onsite fires;
- economic – foreign capital inflow from WWR and potentially other sources;
- social – improved health conditions due to the reduction of gases and the creation of jobs for local residents (www.unfccc.org, 2004, pp. 2–3).

EXHIBIT 19.1 INFORMATION ON WORLD WIDE RECYCLING BV (WWR) – EXCERPTS FROM BROCHURE

World Wide Recycling BV (WWR) is a company that aims to introduce the Recycling Centre Concept worldwide, with an emphasis on Latin America, South-east Asia and former Eastern Europe. The company is owned by Mr. Jan Boone, founder and main shareholder of VAR BV.

Conditions for Success

WWR is convinced that a Public Private Partnership is the most suitable model for operating a recycling centre. After all, waste treatment is a public task that can be executed more efficiently and at lower cost in cooperation with private entities. There are many definitions of a PPP. The one that fits the WWR concept best is:

'. . . an institutional relationship between the public sector and members of the private-for-profit and/or the private-not-for-profit sector, in which the various public and private actors participate in defining the objectives, the methods and the implementation of an agreement of cooperation.'

Investor and Operator

WWR's objective is to participate as an investor as well as an operator. Through the use of its resources, WWR can financially engineer projects, thus underlining its commitment. At the same time, WWR can warrant the performance of the operation by acting as an operator in the project.

The Recycling Centre Concept

The Principle

A recycling centre is a landfill in combination with several recycling installations, each tuned to recover a specific fraction of the incoming waste. Various separate installations can be applied, depending on specific needs and circumstances. In developing a recycling centre, a modular approach is obvious: with reference to local circumstances the recycling centre may start with a single installation, after which the concept may be developed in full over a period of years.

The Set-up: Decentralized

WWR strongly advocates a decentralized set-up, with recycling centres located close to waste producing sources. In this set-up transportation of waste is being minimized. The Recycling Centre Concept warrants a working method that keeps the inconvenience of smell, visual distraction and attracted animals to a minimum. For the implementation of new projects, high standards will be applied. A new recycling centre can easily be built near an existing landfill, extending its lifetime and improving the environmental and social situation.

Source: World Wide Recycling, www.wwrgroup.com, brochure, accessed 6 February, 2006

On 17 September, 2005, the landfill gas recovery project and the composting plant were accepted by the United Nations CDM initiative.

Operations

The site would have two main areas: the landfill gas recovery area and the composting area.

Landfill Gas Recovery

In the landfill recovery zone, methane gas emitted naturally from the decomposing landfill, would be captured and turned into electricity through a gas-powered engine. The electricity would then be used by local power utilities. The teams planned to reshape the current landfill and introduce proper land-filling techniques with daily cover of waste as well as a leachate collection and treatment facility to reduce ground water pollution. These actions were aimed at extending the site's lifetime to 2021. The site would require extraction equipment including vertical wells, piping, a condensate separator and compressors. The gas utilization equipment included a flare, dedicated gas-engines, an electric generator and an electric grid connection (www.unfccc.org, 2004, pp. 5–6).

In the first seven-year crediting period, WWR and Waste Concern predicted that the project would recover 50% of the methane gas. This would allow them to convert 566 000 tons of CO_2 equivalents (methane gas) from the landfill gas recovery project alone (www.unfccc.org, 2004, p. 2). The site would have an electricity production capacity of 3–6 megawatts (MW). In the first year, the site would produce 6625 MW hours increasing to over 16 000 MW hours by 2010. Figure 19.6 shows a diagram and more details of the project.

Composting

The composting plant would also be designed to reduce methane gas by avoiding waste land-filling and performing aerobic composting. Waste Concern and WWR developed a new methodology to calculate the reduction of methane emission by composting that was approved by the UNFCCC (United Nations Framework Convention on Climate Change). The compost would be turned into organic fertilizer and made available for sale to the country's four fertilizer companies. The composting plant was significantly different to Waste Concern's small-scale plants. Whereas Waste Concern's smaller plants processed three tons of solid waste per day, the proposed site at Matuail would process 700 tons of solid waste per day. It was estimated that 624 813 tons of CO_2 equivalents would be reduced by composting 700 tons/day of solid waste in the composting plant.

Finances

The total investment to get the project operational was US$10 million. Approximately US$4.9 million was for the establishment of the composting area and US$3.5 million for the gas extraction and electricity generation portion of the project. Using a 12% discount rate to reflect commercial lending fees in Bangladesh, the team had calculated that the gas extraction portion of the site would create a negative net present value of US$–4.2 million over 15 years without CERs. However, with CERs, the project would produce a positive net present value. Under this scenario, revenues would be generated from the sale of electricity only.

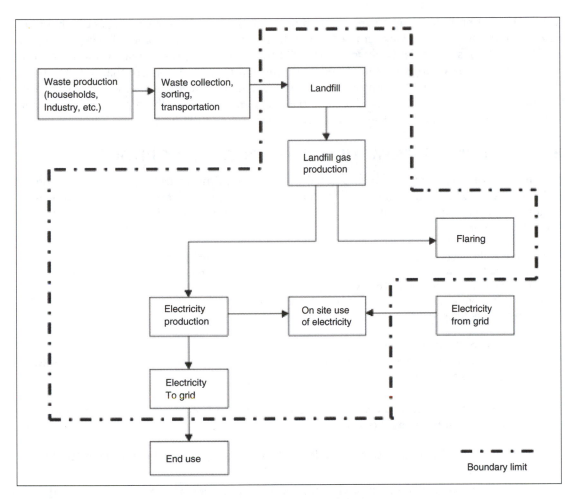

Details of CDM Project

Emission reductions in first crediting period

Year	Net electricity delivered to grid by combusting extracted methane in gas engines MWh	CERs (net) related to prevented electricity generation in the grid (elsewhere) tons (1000 kg)
2006	6625	4185
2007	13976	8829
2008	14723	9301
2009	15492	9787
2010	16284	10287

Proposal to CDM, p. 31.

Figure 19.6 Diagram of landfill area

Source: Project Design Document Form, Proposal to CDM, p. 14

WWR would contribute the financing for both projects. Both sides were seeking additional funding in the form of a grant or long-term loan from the Netherlands Development Finance Company (FMO), which was a special bank set up in 1970 by the Dutch government for the purpose of assisting developing countries. FMO carefully scrutinized projects to ensure that they fell under strict guidelines such as public-private involvement, corporate governance, environmental details and social policies. The FMO offered a grant to a maximum of 45% of the project on a maximum project cost of €45 million (US$54 million) (www.unfccc.org, 2004, p. 6).

SEEKING APPROVAL FROM THE DCC AND POTENTIAL OPTIONS

Even though Waste Concern had been given the green light by the CDM Board of the Government of Bangladesh in 2004 (see Figure 19.7 for a copy of the approval letter), they were still waiting for approval from the municipal DCC. The DCC owned and operated the Matuail landfill site. Enayetullah commented:

> We were authorized to go ahead with the project from the national government, but then the municipality did not give their authorization. They were a little concerned that they were handing over control of the landfill site to us. That was the point where we said, 'maybe we can separate the landfill site from the composting activity and change our approach'. It's not necessary to keep the landfill and composting site together. We would just have to think of another plan.

Enayetullah and Sinha made the decision to continue seeking approval from the DCC for the landfill recovery site because they needed an established landfill site with a minimum of 5–8 m³ of waste in order to capture sufficient gas.

The major question was what should be done with the composting site. Enayetullah and Sinha believed there were three central options:

- continue with the original plan whereby DCC would supply the land and the waste for the composting site;
- Waste Concern would purchase the land for the composting site and the DCC would supply the waste;
- Waste Concern would purchase the land for the composting site and look after the collection of waste.

Option 1: DCC to Supply the Land and Waste

Under this option, the DCC would supply both the land and waste for the composting site. WWR and Waste Concern would be responsible for designing, constructing and operating the site. The fixed cost of constructing the composting site was estimated at US$4.9 million and annual operating costs were projected to be US$1.22 million. Revenues from the sale of compost were predicted to be US$3.11 million per year and the sale of tradable certificates would bring in US$560 000 per year. In exchange for using the DCC's land and waste, Waste Concern would pay a 20% royalty fee on the overall revenues of the composting site per year.

Enayetullah and Sinha predicted a delay to the project of 7–12 months before receiving approval from the DCC. In addition, Enayetullah and Sinha were uncertain of changes to the contract in the future.

এই জমি ও গৃহের লিখিত হয়

Government of the People's Republic of Bangladesh
Department of Environment
Paribesh Bhaban, E/16 Agagaon,
Sher-e-Bangla Nagar, Dhaka 1207
www.doc-bd.org

Ref.: Paribesh/Tech. (Int. Con.)/350/2003/2632   **Date:** 16/09/2004.

Sub.: Host Country Approval to two CDM projects (1) "Landfill Gas Extraction and Utilization at Matuail Landfill Site in Dhaka and (2) Composting of Organic Waste in Dhaka" of World Wide Recycling BV of the Netherlands and Waste Concern of Bangladesh.

This is to inform you that the Project Idea/Concept Note and Project Design Document for two CDM projects (1) "Landfill Gas Extraction and Utilization at Matuail Landfill Site in Dhaka and (2) Composting of Organic Waste in Dhaka" of World Wide Recycling BV of the Netherlands and Waste Concern of Bangladesh, was considered by the Designated National Authority (DNA) in its Meeting of 08 August 2004. The DNA approved the above mentioned projects. The DNA confirms that:

i.   The projects will contribute to sustainable Development in Bangladesh.

ii.   This approval is for the voluntary participation in the proposed CDM project activity.

It may be further noted that the Government of Bangladesh has ratified the Kyoto Protocol on 22 October 2001.

(Mohammad Reazuddin)
Director (Technical 1)
&
Member Secretary
National CDM Committee

Mr. Maarteen (J.M.W.) Van Dijk
Managing Director
World Wide Recycling B.V.
Rijksstratweg 102, 7383 AV Voorst,
P.O. Box 90, 7390, AB, Twello,
The Netherlands.

Figure 19.7 Letter of approval from the government of Bangladesh

Source: Company documents

Option 2: Purchase the Land for Composting and DCC to Supply the Waste

The second option was to purchase a plot of land for the composting site but use the waste collected by the DCC. Enayetullah and Sinha estimated that the cost of a suitable piece of land would be US$514 000. The fixed cost of constructing the site, the annual operating costs and all revenues would be the same as in the first option. Waste Concern would pay 10% of all the revenues to the DCC in exchange for supplying the waste.

Option 3: Purchase the Land and Collect the Waste

Under the third option, Waste Concern would collect the waste directly from individuals at pre-determined quantities, qualities and in accordance with a pick-up schedule. Owning the land and collecting the waste would alleviate any royalty payments to the DCC. Enayetullah and Sinha estimated waste collection would cost an additional US$780 000 per year beyond the annual operating costs of $1.22 million for the site. All other fixed costs and revenues would be the same as the other options.

THE DECISION

Enayetullah and Sinha thought about what had been achieved in 10 years. Their list of achievements was long – through their efforts of setting up numerous decentralized composting sites, they had successfully achieved one of their key goals of turning waste into a resource. This, in turn, had improved soil quality, created employment, enhanced social standards, reduced sickness and disease, attracted international acclaim, spurred foreign investment and saved money for government bodies such as the DCC and the Bangladesh Ministry of Environment.

Now they were embarking on a major project that involved several international stakeholders and millions of US dollars of investment. They had several considerations. Which option for the centralized composting site would be the best for the future of Waste Concern? How could learning be exchanged between the centralized and decentralized composting models? What structure would be the most appropriate for Waste Concern? How should Waste Concern include all of the stakeholders in the impending change?

NOTES

1. The case is intended to be used as a basis for class discussion rather than to illustrate either effective or ineffective handling of an administrative situation.
2. Greenhouse gases include carbon dioxide, methane, nitrous oxide, hydrofluorocarbons, perfluorocarbons and sulphur hexafluoride. They prevent heat from escaping from the atmosphere and thus contribute to a 'greenhouse' effect by warming the earth's surface.
3. The Kyoto Protocol is an international agreement that called for 39 developed countries to reduce greenhouse gases by 5.2% over 1990 levels. CERs were one mechanism developed by the Kyoto Protocol.

REFERENCES

CIA World Factbook (2006), Bangladesh, www.cia.gov/cia/publications/factbook/geos (accessed 1 February, 2006.

Country Paper Bangladesh (2004) SAARC Workshop on Solid Waste Management, Department of Environment, Waste Concern, October.

Hiller, L. (2002) Cash for trash in Bangladesh, Choices, August 2002.

Sinha, A.H.Md. Maqsood and Enayetullah, I. (1999) Community based decentralized composting, *Urban Management Programme for Asia and the Pacific*, 8–9.

Sinha, A.H.Md. Maqsood and Enayetullah, I. (2002) Team's entry to the Fast 50 Social Entrepreneurs, *Fast Company*, 2002.

Waste Concern (2004) Community based decentralized composting in Dhaka, Presentation by Waste Concern, Dhaka, 13–17 September.

www.unfccc.org, Version 2, Clean Development Mechanism Project Design Document Form, UNFCCC, 1 July, 2004 (accessed 22 January, 2006).

www.wasteconcern.org (2004) MOU signed by Waste Concern and WWR, September (accessed 28 December, 2005).

Zurbrügg, C., Drescher, S., Rytz, I., Sinha, A.H.Md. Maqsood and Enayetullah, I. (2004) Decentralised composting in Bangladesh, a win-win situation for all stakeholders, *El Sevier*, 16 June.

CHAPTER TWENTY

Corporate Responsibility in Marketing

C.B. Bhattacharya, Boston University and Sankar Sen, Baruch College, City University of New York

INTRODUCTION

Few notions have so fully captured the imagination of businesses today as that of corporate social responsibility (CSR). Though by no means a new idea (see Smith, 2003), CSR, or a company's status and activities with respect to its perceived societal obligations (Brown and Dacin, 1993, p. 68), is due to a confluence of forces, now front and centre of the global business landscape. A majority of the top global companies not only engages in social responsibility initiatives, but also devotes considerable resources to reporting CSR activities to a wide array of corporate stakeholders (KPMG, 2003).

A recent McKinsey & Company survey of corporate executives (2006) suggests that companies engage in CSR in large part because executives believe that such activity will elicit company-favourable responses from important stakeholder groups. Another McKinsey survey (2007) of the companies that have signed on to the UN Global Compact reveals that of the different stakeholder groups, the participant CEOs expect a firm's customers to have the greatest influence on the way in which companies manage societal expectations in the next five years. Yet, poll upon poll (Boston College Centre for Corporate Citizenship, 2008) reveal that except for a few pioneers, most companies are still struggling to understand and buy into the demand to be socially responsible, let alone reconciling it with the realities of today's global, hyper-competitive marketplace. In this chapter, we take a marketing perspective on CSR to present a model of how, when and why CSR can produce coveted marketing outcomes.

What is Marketing?

Although definitions of marketing abound, the American Marketing Association conceptualizes it as 'the activity, set of institutions, and processes for creating, communicating, delivering, and exchanging offerings that have value for customers, clients, partners, and society at large' (American Marketing Association, 2007). Clearly then, the creation of value for the customer is at the heart of marketing and our research (e.g., Bhattacharya and Sen, 2004; Du, Bhattacharya and Sen, 2007; Sen, Bhattacharya and Korschun, 2006) over the last decade suggests that understood and done correctly, a firm's CSR activities can create immense value for its customers, yielding enviable long-term returns to the company as well as benefits to society at large.

Why Should Marketers Care about CSR?

In line with the definition of marketing, the success of marketers hinges on their ability to create meaningful, sustained and inimitable value for their customers. More specifically, more and more marketers, academic and practitioner alike, agree that building and maintaining consumer relationships is crucial to a firm's financial performance and long-term survival (Oliver, 1999; Reichheld, 2003). This thinking has unleashed a plethora of relationship marketing programmes, such as loyalty programmes and direct mailings, which seek to strengthen consumer-company relationships and engender consumer loyalty. However, for the most part, these efforts have not delivered on their promise: by and large, empirical studies on the impact of relationship marketing programmes reveal either small positive or even negligible effects (De Wulf, Odekerken-Schroder and Iacobucci, 2001; Verhoef, 2003).

In summary, whereas the need to connect with consumers, in this era of diminishing product differentiation and heightened competition, has never been greater, marketers are disillusioned with the performance of economic incentives-based loyalty programmes and continue to search for effective ways to nurture lasting, meaningful relationships with their consumers. In fact, the Marketing Science Institute (2006) has listed 'connecting customers with the company' as one of its capital research topics, calling for more research that 'explores new ways to create and sustain emotional connections with the brand'.

Our basic assertion in this chapter is that a company's actions in the CSR domain, carried out correctly, can offer the kind of value on which these strong, sustained and secure consumer-marketer connections are built. Specifically, research suggests that a company's CSR, by revealing its values, 'soul,' or 'character' (Brown and Dacin, 1997; Sen and Bhattacharya, 2001), can be extremely effective at forging deep meaningful connections with its consumers. It is worth noting that these returns to the company go beyond mere patronage, which is the focus of recent marketplace polls. For example, according to a Cone research study (2007), 87% of American consumers are likely to switch from one brand to another (price and quality being equal) if the other brand is associated with a good cause, an increase from 66% since 1993. Even though research in marketing does attest to such transactional returns to CSR, the true benefit appears to lie in its ability to transform consumers into company/brand[1] champions, who act in the company's best interests, being not only loyal but also actively promoting the company within their social networks.

Clearly, however, these coveted outcomes of CSR are not a given, as is evident from the experience of most marketers. This is because, put simply, as in the case of products and services, 'one size does not fit all'. In fact, our research suggests that consumer reactions to CSR are not as straightforward or evident as the above marketplace polls suggest; there are numerous factors that affect whether a firm's CSR activities translate to strong consumer-marketer relationships. In fact, it is this contingency that may in part be responsible for the lack of clear evidence, at the aggregate level, of the financial returns to CSR. For instance, a recent meta-analysis of 167 studies linking companies' CSR performance (both positive and negative) with their financial performance (Margolis, Eflenbein and Walsh, 2007) finds the relationship to be non-significant in 58% of the cases, positive in 27% and negative in 2% (the remaining 13% did not report sample size and hence could not be analysed).

How then can marketers harness the strategic power of CSR (e.g., Porter and Kramer, 2006) to create the mutually beneficial value that we have been discussing? Based on our research across a variety of CSR contexts with a range of consumer types, we suggest that to do so, marketers need to understand when, how and why consumers respond to both positive CSR initiatives as well as CSR failings (i.e., corporate social irresponsibility; Klein, Smith and John, 2004; Sen, Gurhan-Canli and Morwitz, 2001). We present an input-process-output framework that can provide marketers with a template for the optimal formulation, implementation and measurement of their CSR actions.

Although our focus in this chapter is on showing how positive CSR initiatives can help the firm as well as society, we note that our framework can be applied to understand the ramifications of corporate irresponsibility as well. The central premise underlying our framework is that the ability of CSR to engender coveted marketing outcomes such as loyalty and advocacy hinges on the extent to which it, like other aspects of the marketers' value propositions (e.g., product attributes), satisfies key needs of its consumers. At the same time, unlike most other aspects of the marketers' value proposition, the CSR actions also have the potential of generating returns in the societal domain, which, in fact, often become the basis for consumers' need satisfaction. Again, while our focus in this marketing chapter is on CSR's ability to satisfy consumers' needs, we note that there are many other drivers of company attention to CSR including demands from employees and investors as well as non-instrumental, normative motivations of managers.

AN INPUT-OUTPUT MODEL FOR UNDERSTANDING CONSUMER RETURNS TO CSR

Overall, the framework (shown in Figure 20.1) describes how CSR activity is perceived by individual consumers, satisfies their needs and results in behavioural outcomes directed towards the marketer and the issue at the heart of the CSR activity. The framework also delineates key contingency factors that moderate these primary relationships.

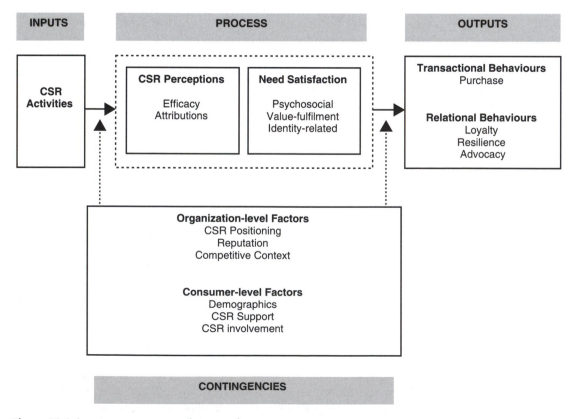

Figure 20.1 Input-process-output framework

CSR Inputs

According to *Socrates: The Corporate Social Ratings Monitor* (a database that describes and rates the largest 3000 US companies in terms of their CSR records, both strengths and weaknesses; see www.kld.com), companies undertake CSR activities in one or more of seven broad domains:

- community (e.g., charitable giving, volunteer programmes);
- diversity (e.g., board of directors, gay and lesbian policies);
- employee relations (e.g., health and safety, retirement benefits);
- environment (e.g., clean energy, recycling);
- corporate governance (e.g., compensation, ownership, transparency);
- product (e.g., quality, safety);
- human rights (e.g., labour rights, relations with indigenous people).

A company's CSR efforts in these domains can take many forms (e.g., cause-related marketing, corporate social marketing and socially responsible business practices), which vary in their objectives and implementation. Naturally, the nature and amount of company resources (e.g., money, goods, employee time and expertise) devoted to a CSR issue varies with the type of initiative through which it is implemented.

Process

Consumer Perceptions

Notably, objective measures of the level of CSR activity are different from the perceptions held by consumers regarding the company's CSR initiatives. And unlike the objective measures, perceptions of even a single initiative can vary greatly across consumers. In other words, consumer evaluations of the company's CSR initiatives are tied to, yet often entirely distinct from, the absolute level of CSR activity at the company.

Recent research indicates that there are at least two aspects to these perceptions. First, stakeholders evaluate CSR initiatives based on the degree to which initiatives are successful in improving the lives of the intended beneficiaries. In other words, they perceive initiatives in relation to the stated objectives of the initiatives (e.g., Du, Bhattacharya and Sen, 2007) and are sensitive to both positive and negative deviations from these objectives (Klein and Dawar, 2004). Second, prior research (Ellen, Webb and Mohr, 2006; Forehand and Grier, 2003) suggests that consumers respond to CSR based on the motives they attribute to the participating company. These motives can be (Batson, 1998) *extrinsic*, in which the company is seen as attempting to increase their profits, and/or *intrinsic*, in which it is viewed as acting out of a genuine concern for the focal issue (Lichtenstein, Drumwright and Braig, 2004). Consumers are often, and increasingly so, tolerant of extrinsic motives as long as CSR initiatives are attributed to intrinsic motives as well (Sen, Bhattacharya and Korschun, 2006).

Consumer Needs

The fundamental mediating construct in our model comprises the consumer needs met by a company's CSR initiatives. Extending the means-end perspective on consumer benefits (for an overview of the means-end chain, see, e.g., Gutman, 1982; Reynolds and Olson, 2001) to the CSR realm, we view CSR initiatives as attributes of the company that are only meaningful to consumers when these produce self-relevant benefits, allowing them to achieve personal goals (Gutman,1997). Importantly, however, the benefits of CSR to consumers are different from those typically associated with normal products and services in that they are less concrete and functional (e.g., a cell phone allows communication) and more abstract and psychological, occupying the higher levels of the means-end chains. These benefits typically pertain to the satisfaction of certain fundamental self- and identity-related needs (e.g., feeling good about oneself and one's place in the world).

CSR's satisfaction of such needs can occur in two ways. First, consumers are able to fulfil certain values or important life goals, such as social connectedness, self-esteem and a sense of harmony through their direct involvement with a company's CSR efforts (e.g., participating in Avon's Race for the Cure, a programme whereby consumers run or walk to raise awareness as well as funds for breast cancer research) or through the mere knowledge, based on their subjective perceptions, of such initiatives. For instance, we studied a corporate oral care initiative where, expectedly, consumers at large (i.e., the non-participants) do not receive any concrete benefits per se (Du, Bhattacharya and Sen, 2008). However, based on their memberships in the partner organizations responsible for implementing the programme (e.g., the Boys and Girls Clubs of America) or even just their awareness and perceptions of the initiative, consumers-at-large do fulfil their psychosocial need to help others in need, through either their enactment of the programme or purchases of the brand that sponsors the initiative. In turn, such actions foster a sense of wellbeing and harmony. Similarly, consumers feel better about purchasing a product that has been made in model manufacturing conditions (Sen and Bhattacharya, 2001), such as those better exemplified by Nike after they revamped their global supply chain operations (Zadek, 2004).

Second, and somewhat different from such value-satisfaction through direct or 'indirect' participation in a company's CSR programmes, is the fulfilment of consumers' higher-order self-definitional needs through their identification with a company engaging in CSR. Research on social identity (Tajfel and Turner, 1985) and, more specifically, organizational identification (Bergami and Bagozzi, 2000) suggests that individuals often identify with organizations to which they belong (e.g., employees with employer organizations), incorporating favourable aspects of the organizational identity into their own identity to satisfy certain basic, higher-order self-related needs (Dutton, Dukerich and Harquail, 1994). These include the needs to know oneself (i.e., self-definition), to feel good about oneself (i.e., self-enhancement) and to feel special (i.e., self-distinctiveness). Historically, identification has been examined primarily in the context of formal organizational membership. However, recent thinking (Bhattacharya and Sen, 2003; Scott and Lane, 2000) argues that in today's consumerist world, as consumers learn more about and develop relationships with not only products but also the organization or people behind the products (McAlexander, Schouten and Koenig 2002), they are drawn to identify, volitionally, with a select few of such organizations (i.e., the companies) even though they are not formal members.

The basis for such identification, or consumers' perceived sense of overlap between their own identity and that of the company, are the company-related associations that make up its perceived identity. This identity typically comprises of consumers' knowledge about two basic aspects of the company: its expertise in producing and delivering its products/services (hereafter Corporate Ability (CA) associations) and its activities with regard to important societal issues (i.e., CSR associations; Brown and Dacin, 1997). In our research, we argue that consumers' identification with a company is more likely to be based on its CSR rather than on CA associations because CSR associations provide consumers with insight into its 'value system', 'soul' or 'character' (Brown and Dacin, 1997; Sen and Bhattacharya 2001). In other words, a company's character as revealed by its CSR actions is not only fundamental and relatively enduring but also often more distinctive by virtue of its idiosyncratic bases (e.g., sponsorship of social cause, environmentalism) than other CA-based aspects of company schema. Therefore, a company's CSR activities are likely to constitute the core, defining characteristics of its corporate identity, triggering a consumer's identification with the company (hereafter C-C identification).

CSR Outcomes

When a company's CSR initiatives fulfil some or all the consumer needs described in the preceding section, consumers are more likely to engage in behaviour that is beneficial to both company and the cause.

Company-directed Behaviours

When a company meets higher-level, identity-related (rather than lower-level functional) needs of consumers, the latter often wish to reciprocate in kind. In fact, such reciprocation is often an integral part of need-satisfaction itself, particularly those pertaining to self-definition and self-enhancement. In particular, identification with a company based on its CSR actions aligns consumers' self interests with the interests of the company (Dutton, Dukerich and Harquail, 1994), triggering a multitude of pro-company behaviours. Research indicates that these behaviours range from short-term, transactional ones such as purchasing, to longer-term, relational ones including consumer loyalty, resilience to negative information and advocacy behaviours (see, e.g., Du, Bhattacharya and Sen, 2007).

Cause-directed Behaviours

The same effects that are found on corporate outcomes as a result of reciprocally beneficial consumer-company relationships can be found in the cause domain as well. Specifically, when consumers' needs are met through a CSR initiative, they are likely to respond positively to the cause at its heart, supporting it and promoting it to others. It is worth noting, however, that such changes are likely to be at least partially mediated by consumers' feelings of reciprocity and connection with the company itself, as opposed to their direct relationship with the cause. In other words, the quality of the relationship with the company influences behaviours towards the cause. Perhaps the best example of this is Lichtenstein, Drumwright and Braig's (2004) finding that consumers donate to charities that are sponsored by the company from which they purchase; this occurs as part of a desire to express the values that they share with the company.

Contingencies

One of the most important lessons to emerge from recent CSR research (e.g., Bhattacharya and Sen, 2004) is that the degree to which the CSR activity influences perceptions of CSR programmes and CSR-based need satisfaction is critically contingent on a host of factors that manifest at either the *organizational level* or the *consumer level*.

Organizational Level Contingencies

Organizational level contingency factors moderate the links between the level of CSR activity and both perceptions of CSR initiatives and needs satisfied by such activity. These factors include characteristics of CSR initiatives, the company and competitors. First, benefits generated by CSR are dependent upon characteristics of the initiative itself, including the issue domain (Bhattacharya and Sen, 2004) and CSR-company fit (Bloom *et al.*, 2006; Pracejus and Olsen, 2004; Sen and Bhattacharya, 2001). CSR-company fit is defined as the 'perceived link between a cause and the firm's product line, brand image, position and/or target market', and is determined by the company's operations, positioning and/or organizational objectives (Becker-Olsen, Cudmore and Hill, 2006, p. 47). Fit reinforces (or diminishes) what consumers believe is central, enduring and distinctive about the company (Albert and Whetten, 1985), magnifying the effect the CSR activity has on their positive pro-company perceptions (e.g., attributions) and behaviours.

Second, characteristics of the company also moderate the consumer returns to CSR. For instance, company reputation can amplify or dampen the positive effects of CSR (Bhattacharya and Sen, 2004; Yoon, Gurhan-Canli and Schwarz., 2006) because it influences consumer attributions, efficacy perceptions and identification. The industry in which a company operates is also a moderator of these relationships (Bhattacharya and Sen, 2004). Stakeholders are often suspicious of companies in certain industries (e.g., tobacco, oil), which can diminish both the ability of CSR to satisfy consumer needs as well as their consequent evaluations of the initiatives and companies.

Third, consumers do not evaluate CSR initiatives in a vacuum but through relative comparisons, both within and across industries. Related to company perceptions is the moderating influence of competitor CSR initiatives. Consumers evaluate CSR initiatives relative to expectations and these expectations are often based on their knowledge of the CSR initiatives of not just one but multiple companies (Bhattacharya and Sen, 2004). For instance, companies positioned on CSR, relative to those merely engaging in it, can enhance consumer perceptions, need fulfilment and pro-company relational behaviours (Du, Bhattacharya and Sen, 2007), but on the flipside such companies are also more likely to be subject to scrutiny and CSR backlash.

Consumer Level Contingencies

Consumer level contingencies include characteristics of the consumer and their level of involvement in CSR initiatives. In particular, both the demographic profile of consumers as well as their preferences/support for the issues at the heart of a company's CSR initiatives will impact the magnitude of the effects in our framework, because these characteristics reflect both the needs and values of the individual stakeholder. For instance, research suggests that gender may play a role in consumers' responses to CSR (Wehrmeyer and McNeil, 2000).

Another important moderating factor is the consumers' involvement in the process of enacting social responsibility. The effects of CSR are naturally most powerful when consumers become active enactors of CSR programmes (Bhattacharya, Korschun and Sen, 2009) because they are most able to use the programmes to express and enhance their identity. Further, highly involved consumers are increasingly able, by tailoring their CSR experiences, to co-create the value that programmes provide them (Prahalad and Ramaswamy, 2000; Vargo and Lusch, 2004). Consumers involved in creating, supporting and sustaining CSR programmes also derive a sense of accomplishment, learn skills and encounter other like-minded individuals, each of which has the potential to satisfy important needs, thus fostering a sense of identification with and trust in the company.

Where in the Marketing Course Should we Talk about CSR?

In our view, CSR is an innovative addition to the array of strategic levers that companies can use to be more customer-centric. As such, it is best to discuss the role of CSR in marketing towards the end of the course after the '4P's' and positioning have been discussed. A discussion of CSR might fit nicely into a module that also discusses other 'beyond the marketing mix' topics, such as consumer-company co-creation and brand communities that marketers can use to build meaningful stakeholder relationships as well as effect positive social change.

CONCLUSION

Traditionally, CSR has been viewed as an activity that is peripheral to the core purpose of the firm. However, we believe that by understanding when, why and how CSR works at the level of the individual consumer, managers can not only add a powerful lever to their marketing strategy but also make a positive difference to society.

NOTE

1. In this chapter, we use the terms 'company' and 'brand' interchangeably.

REFERENCES

Albert, S. and Whetten, D.A. (1985) Organizational identity, *Research in Organizational Behavior*, **7**, 263.

American Marketing Association (2007) Available at http://www.marketingpower.com/AboutAMA/Pages/DefinitionofMarketing.aspx (accessed 6 March 2009).

Batson, C.D. (1998) Altruism and prosocial behavior, in *The Handbook of Social Psychology* (eds D.T. Gilbert, S.T. Fiske and G. Lindzey), McGraw-Hill, New York.

Becker-Olsen, K.L., Cudmore, B.A. and Hill, R.P. (2006) The impact of perceived corporate social responsibility on consumer behavior, *Journal of Business Research*, **59** (1), 46–53.

Bergami, M. and Bagozzi, R.P. (2000) Self categorization, affective commitment and group self-esteem as distinct aspects of social identity in the organization, *British Journal of Social Psychology*, **39** (4), 555–77.

Bhattacharya, C.B. and Sen, S. (2003) Consumer-company identification: A framework for understanding consumers' relationship with companies, *Journal of Marketing*, **67** (April), 76–88.

Bhattacharya, C.B. and Sen, S. (2004) Doing better at doing good: When, why, and how consumers respond to corporate social initiatives, *California Management Review*, **47** (1), 9–24.

Bhattacharya, C.B., Korschun, D. and Sen, S. (2009) Strengthening stakeholder-company relationships through mutually beneficial corporate social responsibility initiatives, *Journal of Business Ethics*, forthcoming.

Bloom, P.N., Hoeffler, S., Keller, K.L. and Meza, C. (2006) How social-cause marketing affects consumer perceptions, *MIT Sloan Management Review*, **47** (2), 49–55.

Boston College Center for Corporate Citizenship (2008) What do Surveys Say About Corporate Citizenship? http://www.bcccc.net/index.cfm?fuseaction=Page.View&PageID=1794

Brown, T.J. and Dacin, P. (1997) The company and the product: corporate beliefs and consumer product responses, *Journal of Marketing*, **61** (January), 68–84.

Cone (2007) Cause Evolution Survey, Available at http://www.coneinc.com/content1091 (accessed 19 May, 2008).

De Wulf, K., Odekerken-Schroder, G. and Iacobucci, D. (2001) Investments in consumer relationships: A cross-country and cross-industry exploration, *Journal of Marketing*, **65** (October), 33–50.

Du, S., Bhattacharya, C.B. and Sen, S. (2007) Reaping relationship rewards from corporate social responsibility: The role of competitive positioning, *International Journal of Research in Marketing*, **24** (3), 224–41.

Du, S., Sen, S. and Bhattacharya, C.B. (2008) Exploring the social and business returns of a corporate oral health initiative aimed at disadvantaged Hispanic families, *Journal of Consumer Research*, **35** (3), 483–94.

Dutton, J.E., Dukerich, J.M. and Harquail, C.V. (1994) Organizational images and member identification, *Administrative Science Quarterly*, **39** (34), 239–63.

Ellen, P.S., Webb, D.J. and Mohr, L.A. (2006) Building corporate associations: Consumer attributions for corporate socially responsible program, *Journal of the Academy of Marketing Science*, **34** (2), 147–57.

Forehand, M.R. and Grier, S. (2003) When is honesty the best policy? The effect of stated company intent on consumer skepticism, *Journal of Consumer Psychology*, **13** (3), 349–56.

Gutman, J. (1982) A means-end chain model based on consumer categorization processes, *Journal of Marketing*, **46** (2), 60–72.

Gutman, J. (1997) Means-end chains as goal hierarchies, *Psychology & Marketing*, **14** (6), 545–60.

Klein, J.G. and Dawar, N. (2004) Corporate social responsibility and consumers' attributions and brand evaluations in a product-harm crisis, *International Journal of Research in Marketing*, **21**, 203–17.

KPMG International Survey of Corporate Responsibility Reporting 2005, KPMG Global Sustainability Services, University of Amsterdam.

Klein, J.G, Smith, N.C. and John, A. (2004) Why we boycott: Consumer motivations for boycott participation, *Journal of Marketing*, **68** (July), 92–109.

Lichtenstein, D.R., Drumwright, M.E. and Braig, B.M. (2004) The effects of corporate social responsibility on customer donations to corporate-supported nonprofits, *Journal of Marketing*, **68** (October), 16–32.

Margolis, J.D., Eflenbein, H.A. and Walsh, J.P. (2007) Does it pay to be good? A meta-analysis and redirection of research on the relationship between corporate social responsibility and financial performance, Harvard Business School working paper.

Marketing Science Institute (2006) *Research Priorities: 2006–2008 Guide to MSI Research Programs and Procedures*, Marketing Science Institute: Cambridge, MA.

McAlexander, J.H., Schouten, J.W. and. Koenig, H.F. (2002) Building brand community, *Journal of Marketing*, **66** (January), 38–54.

McKinsey & Company (2006) Global survey of business executives, *The McKinsey Quarterly*.

McKinsey & Company (2007) *Shaping the New Rules of Competition: UN Global Compact Participant Mirror*.

Oliver, R.L. (1999) Whence consumer loyalty? *Journal of Marketing*, **63** (Special Issue), 33–44.

Porter, M.E. and Kramer, M.R. (2006) Strategy & society: The link between competitive advantage and corporate social responsibility, *Harvard Business Review*, **84** (12), 78–92.

Pracejus, J.W. and Olsen, G.D. (2004) The role of brand/cause fit in the effectiveness of cause-related marketing campaigns, *Journal of Business Research*, **57** (6), 635.

Prahalad, C.K. and Ramaswamy, V. (2000) Co-opting customer competence, *Harvard Business Review*, **78** (1), 79–88.

Reichheld, F.F. (2003) The one number you need to grow, *Harvard Business Review*, **81** (12), 46–54.

Reynolds, T.J. and Olson, J.C. (eds) (2001) *Understanding Consumer Decision Making: The Means-End Approach to Marketing and Advertising Strategy*, Lawrence Erlbaum Associates, Mahwah, NJ.

Scott, S.G. and Lane, V.R. (2000) A stakeholder approach to organizational identity, *Academy of Management Review*, **25** (1), 43–62.

Sen, S. and Bhattacharya, C.B. (2001) Does doing good always lead to doing better? Consumer reactions to corporate social responsibility, *Journal of Marketing Research*, **38** (May), 43–62.

Sen, S., Gurhan-Canli, Z. and Morwitz, V. (2001) Withholding consumption: A social dilemma perspective on consumer boycotts, *Journal of Consumer Research*, **28** (December), 399–417.

Sen, S., Bhattacharya, C.B. and Korschun, D. (2006) The role of corporate social responsibility in strengthening multiple stakeholder relationships: A field experiment, *Journal of the Academy of Marketing Science*, **34** (2), 158–66.

Smith, N.C. (2003) Corporate social responsibility: Whether or how? *California Management Review*, **45** (4), 52–75.

Tajfel, H. and Turner, J.C. (1985) The social identity theory of intergroup behavior, in *Psychology of Intergroup Relations* (eds) S. Worchel and W.G. Austin), Nelson-Hall, Chicago, pp. 6–24.

Vargo, S.L. and Lusch, R.F. (2004) Evolving to a new dominant logic for marketing, *Journal of Marketing*, **68** (1), 1–17.

Verhoef, P.C. (2003) Understanding the effect of customer relationship management efforts on customer retention and customer share development, *Journal of Marketing*, **67** (October), 30–45.

Wehrmeyer, W. and McNeil, M. (2000) Activists, pragmatists, technophiles and tree-huggers? Gender differences in employees' environmental attitudes, *Journal of Business Ethics*, **28** (3), 211.

Yoon, Y., Gurhan-Canli, Z. and Schwarz, N. (2006) The effect of corporate social responsibility (CSR) activities on companies with bad reputations, *Journal of Consumer Psychology*, **16** (4), 377–90.

Zadek, S. (2004) The path to corporate responsibility, *Harvard Business Review*, **82** (December), 125–32.

CHAPTER TWENTY-ONE

Bounded Goodness: Marketing Implications of Drucker on Corporate Responsibility

N. Craig Smith, INSEAD

INTRODUCTION

It should come as no surprise that the immense contribution of Peter Drucker's writing to the thinking and practice of management extends to social responsibility in business. What is surprising, perhaps, is that his writing on this topic goes back more than half a century (e.g., Drucker, 1955) and consistently endorsed the idea of corporate social responsibility (CSR), long before it became fashionable. Hardly a follower of fashion, Drucker wrote incisively on its philosophical underpinnings as well as the social responsibility issues of the day, expressing a belief in CSR that was often in sharp contrast to the zealously dismissive views of other contemporary thought leaders such as Milton Friedman (1962; 1970), Alfred Sloan or marketing's own Theodore Levitt (1958).

The significance of Drucker's work in this area goes beyond his early identification of the social responsibilities of business. It still has currency today and the underlying principles may well prove more timeless than some of his other writing. Drucker is particularly insightful in relation to marketing (Day, 1990) and his work on CSR as it relates to marketing is no exception. However, he also exposes a more widely sensed uncertainty about the scope of CSR – especially now, given demands for social responsibility in the context of globalization and the challenges posed by climate change. A fundamental question posed for business nowadays is how much is enough? Hence the purpose of this chapter is to examine the implications of Drucker's CSR 'principles' for marketing practice today. As well as revealing their relevance, it also considers Drucker's views on the limits of social responsibility, referred to here as 'bounded goodness'.

Social responsibility of business is not a new idea, as Drucker (1974) recognized.[1] It has been traced back at least as far as the paternalistic capitalists of the 19th century (Smith, 2003). However, it has never been more prominent on the corporate agenda than it is today. This is evidenced, for example, in the dramatic growth in corporate social and environmental reporting (KPMG, 2005) and its frequent inclusion as a key topic in high profile meetings such as the World Economic Forum or the Clinton Global Initiative. A 2005 McKinsey survey found that 'Business executives across the

Originally published by the *Journal of the Academy of Marketing Science*, 2009, in a special issue devoted to the contributions of Peter Drucker (1909–2005) to marketing thought. Reproduced with kind permission from Springer Science & Business Media.

world overwhelmingly believe that corporations should balance their obligation to shareholders with explicit contributions to the broader public good' (McKinsey Quarterly, 2006, p. 33), and a cover story in *BusinessWeek* reported many examples of how companies are rising to the challenge (Engardio, 2007). Marketing is increasingly involved, be it in the development of new eco-friendly products or new markets (e.g., at the 'bottom of the pyramid' in developing countries) and in relation to a range of issues, from fair trade to sweatshop labour in the supply chain.

Until quite recently, marketing researchers gave relatively modest attention to CSR and most notably in the 1960s and 1970s, such as Andreasen's (1975) work on the disadvantaged consumer, empirical studies of socially responsible consumers (e.g., Miller and Sturdivant 1977) and more general analyses of the relevance of CSR to marketing (e.g., Patterson, 1966; Webster, 1974). Research in this area has increased substantially in the last few years (e.g., Bhattacharya, Smith and Vogel, 2004; Ellen, Webb and Mohr, 2006; Klein and Dawar, 2004; Maignan and Ferrell, 2004). In the interim, cause-related marketing received considerable attention, from Varadarajan and Menon's (1988) seminal piece onwards, but this topic has more to do with corporate philanthropy than CSR. Likewise, social marketing (e.g., Andreasen, 1995), though concerned with the use of marketing to address social issues, is not CSR. In some cases, writers in marketing still appear to mistake philanthropy and corporate social initiatives for corporate social responsibility (see Kotler and Lee, 2005).

Marketing practitioners also have tended to give little attention to CSR in the past, if not dismiss it (Curtis, 2006; Gidengil, 1977; Robin and Reidenbach, 1987). However, this too is changing, as marketing is increasingly involved in social responsibility issues, if not found in the firing line for social responsibility failings (e.g., obesity and advertising) and marketing budgets are diverted to CSR campaigns. More positively, marketers are responding to consumers' CSR concerns (Bhattacharya and Sen, 2004) and are increasingly developing products, brands and marketing communications that reflect company and product commitment to CSR (e.g., Wal-Mart, BP) and in some cases are centred on a social responsibility proposition (e.g., Toyota Prius, the Co-operative Bank).

Given these trends in marketing research and practice as well as the importance of paying tribute to Drucker and preserving his legacy, it is especially timely to consider the relevance of his work on corporate responsibility to marketing. First, I review Drucker's writing on CSR to identify what can be considered CSR 'principles'. These principles are applied to common CSR issues in marketing, demonstrating their usefulness to marketing practitioners today. I then look at Drucker's writing on the limits of CSR, explaining his position on bounded goodness while showing that it presents marketers and business generally with a conundrum.

This chapter concludes by suggesting that there is no easy answer to the question 'How much is enough?' when applied to CSR. Nonetheless, Drucker has helped us better frame this problem and his thinking will no doubt continue to stimulate further debate on marketing and corporate responsibility.

DRUCKER'S BELIEF IN SOCIAL RESPONSIBILITY

Drucker has consistently affirmed his belief in social responsibility in business (and other institutions). In *The Practice of Management* (1955), having ended his penultimate chapter by observing that integrity will always be central to what it means to be a manager, Drucker devotes his concluding chapter to the responsibilities of management. He writes, '[But] society is not just the environment of the enterprise. Even the most private of business enterprise is an organ of society and serves a social function . . . the very nature of the modern business enterprise imposes responsibilities on the manager' (Drucker, 1955, p. 375). Later, he observes:

> [But] what is most important is that management realize that it must consider the impact of every business policy and business action upon society. It has to consider whether the action is likely to promote the public good, to advance the basic beliefs of our society, to contribute to its stability, strength and harmony.
>
> Drucker, 1955, p. 382

Drucker's earliest writing also affirms this view of the social purpose of business and, through his examination of the grounds for corporate legitimacy, the social responsibilities of management. His first two books in English, *The End of Economic Man* (originally published 1939) and *The Future of Industrial Man* (originally published 1942) together assert that 'economic performance and social responsibility must be considered in establishing business purpose' (Flaherty, 1999, p. 46). *Concept of the Corporation* (Drucker, 1993a, first published 1946), Drucker's hugely influential study of General Motors (and informed by the two previous books), has been credited with establishing management as a field of research and practice (Flaherty, 1999). It was embraced by many companies and their leaders, including Ford, but rejected by GM's top executives. Drucker (1993a, p. 305) explains in his 1983 epilogue that the most fundamental issue in contention was that the book treated the big business corporation as 'affected with the public interest'. He describes how GM was among the first large American companies to accept responsibility for the impact of its activities on society; for example, it introduced and held supervisors responsible for a 'zero accidents' policy inside its plants, and it staggered work hours to reduce traffic jams outside. However, Sloan and other GM executives 'objected to anything that would give the corporation rights, authority and responsibility beyond its economic function' (1993a, p. 306), an argument still occasionally played back today by critics of corporate social responsibility (e.g., *The Economist*, 2005a). He continues:

> They therefore rejected out of hand the suggestion . . . that their company concern itself with what we would now call 'social responsibility' . . . They knew that there is no such word as 'responsibility' in the political dictionary. The concept is 'responsibility and authority' . . . authority without responsibility is tyranny, and responsibility without authority is impotence.
>
> Drucker, 1993a, p. 306

As well as questioning whether GM had legitimate authority to assume social responsibilities, GM executives also questioned whether they had the competence – two important critiques of CSR that Drucker revisited in his later works (discussed below). For these reasons, they considered the book 'anti-GM, anti-business, and indeed subversive' (Drucker, 1993a, p. 307) and Drucker's description led in part to Sloan writing his classic account in 1964, *My Years with General Motors*.

Writing in 1983, Drucker (1993a, p. 310) observed: 'We know today that GM's position is inadequate, no matter how strong its logic.' He concluded that GM's problems of the intervening years were attributable at least in part to a failure to address its societal relationships and responsibilities. He cited employee relations policies that resulted in unprecedented product quality problems and the campaign against GM for improved product safety initiated by Ralph Nader with the publication of his 1965 book *Unsafe at Any Speed*. GM's decision to hire private investigators to spy on

Nader led to a legal settlement that funded Nader's future campaigning for consumer rights, further harmed GM's reputation and contributed to enactment of restrictive product safety legislation – as well as a classic illustration of the 'business case' for CSR. Drucker believed that GM had, by 1983, realized the validity of his concept of the corporation and adopted more appropriate approaches to its business, but felt that it would remain in a defensive position for years to come.

Management, Drucker's (1974, originally published 1973) 800-page treatise on the tasks, responsibilities and practices of management, contained five chapters in an entire section on social impacts and social responsibilities (and no doubt the increased attention reflected the social turmoil of the time, that was a response in part to the Vietnam War and Watergate). Here, Drucker expounded on the ideas originally presented in one chapter in his 1955 book and they provide the basis for the 'principles' described in the next section. However, his arguments are largely the same and his belief in social responsibilities of business. He wrote:

> The quality of life is the third major task area for management. Managements . . . are responsible for their by-products, that is the impacts of their legitimate activities on people and on the physical and social environment. They are increasingly expected to anticipate and resolve social problems.
>
> Drucker, 1974, p. 312

Drucker's later writing remained consistent with these beliefs. In some cases, he addressed social responsibility directly (e.g., Drucker 1984; 1992; 1993b), in other cases more indirectly by describing his humanistic conception of management and his concern for the social role and responsibilities of business, as in his last book, *Management Challenges for the 21st Century* (1999).[2]

DRUCKER'S CSR 'PRINCIPLES'

The Meaning of Social Responsibility

Although Drucker was in some respects more provocative in his discussion of social responsibility in *Concept of the Corporation* (first published 1946), eliciting his CSR principles here will rely on his detailed treatment in *Management* (1974), together with some of his later refinements (e.g., Drucker, 1984). His starting point was to observe that until the 1960s, discussion of social responsibility was generally concerned not with 'the social responsibility of business, but with the social responsibility of businessmen' (Drucker, 1974, p. 314), especially their contributions to the community. The shift in emphasis (arguably anticipated in Drucker's earlier work) was to 'what business should or might do to tackle and solve problems of society' (Drucker, 1974, p. 314). He attributed this shift not to the development of an anti-business attitude but to heightened expectations as a result of the success of business in improving quality of life and growing doubt in the ability of government to solve social problems. He writes in ways that resonate today in relation to climate change, for example:

> [Managers] command the resources of society. But they also command the competence. It is, therefore, only logical that they are expected to take the leadership role and take responsibility for major social problems and major social issues.
>
> Drucker, 1974, p. 319

Drucker (1974, p. 319) identified a shift from an expectation that business minimize its impacts on society to one where business was expected to 'produce the good society'. This required new thinking and new action and could not be left to public relations, which Drucker considered an adjunct to marketing: 'The relevant questions are: "Can business tackle these huge problems?

How? Should business tackle them?" These are not questions which public relations is equipped to handle' (p. 319). The example Drucker gives is of the problems of American inner city ghettos. Today, it might be the 'bottom of the pyramid' in developing countries or AIDS in Africa. Drucker's point still holds. While companies are criticized for rhetoric over substance – if not faced with a backlash (Ellen, Webb and Mohr, 2006) – the requirement is for new thinking and new action (e.g., Prahalad and Hammond, 2002; Vachani and Smith, 2004).

Drucker was less concerned by problems of corporate irresponsibility, greed and incompetence. He didn't doubt they existed, he simply saw the solution as relatively straightforward: 'set forth standards of conduct and hold business to them' (1974, p. 320). The scale of recent business misconduct, exemplified by Enron, WorldCom and too many others to mention (Sorkin and Bayot, 2005), calls this perspective into question, or at least the idea that there is a readily workable solution. Some suggest that a misplaced reliance on the law holding business to standards of conduct contributed to the ethics failings reported in the early 2000s.[3] It is certainly the case that recent attention by business to CSR is in part inspired by diminished public trust in business, following repeated stories of ethics scandals at leading companies.

Nonetheless, although Drucker appears to understate the challenges associated with business misconduct, he was correct in suggesting that it is particularly difficult to determine what business should do to address social problems more proactively, especially those not directly related to its legitimate business activities. Indeed, he offers 'cautionary tales' of good intentions gone wrong that are familiar today.

The Case for Social Responsibility

Although companies clearly can get things wrong, this does not mean that they should not try or, indeed, that they should reject the calls for action on social responsibility as misplaced. Particularly compelling for many businesspeople in the 1970s – and remaining so for a not insignificant minority today – were the ideas of Milton Friedman (1962, 1970).[4] He wrote of social responsibility as a fundamentally subversive doctrine, saying: 'there is one and only one social responsibility of business – to use its resources and engage in activities designed to increase its profits so long as it stays within the rules of the game, which is to say, engages in open and free competition, without deception or fraud' (Friedman, 1962, p. 133).

Drucker (1974) accepted Friedman's argument that business as an economic institution should stick to its task and that there was a risk that social responsibility could undermine economic performance and thus society. He also shared Friedman's concern that social responsibility could entail managers usurping power in areas where they had no legitimate authority (managers are not elected and could become engaged in activities that are more properly the role of government). However, he chided Friedman for rejecting social responsibility and while accepting Friedman's concerns, said:

> [But] it is also clear that social responsibility cannot be evaded. It is not only that the public demands it . . . [and] that society needs it . . . in modern society there is no other leadership group but managers. If [they] . . . do not take responsibility for the common good, no one else can or will. Government is no longer capable . . . managers . . . whether they like it or not – indeed whether they are competent or not – have to think through what responsibilities they can and should assume, in what areas, and for what objectives.
>
> Drucker, 1974, p. 325

Drucker (1974) was forthright in asserting that social responsibility is a management task: 'Social impacts and social responsibilities have to be managed.' Arguably, this proposal has proved less evident in business practice than some of Drucker's other ideas. However, it is increasingly expressed today, drawing especially on the corporate responsibility implications for business of globalization (Bonini, Mendonca and Oppenheim, 2006; PricewaterhouseCoopers, 2007).

Responsibility for Social Impacts

Drucker differentiated between two types of social responsibilities: those to do with social impacts or what business does *to* society and those to do with social problems or what business can do *for* society. Social impacts go beyond the specific contribution the company exists to make, such as providing needed products and services. They are often unintended but inescapable by-products of business as part of, and serving, society. Drucker was clear about the responsibility of business for its social impacts:

> One is responsible for one's impacts, whether they are intended or not. This is the first rule. There is no doubt regarding management's responsibility for the social impacts of its organization . . . Because one is responsible for one's impacts, one minimizes them.
>
> Drucker, 1974, pp. 327–328

Drucker's (1974, p. 330) view on minimizing impacts extended to those that are ostensibly beneficial: 'If an activity is not integral to the institution's purpose and mission, it is to be considered as a social impact and as undesirable.' This might preclude many activities that few would question today, such as the employee volunteering programmes championed by Timberland, for example. However, they have demonstrated business benefits (e.g., team-building). Perhaps Drucker would have argued that they are integral to the company's purpose.

Drucker noted that it is difficult to determine social impacts. It is also difficult to be certain about their relevance to the core activities of the company. Drucker would likely have been more sceptical of seemingly beneficial social impacts to the extent that they are unrelated to the business. Today, stakeholder engagement is a widely regarded tool for identifying and assessing relevant social impacts (Partridge *et al.*, 2005).

Drucker advised that, once identified, social impacts are best eliminated. The ideal approach, he suggested, is to convert the impact into a profitable business opportunity. Drucker offered Du Pont's Industrial Toxicity Laboratory as an example and Du Pont also provides a more recent example in its successful and highly profitable development of CFC-free agents (e.g., for use in automotive air conditioning systems) well in advance of any regulatory requirement.

Seeking regulation to minimize competitive disadvantage

Drucker acknowledged that business often has a knee-jerk reaction opposed to any regulation of its activities. He questioned this response in relation to social impacts of business:

> Whenever an impact cannot be eliminated without an increase in cost, it becomes incumbent upon management to think ahead and work out the regulation which is most likely to solve the problem at the minimum cost and with the greatest benefit to public and business alike . . . [and] work at getting the right regulation enacted.
>
> Drucker, 1974, p. 334

Eliminating social impacts that cannot be turned into business opportunities essentially means that the costs associated with externalities become internalized as business costs (consider, for example, the use of currently more costly biodegradable or recyclable packaging). Drucker argued that the company is put at a competitive disadvantage unless its competitors do the same and so it should seek regulation to 'level the playing field'.

Moreover, Drucker argued that shunning this responsibility – with advocates of regulation discouraged from rocking the boat – could well lead to a crisis and scandal with regulation introduced rapidly and in a heavy-handed way that overly constrains business. Drucker cited by way of example the impact of the Thalidomide scandal on legislation governing drug safety and testing. A prominent current example is the Sarbanes-Oxley legislation introduced in 2002 in response to accounting scandals, which included measures the industry had resisted for years and, now enacted, is widely criticized as adding unnecessarily to business costs and reducing the international competitiveness of US companies (*The Economist*, 2006).

As Drucker observed (1974, p. 336), there is an optimal tradeoff in the costs and benefits involved: 'Beyond a certain level elimination of an impact costs more in money or in energy, in resources or in lives, than the attainable benefit.' These tradeoffs, he argued, are likely to be better understood within the industry than externally, but while the public might be sympathetic prior to any scandal, such sympathy evaporates when evidence emerges of an industry's disregard for its social impacts. Although Drucker doesn't make the point explicitly, it is clear that this argument extends to industry self-regulation. Thus we see industry initiatives around marketing issues as diverse as privacy on the Internet, the advertising of foods implicated in obesity and product placement in movies and computer games. The principle is clear: identify and address if not eliminate undesirable social impacts of business activities and, if they cannot be turned into profitable business opportunities, seek a regulatory solution (industry self-regulation or government regulation) that creates an optimal tradeoff for all involved.

Responsibility for Addressing Social Problems

Drucker (1974, p. 337) differentiated between social impacts of the business itself and social problems, the 'dysfunctions of society'. He viewed (1974, p. 337) social problems as sources of opportunity: 'It is the function of business . . . to satisfy a social need and at the same time serve their institution, by making resolution of a social problem into a business opportunity.' Not all social problems can be solved this way, however. Drucker (1974, p. 341) referred to the 'degenerative diseases' of society (e.g., American racial problems) and asserted that they are management's problems because 'healthy businesses require a healthy, or at least functioning, society'. The starting point, he said, is to establish if workable solutions have been identified by other institutions. Ultimately, this line of thinking raises the question of the extent to which business should address social problems that do not arise as a result of the social impacts of business and do not represent business opportunities. Drucker suggested that business has responsibilities in relation to these social problems, but there are limits to social responsibility. So, for example, how far should marketers go to develop products with reduced (or eliminated) greenhouse gas emissions in manufacture, distribution and consumption? As well as raising the question of how far marketers should go, this example also illustrates the possible difficulty in differentiating between social impacts and social problems. Climate change is a social problem but there are company-specific impacts, close to negligible for some firms, but huge for others, such as utilities.

In his later writing on social responsibility, Drucker essentially returned to the principles laid out in *Management*, but with a slight shift in emphasis. 'The New Meaning of Corporate Social Responsibility' (Drucker, 1984, p. 59) built on his belief that there are economic opportunities in social problems and noted that in 'discussion of the "social responsibility of business" it is assumed . . . that making a profit is fundamentally incompatible with "social responsibility"'. He predicted (1984, p. 59) that 'it will become increasingly important to stress that business can discharge its "social responsibilities" only if it converts them into "self-interest", that is, into business opportunities.' His exemplar was Julius Rosenwald, whose innovation of the county farm agent system turned mail order company Sears Roebuck into America's first national retailer while developing the skills, knowledge and productivity of US farmers. A modern day example might be General Electric's efforts to address climate change by identifying profitable business opportunities for its multibillion dollar Ecomagination initiative (Engardio, 2007).

APPLYING DRUCKER'S CSR PRINCIPLES TO MARKETING

Drucker's assertion of social responsibility as a major task of management clearly applies to marketing managers and in specific ways relative to core marketing activities.

Marketers typically have responsibility for company impacts on an array of stakeholders, but especially customers. In some industries, such as healthcare, this is made paramount. For example, the opening line of Johnson and Johnson's famous Credo states: 'We believe our first responsibility is to the doctors, nurses and patients, to mothers and fathers and all others who use our products and services.'[5]

In some cases, the industry itself raises profound issues of marketing's responsibility to its customers, as in the marketing of 'sin' products (Davidson, 2003). Many other examples of marketing's responsibility for its social impacts can be found across a range of marketing activities and industries:

- *Product safety and product recalls.* Marketers have a responsibility for product safety and to recall unsafe products. This is evident in the recent recall of exploding Sony laptop batteries (Nakamoto and Nuttall, 2006). Safety-related recalls are generally a legal requirement. However, regulations are often inadequate in ensuring satisfactory recall response rates (Smith, Thomas and Quelch, 1996). This is illustrated by the death of children due to recalled products that remain in use, such as Danny Keysar, who died trapped in the 'V' of the folded rails of his Playskool crib, a product that had been recalled five years earlier (Felcher, 2001).

- *Obesity and advertising.* Masterfoods (brands include Mars and Snickers) announced a global ban on advertising of all its core products to children under 12 in the light of evidence linking advertising to obesity. Coca Cola also has a global ban on advertising sodas to children under 12 (Wiggins, 2007).

- *Market selection and targeting of vulnerable consumers.* Concern has been expressed in the past over the marketing of high octane malt liquors to poor inner-city residents, 'alcopops' to teens and, most recently, energy drinks to young children (Brenkert, 1998; Sebor, 2006; Smith and Cooper-Martin, 1997).

These examples clearly reflect what Drucker had in mind in referring to social impacts. They are responsibilities arising from what marketers do to their customers – and there is a long history of questioning these impacts (e.g., Farmer, 1967; Packard, 1957).

Marketing also has impacts on other organizational stakeholders (Maignan and Ferrell, 2004). The impact on other stakeholders might be through customers in the first instance, such as encouraging recycling or responsible consumption of products such as alcohol and thereby reducing negative impacts on others. Or it might be more indirect, such as branding communications that increase employee identification with the organization through sustainability positioning (Sen, Bhattacharya and Korschun, 2006) or suppliers obliged to meet labour rights requirements that are intended to protect the brand and company reputation as well as their workers (e.g., Wal-Mart; see Fishman, 2006).

More challenging are marketing's social responsibilities arising from social problems. In some cases, these problems are relevant to customers and can become influences on their purchase and consumption decisions (Bhattacharya and Sen, 2004). This is evident, for example, with Fair-trade products, where consumers' purchase decisions reflect a concern for the farmers producing products such as coffee or tea. These examples of ethical consumerism are consistent with Drucker's (1984) view that social problems can be converted into profitable business opportunities – as well as his more fundamental assertion that the purpose of a business is 'to create a customer' (Drucker, 1955, p. 35). Examples increasingly abound, such as eco-friendly products like the Toyota Prius, the hybrid gas-electric vehicle that has sold around one million units worldwide since introduction in 1997 and was expected to sell 250 000 units in 2009 alone (Engardio, 2007).

What if the consumer does not care? An interesting test case is the '(RED)' brand, launched by rock star Bono in February 2006. The focal issue is the major social problem of AIDS in Africa, responsible for more than two million potentially preventable deaths a year. (RED) is an innovative combination of umbrella social-cause marketing and ingredient branding. It extends the long-standing idea of cause-related marketing (Varadarajan and Menon, 1988) to a family of brands under the (RED) umbrella, including American Express, the Gap, Motorola, Converse, Armani and Apple. The brands and products involved are not especially relevant to the social problem other than through their (RED) branding. A proportion of profits from sales of the (RED) branded products offered by these companies goes towards the Global Fund – over US$10 million by September 2006 used to buy drugs for AIDS victims in Rwanda and Swaziland.[6] However, the jury is out on whether it will succeed (Beattie, 2007). (RED) as a corporate response to the problem of AIDS in Africa is up against the limits of corporate responsibility.

Drucker's Bounded Goodness

One limitation to social responsibility Drucker identified (1974, pp. 343–344) is the requirement to fulfil the organization's primary social function:

> The institution's performance of its specific mission is also society's first need and interest . . . Managers need to be able to think through the limits on social responsibility set by their duty to the performance capacity of the enterprises in their charge.

Drucker (1974) suggested that to jeopardize performance capacity is irresponsibility and managers need to know the minimum profitability necessary for the business to sustain the activities required to realize its mission. Thus Drucker (1984, p. 62) wrote: 'The first "social responsibility" of business is then to make enough profit to cover the costs of the future. If this "social responsibility" is not met, no other "social responsibility" can be met.' As he explained (1984, p. 62), 'Decaying businesses in a decaying economy are unlikely to be good neighbours, good employers or "socially responsible" in any way.' Drucker (1974) asserted that a business must do well to do good and offered examples of companies that got into trouble because they assumed social responsibilities which could not be supported economically. Later, Drucker (1984) stressed the importance of turning social problems into economic opportunities.

To put into context Drucker's view on the relative importance of company profitability and social responsibility, it is important to first be clear on the type of social responsibility under consideration. Drucker rightly differentiated between social impacts (of the company on society) and social problems, ascribing a greater obligation to attend to the former. Second, Drucker (1992, p. 99) rejected profit maximization: 'It is futile to argue, as Milton Friedman . . . that a business has only one responsibility: economic performance. Economic responsibility is the first responsibility of a business . . . Economic performance is the base without which a business cannot discharge any other responsibilities . . . But economic performance is not the only responsibility of a business.' In this way, though Drucker clearly agreed with Friedman on the importance of economic performance as a necessary condition for survival of the business, he did not subscribe to Friedman's view of the supreme importance of profit maximization.

His first limitation is relatively straightforward in relation to social problems that the firm has not caused. What Drucker left unclear is how this limitation applies in relation to social impacts that he has earlier established are the company's responsibility and must be minimized if not eliminated. Must these social impacts be minimized regardless of the impact on company economic performance? Or do we take Drucker to mean that these responsibilities are to be managed only to the point that profitability permits? For instance, would it allow an apparel company sourcing clothing from suppliers using sweatshop labour to continue to do so if alternative suppliers known not to violate labour rights are more expensive and going to these suppliers would reduce profitability to below the estimated minimum required? To speculate, perhaps where company survival is at stake, a case-by-case approach is demanded, requiring an assessment of the specific social impact (how egregious are the sweatshop labour conditions?).

Drucker identified two further limitations: the limits of competence and authority. He wrote (1974, p. 345): 'To take on tasks for which one lacks competence is irresponsible behaviour. It is also cruel. It raises expectations which will then be disappointed.' Here he was at one with Friedman (1962). However, he approached the problem of determining competence differently; not by restricting the company only to that which it is clearly competent to do but by starting with where the company would be incompetent. Thus, even in areas where in many respects business is out of its depth – his example is training hard core unemployed minorities – it is possible to take on specific partial tasks that start to address the bigger problem. Thus Marriott's Pathways Program, a successful welfare-to-work initiative started by the hotel chain in 1990, is run in partnership with organizations able to provide the elements Marriott cannot.[7]

Drucker (1974, p. 350) asserted that the limitation of authority is a key constraint and wrote that, 'Demands for social responsibility which . . . usurp authority are to be resisted.' However, he was clearly referring only to responsibility in relation to social problems; social impacts are the result of an exercise of authority (thus responsibility follows). He asserted (1974, p. 347) that to 'assume social responsibility . . . always means to claim authority'. He cautioned (1974, p. 348) that one should ask when business is faced with social demands: 'Does business have the authority and should it have it?' Again he was aligned with Friedman (1962; also Levitt 1958), suggesting that

Friedman's position is the only consistent position in a free society, but he rejected it as untenable when faced with desperate social problems. Later, Drucker (1992) anticipated that society would increasingly look to business to tackle social ills. However, he still cautioned against business taking on responsibilities that would undercut its primary purpose or where it lacked competence.

To summarize, Drucker urged action by business on both its social impacts and on social problems, but did identify limits to social responsibility. In answer to the question 'when to say no?', Drucker (1974, pp. 350–351) suggested demands for social responsibility in response to social problems be resisted when this would impair the performance capability of the business, exceed its competence and when it would usurp legitimate authority (e.g., of government) or would involve illegitimate authority.

HOW MUCH IS ENOUGH?

Business and society are now far more interconnected than in Drucker's day. He wrote of companies as largely private enterprises but few big corporations at least can afford to lie low today and not engage with society. This is aptly illustrated by ExxonMobil's recent about-face on climate change and attention to corporate responsibility since the departure of former CEO Lee Raymond (*The Economist*, 2005b).[8] The social contract between business and society has changed and more is expected of corporations than ever before (Bonini, Mendonca and Oppenheim, 2006).

Moreover, corporate responsibility has gone global since Drucker's contributions on the topic. No longer is the agenda limited to the regional or even national problems of the communities in which a company is based, such as we find in the examples of social responsibility discussed by Drucker (e.g., American inner city ghettos). Today, the global scope of the typical multinational enterprise means that the world's problems are placed at its door. Globalization has substantially increased both the pressure on companies to address corporate responsibility and the range of issues to which they must give attention, as recognized, for example, in a global survey of over 1000 CEOs by PricewaterhouseCoopers (2007, p. 43):

> The idea that responsible business is good business is not new . . . However, the observations from CEOs in this year's survey on the need to reorientate their business around this principle reflect the fact that globalization, coupled with continuing distrust of the business community in many parts of the world, makes responsible business even more of a priority.

It is increasingly claimed that business must be a force for good in the face of massive global challenges, evident in the Millennium Development Goals in particular.[9] Business is not responsible for causing most of the challenges associated with extreme poverty and hunger, child mortality, climate change, and HIV/AIDS. However, just as Drucker (1974) argued regarding social problems American society faced in the seventies, it is claimed today that business has a responsibility to help fix many of these problems and, indeed, may be the only institution capable of addressing some of them to any significant extent (Globally Responsible Leadership Initiative, 2005). This is not to suggest that business can or should act alone. But it highlights a fundamental challenge at the core of Drucker's thinking on corporate responsibility – and business practice today – how much can society reasonably expect of business?

Flaherty (1999, pp. 38–39) concluded that 'throughout his career Drucker wrestled with the dilemma of balancing the requirements of corporate economic performance with societal demands, recognizing that either alternative taken to an extreme could threaten the viability of both an autonomous corporation and a free society.' Globalization has brought many opportunities for business, particularly in the form of new market opportunities, but as business has become more global it has been confronted with far more demands that it address social and environmental problems, many of which are not of its making. What should it do in response to these demands? How much is enough?

For instance, with demand for oil outstripping supply and ever more compelling evidence of climate change, oil companies face increasing problems of human rights and political activism in places where oil can be found, while also having to explore alternative energy sources that are many times more expensive than environmentally problematic carbon fuels.

Pharmaceutical companies are being asked to cut the cost of essential medicines for developing countries, such as antiretrovirals for AIDS victims, while also facing growing downward pressure on pricing in the developed world. While millions around the world go hungry, food companies are being blamed for the alarming rise in obesity in developed countries (and many LDCs) and yet consumers are mostly free to choose dietetic alternatives to unhealthy products – and more exercise.

As Drucker discussed (1974; 1993a), a frequent response by business is that attention to such social and environmental problems is inconsistent with the purpose of business, typically defined narrowly and in purely financial terms, such as the maximization of shareholder value. Drucker clearly rejected this argument out of hand. Flaherty (1999, p. 66), writing of Drucker's disagreements with Sloan, observed that Drucker 'argued that fulfilling the corporation's economic task was the corporation's dominant social responsibility but not the sole one. Whether management liked it or not, there was an inescapable accountability to the quality of life.'

In certain respects, Drucker was proved right in his dispute with Sloan and his critique of GM. Its failure to meet societal expectations and obligations led to its loss of public esteem and, more generally, its lack of attention to so-called noneconomic factors contributed to its lacklustre long-term economic performance (Drucker, 1993a; Flaherty, 1999). Similarly, to take a contemporary example, Wal-Mart's failure to consider its social and environmental impacts until quite recently is said to have impaired its financial performance – lowering its market capitalization by US$16 billion – and has led to initiatives ranging from sourcing sustainably-farmed fish to promoting energy efficient light bulbs (Engadio, 2007; Fishman, 2006).

In practice, for many companies today, shareholder value maximization is considered an unrealistic mantra. This is obvious with firms that espouse a social purpose, such as Stonyfield Farm, Tom's of Maine or The Body Shop. But for firms such as Rio Tinto, Shell and BP, it has become evident in the last decade that they must operate in ways that fulfil perceived societal and environmental obligations and protect their 'licence to operate' (Smith, 2003). This argument increasingly extends beyond the resource-extraction industries to other global businesses (Bonini, Mendonca and Oppenheim, 2006; Smith, 2003).

Sometimes the response by business to today's social and environmental challenges is to say that they are not its problem and, even where it is to blame, it is the job of government to address them via regulation. This response is consistent with Drucker's view on the role of regulation to address social impacts and his concerns about corporate legitimacy and business usurping the authority of government. However, this response often carries far less weight in the global context (aside from the fact that Drucker still urged action in the face of major social problems). Globalization continues apace, but global regulation has fallen well behind. Global business cannot look to national governments for regulation on many of the issues that cross national borders. For example, consider child workers and other manifestations of sweatshop labour found in developing countries supplying clothing to the developed world. As Nike found, it is difficult to argue that this is not the problem of the firms sourcing the clothing (Zadek, 2004). Government action to prevent abuse of factory workers is often nonexistent in many textile-exporting countries.

Nike initially argued that it could not be responsible for the actions of independent contractors supplying its sneakers, despite documented evidence of abuse of factory workers (Zadek, 2004). Extensive criticism followed, including a consumer boycott. Nike's response, not least given the threat to its brand and corporate reputation, was to accept that, in the words of Phil Knight, co-founder and (then) CEO of Nike, who said 'good shoes come from good factories and good factories have good labour relations'[10]. It put in place a major monitoring programme intended to cover the 650 000 workers in the factories that supply its products. Yet it is still left with the challenge of how much is enough? How much should Nike invest in monitoring the 800 factories of its independent suppliers in developing countries? This question is all the more pertinent in light of reports of fraudulent audits and supplier factories coached in how to pass inspection (Roberts and Engardio, 2006). At the extreme, to be fully certain of the integrity of its product, Nike could buy the factories that make the shoes and thus have control over labour standards. Is this what is called for?

GlaxoSmithKline (GSK) became the first major drug maker to sell its AIDS medicines at cost in 100 countries worldwide (Engardio, 2007). With millions dying of AIDS in Africa alone, how much more should GSK do to increase access to its antiretrovirals (ARVs)? Should it price below cost? Should it give the drugs away? Should it invest in the healthcare infrastructure needed for drug delivery? Less than 1% of the 4.1 million HIV/AIDS victims in Africa in 2002 who required ARV treatment were receiving it (WHO, 2003). Analysis by Vachani and Smith suggested that although pharmaceutical companies could be criticized for not doing enough to create access to ARVs for AIDS victims in developing countries – many of whom have since died – there were limits to how much the companies could have done to maximize social welfare by getting drugs to all who needed them: 'the economic costs would have been so high . . . running into billions of dollars, that multinationals alone could not reasonably have been expected to bear them' (Vachani and Smith, 2004, p. 132). This is aside from whether the drug companies could have addressed other obstacles to access, beyond price (such as inadequate healthcare infrastructure, lack of AIDS awareness etc.).

Similarly, when it comes to obesity, how much more should food companies do to rein in marketing? Should advertising restrictions extend beyond children to adults? Should other forms of marketing communications and promotion be restricted? Should companies develop alternatives to unhealthy foods or programmes to encourage exercise? How much should be spent?

THE BOUNDED GOODNESS OF CSR

So, how much is enough? Drucker's CSR principles would suggest the following in relation to our obesity, AIDS, and sweatshop labour examples.

Social Impacts or Social Problems?

Food companies certainly have a responsibility to act to eliminate the negative social impacts evident in their contributions to obesity in children if, indeed, obesity can be attributed (in part) to advertising. Arguably with both the Nike and GSK examples (and the food companies absent any effects of their marketing on obesity), the social issues described are what Drucker would term social problems rather than social impacts. It is not Nike's employees who are subject to labour rights abuses (though critics argued that Nike procurement practices put pressure on suppliers to cut corners) and GSK is not responsible for the limited healthcare budgets of developing countries that preclude purchase of ARVs at developed country 'market prices' (see Vachani and Smith, 2004, for discussion of pharmaceutical pricing). In which case, the requirement to act is less or, at least, constrained by the following considerations.

Corporate purpose

The company's first responsibility is to its primary purpose. Company action on social problems must not fundamentally undermine the company's economic health or detract from its social function. Here GSK's mission ('committed to improving the quality of human life by enabling people to do more, feel better and live longer') heightens the requirement for action on access. However, it is lessened by obligations to other customers (including possible future customers for whom it is developing new drugs and needs to invest in R&D). In contrast, Nike's purpose is less obviously linked to human welfare. However, its proximity and capacity to act on the issue might speak to greater rather than less involvement.

Regulatory intervention

The global scope of the GSK and Nike examples reduce the possibility of regulatory intervention, though in the case of GSK, much has been done to improve access to ARVs in developing countries through initiatives involving governments, the WHO, the United Nations, NGOs and others.

Corporate competency

Both Nike and GSK were capable of action. GSK was able to act on pricing, but also on related issues such as HIV/AIDS education, in partnership with NGOs (Vachani and Smith, 2004). It would be far less competent to act on healthcare infrastructure shortcomings (e.g., getting doctors to remote rural areas). Nike likewise demonstrated that some level of monitoring was feasible. However, as a marketing company, with no expertise in manufacturing, it would be far less competent to take ownership of production facilities and thereby control labour standards.

Corporate authority

It is difficult to argue that Nike's monitoring would be usurping government authority, though in some instances Nike's demands of factories might be at odds with government policy (in China, for example). Similarly, GSK lowering prices is unproblematic, but involvement in HIV/AIDS education might present difficulties in some countries because of religious and other beliefs.

Drucker's CSR principles clearly help, but adequate answers to the fundamental question of 'how much is enough?' may only be found on a case by case basis. The answers are also likely to change over time and vary from issue to issue and industry to industry. It is likely that there would have been far less requirement for the actions taken by Mars, Nike and GSK only 10 years ago; for what is responsible and what is enough will in large part be dictated by social norms and pressures. It turned out that there was both a compelling moral and business case for GSK to lower the price of its AIDS drugs to a not-for-profit level in developing countries (Vachani and Smith, 2004). The same argument applies to many other corporate responsibility issues. The expectations of employees, consumers, investors, local communities, NGOs and other stakeholders can quickly translate into pressure on the firm that can at minimum damage its reputation, if not harm sales and lower its share price. Maybe avoiding disincentives is not entirely what Drucker had in mind, but this is certainly consistent with the idea that addressing social responsibilities is in the economic self-interest of business. In contrast, positive examples are to be found in the growing interest in ethical consumerism, such as Fair trade or (RED).

CONCLUSIONS

Peter Drucker is without doubt the William Shakespeare of business literature. Just as Shakespeare wrote prolifically and with profound insight on the human condition, Drucker's writing richly and extensively sheds immense light on business and other institutions and their management. His work in many respects remains as fresh and relevant today as it did decades ago. This is no less true of his writing on social responsibility as it relates to marketing. In some respects, his insights might be taken for granted and they are far from a complete understanding of social responsibility as it is conceived today. However, Drucker's distinction between social impacts and social problems, for example, remains a key consideration, and his three limits on CSR in response to social problems (performance of the firm's specific mission, competence and authority) still have validity even if they only provide a foundational understanding and not a sufficient answer to the question, 'how much is enough?'. Marketers would be well advised to heed Drucker's CSR principles as described here and, more fundamentally, his humanistic view of the business enterprise and the role of marketers within it.

NOTES

1. Drucker generally referred to 'social responsibility' and 'corporate social responsibility' in his writing. These terms remain in use today but various other terms are also used, such as 'corporate responsibility' (because it doesn't appear to preclude environmental impacts), 'corporate citizenship' (a term preferred by US corporations, but often used largely in relation to philanthropic activities), 'sustainable development' (a term seen to better capture environmental considerations and thus favoured by resource extraction companies) and the 'triple bottom line' (the idea of giving attention to a nominal social and environmental as well as economic bottom line). This article mostly retains Drucker's language and the abbreviation CSR and uses the term corporate responsibility in reference to more contemporary thinking on corporate social and environmental responsibilities.

2. Although there are various compilations of his work, Drucker's own (2001) collection of 60 years of writing on management, *The Essential Drucker*, contains a chapter on social impacts and social problems that is an edited version of the five chapters in *Management* (1974).

3. In contrast to his endorsement of social responsibility in business, Drucker expressed doubts about business ethics. This has been traced to his experience of the Arbeitsfreude movement in Nazi Germany (Schwartz, 1998).

4. The 2005 McKinsey survey, mentioned earlier, found 'one in six agrees with the thesis, famously advanced by Nobel Laureate Milton Friedman, that high returns should be a corporation's sole focus' (*McKinsey Quarterly*, 2006, p. 34).

5. *Source:* http://www.jnj.com/our_company/our_credo/index.htm (accessed 6 February, 2007).

6. *Source:* www.joinred.com (accessed 19 January, 2007).

7. See Center for Workforce Preparation, Welfare to Work: An Economic Boost at: http://www.dol.gov/cfbci/.

8. For information on Exxonmobil's corporate responsibility activities today, see: http://www.exxonmobil.com/Corporate/community.aspx (accessed 20 November, 2007).

9. For further information on the Millennium Development Goals, see: http://www.devinfo.info/.

10. http://business.nmsu.edu/~dboje/NIKknightmeetingse2297.html (accessed March 4, 2009)

REFERENCES

Andreasen, A.R. (1975) *The Disadvantaged Consumer*, Free Press, New York.

Andreasen, A.R. (1995) *Marketing Social Change: Changing Behavior to Promote Health, Social Development, and the Environment*, Jossey Bass, San Francisco.

Beattie, A. (2007) Spend, spend, spend. Save, save, save, *FT Magazine*, **27**, January, 24–29.

Bhattacharya, C.B. and Sen, S. (2004) Doing better at doing good: When, why and how consumers respond to corporate social initiatives, *California Management Review*, **47** (Fall), 9–24.

Bhattacharya, C.B., Smith, N.C. and Vogel, D. (2004) Integrating social responsibility and marketing strategy: An introduction, *California Management Review*, **47** (Fall), 6–8.

Bonini, S.M.J., Mendonca, L.T. and Oppenheim, J.M. (2006) When social issues become strategic, *McKinsey Quarterly*, **2**, 20–32.

Brenkert, G.G. (1998) Marketing to inner-city blacks: Powermaster and moral responsibility, *Business Ethics Quarterly*, **8** (January), 1–18.

Curtis, J. (2006) Why don't they trust you with CSR? *Marketing*, **13** (September), 30–31.

Davidson, D.K. (2003) *Selling Sin: The marketing of socially unacceptable products*, Praeger, New York.

Day, G.S. (1990) *Market Driven Strategy*, Free Press, New York.

Drucker, P.F. (1955) *The Practice of Management*, Heinemann, London.

Drucker, P.F. (1974) (first published 1973) *Management: Tasks, Responsibilities, Practices*, Heinemann, London.

Drucker, P.F. (1984) The new meaning of corporate social responsibility, *California Management Review*, **XXVI** (Winter), 53–63.

Drucker, P.F. (1992) The new society of organizations, *Harvard Business Review*, September-October.

Drucker, P.F. (1993a) (first published 1946) *Concept of the Corporation*. Transaction Publishers, New Brunswick.

Drucker, P.F. (1993b) *Post-capitalist Society*, HarperCollins, New York.

Drucker, P.F. (1999) *Management Challenges for the 21st Century*, Butterworth-Heinemann, Oxford.

Drucker, P.F. (2001) *The Essential Drucker*, Butterworth-Heinemann, Oxford.

The Economist (2005a) The good company: A survey of corporate social responsibility, 22 January.

The Economist (2005b) Life after Lee, **24**, December, 87–88.

The Economist (2006) The trial of Sarbanes-Oxley, **22**, April, 69–70.

Ellen, P.S., Webb, D.J. and Mohr, L.A. (2006) Building corporate associations: Consumer attributions for corporate socially responsible programs, *Journal of the Academy of Marketing Science*, **34** (Spring), 147–158.

Engardio, P. (2007). Beyond the Green Corporation, *BusinessWeek*, 29 January, 50–64.

Farmer, R.E. (1967) Would you want your daughter to marry a marketing man? *Journal of Marketing*, **31** (January), 1–3.

Felcher, E.M. (2001) *It's No Accident: How corporations sell dangerous baby products*, Common Courage Press, Monroe, ME.

Fishman, C. (2006) The Wal-Mart effect and a decent society: Who knew shopping was so important? *Academy of Management Perspectives*, **20**, 6–25.

Flaherty, J.E. (1999) *Peter Drucker: Shaping the Managerial Mind*, Jossey-Bass, San Francisco.

Friedman, M. (1962) *Capitalism and Freedom*, University of Chicago Press, Chicago.

Friedman, M. (1970) The social responsibility of business is to increase its profits, *New York Times Magazine*, 13 September.

Gidengil, B. Z. (1977) The social responsibilities of business: what marketing executives think, *European Journal of Marketing*, **11** (1), 72–86.

Globally Responsible Leadership Initiative (2005) *Globally Responsible Leadership: A Call for Engagement*, European Foundation for Management Development, Brussels.

Klein, J. and Dawar, N. (2004) Corporate social responsibility and consumers' attributions and brand evaluations in a product-harm crisis, *International Journal of Research in Marketing*, **21** (September), 203–17.

Kotler, P. and Lee, N. (2005) *Corporate Social Responsibility: Doing the most good for your company and your cause*, John Wiley & Sons, Inc., New York.

KPMG (2005) International Survey of Corporate Responsibility Reporting 2005, at http://www.kpmg.com/Industries/IM/Other/CRSurvey.html (accessed 20 November 2007).

Levitt, T. (1958) The dangers of social responsibility, *Harvard Business Review*, (September-October), 41–50.

Maignan, I. and Ferrell, O.C. (2004) Corporate social responsibility and marketing: an integrative framework, *Journal of the Academy of Marketing Science*, **32** (Winter), 3–19.

McKinsey Quarterly (2006) The McKinsey Global Survey of Business Executives: Business and Society, *McKinsey Quarterly*, **2**, 33–9.

Miller, K.E. and Sturdivant, F.D. (1977) Consumer responses to socially questionable corporate behavior: an empirical test, *The Journal of Consumer Research*, **4**, (June), 1–7.

Nakamoto, M. and Nuttall, C. (2006) Sony battles to restore credibility after recall warning, *Financial Times* (North American Edition), **4** (October).

Packard, V. (1957) *The Hidden Persuaders*. Penguin, Harmondsworth.

Partridge, K., Jackson, C., Wheeler, D. and Zohar, A. (2005) *From Words to Action. The Stakeholder Engagement Manual Vol. 1: The Guide to Practitioners' Perspectives on Stakeholder Engagement*, Stakeholder Research Associates Canada Inc., Cobourg, Ontario.

Patterson, J.M. (1966) What are the social and ethical responsibilities of marketing executives? *Journal of Marketing*, **30** (July), 12–15.

Prahalad, C.K. and Hammond, A. (2002) Serving the world's poor, profitably. *Harvard Business Review*, **80** (September), 48–57.

PricewaterhouseCoopers (2007) 10th Annual Global CEO Survey. Available at www.pwc.com/extweb/home.nsf/docid/2AE969AC 42DD721A8525725E007D7CF2 (accessed 20 November 2007).

Roberts, D. and Engardio, P. (2006) Secrets, lies and sweatshops, *BusinessWeek*, **27** (November).

Robin, D.P. and Reidenbach, E.R. (1987) Social responsibility, ethics, and marketing strategy: closing the gap between concept and application, *Journal of Marketing*, **51** (January), 44–58.

Schwartz, M. (1998) Peter Drucker and the denial of business ethics, *Journal of Business Ethics*, **17** (November), 1685–92.

Sebor, J. (2006) Seeing red over broken wings, *Customer Relationship Management*, August, 13–14.

Sen, S., Bhattacharya, C.B. and Korschun, D. (2006) The role of corporate social responsibility in strengthening multiple stakeholder relationships: A field experiment, *Journal of the Academy of Marketing Science*, **34**, 158–66.

Smith, N.C. (2003) Corporate social responsibility: Whether or how? *California Management Review*, 45 (Summer), 52–76.

Smith, N.C. and Cooper-Martin, E. (1997) Ethics and target marketing: the role of product harm and consumer vulnerability, *Journal of Marketing*, **61** (July), 1–20.

Smith, N.C., Thomas, R.J. and Quelch, J.A. (1996) A strategic approach to managing product recalls, *Harvard Business Review*, 74, 102–112 (September-October).

Sorkin, A.R. and Bayot, J. (2005) Ex-Tyco officers get 8 to 25 years, *The New York Times*, 20 September, A1.

Vachani, S. and Smith, N.C. (2004) Socially responsible pricing: lessons from the pricing of AIDS drugs in developing countries, *California Management Review*, **47** (Fall), 117–44.

Varadarajan, P.R. and Menon, A. (1988) Cause-related marketing: a coalignment of marketing strategy and corporate philanthropy, *Journal of Marketing*, **52**, (July), 58–75.

Webster, F. E. (1974). *Social Aspects of Marketing*, Prentice-Hall, Englewood Cliffs, NJ.

WHO (2003) Global AIDS Treatment Emergency, Fact sheet 274 (September), World Health Organization, Geneva.

Wiggins, J. (2007) Mars to axe child-targeted adverts, *Financial Times* (North American Edition), **5** (February), 1.

Zadek, S. (2004) The path to corporate responsibility, *Harvard Business Review*, **82** (December), 125–32.

CHAPTER TWENTY-TWO

Norsk Hydro ASA: Sustainable PVC at Hydro Polymers?[1]

N. Craig Smith, INSEAD and Josephine Brennan, London Business School

INTRODUCTION

On 21 March, 2006, Hydro Polymers Limited, a division of Norsk Hydro ASA, the fourth largest polyvinyl chloride (PVC) manufacturer in Europe and one of only two in the UK, brought its key UK customers together to showcase its strategy for sustainable PVC. Led by Group Sustainability Manager, Dr Jason Leadbitter, Hydro Polymers had been working since 2001 to address an industry-wide threat of end-users de-selecting PVC products because of environmental concerns. By 2006, the time had come to engage the PVC supply chain and gain key customer support for the long-term development of sustainable PVC. In Hydro Polymers' opinion, it would be impossible to address sustainability in isolation; all the supply chain needed to work together.

There was a 10-year history to this initiative (see Exhibit 22.1). Sustainability had been a priority on Hydro Polymers' agenda since 1996 when Greenpeace UK, a non-governmental organization (NGO), had run a national campaign targeting retailers to 'Buy PVC-Free'.[2] Norsk Hydro had just launched a €90 million investment in 1995 to expand and modernize the largest European PVC resin manufacturing plant at Newton Aycliffe in the UK. Meanwhile, the Greenpeace campaign bolstered widespread public opinion that, like chlorofluorocarbons (CFCs), PVC should be totally phased out, leaving the European PVC industry, representing 25% of a global PVC market worth €20 billion, fighting multiple threats to de-select PVC products.

In response to the campaign, a UK PVC Retail Working Group was set up to investigate the scientific validity of the claims by Greenpeace. An independent assessment concluded that with careful manufacture, use and disposal, the downstream environmental impacts of PVC could be managed. By late 1999, however, tensions still ran high between environmentalists, frustrated by incremental change and lobbying for an EU ban on PVC, and industry scientists backing the wide application of PVC in society. To break the gridlock, a further in-depth study was commissioned to determine whether PVC could ever be fully sustainable. This assessment focused on upstream root causes of environmental impacts using The Natural Step (TNS) Framework, developed by an international nonprofit organization promoting a scientific, whole-systems approach to sustainability.

There were concerns in the industry about the TNS methodology because the furniture retailer IKEA had worked with TNS and subsequently removed PVC from all its product lines. Meanwhile, in

EXHIBIT 22.1 HYDRO POLYMERS' SUSTAINABILITY JOURNEY

August 1996

Greenpeace UK launched its high-profile anti-PVC campaign, targeting end-users of PVC products, distributing its 'Saving our skins' flyers outside retail outlets. Retailers responded by establishing a UK PVC Retail Working Group to understand the environmental issues.

September 1997

The UK PVC Retail Working Group received the impact assessment report from the National Centre for Business and Ecology, concluding that with careful manufacture, use and disposal, negative environmental impacts of PVC could be reduced.

September 1999

The PVC Retail Working Group was expanded to include representatives from the two UK producers of PVC, Hydro and EVC (Ineos), establishing a new UK PVC Co-ordination Group. Unable to resolve the conflict between Greenpeace and the producers, the retailers invited Jonathon Porritt to chair the co-ordination group.

March 2000

The European PVC Industry launched its Vinyl 2010 programme, a voluntary commitment undertaken by members to continuous improvement of their environmental impacts.

July 2000

The Natural Step published its report entitled 'PVC: An Evaluation Using The Natural Step Framework', and held a multi-stakeholder visioning workshop entitled: 'Vision 2020 Series: PVC and Sustainability'.

December 2000

TNS founder Karl-Henrik Robèrt met Hydro President Anders Hermansson, who commissioned Robèrt and TNS to conduct a deeper analysis into Hydro's business by touring all Hydro Polymers' sites, and educating all employees in the TNS approach.

October 2001

Hydro's core leadership team attended extended strategic planning workshop on 'Strategy for Sustainable Business' led by Robèrt and TNS.

March 2002

Hermansson defended Hydro's sustainability strategy against dissenters at Norsk Hydro's annual strategy meeting, allocating an additional corporate budget of NOK25 million (€3 million) annually for three years to kick-start projects.

(Continued)

EXHIBIT 22.1 (*Continued*)

September 2003

Hydro launched its 'Sustainability is Good for Business' campaign and new vision statement, 'To be the Preferred and Sustainable Supplier of Vinyl and Caustic Products'.

September 2004

Jan Sverre Rosstad joined Hydro as Senior Vice President, while Hydro celebrated reaching 12.5% reductions in carbon dioxide emissions within four years, and its annual employee survey showed a 15% increase in employees recognizing Hydro's commitment to environmental issues.

April 2005

Hydro launched its first supplier event to communicate its approach to sustainability and invited suppliers to adopt a similar strategy.

August 2005

Hydro opened its new state-of-the-art membrane technology chlorine plant at Rafnes in Norway, a €200 million investment.

March 2006

Hydro launched its sustainability strategy to key customers, inviting reflections and criticisms to its approach.

Source: Hydro Polymers

March 2000, the European PVC industry launched Vinyl 2010, a voluntary programme committed to continuous improvement of environmental impacts, as a pre-emptive strike against the pending EU legislation. By July 2000, TNS findings had identified five major systemic challenges for PVC to become a sustainable material, requiring major transformation within the industry to address energy emissions, end-of-life recycling, the elimination of toxic by-products and the substitution of toxic additives, and to secure industry-wide commitment to a long-term transformation process.

Although complementary to the industry's own Vinyl 2010 commitment, the TNS challenges went much further in defining the endpoint of sustainability for PVC. Since none of the challenges was technically insurmountable, the industry was left with two major considerations. First, given the risks and cost implications, could it be commercially viable to produce sustainable PVC? Second, could end-product specifiers be convinced that sustainable PVC was a product worth waiting for and defer any deselection decisions in the meantime? Leadbitter saw a real opportunity for Hydro Polymers to be the first producer to integrate these fundamental challenges for the PVC industry ahead of future regulation and key competitors. The biggest challenge, as he saw it, was to communicate

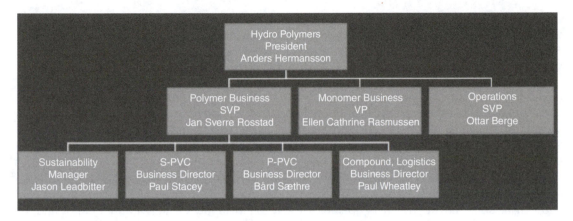

Figure 22.1 Hydro Polymers' organization chart 2005

convincingly to specifiers and end-users that sustainable, non-toxic PVC was achievable within a secure transition time.

Between 2001 and 2004, Hydro Polymers employees identified and implemented numerous internal initiatives, generating cost savings to the business while making tangible progress on each of the first four challenges. Investments in green energy alone achieved a reduction in carbon dioxide (CO_2) emissions of more than 12.5%, reaching Kyoto Protocol targets for 2012 in the first four years. By 2005, Hydro Polymers had proved to itself that the sustainability challenges could be met. Incoming Senior Vice President, Jan-Sverre Rosstad (see Figure 22.1, which shows Hydro Polymers' organization chart for 2005), felt the time had come to take Hydro Polymers' successes to the marketplace and generate support for its endeavours. However, in spite of overall market growth, China had become a key driver of a now €36 billion global PVC industry, with new PVC production capacity based on cheap labour and more energy-intensive and polluting technologies that had been banned in the EU.

The launch of Hydro Polymers' sustainability strategy on 21 March 2006 would put the real business dilemma to the test. As customers weighed up the implications of the sustainability challenges for the industry, would they consider a transition to fully sustainable PVC a realistic future scenario or would they dispute its viability on commercial grounds? In view of the rapid rise of what was believed to be highly unsustainable PVC manufacture in China, would customers feel that PVC was a losing battle and start devising exit strategies to cut their losses in PVC-based applications? Given the availability of alternative materials for their end products (e.g. window frames), would they switch investments to manufacturing substitutes (e.g., wood) and slowly exit PVC-based manufacturing ahead of pending REACH regulation?[3]

Even if customers believed that an industry-wide transition to sustainable PVC was possible, would they be willing to support Hydro Polymers' approach given that the rest of the European PVC producers were taking a less radical approach? Would customers choose to wait and see, believing there was a cost advantage to the more incremental approach (despite Hydro Polymers' experience to the contrary)? Would they see real value in Hydro Polymers' tangible progress to date and accelerate the pace of change within the PVC industry? Would they perceive added value for their own customers and join the industry process towards full sustainability? Customer reactions would give Hydro Polymers a clear signal as to what the future held for its gamble on sustainability.

HYDRO POLYMERS AND POLYVINYL CHLORIDE (PVC)

Hydro Polymers Limited was a subsidiary of Norsk Hydro ASA, the Scandinavian oil and gas major and Norway's second largest publicly quoted company. Founded in 1905, Norsk Hydro focused on natural resources for energy and materials (initially fertilizers and aluminium followed by oil/gas and PVC), with operating revenues of €1.96 billion and over 33 000 people employed in 40 countries by 2005.[4] Hydro Polymers, the petrochemicals division of Norsk Hydro, with operating sites at Newton Aycliffe (UK), Rafnes (Norway), Stenungsund and Helsingborg (Sweden), focused on the production of PVC, its intermediary or 'feedstock' product vinyl chloride monomer (VCM) and caustic soda. Hydro Polymers operated an integrated supply chain, with the Rafnes and Stenungsund sites using Norsk Hydro gas supplies to produce VCM to feed the three resin producing sites in Norway, Sweden and the UK (see Figure 22.2).

The PVC manufacturing process first combined ethylene derived from natural gas with chlorine derived from the electrolysis of salt to produce an intermediate product known as ethylene dichloride (EDC). This was again 'cracked' during a chemical process to produce vinyl chloride monomer (VCM), which was polymerized in water to produce PVC resin. The PVC resin would then be combined with additives to form PVC compounds, or directly processed with additives into products tailored for different applications, and sold on to customers as raw materials for their end products (see Figure 22.3). All sites operated environmental management systems to monitor and evaluate ongoing impacts, and were compliant with reputable standards, notably ISO14001[5] and EMAS (Eco-Management and Audit Scheme).

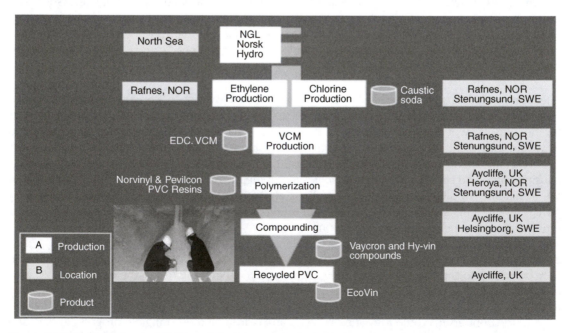

Figure 22.2 Hydro Polymers' PVC – a fully integrated supply chain

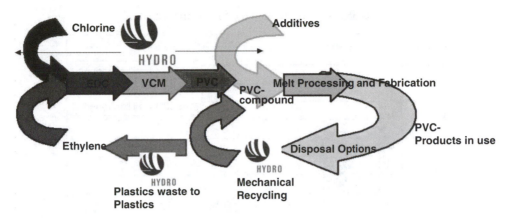

Figure 22.3 Hydro Polymers' PVC production process

Source: Hydro Polymers

PVC Applications

Since its first commercial applications were discovered, PVC had become ubiquitous in everyday life as one of the few plastics that could be used for both rigid and flexible end products. The majority of PVC was consumed in the construction industry where it was used in window frames (profiles), pipes, flooring and cabling applications. PVC was also used widely for food and drink packaging due to its ability to protect against contamination and breakage throughout the product life cycle from factory to table. In the medical sector, PVC was widely used for disposable medical devices including blood bags, catheters, gloves, oxygen masks and tubing. PVC was also used for the production of automotive parts, sporting equipment, credit cards and many other applications.

PVC was lightweight, durable, fire-, shock- and corrosion-resistant, chemically inert, non-toxic, insulating, weather resistant, impermeable, relatively scratch resistant, and could have an opaque or transparent, coloured or colourless finish. Its versatility and cost-effectiveness gave PVC a considerable advantage over competing plastics. Also, whereas most plastics were produced from 100% hydrocarbons derived from oil and natural gas reserves, over 57% of PVC was made up of chlorine derived from common salt, providing unique performance properties and requiring less than half the hydrocarbon (oil) per tonne of product compared to plastics such as polyethylene. Furthermore, PVC's compatibility with a wide range of additives (stabilizers, plasticizers, lubricants, fillers, pigments, etc.) created scope for a virtually unlimited range of applications.

Hydro Polymers in the Marketplace

By 2005, the global PVC market was worth over €36 billion per annum with PVC consumption exceeding 36 million tonnes. Over 60% of production was used in the manufacture of pipes and window profiles for the construction sector. Although PVC was losing ground across some product applications, expansion of global production capacity was on course to exceed estimates of 40 million tonnes by 2010, driven by rapid demand increases from Asia, particularly China (see Figure 22.4, which shows the global PVC market). Between 1998 and 2005, China's annual

Global PVC Production by Region 1980–2010

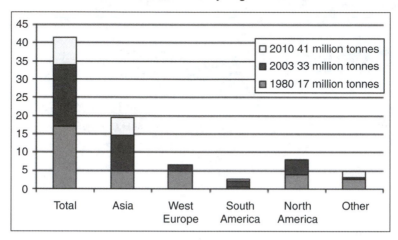

Global PVC Demand by Region 2006

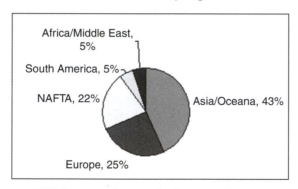

PVC Consumption per Capita by Region 2006

	2001	2006	2011
North America	15.4	16.7	17.5
Europe	7.9	8.6	10.5
North East Asia	5.9	6.9	9.5

Global Demand by Application (%) (2001–2011)

	2001	2006	2011
Pipes/Fittings	38	39	45
Profiles Rigid	14	14	12
Film/Sheet Flexible	17	17	16
Cables/Electric Wires	7	7	7
Tubes/Profiles Flexible	4	4	4
Other	20	19	16

Figure 22.4 Global PVC market – production and demand

Source: CMAI/Hydro Polymers

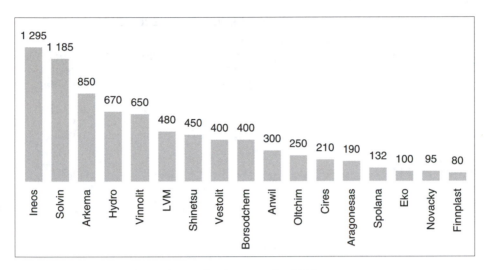

Figure 22.5 European PVC producers by production capacity 2005

Source: CMAI/Hydro European (WE+CEE) PVC Capacity by Producer

PVC consumption increased from one million to over seven million tonnes. With major use in the rapidly growing construction industry, and 48 new airports planned, PVC imports were set to increase until domestic production could catch up with demand.

The European PVC market represented over 25% of global consumption in 2005, supplied by 10 major European producers (see Figure 22.5). Hydro Polymers was the fourth largest producer by volume, and also the lowest cost producer in Europe, benefiting from its integrated supply chain as part of Norsk Hydro. Given the capital-intensive and relatively low-margin nature of the mature PVC production sector, this low-cost position gave Hydro Polymers a significant advantage. In 2005, Hydro Polymers' operating income was €8.6 million (see Figure 22.6) while competitor EVC/Ineos reported losses of €13.2 million for the same period.

Between 1995 and 2000, parent company Norsk Hydro had invested over €90 million expanding and modernizing the PVC resin and compound manufacturing plant at Newton Aycliffe, almost doubling the scale of the operation. Newton Aycliffe began producing PVC in the 1940s and by 2000 had become the largest single-site PVC compounder in Europe. By 2005, the first state-of-the-art membrane technology chlorine plant had also been completed at Rafnes, with the second plant due for completion in 2006 at a combined cost of around €200 million.

Hydro Polymers' main branded products were Norvinyl, a suspension-PVC resin (S-PVC) used in windows and pipes, and Pevikon, an emulsion/paste-PVC resin (P-PVC) used in flooring and wall covering.[6] Other Hydro Polymers products included PVC compounds and caustic soda (supplied to the aluminium, paper and pulp industries and many others) and, since 2003, recycled PVC trading under the brand name EcoVin®.

Between 2000 and 2004, demand for S-PVC had risen across most European markets (with the exception of France and Scandinavia where demand had contracted), notably Poland (8%), Hungary

Hydro Polymers – Financial Information (2001–2005)

	2005 NOK million	2005 € million	2004 NOK million	2004 € million	2003 NOK million	2003 € million	2002 NOK million	2002 € million	2001 NOK million	2001 € million
Operating Income	69	8.6	254	30.33	**(8)**	(0.9)	**(35)**	(4.7)	**(101)**	(13.4)
EBITDA*	564	70.3	774	92.4	401	47.4	320	42.6	363	48.3
Number of employees	1167		1193		1200		1227		1690	

*Earnings before Interest, Tax, Depreciation and Amortization

Hydro Polymers – PVC Production Volumes (2002–2005)

Production outputs	Tonnes 2005	Tonnes 2004	Tonnes 2003	Tonnes 2002
VCM	**566,300**	541,000	575,000	540,000
Caustic soda	**305,700**	260,300	281,000	262,000
Suspension PVC	**483,600**	496,000	507,000	458,000
Paste PVC	**85,200**	82,200	81,000	70,000
Compounds	**119,900**	132,000	129,000	128,000
Total	**1 560 700**	1 511 500	1 573 000	1 458 000

Figure 22.6 Hydro Polymers' financial and production data 2005

Source: Extract from Norsk Hydro Annual Report 2005

(6%) and the Czech Republic (5%). The UK, Hydro Polymers' largest single market, had been experiencing steady decline since 1995 (tracking the construction sector) but by 2005 had stabilized. Over this period, Hydro Polymers had consolidated its UK market share at 42% of the S-PVC market and 18% of the P-PVC market (see Figure 22.7). With positive signs of market growth in the UK due to the resurgence of the building and construction industries, and emerging demand in Eastern Europe, Hydro Polymers was well positioned to take advantage of the upturn.

WHAT FUTURE? PVC VERSUS SUSTAINABILITY

In spite of its ubiquity, PVC was highly controversial (Thorton, 2002). PVC production consumed over one-third of global chlorine gas production, an energy-intensive process requiring 1% of global electricity production (mostly carbon-based), while some of the older plants were based on mercury cell technology, which released quantities of mercury into the environment. Environmentalists argued that certain PVC additives (plasticizers and stabilizers), the ingredients responsible for many of PVC's highly valued properties (e.g., flexibility, light weight, etc.), and

S-PVC by Application

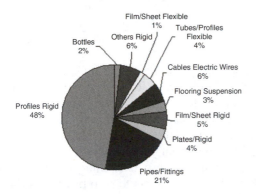

Hydro Polymers Market Share by Volume (1997–2005)

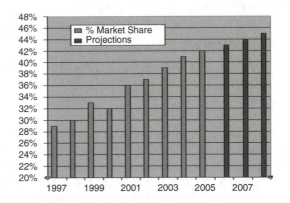

P-PVC by Application

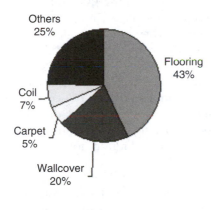

Hydro Polymers Market Share by Volume (1999–2008)

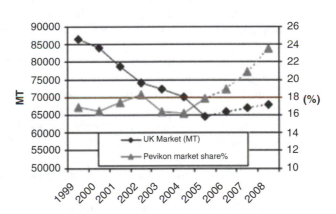

Figure 22.7　UK PVC market data (2005)

Source: Hydro Polymers

by-products from the manufacturing processes (primarily dioxins), were also highly unsustainable, emitted into the air, soil and water through the PVC production process, PVC waste incineration and leakage from landfill sites. Resistant to natural degradation, they built up as global pollutants, were absorbed into living systems and accumulated in the food chain; they were accused of damaging ecosystems and human health, disrupting the endocrine, reproductive, nervous and immune systems.

What little post-consumer PVC that was being recycled in the 1990s was in some cases 'down-cycled' into other products, such as traffic cones, with limited net reduction in virgin PVC production. The unique mix of additives found in each PVC product made post-consumer recycling of mixed PVC products difficult and costly compared to the low cost of virgin PVC.

Given PVC's varied and dispersed uses worldwide, prospects for large-scale recycling efforts appeared limited.

Deselection Threat

These concerns had been the focus of environmental campaigns since the early 1980s. However, in August 1996 Greenpeace UK raised the stakes with its 'Go PVC-Free' campaign. Founded in Canada in 1971, Greenpeace was an independent global campaigning organization, spread across 38 countries by 2005, which used confrontational yet non-violent tactics to focus public attention on a particular environmental issue, demanding an immediate ban of the offending, usually industrial, activity. With limited leverage over PVC producers, Greenpeace targeted retailers on the issue of packaging, staging demonstrations outside stores to raise public concern. Launching a pamphlet – 'Saving our skins' – in the national press, Greenpeace challenged retailers to stop buying products containing PVC, arguing that the health and environmental damage done far outweighed any benefits of PVC to society (see Figure 22.8).

In response to the campaign, a number of leading UK retailers formed the PVC Retail Working Group with representatives from retail majors Asda, Tesco, Co-operative Group and Waitrose, along with cosmetics retailer The Body Shop and Greenpeace. They quickly realized that they had insufficient scientific knowledge to make an informed judgement about the validity of the Greenpeace claims, and so the working group commissioned the National Centre for Business and Ecology (NCBE), a partnership between the Co-operative Bank and four UK universities, to investigate the issue. NCBE published its findings in September 1997 in a report on 'PVC in packaging and construction materials' (National Centre for Business and Ecology, 1997), concluding that with careful manufacture, use, recycling and disposal, it was possible to mitigate the environmental risks associated with PVC. Press headlines reported these findings as: 'PVC Industry told: Clean Up or Phase Out' (Retailer Working Group, 1997).

The UK PVC Retail Working Group invited the two UK PVC producers, Hydro Polymers and EVC/Ineos, into the dialogue, and the expanded PVC Co-ordination Group set out to establish an Environmental Charter and Code of Practice for PVC. By late 1999, however, tensions still ran high, with Greenpeace arguing PVC should be banned alongside toxic wastes such as lead, mercury and other heavy metals, while industry scientists remained convinced that technological solutions could mitigate environmental impacts. Caught in the middle, the retailers asked Jonathon Porritt, founder and chairman of leading UK environmental think-tank Forum for the Future, to intervene. Porritt agreed to chair the PVC Co-ordination Group on condition that they commission a full gap analysis of PVC using science-based principles for long-term sustainability developed by The Natural Step (see Exhibit 22.2).

The Natural Step Evaluation of PVC

The Natural Step Framework was developed in Sweden in 1989 by oncologist Dr Karl-Henrik Robèrt. Frustrated by the piecemeal approach to addressing environmental problems that he saw around him, Robèrt brought leading scientists together to develop a consensus on basic requirements for a sustainable society. Through this consensus-building process, he established basic scientific principles for socio-ecological sustainability, known as 'The System Conditions'.[7] By linking this clear goalpost for global sustainability with systems thinking and strategic planning,

August 1996

Saving our skins

Skincare products
Alternatives to PVC packaging

If you are buying skincare products, think about the packaging too. If you see that the container is marked with: ⚠3▽ then avoid it and choose an alternative instead.

If you shop at the Body Shop you can be sure of avoiding PVC packaging as they don't use it at all. Don't, however, be fooled by other similar 'natural' ranges sold in other places. Our research showed that some of those were packaged in PVC plastic.

The following lists show products that we found packaged in PVC and those that we found packaged in alternative materials. Choose the alternatives.

It's a simple switch – go PVC free!

 Skincare products which we found packaged in PVC plastic

Banana Boat skin care gel range
Boots Natural Collection sunflower
   body lotion
   royal jelly moisturising body spray
Carex antibacterial moisturising hand
   wash
Galenco antibacterial creme handwash
   peach creme handwash
Garnier Nutralia soap free hand wash
Marks & Spencers moisturising body
   lotion range
   royal jelly & honey moisture
   replenishing body milk
Sainsburys moisturising handwash
   Natures Compliments body mist
   Natures Compliments eye make-up
   remover
   Natures Compliments facial toner

Natures Compliments foot lotion
Natures Compliments gentle
   cleansing milk
Natures Compliments light body
   moisturiser
Natures Compliments light
   moisturising lotion
Natures Compliments massage oil
Natures Compliments rich body
   moisturiser
Simple moisturising hand wash
St. Ives chamomile face wash gel
Superdrug moisturising cream wash
   range
   moisturising hand & body lotion
Synergie eye make up remover
Ten-O-Six deep cleanser
   medicated cleanser

Tescos Active Response revitalising
   cleanser
   Active Response refreshing toner
   antibacterial moisturising
   handwash
   camellia moisturising cream wash
   Mild & Gentle pure wash gel
   rose moisturising cream wash
Tisserand face lotion
Waitrose Natural Extracts elderflower &
   yarrow cleanser
   Natural Extracts mallow & almond
   moisturiser
   Natural Extracts willow & mountain
   clover toner

Figure 22.8 Greenpeace anti-PVC campaign

a management framework emerged for integrating sustainability into core business strategy and operations, known as The Natural Step Framework (see Exhibit 22.3).

The Natural Step International (TNS) was established as a nonprofit NGO to develop and share this common framework, with representative offices in Sweden, United Kingdom, United States, Canada, Brazil, Japan, Australia, New Zealand, South Africa and Israel. The Natural Step Framework was used by over 60 leading companies such as IKEA, Electrolux, Interface and McDonalds, as well as by many governments, SMEs and local communities to chart their course towards full sustainability.

EXHIBIT 22.2 THE NATURAL STEP SUSTAINABILITY PRINCIPLES

Basic Science and Sustainability

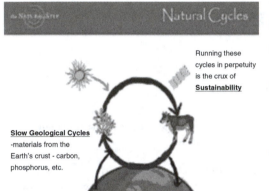

The basic science of sustainability is that natural cycles are out of balance.

- The Earth is a closed system to matter, and open to energy.
- Slow geological cycles of sedimentation and weathering deposit materials into the Earth's crust, and introduce materials into the biosphere.
- Running these cycles in perpetuity is the crux of sustainability.

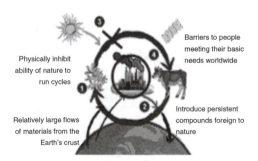

The impact of our collective global society today is such that we are undermining nature's capacity to run these cycles by

- introducing large flows of materials from the Earth's crust at a much faster rate than natural cycles
- introducing persistent compounds that are foreign to nature (cannot be cycled), and natural compounds in volumes far greater than background levels that natural cycles cope with
- inhibiting nature's physical ability to run these cycles through manipulation of eco-systems.

Furthermore, socio-economic barriers, which undermine people's capacity to meet their basic human needs, further reinforce this impact on natural cycles.

In a sustainable society, nature is not subject to systematically increasing

1. Concentrations of substances from the Earth's crust

2. Concentrations of substances produced by society

3. Degradation by physical means

And in that society, people are not subject to

4. Conditions that systematically undermine their capacity to meet their basic needs

The system conditions are the minimum constraints within which to create a sustainable society. For an organization or community to be sustainable it must eliminate its contribution to violating these system conditions.

In a sustainable society, nature is not subject to systematically increasing

- concentrations of substances from the Earth's crust
- concentrations of substances produced by society
- degradation by physical means.

And in that society, people are not subject to

- conditions that systematically undermine their capacity to meet their basic needs.

The System Conditions*

In order for a society to be sustainable, nature's functions and diversity are not systematically subject to increasing:

Concentrations of Substances Extracted from the Earth's Crust

In a sustainable society, human activities such as the burning of fossil fuels, and the mining of metals and minerals, will not occur at a rate that causes them to systematically increase in the ecosphere. There are thresholds beyond which living organisms and ecosystems are adversely affected by increases in substances from the earth's crust. Problems may include an increase in greenhouse gases leading to global warming, contamination of surface and ground water, and metal toxicity which can cause functional disturbances in animals. In practical terms, the first condition requires society to implement comprehensive metal and mineral recycling programs and to decrease economic dependence on fossil fuels.

Concentrations of Substances Produced by Society

In a sustainable society, humans will avoid generating systematic increases in persistent substances such as DDT, PCBs etc. Synthetic organic compounds such as these can remain in the environment for many years, bio-accumulating in the tissue of organisms and causing profound effects on predators in the upper levels of the food chain. Freon, and other ozone depleting compounds, may increase risk of cancer due to added UV radiation in the troposphere. Society needs to find ways to reduce economic dependence on persistent human-made substances.

(*Continued*)

EXHIBIT 22.2 (*Continued*)

Physical Displacement, Over-Harvesting, or Other Forms of Ecosystem Manipulation

In a sustainable society, humans will avoid taking more from the biosphere than can be replenished by natural systems. In addition, people will avoid systematically encroaching upon nature by destroying the habitat of other species. Biodiversity, which includes the great variety of animals and plants found in nature, provides the foundation for ecosystem services which are necessary to sustain life on this planet. Society's health and prosperity depends on the enduring capacity of nature for self-renewal and to rebuild waste into resources.

And in this society, people are not subject to:

Conditions That Systematically Undermine Their Capacity to Meet Their Needs

All human beings have intrinsic needs. The goal of the social system is to provide the opportunity for all to meet those needs, as a precondition to a dignified way of life for everyone. 'What' we do and 'how' we do it matters. To make decisions which take us toward this goal, in consideration of any policy, product, marketing or investment, we should always identify in advance the people who are going to be affected, taking the widest possible systems view. We should ask ourselves: 'Would we like to be subjected to the conditions we create?' In addition, decisions should allow for participation, be transparent, hold actors accountable and be honest.

* In 2002, a study of various sustainability tools and frameworks was undertaken by their pioneering founders, to understand the relationship between The Natural Step, and other approaches to sustainability, namely Natural Capitalism, Ecological Footprint, Factor 10, Sustainable Technology Development, Zero Emissions, and Cleaner Production (Robèrt, *et al.*, 2002). The study concluded that although each of these tools was complementary in terms of application and identification of second order principles for achieving sustainability, The Natural Step 'System Conditions' laid out the end goalpost, acting as overarching socio-ecological principles or minimum constraints for sustainability.

Source: The Natural Step

Backed by the UK Environment Agency, TNS initiated a lengthy and detailed study of PVC asking the question 'Does PVC have a place in a sustainable society?' The study engaged all key stakeholders, including the manufacturing chain, end-users, regulators and NGOs, and tested PVC for violations of the TNS System Conditions (see Exhibit 22.2). Although confident in PVC, Leadbitter and his colleagues at Hydro Polymers had serious concerns about TNS because other organizations had used its methodology as the rationale to phase out PVC. Hydro Polymers accepted that it had little choice but to proceed with the investigation and await the outcome, heartened by the fact that the TNS principles were based on science and that, to date, Porritt had taken a fair stance.

EXHIBIT 22.3 INTRODUCTION TO THE NATURAL STEP FRAMEWORK

The Funnel Metaphor

The practice of sustainability is about creating new ways to live and prosper while ensuring an equitable, healthy future for all people and the planet. Current scientific consensus states that we are currently consuming 25% more of the Earth's natural capital than it is able to regenerate. At the same time, society's demand for these resources is increasing. Metaphorically, this current situation for people on the Earth can be viewed as a funnel where the walls are nearing the intersection, and room to manoeuvre is diminishing (see Figure 22.9). With this awareness that we are all living in this funnel we have the opportunity to change this impact. However, increased awareness is not enough on its own. While we can all agree that sustainability is a noble pursuit, when it comes to making practical decisions in everyday life, there is still very little action being taken in the right direction. Sustainability covers such a vast range of issues, how do you begin to integrate it into core organizational practice?

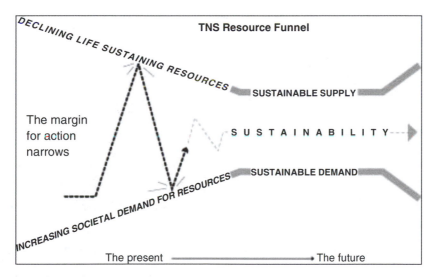

Figure 22.9 TNS Resource Funnel

Principles for Sustainability

The Natural Step (TNS) has identified four scientific principles that lead to a sustainable society, providing a clear definition of sustainability that serves as a compass for navigating the path towards sustainability. These principles, referred to as the 'system conditions', provide a practical set of criteria to diagnose easily the organizational gap with respect to sustainability and can be used to transform debate into constructive dialogue to direct strategic social, environmental and economic actions.

Implementation Methodology

The TNS Framework is based on a planning process called 'Backcasting from Principles', which uses a scientific compass to navigate towards sustainability and an organizational

(Continued)

EXHIBIT 22.3 (*Continued*)

process for developing strategic pathways to get there. The ABCD Process is a four-stage strategic tool for backcasting from sustainability principles (see Figure 22.10), which enables the organization to:

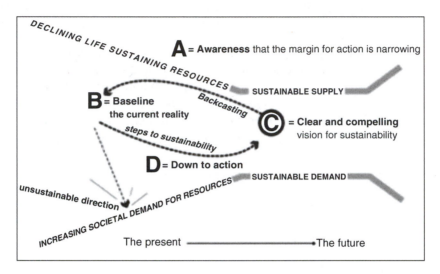

Figure 22.10 TNS A-B-C-D analysis

(A)wareness. Establish a common understanding of sustainability and the 'whole-systems' context.

(B)aseline Mapping. Conduct a gap analysis of major flows and impacts of current business activities against the System Conditions.

(C)reating a Vision. Identify creative solutions in compliance with the System Conditions.

(D)own to Action. Prioritize based on (i) steps in the right direction, (ii) a flexible platform for future moves and (iii) good ROI to support further moves.

By being more strategic when making choices and long-term plans, organizations can become restorative, widening the walls of the funnel while simultaneously increasing the prosperity of all stakeholders (see Figure 22.11). This enables leaders to take strategic and profitable steps towards sustainability by:

integrating environmental considerations into strategic decision-making

incorporating environmental concerns into daily operations and the workplace

reducing operating costs and environmental risk

getting ahead of regulatory frameworks

differentiating their products and services and building a positive brand image

enhancing stakeholder relations.

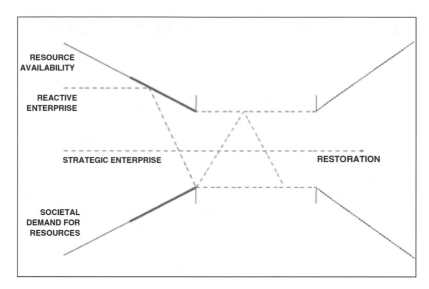

Figure 22.11 Widening the walls of the funnel

Companies that had embraced the TNS Framework by incorporating sustainable practices into their core business processes included:

IKEA (Sweden). The largest furniture company in the world adopted the TNS framework in 1991 in response to consumer pressure against rain-forest wood. Its four-year environmental plan called for implementing the TNS Framework throughout the company. IKEA began its TNS journey by redesigning one furniture line to eliminate metals, persistent glues and toxic dyes, reducing energy consumption and increasing material efficiency. By applying this experience company-wide, IKEA was said to have become more profitable as well as more sustainable.

Electrolux (Sweden). Electrolux adopted the TNS Framework in 1992 after it lost a multi-million-dollar deal because it did not offer a refrigeration system without chlorofluoro-carbons (CFCs). The company used TNS principles to phase out CFCs and won back that customer. But it didn't stop at refrigerators. It introduced washing machines that used 12 gallons of water instead of 45, and substituted canola oil for petroleum-based oil in its chain saws – all while reducing total energy consumption and hazardous waste.

Interface (US). Georgia-based Interface, the world's largest commercial-flooring company, became the first US company to adopt the TNS Framework in 1996. The goal of CEO Ray Anderson was to produce zero waste and to 'never take another drop of oil from the ground'. Innovations included leasing carpets instead of selling them and powering a factory with solar energy. In 1996 company sales increased by $200 million even though Interface used no more raw material than in 1995.

The Natural Step, through its founder Dr Karl-Henrik Robèrt, has been recognized for its contribution to sustainability by the Blue Planet Prize in 2000, and the KPMG International Business Ethics Award for contributions to Social Responsibility in 2005.

Source: adapted from The Natural Step

EXHIBIT 22.4 VINYL 2010 VOLUNTARY COMMITMENT 2000

In 2000, company participation in *Vinyl 2010* represented a commitment to undertake the following key activities:

- Compliance with European Council of Vinyl Manufacturers (ECVM) charters regarding PVC production emission standards.
- A plan for full replacement of lead stabilizers by 2015, in addition to the replacement of cadmium stabilizers, which was achieved in March 2001.
- Recycling of 200 000 tonnes of post-consumer PVC waste per year by 2010 [equivalent to 3% of annual European PVC consumption]. This objective was in addition to 1999 post-consumer recycling volumes and to any recycling of post-consumer waste as required by the implementation (after 1999) of EU directives on packaging waste, end-of-life vehicles and waste electronic and electrical equipment.
- Recycling of 50% of the collectable available [for recycling] PVC waste for window profiles, pipes, fittings and roofing membranes by 2005, and flooring by 2008.
- A research and development programme on new recycling and recovery technologies, including feedstock recycling and solvent-based technology.
- Implementation of a social charter signed with the European Mine, Chemical and Energy Worker's Federation (EMCEF) to develop social dialogue, training, health, safety and environmental standards, including transfer to EU accession countries.
- A partnership with local authorities within the Association of Communes and Regions for Recycling (ACRR) for the promotion of best practices and local pilot recycling schemes.

Source: Adapted from Vinyl 2010 Programme (www.vinyl2010.org/home/home/Our_Voluntary_Commitment/)

Meanwhile, in March 2000, the European PVC industry launched a voluntary commitment programme known as 'Vinyl 2010' (see Exhibit 22.4), as a pre-emptive strike against pending EU legislation threatening to add PVC to the list of banned toxic waste substances. Focused on continuous improvement targets to reduce PVC's environmental footprint, Vinyl 2010 rapidly became the reference 'industry sustainable development plan', and the proposed phase-out of PVC in the draft EU directive on end-of-life vehicles was overturned.[8]

Sustainable PVC – Tough Challenges Ahead

In July 2000, TNS produced a report identifying five major systemic challenges for PVC to become sustainable (see Exhibit 22.5):[9]

- *Challenge No. 1: The industry should commit itself long term to becoming carbon neutral.* PVC consumes large quantities of hydrocarbons, which end up as CO_2 and water with respect to energy, and in landfill with respect to the hydrocarbon inherent in the products. To achieve the challenge, the industry would need to maximize energy efficiency and find cost-effective and renewable sources of power, as well as conduct a life cycle analysis (LCA) of changing feedstock from hydrocarbon to biomass or other sources.

- *Challenge No. 2: The industry should commit itself long term to a closed-loop system of PVC waste management.* If all PVC is recycled, none is lost to landfill, and the material can be re-used. In a fully closed-loop system, the recycled PVC could be re-used in similar applications, saving production of more virgin PVC and avoiding depletion of the earth's resources.

- *Challenge No. 3: The industry should commit itself long term to ensuring that releases of persistent organic compounds from the whole life cycle do not result in systematic increases in concentration in nature.* These pollutants build up in nature because natural processes cannot break them down. This applies particularly to dioxins, a by-product of chlorine production.

- *Challenge No. 4: The industry should review the use of all additives consistent with attaining full sustainability, and especially commit to phasing out long-term substances that can accumulate in nature or where there is reasonable doubt regarding toxic effects.* Current non-sustainable additives such as lead would need to be phased out and sustainable alternatives found that impart the desired properties to the finished product.

- *Challenge No. 5: The industry should commit to the raising of awareness about sustainable development across the industry, and the inclusion of all participants in its achievements.*

EXHIBIT 22.5 PVC – AN EVALUATION USING THE NATURAL STEP FRAMEWORK

the NATURAL STEP

July 2000

Dear

The public profile and interest about issues relating to PVC have steadily increased in recent years. Mounting concerns have meant that the PVC industry has come under a lot of pressure. A huge amount of data has been generated; opinions flow back and forth, with experts as divided as the general public.

The PVC Coordination Group was set up in 1997 to help shed some light on this contentious area. It comprises representatives of major retailers and the two UK PVC manufacturers, as well as a representative of the Environment Agency, and is chaired by myself.

One of the most important projects it has initiated has been a large-scale research project with The Natural Step (TNS) in the UK to evaluate the manufacture, use and disposal of PVC against a set of strict sustainability criteria. The attached documents represent the principal outputs of that research. The full report (*PVC: An Evaluation Using The Natural Step Framework*)

(Continued)

EXHIBIT 22.5 (*Continued*)

contains details of both the research and the consensus-building work that went on around it. The brief summary report (*2020 Vision Series No. 2: PVC and Sustainability*) seeks to capture in plain English the key issues and implications arising from the research and consensus-building. (2020 Vision is a process initiated jointly by TNS and the Environment Agency to help create a vision of a genuinely sustainable future.)

Among the key outcomes of this work is a set of challenges setting out what it would take for PVC to become truly sustainable across its entire life cycle. Representatives of the UK PVC industry participating in this research recognize the magnitude of these challenges, but accept that they are ultimately unavoidable and that they therefore provide a helpful agenda for actions.

It's a tough challenge. But not that dissimilar from the challenge that confronts all plastics. It serves little purpose arguing for the elimination of PVC without first assessing the degree to which any substitutes would have a lower 'sustainability footprint'. PVC may or may not have a place in a genuinely sustainable future (depending on whether or not it can meet the challenges outlined in our evaluation), but exactly the same questions must be asked of all materials, man-made or natural, before leaping to what are often ill-judged and unscientific conclusions.

I very much hope that this report will be of use to you, and will help inform your thinking on this controversial issue.

Yours sincerely,

JONATHON PORRITT
Chairman

9 IMPERIAL SQUARE, CHELTENHAM, GL50 1QB
TEL: 01242-262744   FAX: 01242-524445
info@tnsuk.demon.co.uk   www.naturalstep.org.uk

The Natural Step is a Forum for the Future activity
Charity Number 1040519

Sustainability Challenges for the PVC Industry (from 'PVC: An Evaluation using the Natural Step Framework,' p. 17)

At present, PVC production and usage, particularly at end-of-life, breaches the System Conditions of TNS in a number of significant ways. It is therefore clearly unsustainable taking into account current methods of manufacture, conversion, use and disposal, and this despite the considerable eco-efficiency improvements that have been made over recent years. The challenge of achieving sustainability should not be seen solely as a longer-term issue. Global and national commitments to reductions in greenhouse gas emissions, legislation concerning packaging waste, and public concerns about the fate of PVC in incinerators all indicate the accelerating trend of restrictions on PVC, acting like a 'funnel' constraining industry's room for manoeuvre. This in turn signals the business advantages of addressing sustainable development as a business priority.

Based on the System Condition analysis, five key challenges emerge for the PVC industry. If accepted and addressed proactively, they would mark a major shift towards sustainability and should yield clear business benefits.

CHALLENGE No. 1

The industry should commit itself long term to becoming carbon neutral.

CHALLENGE No. 2

The industry should commit itself long term to a closed-loop system of PVC waste management.

CHALLENGE No. 3

The industry should commit itself long term to ensuring that releases of persistent organic compounds from the whole life cycle do not result in systematic increases in concentration in nature.

CHALLENGE No. 4

The industry should review the use of all additives consistent with attaining full sustainability, and especially commit to phasing out long term substances that can accumulate in nature or where there is doubt regarding toxic effects.

CHALLENGE No. 5

The industry should commit to the raising of awareness about sustainable development across the industry, and the inclusion of all participants in its achievement.

Source: The Natural Step

To the enormous relief of the PVC producers, the TNS study concluded that although PVC was currently unsustainable, none of these five challenges was technologically insurmountable. PVC could become a sustainable material; however, the industry would need to assess carefully whether, practically speaking, the challenges could be met in a commercially viable way. For example, given the energy intensity of the industry, would becoming carbon neutral push costs too high for a low-margin industry (particularly given the competition from the Chinese, who were considered unlikely to adopt the challenges, at least in the short term)? Would the construction industry embrace the recycling of PVC windows and pipes? Could sustainable and cost-effective alternatives be found that reproduced the attractive product qualities provided by current additives? How long would the transition take and would material specifiers switch to alternatives in the interim?

Stakeholder Reactions

Greenpeace concluded that the challenges were unattainable and left the PVC Co-ordination Group. However, other key industry stakeholders held a workshop on the future of sustainable PVC.[10] The TNS challenges led stakeholders to realize that no material was inherently sustainable or unsustainable outright and that it was the sourcing and management of a material across its whole life cycle that determined its long-term sustainability impact. Furthermore, a full life cycle comparative evaluation could give PVC fair consideration against alternative materials such as wood, aluminium and other plastics. By translating sustainability from a vague definition into science-based, concrete and actionable targets in the form of these five challenges, environmentalists were in a much stronger position to hold the PVC industry genuinely accountable, whereas producers were able to refute emotionally-charged criticisms.

Most of the European PVC industry was oblivious to the TNS evaluation but because of the huge political interests was fully aware of the Vinyl 2010 commitments. Although some stakeholders began to see potential for competitive advantage by integrating sustainability into core business planning, others felt unable to tackle such a comprehensive programme, and several did not believe that climate change was a major issue. Hydro Polymers supported the broad Vinyl 2010 approach of uniting the whole of the European PVC Industry; however, Leadbitter also understood the need for a more deep-seated understanding of sustainability that was not politically driven, because the underlying demand for full sustainability would always be there. He was convinced that embracing the sustainability challenges would enable Hydro Polymers to pre-empt future regulation and seize competitive advantage as the first mover. Porritt later echoed this sentiment at the PVC industry conference in Brighton in 2002:

> There is a world of difference literally. I'm not attacking incremental efforts to reduce your environmental footprints, but I question if this is a good use of a company's resources and creativity if the final goal is not sustainability. Merely being less damaging is never going to be enough.

WALKING THE TALK

In 2000, Leadbitter had seen the problem with the retailers and Greenpeace as specific to the UK PVC industry. However, executive management at Norsk Hydro had begun to take its own interest in sustainability. Dr Per Sandberg, an internal consultant and senior researcher on sustainability and ethics, was appointed to investigate the various models of sustainability and make a recommendation that Norsk Hydro might adopt company-wide.

Leadbitter heard about the initiative and invited Sandberg to come to Newton Aycliffe to sit in on his interview with TNS for the PVC Co-ordination Group's study. The interview took a full day and both Leadbitter and Sandberg were impressed by its thoroughness in exploring the entire PVC manufacturing process, looking at all the additives and by-products, and at what happened both upstream and downstream to understand which System Conditions were being breached throughout the entire PVC supply chain.

Sandberg went back to Oslo with a better understanding of the TNS Framework, and after looking at a variety of ethics and corporate responsibility models, concluded:

> The Natural Step Framework impressed us, being both the most radical model ('the real thing') and by having an explicit educational logic. It works because it identifies the gap between our current position and a fully sustainable position. By adapting to the TNS framework, Hydro Polymers' UK operation is by far the leading role model for sustainability within Norsk Hydro.

In spite of considering the framework too tough for an oil and gas company, Norsk Hydro fully endorsed The Natural Step and its application to PVC.

Hydro Polymers' President Becomes Involved

Following publication of the PVC evaluation report, Hydro Polymers' President, Anders Hermansson, was keen to meet Dr Karl-Henrik Robèrt, founder of TNS. The principle of consensus building that Robèrt had used to develop The Natural Step, involving the scientific community to uncover basic scientific principles of sustainability, was deeply rooted in Swedish culture. Hermansson, who was also Swedish, understood the value of the scientific consensus on which this PVC evaluation was based, and invited Robèrt to meet him in Oslo in December 2000.

The two men hit it off immediately. Robèrt's position on PVC was that, like any product, it had a journey to travel to become sustainable, and rather than automatically assuming that the PVC material should be banned in favour of alternatives, the real question was whether the journey itself was commercially viable. Hermansson recognized that the journey ahead for Hydro Polymers required consensus building both within the company and with its suppliers, customers and the public at large, and was keen to kick-start the process by engaging his senior management team.

One of the outcomes of this meeting was a decision to bring in a wider group of managers involved in the PVC production process. Robèrt and his team at TNS were commissioned to tour all Hydro Polymers' plants to undertake a deeper analysis of what it would take to create a sustainable PVC business and to educate the top 40 senior and middle managers in the TNS framework and the five challenges for PVC so that they really understood the scale of the task. Robèrt commented:

> I was shocked to realize how the PVC industry was not on top of how to communicate about this. Every industry has a distance to go to achieve full sustainability. It's a journey with many steps. TNS provides a rigorous and scientific, yet non-prescriptive and non-adversarial approach to developing a strategic roadmap of the way forward. So long as you are moving in the right direction, you are not the bad guy.

In October 2001, Robèrt attended Hydro Polymers' annual strategy meeting in Norway together with Hermansson, Leadbitter and Senior Vice-President of Hydro Polymers, David Summerbell. He was subsequently asked to gather Hydro Polymers' site directors and the rest of the senior management team at Sånga-Säby, a Swedish farmhouse retreat, to lead an extended two-day strategic planning workshop on sustainable business using the TNS Framework (see Exhibit 22.3).

Getting Down to Work

For Leadbitter, the management retreat and Robèrt's involvement could not have come at a better time. Hermansson agreed with Leadbitter on the long-term opportunity the challenges presented, and infected by Robèrt's positive approach to PVC, launched 'PVC for Tomorrow', a programme to bring all employees into the process. Fully supported by Hermansson, divisional teams were set up, working across all sites to pool ideas on how to address the five challenges. Out of a total of 1400 employees, about 140 became actively involved in the process, with each site competing to present their best ideas. In order to help employees understand how the challenges could be addressed, Leadbitter produced a comprehensive paper entitled 'PVC and Sustainability', which could be used by all stakeholders to see a way forward (Leadbitter, 2002). The paper described the sustainability journey and offered solutions to how the challenges could be addressed. Initially, some employees doubted the integrity of this management initiative. However, once they got to grips with the framework as a means to understand the end-goal of sustainability, employees took pride in what was being achieved, which was a significant shift from the frustration of always being attacked by pressure groups such as Greenpeace.

Eager to inject a stimulus to help to get a number of sustainability projects off the ground (especially the energy reduction projects) and convince one or two active dissenters at the annual strategy meeting, Hermansson guaranteed to contribute NOK 25 million (approximately €3 million) per year for three years from 2002, in addition to normal capital expenditure. Each site generated floods of ideas and a cross-functional divisional team selected the best projects based on the highest CO_2 savings per NOK invested. A number of employees had been thinking about these ideas for some time but there had never been the opportunity for such creative thinking and investment until carbon neutrality became a strategic priority. The challenges generated a sense of purpose and achievement among employees, accelerating the implementation process.

Progress on Sustainability Challenges

Between 2001 and 2004, sustainability innovation projects reduced Hydro Polymers' CO_2 emissions by more than 12.5%, meeting Kyoto Protocol targets within the first four years[11] (see Exhibit 22.6). Installation of adiabatic volume pipes used on the chemical 'cracking' process saved on average 8000 tonnes of CO_2 per year while reducing the need for additional energy input. Further savings were generated by the installation of heat exchangers, the move from AC to DC drives and the purchase of two wind turbines. More ambitious projects included the utilization of the hydrogen produced as a by-product in the chlorine process as a fuel for a new sustainable transport project within the Grenland district of Norway. Energy efficiency gains had translated into tangible savings for Hydro Polymers, such as the energy reduction projects, which alone were saving around €3.5 million per annum. Demonstrating savings on the other challenges proved harder, however, as the challenges presented were more complex.

In the meantime, the rest of the PVC industry remained fairly nonchalant about Hydro Polymers' initiatives. Greenpeace and other activist groups were not pressing the industry on its carbon footprint, and so the rest of the industry could not understand why Hydro Polymers was bothering to invest in seemingly unnecessary reductions. In contrast, Robèrt strongly supported Hydro Polymers' approach, highlighting that many alternatives advocated by Greenpeace and others could have far bigger footprints and that reducing CO_2 emissions was crucial to long-term sustainability.

To address the second challenge of closed-loop recycling, Hydro Polymers launched a new, recycled PVC product line under the trademark EcoVin®. Initially recycling its own customers' PVC waste product (post-industrial waste) that at the time was going to landfill, Hydro Polymers saw a future opportunity in recycling post-consumer waste. Although it was possible to produce EcoVin as cheaply as virgin PVC compound, this was only achieved by taking as many costs out of the process as possible. For example, the product was only sold in recycled bags using recycled pallets. However, there were indications that a market was developing for recycled PVC compounds, especially where surface finish was less critical, such as in certain building and construction products. Initial volumes were relatively low but by 2005 had grown to around 4000 tonnes of total production, with several new markets and applications under development.

Hydro Polymers also worked with the industry on recycling, because the Vinyl 2010 initiative had set a target to recycle 200 000 tonnes of post-consumer PVC waste by 2010. With 17 million tonnes of plastics entering the waste stream within Europe, and landfill constraints developing in many member states, further pressure to recycle more PVC was expected. Because recycling was both expensive and risky for a single player, it was preferable to work with partners in the industry and with specialist waste management companies. However, one such recycling initiative had failed. Stignaes was a PVC waste-recycling centre with a 50 000 tonne capacity established in Denmark in 2003. Operational costs were much higher than expected, making the plant uneconomic to run, and with a prohibitive gate fee, the centre was never fully opened.

EXHIBIT 22.6 HYDRO POLYMERS' PROGRESS ON SUSTAINABILITY CHALLENGES 2005: AN EXTRACT FROM HYDRO POLYMERS' ENVIRONMENTAL NEWSLETTER – OCTOBER 2005

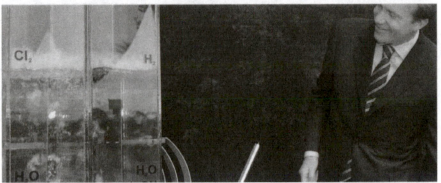

With the switch on of a symbolic chlorine cell, this September Norwegian Trade and Industry minister Børge Brende officially opened Hydro Polymers' new membrane chlorine plant at Rafnes in Norway. This important development takes the business another step closer to its vision of one day being carbon neutral.

Progress on Sustainable Development

As well as supporting the Vinyl 2010 initiative, Hydro Polymers firmly believes that contributing towards achieving sustainability within our industry makes good business sense. For this reason a number of strategic projects have now been completed that directly address the sustainability challenges set out in a report published by scientists from The Natural Step. These projects have also required significant financial investment and are summarised below.

Challenge No 1
Carbon Neutrality
- the industry should commit itself long-term to becoming carbon neutral

Significant progress has been made over the last 4 years to reduce our CO_2 emissions from our manufacturing processes.

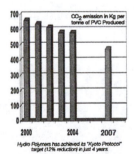

Hydro Polymers has achieved its "Kyoto Protocol" target (12% reduction) in just 4 years.

To date this has led to over 80Kg of CO_2 reduction per tonne of PVC produced. To put this reduction into perspective it means that Hydro Polymers has achieved our "Kyoto Protocol" target (12% reduction) in just 4 years - an excellent achievement for any industry. Furthermore, with the introduction of our new chlorine plant at Rafnes using state-of-the-art technology and the

modernisation of the existing plant we expect further progress in our quest for carbon neutrality. The predicted reduction by 2007 will be 28% lower than the CO_2 emissions in 2000. New green energy projects include the potential for the construction of a hydrogen fuelling station within the Grenland area in Norway, thereby better utilisation of the hydrogen produced from our chlorine plants. In addition, local planning applications have just been granted for the construction of 2*250KW wind turbines at our Newton Aycliffe plant in the UK.

Challenge No 2
Closed-Loop Recycling
- the industry should commit itself long-term to a closed-loop system of PVC waste management

Steady progress has been made on developing our EcoVin® product line. The compound is manufactured from post-industrial scrap and to date we have had nearly 2500 tonnes of sales that could have otherwise been destined to landfill. Our customers have developed novel applications for this product line for use in long-term construction applications that require good physical properties yet the aesthetics of the finished product are not deemed to

be critical compared to their application. There are commercial sensitivities of some of the applications but we are delighted to report that one customer PAL extrusions is prepared to share one such application with our readers. The product is used in a roofing application and is used as an eaves protector under a slated roof. It is not visible yet offers important protection to the elements thereby protects the wooden eaves.

Pictured: An Eaves Protector manufactured from EcoVin®, courtesy of Pal Extrusions.

To date Hydro Polymers has already recycled the equivalent of more than 170,000 windows

(Continued)

EXHIBIT 22.6 (*Continued*)

Challenge No 3
Elimination of Persistent Organic Pollutants
- the industry should commit itself long-term to ensuring that releases of persistent organic compounds (POPs) do not result in systematic increases in concentration in nature.

The reported dioxin levels across the whole of our operations continue to reduce as shown in the graph below. A new research project is underway to evaluate and report on any dioxin emissions for the newly constructed chlorine plant. Levels are anticipated to be extremely small on the basis that the new plant utilises new materials that

Karl Henrik Robert of the Natural Step explaining the TNS Framework Model at Hydro Polymers' Strategic Raw Material Supplier event at Stenungsund in Sweden in April 2005

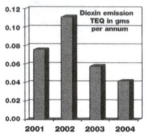

Dioxin emission TEQ in gms per annum

Year	2001	2002	2003	2004
TEQ	0.076	0.11	0.056	0.042

have less propensity for catalysing dioxin formation. Results from this study will be available in 2006.

Challenge No 4
Sustainable Additives
- the industry should review the use of all additives consistent with attaining full sustainability.

Lead Stabiliser Phase Out Programme Hydro Polymers reported at PVC 2005 through the paper given by Jan Sverre Rosstad, Senior Vice President, Polymers that our company will be lead-free by the end of 2007. This is a very challenging target but one that we believe to be important in our drive towards sustainability within European PVC Industry. Whilst we appreciate that the Vinyl 2010 phase-out will see the sun-setting of lead stabilisers by 2015, the developing legislation on REACH could quicken the pace of this commitment. The main stabilisers used to replace lead will be based either on Calcium/Zinc and/or OBS® based systems. The strategy behind our evaluation of the alternative stabilisers was presented by Kristin Eide Lunde from Norsk Hydro's Corporate Research Centre and was also delivered at PVC 2005. The report will shortly be published online in

Plastics, Rubber and Composites: Macromolecular Engineering. at **www.ingentaconnect.com/content/maney/prc**

In addition to the work on lead, our strategic raw material suppliers were invited to a Sustainability Workshop in April held at our Stenungsund plant in Sweden. This workshop was a first for Hydro Polymers, bringing together the key additive suppliers within our industry to participate in a one-day workshop on the theme of sustainability.

Kristin Eide Lunde from Norsk Hydro's Corporate Research Centre presenting a paper on Hydro Polymers strategy for alternative stabilisers at the PVC 2005 conference in Brighton

In view of the importance of this event, and the understanding that not all our raw material suppliers were able to participate, the key presentations at the event were filmed and are now available on DVD. Copies of this DVD can be obtained on request from Hydro Polymers' communications manager Chris Welton either by returning the enclosed request form, or via an e-mail request to: **chris.welton@hydro.com**.

Challenge No 5
Raising awareness across the Industry

Complementing the raw material supplier event in April, invitations were also extended to our customers to attend a Marketing/Sustainability workshop during the official opening of the new chlorine plant at Rafnes in Oslo at the end of August. The main purpose of this event was to both communicate Hydro Polymers Sustainability Strategy and to build a flexible platform for customers and other stakeholders on sustainability issues. The feedback from our customers was very positive and there is now an expectation of follow-up activities. For example we expect to see progress on a Centre of Excellence on a Sustainable PVC set up in partnership with The Natural Step International. We would like to extend the business benefits of addressing sustainability implications on PVC to a wider range of stakeholders. In this way we believe that we can demonstrate PVCs long-term ability in becoming a fully sustainable material.

For more information on Hydro Polymers sustainability initiatives please contact:

Dr Jason Leadbitter
Sector Sustainability Manager
Hydro Polymers
e-mail:jason.leadbitter@hydro.com

Source: Hydro Polymers

Waste collectors found cheaper ways to recycle, in mainland Europe or in some cases sending PVC waste to China.

To make progress towards the third challenge of eliminating dioxins and other persistent chemicals, Hydro Polymers initiated research and development activities in 2002 to understand how dioxins were formed in the first place, committing several human-months per annum over a three-year period. This led to an understanding of the mechanism of formation and consequently, based on these research findings, further expansion and modernization investments of approximately €200 million were made at Hydro Polymers' chlorine plant at Rafnes in Norway. By 2006, Hydro Polymers would be able to use substitute gasketing materials within its chlorine plant, resulting in significant reductions in the formation of dioxins and other chlorinated hydrocarbons as well as significant reductions in CO_2 emissions.

The fourth challenge was to remove all non-sustainable additives, the main one of which was lead, a uniquely efficient stabilizer. In 2002, Hydro Polymers launched a three-year €200 000 research and development investigation into lead and its alternatives using the TNS Framework. Hydro Polymers adopted the challenging target of being lead-free across all sites by the end of 2007. Significant progress had been made on evaluating alternatives to lead stabilizers, with one major raw material supplier, Chemson, disclosing confidential formulation to allow full sustainability analysis of the alternatives. Although alternatives were available, none was found to be fully cost-effective. Hydro Polymers realized that in order to meet its target for phasing out lead, it would have to fund alternatives from some of its savings from energy efficiency projects.

As one of the major issues, the industry was also focusing on lead through the Vinyl 2010 initiative. This set a voluntary target for the industry to be lead-free by 2015. By 2003, however, it was clear to Hydro Polymers that the draft European legislation on chemical safety (REACH) was likely to set a much earlier date for substituting lead stabilizers. Leadbitter felt this would vindicate Hydro Polymers' pre-emptive action, driven by its commitment to be a sustainable producer as rapidly as possible, compared to a more reactive industry position.

From 2001 to 2004, senior management gave high priority to sustainability and maintained a close interest, inviting Robèrt and TNS back regularly to scrutinize investments, run further workshops and education sessions, and provide assurance on steps being taken. Sustainability was no longer treated in isolation and its targets were fully integrated into the traditional business planning process. Various newsletters were periodically circulated to employees, customers and raw material suppliers, highlighting the progress that had been made on the five challenges.[12]

'Sustainability is Good for Business'

In early 2003, Hydro Polymers launched its new vision statement: 'To be the preferred and sustainable supplier of vinyl and caustic products' as part of a 'Sustainability is Good for Business' campaign. Speaking about Hydro Polymers' new philosophy, Hermansson commented:

> We have recognized that each of our stakeholders – our owners, our customers, our employees, our partners and suppliers, and society as a whole, all have differing needs. Our challenge for the future is to reconcile the achievement of genuine sustainable development with practical economics – to help meet the needs of society through harnessing the benefits of an amazingly useful polymer, whilst leaving a minimal environmental footprint and meeting our commercial need to operate as a profitable business.

This represented a significant shift in internal culture, confirmed by the annual employee survey in September 2004, highlighting a 15% increase in employee recognition of the company's environmental commitment, in response to the question 'Does Hydro Polymers put the environment first?'. Since the days of the Greenpeace deselection campaign targeting retailers to 'Go PVC-Free', Hydro Polymers was able accurately to specify the gap between the current position of PVC in relation to the end-goal of sustainability and spell out how it was systematically closing this gap. Management believed that employees were buying into the process as a direct result of actions they saw firsthand, with the visible support of top management, and that the resulting sustainability innovations had reduced risks to which competitors were now being exposed.

THE FIFTH CHALLENGE

In the summer of 2004, David Summerbell, Senior Vice-President of Hydro Polymers, retired. He was succeeded by Jan-Sverre Rosstad. Unlike his predecessor, until now, Rosstad was known to hold a sceptical position on the future of PVC. Back in the mid to late 1990s, Rosstad had been CEO of a plastic pipe company (then owned by parent company Norsk Hydro). The company had been a market leader in Norway, having built its success on polyethylene and polypropylene, both competing materials with PVC. The enormous environmental pressures facing PVC, coupled with the availability of competing plastics, made Rosstad sceptical about its survival. He was head-hunted by Hydro Polymers in 2004 and once he came to understand the science and strategy behind Hydro Polymers' approach he saw the PVC situation in a different light, in spite of his experience with competing plastics that continued to thrive in the marketplace:

> This is a survival game. It was then (1996) as it is today; however we are in a far more proactive situation today because of our journey from deselection to preferred supplier. Finding The Natural Step Framework to define sustainability in clear terms we could act on was no small feat. Understanding what this means for our business took a huge amount of work. Reframing our approach from add-on activities to the core business model, implementing these activities and remaining focused was very important. We are well positioned for this next phase of the challenge, gaining momentum in the market place which will hopefully translate into a snowball effect.

Rosstad saw that Hydro Polymers' unique approach was responsible for pioneering innovations to address the challenges, well ahead of competitors and regulation. In the meantime, the European Commission had been preparing the new REACH directive on the safety of chemicals, with the major implication to switch the onus of proof from regulators to the chemicals industry. The EU's draft proposal, published in October 2003, was expected to be enacted in legislation by 2007, when industry would be expected to bear the costs of achieving the necessary targets, and materials suppliers would need to demonstrate that the chemicals they were producing posed no risk to downstream users, consumers and the environment. Rosstad concluded that although good progress was being made on the first four challenges, it was time to embark on the fifth challenge and start to engage the rest of the industry to move towards complete sustainability.

In April 2005, Hydro Polymers invited its 10 top strategic raw material suppliers – Rohm & Haas, Omya, Kronos, Chemson, Akzo Nobel, Perstorp, Synthomer, Unger, and Exxon and Eliokem – to a supplier event in Stenungsund, Sweden, to expose them to the sustainability challenges facing PVC, and communicate Hydro Polymers' sustainability strategy. Leadbitter believed it was vital for key suppliers to have the opportunity to understand Hydro Polymers' approach to sustainable PVC based on the TNS Framework, if future partnerships to address the challenges were to succeed. Meanwhile, suppliers grappled with the sustainability implications for their own product development against the practical reality of achieving them in a commercially viable timeframe.

Feedback from all those attending was very positive, and the professionally recorded DVD of the event achieved far wider circulation than just among direct stakeholders. Although Hydro Polymers continued to receive positive press for its efforts, some dissenters remained. In October 2005, *Green Futures Magazine*[13] interviewed Mark Strutt of Greenpeace UK, who had left the PVC Co-ordination Group back in 2000 and whose position was unchanged:

> Unless Hydro can show it can make PVC without chlorine, and without using toxic and persistent additives, then we are not interested in small improvements. We still believe that PVC is inherently unsustainable and completely unnecessary, as alternatives exist for virtually all its applications.

Leadbitter, interviewed alongside Strutt, responded:

> We've nearly met the Kyoto target in four years, which is impressive for any industry. Alternatives to PVC were used before PVC was invented, but they do not measure up to the combination of light weight, durability and cost/performance benefits. On chlorine, this adds one of the huge advantages [of PVC] compared to alternatives. Over half of PVC is derived from natural salt and less than half from fossil fuels at a time when we need to reduce carbon. Greenpeace has unwittingly done our industry lots of favours. We have a much better understanding of sustainability and what challenges lie ahead compared to producers of competing materials that have yet to embrace full sustainability.

The Innovators' Dilemma

In 2005, Hydro Polymers' profit was only €8.6 million while key competitor EVC lost €13.2 million. For decades, market growth in Western Europe had been driven by applications for door and window profiles and pipes. The PVC market was maturing and growth of these installations was sluggish, projected to be only 0.5% per annum to 2008. With profitability in the sector almost uniformly poor and running on very tight margins, many players were asking how sustainability could be good for business when the priority was survival. Furthermore, rapidly increasing demand in China was driving a ramp up in domestic PVC manufacturing capacity, with little concern about sustainability. China was preparing to increase production by one million tonnes year-on-year from 2006 to 2010, using large coal feedstock and old, much more energy-intensive and polluting technologies that had been phased out in the EU in the 1960s.[14] Although intended for domestic consumption, Chinese PVC containing additives phased out in the EU could well enter Europe in imported finished products or packaging, at the risk of re-energizing the deselection campaign in Western Europe because, in the majority of cases, REACH legislation would not apply to these finished articles.

For PVC to achieve the complete sustainability that Hydro Polymers envisaged, the entire value chain would need to align with the sustainability challenges over time. In the past, industry competitors had stood shoulder to shoulder against the environmentalists and Vinyl 2010 specifically targeted some of the issues raised by Greenpeace and others. Now Hydro Polymers' more radical approach was being highlighted in the leading environmental journal, *Environmental Data Services* (ENDS, 2005, pp. 25–28):

[Vinyl 2010] could be more ambitious – after all, if Hydro Polymers can go lead-free by 2008, why can't others? If the less fraught atmosphere is making the industry feel more relaxed, now is the time for more open, inclusive discussions with retailers and environmental groups about how to overcome the barriers to reducing the polymer's environmental impacts – and thereby reduce the business risks for downstream users.

Hydro Polymers believed the ongoing deselection threat could only be fully addressed by effective communication about the steps being taken by the industry to address these fundamental challenges as part of a long-term commitment. However, too much high-profile communication about this complete, systems-based approach to sustainability could potentially undermine the importance of bringing the industry together to take early collective action, as Vinyl 2010 was doing about recycling.

Given this overall market climate, the real question on Rosstad's mind was how to keep capitalizing on Hydro Polymers' sustainability initiatives, as the early wins dried up and more bold investments were required. The time had come to engage Hydro Polymers' own customers, the manufacturers of PVC products such as flooring, pipes and window profiles, to support the process. Engaging raw material (additive) suppliers back in April 2005 had been a low-risk strategy to test external reactions to Hydro Polymers' unique, strategic approach to sustainability. Supplier reactions had been favourable, considering that Hydro Polymers' full commitment to sustainability represented virtually guaranteed demand for their sustainable product innovations. Hydro Polymers needed to convince its own customers that sustainable PVC was a viable long-term strategy over alternative materials such as wood, plastics or aluminium, as well as demonstrate tangible added value in its own increasingly more sustainable PVC product – which could position Hydro Polymers' brand so as to command a price premium over competing commodity brands.

Getting Customers on Board

On 20 March 2006, Leadbitter and Rosstad were sitting in Rosstad's office preparing for their crucial meeting with their key UK customers the following day (see Exhibit 22.7). They both felt it was time to talk more openly about what Hydro Polymers had achieved and create demand for further innovations by showcasing Hydro Polymers' strategy for sustainable PVC and progress to date. The most important question was whether their customers would really understand the process the company had embarked on in 2001, and appreciate the advantage of planning for full

---

EXHIBIT 22.7 BACKGROUND ON KEY CUSTOMERS ATTENDING THE SUSTAINABILITY WORKSHOP

The key customers attending the workshop included the following major product areas.

Building and Construction

The highest number of participants in terms of volumes sold by Hydro Polymers in the UK was suppliers to the construction industry. These customers purchased either PVC resin and/or PVC compounds to fabricate extruded profile in applications such as pipes, window frames, facia and soffit boards.

They were faced with increasing pressures to demonstrate the sustainability of their products through increased regulation, especially in relation to social housing, including new drivers being developed from the Office of the Deputy Prime Minister (ODPM), requirements from bodies such as English Partnerships, and private finance initiatives. In addition, they faced pressure from many of their own customers, house builders and architects faced with increasing pressures to demonstrate that they were using sustainable materials in construction.

Their expectations of the workshop were to learn how sustainability could be implemented within their businesses – more especially whether it could help towards the increasing requests for 'sustainable materials'. They were also looking towards collaboration with their suppliers and across the industry over recovery of PVC for recycled applications. For most participants, the workshops were seen as a new way of looking at their respective businesses and most were keen to learn from the experience.

These customers were heavily dependent upon PVC, which remained the only viable plastic for use in window frames and plastic profiles. On that basis any loss of PVC markets would be a direct loss of business to them. Alternative products for use in window frames (timber and/or aluminium) required vastly different processes of fabrication from the invested infrastructure in their own companies already dedicated to processing PVC.

Flooring

Other participants were manufacturers supplying vinyl-based systems to a diverse range of customers in the flooring industry. They had many of the same issues as participants in building and construction. However, unlike construction, these manufacturers could offer alternatives such as linoleum and wood laminate to their customers. Nevertheless, PVC (or vinyl as it is usually referred to within the flooring industry) remained a hugely important material in their portfolio, offering advantages over the alternative materials. These participants were under increasing pressure to demonstrate the recycling potential of their products. For them the workshop served as an opportunity to highlight the need for supply chain engagement in order to address the recycling challenge jointly.

Medical

There were several participants from the medical industry, supplying PVC-based devices for use in a wide range of disposable but critical healthcare applications, such as blood tubing and containers for blood and intravenous solutions. Their main expectations were to gain a better insight into the sustainability implications for PVC. In the main, the threats to their business came from one of the additives used within the PVC rather than the PVC itself, i.e., the plasticizer known as DEHP (di 2-ethylhexyl phthalate, the softening agent to make PVC flexible). While there have been many attempts by other material producers to provide PVC alternatives based on other plastics, PVC still offered the best overall combination of properties and was cost-competitive.

(*Continued*)

EXHIBIT 22.7 (*Continued*)

Moulding Products

Several participants supplied the industry with mouldings for a wide range of applications. Unlike profile manufacturers, who extrude PVC into continuous lengths, these manufacturers processed PVC for a diverse range of applications using injection moulding. They also used a range of other thermoplastic materials and were less dependent on PVC than profile producers. Like flooring, PVC offered some advantages for certain applications compared to alternative thermoplastics. It cost less and, unlike other thermoplastics, did not require the use of anti-flammables such as brominated fire retardants. These participants saw the sustainability workshop as a mechanism to learn more about the positive aspects of addressing sustainability. They planned to use these in their promotional literature.

sustainability, as opposed to the issues-driven approach adopted by Vinyl 2010. How could this event enhance customers' perception of Hydro Polymers' brand, rather than alienate them further, if they considered sustainability to be a lost cause?

As customers weighed up the implications of the sustainability challenges for the industry, would they consider a transition to fully sustainable PVC a likely future scenario or would they dispute its viability on commercial grounds? In view of the rapid rise of highly unsustainable Chinese manufacturing, would customers feel that PVC was a losing battle, and devise exit strategies to cut their losses in PVC-based applications? Given the availability of alternative materials for their end products (e.g., window frames), would they switch investments to manufacturing substitutes, and slowly exit PVC-based manufacturing, ahead of pending REACH regulation? (see Exhibit 22.8).

EXHIBIT 22.8 SUSTAINABLE PVC VERSUS COMPETING MATERIALS

Hydro Polymers had recognized the need to accelerate the pace of change of addressing sustainability within the PVC industry. One of the key drivers in the United Kingdom had been the increasing pressure from a body known as BRE (Building Research Establishment) whose model, the 'Green Guide on Construction Materials', was starting to appear everywhere. The guide, initially designed for the Post Office to rate materials in specific applications, was based on a complex set of environmental profiles, yet the outcome from the model was a simple rating of either A, B or C, where A was good and C poor from an environmental profile perspective. Architects, construction companies and other specifiers turned off by the complexities of life cycle analysis could see the benefit of using such a tool as a simple means of materials selection.

At the time of the workshop, the generic rating for PVC for use in window profile was C, while timber windows had an A rating. For other applications such as flooring, PVC scored favourably and so the BRE rating was not seen as a threat. Hydro Polymers' window customers had highlighted that the threat of a poor rating was directly impacting on their business, while the threat itself was likely to increase. Other influential bodies such as English Partnerships had already decided that they would not use C-rated materials for new build applications. PVC was losing market share as a direct result of this rating. There was clearly a pressing need to undertake a review on improving the rating of PVC for use in windows and this was being addressed by a joint effort across the industry. The main options to improve the rating were identified by Hydro Polymers as:

- extend the life of PVC windows within the Green Guide from its current estimated length of 25 years (an estimate the industry was confident was wrong);
- reduce the environmental footprint of PVC;
- introduce recycled PVC into new profile.

The first option was being tackled across the UK industry via demonstrations to BRE that PVC windows lasted significantly longer than 25 years, i.e., at least 35 years. However, the second and third options were clearly the stuff of sustainability and demonstrated the need to address sustainability challenges from a real business perspective.

So while the BRE assessment was clearly a threat to the industry, Hydro Polymers also saw it as an opportunity ultimately to improve PVC's rating versus competing materials such as timber. If the industry generic rating was insufficient and PVC continued to lose ground to competing materials, there was still the option of a specific rating for Hydro Polymers' own PVC – not its first choice but a shrewd business differentiator if push came to shove.

Even if they believed an industry-wide transition to sustainable PVC was possible, would customers be willing to support Hydro Polymers' approach, given that the rest of the European PVC producers were taking a less radical approach? Would the customers think that there was a cost advantage to the more incremental approach (despite Hydro Polymers' experience to the contrary)? Would they choose to wait and see, or would they perceive added value for their own customers and join Hydro Polymers and its suppliers in the process towards full sustainability?

As they pondered these questions, they knew that they had to give this meeting their best shot. Getting just one or two big customers to buy into the sustainability initiative would be critical if Hydro Polymers was to embark on the next stage of its journey.

NOTES

1. This case was written by Josephine Brennan under the supervision of Professor N. Craig Smith, INSEAD Chaired Professor of Ethics and Social Responsibility. It is intended to be used as a basis for class discussion rather than to illustrate either effective or ineffective handling of an administrative situation.
2. Sustainability had been broadly defined as meeting the needs of the present generation without compromising the ability of future generations to meet their needs.
3. REACH was the acronym for new European legislation regarding the Registration, Evaluation and Authorization of Chemicals. REACH objectives were to enhance the protection of people and the

environment by providing a consistent approach to the screening and risk assessment of chemicals and a common legislative framework across the EU.

4. EUR 1 = NOK 8 (2005),

5. An international standard that specifies a process for controlling and improving a company's environmental performance.

6. PVC is a polymer that has a carbon backbone with hydrogen and chlorine atoms attached to it. S-PVC is produced by polymerizing vinyl chloride monomer in the form of fine droplets suspended in water, whereas P-PVC is a fine resin powder.

7. Minimum conditions for non-destruction of the system of life on Planet Earth.

8. Directive 2000/53/EC Official Journal of the European Communities on end-of-life vehicles.

9. July 2000, 'PVC: An Evaluation Using The Natural Step Framework', The Natural Step.

10. July 2000, 'Vision 2020 Series: PVC and Sustainability Report', The Natural Step, (see http://www.naturalstep.org.uk).

11. CO_2 footprint reduced by 80 kg per tonne of PVC produced – 2000 baseline.

12. See http://www.hydropolymers.com/en/media_room/library/publications/environmental_news/index.html.

13. A Forum for the Future publication.

14. Known as the acetylene process.

REFERENCES

ENDS (Environmental Data Services) (2005) Hydro Polymers: Searching for a more sustainable PVC, *Environmental Data Services*, May, Report 354, 25–28.

Leadbitter, J. (2002) PVC and sustainability, *Progress in Polymer Science*, **27**, 2197–226 (see http://www.hydropolymers.com/library/attachments/en/media_room/publications/pvc_sustainability_en.pdf).

National Centre for Business and Ecology (1997) PVC in Packaging and Construction Materials: An Assessment of their Impact on Human Health and the Environment', Ref C77/38/23, September.

Retailer Working Group Press Release (1997) Clean up or phase out, retailers tell PVC makers, available from Tesco PO Box 44, Cirrus Building C, Shire Park, Welwyn Garden City, Herts AL7 1ZR.

Robèrt, K-H., Schmidt-Bleek, B., Aloisi de Larderel, J., Basile, G., and Jansen, J.L. (2002) Strategic sustainable development – selection, design and synergies of applied tools, *Journal of Cleaner Production*, **10**, 197–214.

Thorton, J. (2002) *Environmental Impacts of Polyvinyl Chloride (PVC) Building Materials*, Healthy Building Network Report.

CHAPTER TWENTY-THREE

GlaxoSmithKline and Access to Essential Medicines[1]

N. Craig Smith, INSEAD and Anne Duncan, London Business School

> Shareholders will be aware that the creation of GlaxoSmithKline has coincided with an upsurge of public comment and concern on two issues in particular: the use of animals in the discovery and testing of medicines and access to medicines in the developing world.
>
> Jean-Pierre Garnier and Sir Richard Sykes
> Joint Statement by the Chief Executive Officer and Chairman[2]

INTRODUCTION

On 17 January, 2000, the Boards of Glaxo Wellcome (Glaxo) and SmithKlineBeecham (SmithKline), two of Europe's leading pharmaceutical companies, announced proposed terms of a merger; a deal that would create the second largest research-based pharmaceutical and healthcare company in the world, with a global workforce in excess of 100 000 and a combined market capitalization of £114 billion. Only US-based pharmaceutical giant Pfizer would be in a position to rival GlaxoSmith-Kline's (GSK) £18.1 billion (US$27.5 billion) in global sales, R&D capabilities, extensive development pipeline and product range (see Exhibit 23.1 for an overview of GSK).

The strategic logic behind the merger appeared clear. Both companies had a number of country-level operations, offering a merged GSK significant scope to reduce costs and to benefit from potential synergies in areas such as marketing, administration and R&D. The proposed cost savings from the merger, combined with savings from manufacturing restructuring efforts that were already underway within the two companies, were estimated to reach around £1.6 billion (US$2.28 billion) by 2003. The aim was to reinvest those savings in the critical area of R&D, which would in turn enhance the merged company's product pipeline.

On 27 December, 2000, Glaxo and SmithKline officially became one company, with Glaxo and SmithKline shareholders holding approximately 58.75% and 41.25% of the share capital of GSK respectively. Dealings in GSK shares commenced on the London Stock Exchange on the same day. On 11 January, 2001, the new CEO, Jean-Pierre Garnier, made his first in-house speech broadcast by satellite to employees around the world. Describing his aspirations for the company, Garnier said: 'The pharmaceutical industry today sells 80% of its products to 20% of the world's population.

EXHIBIT 23.1 GSK'S MISSION AND KEY FACTS

Mission

GlaxoSmithKline – one of the world's leading research-based pharmaceutical and healthcare companies – is committed to improving the quality of human life by enabling people to do more, feel better and live longer.

Overview

Headquartered in the United Kingdom and with major operations based in the United States, GSK is one of the industry leaders, with an estimated seven per cent of the world's pharmaceutical market.

GSK also has leadership in four major therapeutic areas – anti-infectives, central nervous system (CNS), respiratory and gastro-intestinal/metabolic. In addition, it is a leader in the important area of vaccines and has a growing portfolio of oncology products.

The company also has a Consumer Healthcare portfolio comprising over-the-counter (OTC) medicines; oral care products and nutritional healthcare drinks, all of which are among the market leaders.

Based on 2000 Annual Results, GSK had sales of £18.1 billion (US$27.5 billion) and profit before tax of £5 billion (US$8.1 billion). Pharmaceutical sales accounted for £15.4 billion (US$23.5 billion), 85 per cent of the total.

GSK had four products with sales of over US$1 billion and a total of 16 products with sales in excess of US$500 million.

GSK has over 100 000 employees worldwide. Of these, over 40 000 are in sales and marketing, the largest sales force in the industry.

R&D

GSK R&D has over 16 000 employees based at 24 sites in 7 countries. The company has a leading position in genomics/genetics and new drug discovery technologies. The GSK R&D budget is about £2.4bn/US$4bn.

Global Manufacturing & Supply

GSK has 104 manufacturing sites in 40 countries with over 42 000 employees. The sites within the GSK manufacturing network . . .

- supply products to 191 global markets for GSK
- produce over 1200 different brands
- manufacture almost 4 billion packs per year
- produce over 28 000 different finished packs per year
- supply around 6000 tonnes of bulk active each year
- manage about 2000 new product launches globally each year

GSK 'In Time':

Every second, more than 35 doses of vaccines are distributed by GSK.

Every minute, more than 1100 prescriptions are written for GSK products.

Every hour, GSK spends more than £277 000/US$450 000 to find new medicines.

Every day, more than 200 million people around the world use a GSK brand toothbrush or toothpaste.

Every year, GlaxoSmithKline donates more than £55 million/US$90 million in cash and products to communities around the world.

I don't want to be the CEO of a company that only caters to the rich . . . I want those medicines in the hands of many more people who need them.'

Garnier's statement struck a chord with GSK employees, many of whom wanted to work for a company committed to improving the health and lives of *all* the world's people. However, it was becoming more and more difficult to see how any pharmaceutical company could deliver on such a promise in the evolving socio-political and competitive business environment.

GSK: A NEW COMPANY FACING NEW CHALLENGES

A personal reminder for GSK employees of the increasingly cynical view that some people held of the pharmaceutical industry was often revealed in negative reactions in social situations when they mentioned the name of their employer. Indeed, within the first week of the new company's existence, GSK had effectively become *the* primary target of activists' intent on vilifying the pharmaceutical industry. Oxfam International, a confederation of 12 non-governmental organizations (NGOs) formed in an effort 'to find lasting solutions to poverty, suffering and injustice', was preparing to launch a new campaign entitled 'Cut the Cost' aimed at pressuring pharmaceutical companies to make HIV/AIDS treatments available and affordable for people in least developed countries (LDCs).

The day before Garnier's speech, Oxfam had provided GSK with a draft of a briefing document criticizing GSK and inviting it to comment. The briefing, intended to be launched alongside the Cut the Cost campaign, argued that enforcement of global patent rules had the effect of keeping drug prices high in LDCs; that this situation was wrong; and that GSK could and should do more to resolve the situation. Focusing on the HIV/AIDS crisis in LDCs, Oxfam challenged GSK to develop and deliver a comprehensive 'access to essential medicines' policy that would help address the imbalance between treatment in the developing and the developed world.

In response to Oxfam's challenge, GSK's policy staff reviewed the draft briefing and alerted Oxfam to a number of errors that they believed existed within the document. However, Oxfam had already contacted one of GSK's institutional investors, Friends Ivory & Simes (FI&S), which expressed concerns at the contents of the Oxfam briefing and invited a response from Garnier. On 12 February, 2001, earlier than GSK had expected and two days before FI&S was due to host a meeting for Oxfam, GSK and other institutional investors to discuss the Oxfam briefing, Oxfam made its report public. The report received significant media attention and now anything GSK did would seem to be in response to the challenges by Oxfam in its report. It was becoming increasingly apparent that Oxfam, together with other prominent NGOs such as the Nobel Prize-winning

Médecins Sans Frontières and Treatment Action Campaign (a leading NGO on the access issue in South Africa), intended to mount a campaign challenging the pharmaceutical industry's traditional business model.

The South African Court Case

Events came to a head in a Johannesburg courtroom on 5 March, 2001, when opening arguments began in a high profile court case between South African President Nelson Mandela (as well as other parties) and a consortium of 40 pharmaceutical companies, including GSK. The case, which had been filed in April 1998, originally arose from disputes between the industry and the South African government over the 1997 Medicines and Related Substances Control Amendment Act. The industry had criticized the legislation over key issues such as labelling requirements, compulsory licensing of generic drug substitutes and parallel importing (imports of drugs sourced from other countries and not authorized for distribution by the manufacturer), and had claimed that it provided inappropriate discretionary powers to the South African Health Minister. By 2000, AIDS activists and public opinion viewed the dispute as primarily involving a conflict between intellectual property (IP) rights and access to essential drugs. The South African government, under intense public pressure and facing a devastating HIV/AIDS epidemic, had responded by empowering the Health Minister to allow generic versions of patented drugs to be manufactured or imported and distributed in South Africa, though the government stated that it did not have the financial resources to buy HIV/AIDS drugs itself at this time, even at generic prices.

Activists suggested that the prices of generic drugs that might become available for sale in South Africa could be 98% below those of the US patented versions (that were averaging US$12 500/patient/year). The industry consortium argued that the South African government would be acting in violation of the World Trade Organization's (WTO) *Trade-Related Aspects of Intellectual Property Rights* (TRIPS) agreement. As a signatory to the agreement, South Africa was among the countries where the TRIPS rules would be going into force in 2000. In addition to concerns about the regulatory environment within South Africa, the industry consortium believed that any action that might weaken the wider establishment and enforcement of IP protection would threaten the industry's business model by cutting the financial incentives necessary to ensure pharmaceutical innovation. It feared that the government's intention to allow the distribution of generic versions of patented drugs could start a chain reaction involving other countries that would render the TRIPS agreement meaningless.

For several years, AIDS and anti-poverty activists had been trying to focus the world's attention on the price of HIV/AIDS drugs in LDCs. They argued that patent protection resulted in premium prices that restricted access to essential drugs and thus perpetuated unnecessary suffering and deaths of millions of AIDS-affected people in the developing world. Since 1997, Glaxo had tried to be responsive to these pricing concerns by offering lower prices for its AIDS drugs in Africa. In May 2000, the company helped create the Accelerating Access Initiative (AAI), a partnership involving four other pharmaceutical companies, the World Health Organization (WHO) and the United Nations Joint Program on HIV/AIDS (UNAIDS). As part of the AAI, Glaxo had worked voluntarily with LDC governments to reduce prices progressively on HIV/AIDS drugs on a country-by-country basis. It even published its discounted price list, while other companies kept their lists confidential.

However, these actions had proved insufficient to stem the criticism directed at Glaxo and other pharmaceutical companies. Critics argued that the price reductions were small and did not constitute a long-term framework that would ensure that essential drugs reached the world's poor. Graphic photographs showing sick and dying men, women and children with HIV/AIDS were being used to bring home the human cost of AIDS and were capturing the attention of people around the world. Public health experts framed the issue as one of ensuring universal 'access to essential medicines', even though they realized that solving the HIV/AIDS crisis and ensuring universal access involved much more than drug prices. Support was increasing for the activists' message that wealthy drug companies were letting people suffer and die just to preserve their profits.

Garnier knew that the South African court case could mark a major turning point both in terms of the battle between business, government and NGO leaders over how to address the international HIV/AIDS crisis and in defining the nature of the relationship between the pharmaceutical industry and society. Prior to the merger, Garnier had asked Howard Pien, then President of SmithKline's worldwide pharmaceuticals business, to take executive responsibility for the access issue within GSK. Pien's familiarity with many of the issues involved in the access debate would prove critical to the development of GSK's future policy (Pien became head of GSK's international pharma division after the merger). Pien believed that the intersection of the HIV/AIDS crisis with the access issue could prove to be the biggest challenge ever faced by the pharmaceutical industry and that determining how to respond would have profound strategic implications for GSK and the industry as a whole. As Pien explained: 'There was a clear business imperative for doing good. Our ability to do well as a company was predicated on the perception that we were capable of doing good.'

HIV/AIDS AND ACCESS TO ESSENTIAL MEDICINES

First identified in the 1970s, Human Immunodeficiency Virus (HIV), the virus that can lead to Acquired Immune Deficiency Syndrome (AIDS), was believed by scientists to have crossed over to humans from chimpanzees in the 1940–1950s in the Republic of Congo. Infection occurred when HIV was passed from one person to another through blood-to-blood or sexual contact. Pregnant women infected with HIV could also pass the virus to their child during pregnancy, delivery or breast-feeding, a form of infection known as 'mother-to-child transmission'. As an example of a 'retrovirus' (from the Latin 'retro' meaning 'reverse'), HIV's genetic information was stored on single-stranded 'RNA' rather than the double-stranded 'DNA' found in most organisms. In order to replicate, HIV used an enzyme known as 'reverse transcriptase' to convert its RNA into DNA, enabling the virus to enter the nucleus of the host's healthy cells, insert itself into the cell's DNA and instruct the cell to make copies of the original virus. Having identified the mechanism for replication, researchers began to search for ways to interfere with this process. The first 'anti-retro-viral' drugs aimed at preventing the replication of the HIV virus by either binding directly on to the reverse transcriptase enzyme, thus preventing the conversion of RNA to DNA, or by incorporating themselves into the DNA of the virus, thereby stopping the building process.

Although it could take several years, most people who became HIV-infected would ultimately develop full-blown AIDS, resulting in eventual death as the body's immune system became unable to function properly or fight off the daily attacks from even the most common bacteria and viruses such as the common cold. There was no cure for AIDS and like other pandemics such as the global influenza pandemic of 1918–1919 (which may have killed as many as 40 million people), HIV/AIDS spread rapidly, aided by the extent and ease of global movement of people. By 1995, 14 500 new cases of HIV were occurring daily, particularly in the developing world, with 95% of HIV/AIDS sufferers living in the least developed countries. By 2001, it was estimated that more than

53 million men, women and children had been infected worldwide and in 2001 alone five million people became infected with HIV, three million died of AIDS, and 40 million were living with the AIDS virus on a daily basis.[3] Two-thirds of those infected lived in sub-Saharan Africa.

As a slow killer, AIDS was taking a devastating toll, both on afflicted individuals and their families and on the societies in which they resided. The toll on LDCs was particularly acute, crippling their economies and destroying communities by depriving them of millions of productive employees and making orphans out of millions of children.[4] The virus represented the most significant threat to the long-term growth prospects and social progress of countries in the developing world. James Sherry, director of programme development for UNAIDS commented: 'I can't think of the coming of any event which was more heralded to less effect . . . In terms of real redeployment of resources, it hasn't changed. The bottom line is, the people who are dying from AIDS don't matter in this world' (Gellman, 2000a, p. A1).

HIV/AIDS in the Developed World

In the United States, the HIV/AIDS crisis began to emerge in the 1980s, when outbreaks of two rare illnesses typically affecting older men (*Pneumocystis carinii* pneumonia, a respiratory illness and *Kaposi's sarcoma*, a cancer) were found to be increasing among young homosexual males. Medical professionals also started to notice a number of mysterious deaths, primarily among gay males. By 1984, researchers had isolated the virus and identified the disease. However, developing ways to treat its symptoms would take time and money; finding a cure could take decades. Gay activists argued that HIV was receiving insufficient attention because of its label as a 'gay man's disease'. But by the mid-1980s, wider concern intensified when statistics indicated the rate at which the virus was spreading, across the country and to heterosexual as well as homosexual Americans.

As politicians, health experts and NGOs in the United States and increasingly in Europe rallied behind the call for more action, millions of dollars were being poured into developing drugs to treat and eliminate HIV and AIDS. In March 1987, the anti-retroviral (ARV) treatment drug, zidovudine (AZT), was introduced by Wellcome (prior to its merger with Glaxo) under the brand name Retrovir. It was licensed for patients with advanced AIDS. Other anti-retroviral drugs followed. In the United States, each received fast track regulatory approval from the Food and Drug Administration (FDA), though this meant that the potential benefits and risks of these drugs could only be known after they were on the market. Further clinical trials in less sick patients were conducted and in 1995 a study showed that administering AZT during pregnancy and to the newborn infant, reduced the risk of mother-to-child HIV transmission by up to two-thirds.

Between 1995 and 1997, Roche, Merck and Abbott Laboratories introduced new drugs and data emerged indicating that drug combinations delayed the onset of AIDS for those with HIV and reduced the symptoms for those with full-blown AIDS. By 2001, the FDA had approved some 23 HIV/AIDS drugs aimed at increasing the quality and duration of life for HIV-infected individuals. However, the drugs alone cost US$10 000–15 000/patient/year and their administration also required ongoing medical supervision – particularly for the complex 'triple drug cocktails'. The expense involved was an enormous financial burden for healthcare providers, insurance companies and governments, even in wealthy developed countries and though many of the latter victims had access to drugs, this was not guaranteed. The cost of HIV/AIDS treatments, however, seemed entirely out of reach to those living in LDCs. According to the UN, more than 1.2 billion people, 291 million in Sub-Saharan Africa alone, were living on less than US$1/day.[5] Less than 1% of HIV/AIDS victims in need of anti-retroviral treatment in Sub-Saharan Africa were receiving it.

A Pandemic of Tragic Proportions

Experts agreed that treatment of HIV positive patients was only a temporary measure – for most, death remained the ultimate consequence of infection. For those who lacked access to the expensive treatments, death could occur within six months of infection. Efforts at finding a long-term solution needed to focus on prevention and cure. Medical experts believed that it would take at least 10 years before a preventative vaccine would be discovered and finding a cure would take even longer. Educating people to take responsibility for preventing their own infection remained the only proven method to ensure safety. Prevention was also the most cost effective means of forestalling the spread of HIV/AIDS. With so many people around the world still lacking access to basics such as food, clean water and adequate shelter, governments and institutions such as the World Bank were reluctant to channel precious resources into expensive AIDS treatment regimes. They considered preventative approaches to be more cost effective over the long term. As Jeffrey Harris (Center for Disease Control, formerly of USAID and a former head of the US government's overseas AIDS assistance programme), remarked: 'Our experience, and I think *the* experience, is that treatment always drives out prevention. We were afraid that if we opened the door on treatment at all, then all of our money would be drawn away. You get into paying for commodities that have to be supplied, supplied, supplied, to the end of time' (as cited in Gellman, 2000b).

The attention finally being directed at HIV/AIDS in the developed world meant that it was no longer considered to be a disease that attacked only the poor or homosexual communities. HIV was recognized as posing a real threat to the social and economic prospects of people around the world, including those in developed countries. The US government declared the crisis to be a threat to international security. The sheer scale of the pandemic was also beginning to be quantified. Pien observed that 'the problem of HIV/AIDS is going to peak at the current trajectory in 2060 . . . and that is going to impact upwards of 60% of the world's population. This is what is harrowing to me . . . if we are not going to see the crescendo of the crisis in our own lifetime, our children will.'

Although the scale of the crisis served to capture attention, development experts recognized that saving people from HIV/AIDS would be futile if other major killers such as malaria and tuberculosis (TB) were ignored (see Figure 23.1 for data on major infectious diseases). With increasing global awareness of the health conditions of people in the developing world, even pharmaceutical companies that were not active in the HIV/AIDS category found they had to consider their position on the access issue.

HIV/AIDS IN SOUTH AFRICA

The emergence of the South African HIV/AIDS crisis was perhaps the most significant catalyst in the shift of global public opinion about the role of pharmaceutical companies in the advancement of human health and welfare. Only 1% of the adult South African population was believed to have been HIV infected in 1990. By 2000, that number had increased to 20%. More than four

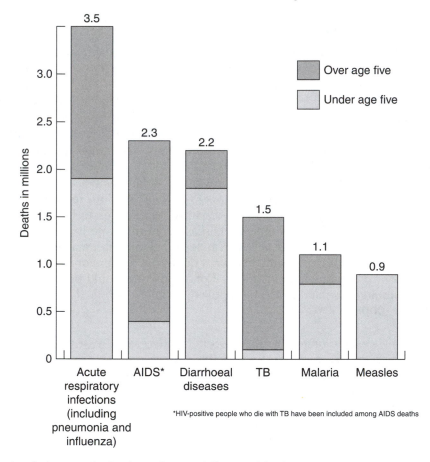

Leading infectious killers

Millions of deaths, worldwide, all ages, 1998

Over age five

Under age five

Deaths in millions

Acute respiratory infections (including pneumonia and influenza)   AIDS*   Diarrhoeal diseases   TB   Malaria   Measles

*HIV-positive people who die with TB have been included among AIDS deaths

Figure 23.1 Graph showing the leading infectious killers worldwide (Source: WHO, 1999)

million people – the largest number of any country in the world – were infected, though only a small number were aware of their HIV status. However, for economic and complex socio-cultural reasons, a frequent response within South Africa had been to ignore the looming crisis.

Many South Africans were uncomfortable talking about the disease or methods of prevention. For cultural reasons, many HIV-infected South African men refused to wear condoms and thus knowingly infected their wives, partners, prostitutes and even rape victims. The myth that having sex with a virgin could cure AIDS drove men to engage in unprotected sex with girls. Infants could avoid infection from their HIV-positive mother during pregnancy and birth, but the public shame associated with failing to breastfeed one's own child led many mothers to do so regardless of the risk of HIV infection (and despite the alternatives of a non-infected wet nurse or bottle-feeding with formula). It was clear that efforts to increase access to HIV/AIDS drugs would be insufficient without corresponding efforts to address certain cultural and behavioural issues.

The problem was exacerbated by the fact that many South African leaders appeared to share these cultural beliefs. At the UN Conference on HIV/AIDS held in Durban, South Africa, in June 2000, South African President (and former Health Minister) Thabo Mbeki angered many people by appearing to support the theory, circulated over Internet rumour pages, that HIV did not cause AIDS. However, UN delegates remained undeterred and UNICEF called for a worldwide 'mobilization' to address the AIDS crisis. An International Labour Organization report released for the conference predicted that by 2020 the economic growth rate in certain sub-Saharan countries would be cut by 25% as a result of AIDS. South African employers were also concerned about the significant negative impacts that the epidemic would have on their workforce. Even South Africa's leading research institution, the Medical Research Council, believed the government's approach was unconscionable. Its research found that AIDS was the leading cause of death in South Africa.

The context for the court battle had been set before the government came to power. In 1995, officials from Glaxo and the British Government provided assistance to the African National Congress (ANC) as it developed its ideas on the type of healthcare system that could be created in South Africa. However, when the ANC was elected, many of those suggestions were not adopted and the new government dismantled many drug licensing laws and the drug safety testing council.

As South African AIDS activists started mobilizing under the banner of the NGO, Treatment Action Campaign, they lobbied the government to disregard patent rights of specific AIDS drugs to allow generic copies to be made in South Africa, even though this would contravene the TRIPS agreement that was to take effect from 2000. Sympathetic government officials grumbled that any changes in government policy would have little effect on South Africa's capacity to treat AIDS sufferers; this was simply out of the question for the debt-ridden South African economy. Thus activists' attention turned to the pharmaceutical industry, focusing not only on the price of drugs but also the claim that it was a social responsibility of the industry to help ensure universal access to essential medicines.

THE PHARMACEUTICAL INDUSTRY

The pharmaceutical industry had global sales of more than US$220 billion in 1999, with 41% of sales and 60% of industry profits coming from the United States, where healthcare was largely based on market principles and drugs expenditures covered mostly by private sector insurers (*The Economist*, 1998). The industry was intensely competitive with no single company capturing more than 7% of the global market (IMS Health, 2001).[6] Nonetheless, it was one of the most profitable; according to *Fortune*, the pharmaceutical industry in 2001 continued to hold the top ranking position with an average industry profit of 18.5% as a percentage of revenues, compared to a median 5% return for all industries surveyed.[7]

The pharmaceutical industry was highly regulated and its business model was based on strict enforcement of IP rights. Industry and economic experts argued that this highly institutionalized legal and market-based structure benefited consumers and society at large because it provided incentives for innovation. Pharmaceutical companies could take advantage of monopoly rights on the sales of their patented products over a 20-year period. The equation was simple: the high risk associated with drug development was balanced by assurances of greater profit potential. A healthy, profitable pharmaceutical industry could attract capital to be invested in continuous innovation. The incentives-based structure benefited society by providing a constant stream of new drugs, treatments and cures that enhanced and saved lives.

Countering this logic, critics argued that although innovation was clearly desirable, the industry enjoyed excess profits at the expense of many of the most vulnerable people in society. Some asserted that the length and universality of many of the patents were indirectly infringing on the universal human right to good health. They suggested that drug prices were far higher than they should be, resulting in access to the drugs being limited to those with good healthcare coverage in the world's richest countries. Even those critics who agreed that some form of market-based system was necessary, acknowledged that the costs of most drugs put them out of reach of most of the world's people.

The General Assembly of the United Nations adopted and proclaimed the *Universal Declaration of Human Rights* on 10 December, 1948. Several articles of the Declaration were offered as the basis for the argument that people have a right to good health, including Article 25, of which Paragraph 1 stated: 'Everyone has the right to a standard of living adequate for the health and well-being of himself and of his family, including food, clothing, housing and medical care and necessary social services, and the right to security in the event of unemployment, sickness, disability, widowhood, old age or other lack of livelihood in circumstances beyond his control.' Paragraph 2 stated: 'Motherhood and childhood are entitled to special care and assistance. All children, whether born in or out of wedlock, shall enjoy the same social protection.'

The industry was doing its part to address the access issue, according to trade associations such as the Pharmaceutical Research and Manufacturers of America (PhRMA), who pointed to the philanthropic activities supported by pharmaceutical companies over many years. In particular, the industry supported foundations investing in research and basic health initiatives and donated drugs for programmes targeted to treat the poor. In addition, companies typically charged less for drugs sold in developing countries and as some drugs moved through the commercial life cycle and new ones were launched in their place, pharmaceutical companies would often significantly reduce prices in LDCs to levels at, or in some cases below, cost. While PhRMA and others argued that the industry was doing what it could to help bring drugs to people who needed them, they also asserted that the problem was one for governments and society, not the industry, to solve. In any event, as noted by many healthcare professionals as well as industry representatives, the most serious constraint that prevented the provision of adequate healthcare for the world's poor was the severe lack of healthcare infrastructure in LDCs. The financial cost of a drug was only one potential obstacle to patient treatment. In fact, 95% of the drugs on WHO's list of essential drugs were not even under patent. Despite their lower prices, many patients in LDCs remained untreated because of the lack of an infrastructure to deliver and administer these non-patented medicines.

Drug Development and Industry Profitability

Drug development involved a significant degree of failure – the average approved drug required more than 10 000 molecules to be vetted before a single molecule emerged successfully from the development process. Only 1 in 5000 compounds ever reached the market as a finished product and only 30% of those would turn out to be commercially successful.[8] An approved drug took an average of 13 years from the time of initial molecular screening through clinical developments and approval processes before finally reaching its market. Thus, although patent protection generally ran for 20 years, patent protected exclusivity on marketing and sales averaged only 10–12 years.

Bringing a new drug to market was capital intensive, costing an estimated US$400–800 million on average, including expenditures on drug development, marketing and regulatory approval and the sunk costs associated with drug failures[9]. Critics disputed the upper limit of the industry's estimate, claiming that it did not take account of various tax deductions and government research contributions common to many drugs that reached the market. NGO Public Citizen asserted that the out-of-pocket drug development cost figure was actually closer to US$240 million because 50% of the Tufts Report total (US$399 million) used in the industry estimate was the opportunity cost of capital, which Public Citizen considered a debatable 'theoretical calculation of what R&D expenditures might be worth if they were invested elsewhere'.[10] Critics also asserted that the costs of bringing a drug to market were not the same for all drug categories and that many costs were the result of the industry's own actions. To illustrate the point, critics attacked marketing expenses and the shift towards a 'pull' strategy, which involved targeting consumers with television advertising (where legally permissible) that encouraged asking consumers to ask their doctor about a drug treatment. However, even at the lower end estimates, the fact remained that drug development was expensive.

During the 1990s, demand for new drugs combined with major scientific advances presented the industry with fresh challenges. Emerging DNA-based approaches to treatment had led to venture capitalist backed biotechnology firms outside the more established industry. The large pharmaceutical companies believed that they needed to invest heavily in these new areas to remain competitive. Profits from existing portfolios of drugs were critical to the ability of the industry to generate capital for long-term investments in new drugs. Thus, any weakening of IP rights was seen as likely to erode profits and prevent the industry from continuing to invest in necessary R&D.

Drug Pricing, Generics and Parallel Trade

Drug prices varied around the world. Even within the developed world, variations were significant due to different pricing mechanisms. In the United States, drug prices tended to be set by the market. In Canada, Mexico and most European countries, state-funded healthcare systems meant that prices were usually negotiated at the national level. In the United Kingdom, the government placed limits on the overall allowable level of profit made by a pharmaceutical company on drug sales to the National Health Service. In other countries such as France and Japan, prices were regulated on a product-by-product basis. In LDCs, private and public funds were limited and drug prices were heavily influenced by the priorities, tendering processes and the subsequent aid provided by international donors, including national aid agencies, global health organizations such as WHO and private sector foundations and NGOs such as Oxfam and Médecins Sans Frontières.

Drug prices also reflected the competitive pressures of generic products, substitutes and parallel trading. Once a drug's patent expired, generic drug manufacturers, who did not face the same lengthy and expensive R&D costs as the original manufacturer, would quickly enter a market at lower prices. In countries that did not honour IP rights, generic versions of patent-protected drugs were manufactured or imported and sold at deeply discounted prices. These lower prices often outweighed possible concerns about the quality of generic drugs, some of which were not monitored and thus had safety and efficacy that was less certain.

Drugs were frequently misappropriated or purchased by a client or government at a discounted price and rather than being used to treat the intended population, were instead resold at a higher price to generate cash. Frequently, there was both a domestic and an export market for this parallel trade and the amounts resold were often significant. In South Africa, GSK estimated that 30% of drug stocks in the National Health Service was stolen and sold into the private sector.

International Trade Rules: TRIPS

The events that led to the South African court case were to some degree by-products of the liberalization of international trade that had occurred under the General Agreement on Tariffs and Trade (GATT) and associated WTO rules. Attempting to use 'free trade' as the primary catalyst for lifting developing countries out of poverty had dominated much of economic development thinking and efforts over the past decade. Experts argued that both developing and developed countries stood to benefit from greater openness of their markets to competition. However, as open trade policies began to take effect, respected analysts and NGOs challenged the assumption that 'free trade' should dominate all other agendas. They pointed to imbalanced outcomes for many countries. For example, some international trading rules such as those involving IP rights could generate benefits but also unfair outcomes for poorer countries coerced into accepting the rules by the threat of being prevented from trading with other countries. Often labelled 'anti-globalization activists', not all NGOs were against global trade, but many wanted to ensure that overall social, health, economic and environmental impacts were considered in parallel with economic free trade objectives.

The South African court case presented an early opportunity to test provisions in TRIPS. The TRIPS agreement had emerged from the 1986–1994 Uruguay round of international trade negotiations and was designed to provide an international standard for the laws and enforcement of IP rights. When future trade disputes over IP rights arose, it was intended that the WTO dispute settlement system would be used to determine outcomes. However, the WTO rules did not provide the flexibility to consider the merits of other needs that a country might have beyond international trade. Only a vague provision in TRIPS allowed a country to waive IP rules in the case of a 'national emergency', under which the country could invoke 'compulsory licensing'; in effect, licensing low cost manufacturers to ignore patents and produce generic versions of essential drugs.

What constituted a national emergency under TRIPS was undefined. In 1997, Brazil launched a controversial programme invoking the provision and authorized state laboratories to manufacture generic versions of all but four of the twelve leading patented HIV/AIDS drugs. The government threatened to license the manufacture of the four remaining drugs unless the pharmaceutical companies radically reduced their prices. The outcome was that the price of HIV/AIDS anti-retroviral treatment was reduced by two-thirds to an average of US$4500 per patient, saving Brazil US$472 million in just three years. Although there were positive health (and economic) results for Brazil, the United States filed a WTO complaint against the Brazilian government for its actions. Even so, other countries soon became interested in following Brazil's example, determined not to allow international trading rules to override public health concerns.

In addition to compulsory licensing, it was also possible to purchase generic versions of patented drugs from companies operating in countries that had not yet implemented TRIPS. Cipla, one of India's generic pharmaceutical companies, was among the most prominent of these 'pirate companies', manufacturing copies of patented HIV/AIDS drugs and selling them at around 2% of the cost of US patented versions.

NGOs were particularly concerned at the potentially unfair outcomes that could result from international trading rules. Many believed that pharmaceutical companies had a *moral* duty to do more to fulfil their societal obligations. Some organizations acted with protests. In March 2000, activists from American NGO, ACT UP (The AIDS Coalition to Unleash Power) stormed the New York offices of Pfizer CEO Bill Steere, demanding that the company provide South Africans with cheap access to Diflucan, a drug used to treat cryptococcal meningitis, one of the diseases associated with AIDS. The following day, Pfizer announced that it would supply the drug free of charge to South African patients.

Other NGOs such as Médecins Sans Frontières and Oxfam had been lobbying governments to address the negative impacts of trade rules long before the widely publicized disruption of the 1999 Seattle meetings of the WTO by anti-globalization protestors. These NGOs wanted the ambiguity within TRIPS to be clarified at the follow-up WTO meetings in Doha, due to be held in November 2001. In late 2000, just before the powerful WTO trade rules were to come into force in many countries, a bloc of NGOs joined together to challenge the pharmaceutical companies to radically reduce drug prices or to waive drug patent rights to allow generic copies of essential medicines to be supplied by low cost manufacturers within developing countries.

THE EVOLUTION OF GSK'S ACCESS POLICY

Both Glaxo and SmithKline had long histories of philanthropic activities prior to their merger. However, many employees felt that little credit had been given to the success of these efforts. One particularly significant programme was a partnership formed in 1997 between the WHO and SmithKline targeted at eliminating *lymphatic filariasis* (LF) by 2020. LF, caused by a parasitic worm found mainly in the developing world, was a crippling and disfiguring disease commonly known as 'elephantiasis' that could lead to the arms, legs or genitalia swelling to several times their normal size. With more than 120 million people suffering from LF in 1997, the disease was the second leading cause of permanent disability in the world. By 2001, the LF Global Alliance, now involving GSK, the WHO and 28 other organizations, was a major initiative, having brought about the most significant drug donation in history and working to create effective distribution systems to reach affected populations once a year for five years. It was estimated that GSK would provide five to six billion treatments to prevent LF infection as part of this programme.

Building upon such programmes, GSK's Global Community Partnerships function, led by Justine Frain (see Figure 23.2 for GSK's organization chart), was working to expand GSK's Positive Action programme. Initiated in 1992, Positive Action had been transformed into an international programme of HIV education, care and support, in partnership with community groups, healthcare providers, governments, international agencies and others.

Glaxo and HIV/AIDS

At the time of the merger, GSK held a dominant position in the global market for HIV/AIDS therapies with a 40% market share. This was due largely to Glaxo's purchase of Burroughs Wellcome in 1995, which brought with it the ground breaking AZT treatment. Glaxo and Wellcome also had

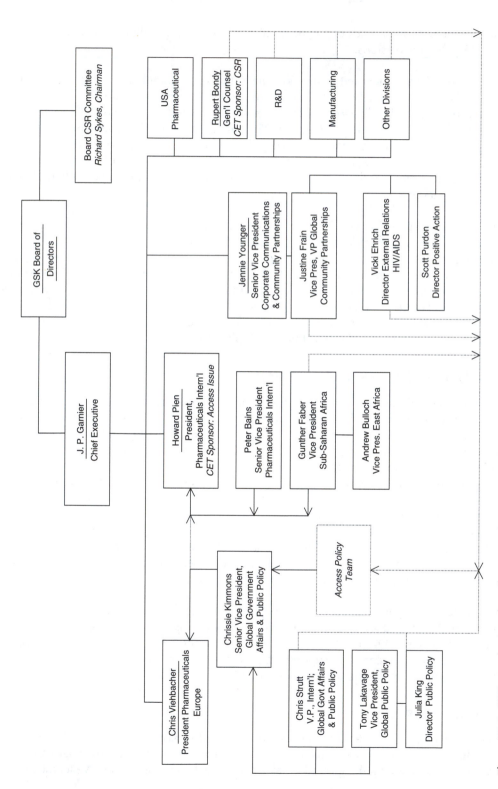

Figure 23.2 GSK organization chart (for access issue)

collaborated on Epivir, an enzyme blocker that prevented the AIDS virus enzyme from replicating itself. After Glaxo and Burroughs Wellcome merged, the new management had considered dropping out of the AIDS market because of its potential political ramifications (not least as a result of protests over LDC pricing of AIDS drugs). However, internal lobbying from the clinical products division resulted in a rethink and the newly merged Glaxo Wellcome continued to develop market, and sell HIV/AIDS treatments. In May 2000, GlaxoWellcome joined five other companies in a partnership with WHO and UNAIDS to create the Accelerating Access Initiative. The aim was to enhance access to HIV/AIDS drugs in LDCs by creating a tri-sector platform to establish national and local level HIV/AIDS treatment plans and delivery systems, to improve access to essential drugs and to lower the ultimate cost of treating more people.

As manufacturing costs came down, so did the prices of Glaxo's HIV/AIDS drugs. However, price was only one factor. The need for lifelong therapy and the scale of the HIV/AIDS pandemic meant any successful long-term AIDS treatment programme would have to take into account the complex process of ongoing treatment and patient management by trained clinicians. As Howard Pien explained: 'HIV and AIDS is a problem that will not go away for a long time. It is a problem that is far bigger than any national government, and is therefore far bigger than any multinational company. The only way to address it is through the involvement of all of us.'

Pre-Merger: Evaluating Options and Building Bridges Across the Two Companies

Garnier was favourably predisposed to addressing the HIV/AIDS crisis and the issue of access generally. As the incoming CEO of the merged GSK, he inherited a portfolio of HIV/AIDS medicines from Glaxo and he wanted to make the most of that opportunity. During his tenure at SmithKline, the company had introduced a tiered pricing model for many of its vaccines, selling them at a market price in countries where healthcare systems could afford to pay for them and providing them heavily discounted in LDCs. Vaccines were very different from long-term treatments, but the success of the vaccines pricing model had been acknowledged.

In advance of the merger, Garnier took a keen interest in the views of various stakeholders including public health experts and NGO leaders, to gain a better understanding of their concerns, together with related analyses from his SmithKline corporate policy team, headed by Chrissie Kimmons. The policy team, working closely with other divisions of SmithKline, had been tracking the HIV/AIDS and global trade rules issues, and representing the company's interests at various international forums, including the Seattle WTO meetings. Protests at Seattle and subsequent events suggested that the new company's reputation could be threatened and it might have to act in response to direct action pressure rather than out of strategic choice. Nonetheless, Kimmons, like Pien, believed that both SmithKline and Glaxo were industry leaders in developing approaches to the access problem, even though this had not been widely recognized.

Garnier asked Kimmons to bring together a team to further analyse the situation and propose specific approaches that GSK could take. Briefing papers developed by the team discussed the access issue, stakeholder and activist concerns, and broader issues associated with corporate social responsibility and global trade. These documents provided a basis for engaging senior managers within both SmithKline and Glaxo in a conversation about these issues in the merged company.

In August 2000, Garnier invited the proposed GSK Corporate Executive Team (CET) to meet and identify key issues that would require management's attention once the merger took place. Corporate social responsibility, including the access issue, was identified as one of the top six topics for attention. GSK would assume global R&D and market leadership in drugs for the three leading diseases in LDCs: HIV/AIDS, tuberculosis and malaria. The CET agreed that GSK's approach to access could thus have significant strategic, commercial, operational and reputation impact.

It was at this meeting that Garnier had asked Pien to lead efforts to develop a GSK access policy that would be responsible and sustainable. Pien observed that the CET

> came to recognize that the ultimate creation of the merged company required among other things, shareholders' support, regulatory authorities' approval and articulation of the vision of what this company was about—things we couldn't do without the encumbrance of the huge amount of pressures that were coming in our direction. I give a huge amount of credit to JP [Garnier] for crystallizing the issue; namely, the moral legitimacy of the innovation-based pharmaceutical industry.

Noting that NGOs had been quick in writing to Garnier as the CEO presumptive and asking to meet with him, Pien said, '. . . and did he do it! In contrast to the bunker mentality of many CEOs, he was very active in engaging these people and thinking through the issues. He became the force that made this a paramount issue for GSK as a new company.'

Garnier and Pien were keen to advance some of the more radical ideas recommended in the internal report on the access issue, released prior to the meeting of the CET presumptive. Garnier thought the industry could do more in partnership with governments and he wanted GSK to be at the forefront of such an initiative. He saw an opportunity in a speech he was to make to the European Union's High Level Roundtable on HIV, Malaria and Tuberculosis on 28 September, 2000. Kimmons and her colleagues were asked to develop a policy statement for the speech. Their draft was not as far-reaching as Garnier had intended. It reiterated the view that drug prices were only one part of the problem. Garnier wanted to suggest a significantly new approach for GSK that would set the company and the industry on a different path. Infrastructure and funding problems in LDCs notwithstanding, Garnier believed that prices were still a serious issue, impacting directly on the ability of governments and NGOs to treat people, and indirectly in preventing resources from being reallocated towards building necessary infrastructure.

In his speech to the EU Roundtable, Garnier, as CEO of SmithKline and GSK's CEO presumptive, made an unprecedented offer. He signalled a desire to consider a new way forward including a willingness on the part of GSK to reduce prices in LDCs to a not-for-profit level. Garnier stated that in return, governments would need to ensure the innovation-based industry's viability by agreeing to protect the existing IP rights and pricing mechanisms in the lucrative North American, European and Japanese markets. It was the first time that such an offer had been made by the CEO of a leading pharmaceutical company and Garnier's statement opened the door for discussions about a new industry-wide approach. However, these ideas were not universally welcomed within the industry and some pharmaceutical companies resolved to defend the prevailing industry position.

Post-Merger: Developing a Detailed and Sustainable Policy

Garnier, Pien and the rest of the incoming CET had agreed that GSK's access policy needed to be in place within six months of the merger being completed. But until the merger became official in December 2000, it had not been possible to engage in the detailed discussions and sharing of product and pricing information that was critical to any specific policy GSK would put in place. That month, Garnier and Pien signed off on the creation of the Access Policy Team, to be sponsored by Pien as a member of GSK's CET. Kimmons, now GSK's Senior Vice President, Global Public Affairs & Public Policy, was made responsible for the policy's development along with a team of key people from across the newly merged company. On the commercial side, Gunther Faber, Vice President of Sub-Saharan and South Africa, and Peter Bains, Senior Vice President of Commercial Development International, assumed responsibility for working out how the policy would be implemented. Chris Strutt, a Vice President and Access Alignment Master, reported to Kimmons and would be responsible for coordination, to ensure the alignment of specific activities and functional areas. Other managers involved included Julia King, Director of Public Policy and CSR, Justine Frain, Vice President, Global Community Partnerships, Vicki Ehrich, Director of HIV External Relations and a former Glaxo spokesperson in South Africa, together with other team members from manufacturing, legal, corporate communications, IP and R&D. Unable to share critical information prior to the merger, the team now had six months in which to develop a specific company-wide policy that could be announced to the world.

The team debated the best approach. Should GSK radically reduce prices and/or donate HIV/AIDS drugs even though there was inadequate healthcare infrastructure in South Africa and other poor countries to support distribution and long-term monitoring? Should it ignore patent infringements in South Africa given that so little profit was derived in such countries anyway? What would be the effect of such decisions on GSK's operations in other countries and on the existing business model? Would pressure continue no matter what the company did? How would the company finance new drug innovation if the existing patent regime could be selectively ignored? Over the long term, should GSK consider withdrawing from the developing world entirely, abandoning expensive operations in LDCs or reducing R&D on developing world diseases?

GSK's tuberculosis and malaria drugs made the company an easy target for activists who had widened the access issue beyond HIV/AIDS drugs. A major concern was that even if GSK continued to reduce prices in the developing world, what was to stop activists in the United States or Europe exerting pressure on their own politicians to force down prices to match those in LDCs, and not just for the HIV/AIDS category? Could they argue that the best interests of shareholders ultimately would be served by the access policy?

On 21 February, 2001, as part of the announcement of GSK's first results, Garnier responded to the charges in the Oxfam report, released just days earlier, that the company was not doing enough. He stated that GSK, a new company, had been working out details of a sustainable pricing model and that it was 'determined to build a long-term viable framework which will enable GSK to offer our best prices in developing countries on a sustainable basis'. He promised that GSK would make further specific announcements in June 2001.

WITHDRAWAL FROM THE SOUTH AFRICA COURT CASE

The ongoing case in South Africa, combined with a joint WTO-WHO conference in Norway, gave many of the activists and NGOs such as Oxfam an ideal platform from which to press their views. On 13 March, 2001, facing rising criticism and reflecting the new approach within GSK, Garnier contacted his counterparts at Roche, Boehringer Ingelheim and Merck to explore how they might withdraw their case against the South African Government, even though other companies wished to proceed. The industry coalition was no longer united and there were now alternative views on how to proceed on the access issue.

On 5 April, 2001, UN Secretary General Kofi Annan hosted a meeting of seven pharmaceutical company CEOs, along with the heads of WHO and UNAIDS. Annan's intention was 'to establish a new and constructive partnership with the research based industry'. The meeting opened a dialogue, with the company leaders signalling a willingness to drop their case in South Africa and Annan indicating his intention to try to focus UN member governments' and the world's attention on the need for vastly more resources for the treatment of HIV/AIDS in LDCs. Two weeks later, the drug companies dropped their case. Considered a victory for their critics, the industry saw it as a major setback in its defence of IP rights. The *Boston Globe* commented, 'With their board-rooms raided and their executives being hounded in the streets, 39 of the world's largest drug makers caved to public pressure . . . It was hailed as a stunning triumph for the developing world: A US$360 billion industry was brought down by a country that represents just half of one percent of the pharmaceutical market' (Shillinger, 2001, p. A8). Pien observed that 'the geographies have become intermingled and the South African court case made it so. Opinion leaders in the U.S., Europe and the developing countries have shifted their focus of concern. Availability of a drug was not the core of the problem, but how a company behaved as a corporate citizen. That was the real problem.'

Justine Frain described the South Africa case as the pharmaceutical industry's 'Brent Spar' (alluding to the controversy over Royal Dutch/Shell's attempt to dump an oil platform in the North Sea). The South African court case had originally started in 1998 as a dispute about the framework and enforcement of drug licensing and regulatory systems in South Africa. However, by April 2001, the case had come to be seen as being exclusively about HIV/AIDS drugs, patent infringements and life or death choices for sick people. It appeared to mark a turning point for the industry, offering a new scenario with far less predictable consequences. As Pien commented: 'what seemed like a long time ago, this issue was principally a staff issue – to do with communication and social responsibility – rather than a business issue. Now it was both.'

Both GSK and Merck announced significant price reductions on their HIV/AIDS drugs to LDCs (though their prices were still two-to-three times those of generic equivalents selling at around US$250–$350/person/year). GSK had signalled its intentions to deliver on Garnier's earlier promise of action. Announcing Merck's price reductions, Raymond Gilmartin, Merck's CEO, reiterated the industry-wide concern that lowering drug prices in LDCs might trigger pressure to lower prices in the developed world, thus rendering the tiered pricing model unsustainable. In a worst case scenario, he suggested, those reductions might trigger a downward spiral, destabilizing the industry's business model, threatening innovation and challenging the viability of the industry. At the very least, the radical cuts could prove to be a double-edged sword, forcing pharmaceutical companies out of controversial areas of health treatment into more neutral and potentially lucrative areas such as 'lifestyle drugs' (e.g., Prozac, Viagra). Gilmartin's remarks largely echoed the concerns that Garnier had expressed at the EU Roundtable six months previously and in February. With GSK's leadership, the industry had been the first to give way. Would governments, NGO's and other stakeholders keep up their end of the deal?

A welcome response to the withdrawal of the South African court case came from Kofi Annan. He used the occasion to emphasize the need for shared responsibility for tackling the HIV/AIDS pandemic. Rather than focusing on drug prices, Annan called for governments, intergovernmental organizations, NGO's and businesses to expand vastly the resource pool and to work in partnership to address the global HIV/AIDS crisis. Addressing a forum of African leaders in Abuja, Nigeria, Annan called for the creation of a global HIV/AIDS and health fund, with an annual 'war chest' of US$7–10 billion to address HIV/AIDS, tuberculosis and malaria in LDCs. This figure (which was similar to the US$7.5 billion/year previously suggested by policy analysts Amir Ataran and Jeffrey Sachs of Harvard University) represented little more than 1% of global military expenditures, according to Annan. However, the world had never united to fund any public health initiative on this sort of scale. Moreover, Annan's announcement and the withdrawal of the court case did not mean that pressures on GSK and the rest of the industry to do more on access would disappear.

Defining a Detailed Access Policy

GSK's managers remained acutely aware that the industry's business model and its reputation remained under threat. Although the long-term hope (at least with respect to HIV/AIDS) continued to be the discovery of an HIV vaccine, in the short term GSK needed to come up with a detailed access strategy and to implement it in a way that would meet GSK's business and ethical imperatives while protecting the company's image and reputation. In early May 2001, just five months after the merger, Kimmon's Access Policy Team was preparing to submit final and specific recommendations to Garnier, Pien and the CET.

NOTES

1. Anne Duncan, NatWest Ph.D. Fellow at London Business School prepared this case study under the supervision of Professor N. Craig Smith, as a basis for class discussion rather than to illustrate either effective or ineffective handling of an administrative situation. Financial assistance provided by Accenture for the development of this case study is gratefully acknowledged.

2. *GSK Annual Report,* December 2000, p. 3. The terms 'developing world' and 'developing country' are used to refer to the world's poorest countries. The United Nations Conference on Trade and Development maintains a list of Least Developed Countries based upon criteria such as GDP per capita of less than US$800/year; low life expectancy, literacy and caloric intake; and low levels of economic diversity. As of 2001, the UN had designated 49 countries as developing countries, 34 of which were located in Africa.

3. International AIDS Vaccine Initiative (IAVI), 2001.

4. AIDS in Africa: the Orphaned Continent, BBC News Report at http://news.bbc.co.uk.

5. *United Nations Basic Facts,* December 2000.

6. Based upon 2000 data.

7. *Fortune,* (2002) 15 April. The pharmaceutical industry performed well ahead of other profitable industries including commercial banks, ranked second at 13.5% return on revenues, diversified

financial institutions (10.5%), mining and crude oil producers (8.6%) and computers, office equipment and computer/data services (2.3%).

8. PhRMA 1997 Annual Report.

9. PhRMA, *Pharmaceutical Industry Profile*, 2000, p. 20. Tufts Center for the Study of Drug Development (2001), Tufts Center for the Study of Drug Development Pegs Cost of a New Prescription Medicine at $802 million, 30 November.

10. Public Citizen (2002) Pharmaceuticals Rank as Most Profitable Industry Again, Washington DC.

REFERENCES

Gellman, B. (2000a) The belated global response to AIDS in Africa, *Washington Post*, 5 July, p. A1.

Gellman, B. (2000b) An unequal calculus of life and death, *Washington Post*, December 27.

IMS Health (2001) Pfizer still ahead following GlaxoSmithKline merger, 4 January.

Shillinger, K. (2001) AIDS drug victory sours in South Africa: Government still refusing to supply AZT, *The Boston Globe*, 23 April, p. A8.

The Economist (1998) Industry survey, 21 February.

CHAPTER TWENTY-FOUR

Corporate Responsibility in Organizational Behaviour

Mette Morsing, Copenhagen Business School, Denmark

INTRODUCTION

In this chapter, I shall argue how the onset of corporate responsibility (CR) holds a strong and powerful potential for improving motivation, commitment and identification among the workforce. In addition, I shall point at how CR may contribute in challenging and developing Organizational Behaviour (OB) in ways that will address the managerial complexity involved in unfolding CR strategies into corporate practice.

Organizational Behaviour is about the behaviour of individuals and groups at work and the OB field provides explanations for behaviour and solutions for improvement of such behaviour. The overall interest of OB scholars is to assist managers in managing people towards achieving the organization's goals. Managing people is the most critically important element in achieving any organization's goal according to OB scholars (French *et al.*, 2008). The field of OB is grounded in psychology, sociology and anthropology in its focus on processes, tools and techniques to motivate individual and group performance inside the organization. From its outset in the 1960s, OB has been characterized by an applied focus and a contingency orientation. Rather than assuming that there is one way to manage people and organizations, OB scholars generally agree that behaviour may vary according to circumstances and people involved.

Departing from the acknowledgment that human beings cannot be managed and controlled to improve their performance in a machine-like 'Tayloristic' mode, OB builds on the tradition of the human relation school's appreciation that people work more efficiently when they are personally motivated, committed and identify with the organization. OB generally promotes a humanistic orientation and consensus-seeking ideal to manage diverse workforces in changing contexts. The underlying assumption in OB remains a strong belief in top down approaches to enhance motivation and improvements among the workforce. Hence, the ways in which the workforce is motivated, committed and identified with the organization is a matter of leadership.

A basic assumption in OB is that leadership requires an understanding of psychological and social dynamics so as to be better prepared to know what to look for in daily work situations to help others take the required action. OB provides managers with techniques, processes and tools to reflect on their own experiences of work in organizations and ideally lead to a new self-awareness. According to OB scholars a key aspect of managing organizations successfully requires that managers are willing to learn and change, and to ask themselves frequently those self-reflective identity questions about 'who are we?' and 'where are we going?' as individuals in the organizational context.

Today, managers face new challenges, as social and environmental concerns have entered the organization. Although it is still important for managers to understand psychological and social dynamics, it is no longer sufficient. Managers need to understand how economic and political dynamics influence Organizational Behaviour and OB needs to develop an understanding of how to respond and adjust to these changes. In particular, OB must address new expectations of ethical organizational behaviour. The recent corporate scandals including the 2008 financial crisis, the new focus on ethical rankings of corporate behaviour, the growing number of critical documentaries on unethical corporate behaviour and the increased amount of media attention to issues of ethics and CR (Buhr and Grafström, 2004; Guthey *et al.*, 2006) have accentuated the need for managers to understand how ethics has become a global concern with serious implications for Organizational Behaviour.

OB AND CR: ISOLATED FIELDS

From the perspective of OB, corporate responsibility holds a strong and powerful lever for contributing to a more motivated, committed and loyal workforce in the same way as, for example, marketing scholars argue that CR contributes to improved relations and loyalty among consumers (Brown and Dacin, 1997; Sen and Bhattacharya, 2001). Interestingly, neither the OB nor the CR literature has paid much attention to how managers and employees relate to CR. OB pays attention to the 'inside' of the corporate body while CR analyses its 'outside' relations: OB is about the analysis and development of psychological competences and interpersonal skills in the organizational context, and CR analyses how companies manage their relations with external stakeholders.

Only recently have a few papers emerged on OB and CR as interrelated issues, for example two empirical case studies demonstrate how structures and cultural norms are aligned in Shell (de Wit, Wade and Schouten, 2006) and Novo Nordisk (Morsing and Oswald, 2009) with the purpose of embedding CR among managers and employees. Also, in Academy of Management's special issue on corporations as social change agents in 2007, a few papers provided theories on how internal processes and motives of organizational members determine how organizations shape action and relate to external stakeholders (Aguilera *et al.*, 2007; Brickson, 2007), and one study explores how certified management standards shape socially desired firm behaviour (Terlaak, 2007). Yet, this research says very little about leadership with respect to social action (Bies *et al.*, 2007), and although it takes in theories of management accounting and culture (Morsing and Oswald, 2009), organizational justice (Aguilera *et al.*, 2003), institutional theory (Terlaak, 2007) and social identity (Brickson, 2007), the research does not link to the extensive field of OB.

One of the conspicuous implications of the isolation of OB and CR is that much CR literature implicitly assumes seamless integration of the corporate CR strategy. It is assumed that managers and employees accept and adopt the CR strategy unchallenged. A corporate engagement in social and environmental concerns such as human rights and climate change is presumably seen as sufficiently motivational *per se*. Moreover, from CR practice we understand that organizational members' competence to identify and learn intelligently about issues, concerns and expectations among stakeholders is one of the most important aspects of successful development and unfolding of a CR programme. For example, engagement in stakeholder dialogue and corporate responsibility is extremely important in Novo Nordisk A/S, a world leader in diabetes care. Top management believes that the Triple Bottom Line is imperative and the company continuously nurtures its strong tradition of empowerment, innovation, coaching and learning to achieve its CR ambitions[1].

Whereas the organizational integration of CR is assumed in research, companies work hard in practice to achieve such integration.

From OB we know how to develop individual and organizational skills to change and learn and that these are vital for organizational success in the context of integrated and coordinated organizational systems and structures. From OB we also know that smooth integration of corporate strategies is the exception rather than the norm. Although a corporate engagement in global concerns is highly attractive and may even be expected as an institutional norm by managers and employees, a CR programme may not be welcomed by all individuals or fit painlessly into all groups of the organization. A CR programme may not be interpreted by the same values and attitudes throughout a globally operating organization, and it may even be perceived as counterproductive to existing local performance and reward systems. If the reward system is not adapted to reward engagement in CR, will this motivate managers and employees sufficiently to pursue such engagement? From the perspective of OB, it is a managerial responsibility to align goals, values, systems and routines across the company to support a corporate responsibility strategy.

Apart from a few case studies (such as 'betapharm' – see Chapter 25), the OB literature does not lend its body of knowledge generously to the CR literature. Equally, the CR literature does not provide much insight into how such organizational implementation and identification processes occur. Arguably, OB provides some answers to some of the challenges of CR. Yet, OB is also itself challenged by the introduction of CR. In this chapter, I focus on the levels of the individual, the group and the organization as I demonstrate how CR is relevant to OB while also suggesting how CR challenges and stimulates the field of OB. The chapter concludes by encouraging the fields of CR and OB to meet more systematically in future research and practice.

TRADITIONAL IDEALS AND CONTEMPORARY CHALLENGES OF OB AS CR ENTERS

There are three levels of analysis in OB: the individual, the group and the organization. The first level focuses on individual perception, competency characteristics and personality characteristics and seeks to develop an understanding among managers and individuals about their own values and how they differ from those of others. The second level focuses on the group effectiveness, team building and group dynamics and seeks to develop an understanding of how coordination and cooperation is achieved and changed in groups and teams. The third level focuses on the organization and deals with structure, culture, leadership, power and conflict, and seeks to understand how the organization can develop consistency between structure and operations and develop interaction between the organization and its environment.

The Individual

The focus on the individual in OB is on understanding individual attributes and their effects on behaviour at work. OB issues at the level of the individual deal with personality, learning and motivation, and include areas such as individual attributes in relation to job performance, learning and self-management, empowerment, job design and other areas related to psychological perspectives. This level of analysis within OB assumes that if individual needs, expectations and values are aligned with the organization's means and goals, this will constitute the best possible environment for organizational success. Ensuring such alignment is the responsibility of the manager.

How is CR relevant to OB at the level of the individual? First, CR provides a powerful lever for OB in improving individual motivation, commitment and identification. Recently, there has been an increased focus on how employees are attracted to and retained in organizations that have a reputation for CR. Companies design employer branding campaigns with CR as a key component. In fact, surveys show how students at business schools and technical universities want to work for companies with explicitly formulated CR policies[2] and it has been suggested that one of the most important aspects of the CR engagement is the organization's ability to attract and retain highly qualified managers and employees (Morsing, 2006). In line with OB, theories of social identity and organizational identification have shown how strong identification with an organization's social responsibilities strengthens individuals' desire to actively contact and support the organization (Dutton and Dukerich, 1991; Sen and Bhattacharya, 2001).

Today, people's worklife has become a strong demarcation of their social identity and many people like to be perceived as belonging to a social category that pays attention to the future sustainability of the world. In other words, a corporate concern for social and environmental improvements in global society is likely to create more personal meaning across the entire workforce than a corporate brand known for its effective lean strategies or extremely efficient pricing policies. A corporate brand that convincingly demonstrates how the company takes a responsibility for human rights and climate change is more likely to create meaningful relationships to its workforce and attract skilled workers, and thereby boost organizational performance (Greening and Turban, 2000).

Next, the challenge for OB is to adjust the OB processes, tools and techniques to the CR ambitions and ideals. Although normative in its managerial ambitions to change organizations towards more effective performance, OB is neutral in a political sense. This neutrality is challenged when CR enters. Moreover, OB's ideal of a self-managing – or self-leading – team where the individual has 'more freedom and authority to make decisions, independent of external supervision' (French et al., 2008, p. 296) may find counterproductive dynamics in corporate practice where individuals may be restrained in their behaviour at the onset of corporate responsibility, because a CR commitment is also enthused through processes of normative control. For example, a CR promise about 'non-discriminative behaviour' may, in fact, entail close supervision of individual behaviour in order to ensure that no single manager or employee trespasses such a promise by at any time discriminating against colleagues, customers or other stakeholders.

Corporate Codes of Conduct are but one example of new CR tools and techniques established to ensure that individuals in the workplace react in standardized and similar ways to ensure fulfilment of the CR policy. IKEA's CR policy emphasizes diversity management and has strongly promoted an inclusive labour policy and advanced its anti-discrimination position by inviting Muslim women to work in the IKEA stores in Denmark wearing their scarves (Morsing and Roepstorff, 2008). Although this is an appealing anti-discrimination message, it may also be interpreted as a political message about pro-immigration, which employees must accept, adopt and commit to if they want to continue as part of the IKEA workforce. The desire to manage behaviours, thoughts and feelings is central for the OB project, and yet the entry of CR radicalizes the notion of employee dedication by making commitment to moral and political agendas an explicit precondition of the professional affiliation. On the one hand, CR engagement may strongly motivate individual ideals of contributing to a greater, global, worthy cause at their workplace. On the other hand, the CR engagement may also enforce constraints and discipline individual behaviour and thereby counter the OB ideals of individual learning, empowerment and self-managing individuals.

The Group

The focus on groups and teams in OB deals with how most activities in work organizations depend on coordination and cooperation that can only be achieved by people working together. In-group and inter-group dynamics are explored and explained in terms of how they affect performance and cohesion. Formal and informal groups, group size, nature of the task and goals, rewards and resources are examples of issues that are dealt with as important aspects for group performance. As at the individual level of analysis, the ambition is to understand how groups and teams may seamlessly coordinate their efforts to experience the least possible dissonance, or at least to reduce dissonance or 'disruptions' to achieve high performance.

First, CR profoundly contributes to enlarging the argument and the scope for why horizontal and vertical coordination among groups and teams across the organization matters. CR inherently needs the attention of the entire organization. One of the typical reactions as companies produce a CR policy is to delegate the CR engagement to a particular CR unit and leave the unfolding of the CR policy within that unit. This may imply that the CR unit is trusted to ensure the unfolding of the CR policy and perceived to be in charge of the entire organization's ethical behaviour. However, as companies purchase from new economies such as China and India and employ global and diverse workforces, the organization's ethical responsibilities are enlarged and changed in unpredictable ways. Although suppliers in China are not in any legal sense part of the firm, nevertheless the company may be held morally responsible for poor working conditions among Chinese suppliers. A (small) compartmentalized CR unit cannot possibly foresee the potential strategic implications of the CR engagement for the company in all areas, and the CR unit will have to engage systematically with the relevant organizational players. In line with OB ideals, to unfold and develop a CR strategy, the organization must involve effectively many organizational groups from product development, design, logistics, finance, accounting, marketing, sales and possibly external stakeholder groups to ensure an alignment with their expectations. While CR presents the very concrete and urgent challenge for vertical and horizontal integration and coordination, the OB discipline provides some of the tools, techniques and processes.

Next, the challenge for OB is to define a new role as organizational boundaries are blurring and increasingly 'non-members' are perceived as integrated parts of the organization. Suppliers in, for example, China or India represent one important non-member, but also end-users may contribute the same kind of challenge, as management of the chemical producer Cheminova realized when they were held accountable for Brazilian farmers spraying pesticides on the banana plants without safety dress while children were playing nearby (Olesen, 2008). Although Cheminova's behaviour was *legally accountable* because the company obeyed all regulations and provided all the required information and warning on the pesticide barrels, the company was still held *morally accountable* for the behaviour of farmers in Brazil (Christensen, Firat and Torp, 2008).

Moreover, on-line communities have contributed to a virtual expansion of the corporate body, as for example in the way on-line brand communities show strong identification with the corporate brand to the extent where external observers do not know the difference between company and brand community, as Lego Group experienced with their adult fans of Lego online brand communities (Antorini, 2007). As profound changes in the global business environment emerge, all group managers must understand how political and economic changes affect the way that organizational groups view and influence each other and understand that 'non-members' such as Brazilian farmers or Chinese suppliers suddenly are perceived to be within the company's 'sphere of influence' and therefore in a certain sense regarded as part of the organization. To what extent can OB contribute to improve the behaviour of such groups of non-members who are outside corporate control? Although the OB discipline today has expanded its domain to many aspects of organizational life, it has generally failed to integrate OB issues outside the organizational 'container'. With the entry of CR, new technologies and globalization, OB needs to step outside the container and address its role vis-á-vis new non-member groups.

The Organization

At the organizational level of OB, issues such as structure, culture, leadership and power come into play. Also, this level of analysis insists on a contingency approach arguing that each organization is unique and that its values and beliefs will have been developed by individual actors through a process of dialogue and negotiation (French and Bell, 1995). Yet, it is assumed that managers can change and manage structure, culture and even leadership styles and develop processes and systems to most effectively manage the organization. Although change is key to mainstream OB literature, change management has its own body of literature (Burnes, 1996; Carnall, 2003; French and Bell, 1995). In line with OB thinking, change management focuses on how people at work are being forced or encouraged to adapt their norms and routines, and to accept changing modes of organizing and being managed to align to the corporate goals in order for the organization to gain a competitive advantage. From a top management perspective, change management focuses on how managers can develop skills for involvement, participation and learning among employees. Although the interplay with the wider society is acknowledged in OB and the change management literature, the focus remains on the interplay and negotiations between members of the organization organized by top management.

CR brings a request for a new kind leadership to the OB discipline. Although issues of CR have started to emerge in the OB literature at the organizational level, interestingly enough issues of social responsibility at the workplace were already an inherent part of leadership a century ago. Enlightened industrialists, such as the Cadbury, Lever and Boot families in the United Kingdom, and the families behind Danfoss, Lego and Carlsberg in Denmark, recognized that health, housing and working conditions of their employees needed improvement and that such improvements could benefit the companies themselves. Factory workers were offered decent and affordable housing, recreational and health facilities, and improved working conditions to keep workers out of poverty and sickness (Marchand, 1998). Although such initiatives did of course reflect a highly paternalistic leadership style, they also offered improvements to workers and organizations alike.

Today, corporate responsibilities stretch far beyond the organizational borderline and CR programmes extend beyond focusing on the improvements of life for its own workforce. Yet, the workforce is still at the core of the CR project. Any CR policy depends on its workforce to provide the organizational platform for its successful implementation. The way managers are able to create an organizational context in support of the CR policy by facilitating systems, structure and culture allows employees to feel personally motivated by the CR ambition as well as make employees understand the economic and political implications of the CR engagement. CR calls for the kind of consensus-seeking managers promoted by the OB school that also understand how to translate economics and politics into organizational values and action. Leadership for facilitating such engagement and understanding is vital for how the CR policy develops from plans and programmes into integrated organizational practice.

However, scholars have argued that although CR calls for a new kind of leadership able to integrate the CR rationale into all areas of the company, most ethical programmes are enacted as decoupled strategies – isolated and disconnected to the rest of the organizational activities. Weaver, Trevino and Cochran (1999) distinguish between 'coupled strategies' and 'decoupled strategies' to differentiate between those ethical programmes that are integrated in the organizational veins through job performance, empowerment, job design and reward systems (coupled strategies), and those ethical programmes that are only superficially articulated by top management but added ad-hoc to existing systems and routines (decoupled strategies). The CR perspective will find much experience and advice in the OB literature on how to integrate a CR policy into organizational norms, values and practice.

The challenge for OB at the organizational level is to appreciate flexibility and 'disturbances' that will serve to ensure development of the CR policy. Whereas OB pursues an ideal of the effectively integrated and coordinated organization, organizational practice shows how people sometimes behave in unpredictable and illogical ways. And whereas the OB ambition is to manage unpredictable behaviour into predictable action, allowing for such unpredictable and illogical behaviour may in fact be a precondition for the development of a CR policy. The strong culture of high quality and predictability among engineers in Shell in the mid-1990s contributed exactly to these intelligent engineers not foreseeing that decision-making in engineering is not only a matter of high quality, economy and following the rules. Greenpeace managed to create a worldwide scandal for Shell, when it demonstrated to the world that engineering is also about taking the environment into consideration, and perhaps more importantly, taking the stakeholders into consideration. Shell's effectively integrated and coordinated, engineer-oriented organization made the organization turn to routines and not even consider that the dumping of the Brent Spar into the Northern Sea could be a problematic issue. Shell learned the hard way to develop a CR policy and to prepare for the unexpected.

The definition of CR changes and organizations need constantly to acknowledge and address such changes. Ten years ago unethical corporate behaviour was primarily related to 'sin stocks', that is, petro-chemical industry, tobacco, pharmaceutical industries, etc. Today unethical behaviour may in principle be related to any kind of corporation on issues such as child labour, sweatshops and CO_2 emissions. To identify and understand such changes and how they influence organizational behaviour, organizations need to be adaptable to changes in their surroundings, sensitive and receptive to new trends, and able to learn fast and rapidly transform new input into changed procedures; in other words to be able to demonstrate responsiveness at all organizational levels. Yet, these characteristics do not necessarily match the qualities endorsed by OB's ambition to integrate and coordinate all organizational levels to adhere to the corporate goals.

Implicitly behind the ambition of integration lies the risk of rigidity – that is, the integrated system's inability to handle change and dynamic competitive forces (Christensen, *et al.,* 2008). Integration requires much planning and management, and this need for strong coordination forms an Achilles heel for development of an ongoing sensibility towards changes on the CR scene. So, when OB suggests tools, techniques and processes to overcome 'resistance to change', 'barriers' and 'disturbances' for the enactment of a corporate strategy, it is a challenge for OB to teach the organization to appreciate – not overcome – resistance to change, barriers and disturbances that may actually provide valuable input. Instead of regarding the organization as a resource for the accomplishment of the CR policy, the OB rhetoric of resistance, barriers and disturbances tends to approach the organization as 'something' that must be seduced, taught or disciplined to adhere to the corporate strategy. When it comes to CR, it is an open question to what extent seduction, teaching and disciplining will do the job. This is another challenge for OB.

SUMMARY

Today, with the growing expectations of organizational responsibilities as a consequence of social and environmental challenges becoming a global concern for everyone, CR in the workplace has become a major issue. How a CR policy is unfolded and developed depends to a high degree on its managers and employees. How they are able to identify and understand the economic and political changes and translate them into organizational norms, values and practices that will support the CR ambitions. In this way, CR and OB become intertwined.

By letting the fields of CR and OB meet, a number of pragmatic questions emerge in search of answers: How are the CR activities designed to improve and develop individual attributes and job performance – and vice versa? How do organizational processes of learning, motivation and empowerment support – or counteract with – the CR plans? To what extent does CR seem relevant to groups across the organization? What role does OB play for the new non-member groups? And to what extent can managers act as leaders in integrating organizational efforts to support the CR policy without making integration a new point of discipline and control at the expense of motivation and personal commitment?

Although the literature and practice of OB has been dominated by an inside-out perspective in its approach to the business and policy environment as a context for internal motivation and development, CR brings an outside-in perspective to OB scholars and practitioners, in which the global economic and political environment becomes much more formative for the motivation and activities occurring inside the organization.

NOTES

1. See 'Novo Nordisk Way of Management', January 2007.
2. See, for example, http://ing.dk/artikel/88192 and http://www.jobzonen.dk/For%20jobsoegere/ Inspiration/NyeIndlaeg/MomentAnalyse.aspx.

REFERENCES

Aguilera, R.V., Rupp, D.E., Williams, C.A. and Ganapathi, J. (2007) Putting the S back in corporate social responsibility: A multilevel theory of social change in organizations, *Academy of Management Review*, **32** (3), 836–63.

Antorini, Y.M. (2007) *Brand Community Innovation: An Intrinsic Case Study of Adult Fans of Lego*, Copenhagen Business School Press, Copenhagen.

Bies, R.J., Bartunek, J.M., Forth, T.L. and Zald, M.N. (2007). Corporations as social change agents: Individual, interpersonal, institutional and environmental dynamics, *Academy of Management Review*, **32** (3), 788–93.

Brickson, S. (2007) Organizational identity orientation: The genesis of the role of the firm and distinct forms of social value, *Academy of Management Review*, **32** (3), 836–63.

Brown, T.J. and Dacin, P.A. (1997) The company and the product: Corporate associations and consumer product responses, *Journal of Marketing*, **51**, January, 68–84.

Buhr, H. and Grafström, M. (2004) The making of meaning in the media: The case of corporate social responsibility in the Financial Times, in *Managing Corporate Social Responsibility in Action. Talking, Doing and Measuring* (eds F. Hond, F.G.A. de Bakker and P. Neergaard), Ashgate Publishing Company, Hampshire, pp. 15–32.

Burnes, B. (1996) *Managing Change. A Strategic Approach to Organizational Dynamics*, Pitman Publishing, London.

Carnall, C.A. (2003) *Managing Change in Organizations*, Prentice Hall, Dorset.

Christensen, L.T., Firat, A. and Torp, S. (2008) The organization of integrated communications: Toward flexible integration, *European Journal of Marketing*, **2** (3/4), 432–52.

Christensen, L.T., Morsing, M. and Cheney, G. (2008) *Corporate Communications: Convention, Complexity and Critique*, Sage Publications, London.

de Wit, M., Wade, M. and Schouten, E. (2004) Hardwiring and softwiring corporate responsibility: a vital combination, *Corporate Governance*, **6** (4), 491–505.

Dutton, J.E. and Dukerich, J.M. (1991) Keeping an eye on the mirror: Image and identity in organizational adaptation, *Academy of Management Journal*, **34** (3), 517–54.

French, R., Rayner, C., Rees, G. and Rumbles, S. (2008) *Organizational Behaviour*, John Wiley & Sons Inc., New York.

French, W.L and Bell, C.H. (1995) *Organization Development*, Prentice Hall, NJ.

Greening, D.B. and Turban, D.W. (1997) Corporate social performance and organizational attractiveness to prospective employees, *Academy of Management Journal*, **40**, 658–72.

Guthey, E., Morsing, M. and Langer, R. (2006) CR is a management fashion. So what?, in *Strategic CR Communication* (eds M. Morsing and S.C. Beckmann), DJØF Publishers, Copenhagen, pp. 39–60.

Marchand, R. (1998) *Creating the Corporate Soul: The Rise of Public Relations and Corporate Imagery in American Big Business*, The University of California Press, Berkeley, CA.

Morsing, M. (2006) CR as strategic auto-communication – on the role of external stakeholders for member identification, *Business Ethics: A European Review*, **15** (2), 171–82.

Morsing, M. and Oswald, D. (2009) Sustainable leadership: management control systems and organizational culture in Novo Nordisk A/S. *Corporate Governance* (in press).

Morsing, M. and Roepstorff, A.C. (2008) CR as organization development – construction and reconstruction of identity at IKEA. Paper presented at the 7th Colloquium of the European Academy of Business in Society, Cranfield, September 10–12.

Olesen, T. (2008) Activist journalism? The Danish Cheminova debates, 1997 and 2006, *Journalism Practice*, **2** (2), 245–63.

Sen, S. and Bhattacharya, C.B. (2001) Does doing good always lead to doing better? Consumer reactions to corporate social responsibility, *Journal of Marketing Research*, **38**, May, 225–43.

Terlaak, A. (2007) Order without the law? The role of certified management standards in shaping socially desired firm behaviours, *Academy of Management Review*, **32** (3), 968–85.

Weaver, G.R., Trevino, L.K. and Cochran, P.L. (1999) Integrated and decoupled corporate social performance: Management commitments, external pressures, and corporate ethics practices, *Academy of Management Journal*, **42** (5), 539–52.

CHAPTER TWENTY-FIVE

betapharm: Be Different or Die[1]

Andre Habisch and Stephan Kaiser, Ingolstadt School of Management and Nigel Roome, Erasmus

> Companies are there to serve people, not the other way round.
>
> Peter Walter, founding CEO, betapharm

INTRODUCTION

After a two-day workshop in 2005 with his top management team, Peter Walter, the founding CEO of betapharm, was wondering what he should do. betapharm, he knew, was a different kind of company: during the last 10 years, the generic-drug company had developed and been celebrated as a model corporate citizen and a socially responsible company. This recognition had positively reinforced betapharm's culture and was a major source of inspiration for its employees. However, market conditions changed. Decision-making power started to shift from doctors and pharmacists towards institutions such as healthcare insurances, clinics and polyclinics with different requirements in procurement. At the same time market prices for generic drugs continued to erode. The changing circumstances caused cost and marketing challenges to arise as well as new business opportunities. The owner of betapharm, 3i, was calling for a clear strategy, which the workshop was designed to find. Walter was uncertain what that strategy should be: not only did he need to preserve the values that underlay the company's culture and unique morale, but he had to do it in a profitable way both for the generic drug business and potential new business opportunities. While he discussed the threats and opportunities with his team, it became clear that more work had to be done to explore the several options.

BACKGROUND

Germany had a dual healthcare system. On the one hand, approximately 90% of all Germans were insured through the national healthcare system. As a general rule, every employee in Germany with a gross salary of less than €45 900 per year was obliged to choose the public health insurance. This also applied to expatriates and guest workers in Germany. On the other hand, the remaining 10% of the population purchased private health insurance though various health insurance plans.

The public healthcare system in Germany was based on the concept of 'solidarity'. Patients requiring treatment could receive it regardless of their prior financial contribution. Employer and employee shared the monthly insurance premium. In practice, the employer paid the monthly premium in full to the insurance company and deducted 50% of the premium from the employee's monthly salary. In the late 1980s the escalating cost of the German healthcare system became a critical public policy issue. As a result, the government introduced a healthcare act in 1993 promoting the use of generic drugs (generics).

Generics were exact copies of the original patent-protected drug, which could be produced and sold after the original patent had expired. The principal requirement of the generic pharmaceutical business was the complete inter-changeability of the generic produced by different companies with one another and with the original product (they all had to be equivalent in efficacy, safety and quality). Once the patent on a drug expired, it was possible to produce generic equivalents subject to the supervision and approval of the public drug authority (BfArM – Bundesinstitut für Arzneimittel und Medizinprodukte). The approval process took approximately two years.

Producers of generic drugs generally did not pursue R&D activities in basic research, which significantly lowered their costs in comparison to so-called 'Big Pharma', that is, the global pharmaceutical companies that maintained R&D capabilities. Once approved, generic drugs were sold at prices ranging from 50 to 80% of the original. By the beginning of the 21st century, more than 300 active substances were patent-free and thus eligible for generic provision. The generics market in Germany represented 70% of units sold and 40% of the value of sales on the pharmaceutical market; the remainder were patent-protected drugs.

Ratiopharm, the first generics company on the German market, was founded in 1974. After Stada and Azu (today part of Sandoz), came Hexal, which was founded in 1986. Ratiopharm and Hexal benefited from first-mover advantage and became the two major players in the country with a combined market share of roughly 40% of the generics market. In the late 1980s and early 1990s many more generics companies entered the market. By 2006, more than 60 generic drug companies operated in the German market.

Strategic Positioning of betapharm up to 1998

betapharm was founded in Augsburg (Bavaria, Germany) in 1993, from where its corporate headquarters operated. The company marketed and sold pharmaceuticals to the German market. Its product portfolio consists of top-quality generic medicines, to treat conditions ranging from the common cold to serious cardiovascular diseases. 95% of these products require prescriptions. Direct customers are physicians and pharmacists, although generic drugs are ultimately used by their patients. The pharmaceuticals were distributed through specialized wholesalers to the pharmacies, and physicians prescribe the products.

In its first five years, betapharm achieved significant annual growth rates in sales (Table 25.1). In a market with average annual growth rates of approximately 10%, the company's annual sales growth reached 20–30%. The company managed to climb to 15th in the industry as measured in sales. This initial success derived from betapharm's original business model (Figure 25.1) and strategy which was based on:

- price leadership;
- being first to market once a drug becomes patent-free;
- brand recognition.

Table 25.1 Sales and Turnover of betapharm Drugs from 1993 to 2002

Sales in DM							Sales in Euro		
1993	1994	1995	1996	1997	1998	1999	2000	2001	2002
1 524 626	9 120 211	22 986 737	38 358 227	64 162 431	71 500 176	95 452 112	62 010 732	74 799 955	95 744 679

Turnover in Units									
1993	1994	1995	1996	1997	1998	1999	2000	2001	2002
176 882	1 049 465	3 005 436	4 895 488	7 264 797	7 458 924	8 900 884	10 324 678	11 311 761	13 843 990

Source: DPM/IMS

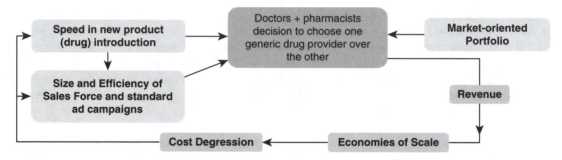

Figure 25.1 betapharm business model of 1998

Source: betapharm

Price Leadership

betapharm guaranteed that all products in its portfolio could be bought at the lowest price. When competitors lowered their prices betapharm immediately followed. betapharm also strove to convince customers that its claims were reliable, providing complete transparency on the price of its product range as well as the price of its competitors.

First to Market

After a patent expired, betapharm consistently brought generics to the market as soon as possible. This first-to-market strategy enabled the company to gain market share, grow and enhance brand recognition. This key strategic goal required betapharm to monitor closely the regulatory authority BfArM (Bundesinstitut für Arzneimittel und Medizinprodukte) to discover which patents were about to expire, what their active ingredients were, what indications were relevant, etc. Special attention was given to the patent expiration-date of the active ingredients. betapharm's marketing strategy also provided timely information regarding new release of generics.

Brand Recognition

betapharm targeted its marketing strategy on two types of clients: physicians and pharmacists (Table 25.2). Physicians often prescribed the active ingredient of a product to patients, regardless

Table 25.2 Market Research Data, Development of Awareness of Physicians and Pharmacists for the betaCare Services Over the Years

Year	'betaCare' known by		'betaListe' known by		'betafon' known by		'betanet' known by	
	Physicians	Pharmacists	Physicians	Pharmacists	Physicians	Pharmacists	Physicians	Pharmacists
2003	29%	40%	52%	74%	46%	63%	25%	40%
2004	46%	63%	60%	84%	49%	63%	31%	35%
2006	67%	79%	72%	87%	56%	67%	40%	54%

Source: Medupha

of the manufacturing source. In this case, the pharmacist was free to choose and dispense any branded product, as long as it was in a so-called low price-segment. However, physicians could also prescribe a specific product. The sales reps' job was to convince both doctors and pharmacists that betapharm products were as good as the patented product or other generic brands. In other words, the job of the betapharm sales force, which was known for its sincere enthusiasm, was to promote brand recognition as the way to sales growth. This reflected the leadership skills of the founding CEO, Peter Walter.

Walter was an early believer in employee empowerment. His vision and guiding principle (Exhibit 25.1) was to build the company around the notion that people and the quality of their relationships with colleagues and others would create the conditions for future success. Regardless of rank or title, he strove to ensure that his employees felt happy, trusted and safe, which in his view would unleash their creativity and play to their strengths. His employees, he stressed, should feel personally responsible for the company's success. To communicate his approach, he developed slogans, such as, 'our cleaners are as important as the managing director' or 'the spirit of healthy companies is that of learning, development and self-organization'.

EXHIBIT 25.1 MISSION STATEMENTS FROM 1994 ONWARDS

Mission Statement 1994:

'At the centre of our concern is the trust of people that build on our enterprise, like customers, employees, business partners and shareholders.

With our customers we have an open dialogue, we want to care about their problems and we hope to exceed the expectations of customers.

We are founded on the idea of learning, development and self-organization. We promote the independence of our employees and their courage to take own responsibility. Failures help us to improve ourselves.

betapharm is a community in which every member sees itself as a part of the whole and should have pleasure in working. Our relationships are colleague-minded, open and everybody works together as partners. Success through trust is our goal.'

(Continued)

EXHIBIT 25.1 (*Continued*)

Mission Statement 1999:

'betapharm is a community in which every member should see him/herself as part of the whole and is able to enjoy his/her work.

At the centre of our concern is the trust of people in our reliability. We see ourselves as partners for health.

We have a holistic view on health. Therefore we take social responsibility and care about issues in psycho-social healthcare.

We seek success in business. In doing so we build on creativity and performance and additionally on the own responsibility of employees.

Our relationships are open and we work together as partners. Success through trust is our goal.'

Mission Statement 2000:

'At betapharm everybody should feel as being a part of the whole and find joy and meaning in his/her work. We are open to each other, reliable and work together as partners, within our organization and with our customers.

Total health considers more than medicine-technology and pharmaceuticals. Therefore we also consider the psycho-social questions concerning healthcare and develop socio-medical future-projects in research and practice.

On the basis of our business success, we further develop our values. Thereby we trust on creativity, performance and the own-responsibility of our employees.'

Mission Statement 2002:

'We want betapharm to be a community where everyone feels they belong, finding a sense of purpose in their work and taking pleasure in it. We deal honestly with each other; we are reliable and work in a spirit of partnership and cooperation – with colleagues and customers alike.

We take social responsibility seriously. That's why we also take an active interest in addressing the psycho-social problems facing the healthcare system and give our support to forward looking social-medical projects.

We see our economic success as a basis from which to develop our values further. This is a sign of our trust in the creativity, effectiveness and personal responsibility shown by our colleagues.'

Source: betapharm

Early Need for a New Strategy

During the 1990s, several of betapharm's competitors began to pursue a hyper-competitive pricing strategy. With roughly 30 competitors of equivalent products, betapharm could no longer sustain its guarantee to be a low-cost provider across all the products in its portfolio. This undermined the basis for its brand recognition, which began to erode betapharm's market position. By 1998, year-on-year growth had dwindled to near zero (see Tables 25.1 and 25.2). The morale of the sales force, so confident and motivated during the years of growth, plummeted. A new strategy was required.

Nonetheless, the hyper-competitive market did not undermine Peter Walter's original vision, that is, that people provided the secret to success. As such, his new strategy hinged on the motivation of his employees, sales force and support teams at headquarters in Augsburg – their satisfaction and happiness, in his view, would lead to happy and loyal customers. How, he wondered, could he accomplish this in a hyper-competitive market?

Der Bunte Kreis

In 1997, betapharm won a regional marketing prize for private sector organizations. At that time, 'Der Bunte Kreis' (DBK) – a charitable organization working to develop and provide care to families with severely and chronically-ill children – won the marketing prize in the non-profit organization category of the same competition. Founded in 1992 in Augsburg by a group of hospital staff working with parents and self-help groups, DBK sought to address the daily problems experienced by families with chronically and severely ill children. The problem, as DBK's founders saw it, originated in the highly fragmented German healthcare system, which many families found confusing to the point of incomprehensibility. DBK built a network between institutions, which enabled healthcare professionals and helpers to exchange information in an ongoing dialogue.

The DBK approach was patient-focused rather than disease-focused. DBK appointed trained 'case managers', usually experienced nurses, to take care of the patients' family from their first hospital visit, liaising with other care professionals on their behalf. For example, they organized care for siblings during the time that the parents spent in the hospital with their sick child. In addition, family members were trained to take care of patients released from hospital, in a similar way to the traditional practice of midwives, who provided support for mothers and their newborn babies at home. In cases where families needed to buy a new car or modify their house due to their child's physical handicap, DBK raised funds.

As betapharm management learned more about DBK, they became deeply impressed by its approach and achievements. In 1998, betapharm decided to sponsor DBK's work. Though some DBK activists initially feared that DBK might be pressured to favour betapharm products, betapharm donated only general support funds to DBK; this demonstrated, to many sceptics in DBK, that the two organizations shared a similar philosophy. Finally, betapharm management answered DBK's concerns with openness and transparency.

Peter Walter and Horst Erhardt, the managing director of DBK, began to build a warm professional relationship. Both believed in the potential for collaboration between the two organizations. Walter created a new position at betapharm to foster the collaboration with DBK. In autumn 1998, betapharm introduced its employees to the work of DBK to equip them with background information on the sponsorship; tours to DBK followed. In addition, betapharm began to establish media contacts on behalf of DBK.

As the relationship between the two organizations developed, it became clear that both benefited from the sponsorship: betapharm employees, disappointed by the downturn in sales, began to show increasing interest and pride in the company's support for DBK activities. Moreover, betapharm sales representatives reported that, when they visited physicians, they could open conversations on the company's sponsorship for DBK; physicians then asked them to provide more information on DBK's approach. Often, this enabled betapharm sales representatives to spend time with physicians who previously had refused to see them. Others reported that they could engage in longer conversations with their clients, often up to 30 minutes, compared to earlier contacts of five minutes or so. As a result, betapharm's sponsorship of DBK enhanced the company's visibility as well as its reputation for trust and credibility. Because of their support for DBK, it appeared, physicians and pharmacists had begun to perceive betapharm to be an *exception* to other drug companies.

Foundation of beta Institut

Despite the improvements in employee morale and the visibility of the company, betapharm was still going through a sales crisis. This required a new strategy, ideally based on the existing patient-oriented values and mission of fulfilling unmet needs. A few months after the sponsorship with DBK began, betapharm created the 'betapharm After-care Foundation'. Its aim was to develop and spread the DBK approach throughout Germany, based on DBK's pioneering work in Augsburg. However, when betapharm and DBK attempted to introduce the Augsburg Aftercare Model into other parts of Germany, they confronted objections regarding the scientific basis of their approach. To ground DBK's work on a firmer scientific foundation, betapharm and DBK established the beta Institut for sociomedical research and development.

In 1999, betapharm provided a donation of €1 million to the beta Institut, which was incorporated as a charitable organization. The vision of the beta Institut was to develop a more holistic and human-oriented healthcare model. The Institut developed the themes of 'patient-oriented case management', 'disease management' and 'total sickness management'; they were designed to investigate how the psycho-social health of patients and their families could be maintained and improved.

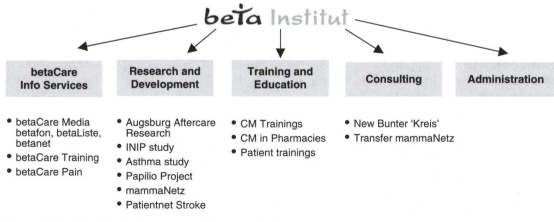

Figure 25.2 Organizational structure of beta Institut in 2006

Source: betapharm

DBK's approach was incorporated into the activities of the beta Institut. The Institut's principal aim was to place the patient at the centre of the German healthcare system, which was notorious for artificial divisions between specialized doctors, hospitals, after-care health professionals and pharmacists. A stronger relationship between these healthcare professionals and the patients moving though the system, in this view, would improve the quality of a patient's life and cut costs. The secondary aim was to improve patients' well-being and recovery in a way that contributed to the prevention of future illness. Furthermore, the beta Institut worked on primary prevention: the direct improvement of psycho-social health, preventing people from becoming sick by avoiding illness-generating situations and life-styles.

The beta Institut disseminated its knowledge and experience to healthcare professionals through lectures, workshops, seminars and publications, and also provided consultancy services to support hospitals and other institutions (Figure 25.2). It worked in partnerships with a number of hospitals and universities and received grants from government foundations and businesses. As the beta Institut developed its network and social capital, these also became available to betapharm.

IMPLEMENTING THE NEW STRATEGY

Based on these developments, Peter Walter formulated a new mission statement (see earlier Exhibit 25.1), which reflected the company's core values as guidelines for success. Walter pointed out that

> number crunching and conventional market research are no prerequisites for a successful business. You see a central demand in a market and you need to find a better solution for that problem. If you have it, you need to make it visible. Success will then follow automatically. You do not need numbers for that purpose at all. You simply need to listen and talk to people and you will find your way. The numbers will follow the things you have done.

Walter also developed his idea that business success must address an 'unmet need' (Figure 25.3). In the early years, betapharm addressed the unmet need of the market's demand for price transparency combined with low prices. Marketing based on honesty and trustworthiness, according to this business model, ensured the clients' confidence in the brand's quality and low prices. betapharm customers remained aware of the distinct company culture that emanated from Walter's philosophy prior to the crisis phase in 1997/1998.

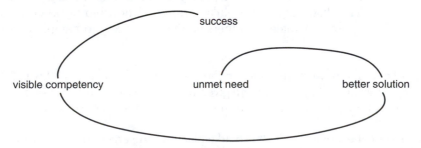

Figure 25.3 betapharm's approach to creating success (1998)

Source: betapharm

The New Strategy

In formulating a new strategy, Walter emphasized that 'the spirit of healthy companies is that of learning, development and self-organization' and these elements were seen as central to the new strategy. The new strategy was based on

- trust, transparency and authenticity;
- branded added-value for sociomedical unmet needs;
- low-prices (but not total low-price leadership).

Not just any unmet need was tackled, but rather the strategy was focused on the sociomedical needs of the healthcare system. The instruction of beta Institut was to develop solutions for the healthcare system in that respect. Before 1998, branding could only be understood in terms of low price brand. But pricing became less important and instead represented an entrance ticket to play on the market. Everybody could offer the same low prices at that time.

The practical outcome of the strategy was that a significant part of the company's marketing-budget was devoted to innovative social structures and healthcare research projects by sponsoring the betapharm After-care foundation and beta Institut. However, given the size of these expenditures (3–4% of sales), betapharm's sales representatives began to ask for more material benefit for the company from this investment.

Therefore, in 1999 the beta Institut started to design and put new services in place: among these was a database for sociomedical information available as a telephone hotline (betafon) for physicians and pharmacists. In 2001, the Institute also developed a reference book (betaListe) and an Internet search engine (betanet). Initially, the phone hotline was marketed by the beta Institut itself, albeit with limited success. betapharm management believed that these services would support its holistic notion of health.

betapharm Takes Over Marketing of Social Services

In 2000, betapharm took over the marketing of these social services completely. The company set up a team to manage all aspects of its social investment and to serve as the interface between betapharm and the beta Institut. The team leader was a member of the management board, who reported directly to the CEO. In addition, betapharm started to train its sales representatives in these new services. What had begun as a philanthropic relationship between betapharm and DBK was now evolving into a strategic partnership that was a key to betapharm's competitive strategy.

All employees of betapharm were instructed in the corporate social responsibility (CSR) strategy as a basis for competitive advantage. They were given the chance to discuss and study systematically the ethical aspects of the pharmaceutical business as well as betapharm's attitude and practices.

The performance of the company in the marketplace improved: customers began to trust the strategy and believe in the social services under development. For their part, employees wanted to explain the new business strategy to outsiders because of their pride in the values it embodied; they were given tools to explain what the company was doing. In what came to be viewed as a

Table 25.3 Annual Employee Figures at betapharm and beta Institut

| Year | number of employees at betapharm | | | number of employees at beta Institut |
	all other functions	sales force	overall	
1994	13	52	65	
1995	17	68	85	
1996	23	103	126	
1997	29	99	128	
1998	33	86	119	
1999	3	109	112	4
2000	49	112	161	9
2001	57	232	289	16
2002	67	231	298	23
2003	80	236	316	35
2004	102	215	317	41
2005	130	219	349	49
2006	161	235	396	53

Source: betapharm

milestone in 2002, the German Federal President, Johannes Rau, awarded the national CSR award 'Liberty and Responsibility' to betapharm. This reinforced the growing confidence and pride of employees. Meanwhile, the beta Institute expanded its list of innovations, gaining further public recognition including a betapharm-initiated federal law in Berlin, which ensured that after-care according to the DBK model was financed by the German public healthcare system.

betapharm's sales force was increasingly able to disseminate information about the products, services, approach and achievements of the beta Institut (Table 25.3). Many doctors that routinely refused visits from sales reps began to welcome betapharm staff and engage in serious dialogue about beta-R&D projects. Furthermore, because betapharm was increasingly seen as a trustworthy generics company that delivered added value to customers while still offering low prices, discussions and then collaboration with health insurance companies were increasingly undertaken.

Enhanced Performance

betapharm's generic drug sales increased quickly. Annual growth rates in sales returned to double digits, averaging 26%, moving from 15th in sales in 1998 to fourth in 2004 (see Table 25.4 and Figure 25.4). betapharm also became a market leader for sociomedical services. Employee satisfaction was back to its normal level, with the workforce exhibiting a strong identification with their firm. By 2002, the sales force had doubled in size. More than half of the incoming staff were recruited by word-of-mouth, and there was a waiting list of employee candidates hoping to join betapharm. New employees tended to have excellent qualifications and were coming

Table 25.4 Sales and Turnover of betapharm Drugs from 1999 to 2006

Sales in Euro							
1999	2000	2001	2002	2003	2004	2005	2006
48 448 288	64 052 977	78 353 232	98 513 825	149 479 313	163 177 271	191 414 073	184 210 098

Turnover in Units							
1999	2000	2001	2002	2003	2004	2005	2006
8 958 583	10 745 082	11 965 701	14 185 814	16 010 470	15 023 971	18 248 989	20 571 244

Source: NPI/NDC

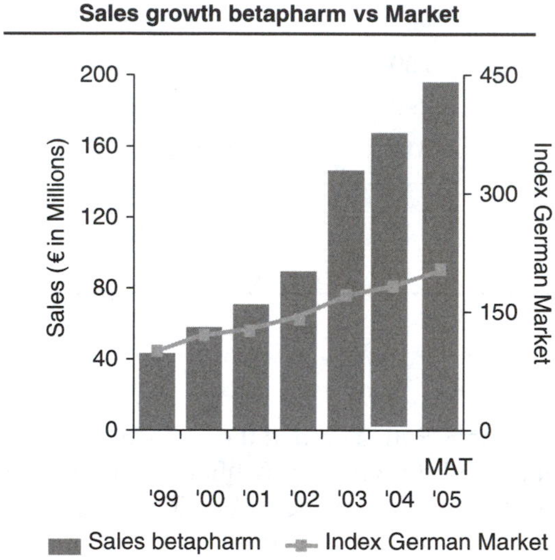

Sales growth betapharm vs Market

Sales growth of Top 10

Rank Generics	Company	'99–'05 Growth Rate
1	Hexal	20.0 %
2	Ratiopharm	15.6 %
3	Stada	22.4 %
4	**betapharm**	**26.0 %**
5	Winthrop	- 2.3 %
6	Neuraxpharm	17.1 %
7	Merck Dura	6.0 %
8	Alpharma Isis	- 4.1 %
9	Heumann	5.4 %
10	TAD	3.7 %

Figure 25.4 Development of betapharm compared to market

Source: NPI.

from large companies with very good reputations. Support staff numbers were recruited with similar ease.

Overall, betapharm's social sponsorship had provided the basis for its new competitive position. In 2004, clients reported, and perception studies confirmed, that the company's activities reflected an appreciation of the role of healthcare professionals greatly superior to that of other drug companies (Table 25.5 and Figure 25.5). Clients pointed out that they felt empathy with betapharm in terms of shared values and identity. The uniqueness and perceived added value of the service appeared to spur customers to identify strongly with betapharm and generated loyalty towards the company and its products. Typical comments were 'I welcome the initiative very much. I feel better using products from a company that cares for humankind just as I do' or 'In contrast to the standard marketing tools of other companies, these are very meaningful and useful tools for my practice' or 'This is a great help to me'. Clients, it seemed, felt that betapharm was 'part' of the healthcare system rather than 'living off' the system.

Table 25.5 Market Research Data Answers from Pharmacists to the Question: 'Do You Know Generic Drug Companies with Social Responsibility and Which Are These?' (More Than One Company Could be Named)

	2000	2001	2002	2003	2004	2005
There are generic companies with social activities	23%	34%	46%	49%	63%	76%
These firms show social responsibility	23%	31%	36%	42%	57%	68%
BETAPHARM	**9%**	**18%**	**21%**	**35%**	**47%**	**51%**
RATIOPHARM	3%	5%	13%	5%	7%	7%
STADA	10%	6%	4%	4%	5%	7%
Others (Merck Dura, Aliud, Hexal, etc)	4%	7%	7%	5%	8%	5%

Source: Medupha

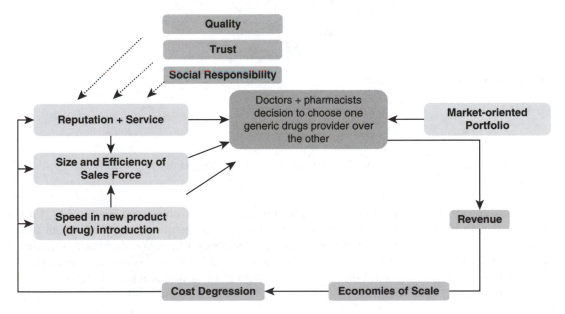

Figure 25.5 Business Model of 2004

Source: betapharm

Transforming Organizational Structure, Culture and Training

As CSR became an integral part of betapharm's business model, the company's organizational structure required changes. As it stood, not even the term CSR was known within the company. At the beginning of 1998, Petra Kinzl was hired as assistant to the managing director for the development of CSR activities, in effect to act as a change agent. Walter defined her job description

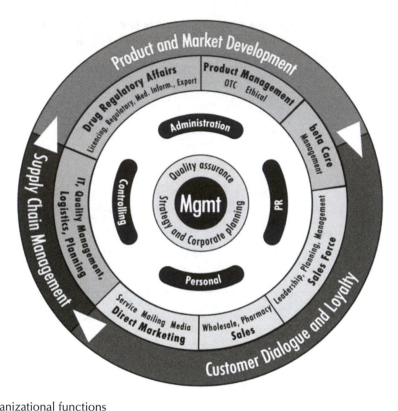

Figure 25.6 Organizational functions

Source: betapharm

to Kinzl as follows: 'I have met the Bunte Kreis, please develop something fruitful out of it'. CSR management was a one-woman-show for the first two years.

In 2000, the organizational structure reflected the company's value chain (see Figure 25.6). Kinzl's team, which would grow into a CSR department with 15 staff members, took care of all issues linked to DBK and betapharm's CSR and its developing strategy. On paper, the work of the team was divided between public relations and the management of betaCare. As the head of the team, Kinzl became a member of the board of management in 2001, a direct acknowledgement of the importance assigned to her activities.

In 2003, the role of the CSR department again expanded (Figure 25.7 and 25.8). The CSR-team at that time was renamed 'Competitive Advantage'; the goal was to underline the competitive importance of CSR in the marketplace. Additionally, the responsibilities were enlarged. The 'brand' would now be developed as a real brand. New departments would be developed: beside communications and betaCare, the team also gained responsibility for such areas as brand development, direct marketing and Key Account management. However, far more important than formal structures was the emergence of 'flexible' responsibilities, according to which every member of the team assumed general responsibility for CSR-related issues rather than solely those in his or her job description.

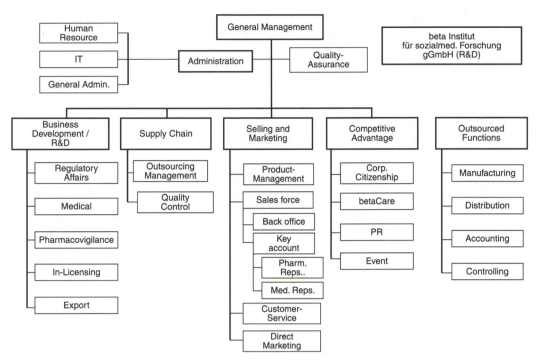

Figure 25.7 Organizational structure of betapharm in 2003

Source: betapharm

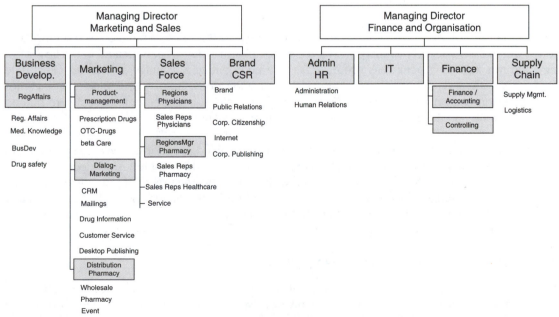

Figure 25.8 Organizational structure of betapharm in 2005

Source: betapharm

In addition to changes in the organizational structure for CSR issues, the corporate culture was reframed to stimulate open dialogue and a sense of belonging to a corporate family. For example:

- Open dialogue and mutual respect were supported throughout the organization and operations. This was designed to achieve a spirit of creativity and courage to undertake new ideas.
- Free, informal employee lunches served as places of dialogue to develop internal cohesion.
- Drinks and small snacks were free for employees.
- For birthdays, every employee received a birthday card personally signed by every employee.
- Every other year, employees got a photograph and picture book to remember events and meetings, sometimes also movies. It was aimed to achieve a family-like cohesion.
- At company parties, employees were encouraged to prepare talent shows themselves (in addition to professional shows). The employee-initiated shows often infused pride into all employees.
- Walter proclaimed a policy of open doors. Everybody was encouraged to step into his office and to speak up freely, without regard to rank.
- In the old office building, there was an open space between the offices, which was called the 'Forum'. The Forum was used for meetings and discussions.
- The new office building, as inaugurated in 2002, was designed with an open architecture without doors. Large windows and removable walls provided for privacy and silence as well as catering to flexibility.

Another important aspect was the training of employees. Formal CSR training focused on the sales force, but it also included the entire workforce of betapharm. They were educated in the CSR strategy and the reasoning behind its use as a basis for competitive advantage as well as 'Der Bunte Kreis', betaCare and the company's mission statement and values. Training took place several times a year, depending on an employee's function. For example, sales force employees were trained more frequently on these topics than those working on regulatory affairs.

The dialogue-oriented culture supported the sharing of knowledge and ideas. Walter continued to question everything, which generated ideas and served as an instrument to test all decisions, processes and opinions. Walter also communicated with everybody, regardless of job function or rank, achieving a wide range of feedback on new ideas and projects. Walter engaged in a particularly close dialogue with the sales force, as a link to the market. He frequently consulted them regarding new market developments, which encouraged a productive and active sales force.

NEW DEVELOPMENTS, NEW CHALLENGES

Having established and implemented a new CSR-oriented strategy and business model, betapharm achieved a growth rate of 39% in 2003. However, two new challenges arose. First, ownership of the company changed. Second, reforms in the German healthcare system created additional pressures.

In summer 2003, the founding owners of betapharm, Santo GmbH, a family holding company, decided to sell. In March 2004, the private equity firm 3i bought the company, in part because of its reputation for a CSR-based strategy. The new owner enjoyed a solid reputation in the healthcare sector, with an international network and expertise.

In 2004, changes in the German healthcare system significantly impacted betapharm's business. Pharmacists were given more latitude over the drugs sold to patients. Because betapharm had concentrated its marketing efforts on physicians, this weakened the company's market position. Sales dropped and growth targets could not be achieved, although 3i expected the company to get back on track with a business plan and financial targets within a few months. Perhaps inevitably, some managers questioned whether CSR activities should be eliminated as a costly indulgence, which had increased too far in recent years. However, 3i maintained a belief in betapharm's business model and intended to enlarge the company and exploit its full business potential, which Walter also believed. 'I always wanted to show,' he stressed, 'that businesses can be successful and at the same time be responsible to humankind. I wanted to develop a company as a place in which people like to work and in which people are allowed their rights even when in crisis phases.' As a consequence, betapharm leaders decided not to cut back CSR activities; instead, they would intensify marketing efforts. For example, the betaCare services, such as patient consulting on sociomedical questions, were offered and promoted to pharmacists as well as physicians; as a result, betapharm suffered less than its competitors from the healthcare system changes.

However, the daily working life in the company changed under the new ownership. Pressure on staff and working hours grew. 3i introduced new evaluation systems with shorter reporting cycles as well as requirements for input from lower management levels than before. betapharm also installed more support functions, particularly in the finance and administrative departments. More-over, because Walter had reached retirement age, 3i hired a successor, Dr. Wolfgang Niedermaier, in June, 2005. Niedermaier was a pharmacist with over 20 years of experience in the national and international pharmaceutical business. He aspired to leverage the brand to a wider group of clients and to enlarge the product portfolio. 'One of my main goals,' he explained, 'was to develop further the exceptional differentiated positioning and well received brand of betapharm.' To that end, both the social services as well as the pharmaceutical products played a critical role in differentiating against competitors and providing unique benefit to the customers.

Only 24 months after taking over betapharm, 3i sold it to the international pharmaceutical com-pany Dr. Reddy's Laboratories for €480 million. Dr. Reddy's was headquartered in Hyderabad, India, operated in more than 100 countries worldwide and employed over 7000 people. The founder, Dr. Reddy, and his family still owned the major stake in the company and remained ac-tively involved in its management. It was listed on the New York stock exchange. Dr. Reddy's busi-nesses range from drug R&D and production (of active pharmaceutical ingredients, final dosage forms and generic products) to marketing and sales of drugs worldwide.

New legislation allowed the statutory sickfunds of the national healthcare system to conclude re-bate contracts with pharmaceutical companies. At the same time pharmacists are forced to substi-tute physicians' prescriptions with rebated generic pharmaceuticals where possible and when not excluded by the physician. Rebate contracts between sickfunds and pharmaceutical companies have evolved as a prerequisite for market access.

The acquisition of betapharm represented Dr. Reddy's first major move into the European market, both as a stake in the largest European, and the world's second largest, generic pharmaceutical market, but also with a CSR-oriented strategy. Not surprisingly, the latest change of ownership brought new challenges to betapharm, in particular the requirements in finance and business administration that were expected of a publicly owned company. Reporting systems had to meet new demands, Sarbanes-Oxley controls were implemented, and business review procedures harmonized with new standards.

During 2006, further reforms in the German healthcare system came into force. A new computer national system would monitor the price of generics and provide pharmacists with information about product prices – pharmacists were obliged to select the lowest priced generic drug shown on the computer. Rebate contracts in connection with the transparency and low-cost principles of betapharm's initial strategy once again became central to the reformed healthcare system's low-cost approach (Figure 25.9). Suddenly, physicians and pharmacists were monitoring price differences of a few cents, even if they existed only for very short periods. In order to maintain sales performance, betapharm was forced to cut prices for a large proportion of

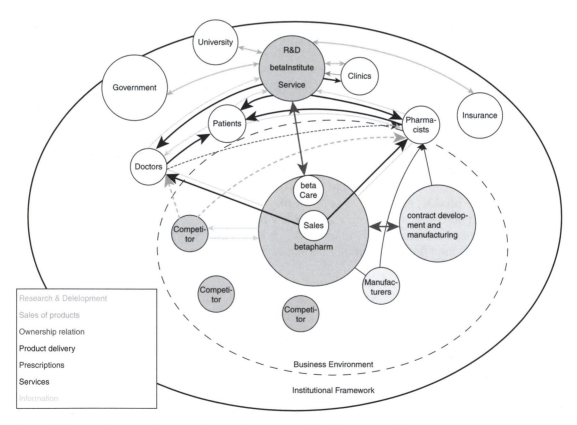

Figure 25.9 betapharm and beta Institut in the context of the German healthcare system

Source: betapharm

its product portfolio. This renewed internal criticisms regarding the costs of betapharm's CSR activities.

Sales and market share were now driven more than ever by price differentials, which were determined by the costs of production, marketing and distribution. Although the company has been successful in providing generics at the lowest possible price, further growth in sales was proving more difficult to achieve. Unfortunately, the company's cost structures remained high, given the price pressures that were expected in the short and medium term. What should management do?

NOTE

1. This case is intended to be used as a basis for class discussion rather than to illustrate either effective or ineffective handling of an adminstrate situation.

CHAPTER TWENTY-SIX

The TPG-WFP Partnership: Looking for a Partner[1]

Luk N. Van Wassenhove and Rolando M. Tomasini, INSEAD

INTRODUCTION

While on a flight to Singapore in November 2001, I read a *BusinessWeek* article about September 11th and its causes and implications. The writer was pointing out the gulf between the rich and the poor. She had worked out that every seven seconds a child dies from hunger. Since then, this horrifying statistic has in fact become closer to every five seconds. The writer's last question was: 'What are you doing for the world after September 11th?' So I began to ask myself that question.

Peter Bakker, CEO, TPG[2]

EXHIBIT 26.1 PERSONAL PROFILES

Peter Bakker, CEO
- Age: 40 at the time the project team started with the research
- Hobbies: golf, music, formula 1 racing
- Profile: very action oriented, easily accessible, 'emailer' with incredible amounts of e-mail, workaholic, ambitious

Ludo Oelrich, Programme Director for Moving the World
- Age: 41 at the time project team started with the research (married, two children, age 6 and 10)
- Company background: TPG Post MD Logistics Netherlands, TNT Logistics Benelux MD, Managing Partner Logispring (venture capital)
- Hobbies: golf, sailing, skiing
- Profile: analytical manager, structured, hard worker, ambitious, sense of humour

EXHIBIT 26.2 COMPANY PROFILES

In 2003, TPG, based in the Netherlands, had built its reputation on its two brands, TPG Post and TNT. The company operated with three divisions: Mail, Express and Logistics. The Mail division focused primarily on the Netherlands and a network of European mail companies. The Express and Logistics divisions operated globally.

TPG

Countries with company-owned operations	62
Employees at end of 2002	150,365

TPGPOST

Depots hubs	845
Postal items delivered in the Netherlands	6,871,000,000
Total tonnes of international mail carried	90,691
Post Offices in the Netherlands (including 300 Bruna outlets)	2,100

TNT Express

Vehicles	31,230*
Aircraft	43*
Depots hubs	891
Countries served by Express	200
Total tonnes carried in 2002	3,322,051
Total consignments carried in 2002	187,206,000
*A substantial number of vehicles and aircraft are not owned by TPG but are leased or subcontracted	

TNT Logistics

Warehouses	415
Square metres managed	6,257,000
Countries with Logistics operations	36
Logistics contracts managed	1,100+

In 2003, WFP food aid reached 110 million people in 82 countries – the highest number in its 40-year history.

In 2002 they distributed food to 72 million of the poorest people in the world:

- 14 million people in development programmes
- 44 million beneficiaries in emergency operations
- 14 million people in rehabilitation operations

(Continued)

EXHIBIT 26.2 (*Continued*)

Of the 3.7 million tonnes of food WFP distributed in 2002:

- 2.244 million tonnes were for emergency operations
- 580 979 tonnes were for development projects
- 918 435 tonnes were for protracted relief and recovery operations

WFP's total operational expenditure in 2002 amounted to US$1.59 billion, of which:

- 88% was spent on relief aid
- 12% was spent on development aid

WFP's total number of employees with contracts of one year and longer in 2002 was 2684, of whom:

- 2063 worked in the field
- 621 worked at the Rome headquarters

WFP's school feeding assisted more than 15.6 million schoolchildren in 67 countries in 2002, thereby supporting increased enrolment in school. Special efforts were taken to close the education gender gap by providing take-home rations to more than 1.1 million girls. In 2002, WFP purchased, by international tender, more than 1.5 million tonnes of food commodities valued at US$307.5 million, 41% of the total tonnage of food provided to beneficiaries. WFP purchased 67% of the food from 57 developing countries. The remaining tonnage was purchased from 20 developed countries. By spending US$204 million in the developing world, of which over 60% was purchased from suppliers in Africa, WFP helped local farmers, agribusiness and the private sector.

Over the next few days, the question persisted in Bakker's mind. As a market leader in the logistics business, TPG was very much part of the globalization process and it was clear to Bakker that the benefit of doing business internationally went hand in hand with the responsibility of acting as a good global corporate citizen.

Back at TPG headquarters in Amsterdam, Bakker called upon a TPG veteran, Ludo Oelrich, Managing Partner of Logispring.[3] Bakker was convinced it was time for TPG to launch a new approach to corporate social responsibility (CSR) and he wanted Oelrich to lead that process. Oelrich was convinced by Bakker's ideas and within two weeks he started working full time on it. He elaborated on the challenge: 'My in-depth knowledge of the logistics business was an asset, but building an engaging corporate social responsibility agenda, a new corporate culture for our company, were uncharted waters for me and the company.'

Focus	Planet	People
Outside TPG	Environmental community investing	Social community investing
Inside TPG	Environmental in-company investing	Social in-company investing

Figure 26.1 Landscape of CSR

SKETCHING THE CSR LANDSCAPE

Over the last five years, TPG had sponsored numerous local, relatively small-scale initiatives. These included community-based programmes in some of the 60 countries in which the company operated, as well as the high-profile annual Dutch Golf Tournament. 'These initiatives had met their objectives and now it was time to operate on a different level, to initiate programmes in line with our global presence,' explained Oelrich. To start exploring the different options, a small team at headquarters made up of strategy, development, corporate communications and human resources specialists began reading up on CSR literature in December 2001, studying examples such as ProbusBNW (UK) and Shell.

'One of our first decisions involved the focus of our initiative. We soon narrowed down the choice to two possible areas: environmental issues or social and humanitarian related issues,' explained Oelrich. As a mail service provider,[4] TPG's success depended on customer satisfaction, the quality of contact and the impact of their service on people's businesses and lives. 'While we all agreed that human related issues seemed more compatible with our brand image, we had to decide on our approach. Should we focus on people close to us, like our employees or our customers, or should we engage these groups to reach out to a wider public?' (see Figure 26.1).

The team discovered that TPG had already sponsored several initiatives focusing on employees. In addition, the company's HR approach was considered very responsive to employee needs. Further research revealed that customer satisfaction levels were good and that business units in different countries were already addressing the needs of the communities they served through targeted needs-based projects. Taking all these factors into consideration, the team concluded that coming up with a CSR initiative that would engage all TPG's (then) 150 000 employees, while winning customer attention and support, would require something of a different order of ambition.

Bakker agreed with the scope and level of ambition envisioned by the team: 'It is not enough to be socially responsible only within our company. We should also strive for social leadership outside our business. If through our business we can help improve people's living conditions, it is our responsibility to do so.'

THE SEARCH FOR THE IDEAL PARTNER

In January 2002, the team moved into the next phase of the operation and started the arduous task of finding a suitable social partner to match TPG's CSR needs. After several months of research and meetings, a shortlist of humanitarian organizations was drawn up. They soon realized that using standard business indicators to compare not-for-profit humanitarian organizations in

Filter	• Neutrality (politics, religion, etc.)	
	• Reputation	
	Criterion	Weight (%)
Selection Criteria	• Matching TPG's core competences	40
	• PR value/their interests & attitude	30
	• Effectiveness, % overhead, tax	20
	• Geographical scope	10

Figure 26.2 Filters and criteria

a fair and objective manner was a challenge. Therefore, the team narrowed its initial screening criteria to focus on the reputation and neutrality of the candidate organizations. The indicators had to ensure that the programme would be well received and adopted in every TPG country context. Consequently, humanitarian organizations with very important missions but a controversial image in areas of the world where TPG was active were carefully put aside.

Once past the filtering stage, the remaining organizations were measured against four selection criteria. The most important of these was organizational fit. Rather than providing cash donations, TPG intended to share its logistics knowledge and capabilities. As such, logistics had to be of great value to the selected partner. Interest and attitude ranked next. The partner's mandate had to match TPG's CSR intentions; the selected organization had to have a vision that the whole TPG family, including its customers, could share. The third criterion was a match between the partner's effectiveness and overhead costs and TPG's culture of successful action-driven operations. 'The last thing we wanted to do was to get involved with an organization consumed by bureaucracy, one that invested largely in its own internal operations rather than the communities they were meant to serve,' emphasized Oelrich. Lastly, to achieve global impact, the partner's geographic scope was taken into account in terms of presence and operations (see Figure 26.2).

The process led to the identification of five finalists:[5] International Federation of Blue Shield (IFBS), Help the Kids (HtK), United for the Children's Future (UCF), Medical Aid (MA) and the World Food Programme (WFP). TPG approached each of these organizations towards the end of January to assess their interest in an eventual partnership. The prospect of being courted by a corporation was a new concept to many of the humanitarian organizations, which posed a number of challenges for the organizations themselves and for TPG. Apart from the language barrier, the motivations behind corporate interest in humanitarian affairs were not obvious or easily understood. In addition, not all the short-listed organizations were familiar with TPG and its range of activities, as Oelrich elaborated: 'We were mainly associated with our mail operations and the general perception was that of an old-fashioned business where the mailman comes on a bike and empties a standing postbox. Rarely did our interlocutors appreciate the very high-tech, extensive, and sophisticated non-stop operations that went on behind the mailman.' To assess the level of interest and coherence between mission statements, the short-listed organizations were asked to complete an information template that expanded on the four selection criteria by February 2002 (see Figure 26.3).

Organization	• Structure
	• Size
	• Operations areas
	• Services provided
	• Yearly costs
	• Income sources
	• Growth
Image	• Image description
	• Political engagement
Marketing	• Types of marketing and communications used
	• Types of marketing and communications allowed to partner companies
	• VIPs connected to the organization
Logistics	• Current practices and structure
	• Skills and knowledge
	• Types of goods distributed
	• Sources used
	• Destinations
	• Types of transport and modalities
	• Timelines involved
	• Overview of logistics flow
	• Current logistics flow
Opportunities	• Possible transportation and logistics services
	• Types of logistics advice required

Figure 26.3 Facts and figures template

GETTING SUPPORT

Unlike any previous CSR initiative implemented by TPG, this one required the early involvement of key staff in order to ensure future contribution and commitment. While Bakker shared his vision of the company's CSR initiative with the company's top management, Oelrich and his team spent time explaining the rationale behind the initiative to the company's business units.

Arguments supporting the initiative were both generic and industry-specific. The Dutch government had a long history of active and generous humanitarian and development aid programmes. TPG's public image as the national mail service provider created expectations among customers and citizens who wished to see TPG address the needs of various communities and engage in CSR programmes. In addition, financial markets were starting to reward socially responsible companies.[6] Finally, there was the growing sentiment among members of the general public and

TPG employees that globally operating corporations had an obligation to try and improve the lives of people in the markets in which they were active. In terms of industry benchmarks, TPG's main competitors also had CSR programmes in place and to many observers it was clear that in order to maintain its position in the top ranks TPG needed not only to match but also surpass these initiatives.

Despite the fact that TPG's motivation was primarily social, the perceived benefits of a successful CSR initiative to its business were multiple. First, it could ensure a more binding and engaging relationship with its employees as well as with society at large. TPG could also enhance its reputation globally by being associated with a leading aid organization. Furthermore, TPG had three divisions – Mail, Logistics and Express – and the CSR drive would add a key issue on which to further build unity. Partnership with a leading aid organization could further strengthen the existing ties between them. Dialogue with the different business units highlighted other benefits and helped to fine-tune the parameters for a good partnership. In retrospect, there was a strong sentiment that the selection process significantly benefited from the participation of a broader-than-usual cross section of TPG colleagues and their varying perspectives.

SURVIVAL OF THE FITTEST

As the parameters for the partnership became more detailed and the plan gained more structure, the profile of the suitable partner became more targeted. In February 2002, much to TPG's surprise, one of the candidates, Medical Aid, voluntarily withdrew from the selection process. 'It was important for us to understand the reasons behind this decision,' explained Oelrich. A meeting sought by TPG with the organization clarified the operational constraints: 'While MA operates globally, the country offices act independently, making a fully-fledged global partnership hard to implement.' Soon after, TPG realized that IFBS had a similar decentralized structure at the country level with independent national societies.

By early March, using a scorecard based on the initial selection criteria, the finalists were narrowed down to UCF and WFP. These two were a better fit than HtK in terms of logistics operations. 'Before making any final decisions and proposals, we wanted to ensure that there was "chemistry" with our future partner. We needed to contrast and juxtapose our gut feelings with and against the results of our analytical approach,' said Oelrich. To this end, Bakker and Oelrich set out to meet the two organizations in person and get a sense of their motivation and commitment.

DINNER IN COPENHAGEN AND LUNCH IN ROME

On 16 May, 2002, Bakker and Oelrich made their first stop in Copenhagen for a meeting with UCF, which ranked highly and seemed very interested. Although clear signs of good collaboration were apparent, UCF was not able to demonstrate the top-level senior management commitment to the almost unconditional worldwide partnership for which TPG was searching.

The next day in Rome, Bakker and Oelrich met with James Morris, the newly appointed Executive Director of WFP. Having spent many years in the corporate environment, Morris had a good understanding of the potential value of a corporate partner for WFP. 'He not only spoke our corporate language but brought to the table WFP's logistics agenda; something which made it easier for us to picture our partnership,' recounted Bakker. 'He showed strong signs of commitment and motivation, pointing out the many areas in which WFP could benefit from our expertise. Most importantly we recognized in him the same driving values and vision that had guided us in our partner search process.' Bakker, convinced of the organizational fit with WFP, shared his vision with Morris: 'I hope this is something that will become the dream of everyone in our company. There are challenges to overcome, but I truly believe that together we can achieve something for the world that our employees and customers can be proud of.'

SHAPING THE INITIATIVE

The meeting between the two executives marked the beginning of a seven-month process that led to a Memorandum of Understanding. To bring content to the partnership and ensure the same level of enthusiasm and commitment among the respective senior management teams, in June 2002 WFP organized a four-day retreat in Tanzania, at TPG's request.[7] The visit brought TPG management in direct contact with the realities of WFP daily operations. In Tanzania, WFP operations centred on school feeding, support to refugee camps and emergency relief. Oelrich related the impressions these different activities made on the TPG team:

> While some of us sat in the classrooms with the children, others helped out in the kitchens. During our visits to homes as well as tents in refugee camps, we had the opportunity to play with the children and listen to the stories of numerous families. It was a powerful experience, our first face-to-face encounter with the realities of the populations addressed by the humanitarian community.

EXHIBIT 26.3 IMAGES FROM TANZANIA

Jim Morris, WFP Executive Director, and Peter Bakker, TPG's CEO, visit the homes of locals in Tanzania.

Karin Waite, a TPG member, playing with the children during the retreat.

The stories spoke loud and clear about the basic needs of the African continent in particular and at-risk populations worldwide. Some people were victims of political unrest, many were infected by HIV-AIDS and hundreds of thousands were orphans of a whole generation of the pandemic's victims. The common denominator was their extreme poverty and the absence of access to vital resources, care and education.

One woman at the refugee camp caught Bakker's attention. He observed, 'Despite her desperate living conditions, she stood firm and strong. Her dignity was her most valuable possession. Her spirit of survival and perseverance were visible to the naked eye.' The woman, captured in a photograph, came to symbolize the motivation behind the partnership under formation.

As the visit progressed, the TPG team was able to relate to WFP's operations and identify areas in which their core competencies could help improve the organization's effectiveness as well as the lives of those they served. On the third night, the small, handpicked TPG and WFP teams gathered for dinner outdoors on wooden chairs and tables at a UNHCR (United Nations High Commissioner for Refugees) compound. 'During the dinner and remainder of the retreat we listened to WFP's main concerns, discussed them, categorized them, and drew up an executable timeframe,' recounted Oelrich. At the end of the Tanzania mission, TPG and WFP agreed to combine their efforts on five initiatives: school feeding support, private sector fundraising, emergency response, joint logistics supply chain and transparency and accountability.[8]

EXHIBIT 26.4 THE FIVE INITIATIVES

The first initiative, School Feeding Support, ties in directly with WFP's Global School Feeding Campaign. By providing food at schools, the campaign aims to create a conducive environment in which children can study and learn, thus simultaneously addressing short-term hunger issues and long-term development goals. The School Feeding Support Initiative has three main components: 1) a TPG cash contribution to the Global School Feeding Campaign, 2) an employee fundraising contribution and 3) first-hand participation of TPG staff in WFP school feeding projects in selected countries.

The second initiative is Private Sector Fundraising. WFP has been historically dependent on government contributions and has had limited experience with the private sector. However, the agency felt the need to diversify its donor base. TPG wants to assist WFP in the development of consumer and corporate fundraising strategies and business plans. The consumer fundraising aims to create brand awareness in specific countries (i.e., the Netherlands, Italy) through cause-related marketing (activities) initiated by different TPG business units. Another goal of this initiative is to help WFP attract new corporate partners. In 2003, the first success was booked when the Boston Consulting Group committed itself to supporting WFP.

The Emergency Response initiative aims to leverage TNT's Express assets, expertise and services at the outset of an emergency. One of this initiative's most prominent sub-projects is the Emergency Response Fund for the delivery of non-food items: transport of critical ICT equipment from WFP depots to emergency locations. Since the initiative's inception, TNT has assisted WFP with emergency shipments to Iran, Chad, Liberia and Haiti. Another sub-project opens up TNT aviation training programmes to WFP air operators. The Joint Logistics Supply Chain initiative will support the common logistics needs and efforts of, in the first instance, WFP, but also the humanitarian community as a whole. Sub-initiatives focus on streamlining and enhancing logistics capabilities in areas related to warehousing, fleet management and joint procurement. One major project in 2003 centred on the development of a Humanitarian Response Network, which aims to create synergies between the logistics activities of various international humanitarian agencies. Another project focused on reorganizing WFP's fleet management systems in countries such as Sudan and Sierra Leone.

The Transparency and Accountability initiative examines the areas of accounting, auditing and human resource management. The initiative encompasses a number of projects involving joint training, best-practice sharing and network activities to help WFP further improve its capacities in these key areas.

Following the retreat, Bakker was even more convinced of the potential for achievement:

> Every night, 800 million people go to bed hungry while there are large surpluses of food in so many areas of the world. In emergency situations it has proven so difficult to get the food where it is most needed. In these emergency situations there is clearly a logistics problem. So if we claim to be leaders in the industry, then we need to make our claim by helping them to solve this.

To move forward with the partnership, however, it was necessary to seek and obtain TPG Board approval.

GOING TO THE BOARD

On 10 July, Oelrich was scheduled to meet the Board members. 'I knew this was my one and only chance to convince our Board of our new CSR vision and agenda,' he recounted. Bakker, together with all those who had been involved at TPG as well as WFP, had gambled on him and he could not let them down. 'I had just one hour to present the case. With little space for error, I had to provide a comprehensive overview of the process that had led to the selection of WFP and the five initiatives.' While preparing his presentation,[9] Oelrich tried to imagine the type of questions that could be raised by the Board. To paint a holistic picture, he went about consulting those present in Tanzania as well as various business units.

Although some of the Board members had been informally advised of the work underway, Oelrich's presentation was to be the first formal introduction to the partnership as well as the first opportunity for Board members to raise questions. Would Oelrich's presentation covering the selection process, the retreat and the five initiatives be sufficient? Or should he provide them with a vision of where things could go after the Board's blessing was given? To strengthen the message and to appeal to the Board's sense of responsibility, should a video with images of the Tanzania mission be projected? Although the outcome of the meeting was unpredictable,

**EXHIBIT 26.5 SLIDES FROM OELRICH'S PRESENTATION
TO THE BOARD OF TPG**

Slide 1

Slide 2

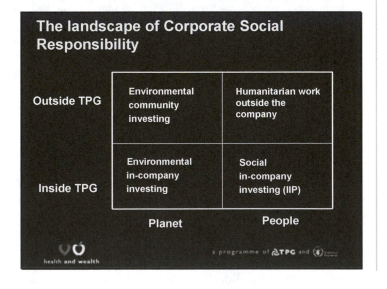

Slide 3

Slide 4

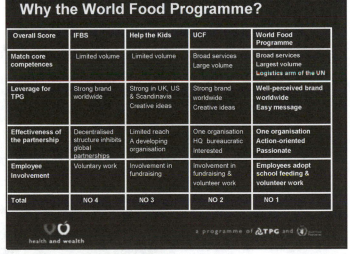

(*Continued*)

EXHIBIT 26.5 (*Continued*)

Slide 5

What is the World Food Programme ?

- UN agency charged with fighting global hunger
- World's biggest humanitarian organisation
- UN's largest budget: €1.7 bn
- Lowest overhead in the UN: < 9%
- Staffing: 2,567 with 90% in the field
- *"WFP is the logistics arm"*, Kofi Annan.
- Spent €500 million on transportation services in 2001
- Global Operations in 2001:   - 77 million fed in 82 countries
                                          - 86% women & children
                                          - 4.2 million tons of food delivered
- On any given day of the year: - 40 ships on the high seas
                                          - 20 planes in the air
                                          - 1,000 trucks on the ground
                                          - Helicopters, donkeys, elephants, canoes...

health **and** wealth   a programme of **TPG** and

Slide 6

So what is this dream ? ....

- Every seven seconds somewhere in the world a child dies of hunger!

- 800 million people go to bed each night hungry

- There is more than enough food in the world to feed all people

- We are just not able to get it to where it is needed

- In emergency situations logistics is a large challenge....

        .... we can help improve the world!

health **and** wealth   a programme of **TPG** and

Slide 7

A Partnership with WFP will move TPG beyond CSR ....

- In all parts of TPG a large number of internal Corporate Social Responsibility Initiatives have started,

- It is my belief that just as TPG is aiming for Industry Leading Positions in its business we should aim for Social Leadership

- If TPG can help improve the world .... our employees and customers will know we are a truly responsible company.

- Companies sponsor people's passions, like sports and art. Social Leadership will prove an even more effective weapon to win (our) people's hearts and minds.

.... towards Social Leadership

health and wealth   a programme of TPG and

Slide 8

What are the external benefits for TPG?

- It has the potential to bring real and lasting improvement to one of the major problems in today's world

- The perception of the value that our industries add to the world will improve

- New discussions with our customers and suppliers on joint programs to help can start

- TPG will be seen as a leading quality company linking up with a leading UN subsidiary

- It might even bring new (direct) business from emergency and other flow of goods

health and wealth   a programme of TPG and

(Continued)

EXHIBIT 26.5 (*Continued*)

Slide 9

What are the internal benefits for TPG?

- Committing ourselves as a Board will be noticed and will enhance our profile as a team
- Our 150.000 employees will be proud to be part of a company that helps improve the world
- Invaluable experience opportunities for volunteers in school feeding projects
- Complex logistics design and fund raising projects provide challenging training ground
- TPG will become a more attractive employer for today's young people

health and wealth   a programme of TPG and

Slide 10

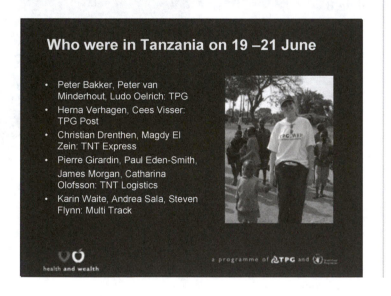

Who were in Tanzania on 19 –21 June

- Peter Bakker, Peter van Minderhout, Ludo Oelrich: TPG
- Herna Verhagen, Cees Visser: TPG Post
- Christian Drenthen, Magdy El Zein: TNT Express
- Pierre Girardin, Paul Eden-Smith, James Morgan, Catharina Olofsson: TNT Logistics
- Karin Waite, Andrea Sala, Steven Flynn: Multi Track

health and wealth   a programme of TPG and

Slide 11

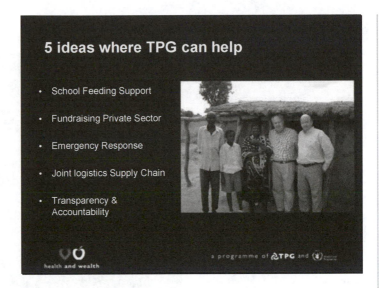

Slide 12

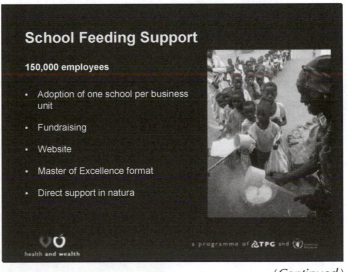

(*Continued*)

EXHIBIT 26.5 (*Continued*)

Slide 13

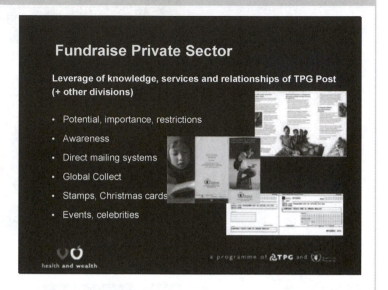

Slide 14

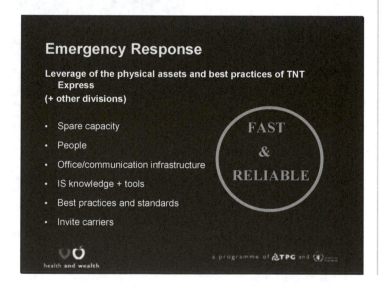

Slide 15

Slide 16

(*Continued*)

EXHIBIT 26.5 (*Continued*)

Slide 17

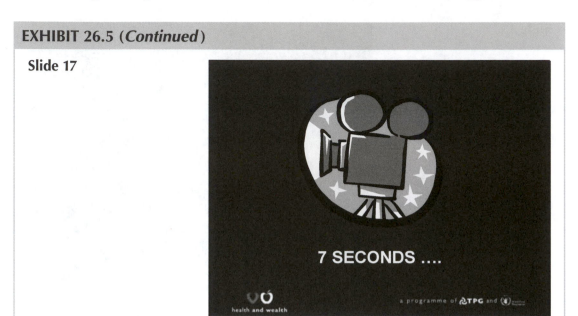

could he call it a victory if the Board gave its approval, or only when the Board members agreed to become personally involved in the five initiatives?

NOTES

1. This case is part of a case study series by the INSEAD Humanitarian Research Group on Moving the World and Humanitarian Private Partnerships. The rest of the cases can be purchased from the European Case Clearing House (ECCH), and their abstracts can be found at www.insead.edu/humanitarian. The case is intended to be used as a basis for class discussion rather than to illustrate either effective or ineffective handling of an administrative situation. The Board of Management of TPG resolved at its annual meeting in 2005 to adopt the name 'TNT'.

2. See Exhibits 26.1 and 26.2.

3. Logispring is a venture capital company independently managed out of Switzerland with funds coming partially from TPG.

4. In 2003, TPG was composed of three divisions: Mail, Express and Logistics. In the Netherlands, the Mail division had a 'public' image given its daily contact with the population and the Dutch government's partial ownership.

5. The names of the finalists other than the eventual partner have been changed in the interests of confidentiality. However, TPG continues to engage in dialogue and projects with each one of the organizations through the partnership and other independent initiatives.

6. According to recent Boston Consulting Group research, 92% of European financial analysts claimed socially responsible investing to be a growing need and 37% put a premium on companies that engaged in successful CSR initiatives.

7. See Exhibit 26.3.

8. See Exhibit 26.4.

9. See Exhibit 26.5.

CHAPTER TWENTY-SEVEN

Corporate Responsibility in Operations Management

Luk N. Van Wassenhove, Henry Ford Chaired Professor of Manufacturing, Academic Director INSEAD Social Innovation Centre, INSEAD

THE FUTURE AIN'T WHAT IT USED TO BE (YOGI BERRA)

The world has changed since the 'Limits to Growth' book of the Club of Rome in the 1970s, and so has the discipline of Operations Management (OM). The 1980s and 1990s brought dramatic innovations such as Total Quality Management (TQM), Just-In-Time (JIT), Business Process Reengineering (BPR) and Time-Based Competition (TBC). These philosophies were mainly imported to Europe and North America from Japan, where they had been refined in the 1960s and 1970s and had formed the backbone of the reconstruction of its post-war economy.

The important point to realize is that these philosophies brought both the tools and the building blocks of the management systems required to integrate them with company strategy.

Operations began its rapid transformation from a neglected stepsister needed to support marketing and finance to a cherished handmaiden of value creation.

Operations became a primary focus of strategic importance for companies around the world.

OPERATIONAL EXCELLENCE: THE ENGINE FUELLING STRATEGIC ATTACKS AND DEFENCES

Processes are the Conduit

Gradually, the whole evolution came to be known as process management, a name that emphasized the crucial importance of processes in value creation and management. Process management was given further impetus by the core competency movement, stressing the need for companies to develop technology-based and organizational competencies that competitors could not easily imitate.

The confluence of the core competency and process management movements caused many of the transformations in the 90s, including the unbundling of value chains, outsourcing and innovations in contracting and supply chains.

People now recognize the importance of aligning strategy and operations, a notion championed by Skinner as early as 1969.

Lean Organizations

As companies developed their core competencies and included them in their business processes, the tools and concepts of TQM and JIT were applied to new product development and managing supply chains, and they typically involved multiple organizations spread across the globe. Often, companies started upstream with JIT supplier relations, subsequently moved downstream to optimized logistics, including Efficient Consumer Response (ECR), and later Customer Relationship Management (CRM). These supply chain trends inspired similar trends at the corporate level as companies moved from lean operations to lean enterprises (Womack and Jones, 2005).

The combination of these process management fundamentals, information and communication technologies and globalization provided the foundations and tools for managing today's outsourcing, contract manufacturing, and global supply chains.

The Supply Chain is the Business Model

Many successful and innovative companies now formulate their strategies and business models in simple operational terms. Asked about ZARA's business model, a senior executive said, 'At ZARA, the supply chain is the business model'. Operations Management has moved from a narrow focus on costs to an appreciation of the customer (service, willingness to pay) and to a closer scrutiny of assets.

OM provides the methods for analysing and improving value drivers at the process level and for measuring and balancing costs, revenues and assets to create economic value. Operational excellence is the engine behind strategic attack and defence.

SO WHAT?

Your € 10 T-Shirt Has Circled the Globe Three Times, Sir

There are two important consequences of the changes in OM described above. First, a simple product such as a handheld electronic device may travel the world multiple times before you buy it at a retail shop. Since these products have become relatively cheap commodities with short lifecycles, there are billions being sold. What happens to them at the end of their short life? Their environmental footprint (extraction, production, use and end-of-life recycling or recovery) may be enormous and all too often society pays for these negative externalities. Scattered supply chains contribute to increased carbon emissions, but also to risks related to poor working conditions in remote areas (social footprint) and even ethical issues (e.g., child labour). And it is not only handheld devices that circle the globe, simple supermarket products such as flowers, shrimp or a T-shirt may have flown multiple times around the world before reaching your home. Despite being cheap and therefore widely affordable, their environmental and social footprint may be pretty abysmal.

The obvious question is whether this is sustainable.

It Wasn't Me!

The second consequence of scattered global supply chains relates to the fact that the original equipment manufacturer (OEM) or the retailer selling the product only 'touches' the product for a very short period of time. A simple electronic product may be in the factories of HP for only a day during its total nine months lead-time from raw materials to final product in the shop. And during that long voyage hundreds of organizations over the globe may have touched (parts of) the product directly or indirectly.

This situation poses a challenge about who is responsible for negative externalities, how are they measured and who should pay for them?

The problem is clearly that today the sheer scale of these environmental and social impacts is so huge that they become a threat to our world (conflicts for access to scarce resources, global warming).

CONVERGENCE OF SOCIAL NEEDS AND COMPETITIVE ADVANTAGE: THE ROOTS AND BRANCHES OF SUSTAINABILITY

The Evolution of Concerns for People and Planet

The transformation of OM was paralleled by a similar rise in importance of *Environmental Management*. While TQM appeared in OM in the 1970s, *eco-efficiency* entered the radar screen with the report of the Club of Rome. In the 1980s, widely reported environmental accidents such as the Exxon-Valdez, shifted the focus to *Environment, Health and Safety (EHS)*. Globalization in the 1990s and the corresponding protectionist quotas led to concerns about *social issues* in poor communities in under-developed countries, bringing *accountability and reporting standards* to the forefront.

In the new millennium, NGOs and pressure groups use the modern media and technology just as creatively as companies, putting corruption and governance centre scene (slavery, child labour). Enter *Ethics*. We have lived through crazy swings of energy prices, shortages of other basic resources (copper, steel) and an increase in natural disasters that have been linked to *climate change*. There has been an avalanche of reports accumulating more and more evidence that human activity is at the origin of the greenhouse effect.

In short, global supply chains were made possible by modern information and communication technologies, but the same technological advances also brought the darker sides (the negative social and environmental externalities) of global growth and development to the forefront.

Enter Sustainability

The World Commission on Environment and Development (1987), aka the Brundtland Commission, defined sustainable development as:

> Development that meets the needs of the present without compromising the ability of future generations to meet their own needs.

Although this definition has been criticized for its all-encompassing scope, the sustainability movement has nonetheless gained traction because of the evident inefficiency of our current products and production processes.

These growing societal concerns mean that businesses are under strong pressure to measure their impacts on the natural and social environment and to engage in triple bottom line reporting to account for the energy and other resources they use, and the resulting footprint they leave behind.

Employees need to take pride in their work and need to believe their companies operate in a prudent and responsible manner and care about employee health and safety. Concerning the planet, aligning sustainability goals with employees (people) and market incentives (profit) can be difficult. That is, profit people and planet are not that easily balanced.

However hard it may be, people can speak up while the planet cannot defend itself.

But community pressures and the threat of liability can drive companies to improve their environmental performance. Clearly, companies are most likely to improve their performance when public pressure results in strong regulations. Sometimes companies lobby for regulations if they have developed an environmentally friendly technology and believe that regulations requiring their technology would give them a competitive advantage.

Does It Pay To Be Green?

Porter (1991) argued:

> The conflict between environmental protection and economic competitiveness is a false dichotomy based on a narrow view of the sources of prosperity and a static view of competition.

Tough environmental standards can trigger innovation. The result in many cases is a process that not only pollutes less but also lowers costs and improves quality.

Since the early 1990s, the debate on whether synergies exist between profits and sustainable practices has become muted, primarily because the public has been largely indifferent to the economic and policy arguments. Throughout the world, the public and its political representatives have been demanding improved performance on environmental, health and safety issues.

The question for companies has become not whether to commit to a strong environmental, health and safety record, but how to do so in the most cost-effective manner.

THE ROLE OF OPERATIONS MANAGEMENT IN THE SUSTAINABILITY MOVEMENT

A Three-Legged Stool

Corporate responsibility needs to become part of the bloodstream of a company. It should be an integral part of normal everyday business. Any employee at any level faces issues where he or she needs to make tradeoffs and allocate scarce resources (time, energy, money and staff). It should not be that these decisions are taken under the profit paradigm with environmental and social concerns being only an afterthought. Any decision at any level in the organization should naturally and properly balance concerns for economic as well as environmental sustainability, natural and social. As any engineer will testify, a stable (sustainable) stool requires three legs. A first crucial leg is tangible top management commitment translated in a clear and operational strategy. The second leg concerns the translation of the sustainable strategy into an execution plan.

Strategies get executed in products and processes (and the corresponding management and information systems, standards, procedures, operating instructions), so this is where Sustainable Operations Management comes in.

The third leg is the individuals who need to carry sustainability in their hearts and minds. This chapter deals only with the second leg. While acknowledging the fundamental importance of the other two legs, we would like to emphasize that perhaps the sustainable management and information systems supporting product development and supply chain execution have not received proper attention.

Indeed, if the appropriate sustainable processes are not in place it is quasi-impossible to implement the sustainable strategy, irrespective of how innovative and great it may be.

Similarly, no matter how much individuals carry sustainability in their hearts, they will not be able to contribute if systems, processes, procedures and standards force them to make the daily tradeoffs while ignoring sustainability considerations.

This explains the central role of OM in moving the sustainability and corporate responsibility agenda.

Operational Excellence and Sustainability

Excellence in operations has gained acceptance as a requirement for business economic performance.

Our research at INSEAD has produced a framework of excellence which essentially reduces to Management Quality applied to Key Processes (Loch et al., 2003).

Management quality is embedded in what the management committee pays specific attention to, and consists of achieving excellence in target setting, delegation, integration, employee development, employee motivation, measurement and communication. This Management Quality should be applied to Key Processes such as new product development, supply chain management and continual improvement of products and processes, but also to the process of policy deployment so all employees pull in the same direction.

Our *Operational Excellence Framework* has been tested extensively and leads to faster improvements in performance, mainly because of its consistent and coherent way of aligning all efforts and focusing them on key objectives.

The Operational Excellence Framework allows a company to translate its business unit strategy into a consistent operations strategy with a paired concrete execution plan at all levels and in all functions. Stated differently, it brings strategic intent into the bloodstream of execution.

For sustainability to be truly integrated in operations, it needs to become a central part of the process described above.

GLOBAL SUPPLY CHAIN EXCELLENCE AND SUSTAINABILITY

Operational excellence as discussed above applies to a single unit or firm. Quite a few sectors have been able to perfectly integrate some elements of sustainability into the bloodstream of how they operate their industrial units. A good example is how Environment, Health and Safety concerns have been integrated into the operational excellence model of many chemical industrial units.

The 3Bs

However, as argued above, units are often a small pawn in a complicated chess game of globe-spanning supply chains involving hundreds of companies and operational units. In our view, supply chains should be viewed from end-to-end and their material (Boxes), information (Bytes) and money (Bucks) flows should be fast and reliable; that is, flawless execution of the 3Bs related to customer orders is paramount for economic survival.

Today, we need to add sustainability to flawless execution: negative externalities should be avoided or at least compensated (e.g., carbon labelling, carbon markets, carbon offsetting). Environmental risks should be minimized.

The 3As

Flawless execution is based on a coherent business model and management quality. Examples of coherent business models can be found in successful firms such as IKEA, ZARA, FedEx, Toyota and many others. At ZARA, the supply chain is the business model and all systems and product design decisions are perfectly aligned with the concept of bringing new designs to the market quickly. This consistency and coherence in the execution of the business model requires the use of enabling information and communications technology to be able to react swiftly to short-term market changes (Agility). It also requires a modular design of products and processes to allow for fast reaction to new market or channel opportunities (Adaptability). Finally, it requires an organization that is in line with the business model and can make fast decisions throughout (Alignment). This is the Triple-A Supply Chain as discussed by Lee (2004).

Triple-A supply chains are powerful translations of an original business model into design and execution (managerial systems and product/process choices). For sustainability to be part of that, it will need to be fully integrated into this Triple-A, modern supply chain thinking.

This situation requires integration in the design of products and processes, organizational structures and systems, and enabling technologies.

The 3Is

The last component of global supply chain excellence concerns organizational alignment, or 'putting all noses in the same direction' as the Dutch expression goes. Alignment requires clear definition of roles along the supply chain to ensure accountability and avoid duplication (Identity). Alignment also requires clear agreements on information to inform all actors quick and precisely, so that wasteful discussions can be avoided (Information). Finally, alignment requires the right measurement and encouragement systems (Incentives).

It takes a high level of Management Quality to 'put all ducks in a row' on matters of Identity, Information is and Incentives.

Although most executives and management scholars put a lot of emphasis on incentive alignment issues, we suggest that too little attention is paid to precise role definition and agreement on what information is to be used when.

Linking the 3Is to sustainability immediately highlights the urgent need for better definition of Identity, Information and Incentives.

For example, how does a company like Nike manage to make all its suppliers abide by the same rules? What is their role in contributing to Nike's sustainability strategy? How can Nike communicate its needs, measure its suppliers' progress and audit them properly? And how does it incite suppliers to improve their sustainability performance?

Sustainable Global Supply Chains

Excellence in sustainable global supply chains, as we defined it above, means applying management quality to a coherent business model in order to obtain flawless execution on profit, people and the planet.

It will require sustainability to be part of the bloodstream of the company; that is, the way the company does things every day and the way its employees make tradeoffs and allocate resources.

One could argue that integrating sustainability into the bloodstream of daily business is yet another complication to an already intricate task. Indeed, in a few decades OM has moved from isolated design and manufacturing to concurrent engineering and design for manufacturing. It has subsequently evolved to three-dimensional concurrent engineering by integrating the design of the product with the design of the manufacturing process, as well as the design of the supply chain. The next logical step is the integration of sustainability concerns at the same time; that is, what we have termed four-dimensional concurrent engineering. For example, as the product, the process and the supply chain are being designed, one should also take care of how components will be sourced from remote suppliers in developing countries (social footprint), how product returns will be handled and how the product will be recycled at the end of its useful life (environmental footprint).

One could argue that this is just too complex, but research and experience seem to indicate that the news is not that bad. The difficulty lies in the quality of management and the management systems it installs, not in adding additional concerns.

If good management systems are being set up for supply chain management from an economic perspective, these same systems can quite easily be adapted to also provide the backbone for handling environmental and social issues.

IS THERE ANYTHING NEW UNDER THE SUN?

No, There Isn't!

One cannot ignore the obvious question of whether there is really anything new in all this. First, there was Quality, and quality needed to be integrated in the bloodstream of the company. In order to get there, the stool needed three legs: top management support through a clear quality strategy, integrating (hard-wiring) quality thinking in process and product design, and winning the hearts and minds of the people (soft-wiring). That is exactly what Total Quality Management means: the word Total is the key.

Then there was Environment, Health and Safety. After implementing TQM and obtaining ISO 9000 certification and European Quality Awards (EFQM), a new wave of environmental ISO 14000 certification hit the industrial world.

Most of the companies who had firmly integrated quality in their bloodstream had very few problems with taking EHS and its corresponding certification on board. They pretty much used the same philosophy, the same systems, and the same processes and information management techniques to ramp up for EHS.

Even better, going for improvement in environmental footprint gave them another wave of cost reductions and quality enhancements, just like the quality movement had allowed them to cut costs and do things faster. It is only the companies who had implemented quality management as a token that found themselves having a hard time taking environmental issues on board.

The point being made is that the current extension to broader sustainability issues (social and environmental footprint) throughout the entire supply chain may not be that hard after all.

At least, not for companies who have already managed to absorb the earlier waves properly and learned how to integrate important new concepts into their bloodstream.

Yes, There Is!

OM is about measuring. You can't manage what you don't measure, as the old quality saying goes. One could argue that cost, speed and quality can be measured, and that they are in modern supply chains. Companies have detailed and precise scorecards with carefully chosen sets of key performance indicators (KPIs) to help them monitor performance throughout global supply chains, and to react quickly to deviations from set targets. These KPI are linked into financial controls to monitor profitability and the whole system is made possible (visible, manageable and timely) by powerful web-based Enterprise Resource Planning (ERP) systems connecting the different players in the supply chain.

But how does one measure environmental impact? Granted, the discipline of Industrial Ecology has given us tools such as Life Cycle Assessment, but LCA analysis is not simple. One has to define the boundaries of the system, measure the different environmental impacts and weigh them against one another. There is very little agreement on how that should be done. Even if one restricts the analysis to a single environmental impact (say carbon emissions), there remains quite a bit of disagreement.

Measuring the environmental impact of global supply chains remains a challenge and good measurement standards are long overdue. Good in this context should be interpreted as simple, verifiable and affordable so that they are practical in a global business environment.

Nevertheless, we have seen the emergence of carbon markets, and carbon offsetting. Quite a few new ventures emerge and do good business. Many offer their own measurement systems and the current situation is pretty chaotic. Standardization is necessary.

Carbon labelling has also become quite fashionable, but can be expensive. Doing an analysis of the carbon footprint of a single stock keeping unit can easily cost €10 000 to a retail company such as Tesco. Not a very attractive prospect if one has 50 000 Stock Keeping Units (SKUs) in portfolio. There is currently no agreement, let alone standardization, on how to do such analyses. So the multitude of carbon labels that will soon appear on the products we are buying may not mean much, or worse, they may not be trustworthy.

Arguably, this may be where the discipline of Operations Management, with its history of measurement and fact-based decision making, may be expected to make the largest contribution. There is an urgent need for clear, verifiable and generally accepted measurement systems.

The picture becomes even gloomier when one considers the social footprint. Measuring the social impact of company activities is very difficult. There are really very few methodologies available and most lack quantification and verifiability. Here again, there is perhaps an even more urgent need for OM to come up with reliable measurement systems that can be developed into standards that can be audited.

A breakthrough in this area would really require several disciplines to work together. Clearly, OM needs to draw closer to fields such as Industrial Ecology. But although this is already happening, the integration of social issues into OM (in a quantifiable and verifiable fashion) is still largely lacking.

CONSEQUENCES FOR OPERATIONS MANAGEMENT

The Call of Duty

We must enlarge our perspective in OM in research and teaching to include people and the planet because companies will be expected to do so. Opportunities to invest in sustainable technologies, operations and supply chains will increase rapidly due to the following factors:

- The costs of materials and energy will continue to grow as the world economy expands and rapidly industrializing countries make strong demands on these resources.
- Public pressure for environmental, health and safety performance will remain strong, leading to strengthened property rights, additional regulations, international agreements on controlling negative externalities and preserving resources, and reductions in subsidies.
- Increasing awareness of triple bottom line issues may lead consumers to select products made by companies with a proven track record.
- People's growing antipathy to globalization is leading to strong non-government organization activity regarding businesses' sustainability performance.

If the discipline of OM does not follow the call of duty, and does not fully engage in sustainability research and teaching, it will lose its relevance and, consequently, its licence to operate.

The World is Flat

Academic disciplines are typically slow to adapt to changes in their environment. It took centuries to accept that the earth is round. Just recently, Friedman's book (2005) argued convincingly that from a global competition perspective, modern technology makes the world flat. How long will it take us to accept the notion this time around?

The world is not only flat for business but even more so for its externalities such as global warming.

Hart (2005) suggests we might expect a slow and grudging acceptance of sustainable OM. Although he does not use the term 'sustainable OM', his framework can easily be adapted to operations:

- *The current internal strategies* in companies are aimed at improving internal operations with continuous process improvements related to sustainability, such as employee involvement, waste reduction, energy conservation and emission control.
- *The current external strategies* are aimed at improving extended supply chains by analysing upstream supply chains to make tradeoffs in the choice of materials and processes and pursuing closed-loop supply chains for remanufacturing and safe disposal.
- *Internal strategies for the future* include investing in capabilities to recover pollution-causing chemicals during manufacturing, to develop substitutes for non-renewable inputs and to redesign products to reduce their material content and their energy consumption during manufacturing and use.
- *External strategies for the future* include developing core capabilities in products, processes and supply chains for long-term sustainability and pursuing strategies to facilitate it.

If companies follow this framework, some areas in OM will become more central and be reinforced. How a specific company evolves will depend on the sector and the company.

Since processes such as new product development and supply chains are crucial to value creation, and value creation will increasingly depend on the right balance between profit, people and planet, the role of OM in sustainable development has to be a central one.

It is clear that companies, policy makers and NGOs will turn to OM academics for adequate training programmes and pedagogical materials covering the new realities. This call of duty should be heard.

The discipline of Operations Management should substantially accelerate the pace of integrating sustainability in its academic research communities (professional societies and journals), its pedagogical offerings (mainstreaming sustainability in education programmes) and its outreach (having a credible voice in the public debate).

This book is a great first step to promote mainstreaming Sustainable Operations Management in teaching.

ACKNOWLEDGEMENT

Parts of this chapter borrow extensively from Kleindorfer, Singhal and Van Wassenhove (2005). The author is grateful to his co-authors for letting him use this material.

REFERENCES

Friedman, T. L. (2005) *The World is Flat*, Farrar, Strauss and Giroux, New York.

Hart, S. (2005) *Capitalism at the Crossroads*, Wharton School Publishing Co., Philadelphia, PN.

Kleindorfer, P. R., Singhal, K., and Van Wassenhove, L. N. (2005) Sustainable operations management, *Production and Operations Management*, **14** (4), 482–92.

Lee, H. L. (2004) The triple-A supply chain, *Harvard Business Review*, (October), 102–12.

Loch, C. H., Van der Heyden, L., Van Wassenhove, L.N., Huchzermeier, A. and Escalle, C. (2003) *Industrial Excellence: Management Quality in Manufacturing*, Springer.

Porter, M. (1991) America's green strategy, *Scientific American*, **264** (4), 96.

Skinner, W. (1969) Manufacturing – Missing link in corporate strategy, *Harvard Business Review* **47** (3), 136–45.

Womack, J. P. and Jones, D. T. (2005) Lean consumption, *Harvard Business Review*, **83** (3), 58–68.

World Commission on Environment and Development (1987) *Our Common Future*, Oxford University Press, New York.

CHAPTER TWENTY-EIGHT

illycaffè: Value Creation Through Responsible Supplier Relationships[1]

Francesco Perrini, Bocconi University and Angeloantonio Russo, Parthenope University

INTRODUCTION

The crisis that hit the coffee market after the International Coffee Organization (ICO) agreement collapsed in 1989 led Italian company illycaffè to look beyond the typical business model that had characterized the coffee industry to date. illycaffè decided to embrace a new strategic challenge and focus on a direct-purchasing model. They would bypass the intermediaries and reward their chosen growers by paying them a premium over the market price.

In the early 1990s, Brazil was the world's largest producer of coffee, but had a reputation for low-quality products and poorly paid producers. But illycaffè prided itself on the high-quality coffee it offered consumers, and so the company had to find a way to overcome the quality problems associated with Brazilian coffee. They had to identify Brazilian coffee producers who were able to supply the high-quality beans the company required. Innovation translated into quality and networking translated into knowledge transfer; thus became the drivers behind illycaffè's strategy, looking for and demanding quality and teaching producers how to deliver that quality. Ultimately, the company had to build a new kind of relationship with relevant stakeholders along the supply chain, starting from the cultivation of coffee, continuing through the purchase and culminating in the roasting, packaging and selling of high-quality coffee blends.

Innovation translated into quality and networking translated into knowledge transfer became, in fact, the main drivers of sustainability, enabling illycaffè to incorporate environmental and social concerns within a strategy of corporate social responsibility (CSR). This strategy produced interesting results in Brazil in terms of company growth, but now management had to assess illycaffè's responsible strategy against the impact of several factors, including the CSR strategies of competitors and market reaction in the long term. They also had to determine whether their own strategy was robust. Was illycaffè's CSR strategy really a key differentiator in the coffee industry supply chain?

THE COFFEE INDUSTRY

Since the 19th century, the coffee industry has suffered from long periods of oversupply and low prices followed by relatively brief periods of short supply and high prices. The 1990s saw a surge in production that substantially altered the global supply structure, causing the worst coffee crisis

EXHIBIT 28.1 THE INTERNATIONAL COFFEE ORGANIZATION

The International Coffee Organization (ICO) is the main intergovernmental organization for coffee, bringing together producing and consuming countries. The ICO was established in 1963, a year after the first five-year International Coffee Agreement came into force in 1962. As of January 2007, ICO members comprise 45 exporting countries and 32 importing countries from all over the world. ICO members have to comply with the International Coffee Agreement. The text of the new International Coffee Agreement was written at a meeting of the 63 Member Governments of the International Coffee Council in London on 27 and 28 September 2000. It was formally adopted by the Council in Resolution 393.

A six-year collaboration to strengthen international cooperation among producing and consuming countries became provisionally operative on 1 October 2001 and definitively on 17 May. 2005. It includes a number of new objectives reflecting the ICO mission, such as encouraging members to develop a sustainable coffee economy, promoting coffee consumption and the quality of coffee, providing a forum for the private sector, promoting training and information programmes designed to assist the transfer of technology relevant to member countries, and analysing and consulting on suitable projects to benefit the world coffee economy.

Source: International Coffee Organization website, 2007

ever in terms of growers' incomes. A number of factors drove this crisis, including the collapse of the International Coffee Organization (ICO) Agreement in 1989 (see Exhibit 28.1), which led to oversupply; the emergence of cost-efficient new entrants such as Vietnam; productivity innovations in Brazil; a lack of technical and financial support for farmers; and tariff and non-tariff barriers imposed by the European Union (EU) trade regime (Golding and Peattie, 2005). The poorly paid coffee farmers at the start of the coffee supply chain (see Figure 28.1) showed enormous resilience,

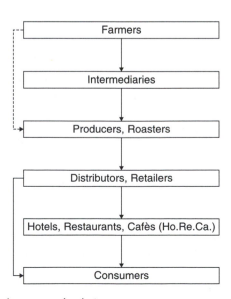

Figure 28.1 The coffee industry supply chain

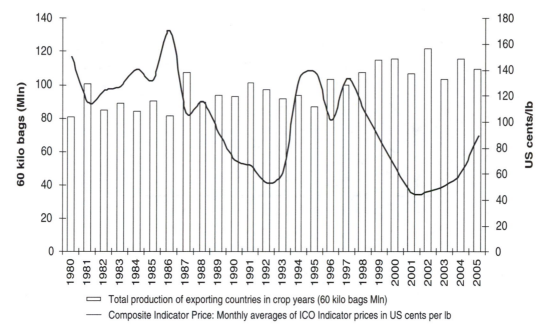

Figure 28.2 Production and market prices for coffee (1980–2005)

Source: Elaboration of International Coffee Organization historical statistics

and one way or another most managed to survive and continue to produce, but this did not make for sustainable development of the coffee industry.

Fluctuations in production and market prices for coffee are shown in Figure 28.2. Between 1980 and 1990, the average production of the main exporting countries was 90 million bags (each weighing 60 kg), increasing to 112 million bags in the 2000–2005 period. In 2006, worldwide production of coffee was 124 million bags against a global consumption estimated at 116 million bags in the same year, compared to 115 million bags in 2005. In general, total coffee production exceeded demand for most of the period from 1997 to 2003 (see Figure 28.3). Consumption showed an increase in some coffee-importing countries during 2002–2005, with per capita consumption rising. In 2005, per capita consumption in the EU was 4.71 kg, and 4.18 kg in the United States.

Coffee-growing countries exported on average about 75% of their total production during the period 1980–2005. Domestic consumption in exporting countries in 2006 was estimated at 31 million bags (30 million bags in 2005), against a consumption of around 85 million bags in importing countries in 2006, basically unchanged compared to 85.5 million bags in 2005.

Meanwhile, market prices were falling. From 1980 to 1990, prices averaged US$1.20 per pound, but fell to an average price of US$0.60 per pound, at a Compound Annual Growth Rate (CAGR) of –22%, for the period 2000–2005.

Brazil unquestionably produced more coffee than any other country. Having contributed more than 42 million 60 kg bags of coffee in the 2006 harvest, Brazil had a market share of 35%, more than one-third of the world's coffee (see Figure 28.4).

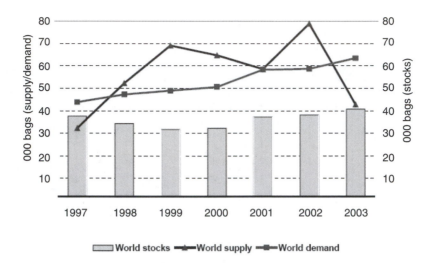

Figure 28.3 World supply and demand for coffee

Source: International Coffee Organizations (ICO), 2004

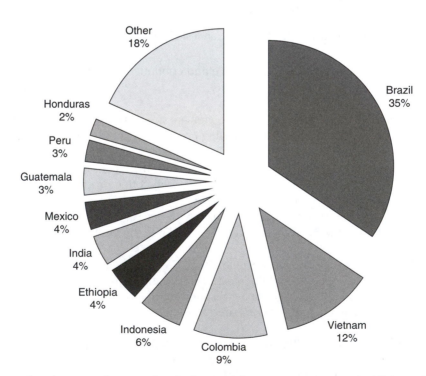

Figure 28.4 Market share (production of 60 kg bags) of the top 10 international coffee producing countries in 2006

Source: International Coffee Organizations historical statistics

The breakdown in the ICO Agreement in 1989 and the economic damage that resulted led to substantial pressure on coffee importers to use their market leverage to alleviate the economic hardships faced by coffee growers and their employees. Leading companies in the coffee industry responded with CSR initiatives. At the same time, several organizations were formed to address particular aspects of the situation. The Brazil Speciality Coffee Association (BCSA) dedicated itself to improving the reputation and quality of Brazilian coffee, the Rainforest Alliance focused on sustainable livelihoods and Utz Kapeh was founded to certify the social and environmental quality of coffee production, identifying responsible coffee producers (for more information on these organizations, see Exhibit 28.2).

EXHIBIT 28.2 CERTIFICATIONS IN THE COFFEE INDUSTRY

The Brazil Specialty Coffee Association

The Brazil Specialty Coffee Association (BSCA) was founded by a group of growers of high-quality coffees to bring to the market their finest specialty products, the very best of Cafés do Brazil. BSCA has members in all areas of Brazil where high-quality Arabica coffees are grown: Sul de Minas, Matas de Minas, Cerrado, Chapadas de Minas, Mogiana, Bahia and Parana.

BSCA's purpose is to obtain thorough research and quality-control techniques that comply with the standards of excellence of Brazilian coffees offered to the international market. Founded in 1991, it has sent representatives to major international events related to the specialty coffees. Since 1992, BSCA has attended all Conferences and Shows of the Specialty Coffee Association of America (SCAA). It has its own booth that exhibits a large variety of Brazilian gourmet coffees, and it organizes lectures and promotional events.

Since 1993, the entity is also responsible for organizing meetings in Europe, together with gourmet roasting companies. Representing Brazilian coffees, BSCA actively participates in congresses and fairs in Germany, Switzerland, Italy, Austria, the United Kingdom, France, Spain and Norway. At these events, it distributes relevant information and promotional samples, as well as tests to demonstrate the quality of its member companies' specialty coffees.

Rainforest Alliance

The Rainforest Alliance works to conserve biodiversity and ensure sustainable livelihoods by transforming land-use practices, business practices and consumer behaviour. Producers who want their farms to be successful, productive, efficient and sustainable follow the farm-management guidelines continuously developed since 1992 by the Sustainable Agriculture Network, a coalition of independent NGOs. By following the guidelines, farmers can reduce costs, conserve natural resources, control pollution, conserve wildlife habitat, ensure rights and benefits for workers, improve the quality of their harvest and earn the Rainforest Alliance Certified seal of approval.

(Continued)

EXHIBIT 28.2 (*Continued*)

Utz Kapeh

The founders created an organization that could stand independently from the producers and the roasters. They chose the name 'Utz Kapeh' which means 'good coffee' in the Mayan language Quichù. An office was opened in Guatemala City in 1999. In 2002, the head office was opened in The Netherlands. In March 2007, Utz Kapeh updated its name to UTZ CERTIFIED, 'Good inside'. This updated name combines confidence in the model and pride in their heritage, with clearer communication for the international market. UTZ CERTIFIED assures the social and environmental quality of coffee production. The idea behind UTZ CERTIFIED is to create recognition for responsible coffee producers and tools for roasters and brands to respond to a growing demand for assurance of responsibly produced coffee.

Source: BSCA, Rainforest Alliance and Utz Kapeh websites, 2007

Commenting on the relationship between the coffee industry and responsible corporate practices, Dr Decio Zylbersztajn, Professor of Economics of Organization at the University of São Paolo and Coordinator of the PENSA, Agribusiness Intelligence Centre (PENSA, Centro de Conhecimento em Agronegòcios), stated:

> Looking at the coffee industry, I have to say that CSR is ignored in general. To the supply process side of the coffee industry in Brazil, CSR is not an issue; most of the companies might not even know what we are talking about. They get their supplies to the market in formalized transactions that can be accomplished through intermediaries. If you have brands, like illycaffè, you might not have to consider CSR as a cost, but as a cost-and-benefit issue, as illycaffè does. You have a market that values CSR. CSR of course can be an expensive strategy, but also, reading the literature, I feel that final consumers recognize the high value of those brands that behave responsibly.

Coffee and Fairtrade

Coffee was the first product to carry the Fairtrade label promoted by the group Fairtrade Labelling Organizations International (FLO). The idea was born when Frans van der Hof, a Dutch missionary living in Mexico, noticed that coffee growers in Oaxaca were selling their coffee to intermediaries at extremely low prices. A plan was developed with Dutch NGO Solidaridad to help the farmers sell their coffee direct to the market.

The Fairtrade movement is described by Wikipedia as a 'market-based approach to alleviating global poverty and promoting sustainability'. Fairtrade coffee sales benefit producers both directly and indirectly. In contrast to Codes of Conduct and other social labels, the Fairtrade Standards are not simply a set of minimum standards for socially responsible production and trade. The Fairtrade Standards go further: they guarantee a minimum price considered as fair to producers. They provide a Fairtrade Premium that the producer must invest in projects that enhance social, economic and environmental development. They strive for mutually beneficial long-term trading relationships. They set clear minimum and developmental criteria and objectives for social, economic and environmental sustainability. Fairtrade Standards must be met by producers, their organizations and the traders who deal with Fairtrade products (see Exhibit 28.3 for more information).

EXHIBIT 28.3 THE FAIRTRADE MOVEMENT

Many definitions of 'Fairtrade' have been proposed, but the following issued by the informal umbrella network, FINE,[2] is widely accepted within the movement.

Fairtrade is a trading partnership, based on dialogue, transparency and respect, which seeks greater equity in international trade. It contributes to sustainable development by offering better trading conditions to, and securing the rights of, marginalized producers and workers, especially in the south. Fairtrade organizations (backed by consumers) are engaged actively in supporting producers, awareness raising and in campaigning for changes in the rules and practice of conventional international trade.

FLO Standards

Trader Standards stipulate that traders that buy directly from the Fairtrade producer organizations must:

- Pay a price to producers that at least covers the costs of sustainable production: the Fairtrade Minimum Price.
- Pay a premium that producers can invest in development: the Fairtrade Premium.
- Partially pay in advance, when producers ask for it.
- Sign contracts that allow for long-term planning and sustainable production practices.

Producers and traders of coffee have to comply with specific Product Standards for small farmers' organizations (such as a cooperative or association).

- **Product description**. The Fairtrade Standards cover two varieties of coffee: Arabica coffee (*Coffea Arabica*) and Robusta coffee (*Coffea Canephora*).
- **Procure a Long-Term and Stable Relationship**. Buyers and sellers will strive to establish a long-term and stable relationship in which the rights and interests of both are mutually respected.
- **International Customary Conditions**. All other customary conditions applicable to any international transaction will apply, such as the conditions of the European Contract of Coffee, unless overruled by any of the special FLO conditions.
- **Pricing and Premium**. Buyers shall pay producer organizations at least the Fairtrade minimum price as set by FLO. The Fairtrade minimum prices vary according to the type and origin of the coffee. In addition to the Fairtrade minimum price, the buyers shall pay a Fairtrade Premium as set by FLO at 5 US cents per pound of coffee. For certified

(Continued)

EXHIBIT 28.3 (*Continued*)

organic coffee, an additional premium of 15 US cents per pound of green coffee will be due, in addition to the Fairtrade minimum price or the market reference price, respectively. If the market price is higher than the Fairtrade minimum price, the market price shall apply. At various times between 1997 and 2003, the Fairtrade coffee price was double that of the world market (see Figure 28.5).

- Prefinancing/credit. The buyer shall make available up to 60% of the contract value, according to what the seller stipulates.

Table 28.1 Fairtrade Minimum Price and Premium Information (December 2005)

| | Fairtrade Minimum Price (US cents/lb) | | | | Fairtrade Premium |
| | Conventional | | Organic | | Conventional and Organic |
Type of Coffee	Central America, Mexico, Africa, Asia	South America, Caribbean Area	Central America, Mexico, Africa, Asia	South America, Caribbean Area	All regions
Washed* Arabica	121	119	136	134	5
Non-washed Arabica	115	115	130	130	5
Washed* Robusta	105	105	120	120	5
Non-washed Robusta	101	101	116	116	5

*Semiwashed or pulped natural coffees are regarded as washed coffee

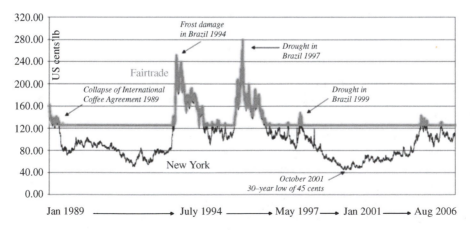

Figure 28.5 The Arabica coffee market 1989–2006: Fairtrade and New York exchange prices

Source: FLO website, 2007

As of October 2006, FLO was working with 586 Fairtrade Certified Producer Organizations representing over one million farmers and workers from more than 50 countries in Africa, Asia and Latin America. Including their dependents, 5 million people were affected, as well as 469 certified traders (consisting of exporters, importers, processors and manufacturers). Between 2004 and 2005, Fairtrade labelled sales across the world grew by 32% to more than 168 863 metric tonnes (MT). In 2005, millions of consumers worldwide bought some €1.1 billion of Fairtrade labelled products, 37% more than the year before. All product lines expanded their markets, especially Fairtrade coffee in the United States (+70.9%) and the United Kingdom (+34%).

Table 28.2 Fairtrade Sales 2004 to 2005

Product	2004	2005	Var.
Bananas*	80 640	103 877	29%
Beer****	62 934	123 758	97%
Cocoa*	4201	5657	35%
Coffee*	24 222	33 992	40%
Cotton*	0	1402	++
Dried fruit*	238	306	29%
Flowers***	101 610 450	113 535 910	12%
Fresh fruit*	5156	8289	61%
Honey*	1240	1331	7%
Juices*	4543	4856	7%
Others*	611	833	36%
Rice*	1384	1706	23%
Sportballs**	55 219	64 144	16%
Sugar*	1960	3613	84%
Tea*	1965	2614	33%
Wine****	617 744	1 399 129	126%

*MT
**Items
***Stems
****Litres

Source: FLO Annual Report 2005

Attracted by Fairtrade's success with consumers, more companies knocked on the door of the labelling organizations. Marks and Spencer, one of the largest food and clothes retailers in the United Kingdom, switched its entire range of coffee and tea to Fairtrade, totalling 38 lines, in a move which was estimated will increase the value of all Fairtrade instant and ground coffee sold in UK supermarkets by 18%, and increase the value of Fairtrade tea by approximately 30%.

Sales of Fairtrade coffee rose by 40% from 2004 to 2005. As of 2007, FLO was working with 248 coffee producers in Africa, Asia and Latin America.

> Worldwide, sales of Fairtrade-certified coffee have increased from $22.5m per year to $87m per year since 1998. This is still only a tiny fraction of the overall world coffee trade, worth $10 billion annually. But there are plenty of other niche markets for high-quality coffee. Some small producers can charge more by marketing their coffee as organic – a switch which takes five years or so – or 'bird-friendly' because, unlike large, mechanized plantations, they have retained shade trees.
>
> 'Fair enough. Taking the quality route to survival',
> *The Economist*, 2006

> The well-known growth of the Fair Trade movement is only the first step toward sustainability, since the fair trade will continue no matter what the quality of its product. My triple concern is, first, that higher prices do not always mean higher value and quality; second, that producers looking for ad hoc certifications have to manage higher costs that spread throughout the supply chain; third, that sustainability does not always last, so that, in the long run, if the fair trade requirements are not met, the market (i.e., producers) might go back to the previous business model very quickly.
>
> Andrea Illy, Chairman and CEO, illycaffè

THE ILLYCAFFÈ GROUP

illycaffè S.p.A. was founded by Francesco Illy in 1933, and was dedicated to providing quality coffee. Francesco was succeeded by his son, Ernesto, soon after World War II, and in 1994, Andrea Illy became Chairman and CEO.

By 2007, illycaffè's distinctive blend of 100% Arabica coffee[3] was available in approximately 130 countries worldwide, and was served in over 50 000 public outlets, including 50 espressamente illy coffee bars in Italy and 100 worldwide. The company's headquarters, including its only roasting, processing and packaging facility, were located in Trieste, Italy, where shipments of green coffee beans arrived. The illycaffè group controlled 10 companies worldwide dedicated to international distribution and maintained relationships within a wider network of companies globally (see Figure 28.6). illycaffè employed over 700 people in 2007, 400 of whom worked in Trieste.

illycaffè ranks among the top performers in the European coffee industry. Among companies in the Processing of Tea and Coffee industry (NACE Rev. 1.1, code 1586), illycaffè had a market share of 2.27% in 2005, ranking it the sixth largest company in terms of turnover in Europe, following larger companies such as Unilever N.V., Sara Lee International B.V., Kraft Foods France, Luigi Lavazza S.p.a. and Kraft Foods Schweiz Ag (see Table 28.3). Turnover for illycaffè increased from €130 million in 1998 to €228 million in 2005, representing a CAGR of 7% over the eight years (see Tables 28.4 and 28.5 for illycaffè's financial results and relevant ratios). illycaffè diversified through acquisitions that built the coffee portfolio and took the company into the tea and chocolate businesses. The company accredits its results to unique managerial practices that mirror its organizational identity. Innovation and quality are critical elements of that organizational identity.

A History of Innovation

illycaffè's dedication to innovation stems from 1935, when Francesco Illy invented the 'illetta', a revolutionary espresso machine that substituted the traditional steam method with compressed air and a system of pressurization to better preserve the flavour of his coffee blend.

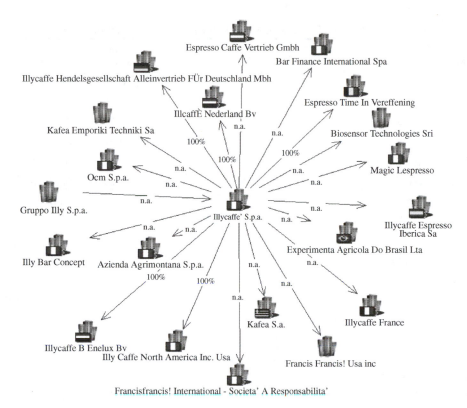

Figure 28.6 The illycaffè group worldwide network (2007)

Source: Amadeus Database

Soon after he took control of the company, Ernesto Illy started a research laboratory that rapidly began to produce a range of products and inventions related to coffee roasting, brewing and drinking. Fourteen new patents were awarded to illycaffè between 1981 and 2006.

Throughout the years, the concept of innovation at illycaffè has been expanded to include a range of projects embracing many different faces of the coffee world. 'illy art collections', 'illywords', 'In Principio' and 'illystories' are examples of the links that illycaffè has built between its network of suppliers, consumers, collaborators and young artists, writers and photographers.

'Excellence and Ethics'

When Andrea Illy took over in the 1990s, he refocused illycaffè's goals towards making it a responsible company, building on existing company values. As he pointed out:

> illycaffè is a stakeholder company, not a shareholder company. We have always paid primary attention to several stakeholders – specifically clients, partners, collaborators, suppliers, local communities, and then shareholders. We manage our relationship with these stakeholders by activating our two main

Table 28.3 European Tea and Coffee Producers, Market Share by Turnover (2005)

Company Name*	Market Share[†] (%)	Country
Kraft Foods France	10.65	France
Luigi Lavazza S.P.A.	8.68	Italy
Kraft Foods Schweiz Ag	2.31	Switzerland
illycaffè S.P.A.	2.27	Italy
Sara Lee Coffee & Tea Belgium	2.25	Belgium
Markus Kaffee Gmbh & Co. Kg	2.24	Germany
Alois Dallmayr Kaffee Ohg	2.15	Germany
Paulig Ab	2.14	Finland
Nestlé Sverige Ab	2.14	Sweden
Drie Mollen International B.V.	2.10	Netherlands
Coop Industria	1.91	Italy
Lipton Limited	1.80	United Kingdom
Oy Gustav Paulig Ab	1.61	Finland
Nevskie Porogi	1.59	Russian Federation
Deutsche Extrakt-Kaffee Gesellschaft Mit Beschränkter Haftung	1.59	Germany
Droga Kolinska, Zivilska Industrija, D.D.	1.59	Slovenia
Nestle Kuban	1.38	Russian Federation
Segafredo-Zanetti S.P.A.	1.30	Italy
Gebr. Westhoff Gmbh & Co. Kg	1.27	Germany
Coffein Compagnie Dr. Erich Scheele Gmbh & Co. Kg	1.24	Germany
Koffie F Rombouts – Cafes F Rombouts	1.16	Belgium
Kraft Foods Cr, S.R.O.	1.14	Czech Republic
Cafè do Brasil S.P.A.	1.11	Italy
Arvid Nordquist Handelsab	1.04	Sweden
Mai	1.01	Russian Federation
Others[‡]	42.33	

*Unilever N.V. and Sara Lee International B.V. are not included, because they are multinational diversified companies for which it was not possible to identify figures related to the coffee industry.
[†]Market share is computed on the total number of companies classified in the 'Processing of tea and coffee industry' (NACE Rev. 1.1, code 1586) for which data were available in 2005 ($n = 1101$).
[‡]'Others' are companies with a market share lower than 1% in 2005.

Source: Amadeus Database

values, excellence and ethics, which drive the company, while striving for perfection in all that we do. Of course illycaffè is a private company that has to manage its cash flows; but cash flows together with environmental and social concerns comprise our approach to sustainability, through which we respond to our stakeholders' needs.

Table 28.4 illycaffè Balance Sheet and Profit and Loss Account (€ Th)

Balance Sheet	2005	2004	2003	2002	2001	2000	1999	1998	Average	CAGR
Fixed assets	66 908	61 416	50 902	44 664	40 646	36 780	29 689	22 997	44 250	14%
Intangible fixed assets	19 078	16 501	8022	6774	6364	5990	4696	2682	8763	28%
Tangible fixed assets	44 437	42 587	37 091	35 337	32 780	28 750	21 245	18 117	32 543	12%
Other fixed assets	3393	2328	5789	2554	1502	2040	3748	2198	2944	6%
Current assets	111 928	87 343	74 660	74 880	80 617	90 620	66 834	53 984	80 108	10%
Stocks	52 320	38 181	30 973	31 664	40 969	46 818	32 247	26 684	37 482	9%
Debtors	48 323	38 925	36 796	34 604	33 427	32 523	27 622	23 620	34 480	9%
Other current assets	11 285	10 237	6891	8612	6221	11 279	6 965	3680	8146	15%
Cash & cash equivalent	3577	4346	1077	4516	3091	3868	3856	2455	3348	5%
Total assets	178 836	148 758	125 562	119 544	121 263	127 400	96 523	76 982	124 359	11%
Shareholders' funds	84 057	75 156	72 523	65 444	57 536	48 721	34 249	24 760	57 806	17%
Capital	6300	6300	6300	6300	6300	5423	5423	1085	5429	25%
Other shareholders funds	77 757	68 856	66 223	59 144	51 236	43 298	28 826	23 675	52 377	16%
Noncurrent liabilities	39 716	32 500	18 395	20 327	46 276	35 072	24 976	21 375	29 830	8%
Long-term debt	0	0	0	0	0	0	0	0	0	n.a.
Other noncurrent liab.	39 716	32 500	18 395	20 327	46 276	35 072	24 976	21 375	29 830	8%
Current liabilities	55 062	41 103	34 645	33 772	17 452	43 656	37 297	30 846	36 729	8%
Loans	15 094	9357	8480	6328	12 676	18 050	9585	13 505	11 634	1%
Creditors	25 727	21 653	17 311	19 448	0	17 467	16 578	10 113	16 037	12%
Other current liabilities	14 241	10 093	8854	7996	4776	8139	11 134	7228	9058	9%
Total shareh. funds & liab.	178 836	148 758	125 562	119 544	121 263	127 400	96 523	76 982	124 359	11%
Working capital	74 916	55 453	50 458	46 820	74 396	61 874	43 291	40 191	55 925	8%
Net current assets	56 866	46 240	40 015	41 108	63 165	46 964	29 537	23 138	43 379	12%
Number of employees	647	590	537	731	678	996	417	385	623	7%

(Continued)

Table 28.4 (Continued)

Profit and loss account	2005	2004	2003	2002	2001	2000	1999	1998	Average	CAGR
Operat. revenue/turnover	228 737	208 188	190 314	193 818	193 845	179 709	154 766	130 596	184 997	7%
Sales	226 907	204 997	189 930	193 113	190 309	175 913	152 584	131 075	183 104	7%
Costs of goods sold	n.a.	n.a.	n.a.	n.a.	n.a.	n.a.	n.a.	n.a.	n.a.	n.a.
Gross profit	n.a.	n.a.	n.a.	n.a.	n.a.	n.a.	n.a.	n.a.	n.a.	n.a.
Other operat. expenses	n.a.	n.a.	n.a.	n.a.	n.a.	n.a.	n.a.	n.a.	n.a.	n.a.
Operating P/L	22 856	17 608	20 357	22 555	19 810	21 081	15 972	12 188	19 053	8%
Financial revenue	1162	433	1997	1588	2508	2203	1920	2131	1743	−7%
Financial expenses	3554	1815	3444	3611	4736	5318	2925	5547	3869	−5%
Financial P/L	−1377	−2127	−1447	−2023	−2227	−3115	−1005	−3416	−2092	−11%
P/L before tax	21 480	15 480	18 911	20 532	17 583	17 967	14 967	8772	16 962	12%
Taxation	9268	7676	8121	8335	7135	7932	6596	4492	7444	9%
P/L after tax	12 212	7804	10 789	12 197	10 447	10 035	8371	4281	9517	14%
Extr. and other revenue	879	967	621	385	804	716	819	417	701	10%
Extr. and other expenses	2487	847	607	1567	1160	328	285	299	948	30%
Extr. and other P/L	−1609	121	13	−1182	−356	387	535	118	−247	n.a.
P/L for period	10 603	7925	10 802	11 015	10 091	10 422	8906	4399	9270	12%
Export turnover	n.a.	n.a.	n.a.	n.a.	n.a.	n.a.	n.a.	n.a.	n.a.	n.a.
Material costs	88 820	73 189	66 113	63 612	76 586	76 242	60 654	56 478	70 212	6%
Costs of employees	39 922	36 734	32 204	30 253	28 067	25 727	23 182	19 671	29 470	9%
Depreciation	14 213	11 620	9 153	8 703	8 533	8 887	6 383	4 220	8 964	16%
Interest paid	2 594	1 813	3 116	3 167	3 925	4 532	2 915	5 395	3 432	−9%
Cash flow	24 816	19 545	19 955	19 718	18 624	19 309	15 289	8619	18 234	14%
Added value	76 600	65 768	63 396	61 473	57 751	57 500	47 982	38 177	58 581	9%
EBIT	22 856	17 608	20 357	22 555	19 810	21 081	15 972	12 188	19 053	8%
EBITDA	37 069	29 228	29 510	31 258	28 343	29 968	22 355	16 408	28 017	11%

Source: Amadeus Database

Table 28.5 illycaffè Ratios

Ratio	2005	2004	2003	2002	2001	2000	1999	1998	Average	CAGR
Current ratio	2.03	2.12	2.16	2.22	4.62	2.08	1.79	1.75	2.35	2%
Liquidity ratio (%)	1.08	1.2	1.26	1.28	2.27	1	0.93	0.89	1.24	2%
Shareholders liquidity ratio (%)	2.12	2.31	3.94	3.22	1.24	1.39	1.37	1.16	2.09	8%
Solvency ratio (%)	47	50.5	57.8	54.7	47.45	38.24	35.48	32.16	45.42	5%
Gearing (%)	65.2	55.7	37.1	40.7	102.5	109	100.9	140.9	81.5	-9%
Share funds per employee (€ Th)	130	127	135	90	85	49	82	64	95	9%
Work. capital per employee(€ Th)	116	94	94	64	110	62	104	104	93	1%
Total assets per employee (€ Th)	276	252	234	164	179	128	231	200	208	4%
Profit margin (%)	9.39	7.44	9.94	10.6	9.07	10	9.67	6.72	9.1	4%
Return on shareholders funds (%)	25.6	20.6	26.1	31.4	30.56	36.88	43.7	35.43	31.27	-4%
Return on capital employed (%)	19.5	16.1	24.2	27.6	20.72	26.85	30.19	30.71	24.48	-6%
Return on total assets (%)	12	10.4	15.1	17.2	14.5	14.1	15.51	11.39	13.77	1%
Interest cover	8.81	9.71	6.53	7.12	5.05	4.65	5.48	2.26	6.2	19%
Stock turnover	4.37	5.45	6.14	6.12	4.73	3.84	4.8	4.89	5.04	-1%
Collection period (days)	76	67	70	64	62	65	64	65	67	2%
Credit period (days)	40	37	33	36	n.a.	35	39	28	35	5%
Net assets turnover	1.85	1.93	2.09	2.26	1.87	2.14	2.61	2.83	2.2	-5%
Costs of employees/oper. rev.(%)	17.5	17.6	16.9	15.6	14.48	14.32	14.98	15.06	15.81	2%
Operat. rev. per employee (€ Th)	354	353	354	265	286	180	371	339	313	1%
Aver. cost of empl./year (€ Th)	62	62	60	41	41	26	56	51	50	2%
Profit per employee (€ Th)	33	26	35	28	26	18	36	23	28	5%
Cash Flow/Turnover (%)	10.9	9.39	10.5	10.2	9.61	10.74	9.88	6.6	9.72	6%

Source: Amadeus Database

The place to start was with quality, a concept basic to illycaffè's business model and the fundamental value that grounded the company's strategies and production processes. illycaffè believed that it could reach its objectives with greater efficacy by means of a business philosophy based on CSR, and developed guiding principles founded on quality and encompassing partnerships and social commitment (see Exhibit 28.4).

illycaffè was the first coffee company in Europe to obtain Quality System ISO 9001 certification from Det Norske Veritas, Italy (DNV). Further certification included ISO 9001:2000, UNI EN ISO 14001 and the environmental ISO 14001 in 2003. In 2004, illycaffè registered with the Eco-Management and Audit Scheme (EMAS), and published its first Environmental Declaration.

EXHIBIT 28.4 ILLYCAFFÈ'S GUIDING PRINCIPLES BASED ON QUALITY

Consumer: the client comes first. The main object of illycaffè's passion for quality is to provide complete satisfaction to clients and consumers. Besides being responsible for the unfinished product that leaves the plant, the company also feels jointly responsible for the finished product – an espresso must always be perfect throughout the world. Toward this goal, illycaffè adheres to and attempts to improve every aspect of the standards of quality, in production, the processes, and in customer services.

Team spirit: care for collaborators. The policy of collaborator growth reaches toward the self-fulfilment and happiness of these people, based on respecting the dignity of others, on professional and personal growth, on their involvement in their work, their sense of responsibility and a system of rewarding commendable work. Indeed, the company's success depends on the skill and contribution of all the collaborators. illycaffè aims at developing the competencies of the collaborators through technical training in each sector and at providing for the necessary resources and a pleasant, stimulating and safe working environment.

Partnership with the supplier. In the area of business ethics, the company policy emphasizes mutual benefits with its suppliers by both selecting and leading them with its values. It fosters long-term collaborations convinced that only a relationship based on mutual interest and growth can guarantee quality and, at the same time, improve the value of the product. In particular, illycaffè provides the producers of green coffee with its acquired know-how and expertise in ways to obtain better-quality coffee, for which it offers a sustainable, above-market price.

Social commitment. illycaffè deeply respects the environment and communities where it works. It undertakes not only to comply with the regulations, but also to implement policies of sustainable development for both the environment and society, by contributing to the development of the territory and the community living there.

illycaffè's commitment with financers. illycaffè's commitment to and its passion for quality and the protection of the shareholders' and financiers' legitimate interests, constantly work toward improving economic performance, aimed at self-financing and the growth of the company's value.

Source: illycaffè website 2005

Making high-quality coffee meant starting at the beginning of the supply chain, and illycaffè recognized that long-term investments were needed to ensure that the company had a sustainable supply of the best Arabica coffee beans for its blends. As Alessio Colussi, Head of the Green Coffee Department at illycaffè, said:

> At illycaffè, we know that value is created on the tree. As you move along the supply chain, starting with the harvest, you lose value and quality. The key skill, therefore, is to capture and preserve the quality you have on the tree. To make this possible, illycaffè has always valued its relationship with farmers. We buy green coffee directly from those growers who produce the highest-quality Arabica coffee beans, rather than purchasing it on the market. The farmers have to work hard to produce the highest-quality coffee, and this involves personal, economic, as well as managerial efforts. But illycaffè remunerates these efforts, we pay about 30–35% more than the market price.

illycaffè established a strong collaborative relationship with its suppliers, starting by selecting the best local growers around the world, mainly in Brazil but also in Central America, India and Africa. illycaffè also began looking for optimum coffee growing conditions in areas not yet planted with coffee trees. According to Marino Petracco, Research and Technical Development Department at illycaffè (and Chair of the Food Products 'Coffee' Technical Committee at ISO), the company was also looking for something else:

> . . . among the others, factors are climate, environment, and techniques, but also love and passion for what you do. If you cannot transfer love and passion in your day-to-day work, you cannot have the highest-quality coffee.

Successful collaboration only works if a long-term, mutually beneficial relationship is established. For illycaffè, this meant finding growers willing to join them in a virtuous cycle of sustainability (see Exhibit 28.5). Alessandro Bucci, Buyer of the Green Coffee Department at illycaffè, described how their grower partnerships were based on trust:

> Throughout the years, illycaffè has worked on building a strong relationship with local growers that is essentially based on trust. If I have to use a Brazilian Portuguese word to describe this situation, I would say 'parceria', which means a partnership between illycaffè and our suppliers, in which both parties

---

EXHIBIT 28.5   SUSTAINABILITY IN ILLYCAFFÈ

Sustainable development and quality: an inseparable pair. To make the best coffee, you need to use the best coffee beans, i.e., the highest-quality Arabica purchased by illycaffè, mainly in Brazil but also in Central America, India and Africa. illycaffè quality begins at its origin, with its cooperative relationship with the cultivators, based on principles of mutual respect and listening to each other's requirements and needs. This company philosophy is consistent with its own strategy and has led illycaffè to work on sustainable development since the end of the 1980s.

100% of illy coffee is purchased directly from the producers. We know each and every one of our suppliers; we educate and train them to produce quality, while protecting the environment; we purchase the high quality our suppliers produce, always paying a price

(Continued)

EXHIBIT 28.5 (*Continued*)

that ensures them a profit: this is at the core of the relationship illycaffè has created and maintained with the growers who supply its raw material. It is a relationship based primarily on trust.

Quality as a tool for enhancing the living conditions of growers over time. The suppliers need to be very carefully selected. This is accomplished through a system of quality-incentive awards established in 1991 in Brazil with the *Prêmio Brasil de Qualidade do Café para Espresso* directed at the best growers in the country. The transfer of know-how begins once the cultivators have been selected. illycaffè agronomists make every effort to transfer knowledge and techniques of cultivation, harvesting and processing. The growers are thus enabled to meet the high standards of quality required by illycaffè. Each year the company team of agronomists dedicate an average of 300 days of training to the growers. Moreover, illycaffè, in conjunction with the University of São Paolo, has created the University of Coffee in Brazil, which offers both practical and theoretical courses for producers.

Fair price. illycaffè calculates a minimum price, below which it never goes, under any circumstances. This price is based on variables such as the country of origin, the type of market, the quality of the product and the cost of production. This minimum price is based on the international market quotations (NYC) and on the cost of production to which a fair margin is added: a margin to reward the producer for the greater care he has taken with his crops and to guarantee him a profit. illycaffè's price policy is based on an empirical approach, built partly through the long-term relationships the company maintains with its producers.

Source: illycaffè website 2007: In Principio Project

gain excellent results. We get the highest-quality Arabica coffee beans we are looking for, they receive knowledge, competences, support and margins of course. Our suppliers often do not bargain over the price, actually, because they know that we are offering the best price they can get. illycaffè pays more than a fair price; illycaffè pays for the effort to produce quality.

When it arrived in Brazil in 1990, illycaffè was almost unknown among Brazilian coffee producers. The company developed specific initiatives to raise awareness and help it to implement its responsible strategy. The first major project was the launch of the illycaffè Brazil Quality Espresso Coffee Award in 1991, the second significant launch was the illycaffè University of Coffee, established in 2000.

illycaffè Brazil Quality Espresso Coffee Award

Brazil's reputation for low-quality coffee presented a challenge, because quality was integral to illycaffè's business model. In order to find the best growers, and therefore to guarantee procurement of high-quality raw material, illycaffè began a competition. The growers would present samples of their coffee, these samples would be analysed by illycaffè, and, if approved, purchased. The illycaffè Brazil Quality Espresso Coffee Award (Prêmio Brasil de Qualidade do Café para Espresso) was created to provide incentives and to recognize growers' efforts to produce high-quality coffee. The best coffee of the year was rewarded through a monetary prize, and purchase of a significant amount of the coffee at prices higher than the market value. The number of participants grew from one year to the next, along with the quality of their coffee.

Evidence that the Espresso Coffee Award improved Brazilian coffee can be seen in the fact that some regions previously thought unfit for coffee cultivation have been discovered and their coffee-growing potential exploited. Such was the case for the Cerrado region, an area that is now producing high-quality coffee. After the first competition, it was discovered that this region had produced some interesting samples. Eventually, a number of growers from the state of Paranà, which had been repeatedly hit by frost, decided to relocate to Cerrado. Other coffee producing areas, such as Sul de Minas and Alta Mogiana, both in the state of São Paulo, subsequently joined the competition seeking to improve the quality of their crops.

In 1999, the success of the illycaffè Brazil Quality Espresso Coffee Award competition led to the creation of Clube illy do Café, a programme through which the best coffee producers reinforced their relationship with illycaffè. The Clube illy do Café was the first example in Brazil of an organization devoted to strengthening relationships between producers and suppliers. Admission to the Clube illy do Café was free, but only to growers who had sold their coffee to illycaffè at least once. New members automatically received the Cartão Clube illy Vermelho, but their position in the club could be reinforced and additional benefits gained if they managed to be suppliers of illycaffè for more than one year (see Table 28.6 for Clube illy do Café benefits). Of course, high quality

Table 28.6 Clube illy do Café Benefits

Card	Benefits
Cartão Vermelho	Supplying illycaffè for one year allows producers to become members of the Clube illy do Café. Members:
	1. receive the Cartão Vermelho and the membership certificate;
	2. preferred access to the Clube illy do Café website;
	3. special offers among illycaffè's products (e.g., coffee, 'espresso' coffee machine, etc.);
	4. periodic information about the Clube illy do Café;
	5. access to the relevant references about coffee;
	6. copy of the movie 'Como Fazer do Café uma Obra de Arte' (How to make coffee a work of art);
	7. opportunity to buy products and participate, as a special benefit, in seminars organized by the Clube with other organizations;
	8. participation in technical workshops with experts identified by illycaffè.
Cartão Prata	Supplying illycaffè for a three-year period allows members to receive the Cartão Prata, which provides additional benefits:
	1. status and reward for receiving a higher-level card;
	2. free participation in courses and workshops at the Universidade illy do Café;
	3. free logo identifying the authorization by illycaffè to analyse the coffee;
	4. reserved Internet channel to exchange information with Dr. Illy, researchers and coffee experts;
	5. annual participation in a holiday in Italy with the full organization.

(Continued)

Table 28.6 (*Continued*)

Card	Benefits
Cartão Ouro	Supplying illycaffè for more than three consecutive years allows members to receive the Cartão Ouro, which provides additional benefits: 1. high status and rewards for receiving the highest-level card; 2. free participation in courses and workshops at the Universidade illy do Cafè; 3. free logo identifying the authorization by illycaffè to analyse coffee; 4. reserved Internet channel to exchange information with Dr. Illy, researchers and coffee experts; 5. technical support with direct visits by illycaffè experts; 6. free copy of the book by Andrea Illy, *Espresso Coffee: The Science of Quality;* 7. participation as special guest in the illycaffè Brazil Quality Espresso Coffee Award Ceremony; 8. annual participation in a holiday in Italy with the full organization.
Award 'Supplier of the year'	Each year, members of the Clube illy do Cafè with Cartão Ouro and Cartão Prata can participate in a cultural trip to Italy. Members of the committee are illycaffè, Assicafè (organization providing quality certification for illycaffè), Porto de Santos (official retailer for illycaffè) and ADS (Assessoria de Comunicaçoes, official communication agency for illycaffè). Requirements to participate in the award are: – loyalty in supplying illycaffè; – efficiency in production; – reliability; – outstanding coffee; – correspondence of the lot with the original sample; – perfect balance sheet; – processing of supplied quantity and subsequent high quality; – relationships: efficiency and reliability in the bargaining process; – participation in the illycaffè Brazil Quality Espresso Coffee Award Ceremony.

Source: Clube illy do Cafè website, 2007

had to be maintained – producers could lose their status within the Clube if they did not maintain a long-term supplying relationship with illycaffè. As Giacomo Celi, Agronomist and Buyer of the Green Coffee Department at illycaffè, highlighted:

> Out of the approximately 450 000 growers in Brazil, illycaffè only buys Arabica coffee beans from about 72 suppliers regularly. Moreover, we only buy 10 to 15 percent of their production on average, as this is the amount of coffee that meets our requirements. Nevertheless, commitment by coffee producers is very high.

The illycaffè Brazil Quality Espresso Coffee Award and the Clube illy do Café built up a mechanism through which Brazilian coffee producers were able to learn and become capable of producing high-quality coffee.

The illycaffè University of Coffee

In 2000, the first academic institution dedicated to coffee producers, the illycaffè University of Coffee (Universidade illy do Cafè), was established in Brazil in collaboration with the University of São Paolo. The goal was to transfer illycaffè's knowledge to current growers, operators and technicians in the coffee supply chain, as well as to future generations, in order to enrich and improve their productivity and managerial skills. Brazil was chosen because it was the largest producer of green coffee in the world, therefore an excellent place from which to harvest the growth that originated the best blends.

The illycaffè University of Coffee was built as a network within which different actors performed specific activities. The network facilitated information exchange between illycaffè, coffee producers, Porto de Santos (illycaffè's official distributor in Brazil), Assicafè (the organization in charge of certifying the quality of coffee for illycaffè) and of course the illycaffè University of Coffee and the Clube illy do Cafè (see Figure 28.7). People who attended the university could improve their skills, and thus their ability to produce high-quality coffee. Everything around the network of the university was based on specific prerequisites, such as passion and competent human resources, which were a cornerstone of the illycaffè University of Coffee values.

The illycaffè University of Coffee helped producers to become entrepreneurs working towards high quality, and facilitated the creation of a useful, direct relationship between coffee growers and illycaffè. *The Economist* (2006) reported in 2006 that more than 1000 growers a year attended a one-day course at the illycaffè University of Coffee in São Paolo, and that a team of nine agronomists had been travelling the world providing training. Dr. Samuel Ribeiro Giordano, Professor of Agribusiness and Environmental Management, Vice Coordinator of the illycaffè University of Coffee and Coordinator of Education of the PENSA, Agribusiness Intelligence Centre, also suggested that:

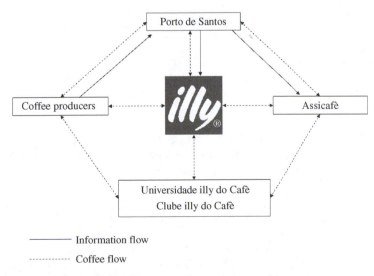

Figure 28.7 The illycaffè University of Coffee network

Source: Adapted from University of Coffee website, 2007

The main objective of the illycaffè University of Coffee is to transfer competences to, and build new professionals among, farmers. The logic that we apply throughout our courses at the university is strictly related to what theorists call stakeholder theory. Growers are not just suppliers, but stakeholders of the firm. Therefore, following a sustainable approach we have to transfer knowledge and techniques to growers wherever they are, even if they do not supply illycaffè.

VOICES FROM THE SUPPLY CHAIN

Josè Carlos Grossi, President of Alto Cafezal, has cultivated 1200 hectares of coffee plants distributed in 11 *fazenda* (farms) in the Cerrado region since 1972, employing between 800 and 1500 employees depending on the season. His company has obtained several certifications, including BSCA, Utz Kapeh and Rainforest Alliance. He has very clear ideas about how CSR must be part of the corporate strategy:

> Since 1990, we have changed the way we produce coffee. Comparing coffee with cars, until that time we didn't know we could produce a Ferrari; we thought that we probably could produce a Fiat. illycaffè told us that our coffee was very good, something we hadn't known. Today, we are very proud to know that we produce the best coffee in the world. We learned a lot from illycaffè about the best way to produce high-quality coffee and obtain certifications, indicating compliance with social and environmental issues; nevertheless, if certifications do not bring in income, they do not produce miracles and are not real. The main issue is that we work to make a profit and we have to care about cash flows.

Ednilson Alves Dutra and Walter César Dutra have owned Fazenda Dutra since 1950. The company has three *fazenda* of about 500 hectares in the Manhuaçu region employing between 200 and 600 people according to season and producing 1500 bags of coffee. Fazenda Dutra is Utz Kapeh and BSCA certified. The Dutras emphasized the benefits of learning how to make high-quality Arabica coffee:

> We learned a lot from the course with illycaffè, and we were able to improve the quality of our coffee. In 1999, we sold our coffee to illycaffè for the first time, the next year, in 2000, we were fourth at the illycaffè Brazil Quality Espresso Coffee Awards. Becoming a supplier of illycaffè helped eliminate the prejudices against our region and local community, which learned to value the quality of our coffee. It was a long process, but now we can sell our coffee, and thanks to illycaffè, which we really think of as our family.

Josè Aparecido Naimeg cultivates 560 hectares of coffee in four *fazenda* in the Cerrado region, produces 2000 bags of coffee a year and has been supplying illycaffè since 1992. He had direct experience of the change in the supply-chain structure:

> Becoming an illycaffè supplier was an opportunity more than a decision. We began in 1992, when we also won first prize at the illycaffè Brazil Quality Espresso Coffee Award competition. The award was satisfying to us of course, but the important thing was joining the illycaffè network. We do not have relationships with intermediaries, we just trust illycaffè, as illycaffè trusts us. It is actually a cooperative relationship. The University is also a network. You can learn, of course, but can also participate in a dynamic exchange of ideas and knowledge, not just between illycaffè and its suppliers, but, most important, between producers.

Francisco Sergio de Assis, who has supplied illycaffè since 1992 from his five *fazenda*, has 50 permanent employees and 250 seasonal employees during the harvest. He suggested how CSR and specific corporate strategies might be related:

> Even small producers can benefit from the corporate strategies that illycaffè brought to Brazil. The first was innovation in our cultivation techniques and technologies, which we learned at the illycaffè University of Coffee. Second, illycaffè changed the history of coffee production in Brazil since they took the responsibility of rewarding our efforts to achieve the quality they required; now they still pay a fair premium that rewards the quality and innovation we have applied to improving our production processes.

Coffee producers clearly understood that recognized certification could become a managerial tool with which to manage their relationships with stakeholders, but there were also broader impacts on sustainability in the supply chain. Public authorities as well as the financial system, for example, have increasingly influenced the operations of coffee producers. Ednilson Alves Dutra again:

> Banks no longer just ask for our financial status. They now require social and environmental responsibility before funding our firms, and the same pressure comes from the Secretary of the Environment and the Ministry of Labour. We joined the certification programme because we aspired to a level of competence that would help us increase our volumes of high-quality coffee and to better structure managerial practices in our firm. That is why we focused our attention on labour conditions, the environment, and health and safety as well, even though keeping up the standards of these certifications is expensive.

Joao Carlos de Souza Meirelles, the Secretary of Agriculture, sees illycaffè's contribution as significant: 'The Illys were pioneers. They helped us learn to produce high-quality coffee, first for them and then for everybody else. Today, we don't think anymore in terms of quantity of production. We think in terms of quality of production.' And this was echoed in a *Fortune* report:

> . . . the indirect benefits illycaffè has brought to Brazil may be even more valuable than the millions of dollars a year the company puts in the pockets of the country's coffee farmers. illycaffè taught Brazilian growers how to produce high-quality coffee, in the process helping Brazil shake its bad reputation among the gourmet coffee crowd. As a result, the Brazilian growers who supply illycaffè – and those who don't – get more for their coffee today, relative to the market price, than a decade ago.
>
> Stein, 2002

OTHER APPROACHES TO CSR IN THE COFFEE SUPPLY CHAIN

Larger players in the global coffee industry have different business models. In 2002, Nestlé stated that only 13% of the estimated 13 million bags of coffee it bought each year came directly from the farm. Sara Lee claimed 10%, and Procter & Gamble (P&G) and Kraft did not buy directly at all. But regardless of their individual commitments, none of the so-called 'Big Four' believed direct purchasing was a long-term solution for ailing growers. 'For us it would be impractical and less financially feasible to manage commercial relationships and bean quality at the farm level,' said P&G spokeswoman Tonia Hyatt. 'We would have to work with one million growers to buy directly' (Stein, 2002). In order to somehow respond to this situation, P&G announced in September 2003 that it would sell Fairtrade coffee through its Millstone label. Sara Lee also later began to sell Fairtrade coffee, but this represented slightly less than 1% of total American coffee consumption (Vogel, 2005).

Projects comparable to illycaffè's responsible strategy included the ¡Tierra! Project of Luigi Lavazza S.p.a., the Nespresso AAA SUSTAINABLE QUALITY™ Program of Nestlé and C.A.F.E Practices by Starbucks, which we discuss in the following sections. The contrast between the Starbucks approach and that of illycaffè was highlighted by Wendy Liebmann, President of market researcher WSL Strategic Retail, who stated that 'Starbucks is less about coffee and more about community. illycaffè is about the elegance of coffee . . . It is elitist' (*BusinessWeek*, 2006).

Luigi Lavazza S.p.a.: ¡Tierra!

(*Source:* Lavazza website, 2007)

Luigi Lavazza S.p.a., established in 1894, had a turnover of over €850 million in 2005 and was the leading Italian coffee producer. The company had seven foreign subsidiaries and a wide-reaching international distribution network. In 2007, more than 16 million families in Italy claimed to buy Lavazza coffee, and the company challenge was to become a worldwide leader in the coffee industry.

Lavazza has always been committed to developing responsible activities to improve social welfare. For three generations, the Lavazza family worked to reach this goal alongside other partners. The company focused its attention on sustainability projects in coffee-producing countries, aware that it was well capable of managing its own agenda in the coffee industry. Lavazza engaged in activities to improve living conditions and social and production structures in countries such as Africa and Central and South America, where coffee production played a crucial role in the national economy.

In 2004, the ¡Tierra! project was conceived, organized and implemented based on the triple-bottom-line approach, which means taking into account the social, economic and environmental impacts of coffee production. As declared by Lavazza:

> The objective of ¡Tierra! is to enable its beneficiaries – communities of small-scale coffee producers who currently live in extremely disadvantaged situations – to improve their living conditions and the quality of their products, to acquire new tools in order to trade under more favourable conditions and, finally, to be truly more competitive and autonomous in their choices and in the economic management of their production.

Implementation was supported by Volcafè, one of the world's leading coffee-exporting groups, and guidelines were drawn up with the help of the Rainforest Alliance. ¡Tierra! aimed at building differentiated operations that involved not just the coffee-production process, but also education, health and homes. The project was rolled out in communities in three different coffee-producing countries, Honduras, Colombia and Peru, and participants were directly involved in the project, bringing in both their direct experience and their needs.

The communities involved aimed to meet the social and environmental requirements for Rainforest Alliance Certification. In its final stage, the communities directly involved in ¡Tierra! were producing 100% Arabica coffee, and the result was a coffee blend of extraordinary quality but at no extra cost to the final consumer, because the costs of the entire project were part of Lavazza's commitment to CSR.

Nestlé: Nespresso AAA SUSTAINABLE QUALITY™

(*Source:* Nespresso website, 2007)

As of 2007, Nestlé, with its headquarters in Vevey, Switzerland, was the world's biggest food and beverage company. Sales for 2006 were CHF98.5 billion, with a net profit of CHF9 billion. Nestlé employed approximately 260 000 people and had factories or operations in almost every country in the world.

Based on its Shared Value approach, Nestlé has always demonstrated CSR in the coffee industry, where it operated through several brands: Nescafé, Taster's Choice, Ricoré, Ricoffy, Nespresso, Bonka, Zoégas and Loumidis. While searching for high-quality coffee, Nestlé realized that only a small percentage of the world's coffee harvest, around 2%, matched the standards required for the Nespresso Grands Crus. Therefore, Nestlé focused on lasting and mutually beneficial relationships with the farmers who produce that coffee.

The Nespresso AAA SUSTAINABLE QUALITY™ Program was launched in 2003. It was based on an extensive collaboration with farmers across the coffee-producing world, as well as on collaborative partnerships with the Rainforest Alliance.

> The AAA SUSTAINABLE QUALITY™ Program is a set of practices that together enable farmers to benefit directly from the cultivation of the highest-quality coffees. It is not a solution to all of the problems affecting coffee producers around the world, but it is our clear commitment to the farmers who produce Nespresso AAA coffees that they benefit from their relationship with us.

Farmers were introduced to the principles of AAA through the Tool for Assessment of Sustainable Quality (TASQ™). In collaboration with the Rainforest Alliance, Nespresso's agronomists set up workshops for farmers and trained them in AAA farm practices. Then the farms were assessed by agronomists, and later on Rainforest Alliance independently verified whether an individual farm management plan conformed to AAA practices.

The Program was based on a few simple principles established at Nestlé:

> First, we pay a premium price for the AAA coffees we buy. Second, we invest in the whole farm assessment and verification process and do not pass this cost on to the farmer. Third, we analyse the data from the TASQ™ assessments and work with the farmers to suggest and make improvements at the farm and regional level. Fourth, we set up technical training and assistance workshops for farmers. Finally, we invest in specific projects in the communities.

The Nespresso AAA SUSTAINABLE QUALITY™ Program has produced interesting results. In 2005, Volluto, one of the most popular brands, became Grands Crus, the first 100% AAA SUSTAINABLE QUALITY™ coffee in the Nespresso range, as independently verified by the Rainforest Alliance. The next year, in 2006, Caffè Forte for the business-to-business market was added to the range of Nespresso Grand Crus sourced 100% from the AAA SUSTAINABLE QUALITY™ Program. In 2007, 30% of the total green coffee beans bought by Nespresso came from the AAA Program, and the objective was to reach 50% by 2010.

Starbucks: C.A.F.E Practices

(*Source:* Starbucks website, 2007, and Starbucks 'Beyond the cup. Highlights of Starbucks Corporate Social Responsibility', 2006)

Starbucks Coffee Company is the leading retailer, roaster and brand of specialty coffee in the world, with more than 6000 retail locations in North America, Latin America, Europe, the Middle East and the Pacific Rim. Born in 1970 in Seattle, Starbucks is committed to offering its customers the world's best coffee and the finest coffee experience, while also conducting its business in ways that produce social, environmental and economic benefits for the communities in which it does business.

CSR at Starbucks runs deeply throughout the company. Starting from its mission statement, several actions are implemented every day for relevant stakeholders: commitment to origins™, environment, communities and partners. Within this mission, the C.A.F.E. (Coffee And Farmer Equity) Practices were developed and launched in 2001. C.A.F.E. Practices evaluated, recognized and rewarded producers of high-quality, sustainably grown coffee. Guidelines were developed in collaboration with Scientific Certification Systems (SCS), a third-party evaluation and certification firm. C.A.F.E. Practices sought to ensure that Starbucks sourced sustainably grown and processed coffee by evaluating the economic, social and environmental aspects of coffee production against a defined set of criteria.

Starbucks buys high-quality Arabica coffee. According to its commitment to origins™, Starbucks pays premium prices that result in a profit for the farmers and their families. In 2005, Starbucks paid on average US$1.28 per pound for high-quality coffee beans. This was 23% higher than the average New York 'C' market price (NYC).

In 2000, Starbucks agreed to sell Fairtrade Certified™ coffee in its retail outlets (Table 28.7). Starbucks purchased 11.5 million pounds of Fairtrade Certified™ coffee in 2005, paying a

Table 28.7 Starbucks's Purchases of Coffee from C.A.F.E. and Fair Trade Systems

	2004		2005	
	Coffee Purchased (lb Mln)	% of Total Coffee Purchases	Coffee Purchased (lb Mln)	% of Total Coffee Purchases
C.A.F.E. Practices	43.5	14.5	76.8	24.6
Fairtrade Certified™ coffee	4.8	1.6	11.5	3.7

minimum of US$1.26 per pound for nonorganic green Arabica coffee and US$1.41 per pound for organic green Arabica coffee. Of all the Fairtrade Certified™ coffee imported into the United States in 2005, Starbucks purchased 21%, becoming the largest purchaser of Fairtrade Certified™ coffee in North America. Considering the rest of the coffee purchased by Starbucks, Mary Williams, a Starbucks senior vice president, said 'We would love to know where all our coffee comes from, but it is very difficult to purchase directly from such small farmers' (Stein, 2002).

THE BUSINESS DILEMMA

If we consider the international coffee industry, we are happy to see that today CSR-related actions are gaining momentum among several organizations, but we believe that more can be done. We believe CSR is not just a matter of social and environmental issues, but strictly refers to companies' responsibility. That is why we manufacture coffee focusing on innovation, that is the quality, and the networking, that is the knowledge transfer, as drivers of sustainability.

Andrea Illy

Managers now need to determine whether the illycaffè CSR concept is different, what impact its initiatives have had on sustainability in the supply chain and whether this approach really is a source of competitive advantage over rivals – is illycaffè's responsible strategy sufficiently differentiated from other business models so that it offers the potential for value creation within the company?

Several other issues must also be explored. What are the future challenges for illycaffè? Are competitors imitating illycaffè's CSR strategy, and if so, how long does it take them to catch up? Is the illycaffè model viable on a larger scale? Is the illycaffè CSR concept the most efficient initiative for emerging markets? Where should illycaffè position itself in the market? Do its sourcing and delivering strategies support the brand? Is illycaffè's business model applicable to other industries?

NOTES

1. The case is intended to be used as a basis for class discussion rather than to illustrate either effective or ineffective handling of an administrative situation.
2. FINE is an informal umbrella network established in 1998 within which representatives of the most important worldwide Fair Trade networks meet to share information and coordinate activities. The acronym FINE stands for the first letters of the following four Fair Trade networks: Fairtrade Labelling Organizations (FLO) International, the International Federation for Alternative Trade (IFAT), the Network of European World Shops (NEWS!) and the European Fair Trade Association (EFTA).
3. Coffee has its peculiarities, and the kind of bean grown and its location determines the flavour of the coffee. Various labels help traders identify the beans used in the coffee, thus assisting them in pricing it. There are about 60 kinds of coffee plant, and each kind comes in several varieties. Of these varieties, only 10 are mass-produced throughout the world, the most popular being Arabica (*Coffea Arabica*) and the well-known Robusta coffee (*Coffea Canephora*). Arabica and Robusta coffees are classified, respectively, as the highest quality and most expensive and the lowest quality and least expensive coffees sold in the international market. The taste of an Arabica bean from Brazil will differ from that of an Arabica bean from Kenya.

REFERENCES

BusinessWeek (2006) Basta with the venti frappuccinos. illycaffè is the anti-Starbucks, and it's out to spread the espresso gospel to java heathens, Global Business, 7 August.

Golding, K. and Peattie, K. (2005) In search of a golden blend: Perspectives on the marketing of fair trade coffee, *Sustainable Development*, **13** (3), 154–65.

Stein, N. (2002) Crisis in a coffee cup. The price of beans has crashed. Growers around the world are starving. And the quality of your morning cup is getting worse. So why is everyone blaming Vietnam?, *Fortune*, 9 December.

The Economist (2006) Face value. Head barista, Business, 30 September.

Vogel, D. (2005) *The Market for Virtue: The Potential and Limits of Corporate Social Responsibility.* Brookings Institution Press, Washington, DC.

CHAPTER TWENTY-NINE

The Co-operative Group Fairtrade Chocolate[1]

Adrian Clarke, Josephine Brennan, Stephanie Robertson and Chris Voss, London Business School

INTRODUCTION

Terry Hudghton, Head of Brand Marketing, and David Croft, Head of Quality and Consumer Care (QACC), were finalizing their presentation to the Co-operative Retail Executive Committee. Since 1999, they had been building the Fairtrade product range across Co-op retail outlets. By 2002, Co-op stores were stocking Fairtrade products ranging from bananas to coffee, tea, wine and chocolate. The introduction of Fairtrade chocolate had been one of the Co-op's most successful product launches ever. David and Terry were hoping to convince the Retail Executive Committee to convert all the Co-op's own-brand chocolate to Fairtrade.

The Co-operative Group resulted from the merger of the Co-operative Wholesale Society with Co-operative Retail Services in 2000. The costs from the merger had resulted in a combined operating loss of £39m for 1999 and many organizational changes. The following year, the new company achieved a remarkable turnaround to which the retail group contributed 45%. By early 2002, the Co-op was in a stronger position to pursue new opportunities, and yet managers were strongly focused on embedding organizational changes and the continued push for profitability.

David, Terry and the Brand Marketing Team had a clear vision of how the Co-operative's brand values complemented Fairtrade principles and believed that the Co-op would benefit commercially from offering a broader assortment of Fairtrade products. However the category management team had not yet expressed its support. Category management had major concerns regarding the impact that further range extension would have on the distribution system and it was far from proven whether the Co-op's customers would support further efforts to extend the Fairtrade range.

THE CO-OPERATIVE MOVEMENT AND THE CO-OPERATIVE GROUP

The worldwide Co-operative movement was founded during the industrial revolution. Consumers began to form co-operatives in response to long-standing exploitation by established retailers. With increased purchasing power behind them, lower prices were negotiated for goods stocked. The co-ops also offered suppliers advanced, repeat purchases with regular deliveries, which benefited the consumer because stocking and distribution costs were kept to a minimum.

The Co-operative Group was founded as the North of England Co-operative Society in 1863 and became the Co-operative Wholesale Society some 10 years later. The merger with Co-operative Retail Services created the Co-operative Group (CWS) Limited ('Co-op'), the world's largest consumer co-operative.

The new Co-op was made up of a variety of businesses, ranging from Co-operative Retail (supermarket outlets), the Co-operative Bank, Farmcare (farming insurance) and Travel Care (travel agencies) to The Co-operative Insurance Society (CIS), (insurance and investment).

In 2001, the Co-operative Retail division made £46 million in operating profit (up 76% from 2000). Co-op food retailing was 5.5% of the UK supermarket sector, and yet accounted for 33% of total group revenues (£5.4 billion) (see Tables 29.1 to 29.6 for detailed figures). This made the division a key contributor to the post-merger turnaround.

Table 29.1 UK Food Retailing Market by Sector for 1998–2001 at Current Prices (£m and %)

	1998	1999	2000	2001	% of total
Supermarkets	55 420	57 477	59 481	62 072	59.8
Discounters	708	725	742	757	0.7
Convenience stores	18 100	19 000	19 200	19 600	18.9
Others	18 472	19 398	20 377	21 371	20.6
Total	93 300	96 600	99 800	103 800	100.0
% change year-on-year		3.5	3.3	4.0	

Source: IGD/Keynote

Table 29.2 UK Food Retailers by Market Share by Value for 2001

	2001 (%)
Tesco	16.5
Sainsbury's	11.6
ASDA	9.6
Safeway	7.5
Co-operatives	5.5
Somerfield (incl. Kwik Save)	4.7
Morrisons	3.4
Marks & Spencer	2.7
Waitrose	2.1
Iceland	1.6
Others	34.8
Total	100.0

Source: IGD/Keynote

Table 29.3 UK Convenience Store Market by Sector for 2000

	Sales (£m)	% of Total	No. of outlets 2000	Average sales per store (£)
Non-affiliated independent stores	8861	46.2	35 500	249 650
Symbol groups	4009	20.9	6961	575 922
Petrol forecourt stores	3168	16.5	9386	337 523
Convenience multiples	2171	11.3	2715	799 632
Co-operative convenience stores	972	5.1	1236	786 408
Total	19 181	100.0	55 798	343 757

Source: IGD/Keynote

Table 29.4 Co-operative Group Turnover by Segment for 2001

Turnover	2001	Proportion* (%)
Food retail	2409	33
Other retail	822	11
Production	1447	20
Federal services	1926	26
Banking	727	10
(Trade between segments)	(1978)	
Total	5354	100

Corrected for trade between segments
Source: Co-operative Group/Keynote

Table 29.5 Co-operative Group Operating Profit for 2001

Operating profit (£m)	2001	Proportion (%)
Retail businesses	58.4	35
Banking	107.5	65
Total	164	100

Source: Co-operative Group

Table 29.6 Co-operative Group Food Retailing Division Turnover and Margin for 2000–2001

	2000	2001	Change (%)
Food retailing turnover (£m)	2266	2409	6
Operating profit (£m)	26	46	76
Operating profit margin	1.2%	1.9%	0.7

Source: Co-operative Group

The group's core objective was 'to optimize profits from businesses where its co-operative values give it a positive marketing advantage, allowing it to serve its members and to deliver its social goals as a successful co-operative, while making a reasonable financial return to its consumer based member-owners . . .'[2].

In 2002, the Co-op had approximately 3 million individual members and more than 140 corporate members. Members had organized opportunities to vote on issues relating to how a division was run, the types of products or services sold, and to hold Co-operative management accountable for the extent to which it was perceived to be living up to Co-operative values (see Exhibit 29.1).

EXHIBIT 29.1   INTERNATIONAL CO-OPERATIVE ALLIANCE: STATEMENT OF IDENTITY

Definition

A co-operative is an autonomous association of persons united voluntarily to meet their common economic, social and cultural needs and aspirations through a jointly owned and democratically controlled enterprise.

Values

Co-operatives are based on the values of self-help, self-responsibility, democracy, equality, equity and solidarity. In the tradition of their founders, co-operative members believe in the ethical values of honesty, openness, social responsibility and caring for others.

Principles

The co-operative principles are guidelines by which co-operatives put their values into practice.

1st Principle: Voluntary and Open Membership

Co-operatives are voluntary organizations, open to all persons able to use their services and willing to accept the responsibilities of membership, without gender, social, racial, political or religious discrimination.

2nd Principle: Democratic Member Control

Co-operatives are democratic organizations controlled by their members, who actively participate in setting their policies and making decisions. Men and women serving as elected representatives are accountable to the membership. In primary co-operatives members have equal voting rights (one member, one vote), and co-operatives at other levels are also organized in a democratic manner.

3rd Principle: Member Economic Participation

Members contribute equitably to, and democratically control, the capital of their co-operative. At least part of that capital is usually the common property of the co-operative. Members usually receive a limited compensation if any on capital subscribed as a condition of membership. Members allocate surpluses for any or all of the following purposes: developing their co-operative, possibly by setting up reserves, part of which at least would be indivisible; benefiting members in proportion to their transactions with the co-operative; and supporting other activities approved by the membership.

4th Principle: Autonomy and Independence

Co-operatives are autonomous, self-help organizations controlled by their members. If they enter into agreements with other organizations, including governments, or raise capital from external sources, they do so on terms that ensure democratic control by their members and maintain their co-operative autonomy.

5th Principle: Education, Training and Information

Co-operatives provide education and training for their members, elected representatives, managers and employees so they can contribute effectively to the development of their co-operatives. They inform the general public – particularly young people and opinion leaders – about the nature and benefits of co-operation.

6th Principle: Co-operation among Co-operatives

Co-operatives serve their members most effectively and strengthen the co-operative movement by working together through local, national, regional and international structures.

7th Principle: Concern for Community

Co-operatives work for the sustainable development of their communities through policies approved by their members.

Membership was encouraged, though not a prerequisite of the dividend scheme that enabled a 1–3% discount on Co-op own-brand goods and a 1% discount on branded products. Co-op membership was encouraged through the Dividend Card. Twice a year shoppers would receive cash vouchers for the equivalent of the discounted savings that resulted from purchases in Co-op stores. Members received additional vouchers during the year.

> We are fundamentally different to other retailers, in that we are a consumer co-operative, so we're owned by our consumer shoppers, we're owned by our membership.
>
> Terry Hudghton, Head of Co-op Brand and Corporate Marketing,
> The Co-operative Group Limited

THE UK FOOD RETAIL INDUSTRY

The UK food retail industry is effectively divided into supermarkets, discounters, convenience stores and other specialist or niche stores. Convenience stores are further segmented into independents, symbol groups[3], petrol forecourts, convenience multiples[4] and co-operative convenience stores.

The major supermarkets such as Tesco, Sainsbury's and Asda/Walmart dominate the top end of the market. Independent retailers dominate the convenience sector, while the smaller supermarkets operate in both sectors and vary their store format accordingly.

Since the mid-1990s, the UK retail market had become more discount-driven. This was not a result of increased market share by the discounter segment, but of product discounting price wars. Over the same time period, the highly fragmented convenience sector was becoming increasingly lucrative as consumer trends moved towards convenience shopping across the food retail industry. As such, the convenience store market was becoming increasingly attractive to the major supermarkets.

The Co-op's Retail Outlets

The Co-op's food retailing stores were generally smaller than the major UK supermarket players, with the average Co-op store size less than 5000 sq ft. By comparison, Tesco stores were an average of 26 000 sq ft and Sainsbury's averaged 31 000 sq ft (see Tables 29.7 to 29.10).

Table 29.7 Grocery Retailer Average Store Size for 2002

Grocery Retail Competitors	Store Numbers	Avg Store Size (sq ft)
Sainsbury's	447	30 800
Tesco	672	25 600
Safeway	528	19 500
Waitrose	138	17 200
Somerfield Group	1310	8100
Co-operative Group	1073	5000
Iceland	764	4900

Source: IGD

Table 29.8 Store Size Category by Retailer for 2002 (% of stores by band)

Category	0–5000 sq ft (%)	5001– 10 000 sq ft (%)	10 001– 20 000 sq ft (%)	20 001– 30 000 sq ft (%)	30 001– 40 000 sq ft (%)	+ 40 001 sq ft (%)	Total stores
Co-operative Group	71	16	10	2	0	0	1 073
Somerfield Group	25	46	27	2	0	0	1 310
Iceland	58	41	0	0	0	0	764
Waitrose	1	6	67	25	0	1	138

Source: IGD

Table 29.9 Store Size Category by Retailer for 2002 (% of sales area by band)

Category	0–5000 sq ft (%)	5001–10 000 sq ft (%)	10 001– 20 000 sq ft (%)	20 001– 30 000 sq ft (%)	30 001– 40 000 sq ft (%)	+ 40 001 sq ft (%)	Total Sales Area '000 sq ft
Co-operative Group	32	23	29	11	2	3	5334
Somerfield Group	11	41	40	6	1	1	10 914
Iceland	50	49	0	0	0	0	3700
Waitrose	0	3	58	34	0	5	2365

Source: IGD

Table 29.10 Co-operative Group Retail Customer Profile

Social class (demographic profile)		% of Co-op customer base	Occupation of head of household	% of UK adult population
A	Upper middle class	1	Higher managerial, administrative or professional	3
B	Middle class	16	Intermediate managerial, administrative or professional	14
C1	Lower middle class	29	Supervisory or clerical and junior managerial administrative or professional	22
C2	Skilled working class	24	Skilled manual workers	32
D	Working class	19	Semi- and unskilled manual workers	19
E	Subsistence Level	11	State pensioners, etc., with no other earner	10

Source: Co-operative Group/www.ipsos-mori.com

The Co-op's smaller store size was due to the neighbourhood market and high-street stores in its portfolio (Figures 29.1 and 29.2). The few larger stores were slowly being divested, and if removed from the overall store profile, would reduce the Co-op's average store size to around 4000 sq ft. The smaller size and more urban location profile impacted on the customer base and product offering. Over 70% of the portfolio was made-up of the community convenience stores (each under 1000 sq ft), and these were stocked with top-up, impulse, distress[5] and emergency purchases (see Tables 29.11 to 29.13).

UK convenience stores generated, on average, 45% of sales from ambient products; that is, tobacco, alcohol, confectionery, newspapers etc. For the majority of Co-op retail outlets, ambient goods represented 63%, with confectionery representing 3% of sales in market town stores, and as much as

Figure 29.1 Co-op retail stores: convenience store format

Figure 29.2 Co-op retail stores: market town store format

Table 29.11 UK Petrol Forecourt Product Mix by Value for 2001

	2001 (%)
Tobacco	37.0
Confectionery and snacks	18.0
Soft drinks	8.0
Groceries	7.0
Chilled and frozen food	6.0
Newspapers and magazines	6.0
Fresh food	4.0
Other (non-food items)	14.0
Total	100.0

Source: Keynote

Table 29.12 UK Convenience Store Best-Selling Categories (in terms of basket penetration) (% people purchasing this category)

	Customers buying this category (%)
Confectionery	22.0
Newspapers	21.0
Milk	17.0
Bread	16.0
Cigarettes	15.0
Chilled foods	13.0
Soft drinks	13.0
Crisps and snacks	10.0
National lottery	8.0
Fresh fruit and vegetables	7.0

Source: Keynote

Table 29.13 Co-op Convenience Store Product Category Mix by Value for 2001

	2001 (%)
Ambient products (Includes confectionery, alcohol, tobacco, newspapers etc.)	63
Fresh foods	20
Frozen foods	7
Non-food Products	10
Total	100.0

Source: Co-operative Retail

4.5% of sales in convenience stores. The remaining shelf space was allocated between fresh and frozen foods (20% and 7%) and non-food products (10%). In a typical store, confectionery would be placed nearest the checkout tills, either in a dedicated aisle or at the actual point of sale.

The Co-op stocked around 14 000 products, of which 4000 (29%) were 'own-brand' products. The Co-op's distribution was organized around one national distribution centre that specialized in slow moving lines and a series of regional centres that stocked more rapidly moving lines.

In the smallest of stores, stocking a new product might require dropping existing stock because space was so limited. Increasing a product range would almost certainly reduce throughput of any given product within that range. These changes required careful consideration, particularly with fresh produce, in order to avoid wastage. In 2002, the Retail Division had set targets to reduce wastage. Given the size of 70% of Co-op retail outlets, this could only be achieved by getting product selection and range right.

The Co-op's Retail Customer Profile

The Co-op's retail customer base reflected all socio-demographic groups, although the Co-op considered its main retail customer as 'Middle Britain'. The C1/C2 demographic profile represented more than 50% (see Table 29.10) of its customer base. 'Middle Britain' was on a limited budget, however, and the Co-op had to achieve the right balance between C1/C2 buying power and its convenience or 'top-up shop' strategy. Convenience retailing is typically less discount-driven, as even price-conscious customers will trade price for convenience to a certain extent. The Co-op's membership was a subset of its customer base.

FAIRTRADE

The Fairtrade concept emerged from within the co-operative movements in Britain and Italy at the end of the 19th century. Originally envisaged as a means to provide jobs and income to marginalized and poor communities, the definition had evolved to encompass providing market access for marginalized producers.

By the late 1980s, the Fairtrade movement was well established in Britain. By the mid-1990s Fairtrade was regularly being brought to the attention of the Co-op through its discussions with NGO groups, and through its more active members. The combination of member activity on these issues and growing awareness among the broader public prompted the Co-op to commit publicly to sell Fairtrade products and to position itself as a key Fairtrade advocate.

The Co-op became the leading retail supporter of the inaugural Fairtrade Fortnight, a two-week long series of events established in 1998 to promote awareness of Fairtrade issues and the range of Fairtrade products available. The event brought together campaigners, farmers, community groups, retailers etc., and subsequently became the busiest period in the Fairtrade calendar.

By 1999, the Co-op had two ambitious targets: to become the leading supermarket supporter of Fairtrade in the UK and to bring Fairtrade into the mainstream of UK grocery retailing. This included a commitment to developing own-brand Fairtrade products. As such, the Retail team had to increase own-brand sales, including Fairtrade products and ensure that the membership's stated interest in Fairtrade products was illustrated through consumer purchasing behaviour.

Terry Hudghton outlined the following necessary steps for the Co-op to achieve the above targets:

- increase public awareness of issues around Fairtrade;
- increase sales of Fairtrade products in the UK;
- increase Co-op's product offering with new Fairtrade options.

The Co-op's challenge was to expand the breadth of its Fairtrade offering while retaining commercial sustainability. Merely stocking additional Fairtrade versions of what was already available (i.e., tea and coffee products), risked cannibalization of existing Fairtrade brand sales and therefore would not assist with the ambitious sales targets that had been set for the Retail Division as a whole.

FIRST STEPS INTO FAIRTRADE PRODUCTS

In January 1999, a small range of branded Fairtrade products was introduced in *all* stores, which established a base from which to market Fairtrade. This included one tea product, one ground coffee, one instant coffee and the Divine block chocolate bar (see Figures 29.3 and 29.4), which

Figure 29.3 Co-op Fairtrade product range 2000

Figure 29.4 Co-branded Co-op/Divine mini bar (launched 2000)

was produced by The Day Chocolate Company.[6] Following this, the Co-op introduced a Fairtrade banana range in January 2000, which generated a significant amount of press and PR coverage. Sales increased rapidly, and the Co-op's sales of Fairtrade bananas soon accounted for 40% of pre-packed bananas, representing 11% of their overall banana sales by 2002. By then, all the major UK food retailers across the UK were selling Fairtrade bananas.

After such success with bananas, the Co-op was looking for another Fairtrade product that would challenge the retailing industry and yet fit with Co-op customer profile and purchasing behaviour.

THE CO-OP AND FAIRTRADE CHOCOLATE

Chocolate consumption in the United Kingdom is among the highest in the world in terms of market share, with British consumers eating an average of one chocolate mini-bar per day.[7] In 2001, expenditure on chocolate alone reached £3.9 billion, which was approximately 4% of the total UK food retail market (for more data on UK chocolate confectionery, see Tables 29.14 to 29.19).

Fairtrade chocolate in a large block format[8] was already available in the United Kingdom through a variety of producers and retailers, but none of the major brands (Mars, Nestle, Cadbury etc.) had any Fairtrade offering. The Co-op saw this as an opportunity to produce and market the first 'own brand' Fairtrade chocolate product in the United Kingdom, provided they could secure their own supplier. The decision was made to test the idea with the mini-bar format.

Table 29.14 UK Chocolate Confectionery Sector Sales for 1998–2001

	1998	1999	2000	2001
Value (£ billion)	3.69	3.73	3.75	3.89
% change year-on-year	–	1.1	0.5	3.7
% share of total market	68.2	68.2	68.2	68.8

Source: Keynote

Table 29.15 UK Chocolate Confectionery Sector by Sub-Sector for 2001

	Value (£ m)	(%)
Countlines*	1615	41.5
Boxed chocolates	1050	27.0
Blocks/moulded chocolate	428	11.0
Bite-size chocolates**	350	9.0
Other	447	11.5
Total	3890	100.0

*Chocolate bars sold by number rather than weight, e.g., Crunchie and Mars Bar
**Sold in bags, tubes or rolls, e.g., Smarties and Maltesers

Source: Keynote

Table 29.16 UK Confectionery Market by Retail Distribution Channel (%) for 2001

	(%)
Multiple grocers and co-ops	43.0
Confectioners, tobacconists and newsagents	18.0
Independent grocers and off-licences	15.0
Forecourts	7.0
Other	17.0
Total	100.0

Source: Keynote

Table 29.17 UK Confectionery Market by Manufacturer's Share by Value for 2001

	(%)
Cadbury Trebor Bassett	28.0
Mars	20.0
Nestle Rowntree	19.0
Wrigley	5.0
Kraft Jacob Suchard	2.0
Haribo	1.0
Own Label	6.0
Others	19.0
Total	100.0

Source: Keynote

Table 29.18 Consumption of Chocolate Confectionery in Selected Countries for 2000 by Volume (kilograms per person)

Switzerland	n.a.
Austria	9.13
Republic of Ireland	8.98
Norway	n.a.
Denmark	9.11
Germany	n.a.
United Kingdom	8.45
Sweden	5.85
Australia	5.89
Belgium	8.12
France	7.06
United States	5.28
Japan	2.11
Brazil	1.89

Source: Keynote.

Table 29.19 UK Confectionery Consumption per Person per Week by Sector (grams)

	1997	1999	2000
Chocolate confectionery	41	38	48
Mints and boiled sweets	13	13	13
Other	3	3	3

Source: National Food Survey, National Statistics website/Keynote

The large chocolate manufacturers were an attractive option as potential suppliers, because the volume of goods already purchased meant that distribution costs would be kept low. However, attempts to encourage them to procure Fairtrade chocolate, and invitations to tender for the Co-op's 'own-brand' business were not successful. Terry understood their concerns as he grappled with the question himself: 'If you say a product is Fairtrade, what does it say about the rest of your range?'

Divine block chocolate was sold alongside Co-op own-brand block chocolate. The Day Chocolate Company was a small Fairtrade chocolate producer primarily supplying the UK network of whole food and organic/Fairtrade shops.[9] Since Day Chocolate manufactured their chocolate in Germany, the Divine chocolate flavour profile was based on the European rather than UK chocolate palate, which were markedly different.

Day Chocolate sourced its Fairtrade cocoa from Kuapa Kokoo, a grower co-operative in Ghana that supplied only 3% of its production as Fairtrade. The other 97% was sold on the global commodities market without the Fairtrade premium even though the production methods for the entire product line were the same.

The supply of Fairtrade cocoa was not going to be a problem should Day Chocolate decide to tender to supply the Co-op's own-brand product. However, management had significant reservations about supplying 'own-brand' products with which supermarkets typically made huge profits at the expense of ethical trading policies. Fairtrade products have a higher cost base, and are therefore less profitable for the retailer, unless the Fairtrade premium is transferred 100% to the consumer, increasing the retail price. Day Chocolate had strong concerns about expanding its production facilities for an own-brand product that a retailer might one day decide to remove from the shelves in favour of more profitable items.

In the summer of 1999, after months of negotiation, it was finally agreed that Day Chocolate would produce a co-branded chocolate mini-bar, labelled with both the Co-op and Divine Chocolate logos. The mini-bar was planned as a niche product that was still geared towards the European palate.

The mini-bar (see Figure 29.4) was launched during the Fairtrade Fortnight of March 2000 to very positive results. In terms of sales, the co-branded bar exceeded 12 month sales expectations in the first eight months and eventually settled at about 10% of total mini-bar sales.

> The Co-op and The Day Chocolate Company have together launched a jointly branded Co-op-Divine 45-gram snack-sized bar – the first supermarket own brand fairly traded product. Since its launch in March 2000 the chocolate bar has consistently out-sold many well known brands in Co-op Stores. Marketing Manager Terry Hudghton says 'We have been stunned; we knew our customers were backing Fairtrade but nobody could have predicted the level of success.' The 45-gram bar is available in almost 2000 Co-op outlets.
>
> www.divinechocolate.com

The mini-bar was sold at a competitive price (39 pence), making it the cheapest Fairtrade product available, and competed with other single chocolate bars in Co-op stores such as Yorkie, Cadbury's and Galaxy, all of which were between 3 and 6 pence more expensive. There was no directly competing Co-op own-brand product, although the larger Divine block chocolate bars from Day Chocolate were also stocked. In the smallest stores where shelf space was an issue, some of the competing chocolate bars were dropped.

In terms of non-financial targets, the mini-bar generated a huge amount of positive PR, estimated to be worth around £1m advertising spend. This benefited the Co-op and Fairtrade brands equally and spilled over to the Divine large block chocolate, doubling Divine sales volume in Co-op stores over a period of 12 months.

Surveys found the accessibility of Fairtrade chocolate brought new customers to Co-op stores and also increased own brand sales. These new customers were still 'Middle Britain', identified strongly with Co-op values, and responded positively to the concept of Fairtrade. Furthermore, because the Co-op had a consumer-based membership, stakeholders saw the move towards Fairtrade as a positive step with regard to living out Co-operative values while increasing the overall value of the company.

This view was reinforced by market research commissioned by the Co-op showing that the level of trust in the Co-op supermarket had increased from 60% in 2000 to 76% in early 2002. This was significant in light of the prevailing climate of consumer mistrust towards the large food retailers generally. David Croft considered this to be a direct consequence of the increase in Fairtrade activities over the period, in combination with the positive PR generated for the Co-op. Moreover, their competitors seemed to be ignoring the Fairtrade agenda.

Taking the Next Step

Co-op sales volumes for Fairtrade products had increased significantly throughout this period, starting from as little as £100 000 in 1998, to £1.8 million by 2001 (see Tables 29.20 and 29.21 for details of UK Fairtrade Product Sales). David and Terry continued to expand the product range throughout 2001 with Fairtrade ground and roast coffee, wine and a Co-op branded chocolate cake using Fairtrade sugar and cocoa (for some examples of Co-op Fairtrade advertising and promotion, see Figures 29.5, 29.6 and 29.7). With these successes in mind, David and Terry were

Table 29.20 Fairtrade Product Sales in the UK

Wholesale value (£ million)	1998	1999	2000	2001
Coffee	8.2	9.0	9.3	11.1
Tea	1.2	2.7	3.0	3.5
Chocolate/cocoa products	0.6	1.4	2.2	3.6
Honey products	n/a	0.1	0.5	1.9
Bananas	n/a	n/a	5.6	10.2
Other	n/a	n/a	n/a	1.3
TOTAL	10.0	13.2	20.6	31.6
Retail value (£ million)*	**1998**	**1999**	**2000**	**2001**
Coffee	13.7	15.0	15.5	18.6
Tea	2.0	4.5	5.1	5.9
Chocolate/cocoa products	1.0	2.3	3.6	6.0
Honey products	n/a	> 0.1	0.9	3.2
Bananas	n/a	n/a	7.8	14.6
Other	n/a	n/a	n/a	2.2
Total	16.7	21.8	32.9	50.5

*assumes a margin of 40% for retailers (30% on bananas)

Source: Fairtrade Foundation website (www.fairtrade.org.uk)

Table 29.21 Co-operative Group Fairtrade Product Sales

Year	Fairtrade sales volume
1998	£100 000
1999	£200 000
2000	£600 000
2001	£1.8 m

Source: Co-operative Group

Figure 29.5 Co-op in-store promotional materials

Figure 29.6 Co-op Fairtrade advertising campaigns

Figure 29.7 Co-op Fairtrade media coverage 1999–2000

ready to make a more significant brand statement about the Co-op's commitment to Fairtrade. Furthermore, Channel 4 television coverage of child labour in cocoa farming had raised concerns in many quarters, not least among Co-op members and executives across the Co-operative Retail Division. David and Terry were sure that the organization, the Co-op's members and customer base would support a bigger commitment to Fairtrade chocolate.

The Co-operative Retail Division and CIS (in their capacities as corporate customers and shareholders respectively) had jointly and individually entered into discussions with the major chocolate manufacturers in order to investigate the potential of a child labour problem and the demand for accountability in the supply chain. Although partly driven by EU legislative pressure, a more traceable route to cocoa sourcing would also create more direct contact with the cocoa producers. This would more naturally enable a review of labour standards and improve the Co-op's ability to trace ingredients to source.

Discussions also included consideration of the price paid to growers and investigating issues behind the financial crisis within the primary cocoa production market. The largest chocolate manufacturers were not enthusiastic about converting to Fairtrade or introducing a limited range of Fairtrade bars. In part, their concerns centred around the difficulties of tracing cocoa to source, ensuring that the cocoa was actually fairly traded and segregating relatively small amounts of Fairtrade cocoa from non-Fairtrade cocoa during production. Their argument was that global commodity market trading mixes the cocoa sources, making identifying individual sources practically impossible and that it was the role of governments, not manufacturers, to address these issues.

During the period of these discussions, a news item commonly known as the 'child slave ship' story hit the headlines (see Exhibit 29.2). The story centred on the discovery of a ship alleged to be carrying 250 children from Benin and Togo who had been sold into slavery and were to be put to

---

EXHIBIT 29.2 ARTICLES ON THE 'CHILD SLAVE SHIP' STORY

Friday, 13 April, 2001, 16:30 GMT 17:30 UK

Sea Ordeal of 'Child Slaves'

A ship carrying up to 250 suspected child slaves is heading back to Benin after being refused entry to two nearby West African states.

The children, from Benin and neighbouring Togo, left port three weeks ago, but their boat was turned away by officials in Gabon and Cameroon.

They are expected to dock in the Benin capital, Cotonou, by Saturday after a round trip of more than 2000 km (1250 miles). A spokeswoman for the United Nations in Benin said that, where possible, the children would be reunited with their families.

> The borders are very porous and the sea is not the only exit for these children
>
> Estelle Guluman of Unicef

'There are centres which have been established in Benin to receive such children where they can be housed temporarily while we establish their identity,' said Unicef's Estelle Guluman.

(Continued)

EXHIBIT 29.2 (*Continued*)

She said that, as in the past, the children were likely to have been taken in by false promises that they would be able to send money home.

But such schemes, she said, were clearly slavery; the children made little or no money, they had no choice where they went, and many never saw their families again.

The BBC West Africa correspondent Mark Doyle says it remains unclear whether the slave ship, which is not being escorted by any naval enforcement vessels, will actually dock in Cotonou. He says the ship's crew may fear being arrested, so the safety of the children is still far from ensured.

Two in five African children are estimated to be working

April 14, 2001 Web posted at: 1:06 PM EDT (1706 GMT)

Benin Searches for Child Slave Ship

COTONOU, Benin (CNN) – Authorities have mounted a search for a ship, believed to contain as many as 250 children intended for slave labour that is expected to arrive in Benin on Sunday.

The ship has been seeking a port on Africa's west coast for more than a week. It was recently spotted off the west coast of Nigeria, said UNICEF spokeswoman Esther Guluma.

The government of Benin requested that Interpol try to locate the boat because it contains a number of children to be taken for forced labour in Gabon, she said.

Benin police said the ship left Cotonou a week ago, bound for Libreville, Gabon, where it was refused entry. It then headed to Douala, Cameroon, but officials there refused to let it dock, so the vessel was on its way back to Benin.

Cotonou police said there were about 250 children on the ship, from Benin and neighbouring Togo, though Douala police said the ship carried 28 children and 148 adults.

Officials from UNICEF were at the port awaiting the ship's arrival, said spokeswoman Esther Guluma. She said the children would be cared for by a doctor while the agency worked to find their parents.

Guluma said police told her they would make arrests when the ship docks.

It was unclear in what capacity the children were travelling. Guluma said it was possible the children were involved in illegal child trafficking.

Often, she said, traffickers will offer poor families money to take their children to other countries. The families accept, believing their children will send money home, but the children are often resold as plantation workers or domestic servants and are never able to send wages to their families.

'Trafficking children . . . is very similar to slavery,' Guluma told CNN, 'because the children are normally not paid and they work very, very hard labour in the plantations and in other areas where they work. The conditions are not the same as slavery, but they work as slave labour, in essence.'

More than 200 000 children in West Africa are involved in this kind of labour, Guluma told CNN.

UNICEF and other organizations have made headway against the problem, by educating parents in rural areas about the dangers and working at governmental levels. Last August, Mali signed an agreement to stop sending children to work on plantations in the Ivory Coast.

work in local industries, possibly including cocoa farming. The story led to international discussion of the extent of child slavery in Africa, further highlighting the situation in places such as Ghana where Kuapa Kokoo (the cocoa growers co-operative supplying Day Chocolate) had been set up. Although this fuelled the Co-op's intentions it did not move the chocolate majors into action. A summary of the various parties' positions in response to the slave ship story is shown in Exhibit 29.3.

EXHIBIT 29.3 RESPONSES TO THE CHILD SLAVE SHIP STORY

Simon Jeffery and Ben Stafford (*The Guardian*)

Thursday 19 April, 2001

Day Chocolate Company, Manufacturers of the Fairtrade Divine and Dubble Bars

'Child slavery is still rife within the cocoa industry in West Africa. Unless western chocolate companies have transparent supply chains and actively monitor their sources, they cannot claim to be using cocoa free from forced labour. The UK chocolate market is worth £4 billion a year – it is dominated by some of the biggest players in the global market. It is up to these companies to implement internal monitoring and standards and to ensure that they only accept cocoa from sources which can guarantee that they are not using child or forced labour.'

Nestlé

'We are deeply concerned about this issue and are actively working with other manufacturers in our trade association to find a solution. These are illegal acts which must be stamped out and we fully support the efforts being made by the governments of Côte d'Ivoire and

(*Continued*)

EXHIBIT 29.3 (*Continued*)

Mali to do so. Slavery is unacceptable and we intend to exert every influence to ensure such practices do not take place. We have been instrumental in getting clauses on working conditions incorporated in the international cocoa agreements and other contracts which are currently being negotiated. However, it is quite wrong to imply that slavery is either widespread or representative of conditions generally on cocoa farms. Members of our industry and the cocoa processors have been visiting the Côte d'Ivoire for decades and working closely with many cocoa farmers. In all that time we simply have not come across such practices. That is why we are confident that whilst illegal practices may exist, this is on a very limited scale indeed and confined to certain areas.'

Fairtrade Foundation

'The debate in the media about this issue unfortunately has missed an important point. While the price of cocoa remains as low as it is, appalling cases like this will continue to come to light. The market price for cocoa now is much the same as it was 30 years ago. Unless chocolate manufacturers are willing to pay more for their cocoa, these conditions will persist. An increasing number of consumers want to be sure that the cocoa used in the chocolate they eat has been produced under decent social conditions – the Fairtrade mark is the only independent guarantee of this.'

Anti-Slavery

'It is difficult to say whether slave labour or other forms of illegal exploitation are used in the production of cocoa. Because of the way that cocoa is bought on the international market, it is difficult to trace which plantation each bag of cocoa comes from. However, a number of cases of forced labour were exposed in a recent Channel 4 documentary but we don't know its extent, because there has been no proper research.

'The chocolate companies could purchase direct from plantations and work with governments and growers to ensure that international labour standards are met. Consumers can write to chocolate companies to voice their concerns over these allegations. They can also write to supermarkets and ask them to stock Fairtrade products, which are guaranteed to be produced without the use of slavery such as forced labour or illegal child labour.'

In America, the chocolate industry agreed to develop the Harkin-Engel protocol (see Exhibit 29.4), a framework to tackle child slavery in the cocoa industry, as an industry-wide initiative; however, no real action was taken.

> The industry protocol didn't solve anything. It was an industry excuse that something was happening, but no real action was taken, just signatures of intent and studies to be done in Cote D'Ivoire. For the Co-op, this is not enough and not happening quickly enough.
>
> David Croft, Head of Quality and Consumer Care,
> The Co-operative Group Limited

EXHIBIT 29.4 US PROTOCOL AIMS TO END CHILD SLAVERY IN COCOA FIELDS

www.antislavery.org
4 October 2001

On 1 October, the international cocoa and chocolate industry signed a Protocol in the United States to eliminate child slavery in the chocolate industry.

The 'Harkin-Engel' Protocol (http://www.antislavery.org/homepage/news/cmaprotocol.pdf) set a four year timetable for all stages of the cocoa industry to comply with standards set by the International Labour Organization's Convention against the worst forms of child labour (No.182) (http://www.antislavery.org/homepage/campaign/childlabourcamp.htm). It has been signed by leading members and companies of the cocoa and chocolate industry, the IPEC programme of the ILO, International Union of Food and Allied Workers, Child Labor Coalition, National Consumers League and Free the Slaves (Anti-Slavery's associate in the USA).

Under the agreement advisory groups have been set up to take responsibility for the investigation of child labour practices in West Africa and to advise on appropriate remedies. The remedies set out will be monitored by a consultative group including trade unions and NGOs.

The chocolate industry will establish a foundation to sustain the efforts to eliminate abusive child labour in the West African cocoa industry, including the development of best practices in the fight against the worst forms of child labour and development of alternatives for children removed from such situations.

Anti-Slavery welcomes the introduction of the Protocol as a positive move by the chocolate industry to take responsibility for labour practices throughout its supply chain. However, we are concerned that it might fail to address the situation of young adults (18 years and older) who may find themselves working under conditions of forced labour. It is vital that any investigation and subsequent strategy tackle all forms of forced labour and also address the conditions that foster trafficking in the region, principally poverty and lack of alternatives.

The extent of forced labour on cocoa farms in West Africa and the numbers of children working in cocoa production is not known. The first large survey to assess labour conditions on cocoa farms in the region will soon be launched by the International Institute for Tropical Agriculture, assisted by the ILO. It will survey 3000 farms across West Africa; the results will inform the future strategy to end child and forced labour in the cocoa industry.

Commercial Risks

Under the umbrella of the Co-op's Responsible Retailing Initiatives the Fairtrade initiative was being complemented by ethical product sourcing.[10] Ethical product sourcing was being reviewed across the broader supply chain for the Co-op's own-brand range of over 4000 products. The push to expand the Fairtrade range began to raise concerns with the category management teams, especially since competitors were not responding to the Fairtrade agenda at this time.

With the Co-op's portfolio of small stores, any Fairtrade range extension would need to address issues relating to volumes, distribution and throughput, in order to protect successful product lines. Concerns had already arisen in relation to the introduction of the Fairtrade mini-bar and were exaggerated by the fact that Day Chocolate was only supplying a small number of products to the Co-op. This meant that it had to be stocked through the national centre, typically used for slow-moving lines.

Since the late 1990s, price competition in supermarkets had become increasingly fierce. Fairtrade products mostly involved higher raw material prices for the producer, which meant higher wholesale prices for the retailer, which were passed on to the consumer if the retailers were to maintain their price margin. In addition to buying costs, range extensions could also carry hidden costs. Price increases might force the customer to switch to branded alternatives depending on whether he or she wanted to pay an increased price for a Fairtrade product. A consumer move to branded alternatives would remove the need to come into the Co-op specifically to make the purchase, losing the Co-op both the individual sale and the sale of the entire product basket to competitors.

Another significant problem was that the historic customer base for the Co-op was of a slightly lower socio-economic profile than those of competitors such as Waitrose and Sainsbury's. Market research on ethical purchasing behaviour indicates that women and those in high-income brackets favour ethical products. National opinion polls in 2000 uncovered that 59% of AB respondents were not prepared to ignore green or ethical issues when making a buying decision, assuming the price was right.[11] However, further surveys also revealed that 80% of respondents claimed to shop ethically, yet only about 30% actually do.

David and Terry were only too aware of the difference between aspiration and action, especially following the recent failure of rival Iceland's '100% Organic' food strategy. In September 2000, Iceland had switched all product lines to organic, taking an ethical stance on the Genetically Modified Food (GMO) debate. By dropping all non-organic alternatives without communicating the new value proposition, Iceland had severely miscalculated customer expectations and saw food sales drop by 1.5%. By January 2001, Iceland was forced to retract the position (see Exhibit 29.5), which only further highlighted the significant risks associated with pursuing the ethical trade agenda more aggressively than a customer base will support.

EXHIBIT 29.5 ICELAND CATCHES A COLD

Johan Bakker
Source: @g Worldwide (Meredith Corporation)
2001-01-23 09:24:32.0

In September of 2000, the chairman of Iceland Group, one of the largest food store chains in the UK, stunned the retail food industry in that country by announcing that Iceland food stores would henceforth stock only organic foods. In a decision which was calculated to involve nearly 40% of the entire world production of organic foods, Malcolm Walker took perhaps the most aggressive step yet seen anywhere to promote the consumption of organics – especially since he made the commitment that organics would be sold at prices comparable to conventional foods. Here at last was the opportunity that the organic food industry has clamoured for years – to break out of its 'niche market' status and go head-to-head with conventionally produced foods in a large-volume market, with previous price disadvantages removed.

Organic Strategy Falls Short

Just four months later, Iceland has been forced to withdraw those commitments. Food sales fell by some 1.5% in the second half of last year, and by as much as 5.5% in the month of December – when traditionally, they would be expected to rise in anticipation of the holiday season. Shares of Iceland Group caught a terrible cold also, falling more than a third in value.

Calling the 100%-organic direction 'bold, but misguided', the new CEO of Iceland Group, Bill Grimsey, announced that Iceland will continue to promote organic foods, but not exclusively. Conventional foods will appear once again on Iceland's shelves, side-by-side with organics. He also admitted that Iceland was unable to meet their commitment to offer organic foods at the same price as conventional foods.

Malcolm Walker was not available for comment – however, it is known that he sold four million shares of Iceland stock – the great majority of his personal holding in the group – prior to the major fall in the stock price, for a total of about £14 million, or about US$22 million.

So – What Can We Learn from This Debacle?

The first thing to consider might be how badly Iceland miscalculated the desires of the consumer. For all of the propaganda about how organic food is more natural, more whole-some, and safer (none of which is necessarily true), when faced with the stuff on the shelves, the average British consumer didn't like what they saw and went elsewhere. It's a fact of life that organic produce does not look as good as conventional produce does – it tends to be smaller, has more blemishes and other imperfections, and is offered in fewer varieties. And the sheer size of the deal, and the promise of comparable pricing, meant that what organic food there was could not be picked over for improved appearance at a higher cost – as is often the case in the more traditional 'niche' market which organics have enjoyed up to now.

The failure of organic foods in a mass market shows that they are still primarily the choice of a very few consumers, who prefer them for a variety of reasons which go way beyond simple issues of nutrition, wholesomeness or safety.

The second thing is that Iceland found out the hard way that organic foods just cost more to produce. Even with the buying power of a food industry giant like Iceland, and the access to a huge market which it provided, the cost of organic foods could not be brought down to a level even comparable to conventional food. Don't believe the hype!

(Continued)

EXHIBIT 29.5 (*Continued*)

The third thing is that Iceland came a cropper because they assumed that consumers would accept the propaganda which they have been fed regarding organic food. They were perhaps persuaded to that viewpoint because of their previous marketing coup in the matter of GM foodstuffs. When the more lurid British tabloid newspapers began putting anti-GMO headlines about 'Frankenfoods' on the front pages, about a year ago, Iceland jumped on the marketing opportunity with both feet and immediately announced that all of their foodstuffs were guaranteed GMO-free – the first UK food retailer of any size to do so. Shoppers frightened by the invisible horrors of GMO food, as described for them in gory detail in the media, flocked to Iceland stores and the result was a gratifying increase in sales. Iceland thought that they could achieve another market first in the matter of organics. Not only did the consumers not like what they saw, they maybe learned a little more about the actual differences between organic and conventional foods – as in, there really are none – and they stayed away in droves. The anti-GMO move played on the fears of consumers about an invisible threat in their food which might have long-term and unknown health effects.

But the push for organics presented consumers with food which just didn't look as good, and claims about nutrition and safety were just a lot easier to assess, without the need for a masters degree in microbiology. Whichever the case, the failure of this attempt to mass-market organics points up a few issues which farmers may want to consider, especially in light of the recently-introduced USDA standards for organic certification and the severe restrictions they impose.

Organic foods cannot be produced at anything near the cost of conventional foods. And the market for them will always be dominated by a relatively small part of the population which has the desire, and the disposable income, to pay premium prices in order to satisfy a personal belief system. It may also be considered that the proportion of the population prepared to pay premium prices will vary with the health of the economy – if people are doing well, they will have money available to indulge their beliefs. But if the economy is doing less well, and disposable incomes are lower, the choice between making the mortgage payment and paying extra for organic tomatoes may become a very real one.

THE FUTURE OF CO-OP CHOCOLATE AND FAIRTRADE

Terry and David started to look at their options regarding next steps for the block chocolate range. Singles and block chocolate together represented an annual turnover of £69 million, 4% of which was derived from Co-op own-brand products (see Table 29.22).

The first possibility was to introduce a Co-op Fairtrade range of chocolate, in addition to existing non-Co-op Fairtrade chocolate. This risked further exacerbating the challenges of the Co-op's distribution system and would require considerable work to establish the new range. The Co-op's

Table 29.22 Co-operative Group Confectionery Retail Sales for 2001

	(£'000)	Share (%)	Change (%)
Block Chocolate Sales	**39 130**	**8.6**	**+12.2**
Cadbury	21 404	54.7	−0.9
Mars	7161	18.3	−0.3
Nestle	6104	15.6	−0.4
Kraft	1448	3.7	+0.7
Co-op Label	2700	6.9	+1.3
Others	313	0.8	−0.4
Singles Sales	**30 000**	**31.7**	**+8.8**
Cadbury	9000	30.0	−2.7
Mars	5880	19.6	+0.8
Nestle	5550	18.5	−0.6
Kraft	810	2.7	−0.1
Co-op Label	300	1.0	+0.1
Others	8460	28.2	+2.5

Source: Co-operative Group

own brand supplier, Kraft-Suchard, declined the Co-op's request to source Fairtrade chocolate, therefore the Co-op would either have to switch or add a supplier.

The option to use The Day Chocolate Company, the Co-op's current Fairtrade chocolate supplier, was a significant risk. Volume estimates for a more substantial switch to own brand Fairtrade chocolate would require a doubling of production for Day Chocolate. In addition, the Co-op would have to invest a significant amount of time to ensure their supplier met the flavour profile of the English palate, since Day Chocolate manufactured their chocolate in Germany with a European flavour profile. The European chocolate palate was markedly different, therefore launching a wider range of products targeted at the UK mass market would require that each product be individually formulated and tested to ensure that it appealed to the UK market.

An alternative strategy would be to cease production of Co-op non-Fairtrade chocolate and to increase the presence of other branded Fairtrade chocolate, such as Divine and Maya Gold. This reduced the risk for the Co-op in that the suppliers would have to deal with sourcing, production and taste issues, although stocking more lines from diverse producers would again impact negatively on the segmentation and distribution aspects of the business.

However, because Fairtrade chocolate products were still typically specialist or niche products, they were created with the European flavour profile. These were far from a mainstream offering, because they did not match the UK flavour palate, and therefore would not compete directly against the mainstream brands. This was not ideal as it limited the Co-op's ability to lead the development of the Fairtrade agenda. David and Terry were seeking a mass-market Fairtrade product, not another specialist or premium chocolate product.

The boldest move would be to move 100% of Co-op own brand chocolate to Fairtrade. On the positive side, there was no risk sourcing Fairtrade cocoa, with Kuapa Kokoo, which produced in excess of 60 000 tonnes of cocoa each year and sold only 3% as Fairtrade. The rest (although produced in the same way) was sold on the global commodities markets without a Fairtrade premium.

The risk of this strategy came from placing the Co-op's entire block chocolate production with the Day Chocolate Company. There was also the possibility of harming or increasing the cost of trade with Kraft Suchard by removing some of its custom. Finally, by removing choice from Co-op customers, leaving them with a more expensive Fairtrade chocolate bar[12] and without an own-brand alternative, the Co-op risked losing the chocolate sale and the entire basket spend. Most of all, retracting this position would be difficult, both operationally and philosophically, if the strategy failed.

There was of course the option to continue with the range as it was, and thus to focus efforts on a campaign to further highlight exploitation in the West African cocoa growing industry. The Co-op had started a well-received campaign to promote these issues during the mini-bar launch, however David and Terry were aware of the contradictions within its current product positioning.

THE BUSINESS DILEMMA

The Brand Marketing team needed to determine the extent to which Fairtrade values would be supported, without risking a public-relations disaster. As proven by Iceland, if high moral claims are not supported in the long run, the impact would be disastrous. Given the small set of active members pushing the Fairtrade agenda versus 'Middle Britain', it was not clear whether David and Terry's proposed strategy might push customers towards low-cost rivals (for example, Lidl, Asda etc.). Could the category management teams cope?

NOTES

1. The case is intended to be used as a basis for class discussion rather than to illustrate either effective or ineffective handling of an administrative situation.
2. Co-operative Group Annual Report and Accounts, 2000.
3. Buying groups offering independent retail outlets a form of 'retailer co-operative', i.e., preferential terms, access to merchandising and IT systems advice, 'own-brand' products, etc.
4. Chains with more than 10 convenience outlets, increasingly dominated by major supermarkets entering the sector with convenience store formats.
5. Refers to essential products such as nappies, toilet paper, etc.
6. Day Chocolate was formed by the Twin Trading group (who also established Café Direct) in conjunction with the cocoa growers co-operative Kuapa Kokoo, Christian Aid and the Body Shop.
7. Mini-bars refer to single-serve or individual size chocolate bars (45–50 grams)

8. Block chocolate refers to the large slabs of chocolate (150–200 grams) usually purchased for sharing.

9. www.divinechocolate.com

10. Unlike Fairtrade, Ethical Trading primarily directs its efforts at improving the conditions of employees, rather than independent and marginalized growers, and it works with employers to ensure basic human and labour rights, develop safe and decent working conditions and improve general standards of living.

11. Keynote Report – Green and Ethical Consumers.

12. To make the bar appeal to consumers, the price would have to be kept below the £1 barrier by dropping the weight of the bar against the standard weight for block chocolate, e.g., 150 grams rather than 200 grams.

CHAPTER THIRTY

The Wal-Mart Supply Chain Controversy[1]

N. Craig Smith, INSEAD and Robert J. Crawford, London Business School

We are not seeking punitive damages or any type of extra compensation. All we want to do is get Wal-Mart to comply with its own Code of Conduct. If it doesn't, then we will get the company to stop saying that it does.

Terry Collingsworth, Executive DirectorInternational Labor Rights Fund[2]

INTRODUCTION

When Hurricane Katrina hit the coast of Louisiana on 29 August, 2005, Wal-Mart was ready to help its many victims. While focusing on helping Wal-Mart's employees ('associates') to cope personally with the immediate disaster as well as re-open affected stores as soon as possible, Wal-Mart also worked to fill the significant gaps in the relief efforts of the various government agencies. Wal-Mart's vehicles were often the first to arrive with emergency supplies such as bottled water, food, clothing and life-saving drugs at distribution centres and shelters in devastated areas. Its accomplishments were almost universally praised, achieving a far more positive response from the public than the fumbling govern-mental authorities. According to Marshal Cohen, industry analyst for the NPD Group: 'Short-term, you could think of all the media exposure as a promotional vehicle for Wal-Mart. But I see longer-term benefits, too. Most people who were dramatically affected were Wal-Mart consumers. They're going to remember Wal-Mart was there' (as cited by Bhatnager, 2005). Even one of the union-backed activist groups, Wake-Up Wal-Mart, wrote in a letter that the Katrina measures 'brought out the best in Wal-Mart and we applaud your hurricane relief efforts' (as cited by McCauley, 2005).

However, there were others who were less impressed. On 13 September, 2005, activist lawyer Terry Collingsworth filed a lawsuit in the California Superior Court in Los Angeles on behalf of Wal-Mart workers from China, India, Indonesia, Nicaragua and Swaziland, as well as California. The plaintiffs accused the company of failing to meet contractual obligations as specified in Wal-Mart's Standards for Suppliers Agreement, under which the company claimed that it monitored and enforced its Code of Conduct. These workers claimed that they were denied their basic minimum wage, were forced to work overtime and in some cases denied their right to organize. Collingsworth and his team at the Washington, DC-based International Labor Rights Fund knew they were in for a long fight, perhaps of 10 years or more, as the case made its way through the US court system. Nonetheless, the attor-neys, who were specialists in human rights, hoped that the lawsuit would test the enforceability of corporate conduct codes. Though Wal-Mart had adopted its supplier standards agreement in 1992, according to Collingsworth, the company had 'never taken it seriously'. He and many others were making it their mission to ensure that the company would (Sevin, 2005).[3]

Collingsworth and his team had long experience with this type of lawsuit. In 1996, they had filed a lawsuit against the Unocal Corp operations in Burma. They charged the company with 'vicarious liability' for the repressive actions of the Burmese military government against conscripted labourers, who were the plaintiffs. 'If we win,' Collingsworth had said, 'we'll make companies rethink the cost of investing in places where there are horrific violations of human rights, or thinking that they can take advantage of looser regulatory environments abroad' (as cited in Kurlantzick, 2002, p. 19). After nearly 10 years of courtroom wrangling, Unocal finally agreed to settle the lawsuit for an estimated US$30 million, though the precise amount was undisclosed due to a gag order (Magnusson, 2005).

For his part, Lee Scott, Wal-Mart chief executive since 2000, had decided to press forward with a series of reforms at the world's largest retailer, including a new public relations strategy. Scott was a 27-year Wal-Mart associate who had held senior roles in distribution and logistics before becoming CEO. He had suggested to investors back in November 2004 that the company's poor reputation posed a threat to the continued growth of the business. How should Wal-Mart respond, not least to the mounting supply chain controversy?

WAL-MART'S BUSINESS MODEL

When Sam Walton founded Wal-Mart in 1962, he did not entertain any dream of becoming the wealthiest man in America or creating the world's largest corporation. Instead, from long experience as the owner of a chain of Ben Franklin discount stores, he wanted to bring big-city discounting to his corner of the rural American South. Walton was a natural salesman, passionate about building his retail business. He enjoyed creating personal relationships with employees and business associates, whom he pushed very hard to meet his standards of excellence. 'I have occasionally heard myself compared to PT Barnum because of the way I love to get in front of a crowd and talk something up,' he said.[4] 'But underneath that [I want] to make things work well, then better, and then the best they possibly can' (as cited in Slater, 2003, p. 30).

Walton's Formula: 'Every Day Low Price'

The idea behind Wal-Mart was similar to other American discount chains created in the 1960s, including Target and Kmart. They were conceived to compete directly with Sears and Woolworth's, the department store chains that dominated retailing in urban areas. What Wal-Mart would do, Walton reasoned, was offer the same range of merchandise found in nearby stores, but at about 20% lower prices – every day, rather than through one-time sales promotions of selected items. Although this lowered profit margins, Walton planned to make up for that in higher volumes of sales, eventually from a large number of retail outlets. He chose to expand locally, opening stores in his native Arkansas and spreading slowly into Oklahoma, Missouri and Louisiana. By 1969, he owned 32 stores (Slater, 2003, p. 31).

The Wal-Mart strategy was simple. To sell cheaply, Walton's company developed a relentless drive to lower costs by going directly to manufacturers and constantly increasing worker productivity; in addition to paying attention to the competition, Wal-Mart workers were also trained to treat customers with courtesy and consideration of their needs (Slater, 2003, p. 34). According to many observers, the company helped to create a new kind of 'culture of consumption', that is, consumers bought more with the expectation of very low prices on a wide array of goods (Strasser, 2006, p. 53).

Walton's formula was a phenomenal success. In 1985, with just under 1000 stores, he was named by *Forbes* as the richest man in America (Slater, 2003, p. 66). Surpassing Kmart and Sears in 1991, the year before Walton died from leukaemia, Wal-Mart was recognized as America's largest retailer as it began to expand overseas. It was repeatedly hailed as the most admired company in America (Slater, 2003, p. 41). By 2004, Wal-Mart had become number one on the Fortune 500 list, as both the world's largest corporation and the largest non-governmental employer. Sales in fiscal 2005 exceeded US$285 billion (US$56 billion outside the United States), with goods sourced from over 68 000 suppliers and 138 million customers served worldwide each week, a net income of more than US$10 billion, and over 1.6 million employees worldwide.[5] Wal-Mart accounted for approximately 10% of all retail sales in the United States (Fishman, 2006, p. 103).

Technology and Globalization

In the aftermath of Walton's death in 1992, the expansion of the company accelerated with a combination of new technologies – the 'logistics revolution' – and the globalization of its operations. Its days as a regional Southern company catering to customers in underserved rural areas were long gone.[6] In 2000, to continue its expansion, Wal-Mart executives decided that the company needed to develop a more urban strategy, with products for upscale customers in addition to lower-price items; Wal-Mart would also enter the grocery sector (see Halkias, 2005). In 2005, 85% of US consumers shopped in Wal-Mart, but the top third of shoppers accounted for 80% of sales and these consumers skewed lower-to-middle income and those under age 55. Lower income consumer spending was typically more volatile, especially for discretionary spending, becoming squeezed when costs of essentials rise, such as petrol or heating fuel.[7]

From the mid-1990s, Wal-Mart became a pioneer in technology-driven productivity enhancement. Elements included:

- point-of-sale data collection, enabling managers to track inventory and demand in real time;
- data mining in order to exploit trends to boost sales via novel merchandising techniques, e.g., placing nappies and six-packs of beer near store entryways on Fridays, to exploit a spike in demand for both items at the end of the workweek (Hoopes, 2006, p. 91);
- establishment of a just-in-time delivery system, which suppliers and distributors were obligated to participate in and obey, in effect joining Wal-Mart's data network (Petrovic and Hamilton, 2006, p. 133).

According to a widely-cited estimate by McKinsey and Co., Wal-Mart alone was responsible for 25% of the gain in productivity of the US economy from 1995 to 1999. Many of these efficiency gains, the company claimed, were passed directly on to consumers in the form of lower prices. Wal-Mart, the company claimed, saved US consumers over US$100 billion per year (Hoopes, 2006, p. 89).

To the mid-1970s, Wal-Mart tended to buy brand-name goods from American manufacturers. However, as the Chinese economy began to position itself as an exporter to the developed economies in the West, Wal-Mart shifted its purchasing policies to that region: the labour was cheaper, though the regulatory environment was far less stringent, with fewer protections for workers and weaker pollution controls. By 2004, with US$18 billion in purchases, Wal-Mart had become the world's largest importer from China, accounting for 10% of everything that China exported to the United States every year and for 30% of Wal-Mart's total supplier purchases. Wal-Mart was also a major purchaser from Bangladeshi and Central American manufacturers (Petrovic and Hamilton, 2006).

A New Kind of Centralization

Combined with its sheer size, Wal-Mart's technological capabilities enabled the company to exert an unprecedented degree of control over not only its employees, but also its business partners (independent manufacturers, suppliers and distributors). According to Lichtenstein (2006, p. 11) 'at individual Wal-Mart stores, thermostats were manipulated from [the] Bentonville Arkansas headquarters'.

On the one hand, managers in Wal-Mart headquarters were able to track the productivity of workers in its individual stores. The centralized management of the stores' budgets and the logistics requirements placed an enormous burden on local managers, many of whom struggled to meet their targets for cost containment and profitability. This led them, many critics charged, to resort to degrading and even illegal practices in the relentless pursuit of 'improvements' in performance, allegedly in the form of unpaid over-time and by refusing to allow breaks for meals or relaxation. Because Wal-Mart managers were unwilling to pay overtime or hire additional workers, Wal-Mart associates bore the brunt of the relentless pursuit of 'productivity gains' in the form of more work for the same amount of pay (Rosen, 2006, pp. 245–246).

On the other hand, Wal-Mart's centralization represented a fundamental shift of market power to the retailer. Up to the early 1980s, retailers had served as outlets for manufacturers, who set prices, created their own unique marketing and brand strategies, and independently gauged consumer preferences for their products. As Wal-Mart grew into the world's largest retail channel, manufacturers increasingly found themselves dictated to by a hard-bargaining buyer that in effect could act like a monopsony. In practical terms, this meant that Wal-Mart could force its partners to set prices at whatever levels the retailer deemed desirable, package goods to fit Wal-Mart requirements and even reconfigure their entire computer systems in a manner compatible with Wal-Mart's. In other words, Wal-Mart gained direct control of both their marketing through its stores and beyond that, the manufacturer's brand. Given the imperative of cost containment, this tended to cut the profit margins of Wal-Mart's suppliers to the bone (Petrovic and Hamilton, 2006, p. 130).

Wal-Mart's pricing policies could entail dire consequences for suppliers. For example, Wal-Mart's treatment of Vlasic apparently led directly to the gherkin company's decline and bankruptcy, according to Vlasic executives (Fishman, 2003, p. 73). Long a premium brand in the US grocery industry, Vlasic recognized Wal-Mart as its most important marketing outlet, in effect accounting for 30% of its gross sales. As such, Vlasic executives felt compelled to obey the conditions that Wal-Mart set. According to reporter Charles Fishman, Wal-Mart tested sales of gherkins by the gallon – a jar large enough to supply an average family for an entire year – at a price of US$2.97, which was less than a third of the price normally charged in grocery stores. It sold so well that Wal-Mart soon required Vlasic to sell the gallon jar at that price in all its stores, cutting Vlasic's profits down to about one cent of gross revenue per jar. Though the gallon jars sold extremely well, they reduced the higher margins that Vlasic enjoyed in US supermarkets, lowering profits by approximately 25%. As one Vlasic executive put it: 'Quickly, it started cannibalizing our non-Wal-Mart business.' As the firm's finances deteriorated alarmingly, the executive said, Wal-Mart refused to allow it to raise prices until it was too late (see Fishman, 2003, pp. 79–83). As a result, not only did Vlasic file for bankruptcy, but the gallon-gherkin jar effectively destroyed the company's marketing strategy, which was based less on low prices than an intangible cachet of high quality. In forcing Vlasic to comply with its pricing policies, the Wal-Mart business model had changed Vlasic from a brand-led business into a commodity discounter, with disastrous results (Hoopes, 2006).

CRITICS AND THE SUPPLY CHAIN

Wal-Mart's size and reach attracted many critics, who condemned its practices and began to mount protest campaigns against the company. Their tactics included: grassroots campaigns to block the establishment of new Wal-Mart Supercenters in their neighbourhoods; consumer boycotts of targeted product lines; a barrage of media attacks (in films and television, on the Internet and in print); and efforts to unionize Wal-Mart associates. In addition, the company became the object of a growing number of lawsuits – on average five new suits were filed per day in the United States – from both current and former employees and customers. At the same time, Wal-Mart faced declining profit margins and a stock price that had lost more than 25% of its value since 2000. Many industry observers believed that the company's old formula of cost-cutting and rural expansion had reached a saturation point. If the company were to continue to grow, it would have to enter more urban markets as well as continue its expansion abroad with the opening of stores in Europe, Asia and Latin America (see Halkias, 2005).

The Critics' General Case

Wal-Mart's critics argued passionately that the company had to change. First, they believed, Wal-Mart had somehow to lessen its impact on the communities that it entered. As things stood, critics charged, Wal-Mart not only destroyed local 'mom and pop' stores that could not compete on price – which sometimes turned traditional downtown shopping areas from vital social centres into ghost towns – but also generated the second-hand effects of increased traffic, reduced demand for other local businesses, such as local newspapers, and additional infrastructure costs that created new tax burdens (see Quinn, 2005, pp. 1–26). Second, Wal-Mart's labour practices, which critics said were brutal and unfair, had to improve. The company, they demanded, must allow associates to unionize, offer better wages and health insurance benefits,[8] and treat them more humanely. Third, they argued, Wal-Mart had to provide a more equitable management of its supply chain, from the treatment of 'sweatshop' workers in China to the company's truckers as well as its manufacturing partners, all of whom faced continuing pressure to lower their costs. This often meant that the company should pay more for the goods and services it bought, which would eat into its razor-thin profits margins as well as force Wal-Mart customers to pay more (see Featherstone, 2005). Although these issues covered a huge range of concerns that many consumer activists found difficult to address in concerted campaigns, their actions ensured that Wal-Mart received constant public scrutiny, in particular with regards to the loss of US manufacturing jobs, sweatshops and environmental degradation.

Job 'Exportation'

According to many critics, Wal-Mart's perpetual search for the lowest possible prices forced many of its suppliers to manufacture outside the US, in effect sending jobs to underdeveloped economies where labour was cheaper and regulations were less stringent. While acknowledging that this was emblematic of the new global economy, critics viewed Wal-Mart as perhaps the most important initiator of this trend (see Quinn, 2005, pp. 90–94). For example, the Huffy Corporation was forced to outsource more and more of its bicycle manufacturing until, by 1999, it had closed all its factories in the United States. To varying degrees, the same story was repeated in many other American manufacturers, from Welch's Grape Juice to Levi Strauss (see Fishman, 2003, pp. 88–93). As one Philips television design engineer summed up: 'the cost pressure was negative . . . They've lowered the price of the TVs to the point where they can't afford to pay US$1 or US$2 an hour they have to pay in Mexico,' which generated pressure on Philips to move its plants to China (Fishman, 2003, p. 100).

Global Sweatshops

In 1996, a sweatshop-related discovery helped to catapult the issue of child labour into the international spotlight: a line of Wal-Mart clothing endorsed by US television personality Kathy Lee Gifford, reporters found, relied on Honduran girls, aged 13 to 15, who were paid only US$0.30 per hour in shifts up to 12 hours in duration; they were also denied the right to take breaks and routinely humiliated by their superiors. It was a galvanizing moment for labour activists, who operated in an arena that had long been the concern of a few politicians and professionals in international organizations; suddenly scores of activists were able to act on their concerns about working conditions in the 'sweatshops' that had become part of the global economy (Duke, 2005; Rivoli, 2005). Though the overwhelming majority of these factories were subcontractors – in 2004, Wal-Mart was supplied by over 5300 factories in 60 countries – outsourcing companies such as Wal-Mart were held accountable for their condition, including such issues as:

- child labour;
- demand-driven production schedules, allegedly up to 90 hours per week at peak times;
- unpaid overtime;
- poverty-level wages;
- dangerous working conditions ranging from degraded environments and fire hazards to poorly designed equipment;
- lack of labour rights guarding against poor treatment by managers, including threats of bodily harm and other forms of reprisal.

For example, in support of the lawsuit filed by Collingsworth and his team, a young Bangladeshi worker (Robina Akther) described her work conditions: she earned US$0.13 per hour for 14 hours of work per day – US$26.98 per month – and was under constant threat of abuse from her supervisors.

'If you made any mistakes or fell behind on your goal,' she said, 'they beat you . . . they slapped you and lashed you hard on the face with the pants [that she was sewing]. This happens very often. They hit you hard. It is no joke' (cited in Fishman, 2003, p. 185). Akther had only 10 days holiday per year, was required to ask permission to go to the toilet and was forbidden even to talk with co-workers. The 15 other workers in the lawsuit offered reports of similar conditions in their respective countries. Although Wal-Mart had adopted its Standards for Suppliers since 1992 (see Exhibit 30.1), the problem lay in their implementation: somehow, the company had to ensure that its subcontractors complied with them (see Fishman, 2003, pp. 185–188).

EXHIBIT 30.1 WAL-MART STORES, INC. – STANDARDS FOR SUPPLIERS

Wal-Mart Stores, Inc. ('Wal-Mart') is successful by adhering to three basic beliefs since its founding in 1962:

1. Respect for the Individual
2. Service to our Customers
3. Strive for Excellence

Wal-Mart strives to conduct its business in a manner that reflects these three basic beliefs and expects its suppliers to adhere to these beliefs in their contracting, subcontracting, and other business relationships. Additionally, because the conduct of Wal-Mart's suppliers can be attributed to Wal-Mart and its reputation, Wal-Mart requires its suppliers, and their contractors, to meet the following standards, and reserves the right to make periodic, unannounced inspections of suppliers' facilities and the facilities of suppliers' contractors to ensure suppliers' compliance with these standards:

Compliance with applicable laws and practices: Suppliers shall comply with all local and national laws and regulations of the jurisdictions in which the suppliers are doing business as well as the practices of their industry. Should the legal requirements and practices of the industry conflict, suppliers must, at a minimum, be in compliance with the legal requirements of the jurisdiction in which they are operating. If, however, the industry practices exceed the country's legal requirements, Wal-Mart will favour suppliers who meet such industry practices.

Wal-Mart expects its suppliers to comply with the following conditions of employment:

Compensation: Suppliers shall fairly compensate their employees by providing wages and benefits which are in compliance with the local and national laws and regulations of the jurisdictions in which the suppliers are doing business, or which are consistent with the prevailing local standards in the countries, if the prevailing local standards are higher.

Hours of Labor: Suppliers shall maintain reasonable employee work hours in compliance with local standards and applicable laws of the jurisdictions in which the suppliers are doing business. Suppliers' employees shall not work more than 72 hours per six days or work more than a maximum total working hours of 14 hours per calendar day (measured midnight to midnight). Supplier's factories should be working toward achieving a 60-hour workweek.

Wal-Mart will not use suppliers who, on a regularly scheduled basis, require employees to work in excess of the statutory requirements without proper compensation as required by applicable law. Employees should be permitted reasonable days off (at least one day off for every seven-day period) and leave privileges.

Forced/Prison Labor: Forced or prison labor will not be tolerated by Wal-Mart.

Child Labor: Wal-Mart will not tolerate the use of child labor. Wal-Mart will not accept products from suppliers or subcontractors who use child labor. No person shall be employed at an age younger than the legal minimum age for working in any specific jurisdictions. In no event shall suppliers or their subcontractors employ workers less than 14 years of age.

Discrimination/Rights: All conditions of employment must be based on an individual's ability to do the job, not on the basis of personal characteristics or beliefs. Wal-Mart favors suppliers who do not discriminate on the basis of race, color, national origin, gender, sexual orientation, religion, disability, and other similar factors.

Freedom of Association and Collective Bargaining: Suppliers will respect the rights of employees regarding their decision of whether to associate or not to associate with any group, as long as such groups are legal in their own country. Suppliers must not interfere with, obstruct or prevent such legitimate activities.

Immigration law and compliance: Only workers with a legal right to work shall be employed or used by a supplier. All workers' legal status must be validated by the Supplier by reviewing original documentation (not photocopies) before they are allowed to commence work. Procedures which demonstrate compliance with these validations must be implemented. Suppliers must regularly audit employment agencies from whom they obtain workers to monitor compliance with this policy.

Workplace Environment: Factories producing merchandise to be sold by Wal-Mart shall provide adequate medical facilities and ensure that all production and manufacturing processes are carried out in conditions that have proper and adequate considerations for the health and safety of those involved. Wal-Mart will not do business with any supplier that provides an unhealthy or hazardous work environment or which utilizes mental or physical disciplinary practices.

Security: Suppliers will maintain adequate security at all production and warehousing facilities and implement supply chain security procedures designed to prevent the introduction of non-manifested cargo into outbound shipments (e.g., drugs, explosives bio-hazards and/or other contraband). Additionally, each production and warehousing facility must have written security procedures and maintain documented proof of the adequate controls implemented to guard against introduction of non-manifested cargo.

Concern for the Environment: We encourage suppliers to reduce excess packaging and to use recycled and nontoxic materials.

(Continued)

> **EXHIBIT 30.1** (*continued*)
>
> **Right of Inspection:** Wal-Mart or a third-party designated by Wal-Mart will take certain actions, such as inspection of production facilities, to implement and monitor these standards.
>
> **Confidentiality:** Suppliers shall not disclose to others and will not use for its own purposes or the purpose of others any trade secrets, confidential information, knowledge, designs, data, skill, or any other information considered by Wal-Mart as 'confidential'. The 'Standards for Suppliers' must be posted in a location visible to all employees at all facilities that manufacture products for Wal-Mart. If you know of a violation of these standards by a supplier, factory, or Wal-Mart associate, please call 1-800-WM-ETHIC (1-800-963-8442). Alternatively, write to: Wal-Mart Stores, Inc., Wal-Mart Ethics Office, 702 SW 8th St., Bentonville, AR 72716-0860 or e-mail to: ethicalstnds@wal-mart.com.
>
> *Source:* http://www.laborrights.org/projects/corporate/walmart/Supplier-Standards-2005.pdf

Secondary Effects

Once Wal-Mart entered a supplier market, the scale of its operations virtually guaranteed that it would have a fundamental impact on supplier communities, ranging from its environmental impact to local working standards. First, according to labour activists, Wal-Mart was viewed as a bellwether: others would wait to see what it did. For example, in the mining industry – Wal-Mart was the largest retailer of gold jewellery in the US in 2005 – other retailers stated that they would not seek to buy from more worker-friendly companies unless Wal-Mart consented to uphold similar standards.[9] Second, because Wal-Mart not only dominated markets but also created entirely new ones, its environmental impact increasingly attracted scrutiny. In the aquatic-farm industry, Wal-Mart created a huge market for inexpensive, de-boned salmon fillets. To supply this market, entrepreneurs in Chile established enormous salmon farms in ocean pens, capable of producing a million pounds of fillets or more per year. Although manageable, the Chilean aquatic farms produced so much waste from faeces and excess feed that huge 'dead zones' around them were observed (see Fishman, 2003, pp. 176–181).

Evidence suggested that criticism of these practices resonated with a growing portion of the public. In 2004, a confidential McKinsey & Co. study reported that 2–8% of the public had ceased to shop at Wal-Mart due to the 'negative press' about the company (Barbaro, 2005). Most alarming to Wal-Mart executives, however, was the growing disapproval of more affluent, middle class consumers in urban areas – they were better educated and more inclined to social activism than Wal-Mart's original consumers in the rural South of the United States. To sustain its growth rate, the urban middle class was the group that the company had identified as the market segment that it must increasingly penetrate (Barbaro, 2005).

WAL-MART BEGINS TO RESPOND

Despite the growing army of critics, Wal-Mart managers tended to perceive themselves as 'consumer advocates', on average saving individuals US$600 per year at the checkout counter (Fishman, 2003, p. 62). Media campaigns against the company grew in 2004–05, including concerted efforts by the union-sponsored organizations Wal-Mart Watch and Wake-Up Wal-Mart, as well as a much-anticipated independent film.[10] Chief executive Lee Scott decided to mount a counter-offensive. His aim to respond directly to the claims of critics represented a major departure for the company. In summer 2005, after hiring the public relations firm Edelman, the company created a rapid-response 'war room' at its Arkansas headquarters as part of a new PR group. Among the tasks of the group was the cultivation of a more positive image of the company – as environmentally aware and more worker friendly – in the minds of the 'swing voters' who had not yet decided against shopping at Wal-Mart (Barbaro, 2005).

Katrina and Its Aftermath

The first big success of Scott's new strategy was the company's relief efforts on behalf of the victims of Hurricane Katrina. According to Scott, this was only the beginning of the company's 'charm offensive'. 'When growth was easier,' he said, 'this idea of critics being ignored was OK. [But] as the share price slows you have to get to this point [reach out to its critics]' (as cited in Berner, 2005). In addition, Scott promised, the company would reduce greenhouse gases produced by Wal-Mart stores by 20% over the next 7 years. Moreover, measures to publicize and improve the treatment of its workers were underway: healthcare coverage would be provided to Wal-Mart associates for US$25 per month. He even called on the US Congress to raise the minimum wage (as cited in Sarkar, 2005).

However, just days after Scott's announcements in October 2005, Wal-Mart Watch provided *New York Times* reporters with a leaked internal memo. Though only a draft memo, it had been written by the Executive Vice President for Benefits, Susan Chambers, to the company Board of Directors. In the memo, Chambers not only described how many Wal-Mart employees were uninsured or on public assistance for health, but also outlined a strategy to 'dissuade unhealthy people from coming to work at Wal-Mart'. This leak ignited a firestorm of criticism, which many observers believed would undermine the company's new public relations strategy (McGinn, 2005).

Wal-Mart's Sweatshop Measures

In its most recent Factory Certification Report,[11] Wal-Mart outlined its inspection processes for compliance, which included visits to factories, meetings with subcontractor managers, interviews with workers and proposals for improvement. In particular, Wal-Mart developed a 'traffic light' system, or hierarchy of violations from 'green' (acceptable or low risk conditions), 'yellow' (medium-risk violations), 'red' (high-risk violations) and 'failed' (child labour, bribery, forced labour, discrimination, human rights abuses, unsafe or hazardous working conditions). A 'red' or 'failed' designation would result in a 'disapproved' status for the factory, which would result in a temporary halt to Wal-Mart orders pending improvement. If a subcontractor failed to improve after several attempts, Wal-Mart would terminate its relations with the factory – 'three strikes and you're out' (Exhibit 30.2).

Many observers took a highly critical perspective. According to Fishman, in 2004, over 2100 (of approximately 5,300) factories were suspended for a certain period, of which only 260 were permitted to return as suppliers. However, in that period, because over 90% of the Wal-Mart inspections were scheduled in advance, that is, they were not the surprise inspections that activists argued were the most revealing and useful. Furthermore, Wal-Mart's interviews with workers were not anonymous, but conducted with the knowledge of local managers. Because this opened

EXHIBIT 30.2 WAL-MART INSPECTION CHECKLIST – SAMPLE VIOLATIONS

Wal-Mart is continually evaluating and updating its inspection checklist. Below is a sample checklist.

Compensation

- non-payment of applicable wages
- wages unverifiable, or wage system unclear
- failure to pay minimum wage
- failure to pay legally required overtime premium
- legally required benefits unpaid
- illegal deductions from pay
- no pay slips for workers
- workers unaware of pay rates and deductions
- lower training wages paid longer than legal length of probation
- training wages paid to skilled labour
- delaying payment of any portion of wages
- unpaid piecework or lack of payment for redoing work
- manipulation of payroll

Working Hours

The facility must post working hours. The supplier must compensate workers appropriately for hours worked in excess of posted hours. Overtime must not exceed the amount permitted by national or local standards, unless the factory possesses a document explicitly granting exemption from this law for a specific period and a specific amount of additional overtime. General exemptions are unacceptable. National and local exemptions must still be in compliance with Wal-Mart standards, as follows:

- Factories must require a day of rest every week.
- They must have an acceptable system to track hours worked, and they must prohibit working off the clock.
- Work weeks exceeding 60 hours are unacceptable and considered a violation. Wal-Mart's maximum tolerance is a 72-hour work week over six days, or no more than 14 hours per calendar day. Factories should be working toward a maximum of 60 hours per work week.

Forced Labour

- workers imprisoned in factory
- use of labourers in bondage
- purchasing supplies from state entities using prison labour
- excessive recruitment fees

- unreasonable access to basic needs (i.e., food, water, toilet, etc.)
- terminating or disciplining workers who refuse to work overtime
- factory holds government-issued identity papers against worker's will
- excessive restrictions on movement – such as prohibiting workers from going out at night, or permitting them to go out on only certain days of the week
- illegal or unreasonable terms in contract or in factory rules and regulations

Child Labour

- no health examination provided to young workers
- no proper breaks for minors of legal working age
- minors with no/expired/incomplete work documents
- minor's age unverifiable because of:
  - no authorizing work document
  - cannot verify age
- under-age workers hired:
  - if worker is found to be below the legal allowable working age (based on the Western birth date) during the inspection, it is a child labour violation
  - if worker is below legal allowable working age (based on the Western birth date) within six months prior to the inspection date, this is also a violation
- under-age workers working 'off the books'
- numerous discrepancies in age verification records
- youth of legal age working in prohibited areas
- workers' children on production floor
- no hiring procedures to ensure compliance
- job applicants falsifying age documentation

Discrimination

- maternity and paternity rights fall short of current national legislation
- pregnancy testing, for reasons other than verifiable legal requirement
- verifiable incidents of pregnant women denied jobs or dismissed
- verifiable incidents of promotions and pay based on race, ethnicity, national origin, gender or age

Workplace Environment (Health & Safety – Dormitories)

- Health & Safety – no inspection and certification by local health authorities
- Health & Safety – insufficient restroom and bathing facilities
- Health & Safety – restricted access

(Continued)

EXHIBIT 30.2 (*Continued*)

- Health & Safety – not segregated by gender
- Health & Safety – unsafe
- Health & Safety – insufficient ventilation
- Health & Safety – insufficient space for number of boarders
- Health & Safety – hazardous chemicals are present
- Health & Safety – lack of access to potable water
- Health & Safety – wiring impedes exit/passage
- Health & Safety – lack of non-slip materials on wet or slick surfaces
- Health & Safety – insufficient restrooms for the number of boarders
- Health & Safety – poorly maintained restroom facilities
- First Aid – empty/no/locked first aid box or kit
- Fire Safety – no emergency evacuation plan posted in native language
- Fire Safety – lack of access to fire protection equipment
- Fire Safety – inadequate number and distribution of fire extinguishers and fire hoses
- Fire Safety – no fire alarms, emergency lighting, or sprinkler system
- Fire Safety – expired fire extinguishers
- Fire Safety – inadequate fire drills
- Fire Safety – no fire evacuation plan marked on floor
- Fire Safety – electrical panel uncovered/electrical cords run through damp or wet areas/ electrical outlet overloaded
- Fire Safety – inadequate/restricted access to staircase
- Exits – exits unmarked
- Exits – locked or fully blocked exits
- Exits – inadequate number of exits based on workforce
- Exits – partially obstructed exits
- Exits – inadequately marked and lit exits

Workplace Environment (Health & Safety – Work Areas)

- Health – lack of access to potable water
- Health – work area poorly ventilated
- Health – factory conditions are crowded, disorganized, and unsanitary
- Health – work area poorly lit
- Health – possible infestations of rodents or insects
- Health – inappropriate trash disposal
- First Aid – empty first aid kit

- First Aid – insufficient or inadequately supplied first aid kits
- First Aid – first aid procedures not posted
- First Aid – injuries not monitored
- Protective Equipment – appropriate personal protective equipment not provided to workers (i.e., lint masks, eye protection, chain gloves)
- Protective Equipment – machinery not fitted with safety features
- Fire Safety – inadequate number and distribution of fire extinguishers and fire hoses
- Fire Safety – fire extinguishers are blocked
- Fire Safety – no posted evacuation plan
- Fire Safety – no fire alarms, emergency lighting, or sprinkler system
- Fire Safety – expired fire extinguishers
- Fire Safety – inadequate fire drills
- Fire Safety – fire evacuation plan not marked on floor
- Fire Safety – storage of finished goods presents fire hazard
- Fire Safety – hanging wires/wiring impedes exit or passage
- Fire Safety – electrical outlets overloaded/electrical cords run through damp or wet areas/ electrical panel uncovered
- Safety – hazardous chemicals stored in work area
- Safety – lack of non-slip materials on wet or slick surfaces
- Exits – locked and/or fully blocked exits
- Exits – inadequate number of exits based on workforce
- Exits – inadequately marked and lit exits
- Exits – partially obstructed exits/excessive work in progress/work station too close/storage in aisles that precludes speedy exit
- Toilets – insufficient restrooms based on workforce
- Toilets – poorly maintained restroom facilities
- Canteen – food preparation and eating areas are unsanitary
- Canteen – food prepared or consumed on the production floor
- Canteen – insufficient canteen capacity
- Canteen – chemicals improperly stored near food
- First Aid – glucose or dextrose noted in first aid kit
- Toilets – failure to provide gender-segregated bathrooms

Workplace Environment (Health & Safety – Harassment or Abuse)

- abuse – corporal punishment/physical abuse
- body search – strip searches

(Continued)

EXHIBIT 30.2 (*Continued*)

- harassment – verbal abuse
- pat down searches by opposite sex
- harassment – sexual harassment

Environmental Concerns

- wilful violation of environmental legal requirements
- workers exposed to toxic levels of pollutants
- inappropriate storing or handling of chemicals

Right of Inspection

- denied access to factory or dormitory
- factory fails to provide factory/production records/contract or any relevant documentation
- worker interviews prohibited
- relevant information withheld
- no business licence
- inappropriate/in process of application of business licence

Subcontracting

- subcontractors used for Wal-Mart production
- home workers used and paid by factory

Standards Posted

- no Wal-Mart standards posted

Source: http://www.walmartfacts.com/docs/131_NewsDeskFactShtSourcingarticle_1161280340.pdf

workers to retaliation, critics claimed it tended to lessen their candour. Finally, Wal-Mart relied almost exclusively on its own inspectors rather than independent third-party auditors, which could compromise their usefulness. While there were 202 full-time Wal-Mart employees involved in compliance issues, they were far fewer than those employed by the Gap and others when compared as a ratio to gross revenues (see Fishman, 2003, pp. 190–191).[12]

Furthermore, in separate instances, there was growing anecdotal evidence that Wal-Mart was not taking its factory-inspection policies 'seriously.' Among the lawsuits, there was the 'unjust termination' case of Jim Bill Lynn, a self-described whistleblower. Although as global services manager he was hired to monitor factory conditions in Central and South America, Lynn claimed that he was fired for bringing evidence of unfair practices to the firm's attention – that is, doing his job. Not only had Lynn discovered conditions that violated Wal-Mart standards, he said, but also he uncovered evidence that factory-certification reports were 'routinely falsified' by the factory owners (Meyerson, 2005, p. 32).

Wal-Mart was also the subject of a growing number of independent investigative reports, which focused on compliance issues related to the corporate code of conduct, its environmental record and its pressure on suppliers to relocate overseas. For example, at the end of 2005, the China Labor Watch and the National Labor Committee issued reports on worker conditions in Chinese factories; allegations included 'sham' work contracts and regulations designed to falsify information about working conditions; works shifts of more than 13 hours; refusal to offer health insurance, and the like.[13] Factory managers in China and elsewhere, it seemed, were becoming expert at falsifying their records in order to create the appearance of compliance with corporate codes of conduct. It was reported that workers were required to punch fake time cards in accordance with mandated 40-hour ceilings for work weeks. In addition, payroll records were doctored to falsify pay levels as well as the number of hours worked per day, with the object of appearing to comply with overtime pay requirements. According to activists with the Asia Foundation: 'In China, it is common for the actual wage to amount to as little as half the legal wage limit' (as cited in Foster and Harney, 2005).

Nonetheless, Wal-Mart asserted that it had instituted a number of positive changes, including the creation of: 1) internal audit teams to evaluate the execution of Wal-Mart's quality assurance programme for factory certifications; 2) training programmes of nearly 11 000 supplier representatives for various factories worldwide; 3) training programmes for Wal-Mart buyers regarding compliance issues; 4) the creation of a team focused on corporate social responsibility and stakeholder engagement. To support the company's claims of improvements, the 2005 report offered statistical evidence. During 2005, Wal-Mart made 13 600 inspections in 7200 supplier facilities, which resulted in 141 permanent bans on factories (primarily because of underage labour violations); the company also increased the number of unannounced visits from 8% to 20% of total inspections (Wal-Mart Stores, Inc., 2005).

Other Initiatives

In spite of these mixed results regarding sweatshops, there were many other activists who decided that they would try to work with Wal-Mart. To them, with the company appearing to seek their advice, they recognized an important opportunity for change. For example, Scott Burns, the Director of Marine Conservation programmes at the World Wildlife Fund (WWF), had begun to work with Wal-Mart on a programme to improve the sustainability of the fisheries that supplied the company. With a team of outside experts, he explained, Wal-Mart had informed its suppliers that they would: evaluate the current environmental impact of their fisheries; report on those that need to improve; and come up with corrective action plans. 'Wal-Mart,' he said, 'expects to see measurable progress and is very clear about what it expects.' Furthermore, according to Burns, the fisheries initiative was one programme among many that the company were contemplating with non-governmental organizations and outside experts.[14]

WHAT WOULD IT TAKE?

Collingsworth's lawsuit was only one in a number of initiatives by activists that targeted Wal-Mart's supply chain. Like many anti-Wal-Mart activists, he was passionately devoted to the cause, even if it took years. 'We have the tenacity and will find the resources to keep going,' he said. He was committed to the case because 'Wal-Mart is the leader of the sweatshop movement. We've gone into a lot of factories in the developing world and whenever Wal-Mart is there, [factory managers] tell us they can't change because Wal-Mart won't pay for it.' While the case was in its early stages – and Wal-Mart lawyers had filed a motion to dismiss it in February 2006 – Collingsworth was confident that the company was courting disaster by its apparent refusal to take the issue seriously. As a retail chain, he explained, Wal-Mart was far more vulnerable to consumer scrutiny than was the case with the oil company and natural gas wholesaler Unocal. Assuming the case would go forward, he continued, 'we would enter the discovery phase. Then I can subpoena documents to get access to internal memos and take depositions from [Wal-Mart] managers.'[15]

As if to address these concerns, Wal-Mart's Scott had begun to speak out on a number of issues in the wake of the praise regarding the company's relief efforts following Hurricane Katrina. Wal-Mart, he said, had to find new ways to provide jobs and healthcare; increase its involvement in the community and its diversity; and improve its environmental impact. '[A]ll the issues,' he stated, 'we've been dealing with historically from a defensive posture. What became clear is that in order to build a 21st century company, we need to view these same issues in a different light.' He went on to ask:

> Katrina asked this critical question, and I want to ask it of you: What would it take for Wal-Mart to be that company, at our best, all the time? What if we used our size and resources to make this country and this earth an even better place for all of us: customers, associates, our children, and generations unborn? What would that mean? Could we do it? Is this consistent with our business model? What if the very things that many people criticize us for – our size and reach – became a trusted friend and ally to all, just as it did in Katrina?[16]

For some, there was room for optimism. WWF's Burns and others hoped that the company (or at least some of the managers in it) was genuinely striving to change. He knew that working with the company would open his organization to charges that they had 'sold out'. What he wanted to do was get things done, to seize the opportunity if indeed it existed. Of course, he acknowledged, it was too early to evaluate Wal-Mart's effort – the proof depended on how the fisheries programme was implemented over the next five years. Nonetheless, Burns concluded, 'I think they are serious, and if they are, it will be possible to have an extremely big impact in creating a sustainable fisheries system' worldwide.[17]

NOTES

1. Robert J. Crawford prepared this case from public sources under the supervision of Professor N. Craig Smith, as a basis for class discussion rather than to illustrate either effective or ineffective handling of an administrative situation. Financial assistance provided by Accenture for the development of this case study is gratefully acknowledged.

2. *Source:* telephone interview with case author, 16 March, 2006.

3. See also www.laborrights.org, Stop Wal-Mart sweatshops globally, complaint.

4. P. T. Barnum (1810–91) was an American showman noted for extravagant advertising, billing his circus as 'The Greatest Show on Earth'.

5. *Wal-Mart Annual Report* 2005, http://walmartstores.com/Media/Investors/2005AnnualReport. pdf. Wal-Mart's fiscal year 2005 ended 31 January 2005. Sales in fiscal 2006 were over US$312 billion worldwide (US$63 billion outside the United States) and net income exceeded US$11

billion. As of year-end January 2006, Wal-Mart had over 1.8 million associates and 6100 stores worldwide.

6. *Wal-Mart Annual Report*, 2005, p. 12.

7. Data from IRI report on Wal-Mart at: http://www.gmabrands.com/publications/gmairi/2006/may/may.pdf.

8. According to Fishman (2003, pp. 240–241), in Tennessee 10 261 children of Wal-Mart employees were enrolled in state healthcare for the poor; in Georgia, 9 617 Wal-Mart associates were provided healthcare by state-aided programmes for the poor. Wake-Up Wal-Mart claimed that one in seven US Wal-Mart employees had no healthcare coverage and that a substantial number earned below the poverty line. See: http://www.wakeupwalmart.com/facts/#healthcare.

9. Case author interview with an anonymous activist.

10. *Wal-Mart: The High Price of Low Cost*, by Robert Greenwald, 2005.

11. Wal-Mart Stores, Inc., Factory Certification Report March 2003–February 2004. See: http://www.walmartstores.com/media/resources/legacydocs/2004SuppStandards_1.pdf.

12. The calculation that Fishman made is as follows: with revenues of US$288 billion in 2004, Wal-Mart's staff of 202 is proportionately smaller than that of the Gap, which had 90 factory inspectors with revenues of US$16.3 billion for the same year; by this calculation, Wal-Mart should increase its factory inspection staff by a factor of nearly six.

13. 'Wal-Mart Sweatshop Toys Made in China' (December, 2005) and 'New Balance Sweatshop Stumble in China No Surprise – Wal-Mart in the Same Factory' (5 January, 2006), www.chinalaborwatch.org.

14. Case author interview with Burns, 17 March, 2006.

15. Case author interview with Collingsworth, 16 March, 2006.

16. 'Twenty First Century Leadership', Lee Scott presentation to Wal-Mart employees, 24 October, 2005. See: http://www.walmartstores.com/Files/21st%20Century%20Leadership.pdf.

17. Case author interview with Burns, 17 March, 2006.

REFERENCES

Barbaro, M. (2005) A new weapon for Wal-Mart: A war room, *The New York Times*, 1 November.

Berner, R. (2005) Can Wal-Mart wear a white hat?, *BusinessWeek*, 3 October.

Bhatnager, P. (2005) Wal-Mart redeems itself, *CNNMoney.com*, 9 September. Available at http://money.cnn.com/2005/09/09/news/fortune500/walmart_image/index.htm (accessed 6 March, 2009).

Duke, L. (2005) The man who made Kathy Lee cry; Labor gadfly Charles Kernaghan busses in, *The Washington Post*, 31 July.

Featherstone, L. (2005) Wal-Mart's P.R. war, *Salon.com*, 2 August. Available at http://dir.salon.com/story/news/feature/2005/08/02/walmart/index.html (accessed 6 March, 2009).

Fishman, C. (2003) The Wal-Mart you don't know: Why low prices have a high cost, *Fast Company*, December.

Fishman, C. (2006) *The Wal-Mart Effect: How the World's Most Powerful Company Really Works – and How It's Transforming the American Economy*, Penguin, Harmondsworth.

Foster, L. and Harney, A. (2005) Doctored records on working hours and pay are causing problems for consumer multinationals as they source more of their goods in Asia, *The Financial Times*, 22 April.

Halkias, M. (2005) Wal-Mart's urban push, *The Dallas Morning News*, 1 November.

Hoopes, J. (2006) Growth through knowledge, in *Wal-Mart: The Face of Twentieth Century Capitalism*, (ed. N. Lichtenstein), New Press, New York, pp. 83–106.

Kurlantzick, J. (2002) Globalism in the dock; Burmese villagers sue Unocal in an L.A. courtroom, *The American Prospect*, 4 November.

Lichtenstein, N. (ed.) (2006) *Wal-Mart: The face of Twentieth Century Capitalism*, New Press, New York.

Magnusson, P. (2005) A milestone for human rights, *BusinessWeek*, 24 January.

McCauley, K. (2005) Katrina relief lifts Wal-Mart's image, *O'Dwyer's PR Services Report*, October.

McGinn, D. (2005) Wal-Mart hits the wall; The No. 1 retailer always had reasons to smile. Now PR problems and a falling stock are giving it headaches, *Newsweek*, 14 November.

Meyerson, H. (2005) Open doors, closed minds; Jim Bill Lynn believed his Wal-Mart bosses when they said he should report unfair practices. He did – and walked into Kafka's castle, *The American Prospect*, December.

Petrovic, M. and Hamilton, G.G. (2006) Making global markets, in *Wal-Mart: The Face of Twentieth Century Capitalism* (ed. N. Lichtenstein), New Press, New York, pp. 107–42.

Quinn, B. (2005) *How Wal-Mart is Destroying America (and the World) and What You Can Do About It*, Ten Speed Press, 2005.

Rivoli, P. (2005) *The Travels of a T-Shirt in the Global Economy*, John Wiley & Sons, Inc., New York.

Rosen, E.I. (2006) How to squeeze more out of a penny, in *Wal-Mart: The Face of Twentieth Century Capitalism* (ed. N. Lichtenstein), New Press, New York, pp. 243–60.

Sarkar, P. (2005) Wal-Mart's world view: Giant retailer says it's ready to tackle hot-button issues, *San Francisco Chronicle*, 26 October.

Sevin, M. (2005) Wal-Mart faces suit by labor group, *Los Angeles Times*, 14 September.

Slater, R. (2003) *The Wal-Mart Triumph: Inside the World's #1 Company*, Portfolio, London.

Strasser, S. (2006) Woolworth to Wal-Mart: Mass merchandising and the changing culture of consumption, in *Wal-Mart: The Face of Twentieth Century Capitalism*, (ed. N. Lichtenstein), New Press, New York, pp. 31–56.

Wal-Mart Stores, Inc. (2005) *Report on Ethical Sourcing*. http://www.walmartfacts.com/global/ WMstoresWeb

Index